The Bristol and Gloucestershire Archaeological Society
Gloucestershire Record Series

Volume 4

A Calendar of the Registers of the Freemen of the City of Gloucester 1641–1838

ed. A. R. J. Juřica

A CALENDAR OF THE REGISTERS OF THE FREEMEN OF THE CITY OF GLOUCESTER 1641–1838

Transcribed by
Peter Ripley
and
revised and edited by
John Juřica

The Bristol and Gloucestershire Archaeological Society

1991

The Bristol and Gloucestershire Archaeological Society
Gloucestershire Record Series

ISBN 0 900197 32 3

This volume was published with the generous assistance of a grant from the Twenty-Seven Foundation

Produced for the Society by Alan Sutton Publishing Ltd., Stroud, Gloucestershire
Printed in Great Britain

CONTENTS

PETER RIPLEY M.A. M.LITT

'The Freemen of Gloucester' was Peter Ripley's last major study in Gloucestershire history; with his death on 29 March 1988 the Bristol and Gloucestershire Archaeological Society lost a long-standing member, and local studies a good friend. He joined the Society in 1970 and in 1987 was elected General Editor of this Record Series, a task he tackled with zest and absolute commitment, achieving a prodigious amount in a very short time. The long term success of the Record Series would be the best appreciation of his service both to the Society and to local history studies in Gloucestershire.

As an undergraduate Peter Ripley studied Modern History at Queen's College, Oxford. After taking his degree in 1951 he entered the colonial education service in Kenya where he worked for twelve years, first as a teacher, then in training teachers, and finally as an inspector. East Africa captured his interest, which led to his writing a textbook for use in African schools, and several monographs. Later he took the opportunity to introduce the subject to students in this country.

He came to Gloucester from Bridlington Grammar School in 1967 to join the History Department at the Gloucestershire College of Education where he worked for eleven years. During that time his fruitful commitment to Gloucestershire history took root. His first major study in this field (outside his work for students) was 'The City of Gloucester 1660–1740', his M.Litt thesis for Bristol University completed in 1977. This was followed by several articles published in the *Transactions*. Though Peter Ripley's career then took him to Kent for two years he was glad to return to this area in 1980 as Head of Humanities and Social Science at Brunel College of Technology, Bristol. In spite of a very busy professional life he again took up the threads of his research and found time to transcribe the registers of the Freemen of Gloucester 1653–1838.

As he had a premonitory indication of heart trouble early in 1988 he decided to retire that summer. He was then looking forward to having more time for his own research and to edit this Record Series for which he had only recently taken responsibility. Sadly those hopes were not to be realised.

E.A.C. Dec. 1990

ABBREVIATIONS USED IN THE NOTES

Alumni Cantab.	*Alumni Cantabrigienses*, ed. J. and J.A. Venn (10 vols. 1922–54)
Alumni Oxon.	*Alumni Oxonienses*, ed. J. Foster (8 vols. 1887–92)
Atkyns, *Glos.*	R. Atkyns, *Ancient and Present State of Glostershire* (1712)
Austin, *Crypt School*	R. Austin, *Crypt School, Gloucester, 1539–1939* (Gloucester, 1939)
B.G.A.S.	Bristol and Gloucestershire Archaeological Society
Bigland, *Glos.*	*Historical, Monumental, and Genealogical Collections Relative to the County of Gloucester. Printed from the Original Papers of Ralph Bigland* (3 vols. 1791–1889, issued in parts)
Complete Baronetage	G.E. C[ockayne], *Complete Baronetage* (6 vols. 1900–9)
Complete Peerage	G.E. C[ockayne] and others, *Complete Peerage* (2nd edn., 13 vols. 1910–59)
D.N.B.	*Dictionary of National Biography*
Fosbrooke, *Glouc.*	T.D. Fosbrooke, *Original History of the City of Gloucester almost Wholly Compiled from New Materials . . . including also the Original Papers of Ralph Bigland* (London, 1819)
GBR	Gloucester Borough Records in Gloucestershire Record Office
Glos. Colln.	The Gloucestershire Collection, in Gloucester Divisional Library, comprising printed works, manuscripts, prints and drawings, etc.
Glos. N.&Q.	*Gloucestershire Notes and Queries* (10 vols. 1881–1914)
Glos. R.O.	Gloucestershire Record Office
Glouc. Corp. Rec.	*Calendar of the Records of the Corporation of Gloucester*, ed. W.H. Stevenson (Gloucester, 1893)
Glouc. Jnl.	*Gloucester Journal*
Gray, *Antiquaries*	I. Gray, *Antiquaries of Gloucestershire and Bristol* (B.G.A.S. 1981)
Heref. R.O.	Hereford Record Office
Hist. MSS. Com.	Royal Commission on Historical Manuscripts
Hockaday Abs.	The 'Hockaday Abstracts', being abstracts of ecclesiastical records relating to Gloucestershire, compiled by F.S. Hockaday mainly from diocesan records, in Gloucester Divisional Library.
Nash, *Worcs.*	T. Nash, *Collections for the History of Worcestershire* (2 vols. 1781–2)
P.N. Glos. (E.P.N.S.)	*Place-Names of Gloucestershire* (English Place-Name Society vols. xxxviii–xli, 1964–5)
P.R.O.	Public Record Office
Rep. Com. Mun. Corp.	*First Report of the Commissioners Appointed to Enquire into the Municipal Corporations of England and Wales*, App. I, H.C. 116 (1835), xxiii (1)

Rudder, *Glos.*	S. Rudder, *New History of Gloucestershire* (Cirencester, 1779)
Rudge, *Hist. of Glos.*	T. Rudge, *History of the County of Gloucester* (2 vols. Gloucester, 1803)
Trans. B.G.A.S.	*Transactions of the Bristol and Gloucestershire Archaeological Society*
V.C.H.	*Victoria County History*
Visit. Glos. 1682–3	*Visitation of the County of Gloucester, 1682, 1683*, ed. T. FitzRoy Fenwick and W.C. Metcalfe (Exeter, priv. print. 1884)
Williams, *Parl. Hist. of Glos.*	W.R. Williams, *Parliamentary History of the County of Gloucester* (Hereford, priv. print. 1898)

INTRODUCTION

The early history of the freedom[1]

By the mid 12th century the leading townsmen of Gloucester were seeking legal and commercial privileges from the Crown. Their efforts were rewarded by Henry II when, soon after his accession, he granted the burgesses their first charter of liberties. In time the burgesses secured additional privileges or freedoms and restricted them to themselves and their sons. They admitted others to their circle, the freeman body, on payment or on completion of a term of apprenticeship. The achievement of liberties and the history of the freedom followed in their broad outlines a pattern common to many boroughs but influenced by local circumstances and considerations. The development of the freedom in Exeter and Oxford, for example, often paralleled its evolution in Gloucester.[2]

The freedoms granted by Henry II to the burgesses of Gloucester were the same exemptions from toll and the same procedures in their courts as the citizens of London and Winchester enjoyed.[3] In 1165 the burgesses acquired the right to collect royal dues arising in the town in return for an annual payment but in 1176 that right was revoked. In the late 1160s some burgesses had attempted to form a commune to gain greater control over the administration of the borough. The right to farm royal dues was conceded anew by Richard I in 1194 and a new charter of liberties was granted by John in 1200. John's charter gave the burgesses the right to elect two bailiffs and four coroners, confirmed their freedom from tolls and, among a number of legal franchises, protected them against pleading in external courts except in cases concerning land outside the borough. It remained the basis of the town's liberties until 1483. Those liberties, though not immune from challenges from the Crown and other authorities, were widened by a number of charters in the 13th and 14th centuries.

By 1200 the town's commercial life was regulated by a merchants' guild. In referring to 'our burgesses of Gloucester of the merchants' guild' John's charter indicates that the guild embraced all the townsmen with full burgess rights. Merchants' guilds in many other towns were similarly constituted though that in Oxford may have had a more exclusive membership in the early 13th century.[4] Further evidence of the close relationship in Gloucester between borough and guild is provided by the inscription 'sigillum burgensium de gilda mercatorum Gloucestrie' on the town's earliest common seals.[5] By 1409 men acquiring the

[1] This section is based on *Victoria History of the Counties of England, Gloucestershire*, iv: *City of Gloucester*, 28–35, 54–9.

[2] Cf. *Exeter Freemen 1266–1967*, ed. M.M. Rowe and A.M. Jackson (Devon & Cornwall Record Society extra series i, 1973), pp. xi–xxxv; *V.C.H. Oxon.* iv. 48–52, 126–30, 151–2, 225–6, 249–51.

[3] Hist. MSS. Com. 27, *12th Rep. IX, Glouc. Corp.* p. 400; *Glouc. Corp. Rec.* p. 3.

[4] *V.C.H. Oxon.* iv. 49; cf. J. Tait, *Medieval English Borough* (1936), 222–34.

[5] *V.C.H. Glos.* iv. 369.

freedom were sworn in as 'burgesses' to the 'merchants' guild' and the earliest surviving text of the freeman's oath, dating from the early 16th century and probably little changed from the late 13th, refers to the burgesses as 'guild brothers'.[1]

The assimilation of borough with guild, or vice-versa, explains early uncertainty over the name of the Boothall, the original seat of town government and a centre of commercial activity. Recorded from 1216, the Boothall stood in Westgate Street on or near the site of a building called the guildhall in 1192. A lease of *c.* 1230 shows that the guildhall and Boothall were parts of the same building but later the two names were used interchangeably, with that of Boothall becoming preferred.[2] The Boothall was the meeting place of the hundred court. The court, so called by the late 12th century, was the main organ of town government until 1483 and under the presidency of the town's bailiffs probably met weekly (as it certainly did later) and held frankpledge sessions twice a year. Apart from the hearing of pleas it probably had an administrative role including regulation of trade and maintenance of burgess rights and duties. Admissions to the freedom were marked by ceremony in the court by the late 13th century. That practice continued after 1483 when a new common council with members co-opted from among the burgesses and a mayor at its head emerged to replace the court as the chief organ of civic government. The volume used to record pleas before the court in the period from 1641 to 1653 also served as a register of admissions to the freedom during those years.[3]

By the late Middle Ages each burgess or freeman belonged to one of Gloucester's trade companies.[4] The appearance of those companies, the earliest known being that of the butchers recorded from 1454, was bound up with the delegation of the regulation of certain trades from the borough to particular groups of burgesses. It is apparent that in the long term the companies failed to ensure that their trades were exclusive to freemen but, as in Oxford and Salisbury, attempts to preserve the interdependence of freeman status and craft guild membership persisted beyond the 16th century.[5] Mid 16th-century Gloucester had at least seven companies, including those of the tanners, the cooks, the cordwainers, the weavers, the bakers, and the tailors and hosiers. In addition to supervising their trades, they protected burgess rights and regulated the apprenticeship system by which men entered those trades and thereby the freedom. By an act of the common council in 1570 membership of the companies was opened to hereditary burgesses, sons born to freemen, who had served apprenticeships in other cities and towns.[6]

The responsibilities and obligations which free status entailed were summarized in the oath sworn by entrants to the freedom.[7] By swearing to forbear acquiring property within the town which might jeopardize the burgesses' exemption from external pleading the new freeman undertook to remain justiciable in the town's courts. In the oath's general clauses was also implicit the privileged position of the burgesses in the economic life of the town. Among their privileges, as reserved to them in 1514, were the rights to buy grain in the corn market for resale and to purchase merchandise, notably wool, cloth, and timber, brought to the town and its

[1] Cf. below, Appendix I.
[2] *V.C.H. Glos.* iv. 248; cf. *Glouc. Corp. Rec.* pp. 122, 346.
[3] GBR G 10/2: register calendared below.
[4] *V.C.H. Glos.* iv. 80.
[5] Ibid. *Oxon.* iv. 127; *Wilts.* vi. 137.
[6] GBR B 3/1, f. 26v.
[7] Below, Appendix I.

quay by visiting merchants.[1] In practice the freemen never had an absolute monopoly of trade in Gloucester. A category of townsmen called 'portmen' (*portmanni*), the term used in the sense of 'citizens' or 'burgesses', existed apparently by the 1260s and enjoyed a limited range of privileges. The portmen, who probably included resident householders and members of the town community, evidently shared some of the trading rights of the full burgesses. They paid a fine for their privileges and took an oath in which, like the burgesses, they were obliged to foreswear trading on behalf of outsiders. That requirement indicates that use by freemen and portmen of their privileges to benefit visiting traders had been a problem. In the late 14th century and the early 15th, when as many as 92 men a year paid to become portmen, many more people, both unenfranchised townsmen and residents of surrounding villages and other towns, traded in Gloucester in return for an annual payment to the bailiffs. The portmen are last recorded in the early 16th century.

Admissions to the freedom

Throughout the period covered by the registers published in this volume entry to the freedom of Gloucester was controlled by the city corporation and was obtained in one of four ways – by patrimony, apprenticeship, fine, or gift. Most entrants qualified by patrimony or apprenticeship, the freedom being open as of right to sons born after their father had become free and to men completing a seven-year apprenticeship in the city to a freeman and having lodged with him during that term. Admission by patrimony was originally without payment but admission by apprenticeship incurred a fee of 4*s* by 1534.[2] While patrimony or apprenticeship provided an automatic entitlement to the freedom, admission under some special circumstance, such as inability to produce indentures of apprenticeship, an apprenticeship not running its full term or served outside the city, and waiving or abatement of fees on the ground of poverty, required the common council's consent.[3]

To gain the freedom by purchase, more usually styled by fine, an entrant made his own agreement with the common council as to the price or fine. The council's acts in the mid 17th century show that residents who had performed loyal service to the city, particularly during the siege of 1643, and to the parliamentary cause during the Civil Wars were allowed to buy their way into the freedom. They also suggest that some purchasers had acquired businesses in the city by marriage to the widow or daughter of a freeman. From 1669, when the intervention of a group of freemen delayed the sale of the freedom to an upholsterer, men wishing to purchase free status had to submit their petition to the common council twice.[4] For much of the period those buying free status were usually innkeepers.[5] In 1762 they included the first female to have her entry to the freedom registered.[6] To control alehouses in the city there were several attempts to restrict licences to freemen or their widows[7] and a move in 1747 to limit the number of licences to 90 prompted a large number

[1] GBR B 2/1, ff. 21v.–22; Hist. MSS. Com. 27, *Glouc. Corp.* pp. 438–40.
[2] GBR C 9/6.
[3] Ibid. B 3/2, p. 877; 3, pp. 51, 212, 456, 834; 7, f. 103.
[4] Ibid. 3, pp. 406, 408–9.
[5] Cf. ibid. 8, pp. 501, 503–4.
[6] Ibid. C 9/8, p. 255.
[7] Ibid. B 3/3, p. 668.

of innkeepers to purchase free status.[1] Among other purchasers of the freedom were farmers and graziers who stood to benefit particularly from the freemen's right to pasture livestock in the city's common meadows.[2] The price of the freedom, which in 1409 had been £1,[3] varied considerably in the mid 17th century. By the mid 1670s it was usually £10[4] and from the late 1740s £20.[5] In 1813 the minimum price, that usually paid, was doubled to £40 but in 1831, parliamentary legislation on the sale of beer having reduced the freedom's value to innkeepers, it was restored to £20.[6]

Freemen by patrimony, apprenticeship, or fine were liable to a number of payments on taking up the freedom. Fees were owed to the mayor and other civic officers taking part in the swearing-in ceremony and a registration fee to the town clerk. In addition new freemen contributed financially towards the provision of buckets for fire fighting.[7] That obligation, similar to one imposed on Oxford freemen in 1590,[8] was established before 1635 and was fixed at 2*s* 8*d*, the price of a bucket, for new freemen by patrimony and apprenticeship and 5*s* 4*d* for those by fine.[9] The payments became known as bucket money and in time became part of the corporation's general revenues along with purchase fines and fees for entry by apprenticeship.[10] The freedom thus ensured a regular income for the corporation, which was an appreciable, if modest, part of the city's revenues in periods when there were large numbers of new freemen.

Like its counterparts in Oxford, Salisbury, and many other places Gloucester corporation had the power to make freemen by the 17th century.[11] A regular succession of men achieved the freedom without payment by its gift. The corporation used its power in a number of ways one of which led to the creation of a large body of honorary freemen from outside the city and enfranchised for political purposes. Before the Restoration most persons given the freedom lived in the city. Some, including several who were indigent, were rewarded with the freedom for service to the city and corporation, especially during the Civil Wars, and some who were sick and elderly were made free to enable them to enter one or other of the city's almshouses.[12] Several national figures were awarded the freedom in token of the corporation's thanks for their part in the military and political life of the city.[13] Those grants suggest that honorary freedom in Gloucester, as in Oxford, originated mainly in the mid 17th century. Later, while beneficiaries occasionally included past servants of the corporation and the needy, the freedom's honorific character was increasingly enhanced. Among recipients were county landowners, noblemen visiting the city, members of the royal family, and distinguished military and naval officers. The corporation also honoured with the freedom those whose political and

[1] Ibid. 10, ff. 92v.–97; cf. ibid. ff. 98–101v., 107v.–110, 116v.–117, 125–6; C 9/8, pp. 171–6.
[2] Ibid. B 3/11, f. 218; 13, f. 200; for the freemen's common rights, below.
[3] *V.C.H. Glos.* iv. 57.
[4] GBR B 3/3, pp. 645, 656, 682, 692.
[5] Ibid. 10, ff. 118, 121, 125–126v., 140, 153v., 163v.
[6] Ibid. 13, f. 131v.; 14, f. 167v.; *Rep. Com. Mun. Corp.* 61.
[7] GBR B 3/2, p. 371.
[8] *V.C.H. Oxon.* iv. 127.
[9] GBR F 4/5, f. 29.
[10] Ibid. f. 171v.; 6, pp. 111, 391; 7, p. 418; cf. *V.C.H. Glos.* iv. 267–8.
[11] Cf. *V.C.H. Oxon.* iv. 128; *Wilts.* vi. 105.
[12] GBR B 3/2, pp. 386, 405, 412, 419, 450, 506.
[13] Ibid. p. 876; 3, p. 131.

religious views it found sympathetic[1] and those who advanced its interests.[2] Honorary freedom was bestowed gratuitously but freemen by gift were expected, according to a common council act of 1717, to pay a fee of at least two guineas.[3]

In its choice of honorary freemen Gloucester's 18th-century Whig oligarchy, while sometimes influenced by persons outside the corporation,[4] was usually guided by the mayor. From 1672 mayors had occasionally been empowered to confer the freedom on distinguished persons accompanying noble visitors to the city[5] and by the 1740s, and probably much earlier, they customarily recommended candidates for honorary freedom at the end of their term of office.[6] Their nominations were rarely, if ever, rejected by the common council. The outgoing mayor in 1782 proposed seventeen new freemen and his successors not uncommonly nominated as many as ten.[7] Mayors used that power in favour of relations, friends, and associates[8] and Samuel Woodcock, elected to the office in 1788 and 1801, secured the freedom for several senior officials of the Post Office, his employer.[9] The power was curtailed in 1808 when the common council limited the number of honorary freemen that each mayor could propose to six.[10] In time that limit was circumvented by a growth in the practice for other members of the corporation, notably the sheriffs, to nominate freemen.[11]

Admissions by fine and gift, authorized by act of the common council, were directly controlled by the corporation. Those by patrimony and apprenticeship were not as readily scrutinized and consequently unqualified men sometimes took one or other of those ways to the freedom. To check such deception, which only took place with the connivance of individual freemen, the freemen registers were occasionally examined and persons found to have gained the freedom by fraud were disfranchised.[12] Resort to that sanction was rare apart from the time of the parliamentary election of September 1727 when thirteen men were deprived of free status and thereby of the right to vote.[13] As the number of freemen living far from the city grew claims of patrimony became difficult to verify and from 1732 they, together with claims of apprenticeship, were registered and vetted by a committee of the common council.[14] The committee's work presumably reduced the number of fraudulent entries[15] but on several occasions, as in 1812, bogus claims were approved.[16]

The apprenticeship system was particularly open to abuse as a way to the freedom. With the declining role of many trade companies in the regulation of the city's economic life, a development under way by the early 17th century, the task of

[1] Ibid. 8, p. 647; 9, f. 9v.; 11, ff. 313v., 350.
[2] Ibid. 11, f. 303.
[3] Ibid. 9, ff. 23, 78v.
[4] Ibid. f. 106.
[5] Ibid. 3, p. 547; 6, f. 249 and v.; 7, f. 128; 8, pp. 455, 506.
[6] Ibid. 10, ff. 12, 56, 72; cf. ibid. 8, p. 565; 9, ff. 48v., 130, 152v.
[7] Ibid. 11, f. 323; 12, ff. 152v., 169, 171.
[8] Ibid. 10, ff. 167, 234v.; 13, ff. 215v., 231v.
[9] Ibid. 12, ff. 115v., 346; *V.C.H. Glos.* iv. 380.
[10] GBR B 3/13, f. 55.
[11] Ibid. ff. 120, 135v., 153, 174v., 195 and v.
[12] Ibid. 8, pp. 244, 334–5.
[13] Ibid. 9, ff. 222–3; for the parliamentary franchise, below.
[14] GBR B 3/9, ff. 325v.–326v., 331, 349v., 362.
[15] Claim books survive for the periods 1732–49 and 1765–1837: ibid. C 9/12–14; P.R.O., PROB 37/1316.
[16] GBR B 3/13, ff. 140, 142 and v.

ensuring that apprentices met conditions for entry to the freedom became more difficult. In 1613 and 1617 the common council had addressed the associated abuses of antedating of indentures and avoidance of a full seven-year apprenticeship by ordering the registration of all apprenticeship indentures to freemen in the city.[1] Disregard of those orders and the practice, causing concern by the 1670s, of some freemen to take apprentices not to teach them their trade but solely to enable them to obtain the freedom, led the common council in 1680 to rule that freedom by apprenticeship was open only to those with indentures registered at the outset of a seven-year term of service.[2] Other conditions for entry, notably the requirements for apprenticeships to be served in the city and for apprentices to lodge with their masters, were also restated by the common council in the early 18th century.[3] The 1680 act, modified by a ruling of 1708 that apprenticeships were to be registered at the Tolsey on Mondays and Fridays,[4] was relaxed in individual cases and by the late 18th century had become a dead letter.[5] In 1818 the corporation invoked it to deny the freedom to a grocer but in 1819, in an ensuing court case, the act was declared legally null.[6]

In the early 17th century apprentices in a dozen or more trades had a right to the freedom of Gloucester. The companies governing these trades included those of the mercers, weavers, bakers, tanners, haberdashers, innkeepers, tailors, butchers, glovers, shoemakers, barbers, metal men, and joiners. Another company, that of the shearmen, was defunct by 1634.[7] The decline of the companies was a symptom of economic developments undermining the relationship between company membership and free status. Many companies' abandonment of a regulatory role in their trades brought about a dwindling in the number of freemen by apprenticeship. Conversely, the growth of trades outside their framework saw a rise in the number of apprentices excluded from the freedom. A solution was not tried until 1755 when the freedom was extended to the trades of *upholder* (dealer in small wares or second-hand articles), bookseller, brushmaker, woolcomber, woolstapler, clock and watchmaker, hatter, currier, vintner, and distiller.[8] The reform proved ineffective in halting the decline in entries by apprenticeship and, even though the mercers' company sought to control the trades of grocer, haberdasher, linen-draper, silkman, and salter,[9] many men continued to be denied the freedom by reason of being in unprivileged trades. The anomaly ended in 1787 when the freedom was opened to the apprentices of all resident freemen.[10]

Rights and duties of the freemen in the 17th and 18th centuries

Freeman status enabled its holders to participate more fully than other inhabitants of Gloucester in the political and economic life of the city. Members of the common council, the most important civic institution, were co-opted from among the freemen and the borough's parliamentary representatives were elected by the

[1] Ibid. 1, ff. 249, 443v.
[2] Ibid. 3, pp. 674–5, 778.
[3] Ibid. 8, p. 275; 9, f. 120.
[4] Ibid. 8, p. 267.
[5] Ibid. 12, f. 38.
[6] *Glouc. Jnl.* 8 June 1818; 22 Feb, 5 Apr 1819.
[7] *V.C.H. Glos.* iv. 80.
[8] GBR B 3/10, f. 200v.
[9] Ibid. 11, f. 278v.
[10] Ibid. 12, f. 86.

freeman body.[1] Freemen's economic privileges included, in theory at least, exclusive trading rights in the city except during the time of public fairs.[2] Their immunity from being sued in courts outside Gloucester was maintained and in the late 18th century on two occasions groups of citizens had to surrender the freedom temporarily to be able to take part in legal proceedings elsewhere.[3]

From the late 16th century the freemen's commercial privileges, protected by the trade companies, were constantly challenged by unfree residents. The companies, faced also with the decline of certain trades and with internal divisions, became less important in the regulation of trade and, although they remained vital institutions, the benefits to freemen of membership were reduced.[4] The increasing political role of the freedom from the later 17th century further hastened the companies' decline. The corporation took some steps to bolster the companies' authority and safeguard their privileges and to ensure that freemen were company members.[5] In 1675 a freeman was ordered to join the tanners' company and, because he lived in Littledean, the company to excuse his attendance at its assemblies.[6] The common council sometimes acted against unfree traders and on a few occasions closed the shops of men expelled from the freedom[7] but the restriction of retail trade and manufacture to freemen became increasingly unenforceable. Some trade companies attempted with help from the corporation to enforce their monopolies well into the 18th century.[8] Such efforts were sporadic yet the existence of restrictive practices enabled the vendor of some houses in the Barton Street suburb in 1736 to point out that their situation just outside the city made them ideal for tradesmen wanting to pursue a business without taking the freedom.[9] In the 1760s and 1770s several companies submitted new bylaws to the common council for approval. The last to do so was the mercers' company, which sought in 1780 to reserve a number of trades to men free of it and of the city. The mercers' abandonment in 1781 of legal proceedings against an unenfranchised linen-draper apparently marked the end of any concerted attempts to preserve the freemen's exclusive trading rights.[10] In Oxford attempts to protect the freemen's trading monopoly continued until at least 1827.[11] In Gloucester, as in Exeter and Salisbury, the relaxation of restrictive practices in the 18th century assisted commercial development,[12] which in other boroughs, notably York, was hindered by resolutions to force all traders and manufacturers to take up the freedom.[13]

A number of the privileges enjoyed by the Gloucester freemen survived the 18th century.[14] They included common rights in a number of meadows by the river Severn on the west and north-west sides of the city, notably in Oxlease, Portham, and Town (formerly Common) Ham on Alney Island and in Archdeacon Meadow,

[1] *V.C.H. Glos.* iv. 84, 86, 152.
[2] Cf. GBR B 3/11, f. 278v.
[3] Ibid. ff. 298v., 344; 12, ff. 219–22, 227v.
[4] *V.C.H. Glos.* iv. 80–1.
[5] GBR B 3/3, pp. 408–9, 668; 7, f. 138v.
[6] Ibid. 3, pp. 635–6.
[7] Ibid. pp. 750–1; 7, f. 226 and v.; 9, f. 312.
[8] Ibid. 10, ff. 135v., 243.
[9] *Glouc. Jnl.* 29 June 1736.
[10] *V.C.H. Glos.* iv. 146–7; GBR B 3/11, f. 278v.
[11] *V.C.H. Oxon.* iv. 225–6.
[12] *Exeter Freemen 1266–1967*, pp. xxii–xxiii; *V.C.H. Wilts.* vi. 137.
[13] *V.C.H. Yorks.* 215–19, 231, 257.
[14] *Rep. Com. Mun. Corp.* 61.

Little Meadow, and St. Catherine's Meadow (formerly Meanham),[1] and freedom from tolls collected by the corporation.[2] Under statutes issued by the common council in 1636 freemen and their wives were preferred as inmates in three almshouses, namely the hospital of St. Bartholomew in lower Westgate Street and the hospitals of St. Margaret and St. Mary Magdalen just outside the city at Wotton. Those hospitals, medieval foundations, had passed under the corporation's control by the late 16th century.[3] Places in Sir Thomas Rich's school, sometimes called the Bluecoat Hospital, were reserved by the corporation for sons of freemen at its opening in 1668.[4]

Freeman privileges were secured by swearing the freeman's oath. Men readmitted to the freedom were expected to take the oath a second time.[5] The oath, of which freemen were given a copy on their certificates of free status, hardly differed in the 18th century from that used in the late Middle Ages. Its text,[6] having the same import as the oaths sworn in Exeter and Oxford,[7] summed up the responsibilities incurred on entering the freedom and perpetuated the notion that the freemen constituted the commonalty of the city. Freemen swore to uphold the liberties and customs of the city and corporation, to assist and obey the mayor and sheriffs, to observe acts of the common council, and to share according to means in the taxation of the city. As earlier the practice of trading on behalf of outsiders was foresworn. Opinion that failure to pay taxes meant loss of the parliamentary franchise led the council to rule in 1677 that all freemen, including those unable to pay through impoverishment or physical incapacity, enjoyed voting rights solely by virtue of having taken the oath.[8]

Actions regarded as prejudicial to the city's interests were punishable by expulsion from the freedom. According to an act of 1625 they included prolonged absence from the city, residence elsewhere, refusal to hold civic office, and failure to pay taxes.[9] In May 1643 several freemen were disfranchised for deserting the city then in imminent danger of attack by royalist forces.[10] There were a few instances when men lost the freedom for failure to share the burden of office. In one, in 1680, a grocer, who had refused several years earlier to be sheriff, was removed from the common council for persistent non-attendance.[11] In the later 17th century failure to submit to the city magistrates and behaviour harmful to the interests of trade companies were also reasons invoked for expulsions from the freedom.[12] The most contentious expulsion, that in February 1685 of the Whig baronet John Guise, marked the culmination of his differences with the Tory dominated corporation and highlighted the passion of contemporary political argument. Guise, who had been M.P. for the county until 1681, was accused of continually slighting the corporation and of having slandered a common councillor in parliament. His expulsion was overturned in November 1686 when Tory influence on the corporation was

[1] Cf. *V.C.H. Glos.* iv. 60, 67, 193–4.
[2] Cf. GBR B 3/3, p. 836; 7, f. 191; 9, f. 437v.
[3] *V.C.H. Glos.* iv. 351–4.
[4] Ibid. 335–6.
[5] GBR B 3/3, p. 890.
[6] Below, Appendix II.
[7] Cf. *Exeter Freemen 1266–1967*, p. xviii; *V.C.H. Oxon.* iv. 126.
[8] GBR B 3/3, p. 673.
[9] Ibid. 1, f. 506v.; cf. ibid. f. 232.
[10] Ibid. 2, pp. 245, 256.
[11] Ibid. 3, pp. 750–1.
[12] Ibid. pp. 332, 481, 674–5; 7, f. 226 and v.

waning.[1] In the 18th century the common council rarely considered individual's actions as meriting loss of the freedom,[2] save when free status was discovered to have been obtained by fraud.

Political importance of the freedom

After the Restoration the freedom of boroughs as far apart as Exeter and York became increasingly political in character.[3] That process, pointing up and contrasting with the divorce between the freedom and the economic life of those towns, was brought about by political factionalism and gathered pace as parliamentary elections became the principal cockpit for clashes between competing interests. Political dissension, which particularly after 1688 mirrored the growth of party divisions nationally, was stimulated in Gloucester by the survival of Civil War loyalties and the growing influence of county landowners in the city's economic, social, and political life.[4]

The retention by the parliamentary party of a strong following in Gloucester after 1660 led the Crown to institute purges of the ruling corporation.[5] Carried out in 1662 and 1663 and in 1672, those purges brought into the city's government a number of men, including some gentry, until then outside the freeman body. The changes of 1672 assured royalist control of Gloucester's politics which lasted until James II's reign. Under James Tory domination of the corporation lessened. In April 1687 the common council offered some resistance to the Crown by seeking clarification of a royal order to admit Anselm Fowler, a Roman Catholic, to the freedom.[6] The following November the Crown replaced leading Tories on the corporation by its own appointees, a handful of whom became freemen shortly afterwards. In the 1690s Whigs came to dominate the aldermanic bench and thereby secured a control of the corporation lasting until the first elections held under the Municipal Corporations Act of 1835 ended Tories' virtual exclusion from the city's government.[7]

In Gloucester the right to vote in parliamentary elections was secured solely by the taking of the freeman's oath.[8] Consequently efforts by factions to influence the outcome of elections were crucial in the history of the freedom from the later 17th century. Candidates including city men and county gentry backed by the corporation or its opponents vied for freemen's votes. The parliamentary franchise, or rather the access it provided to the largesse distributed by candidates, became the primary incentive for many to become freemen. The practice of freemen taking apprentices not to teach them a trade but to enable them to enter the freedom was widespread enough to cause concern by the late 1670s.[9] During election campaigns

[1] Ibid. 3, pp. 876, 915, 918; Williams, *Parl. Hist. of Glos.* 59; cf. *V.C.H. Glos.* iv. 114.

[2] Cf. GBR B 3/9, f. 317v.

[3] Cf. *Exeter Freemen 1266–1967*, pp. xxii, xxvi–xxviii; *V.C.H. Oxon.* iv. 129, 151–2, 249–50; *Yorks.* 166–7, 183, 240–1.

[4] *V.C.H. Glos.* iv. 113–5.

[5] This paragraph is based on ibid.

[6] GBR B 3/6, ff. 153–154v.

[7] *V.C.H. Glos.* iv. 191.

[8] GBR B 3/3, p. 673. The rest of this section is based mostly on the freemen registers; J.A. Cannon, 'Parliamentary Representation of City of Gloucester (1727–90)', *Trans. B.G.A.S.* lxxviii. 137–52; G.L. Goodman, 'Pre-Reform Elections in Gloucester City, 1789–1831,' ibid. lxxxiv. 141–60; *V.C.H. Glos.* iv. 113–5, 152–4; Williams, *Parl. Hist. of Glos.* 199–215.

[9] GBR B 3/3, pp. 674–5.

those qualifying by patrimony or apprenticeship were encouraged to become freemen and may have had their costs paid by factions and candidates. The buying of votes, as well as the organization behind candidates, is suggested by the allegation in 1690 that William Trye, a Tory landowner, had secured his election by mobilizing support among poorer freemen. Trye's return was also contested by the corporation on the ground that he, unlike most of the city's parliamentary representatives, was not a freeman.

As early as 1660 parliamentary elections in Gloucester saw a discernible increase in the number of new freemen. While the elections of April 1675 and February 1681 were both accompanied by an influx of about 30 citizens to the freedom, the first electoral contest to have a marked effect on admissions was that of October 1695 when some 80 new freemen, including several living just outside the city, were created in the few weeks before polling. With the increase in political factionalism after the turn of the century many elections were keenly contested and witnessed much larger influxes to the freedom. Indeed the incidence of political strife before 1832 can virtually be measured by the number of new freemen. In the run-up to the contest of July 1702 there were over 200 admissions by patrimony and apprenticeship and before that of September 1727 well over 300. The latter election, which was fought fiercely, also saw the corporation disfranchise several men found to have obtained the freedom by fraud[1] and enfranchise a much larger number of local landowners and others from outside the city. Earlier the corporation on rare occasions had given the freedom to prospective M.P.s but in 1727 it used its power to create freemen on a massive scale to influence an election's result. On 25 July the common council conferred the freedom on 119 men, a move prompting a complaint from the corporation's opponents that 140 had been made free in one day, and on 9 August a further 25 new freemen were created. Nearly all lived outside the city and many were county landowners, clergymen, or businessmen.[2] Other corporations, including that of Coventry from 1722, also manipulated the freedom of their boroughs for electoral ends[3] and resorted, as in Exeter in 1741, to the expedient of enfranchising large numbers of outsiders.[4]

After 1727 Gloucester's politics alternated between compromise and conflict. Periods of truce when the opposing factions shared the city's two parliamentary seats were punctuated by outbreaks of hostility resulting in elections, such as those of May 1741, March 1761, and September 1780, which saw several hundred admissions by patrimony or apprenticeship to the freedom. A byelection in February 1789, preceded immediately by well over 400 admissions, was won by the corporation's opponent John Pitt by a single vote. The contest was followed by an agreement between the corporation and Pitt to share the city's parliamentary representation. The accord, though interrupted by a byelection in August 1805 after Pitt's death, lasted until a byelection in October 1816. During both by-elections over 300 men took free status. A similar increase in the electorate's size preceded the election of August 1830, the last to see a large influx of new freemen.

The corporation continued to use its power to create freemen with notorious partiality. After the 1761 election there were allegations that it had refused the freedom to its opponents. While only a handful of honorary freemen were admitted during parliamentary elections after 1727, there was a regular succession of new

[1] Ibid. 9, ff. 222–3.
[2] Ibid. ff. 214v.–215v., 218v.
[3] *V.C.H. Warws.* viii. 253.
[4] *Exeter Freemen 1266–1967*, p. xxviii.

freemen by the corporation's gift. An attempt to curb that power by statute foundered in 1780 but the corporation's influence over elections was reduced, albeit minimally, by an Act of 1786, under which new honorary freemen were unable to vote for twelve months. Following the 1816 byelection the city was gripped by political antagonism which continued beyond the next general election in June 1818. During that period the corporation created over a hundred freemen for electoral purposes. That action was contested in law and in 1819 the court of King's Bench ruled illegal the corporation's practice of electing honorary freemen together in groups and not as individuals. The ruling disfranchised 90 men,[1] most of whom were readmitted as freemen in 1820 and 1821.[2]

The consequences of the growth in the freedom's political significance were threefold. Firstly it ensured the survival of an institution increasingly bereft of economic meaning. Exercising a central role in parliamentary elections, the freeman body was continually replenished by new recruits. While it is difficult to be exact about the number of freemen at any one time it has been estimated at 1,400 in the first decade of the 18th century and was well over 1,750 in the early 1740s. The rate of growth in the freeman body evidently increased in the late 18th century and the early 19th and, whereas the Municipal Corporations Commissioners estimated the number of freemen at 1,725 in 1833,[3] the freemen's roll compiled immediately after the passing of the Municipal Corporations Act of 1835 originally contained some 2,790 names.[4]

Secondly the freedom was accorded to men living outside the city, the outvoters, in such numbers that in time they came to constitute a majority of the freemen. That development, which had considerable impact on the conduct and expense of elections, was under way by the late 17th century and was only partly the result of the corporation's practice of making outsiders freemen. Non-residents qualified by patrimony or apprenticeship were encouraged by the benefits accruing from the parliamentary franchise to take the freedom. When outvoters first outnumbered resident freemen is uncertain but their number increased rapidly in the later 18th century. Of the 447 freemen admitted during the 1789 byelection 358 lived outside the city and of the 1,579 voting in the 1816 byelection only 562, just over a third, lived inside it. At first the outvoters were found mostly in the county but later they were spread over a much wider area. The difficulty of verifying claims of patrimony by persons born in distant places was a reason for the establishment of the committee of freedoms in 1732.[5] Freemen living in London were sufficiently numerous by the 1780 election for one candidate's nephew to entertain them and to make arrangements to send them to Gloucester for the poll. Of the freemen admitted during the 1789 contest over 100 lived in or near London, slightly more than the new outvoters with Gloucestershire addresses, and a substantial number lived in Bristol or its suburbs. Several came from Birmingham and a few from places like Worcester, Upton upon Severn, Hereford, Ledbury, Oxford, and Banbury. The number of outvoters grew in the early 19th century and constituted just under two thirds of the electoral body in 1835, when only 965 of the men listed on the freemen's roll had Gloucester addresses.[6] By comparison, in Oxford, where

[1] *Glouc. Jnl.* 28 June, 5 July, 6 Dec 1819.
[2] Cf. *Rep. Com. Mun. Corp.* 61.
[3] Ibid.
[4] GBR C 9/11.
[5] Ibid. B 3/9, ff. 325v.–326v.
[6] Ibid. C 9/11.

the freedom was also taken up for political reasons and especially during elections, the outvoters made up only a third of the freeman body in the early 19th century.[1]

Thirdly Gloucester freemen increasingly came from a much wider section of society. New freemen in the 1660s were mostly from the city and were drawn from some 68 trades, particularly those of cordwainer, pinmaker, tailor, tanner, and butcher. In the 1820s, when a similar number of trades was represented, many more members of the landed and professional classes, including clergymen, lawyers, military officers, and surgeons, were admitted. The enhanced honorific character of the freedom and the creation of freemen for political purposes were crucial in that change and upward social mobility also played its part. Successive members of families prospering and rising in social position did not eschew freeman status, which was recorded on the posthumous monuments to several of its holders.[2]

Reform and after

The course of the freedom in Gloucester in the 17th and 18th centuries was in its essentials one common to the freedom of many English boroughs. The obsolescence of the once vital connexion with economic activity and the acquisition of a mainly political and honorific character meant in Gloucester as elsewhere that the Reform Act of 1832 was to have a more decisive impact on the freedom of the borough than the Municipal Corporations Act of 1835.[3]

When the Municipal Corporations Commissioners visited Gloucester in September 1833[4] they found the freedom there essential for membership of the common council and the freemen entitled to a number of privileges. The Municipal Corporations Act, which vested the city's government in a council elected by some householders and, in abolishing exclusive trading rights, swept away the redundant legal basis of the freemen's economic monopoly, nonetheless left many privileges intact. Those included rights of common in the city's meadows, exemption from a number of tolls levied in the city, and precedence in admission to certain almshouses. Freemen's rights of common, described in 1833[5] as of no great value, remained a source of dispute particularly with the city corporation. A committee appointed in 1848 to look after freemen's interests took over the management of the city's meadows from the corporation in 1875. Following the resolution of remaining disputes in 1899 the corporation resumed management of the meadows and extinguished the freemen's common rights, which had been exercised latterly by a few butchers and cattle dealers, in parts of them. The £7,095 awarded to the freemen in compensation was invested in 1903 for a charity, which from 1906 provided pensions for freemen and their widows. The endowments of the charity, known as the Freemen's Compensation Fund, were augmented as the freemen surrendered their remaining common rights, a process completed in 1942.[6] The benefit of exemption from toll was gradually reduced. In 1867 the corporation abandoned the collection of dues levied on goods moved through the city[7] and in

[1] *V.C.H. Oxon.* iv. 249–50.
[2] e.g. Bigland, *Glos.* ii. 275; mon. to Hen. Bossom (d. 1828) in Mitcheldean church.
[3] Cf. *Exeter Freemen 1266–1967*, pp. xxvii–xxx.
[4] *Glouc. Jnl.* 21, 28 Sept 1833.
[5] *Rep. Com. Mun. Corp.* 60–1; Municipal Corporations Act, 5 & 6 Wm. IV, c. 76.
[6] *V.C.H. Glos.* iv. 193–4, 358–9; G. Whitcombe, *Gloucester Common Meadows* (1897), 7–9.
[7] *V.C.H. Glos.* iv. 193.

1874 the freemen's right to use the city quay free of toll was abolished.[1] The freemen remained exempt from toll in the cattle market in 1950.[2]

By disfranchising all freemen living more than seven miles from the city the Reform Act of 1832[3] reduced the number of freemen voters by more than half. The Act also extended the parliamentary franchise to some householders and the parliamentary borough was enlarged at the same time.[4] In the immediate aftermath of reform freemen voters, numbering perhaps as few as 800, constituted a majority of the electorate and remained a considerable, if declining, force in Gloucester's politics. Under the 1832 Act the voting rights of future freemen were restricted to those qualifying by patrimony or apprenticeship. Continuing corruption in the conduct of the city's elections encouraged such men to enter the freedom. By paying registration costs and adopting a range of electoral malpractices political parties slowed the decline in the number of freemen. In 1859, when a Royal Commission revealed widespread venality within the electorate, there were 534 freemen voters. They included 197 outvoters, a number which in large part probably reflected recent suburban development just beyond the municipal and parliamentary boundary.[5] By the later 19th century entries by apprenticeship had ceased and, the practices of selling the freedom or conferring it for no payment having been ended by the Municipal Corporations Act, patrimony remained the only qualification for freeman status.[6]

Although the reforms of 1832 and 1835 diminished the corporation's direct influence over elections electoral malpractice continued. It led to Gloucester being denied parliamentary representation between 1859 and 1862 and to one of its members being unseated in 1880 and gave the city a reputation for corrupt elections up to the First World War.[7] The political character of the freedom enabled it to survive the reforms of the 1830s and freemen remained a substantial part of the electorate until their voting rights lapsed with the passage of the Representation of the People Act in 1918.[8] In the mid 1890s there had been about 400 freemen.[9] Political disfranchisement ended an historically important aspect of the freedom but the other benefits ensured that free status, open to the children of freemen on coming of age and paying a fee of 13*s* 6*d*, continued to be attractive. In 1950 there were just over 300 hereditary freemen. Nearly half of them lived in the city.[10] The honorific character of the freedom was revived after 1885 when legislation enabled municipal boroughs to establish a new, purely honorary category of freemen.[11] Gloucester first made use of that power in 1906, since when only ten more men and women have been granted the honorary freedom of the city.[12]

[1] Gloucester Extension and Improvement Act, 37 & 38 Vic. c. 111 (Local), s. 12.
[2] *Freemen of City of Gloucester* (1950), 16: Glos. Colln. NQ 12.27.
[3] Representation of the People Act, 2 Wm. IV, c. 45, ss. 27, 32.
[4] Parliamentary Boundaries Act, 2 & 3 Wm. IV, c. 64, sched. (O).
[5] *V.C.H. Glos.* iv. 154, 206.
[6] Whitcombe, *Gloucester Common Meadows*, 6; *Freemen of City of Gloucester* (1950), 7.
[7] *V.C.H. Glos.* iv. 206–8.
[8] Representation of the People Act, 7 & 8 Geo. V, c. 64, ss. 1, 17.
[9] Whitcombe, *Gloucester Common Meadows*, 6.
[10] *Freemen of City of Gloucester* (1950), 15, 17.
[11] Honorary Freedom of Boroughs Act, 48 & 49 Vic. c. 29.
[12] Below, Appendix III.

Freemen registers as historical sources

The register started in 1641 provided a record of those sworn as freemen after the payment of the required fees, including bucket money, and in the case of entrants by purchase the agreed fine. For gauging how far the registers calendared in this volume constitute a complete record of admissions to the freedom in the following two centuries historians have recourse to other sources, notably the common council's act books[1] and the stewards' or chamberlains' accounts.[2] The act books record not actual admissions but decisions authorizing entries by fine or gift and by apprenticeship in special circumstances. They also give details of the amount of fines and often reasons for gifts of the freedom. The accounts, in addition to recording the receipt of fines, fees, and bucket money, contain lists of new freemen, including those by gift.

Comparison of the various sources reveals occasional discrepancies over names, ways in which the freedom was obtained, and levels of fine. Even cursory examination of the act books and accounts also shows that men awarded the freedom by act of common council and, in some instances, having made the required payments were not invariably registered as freemen. While individuals evidently chose not to take up the freedom for one reason or another, it is clear that some omissions in registration were the result of defects in the registers. A number occurred in the period 1671–5 when the keeping of the registers was particularly poor. In those years few dates of registration were recorded. Later omissions were fewer and some, once discovered, were noted in registers. The development of the freedom as an honour had an impact on the frequency of registrations from the late 17th century. Whereas entrants by patrimony, apprenticeship, and fine needed a formal record of their achievement of free status, freemen by gift often had no motive to register and many did not actually take up the freedom by being sworn in formally. The entry of the Pontypool ironmaster John Hanbury, who was given the freedom by act of 10 July 1690,[3] was not registered yet three of his sons became free by patrimony. Similarly Benjamin Bathurst (d. 1767) of Lydney, who like John Hanbury sat in parliament for the city,[4] does not figure as a new freeman in the registers but two of his sons were admitted by patrimony. From 1790 the names of men awarded the freedom by the common council's act were customarily transcribed into the freeman register regardless of whether they took the oath or not. For those who did the date of their swearing in was sometimes added to their register entries.

Despite limitations the registers provide a basic genealogical source and make an important contribution to historical studies in a number of areas. They yield information about the fortunes and duration of individual families over several generations and about the background of families prominent in public life. The Wiltons, who became the most important family in the city's administration in the late 18th century, provide an interesting example. They were descended from Henry Wilton, a pinmaker in Gloucester in 1725. His son Charles followed the same trade but his grandson Henry Wilton, a freeman from 1760, became a solicitor and laid the foundations for the family's involvement in city government.[5] The registers are also a mine of information about careers. They show that Abel

[1] GBR B 3/2–3, 6–15.
[2] Ibid. F 4/5–16; F 5/8–17, 22–7, 82–3.
[3] Ibid. B 3/6, f. 274.
[4] Williams, *Parl. Hist. of Glos.* 205–6, 209.
[5] *V.C.H. Glos.* 145, 192, 380–1.

Wantner (d. 1714), who compiled the first detailed history of the city and county, was an innkeeper in the city in 1709 as his father had been in 1666.[1] Richard Finch and John Blackwell, who were among leading members of the corporation in the 1740s,[2] had much earlier been apprenticed in the city to a bodice-maker and a baker respectively. From the mid 18th century the registers' value in tracing the progress of individual careers is diminished by the practice in some entries by patrimony of copying details from a father's certificate without regard to any change in his circumstances.

The existence of a substantial body of outvoters makes the registers a useful source for internal migration. It also enables the registers to reveal the origins of several men who rose to prominence outside Gloucester. The artist, and later president of the Royal Academy, Sir Thomas Lawrence entered the freedom by patrimony in 1816 when he was living in London. His father Thomas had been a solicitor and his grandfather William Lawrence a Presbyterian minister. William, who lived for a time at Newbury (Berks.), was apparently the son of a baker Thomas. The latter, having completed an apprenticeship in Gloucester by 1684, had moved to Ledbury (Herefs.) by 1707.[3]

The registers, while indicating the range of trades in Gloucester, are not a directory of trades. The exclusion of many trades from the freedom before 1787[4] makes the registers unsuitable for detailed analyses of occupations and of social structure within the city and how they varied from period to period. The freemen registers are, however, an invaluable supplement to the apprenticeship registers[5] for they show how many apprentices on completion of their service took advantage of their right to free status.

While English urban history has benefited greatly from the frequent publication of apprenticeship registers its understanding of the political and economic roles of freemen has been limited by a comparative lack of readily accessible lists of freemen. The registers calendared in this volume illustrate the nature and structure of the freedom of Gloucester in the centuries beginning with the city's active espousal of the parliamentary cause in the 1640s and ending with the reform of its government and the start of its commercial and industrial expansion in the 1830s. They reflect the significance of the freedom where an oligarchical system of government was riven by political divisions in the later 17th century and where a ruling corporation and its opponents vied to influence parliamentary elections well into the 19th century.

Editorial method

This volume contains a calendar of the text of the Gloucester freemen registers covering the period from 1641 to 1838. The registers are contained in four volumes among the Gloucester borough records deposited in the Gloucestershire Record Office. Among the same records is also a roll recording admissions to the freedom in the years from 1534 to 1564[6] but other freemen registers compiled before 1641

[1] Gray, *Antiquaries*, 45–6; cf. *Trans. B.G.A.S.* xcix. 171.
[2] *V.C.H. Glos.* iv. 379.
[3] *D.N.B.* s.v. Lawrence, Sir Thos.
[4] Cf. GBR B 3/12, f. 86.
[5] The surviving apprenticeship registers for Gloucester cover the periods 1595–1742 and 1765–1834: ibid. C 10/1–4.
[6] Ibid. C 9/6.

have disappeared.[1] At the time of his death Peter Ripley was revising a typescript calendar of the registers for the years 1653–1838 which he had made in 1984 with a view to eventual publication. The present editor, who has written a new introduction and added the register for the years 1641–53, has largely adopted his predecessor's practice in editing the manuscripts for publication.

The present text records all entries in the registers and uses English throughout. The manuscript entries are in Latin between 1641 and 1651 and between 1660 and 1732 and usually employ abbreviations, either with or without the customary signs. The original order of entries and their arrangement by mayoral year (beginning the Monday after Michaelmas) are respected and the calendar year, which up to 1752 started on 25 March, is taken to begin on 1 January throughout. The registers' foliation or pagination is indicated by italic figures in the left-hand margin. An asterisk indicates an incomplete entry. Earlier entries in the registers included the names of men acting as pledges for the payment of fees and sometimes fuller particulars of apprenticeships; this calendar has reduced all entries to a few common forms and includes some information recorded originally as marginalia. The form of each entry depends on the way the freedom was obtained. Wherever appropriate consecutive entries are linked by brackets.

Forenames are given in standard, modern forms and surnames are spelt as in the manuscripts. In entries by patrimony the father's surname is omitted except where to do so may cause confusion. Round brackets within a surname indicate variations in its spelling in the entry concerned. The registers almost invariably supply details of fathers' and masters' occupations and residence and from the mid 18th century they increasingly provide similar information for new freemen by patrimony and apprenticeship. In this calendar the trade or occupation of an entrant by apprenticeship is noted only if it differed from that recorded for his master. Place names are given in their modern forms wherever possible. The symbol † indicates that no place of residence is recorded in the register. To avoid repetition the phrase 'of Gloucester' is generally omitted for residents of the city. It has been retained for Gloucester men whose fathers or masters lived elsewhere and for men described as 'late of Gloucester' but not stated to be deceased. Conciseness has also been achieved by omitting an entrant's place of residence if it was given as the same as that for his father or master. Where the calendar indicates that a father or master had changed residence the entrant's residence is included if it was not the later place. Counties are given as in the registers but are omitted for large and county towns and for Gloucestershire towns and parishes. Manuscript readings are given in italics and brackets when renderings of personal and place names are doubtful and when the form is unusual.

Many entries by fine and gift were recorded solely as 'by act of common council'. Information on the method of entry supplied from the common council act books is given in round brackets as are other details collated from the same source. Square brackets enclose other material added by the present editor. Footnotes have been used for textual matters and particulars relevant to the acquisition of the freedom. Biographical information in footnotes is limited to details pertinent to Gloucester such as service as one of its parliamentary representatives or tenure of one of its benefices.

John Juřica
March 1991

[1] Cf. ibid. B 3/3, p. 779.

ACKNOWLEDGEMENTS

In preparing this calendar of the Gloucester freemen registers I have been indebted to David Smith for his encouragement and his invaluable and sensible advice. I am also grateful to Nicholas Herbert for suggestions about the introductory section, to Jeremy Fennell for help with the translation of the oldest surviving text of the freeman's oath, and to Brian Frith and Joyce Popplewell for information about certain freemen. For this project Peter Ripley began a revision of his 1984 typescript calendar of the registers. In completing that task I have had access to his notes and assistance from the staff of the Gloucestershire Record Offfice.

John Juřica

ABBREVIATIONS AND SYMBOLS USED IN THE CALENDAR AND APPENDICES

Adm.	Admiral
ald.	alderman
Alex.	Alexander
And.	Andrew
Ant.	Anthony
app.	apprentice
B.A.	Bachelor of Arts
Beds.	Bedfordshire
Benj.	Benjamin
Berks.	Berkshire
Brec.	Breconshire
Brig.-Gen.	Brigadier-General
Bt.	Baronet
Bucks.	Buckinghamshire
Carms.	Carmarthenshire
Chas.	Charles
Ches.	Cheshire
Chris.	Christopher
Col.	Colonel
Dan.	Daniel
D.C.L.	Doctor of Civil Law
D.D.	Doctor of Divinity
decd.	deceased
Derb.	Derbyshire
Dors.	Dorset
Dr.	Doctor
D.S.O.	Companion of the Distinguished Service Order
Edm.	Edmund
Edw.	Edward
esq.	esquire
Flints.	Flintshire
G.B.E.	Dame Grand Cross of the Order of the British Empire
G.C.V.O.	Knight or Dame Grand Cross of the Royal Victorian Order
Gen.	General
gent.	gentleman
Geo.	George
Geof.	Geoffrey
Glam.	Glamorgan
Glos.	Gloucestershire
Hants.	Hampshire
Hen.	Henry
Herefs.	Herefordshire
Herts.	Hertfordshire
H.M.	His or Her Majesty('s)
H.R.H.	His or Her Royal Highness
Humph.	Humphrey
Jas.	James
Jos.	Joseph
K.G.	Knight of the Garter
Kt.	Knight
Lancs.	Lancashire
Lawr.	Lawrence
Leics.	Leicestershire
Leon.	Leonard
Lieut.	Lieutenant
Lincs.	Lincolnshire
LL.D.	Doctor of Laws
Lt.-Col.	Lieutenant-Colonel
Lt.-Gen.	Lieutenant-General
M.A.	Master of Arts
Maj.-Gen.	Major-General
Mat.	Matthew
Maur.	Maurice
M.B.	Bachelor of Physic or Medicine
M.D.	Doctor of Medicine
Mdx.	Middlesex
Mic.	Michael
Mon.	Monmouthshire
Mont.	Montgomeryshire
M.P.	Member of Parliament
Nat.	Nathaniel
n.d.	no date given
Nic.	Nicholas
Norf.	Norfolk
Northants.	Northamptonshire
Notts.	Nottinghamshire
Oxon.	Oxfordshire
P.C.	Privy Counsellor
Pemb.	Pembrokeshire
Phil.	Philip
R.A.	Royal Artillery
Radnors.	Radnorshire
R.E.	Royal Engineers
Rear-Adm.	Rear-Admiral

Revd.	Reverend	Suff.	Suffolk
Ric.	Richard	Surr.	Surrey
R.M.	Royal Marines	Suss.	Sussex
R.N.	Royal Navy	Thos.	Thomas
Rob.	Robert	V.	Viscount
Rog.	Roger	V.C.	Victoria Cross
Salop.	Shropshire	Ven.	Venerable
Sam.	Samuel	Wal.	Walter
Som.	Somerset	Warws.	Warwickshire
Staffs.	Staffordshire	Wilts.	Wiltshire
Steph.	Stephen	Worcs.	Worcestershire
S.T.P.	*Sacrae Theologiae Professor* (Professor of Divinity, old form of D.D.)	Wm.	William
		Yorks.	Yorkshire

* incomplete entry
† no place of residence given
‡ resigned 21 Jan 1820: GBR B 3/13, ff. 265–6
¶ disfranchised by judgement of King's Bench, Michaelmas 1819
x see footnote

GBR G10/2

3 **City of Gloucester**

The names entered in the guildhall of the said city of the burgesses of the said city made and sworn in the time of John Scriven, esq., mayor . . .

	1641	25 Oct	Hen. Edwards, son of Ric., baker
		n.d.	Wm. Smith, app. of Giles Crumps, cordwainer
		n.d.	Wm. Carter, son of Wm. [?and] app. of Anselm Stallard[1]
		22 Nov	Moses Beaton, app. of his father Moses, plumber[2]
			Thos. Feild, son of Thos., gent., decd.
			Ric. Whitfeild, son of Ric., cordwainer
3v		29 Nov	Rob. Longdan, app. of John Scriven, mayor
		22 Dec	Rob. Knight, app. of Nat. Knight, chandler
		24 Dec	Wm. Wood by fine of 20 nobles[3]
	1642	14 Jan	Wm. Peirson, (public notary), by fine of £5
		17 Jan	Edw. Kemp, son of John, yeoman
		31 Jan	Chris Savorey, app. of Wm. Wantner, blacksmith
4		14 Feb	Edm. Bick by fine of £6 13*s* 4*d*
		28 Feb	Francis Pace alias Panrice, app. of Anne Hayes, baker
		14 Mar	Thos. Iles, app. of John Woodward, blacksmith
		9 May	Thos. Colchester, app. of John Edwards, haberdasher
		16 May	Giles Gilbert, app. of Thos. Cooke, chandler
		23 May	Wm. Wilks, app. of Rob. Brethers, cardmaker
4v		13 June	Jos. Nurse, son of Phil. [?and] app. of Giles Crumpe, husbandman[4]
		20 June	Sam. Taylor, app. of Wm. Jennings, barber-surgeon
		27 June	Thos. Heath, app. of Ric. Heath, pewterer
		1 Aug	Humph. Harris, app. of Wal. Harris, cordwainer
		8 Aug	Rob. Corr by fine of £6 13*s* 4*d*
		22 Aug	Dan. Palmer, (labourer), by fine of £5
5		26 Sept	Edw. Charleton, son of Edw., wiredrawer

Dennis Wise, esq., mayor 1642–3

	1643	30 Jan	Thos. Onyon, son of Humph., sievemaker, app. of Wm. Hale, silkweaver
		23 June	John Gravestock, app. of Wal. Strawford, butcher
		8 July	Rog. Davis by fine of 26*s* 8*d*[5]
			Wm. Madocks, app. of John Whithorne, tailor[6]

[1] By apprenticeship: GBR F 4/5, f. 172.

[2] Entrant or his father disfranchised 3 May 1643 for leaving the city, then preparing for a royalist attack, and readmitted by act of 20 June 1643 by fine of £10: ibid. B 3/2, pp. 245, 256, 266.

[3] Having married a freeman's widow: ibid. p. 204.

[4] By apprenticeship: ibid. F 4/5, f. 172.

[5] For service to the city 'to the hazard of his life': ibid. B 3/2, p. 267.

[6] Entry preceded by note that Madocks had been discharged from serving the last six months of his apprenticeship.

5v			**Nicholas Webb, esq., mayor 1643–4**
	1644	29 Jan	John Hobson, app. of Wm. Fowler, mercer
			John Bingle, app. of Rog. Hill, cooper
		12 Feb	Thos. Mellechep, son of Nic., app. of Humph. Hiron the elder, chandler
		19 Feb	Ric. Cowles, app. of Rob. Cowles, butcher
		18 Mar	Clement Dowle, app. of Dennis Wise, mercer
		15 Apr	Rob. Dobbs, son of Ric., cordwainer
		23 May	Ric. Griffith,[1] cook,† (by gift) at request of (Col.) Edw. Massey, governor of Gloucester
6		n.d.	Wal. Hill the younger, cobbler, by fine of £5*[2]
		29 July	Nic. Webb, son of Nic., esq., mayor
		6 Aug	John Bishop by fine of £5
		12 Aug	Ant. Palmer, son of John, cooper
		26 Aug	Gilbert Jones, son of John, innholder
			Thos. Vaughan, son of Ric., joiner
6v		3 Sept	Nic. Snell, gent., by fine of £10[3]
			Luke Nurse, esq., mayor 1644–5
		7 Oct	Wm. Endall, son of John, butcher
		19 Oct	Nic. Haines late of Bristol by fine of £10[4]
		5 Nov	John Welsteede, blacksmith, by fine of £5 13*s* 4*d*[5]
		11 Nov	John Hunt by gift[6]
		2 Nov	John Elliotts, app. of Arthur Cugley, wiredrawer
7	1645	31 Jan	Thos. Feilding, victualler, by fine of £5[7]
			David Davis, son of Jas., broadweaver, app. of John Payne, feltmaker
		12 May	Thos. Parker, app. of John Pincke, baker
			John Randle by fine of £5
			Abel Lewes by fine of £8
		2 June	Ric. Nelme, son of John, mercer, decd.
		11 Aug	Wal. Vaysey, tailor, by fine of £5[8]
7v			Thos. Pullen, tailor, by fine of 5 marks[9]
		18 Aug	Alex. Neast,[10] app. of Wm. Hichins, silkweaver
		25 Aug	Hen. Anstee,[11] son of Randle, butcher
		1 Sept	Wm. Perry, brewer, by fine of £6 13*s* 4*d*
		18 Aug	Dan. Colericke, bodice-maker, by fine of 4 marks[12]
		15 Sept	Hen. Hayes, son of Hen., shearman
8		22 Sept	Thos. Mason, son of Edw., saddler, decd.
			Augustine Gwyn, son of Augustine, cordwainer

[1] Ric. Griffin: GBR B 3/2, p. 301.
[2] By act of 3 July 1644: ibid. p. 304.
[3] Having married a freeman's daughter: ibid. p. 307.
[4] On undertaking to employ 100 poor inhabitants of Gloucester in making jersey stockings: ibid. p. 316.
[5] By fine of 5 marks and 'to remit 40*s* for screws and 7*s* 8*d* for firing of muskets due unto him from the city': ibid. p. 319.
[6] A freeman's son, who has sustained great losses: ibid.
[7] Having married a freeman's daughter: ibid. p. 322.
[8] Having married a freeman's daughter: ibid. p. 334.
[9] Having married a freeman's daughter and his house having been ruined during the siege of 1643: ibid.
[10] Chris. Neast: ibid. F 4/5, f. 266v.
[11] Hen. Randle: ibid.
[12] Husband of Mary, widow of Toby Kible killed after capture by royalists at Maisemore leaving four small children: ibid. B 3/2, p. 332.

			John Horrald, (tailor), by fine of £6 13*s* 4*d*
		2 Oct	Hen. Browne, servant of Luke Nurse, mayor[1]
			Jas. Ricketts, app. of John Wood, tanner[2]
		28 Oct	Jos. Byford, app. of Phil. Ward[3]
8v			**Lawrence Singleton, esq., mayor 1645–6**
		24 Nov	Giles Reeve, (gunsmith), by fine of 20 nobles[4]
			John Lenthall, esq.,† by gift[5]
			Jos. Edwards,[6] son of Wm., clothier, late of Gloucester
		n.d.	John Luellin, cordwainer, (by gift)*[7]
		15 Dec	John Fones, app. of Edm. Sturmy, glover
			Thos. Steephens by fine of £8
9		n.d.	John Barnewood† by fine of £5[8]
		n.d.	Ric. Cox, son of John, cordwainer
		n.d.	Thos. Jelf, app. of Ric. Herd, baker
		n.d.	John Wyneatt, app. of Rob. Brethers, cardmaker
		n.d.	Thos. Trippett, app. of Ric. Taylor, mercer
9v	1646	19 Feb	Edw. Elliotts, son of Hen., tailor
			Thos. Hall, app. of John Nicholls, tanner
		16 Feb	Ric. Wood† by fine of £5[9]
			Rob. Jones, son of Rob., butcher
		n.d.	Ric. Teeckle, ropemaker, (by fine of 40*s*)[10]
		n.d.	John Milton, son of John, cordwainer
10		2 Mar	Thos. Robinson, son of John, cordwainer
		16 Mar	Thos. Jones, son of Thos., victualler
		23 Mar	Rob. Elme, app. of Chris Hodges, mercer
		24 Mar	Hen. Robins, gent., by fine of £8 6*s* 8*d*[11]
			Giles Badger, app. of Ric. Hayes, cutler
10v		31 Mar	Edw. Grevill, app. of Giles Grevill, mercer, decd.
			Jas. Davis, app. of John Hurte, clothier
		30 Apr[12]	Zachariah (*Esekiall*) Gregory, app. of Hen. Gregory, butcher
		[ ] Apr[13]	Thos. Wright, innholder, by fine (of £10)
			Dan. Birdde, app. of Simon Pryor, feltmaker
		4 June	Ric. Pell,[14] son of Pauncefoot, gent., decd.
10A		22 July	John Marten, app. of John Smith, baker
			Wm. Hayes, son of Ric., cutler

[1] *pays nil fine and for two leather buckets*; admitted at the mayor's request as if an apprentice: ibid. p. 349.

[2] Entry recorded under the following mayoralty in ibid. F 4/5, f. 306.

[3] Entry belongs to following mayoralty.

[4] By fine of £5: GBR B 3/2, p. 356.

[5] Only son of Wm. Lenthall, recorder of Gloucester, 'who has very well merited of us': ibid. p. 358. Entry followed by note that John Lenthall was elected M.P. for the city the following day in place of Hen. Brett, who had defected to royalist Oxford. Wm. Lenthall, Speaker of the Long Parliament, was elected M.P. for Gloucester in 1654 but chose to represent another constituency: cf. *V.C.H. Glos.* iv. 85, 94–5; Williams, *Parl. Hist. of Glos.* 195–6.

[6] Wm. Edwards of London: GBR F 4/5, ff. 305–6.

[7] 'Being a poor impotent man and having a great family': ibid. B 3/2, p. 356.

[8] Having served the city during the siege of 1643: ibid. p. 363.

[9] Having married John Young's widow: ibid. p. 369; F 4/5, f. 306.

[10] By act of 16 Feb 1646, son of Sam., decd., a freeman, on his promise to take one of his brothers as app. and to support another during his minority: ibid. B 3/2, p. 370.

[11] A brewer, having married a freeman's widow: ibid. p. 371; F 4/5, f. 305v.

[12] Day struck through.

[13] *Sworn in court, Apr.*

[14] On his appointment as attorney in the city's courts in place of his father: ibid. B 3/2, p. 374.

			Wm. Baker, app. of Phil. Tilsley, pinmaker
		n.d.	Rob. Atkins, son of John, baker, decd.
		3 Aug	Hen. Purlewent, son of Arthur, yeoman
			Rob. Cowdle, son of Rob., yeoman, decd.
			Hen. Barrett, app. of Thos. Barrett, cutler
10Av		24 Aug	Ant. Savage, app. of John Browne, wiredrawer
		?[1]	John Turner, app. of Thos. Turner, cook
		31 Aug	Ric. Nash, app. of Ric. Window, chandler
		4 Oct	John Saunders, clothworker, by fine of £5
			Thos. Child, maltmaker, by fine of £5
11			Hen. Stephens, gent., by fine of £15[2]
			John Hayward, feltmaker, by fine of £5

Jasper Clutterbooke, esq., mayor 1646–7

		9 Oct	Edw. Mason, son of Edw., saddler
		12 Oct	John Willmotts, app. of Wm. Browne, pewterer
		22 Oct	Rob. Cleevly, app. of Ric. Cooke, chandler
		26 Oct	Wal. Taynton, son of Wal., mercer
			John Jones, son of Rob., butcher
11v			Ric. Greene, son of Hercules, upholsterer
			Sam. Evans, wiredrawer, by gift[3]
		2 Nov	Thos. Fleminge, tailor, by fine of £5
			Isaac Williams, tailor, by fine of £5
			Hen. Elliotts, joiner, son of Hen., tailor
			John Fawlkner by patrimony*
12		3 Nov	Thos. Appowell, app. of Ric. Symons, glover
			Wm. Jelly alias Jollie, glover, by fine of £6 13*s* 4*d*
			Thos. Showell, maltster, by fine of £5
		10 Nov	John Gilberd, app. of Anne Hayes, widow, baker
			Jos. Thomas, son of Wm., cordwainer
12v		27 Nov	Thos. Allen, app. of Edm. Collett, tanner
			Chas. Anstee, son of Randle, butcher
		7 Dec	Ric. Greening, tailor, by fine of £5
			John Dew, victualler, by fine of £5[4]
			Wm. Brimiard by gift
			John Lewes by gift
			Thos. Meriman, carpenter, by gift
13		28 Dec	Hen. Dowdeswell alias Wheeler, app. of Hen. Selwyn, cordwainer
		n.d.	Rob. Symes, app. of Rob. Payne, mercer
		n.d.	John Barrat, app. of his father Thos., cutler
		n.d.	Wm. Fewterell alias Fewterer, son of Wm., tailor
		n.d.	[Lieut.][5] Thos. Barnes, plumber, by fine of 20 nobles[6]
	1647	18 Jan	Edw. Tyther by fine of £10[7]
			John Parrish, app. of Wm. Fewterell, tailor
13v			John Walker, son of Ant.
		23 Jan	Cornelius Plott, tailor, by fine of 20 nobles

[1] *Sworn in court.*
[2] Maltster, having married a freeman's widow: GBR B 3/2, p. 381; F 4/5, f. 303v.
[3] An aged and impotent man, for service to the city: ibid. B3/2, p. 386.
[4] By fine of £8: ibid. p. 390.
[5] Ibid. F 4/5, ff. 304, 306 and v.
[6] By act of 7 Jan 1647, having married a freeman's daughter: ibid. B 3/2, p. 393.
[7] Not to use the trade of mercer or grocer in the city: ibid.

	1 Feb	Geo. Farly, cutler, by fine of 5 marks[1]
	17 Feb	Wal. Beard, tailor, by gift[2]
	1 Mar	Phil. Griffith, yeoman, by fine of £8[3]
		(Captain) Wm. Rissall, gent., by fine of £13 16*s* 8*d*[4]
	n.d.	Thos. Hale, app. of Jas. Freeman, feltmaker
14	1 Mar	Thos. Fletcher, app. of Ric. Nash, tanner
	15 Mar	Jasper Lugg, app. of his father Jasper, tanner
	n.d.	John Gwilliam, son of John, clerk, decd., (by fine of £3 6*s* 8*d*)[5]
	n.d.	John Symons, victualler, by gift[6]
	n.d.	John Baker, son of Jas., butcher
14v	n.d.	Chris. Hayes, son of Hen., clothworker
	n.d.	Wm. Whittington, son of Rob., apothecary
	n.d.	Wm. Cooper, victualler, by fine of 20 nobles[7]
	n.d.	Arthur Ingley, weaver, by fine of 5 nobles[8]
	n.d.	Wm. Lewes, app. of John Craker, garter-weaver
	n.d.	John Symon, app. of John Thomas, cordwainer
	n.d.	Ric. Hancox, weaver, by gift[9]
15	n.d.	Thos. Husse, victualler,[10] by fine of 20 nobles
	n.d.	Thos. Bicke by gift[11]
	21 June	Dan. Welsteed, app. of Rob. Tyther, gent., tanner
	5 July	Thos. Turner, son of Thos., cook, late of Gloucester
	12 July	Jas. Church, carpenter, by gift[12]
	15 July	Steph. Holford, gent., son of Steph., gent., by gift
	26 July	Nat. Burwell, fellmonger, by fine of £5
15v	2 Aug	Wm. Swayne, lantern-maker, by fine of 5 marks
	12 Aug	Geof. Harward, son of Ric., draper
		Peter Haynes, app. of Humph. Hieron, chandler
	16 Aug	Ric. Overton, son of Ric., butcher
16		Brice Barrow, son of Rob., butcher
		Thos. Floucke, app. of Wm. Lugg, tanner, ald.
		Thos. Robinson, butcher
	17 Aug	John Moure, app. of Wm. Packer, tanner
	23 Aug	Wm. Blicke, app. of Geof. Beale, mercer and one of the city's stewards
	26 Aug	Dan. Washborne by fine of £5
16v	n.d.	John Hunt, app. of John Craker, garter-weaver
	10 Sept	Ric. Couper, app. of Thos. Pierce, mercer
	13 Sept	John Sturmy, son of Rob.

[1] Having served an apprenticeship in the city's suburbs and married a freeman's daughter: ibid. p. 396.

[2] On condition he takes a younger child of Joan Holmes as app.: ibid. p. 399.

[3] Having married a freeman's daughter: ibid.

[4] Having married a freeman's daughter: ibid.

[5] By act of 9 Apr 1647, entrant's father, vicar of Down Hatherley at his death in 1640, having often preached in the city: ibid. p. 402; Hockaday Abs. ccxxxvii.

[6] By act of 26 Apr 1647, a sergeant in Thos. Pury's company, having married a freeman's daughter: GBR B 3/2, p. 405; cf. Williams, *Parl. Hist. of Glos.* 198.

[7] By act of 13 May 1647, had had six houses in Southgate Street burned down, presumably at the siege of 1643: GBR B 3/2, p. 412; cf. *V.C.H. Glos.* iv. 94.

[8] By act of 13 May 1647, having married a freeman's daughter and been a soldier in the Gloucester garrison: GBR B 3/2, pp. 411–2.

[9] By act of 13 May 1647, to make him eligible for entry to one of the city's almshouses: ibid. p. 412.

[10] By act of 4 June 1648, soldier: ibid. p. 414.

[11] By act of 13 May 1647, to make him eligible for an almsman's place: ibid. p. 412.

[12] To make him eligible for an almsman's place: ibid. p. 419.

			Jas. Slicer, app. of Wm. Lugg, tanner, ald., decd.
			Sergeant Webb, son of Sergeant
17		17 Sept	John Addames, son of John, broadweaver
		20 Sept	Wal. Whitehorne, app. of John Jordan, baker
		22 Sept	Grey Cox, son of Ric., innholder
		n.d.	John Tarne, son of Thos., glover
		27 Sept	Edw. Abbotts, son of Ric., tailor
		n.d.	Wm. Davis, app. of Francis Baughe, cordwainer
17v		4 Oct	Edw. Aingell, clothworker, [by apprenticeship][1]
			Hen. Prichard, app. of John Bearne, mercer

John Madocke, esq., mayor 1647–8

		21 Oct	Thos. Yate, app. of Jas. Comalyne, apothecary
		22 Nov	(Captain) Wm. Stapp, gent., by fine of 20 marks[2]
	1648	1 Jan	Ant. Hale, carrier, by fine of 20 nobles
18		12 Jan	Hen. Norris, gent., late of Slimbridge by fine of £15[3]
		17 Jan	Wm. Cooke, app. of Anne Hayes, widow
		10 Mar	John Smalewood, app. of Chris. Townsing, barber, decd.
		11 Mar	Wm. Higgs, app. of John Webb, mercer, ald., (decd.), by fine of £10[4]
		20 Mar	Ric. Tayler, app. of Giles Webly
18v			Thos. Prince, gent., late of Hartpury by fine of £5[5]
		17 Apr	Jo(hn) Isold, (millwright), by gift[6]
		24 Apr	Hen. Carter, app. of Lawr. Allen, chandler
		29 May	Hen. Church, tailor, by fine of £5[7]
			Ric. Talbott, app. of Ric. Jeynes, tanner
19		6 June	John Halford, clerk, son of Steph. Holford, gent.
		12 June	Ric. Wells (by fine of £6)
		n.d.	Ric. Smart, app. of Wm. Phelps, shoemaker
		7 Aug	Thos. Aldridge,[8] app. of Wm. Beard, tailor
		11 Aug	Edm. Palmer, son of Edm., baker, decd.
19v		3 July	Wm. Powell, (haulier), by fine of £8 for work he did for the city[9]
		25 Aug	Edw. Fewterell, app. of Wm. Fewterell, tailor
		18 Aug	Rowland Greene (of Churcham)† by fine of £13 6*s* 8*d*[10]
		28 Sept	John Whyte, (one of the city's waits),† by fine of £5
		29 Sept	Thos. Younge, app. of Ric. Humphreyes, tailor
			John Browne, son of John, butcher
20		n.d.	Humph. Wingott† by gift[11]
		n.d.	Sam. Warner (of Haresfield)† by fine of £13 6*s* 8*d*[12]

[1] Ibid. F 4/5, f. 334v. Entry later amended, incorrectly, to become the first of John Madocke's mayoralty.

[2] Lately married Sarah, widow of Wm. Paite, freeman: ibid. B 3/2, p. 439.

[3] Having married a freeman's daughter: ibid. p. 433.

[4] Webb died before Higgs completed his apprenticeship: ibid. p. 447.

[5] At instance of Wm. Lenthall, recorder of Gloucester, for service to the city during the 1643 siege: ibid. p. 445.

[6] For service during the siege: ibid. p. 450.

[7] Had married a daughter of Edw. Harris, master of the tailors' company: ibid. p. 451.

[8] Ric. Aldridge: ibid. F 4/5, f. 363.

[9] For paving the way to Quay Lane at Bearland: ibid. B 3/2, p. 451.

[10] Having married a daughter of Ald. Jas. Stephens: ibid. p. 463; cf. *V.C.H. Glos.* iv. 377.

[11] By act of 25 Sept 1648, having done good service during plague and the Civil Wars whereby he had become disabled: GBR B 3/2, p. 467.

[12] By acts of 25 July and 25 Sept 1648, having married a granddaughter of Ald. John Baugh, decd.: ibid. pp. 463, 467; cf. *V.C.H. Glos.* iv. 377.

		2 Oct	John Danghby by gift
			(Captain) John Evans by fine of 20 marks
			(Henry Cugley, esq., mayor 1648–9)
		n.d.	Morgan Williams by gift[1]
		n.d.	John Milles, app. of Edw. Charleton, cordwainer
20v		n.d.	John Braunch, app. of Ric. Tayler, mercer
		17 Nov[2]	Sam. Pace, app. of Humph. Harris, baker
		n.d.	Rob. Mercer, son of Hen., yeoman
		13 Nov	Humph. Morse, app. of John Taylor, chandler
			Wm. Collyer† by fine of 40*s*[3]
21		n.d.	Wm. Hayward, sievemaker (*siveyer*), by fine of 40*s*
		20 Nov	Rowland Curr by fine of £10
			Edm. Clarke,[4] joiner, son of Hen.
		27 Nov	Thos. Goslinge, app. of his father John
			Ric. Mills, son of Wm., app. of Geo. Willets
21v		4 Dec	Toby Hunt alias Tonne, son of Toby Hunt late of Gloucester
		11 Dec	Thos. Price, victualler, by fine of £5[5]
		18 Dec	Edw. Symonds, app. of Steph. Doughton, wiredrawer†
		22 Dec	John Mathewes, app. of Arthur Cugley, wiredrawer
		23 Dec	Sam. Browster, son of John, ald.
22		26 Dec	And. Stratford, son of Arthur, late of Gloucester
	1649	21 Jan[6]	Wm. Hodges, son of Nat., gent.
		14 Jan	Godfrey Phones, app. of John Atkins, cordwainer
			Hen. Bradley, son of Joan [and] app. of Edw. Sheppard, feltmaker, [by apprenticeship][7]
		26 Jan	Ric. Hands, (mason), son of Wm.,† by fine of £6
22v		26 Feb	Thos. Morse, son of John, broadweaver, late of Gloucester
		26 Mar	Geo. Mitchell, son of Ric., decd., [and] app. of Margaret Craker, garter-weaver, [by apprenticeship][8]
		29 Mar	Thos. Grove, son of Ant., of London
		13 Apr	Edm. Cartwright, son of Edm. [and] app. of John Pinke, baker, [by apprenticeship][9]
			Phil. Hilly, app. of Lawr. Singleton, woollen-draper, ald.
23		30 Apr	Ric. Whittorne, son of John
			Ric. Malson, app. of Winston Coxe, shoemaker
		3 May	Thos. Deane, app. of Wm. Woodward, blacksmith
		10 May	Thos. Mills, app. of Edw. Charleton, wiredrawer
		2 July	Wm. Wintle, app. of John Edwards, haberdasher, and his wife Elizabeth
23v			Thos. Hickes, app. of Thos. Good, tailor
			Rhys (*Riceus*) Nicholls† by fine of £5
		30 July	Thos. Burrowes, son of Nat., cordwainer, decd.

[1] By act of 6 Oct 1648, a poor blind man long resident in the city: GBR B 3/2, p. 472.

[2] Altered from *Oct*.

[3] Son of Ant., gunsmith, decd., on condition he brings up his sister without charge to his parish: GBR B 3/2, p. 475.

[4] Edw. Clarke: ibid. F 4/5, f. 388v.

[5] Possibly had been disfranchised 3 May 1643 for leaving the city while it anticipated a royalist attack: ibid. B 3/2, pp. 245, 256.

[6] Or *1 Jan 1649*.

[7] GBR F 4/5, f. 387v.

[8] Ibid. f. 387.

[9] Ibid. f. 387v.

			John Smith, app. of Eleanor Hill, widow, barber
		n.d.	John Richardson, sawyer, by gift[1]
24		n.d.	Rob. Willmotts, app. of Oliver Stephens, saddler
		n.d.	John Cowcher, app. of John Powell, pinmaker
		n.d.	Thos. Payne, app. of Ric. Wilkins, wiredrawer
		27 Aug	Hen. Phenix, (pinmaker, of Gloucester)† by fine of £5[2]
		n.d.	Wm. Wheeler, (tailor),† by fine of £5[3]
		n.d.	Giles Ockford, son of Giles, weaver, late of Gloucester
24v		n.d.	John Brewster, gent., son of John, ald., decd.
		10 Sept	John Woodward,[4] son of John, gent., late of Gloucester
		20 Sept	Wm. Freeman, app. of Jas. Willis, tanner
		24 Sept	Wm. Tailor, son of Thos., decd.
			John Hathorne† by fine of 20 marks
25			**James Stephens, esq., mayor 1649–50**
		8 Oct	Wm. Aspyn, son of Wm., decd.†
			Ric. Wooley, app. of John Pincke†
		29 Oct	Ric. Tayler, son of Jas., cutler
		12 Nov	Wm. Roberts, son of Wm., decd.
25v		19 Nov	Ric. Ricketts, (cordwainer),† by gift[5]
		3 Dec	Nic. Barnewood, son of Jas., seaman
		10 Dec	Thos. Horsinton, app. of John Shipton, bodice-maker
			Sam King, tailor, by fine of £6 13*s* 4*d*
			Thos. Phelps, son of Wm.
		14 Dec	Ant. Roberts, son of Hen., pewterer
26		24 Dec	Jas. Phillips, son of Wm., haberdasher, decd.
		30 Dec	Wm. Hurleston, son of Giles, of Maisemore, [and] app. of Brian Jennings,† [by apprenticeship][6]
	1650	11 Mar	Hen. Moore, son of Thos., fletcher
		22 Mar	John Gythens, app. of Wm. Singleton, woollen-draper
		1 Apr	Geof. Flecher† by fine of £6 13*s* 4*d*
		27 Apr	Thos. Hill, app. of John Bullricke, garter-weaver
		29 Apr	Thos. Saunders, app. of Jasper Lugg, tanner, decd.
26v		10 May	Wm. Syms, app. of Hen. Prichard, mercer
			Thos. Baily, son of John, glover
		13 May	Francis Bennett, son of Thos., wiredrawer, by gift[7]
		24 May	John Titcombe, son of Ric. plumber
			John Williamson, (serjeant),† by fine of £5[8]
		14 June	Jonathan Thomas, son of Wm.†[9]
			Lancelot Carter, app. of Ralph Butter, currier
			Jonathan Thomas, son of Wm.†[10]
27		26 June	Wm. Stowell, app. of Phil. Tilsy, pinmaker, decd.

[1] By act of 11 June 1649, to make him, an old disabled man, eligible for an almsman's place, his son having been slain during the siege: ibid. B 3/2, p. 506.

[2] For having lived long in the city and kept poor people at work: ibid. p. 500.

[3] By act of 29 Jan 1649: ibid. p. 491.

[4] Allowed the freedom notwithstanding service in the king's army: ibid. p. 516.

[5] An elderly man with an elderly wife and few means, his house and goods having been burned during the siege: ibid. p. 529.

[6] Ibid. F 4/5, f. 402v.

[7] A freeman's son in much want: ibid. B 3/2, p. 550.

[8] On marriage to Elizabeth, daughter of Humph. Beale, decd.: ibid. p. 551.

[9] Entry struck through and repeated below: ibid. G 10/2, f. 26v.

[10] Cf. above: ibid.

		28 June	Thos. Wood, son of John, tanner, decd.[1]
		8 July	Wm. Barnesdale, victualler, by fine of £10[2]
		2 July	Rob. Giddens, brewer, by fine of 20 nobles
		14 July	Jas. King, scrivener, by gift[3]
		1 Aug	Wm. Chaundler, app. of Anne Haies, widow, baker
27v		16 Aug	John Taylor, son of Geo., cordwainer
		19 Aug	Thos. Meeke, app. of Rob. Reynolds, currier
		23 Aug	Hen. Medway† by fine of £5[4]
		2 Sept	Hen. Hunte, (tiler),† by gift[5]
		9 Sept	Thos. Browninge, son of Thos., serjeant
28		16 Sept	Hen. Davis, son of Thos., cobbler
		23 Sept	Edw. Powell, app. of Ric. Wintle, cordwainer
			Thos. Prior, app. of Simon Prior, feltmaker
		21 Oct	Lawr. Horner, son of Wm., decd.[6]
28v			**Anthony Edwards, esq., mayor 1650–1**
		14 Oct	Jeremiah Badger, app. of Albert Addames, broadweaver, decd.
			Thos. Greene, son of Edm., cordwainer
			Wm. Holtham, app. of Ric. Windowe, chandler, decd.
		18 Oct	Thos. Weaver, son of Francis, butcher
29		25 Nov	Wm. Nichols, bricklayer, by fine of £8
			John Wingod† by fine of £15[7]
		21 Oct	Lawr. Horner, son of Wm., decd.[8]
		6 Dec	Chas. Hoare, son of Thos., decd.
		16 Dec	Ric. Eliots, son of Edw., decd.
		n.d.	Ant. Rogers, yeoman, by fine of £15[9]
29v	1651	7 Feb	Ric. Niblet, app. of Wm. Fewtrell, tailor, decd.
		10 Mar	Steph. Downebell, vintner, by fine of £5[10]
		17 Mar	Giles Bishoppe, app. of Ric. Coxe, mercer
		24 Mar	Wm. Seaman† by fine of £20
		14 Apr	John Greene, son of John, cooper
			John Lugge, son of Ric., tanner, decd.
30		21 Apr	Thos. Aram, app. of John Browne, mercer
		25 Apr	Wm. Hore by gift
		28 Apr	Thos. Lamburne by fine of £5[11]
		12 May	Ric. Bosly, app. of Wm. Lane, feltmaker
30v		9 June	Lewis (*Lodwicke*) Gwyn, app. of Thos. Stephens, pinmaker†
			John Beeke, app. of Phil. Tilsey, pinmaker†
		23 June	Thos. Kemply† by fine of £5
			Edw. Eckly† by fine of £6[12]
			Hen. Eckly† by fine of £6[13]

[1] Entry preceded by note that Ric. Wood of Tuffley, gent., undertook that entrant would not be impleaded for any bargain, or contract he made during his minority.
[2] Having married Anne, widow of Edw. Coucher: GBR B 3/2, pp. 554, 556.
[3] By act of 7 Dec 1649, for making a table on which to record names of mayors and sheriffs: ibid. p. 530.
[4] Had married Joan, daughter of John Nicholls, tanner: ibid. p. 562.
[5] Having lived long and done good service in the city: ibid. p. 568.
[6] Entry, belonging to following mayoralty, is repeated below: ibid. G 10/2, f. 29.
[7] Having married the widow of Miles Keene, freeman: ibid. B 3/2, p. 582.
[8] Cf. above: ibid. G 10/2, f. 28.
[9] By act of 13 Dec 1650: ibid. B 3/2, p. 592.
[10] Having married a freeman's daughter: ibid. p. 600.
[11] Having married a freeman's daughter: ibid. p. 607.
[12] Not to use the trade of mercer in the city: ibid. p. 615.
[13] Not to use the trade of mercer in the city: ibid.

		30 June	Edm. Allen, son of Lawr., yeoman, of Maisemore
31		3 July	Edw. Nourse, son of Luke, ald.
		6 Aug	Jacob Cugley, son of Arthur, wiredrawer, decd.
		8 Aug	Rob. Cugley, haulier, by fine of £5
		8 Sept	Hen. Turbervile† by fine of £6 13*s* 4*d*[1]
			John Baker, app. of Ric. Humfris, butcher
31v		22 Sept	Matthias Hutchins, son of Thos., cordwainer
			Thos. Mayo, son of Lawr., late of Gloucester
			John Tyler, son of John, tailor, decd.
			Ric. Frankis, app. of John Galle, shoemaker
		24 Sept	Wm. Lambe† by fine of 20 marks[2]
		26 Sept	Wm. Bicknell, app. of Ric. Beard, tailor
32		2 Oct	Wm. Nicholls, son of John, tanner
		6 Oct	Sam. Rose, gent.,† by fine of 20 marks

William Singleton, esq., mayor 1651–2

		10 Oct	John Bradford, app. of Rog. Hall, cooper, decd.
		3 Nov	Young Hale, app. of Anne Hayes, widow, decd.
		1 Dec	Thos. Baker, son of Thos., weaver, decd.
32v		8 Dec	Rob. Weaver, app. of John Smallman, vintner
		12 Dec	Ric. Cooke, app. of John Salcombe, blacksmith
		15 Dec	John Wells, app. of Wal. Hill, cordwainer
			Rob. Berry, (clothmaker, of Gloucester)† by fine of £5
33		5 Dec	Steph. Davis alias Reese† by fine of £8
	1652	9 Jan	Mat. Smith, app. of Wm. Lugg, ald., tanner, decd.
			John Greening, app. of Thos. Chamlen, sealmaker, decd.
		16 Jan	Ralph Price, app. of Wal. Hill, cordwainer
		23 Jan	Wm. Harris, app. of John Motley, pinmaker
33v			Wm. James† by fine of £13 6*s* 8*d*[3]
		30 Jan	John Salter, (baker, of Gloucester)† by fine of £5[4]
		2 Jan	Geo. Elmes, app. of Edm. Collett, tanner, late of Gloucester
			Thos. Merrett, app. of Francis Yeates, cordwainer
34		9 Feb	Jonathan Griffith, Wm. Merrett, } apps. of Wal. Harris, cordwainer
			Wm. Bramley, son of John, glover, late of Gloucester
			John Boulter, app. of Edm. Palmer, baker, late of Gloucester
		22 Mar	John Wood, son of John, gent., late of Gloucester
34v		26 Mar	Nat. Webbe† by fine of £20
		29 Mar	Geo. Moore, app. of Joan Grave, widow
		10 Apr	Ric. Chaundler, app. of Thos. Pedlingham, saddler
			Ric. Pigg, app. of Ric. Paine, pinmaker
		29 Apr	John Webbe, son of Nic., ald., decd.
		7 May	Wm. Greene, app. of Wm. Harris, pinmaker
35		24 May	Thos. Cugley, son of Thos., cardmaker
		9 June	Wm. Jones, Jonathan Jones, } sons of Emanuel, apothecary, decd.
		10 June	Jas. Robins, app. of Ralph Butterton, currier
		25 June	Humph. Merricke, app. of Chris. Caple, mercer, decd.
35v		5 July	John Skillum, son of Wm., tanner, decd.
			Wm. Parlour, son of Wm., cutler, decd., by gift

[1] Not to use the trade of tanner in the city: ibid. p. 633.
[2] Having married Joyce, widow of Ric. Whithorne, freeman: ibid. p. 637.
[3] Having married a freeman's daughter: ibid. p. 659.
[4] Had married a daughter of John Bulbricke, one of the city's porters, decd.: ibid. p. 653.

12 July Thos. Garrett, app. of Wm. Lugg, ald., tanner, decd.
26 July Geo. Loggins, Augustine Loggins, } sons of Augustine, haulier
9 Aug Ric. Taylor, son of Ric., cordwainer, decd.
36 30 Aug Ant. Walker, son of Ant., clothier, decd.
John Holland, son of John, gent.[1]
John Mathewes, app. of Wal. Straford, butcher, decd.
Geo. Marten, son of Geo., brewer, decd.
3 Sept Thos. Harding, app. of Edw. Bingham, salter, decd.
5 Sept Hen. Thomas, (servant of the mayor), by such fees as apprentices usually pay
36v 13 Sept Thos. Marten, son of Geo., brewer, late of Gloucester
Thos. Collet, app. of Lawr. Allen, chandler[†]
Giles Collings[†] by fine of £3 6*s* 8*d*[2]
25 Sept Edw. Swayne, son of Thos., decd.
27 Sept John Wood, son of John, tanner, decd.
Ric. Hunt, app. of John Bubb, cordwainer, late of Gloucester
37 2 Oct Ric. Pace (of Ashleworth)[†] by fine of £10[3]

William Caple, esq., mayor 1652–3

37v 16 Oct Hen. Bray, app. of Ric. Nelmes, mercer
8 Nov Hen. Partridge the younger, app. of Thos. Partridge, maltster
10 Dec Edw. Elliott, son of Edw., tailor, late of Gloucester
14 Dec Wm. Barrowe, son of Geo., tailor
1653 13 Jan John Screven, gent., son of John, gent.
24 Jan Wm. Gifford, (tailor, of Gloucester)[†] by gift[4]
31 Jan John Paynter,[5] son of Jesse, glazier
38 28 Feb Jas. Miles, app. of Wm. Haynes, baker, decd.
28 Mar Edw. Addis, cordwainer, by gift[6]

GBR C9/7

1

City of Gloucester

The names of the burgesses of the said city made and sworn in the time of William Caple, esq., mayor of the said city . . .

1653 15 Apr John Beard, son of Thos., mercer, late of Gloucester
22 Apr Thos. Thomas, son of Ric., glover, late of Gloucester
25 Apr Thos. Bellamy, app. of Edw. Key, glover, late of Gloucester
Edw. Lugg, app. of Ric. Humphries, butcher, late of Gloucester
29 Apr Rob. Paine the younger,[7] app. of Rob. Paine the elder, mercer
2 6 May Hen. Willoughby, gent.,[†] by fine of £10[8]

[1] Entrant's father, an attorney, had served the town clerk and the city's courts: ibid. 1, ff. 270v., 493, 496.
[2] Had married a freeman's daughter: ibid. 2, p. 680.
[3] On condition he married the widow of Thos. Kinge, freeman, before 3 Oct 1652: ibid. pp. 682–3.
[4] By act of 8 Feb 1650, to make him, a very aged and distressed man, eligible for entry to one of the city's almshouses: ibid. p. 536.
[5] Also spelt *Painter*.
[6] An aged man: GBR B 3/2, p. 700.
[7] M.P. for Gloucester 1695–8: Williams, *Parl. Hist. of Glos.* 204.
[8] Having married a freeman's widow and his ancestors having been benefactors to the city: GBR B 3/2, p. 700.

Geo. Palmer, son of John and app. of John Pearks, baker, [by apprenticeship][1]
14 June Thos. Smith, } sons of Thos., mercer
Wm. Smith, }
17 June Humph. Wood, app. of Wal. Bird, tailor
20 June John Edmonds, app. of Nic. Haynes, milliner
3 18 July Giles Smyth, app. of Alice Jennings, widow
29 July Ric. Colly, app. of Dan. Lysons, woollen-draper
22 Aug Dan. Syre, son of John, tanner, decd.
5 Sept Arthur Corbert, app. of Thos. Burrup, cordwainer
19 Sept Thos. Foord, app. of Wm. Jennings, barber-surgeon
26 Sept John Purlewent, son of John, gent.
4
5 **Thomas Pury, esq., mayor 1653–4**

21 Oct Thos. Pedlingham, son of Thos., saddler
4 Nov Edw. Hill, son of Edw., maltster, late of Gloucester
7 Nov John Ewins, app. of Ric. Harward, woollen-draper
1654 10 Jan Wm. Orchard, app. of Winston Cox, cordwainer
6 23 Jan John Wassfeild, app. of John Wellsteed, smith
Jos. Phelps, app. of Nat. Knight, chandler, decd.
Thos. Kircombe, son of John, smith
26 Jan John Crumwell, carrier, by fine of £10
6 Feb Thos. Mason, app. of Thos. Parker, baker, decd.
13 Feb Humph. Onyon, app. of Humph. Onyon, sievemaker
7 John Bell, app. of Thos. Onion, sievemaker
17 Feb John Rogers† by fine of £6 13*s* 4*d*[2]
Phil Painter, app. of Dan. Clutterbooke, skinner
24 Apr Wm. Partridge, app. of Geof. Beale, mercer
7–8 26 June Ant. White, app. in turn of Ric. Taylor, decd., Thos. Burrup, and John Price, cordwainers
8 John Swayne, son of Thos., brewer, decd.
17 July Wm. Kinge, app. of Sam. Pitt, pinmaker
9 12 July John Elliotts, son of Edw., tailor, decd.
14 July Nat. Dobbins, app. of John Perks, baker
31 July Ric. Fletcher, app. in turn of John Siesmore and John Smallwood, barber-surgeons
10 7 Aug Sam. Jorden, app. of Thos. Cooke, chandler
John Hitchman, app. of John Williams, ropemaker
21 Aug Rob Beale, cordwainer, by fine of 40*s*[3]
11 Lawr. Allen, son of Lawr., cordwainer
Thos. Suckly by fine of 5 marks[4]
John Oker, (late organist), by gift
12
13 **Edmund Collett, esq., mayor 1654–5**

6 Oct John Hardinge, app. of Edm. Sturmy, glover
Jas. Tyler, son of Jas., cordwainer, late of Gloucester

[1] Ibid. F 4/5, f. 474.
[2] Native of Gloucester, who had been in parliament's service in England and Scotland and had married a daughter of Thos. Price, freeman: ibid. B 3/2, p. 752.
[3] Had married Alice, daughter of Thos. Cox, freeman, and been a soldier in the city: ibid. p. 780.
[4] Had married a daughter of Rog. Davis, freeman, and served parliament as a soldier: ibid. p. 784.

		16 Oct	Thos. Browne, app. of Humph. Onion, sievemaker
14			Phil. Ebbs, app. in turn of Margery Bruckbancke, widow, and Rob. Willmotts, saddlers
			Thos. Cowles, (glover), by fine of £3 6*s* 8*d*
		23 Oct	John Thomas, app. of Wm. Lane, feltmaker
15		13 Nov	John Holborne, app. of Edm. Collett, esq., mayor
		20 Nov	Thos. Woolford by fine of £3 6*s* 8*d*[1]
			Wm. Baker by fine of £3 6*s* 8*d*[2]
			Thos. Robins, app. of John Collett, tanner
		27 Nov	Ric. Stephens, son of Jas., ald.[3]
		12 Dec	Lawr. Lugg, son of Lawr., tanner, late of Gloucester
16	1655	5 Jan	Jesse Nash, son of Ric., tanner, decd.
		12 Jan	John Wilkins, son of Ric., wiredrawer
		22 Jan	Rob. Coucher, app. of Thos. Jones, pinmaker
		2 Feb	Jos. Browne, app. of Thos. Trippett, mercer
		29 Jan	Hen. Owen alias Wood, app. of Phil. Tillsley, pinmaker, late of Gloucester
17		9 Feb	Sam. Burroughs, son of Nat., cordwainer, decd.
			Wm. Jordan, son of Wm., maltster
		12 Feb	Thos. Churches, app. in turn of Ric. Wilkins and Thos. Denis, wiredrawers
		26 Feb	Augustine Newman, son of Wm., chandler, decd.
		2 Mar	Wm. Drinkwater by fine of 20 nobles
18		2 Apr	Benj. Cooke, app. of Cornelius Plott, tailor
		25 May	Wm. Hall, glover, by fine of £5
		18 June	Hen. Griffith, app. of Edw. Mason, saddler, decd.
19		16 July	Dennis Falkner, son of Maur., clothier, decd.
		3 Aug	Jas. Holman, son of Hen., brewer, decd.
		13 Aug	John Gregory, son of Hen., butcher, decd.
		27 Aug	Jonathan Sampson, app. of Wm. Sampson, turner
		10 Sept	Ric. White, app. of Sergeant White, cordwainer
20			Sam. Milles, son of Ric., silkweaver, decd.
		2 Oct	Thos. Putley, app. of Edw. Clayfeild, tanner
		24 Sept	John Gransum, app. in turn of Thos. Lugg and Wm. Parker, tanners
21			**Dennis Wise, esq., mayor 1655–6**
		25 Oct	David Griffin, app. of Wm. Beard, tailor
		2 Nov	Wm. Merrett, app. of John Smaleman, innholder, decd.
22		9 Nov	Ric. Webb by gift[4]
		14 Dec	Jos. Cooke, app. of Thos. Jelfe, baker
		28 Dec	Thos. Wilcox, son of John, clothier, decd.
	1656	7 Jan	Giles Crumlum, app. of Augustine Gwyn the elder, cordwainer
23		18 Jan	Arthur Champneys, app. of John Greene the elder, cooper
		1 Feb	John Lane, app. of John Gilbert, baker
			Dan. Collins, app. of John Tomes, gent.
24			Thos. Mills, app. of Ric. Broad, baker
		8 Feb	Wm. Walker by fine of £4[5]
		5 May	Edw. Bicke, app. of Wm. Warwicke, innholder

[1] Having married a freeman's daughter and served parliament as a soldier: ibid. p. 796.
[2] Having married a freeman's daughter and served parliament as a soldier: ibid.
[3] M.P. for Gloucester 1656–8, 1659, and 1660: Williams, *Parl. Hist. of Glos.* 198.
[4] A poor man and a freeman's son, who had served the city during the Civil Wars: GBR B 3/2, p. 845.
[5] Had taken up arms to defend the city during the Civil Wars: ibid. p. 853.

25		2 June	Francis Farmer, app. of David Davis, feltmaker[1]
		9 June	Edw. Norman, app. of Ric. Hughes, butcher
25–6			Thos. Roberts, app. in turn of Ric. Symons and Jas. Cordell, glovers
26		13 June	John Smart, app. of Thos. Hemming, joiner
			Hen. Harris, son of Edw., tailor
		16 June	Rob. Powell, app. of Eleanor Hill, widow, barber-surgeon
27		7 July	Jas. Parker, app. of Thos. Parker, baker, decd.
			Ric. Edwards, son of Ric., baker
		4 July	John Drinkwater, son of Ric., late of Gloucester
			Sam. Hill, son of Edw., late of Gloucester
		11 July	Thos. Chandler, son of Thos., victualler, decd.
			Wm. Dennis, (cordwainer), by fine of £5[2]
28		15 July	Wm. Symonds, app. in turn of Joan Gray, widow, and Rob. Jones, butchers
			Phil. Jones by fine of £5[3]
		1 Aug	Nic. Lane, son of Wal., gent., decd.
		4 Aug	Thos. Selwyn, son of Hen., cordwainer
		11 Aug	Wm. Woolley, } sons of Hen., barber-surgeon, decd.
29			Josiah Woolley, }
			Ric. Bridges, son of Wm., clothier, decd.
		15 Aug	Ric. Barnelme, son of Wm., turner, decd.
		25 Aug	John Jones, (pinmaker), by fine of 40*s*[4]
		19 Aug	Gen. John Disbrowe† [by gift][5]
		25 Aug	John Wood, (button-maker), [by fine][6]
29–30		15 Sept	John Thackwell, app. of Edm. Collett, tanner
30		19 Sept	Jos. Harris, app. of Wal. Harris, cordwainer
		29 Sept	Edm. Palmer by gift[7]
		2 Oct	Arthur Barrett, son of Thos., cutler, decd.
31–2			
33			**Luke Nourse, esq., mayor 1656–7**
		17 Oct	Thos. Goodcheape, app. of Winston Cox, cordwainer
			Geo. Baker, app. of Wm. Cowles, butcher
		20 Oct	John Shipton, app. of Sergeant White, cordwainer
34			John Bennett, app. of Wm. Jennings, barber-surgeon
		31 Oct	John Wintle, son of Ric., cordwainer
		4 Nov	(Captain) Jos. Wallington† (by gift)
			John Hill, gent., son of Thos., ald., decd.
		24 Nov	Wm. Cooke, app. of Wm. Reeve, cordwainer
34–5	1657	23 Mar	Ric. Swett, app. of Chris. Hayes, glazier, decd.[8]
35		3 Apr	Lewis Morse (by gift)

[1] Farmer had served five years as app. to Davis and Ric. Nash and had spent two years in parliament's service.

[2] Has been a soldier for parliament and has lately married a freeman's widow: GBR B 3/2, p. 866.

[3] Had married Sarah, daughter of Steph. Halford, decd.: ibid.

[4] Having served all but two months of his apprenticeship: ibid. p. 877.

[5] Ibid. F 4/6, p. 112; 'for his noble favours to this corporation': ibid. B 3/2, p. 876. John Desborough, attorney and parliamentary soldier, was elected M.P. for Gloucester in July 1656 but represented Somerset: Williams, *Parl. Hist. of Glos.* 196–7; *D.N.B.*

[6] GBR F 4/6, pp. 111–2; a member of the Gloucester garrison taking a poor man's son as app. without payment: ibid. B 3/2, p. 877.

[7] Had been forced to leave Tewkesbury for Gloucester during the Civil Wars: ibid. B 3/2, p. 887.

[8] Entrant had served Hayes and his wife for five years and spent the rest of his apprenticeship as a soldier.

Elisha (*Elizaeus*) Hathaway, son of Ant., ironmonger, decd.
25 May Thos. Lane, son of Wal., baker, decd.
Wm. Gregory, son of Hen., butcher, decd.
8 June Thos. Badger, app. of Eleanor, widow of Rob. Reynolds, tanner
36 15 June Geo. Chestro,[1] app. in turn of Eleanor Bubb, widow, and Toby Bubb, cordwainers
Wm. Phillips, son of Wm., haberdasher, decd.
9 July Chas. Tuffly, app. of Geo. Taylor, barber-surgeon
20 July Ric. Skillam, son of Wm., tanner, decd.
9 Sept Geo. Archard, son of Edw., gent., decd.
37 18 Sept Thos. Silvester, app. of Wm. Sampson, turner
28 Sept Wm. Kayse, app. of Ric. Nash, feltmaker
Thos. Sturmy, son of Rob., glover, decd.
20 Oct Thos. Farly, app. of Thos. Philips, cutler

38

39 **Lawrence Singleton, esq., mayor 1657–8**

9 Oct Ric. Partridge, son of Thos., baker
16 Oct Simon Prytchetts, app. of Wm. Davies, cooper, decd.
19 Oct Giles Woodward, app. of Nic. Phelpes, brewer
6 Nov Edw. Williams (by gift)[2]
19 Nov John Harborne, app. of Giles Lye, chandler
40 20 Nov Edm. Collett, son of Edm., ald.
John Ryland, app. of Edm. Collett, tanner, ald.
27 Nov Ric. Byford, (narrow-weaver),† by fine of £5[3]
11 Dec Jos. Smarte, app. of John Welsteed, blacksmith
21 Dec Ric. Woodward, app. of Ric. Doughton, pinmaker, decd.[4]
1658 8 Jan Wm. Marchant, app. of Thos. Cugly, cardmaker, decd.
41 29 Jan John Burup, son of Thos., cordwainer, decd.
1 Feb Ric. Cooke, app. of Wm. Reeve, butcher
12 Mar Sam. Sturmy, son of Edm., glover
5 Apr Hen. Abbatt, app. of Alice Jennings, widow, baker
30 Apr Wm. Wood, son of John, gent., decd.
4 June Thos. Lugg, son of Thos., gent.
30 May Wm. Cooke, app. of Humph. Morse, chandler
42 4 June John Gardner, app. in turn of Sergeant White and Francis Yates, cordwainers
7 June Thos. Massinger, son of Wm., gent., decd.
14 June Wm. Parker, son of Wm., tanner, late of Gloucester
2 July Thos. Bennett, beadle, by gift[5]
Rob. Mercer, son of Hen., fishmonger
John Marston, app. of Thos. Aram, mercer
43 5 July Wm. Bamford, app. of John Shipton, bodice-maker
16 July Giles Reeve, app. of his father Giles, gunsmith
22 July John Perry, son of Thos.
Jas. Wyniatt, app. of Wm. Beard, tailor
30 July Ralph Rixton, app. of John Branch, mercer
44 27 Aug John Wilse, app. of Isaac Williams, tailor

[1] Disfranchised 22 Oct 1699, having refused to serve as overseer of the poor for St. Nicholas parish, and readmitted by act of 29 Apr 1700: GBR B 3/7, ff. 226 and v., 235.
[2] On his appointment as reader for the city's almshouses: ibid. 3, p. 47.
[3] Having married a freeman's daughter: ibid. p. 51.
[4] Having served Doughton for five years and been a soldier under Thos. Pury for parliament for six years: ibid. p. 55; cf. Williams, *Parl. Hist. of Glos.* 198.
[5] An old servant of the city now much decayed: GBR B 3/3, p. 69.

		10 Sept	Ric. Goodwin, app. of Winston Cox, cordwainer
		13 Sept	Brice Gregory, son of Hen., butcher, decd.
		25 Sept	Peter Smith, carpenter, by fine of £5[1]
			Ralph Wallis by gift
45			Ric. Bond, app. of Ann Harris, widow, baker[2]
46			
47			**Robert Tither, esq., mayor 1658–9**
		18 Oct	Wm. Singleton, app. of Wm. Singleton, ald.
			Wm. Taylor, son of John, mercer
		19 Nov	Ric. Wintle, son of Ric., cordwainer
			Wm. Ham, app. of Nic. Barnard, butcher, decd.
48		22 Nov	Ant. Suffeild, son of Thos., late of Gloucester
		19 Dec	Wm. Lugg, son of Jasper, tanner, decd.
			Ant. Martley, son of Ant., horner
	1659	3 Jan	Ric. Hale,[3] app. of John Tailor, cordwainer
			John Martley, son of Ant., horner
			Thos. Pritchards, son of Thos., gent.
			Wm. Lugg, son of Thos., gent.
49		7 Jan	John Nurse, son of John, cooper
			Edw. Barnelme, son of Wm., turner
			Jesse Whittingham, son of Thos., baker
		10 Jan	Ric. Greene, son of Ric., baker
			John Farmer (by gift)[4]
			Ant. Summers (by gift)[5]
			John Smyth, son of John, baker, decd.
		11 Jan	Wm. Cugley, son of Thos., cardmaker
			Wm. Stephens, son of Mat., cordwainer
50		14 Jan	Ric. Simonds, son of Ric., glover
		17 Jan	Ric. Merrett, son of Thos., cordwainer, decd.
			Edw. Haines, app. of Lawr. Singleton, woollen-draper, ald.[6]
		18 Jan	Hen. Bowdley, app. of Rob. Bullocke, smith, decd.
50–1		28 Feb	Thos. Haines, app. of Nic. Haines, milliner and hosier
51		18 Mar	Wm. Hall, son of Rog., wine cooper, decd.
		21 Mar	Nic. Hieron, app. of Dan. Colericke, bodice-maker
		28 Mar	Wm. Welch, app. of Edw. Charleton, wiredrawer
		8 Apr	Thos. Shayle, app. of Thos. Pierce, mercer
52		11 Apr	Ric. Childe, app. of John Martin, baker
		14 Apr	Sam. Cripps, app. of Chas. Anstee alias Randle, butcher
		2 May	Ric. Jones, son of Thos., baker, decd.
		6 May	Cyprian Clarke, app. in turn of John Collett and Thos. Wood, tanners
53		30 May	John Fleminge, app. of his father Thos., tailor
		17 June	John Little, app. of Ric. Wintle, cordwainer
		21 June	Wm. Cooke, son of Wm., baker
		8 July	John Norris, app. of Wm. Powell, pinmaker
53–4			Sam. Whitle, app. of John Atkins, cordwainer
54			Geof. Webb, carpenter, by gift

[1] Having married a freeman's daughter: ibid. p. 78.

[2] Ann, widow of Wm. Hurlestone, baker, affirmed that Bond had served his apprenticeship.

[3] Disfranchised 7 Feb 1667 for behaviour in contempt of the cordwainers' company: GBR B 3/3, p. 332.

[4] To enable him to take Francis Weaver, son of Francis, decd., as his app.: ibid. p. 92.

[5] Having been a soldier in the time of the garrison and married a freeman's daughter: ibid. p. 93.

[6] M.P. for Gloucester 1659: Williams, *Parl. Hist. of Glos.* 199.

Jas. Cooke, sawyer, by gift[1]
5 Aug Sam. Willets, son of Geo., wiredrawer, decd.
5 Sept Wm. Bennett, son of John, oatmeal-maker, decd.
Rog. Wadman, app. of Geo. Mitchell, garter-weaver
12 Sept Wm. Dewxell, app. of Ric. Massinger, brewer, sheriff
55 23 Sept Rob. Litle, app. of Thos. Burrough, mercer, decd.
26 Sept Rob. Powell, app. of Thos. Burrop, cordwainer, decd., and of his widow Joan
56

57 **Toby Jordan, esq., mayor 1659–60**

24 Oct Thos. Parker, app. of John Jordan, baker
Alex. Bishop, son of Thos., cordwainer
7 Nov Hen. Cox, app. of Wm. Bicknell, tailor
58 Thos. Fletcher, app. of Thos. Fletcher, tanner
14 Nov Phil. Greene, app. of Wm. Swaine the younger, lantern-maker and brickmaker, late of Gloucester
21 Nov Wm. Sparrowhawke, son of Rob., garter-weaver
2 Dec Wm. Vyner, app. of Ric. Bosly, feltmaker
59 1660 19 Mar Sam. Reeve, app. of Giles Reeve the elder, gunsmith
29 Mar Humph. Merry by gift[2]
Jonas Bidle, app. of Ric. Cox, cordwainer
1 Apr Edw. Massie, esq.,† by gift[3]
3 Apr John Ockford, son of John, baker, late of Gloucester
John Lugg, son of Thos., tanner, late of Gloucester
Giles Grevile, son of Giles, gent.
Thos. Goslinge, app. of Wm. Wintle, haberdasher
Thos. Barrett, son of Thos., cutler, decd.
60 Ric. Coucher, app. of John Coucher, pinmaker
John Hinckesman, app. of Wm. Stapp, innholder, decd., and of his widow Sarah
Thos. Prichard, son of Hen., glazier, decd.
Hen. Lea, app. of Francis Lea, cordwainer
John Lane, son of Wal., gent., decd.
John Williams, app. of Wm. Wheeler, tailor
61 Hen. Lye, app. of John Kercombe, blacksmith
Hen. Butterton, son of Rob., decd. Paid nothing[4]
John Hickman, son of John, sievemaker, late of Gloucester
Thos. Danby, son of John, cordwainer
John Childe, app. of Thos. Greene, cordwainer
Edm. Whitfeild, app. of Hen. Davis, cordwainer. Paid nothing[5]
62 John Bennett, son of John, oatmeal-maker, decd.
Thos. Morse, son of Jas., cordwainer
21 May Wm. Franckis, son of Wm., baker, late of Gloucester
12 June John Jordan, son of John, baker
13 June Wm. Harrison by fine of £10
Ric. Ireland, app. of John Jones, innholder
18 June John Lewis, son of Abel the elder, plasterer
63 2 Aug Jas. Payne, son of John, feltmaker

[1] Having spent money on the city's behalf during the 1643 siege: GBR B 3/3, p. 103.
[2] Having been servant to Ald. Hen. Cugley and the city's sheriffs: ibid. p. 130.
[3] Col. Edw. Massey, former commander of the Gloucester garrison, on or just before his election as M.P. for the city: ibid. p. 131; Williams, *Parl. Hist. of Glos.* 199–200; *V.C.H. Glos.* iv. 93–5.
[4] By gift: GBR F 4/6, p. 342.
[5] By gift: ibid.

3 Aug Giles Thorne, son of Giles, clothier, decd.
Wm. Byrt, app. of Jas. Phillips, tailor
10 Aug Luke Pyckeringe, app. of Wm. Smyth, feltmaker, late of Gloucester
20 Aug Ric. Sparkes by apprenticeship*
24 Aug Geo. Paradise by fine of £6 13*s* 4*d*[1]
John Yeates, app. of Francis Yeates, cordwainer
64 28 Sept Rob. Bishop by fine of 20 nobles
10 Sept Toby Tainton, son of a freeman, decd.*
Edw. Jones, son of Wm., cordwainer, decd.
1 Oct Wm. Cleevely, son of Wm., ironmonger, decd.
Lawr. Knott, carpenter, by fine of £5
65–6
67 **Robert Payne, esq., mayor 1660–1**

8 Oct Thos. Chapman, son of Thos., tailor, late of Gloucester
15 Oct Hen. Wintle, app. of John Bingle, cooper
26 Oct Wm. Nash, son of Ric., tanner, decd.
29 Oct John Woolley, son of Thos., gent.
2 Nov John Cawdale, son of John, button-maker, decd.
9 Nov Jas. Woodward, son of Wm., blacksmith
68 19 Nov Ric. Tayler, app. of Rob. Reynolds, currier, late of Gloucester, and his wife Eleanor
Isaac Lumbert, (narrow-weaver), by fine of £5
John Heyward, app. of Rob. Sturmy, glover, decd.
24 Nov John Davis, son of John, cobbler (*translator*), late of Gloucester
26 Nov Ric. Holder, app. of Phil. Tilsley, pinmaker, decd.
30 Nov John Cowles alias Stephenson, app. of Thos. Horsington, bodice-maker
69 Thos. Vaughan, (yeoman), by fine of £5[2]
14 Dec John Price, app. in turn of Jonathan Charleton, decd., and Edw. Charleton, wiredrawers
24 Dec Hen. Clarke, app. in turn of Chris. Hayes, decd., and John Painter, glaziers
28 Dec Ric. Holliday, app. of Alice Jennings alias Pincke, widow, baker
Thos. Greene, app. of Wm. Samson, turner
70 1661 10 Jan John Axton alias Exton, app. of Margaret, widow of Wm. Wantner, farrier, decd.
18 Jan Wm. Baggatt, son of John, cordwainer, decd.
28 Jan Dan. Clutterbooke, son of Amity, tailor, decd.
15 Feb Thos. Owtin by fine of £6 13*s* 4*d*[3]
Lazarus Powell, app. of Mat. Smyth, tanner
Wm. Harris, (late beadle),† by gift
John Bridges, (wiredrawer, of Gloucester)† by gift
18 Feb Ric. Gough, (goldsmith), by fine of £10[4]
Wm. Lewis† by gift
71 25 Feb Evan Seys, serjeant-at-law, recorder of Gloucester, (by gift)[5]
1 Mar Rob. Curr, app. of John Crumwell, carrier (*tabellarii*)

[1] Son-in-law of Mary Barrett, widow: ibid. B 3/3, p. 143.
[2] Having married a granddaughter of John Reade, a former sheriff of the city: ibid. p. 159; Fosbrooke, *Glouc.* 209.
[3] A poor man, having married a freeman's daughter: GBR B 3/3, p. 170.
[4] Having married a daughter of John Purlewent: ibid. p. 169.
[5] Prior to his election, in Apr 1661, as M.P. for Gloucester: Williams, *Parl. Hist. of Glos.* 200–1.

5 Mar Hen. Price, John Price, } sons of Thos., gent., decd.
Wm. Harmer, son of John, gent., decd.
Dan. Comelin, son of Jas., apothecary
Francis Singleton, son of Francis, gent., decd.
Jas. Sace, son of Ralph, pinmaker
Clement Merrett by fine of 5 marks[1]

71–2 4 Mar John Trowe, app. of Wm. Greene, pinmaker, by fine of 2*s* 6*d*[2]
72 8 Mar Wm. Hornedge, app. of Thos. Stephens, pinmaker
7 Mar Thos. Kearsey, app. of Hen. Eckly, milliner
Sam. Comelin, son of Jas., apothecary
Jas. Andros, (glover), by fine of £8
11 Mar Ambrose Evereds, app. of Dan. Lysons, woollen-draper
Edw. Dunn, son of Edw., chandler, late of Gloucester
73 Thos. Summers, app. of Wm. Eldridge, silkweaver, late of Gloucester
Chas. Bower, app. of John Perkes, baker
15 Mar Jas. Dyer, son of a brewer, decd.*
Thos. Hinckesman by patrimony*
Sam. Kent, app. of Wm. Greene, joiner
18 Mar Ric. Pedlingham, son of Thos. the elder, saddler
Edw. Bennett, son of an oatmeal-maker, decd.*
74 Ric. Doughton, son of Ric., pinmaker
22 Mar Sam. Skinner, son of Rob., glover, decd.
Ric. Nelme, app. of Dan. Clutterbooke, furrier, decd.
25 Mar Godwin Pitt, Sam Pitt, Jas. Pitt, } sons of Sam., pinmaker
29 Mar Sam. Roberts, son of Rob., pewterer, decd.
Thos. Rawlins, app. in turn of Jos. Phelpes and Thos. Hale, feltmakers
1 Apr Ant. Howlett, son of Thos., butcher
Dan. Cugley, son of Thos., cardmaker
Jas. Clifford, app. of Hen. Phenix, pinmaker, late of Gloucester
Edw. Jackson, app. of Thos. Baily, pinmaker
75 John Sheppard, app. of Wm. Merrett, cordwainer
Wm. Hartland, app. of John Coucher, pinmaker
John Keare, app. of Thos. Stephens, pinmaker
Sam. Hayward, app. of Rob. Cleevely, chandler
2 Apr John Edwards, clerk, son of John, haberdasher, decd.
75–6 Ric. Lowe, app. of Thos. Davis, wiredrawer
76 Wm. Parkes, app. of Sam. Pitt, pinmaker
15 Apr Ant. Lea, son of Francis, cordwainer
24 Apr John Howe, esq.,[†] (by gift)[3]
26 Apr Thos. Brooke, (trowman, by fine)[4]
3 May Wm. Williams, app. of Hen. Randle alias Ansticke, butcher, late of Gloucester
And. Phelpes, app. of Thos. Flucke, tanner
76–7 20 May John Dobbes, app. of Rob. Dobbes, barber-surgeon, late of Gloucester

[1] Having been lately a soldier in the king's service under the duke of Albemarle: GBR B 3/3, p. 172.

[2] Trowe had been bound app. before Greene became a freeman: ibid. p. 173.

[3] Of Langar, Notts., by act of 1 Mar 1661 admission to the freedom was deferred until after parliamentary elections, in which he was returned for the county: ibid. p. 172; Williams, *Parl. Hist. of Glos.* 58–9.

[4] Having married a daughter of Sam. Chapman, freeman, decd.: GBR B 3/3, p. 177.

77			Mic. Bower, app. of Rob. Plummer, pewterer, by fine of £3 6*s* 8*d*
		24 May	John Bishop, app. of Geof. Beale, mercer
		27 May	Ric. Thomas, app. of his father Ric., cook, late of Gloucester, and mother Joan
		31 May	Ric. Holman, son of Hen., gent., decd.
78		7 June	Thos. Addams, app. of John Greene, cooper
		10 June	Chas. Blunt, app. of Thos. Pedlingham, saddler
			Steph. Doughton, son of Steph., pinmaker
		21 July	Sam. Kenricke, app. of Rob. Longden, ironmonger[1]
		26 July	Hen. Carpenter, app. of Hen. Hayes, cordwainer
79		n.d.	Wm. Hutchins, app. of Wm. Madocke, tailor
		12 Aug	John Blisse, app. of Edw. Clayfeild, tanner
			Rob. Webley, app. of Edw. Elliott, cordwainer
		22 Aug.	Thos. Bancknett, porter (*janitor*), by gift[2]
		26 Aug	John Woodward, combmaker, by fine of £6 13*s* 4*d*
		11 Sept	John Campion (by gift)[3]
80		30 Sept	John Griffin, app. of Thos. Partridge, baker
81			**Thomas Peirce, esq., mayor 1661–2**
		10 Oct	Ant. Robinson, clerk, son of Ant., ald., decd.[4]
		21 Oct	Thos. Gwin, clerk, son of Augustine, cordwainer
		2 Nov	John Linckinholt, son of a wiredrawer, decd.
		5 Nov	John Davis, app. of John Elliotts, wiredrawer
		11 Nov	Jesse Clarke† by gift[5]
		9 Dec	Jas. Walker, son of Ant., broadweaver, decd.
			Edm. Pearce, app. of John Heyward, feltmaker*
82	1662	4 Jan	Wm. Corsly, (goldsmith), by fine of £20
		13 Jan	Ric. Morris, carpenter, by fine of £4
		16 Jan	Alex. Davis by fine of £10[6]
		21 Feb	Wal. Harvey by fine of £5
		3 Mar	Rob. Sparrowhawke, son of Rob., garter-weaver
			Sam. Woodward, son of Wm., blacksmith
		21 Apr	Thos. Witcombe, son of Thos., gent.
83		16 May	Hen. Collett, app. of John Sturmy, glover
		23 May	Geo. Gillman, app. of Ric. Price, pewterer
		12 May	Jas. Prosser, app. of Jas. Stephens, ald.
		26 May	Ric. Weaver by fine of £5
		30 May	Miles Mutley, son of John, fishhook-maker, decd.
			Wal. Lewis, app. of John Jones, butcher, late of Gloucester, and his wife Margaret
84		7 July	Zachariah Heyward, app. of John Perkes, baker
		23 July	Ant. Arnold, gent., by gift
			Hen. Fowler, gent., by gift
		1 Sept	Ric. Dewxell, son of Ant., decd.
		12 Sept	Wm. Cole, clothworker, by fine of £5
		26 Sept	John Hilles, app. of Jos. Phelps, grocer
			Hen. Perry, app. of John Gravestocke, butcher

[1] Freedom granted by act of 22 July 1661: ibid. p. 193.

[2] Having been a servant to the city for about fifteen years: ibid. p. 197.

[3] Having married a freeman's daughter, on his designing and setting up the king's arms at the Tolsey: ibid. p. 200.

[4] M.P. for Gloucester 1620–2 and 1624–5: Williams, *Parl. Hist. of Glos.* 193.

[5] Of Gloucester, having become 'much decayed in his estate': GBR B 3/3, p. 212.

[6] Having married the widow of Simon Hilleyard, button-maker: ibid. p. 215.

3 Oct John Branch, app. of Ric. Broade, baker
85 Rob Feildinge, M.D. (*doctor in physicis*).† Paid nothing[1]
Hen. Ockold, gent. Paid nothing[2]
Thos. Woolley, son of Ric., innholder, decd. Paid [ ]*
86
87

William Russell, esq., mayor 1662–3

24 Nov Albert Badger, app. of Hen. Phenix, pinmaker, decd.
1 Dec Ric. Dewxell, gent., son of Ant. See before, entered twice[3]
15 Dec Florence (*Floritius*) Cowper, app. of Thos. Robins, tanner
31 Dec John Jones, son of Arthur, gent., late of Gloucester
1663 9 Feb Nat. Chaundler, app. of Hester Palmer, widow, baker
13 Mar Jos. Wilton, app. of Jas. Ricketts, tanner
88 27 Mar Jos. Ludlo,[4] app. of Thos. Aram, mercer
30 Mar Ric. Williams, app. of Thos. Pace, cooper, decd.
7 Apr Thos. Croker,[5] app. of Nic. Williams, joiner
15 May John Stephens, app. of Wm. Jennings, barber-surgeon, and son of Thos., pinmaker, by patrimony
5 June Wm. George, app. of Thos. Phelpes and Ric. Bosly, feltmakers
22 June John Ball, app. of Edw. Swayne, collar-maker
Matthias Bower, gent. Paid nothing[6]
89 15 June Sam. Bawry, app. of Jas. Ricketts, tanner
3 Aug Sam. Jones, son of Thos., baker, decd.
25 July Chas. Staniford, app. of Dan. Collins, mercer
Hen. Litle, app. of Thos. Cooke, chandler, late of Gloucester
4 Sept Sam. Hearth, app. of Thos. Onyon, silkweaver
7 Sept Hen. Springe by fine of £10
Thos. Tayloe, app. of John Dewxell*
90 Humph. Hutchins, son of Wm., innkeeper
Wm. Jones, son of Wm., cordwainer, decd., by gift
18 Sept Dan. Bishop, app. of John Horrell, tailor
91–2
93

John Powell, esq., mayor 1663–4

9 Oct Rob. Stephens by fine of £5
23 Oct Rob. Lawrence by fine of £6 13*s* 4*d*
Chas. Mayris, app. of Hen. Knowles, brazier
2 Nov Geo. Powell, son of Wm., pinmaker
John Cox, son of Ric., cordwainer
9 Nov Francis Braban, app. of John Greene the younger, cooper
94 1664 15 Feb Thos. Carpenter, app. of John Nicholls, tanner
4 Apr Nat. Gardner, app. of Margaret Parker, baker
26 Feb Wm. Perris, app. of Ric. Hughes, butcher

[1] Of Gloucester, on his appointment as ald. by commissioners under the 1661 Corporations Act: ibid. C 8/1, f. 16 and v. Disfranchised and removed from the aldermanic bench 7 Aug 1671 for taking apps. contrary to the liberties of the mercers' company: ibid. B 3/3, p. 481.

[2] Following his appointment as common councillor by commissioners under the 1661 Corporations Act: ibid. C 8/1, ff. 7v.–8.

[3] Entry struck through; cf. above: ibid. C 9/7, p. 84.

[4] Disfranchised and excluded from the common council 6 May 1680 for non-attendance and for refusing in 1674 to serve as sheriff and readmitted by act of 16 Aug 1680: ibid. B 3/3, pp. 750–1, 756.

[5] Disfranchised 28 May 1677 for taking Dan. and Seth Blanch as apps. to enable them to gain the freedom: ibid. pp. 674–5.

[6] Following his appointment as common councillor by commissioners under the 1661 Corporations Act: ibid. C 8/1, ff. 18v.–19.

4 Apr John Parke, blacksmith, by gift[1]
8 Apr John Bosly, app. of Ric. Bosly, feltmaker
Edw. Cor, son of Hen., baker, decd.
25 Apr Hen. Smith, son of Ric., gent.
95 9 May Geo. Rudge, app. of Thos. Lucas, farrier, late of Gloucester
20 May Thos. Saunders, son of Wm., fustian-weaver, late of Gloucester
3 June Wal. Gwatkin, app. of Edm. Collett, tanner
6 June Wm. Bishop, app. of Wm. Beard, tailor
Mat. Hill, app. of Edw. Fewtrell, tailor
20 June Sam. Carter, app. of Giles Lye, chandler, decd.
96 27 June Arthur Cam, app. of Rob. Payne the younger, mercer
Dan. Randle, app. of Thos. Hemminge, joiner
11 June Jos. Probert, glover, by gift
1 Aug John Webley, app. of Giles Grevile, mercer
8 Aug Hen. Parlour, son of Wm., cutler, decd.
15 Aug Thos. Rogers, app. of Thos. Mills, baker
22 Aug Wm. Fowler, son of Wm., mercer, decd.
97 John Winston, app. of Sam. Kinge, tailor
25 Aug Ric. Harward, S.T.P., prebendary of Gloucester cathedral, son of Ric., gent., decd.
23 Sept Wal. Barney, tobacco-pipemaker, by fine[2]
26 Sept Hen. Powell, app. of John Fones, glover
Thos. Shewell, app. of Ric. Teeckle, ropemaker, late of Gloucester

98 **Robert Feildinge, M.D., mayor 1664–5**

17 Oct Thos. Cooke, son of Thos., butcher
Thos. Barrowe, son of Geo., tailor
Wm. Watts, app. of Thos. Cooke, butcher
14 Nov Rob. Cheesman, app. of Simon Pritchetts, cooper
21 Nov Hen. Goslinge, app. of Edm. Palmer, baker
Wm. Cowcher, app. of John Cowcher, pinmaker
99 1665 20 Feb Edw. Cripps, app. of Chas. Anstee,[3] butcher
Thos. Hornedge, app. of Dan. Colericke, bodice-maker
Wm. Fones alias Watts,[4] cordwainer, by gift
13 Feb Thos. Belcher, app. of Ann Hurlestone, baker
20 Mar John Witcombe, son of John, cordwainer, late of Gloucester
10 Apr Wm. Wrench, gent., by gift
Dan. Bingle, app. of Wm. Jordan, apothecary
100 Jacob (*Jacobus*) Heagh, app. of Thos. Lane, chandler
24 Apr Ric. Hemminge, yeoman, by fine of £13 6*s* 8*d*
Wm. Eldridge, son of Wm., silkweaver
12 June Edm. Greene, } sons of Edm., cordwainer
John Greene, }
26 June Wm. Ridler, app. of Ric. Greening, tailor, late of Gloucester
John Chamlyn, son of Thos., turner, decd.
30 June Jos. Etheridge, app. of Ric. Nash, grocer
4 Sept Aaron Jaquis, app. of Margaret Parker, baker
101 8 Sept John Adys, app. of Wal. Hill, cordwainer

[1] Excused the customary fees because of his poverty: ibid. B 3/3, p. 177.
[2] Having married a freeman's widow: ibid. p. 248.
[3] Chas. Randle alias Anstee: ibid. p. 300.
[4] Wm. Watts alias Jones: ibid. p. 301.

22 Sept Thos. Marten, son of Thos., brewer, late of Gloucester
Wm. Feild, son of Thos., gent.
25 Sept Sam. Perry, app. of Wm. Angell, merchant
27 Sept Sam. Washborne, app. of Thos. Yate, apothecary, ald.
102

103 **Thomas Yate, esq., mayor 1665–6**

20 Nov John Carell, app. of Nic. Haines, hosier
1 Dec Isaac Comelin, son of Jas., apothecary
8 Dec Thos. Eckly, son of Thos., chandler, decd.
22 Dec Thos. Midlewrite, son of Thos., tanner, decd., by gift
1666 8 Jan Edw. Clayfeild, son of Edw., tanner
15 Jan Arnold Aram, app. of Edw. Hill, haberdasher
29 Jan John Prickett, app. of Augustine Gwin the younger, cordwainer
104 12 Feb Dan. Harris, son of Humph., baker, decd.
12 Mar John Thomas, son of Ric., cook, late of Gloucester
30 Mar Edw. Feild, son of Thos., gent., decd.
John Cawles, son of Wm., butcher
Mat. Walker, app. of Jas. Slicer, tanner
23 Apr Abel Wantner,[1] son of Abel, innkeeper
Wm. Brimyard, son of Wm., wiredrawer
14 May Hen. Eliote, son of Hen., joiner
105 25 May Thos. Cussens, app. of John Greene the elder, cooper
15 June Edw. Hickes, tobacco-pipemaker, by fine of £5[2]
Ric Surman, app. of Thos. Burrup, cordwainer, decd.
John Belcher, app. of Wm. Berrowe, tailor
9 July Abraham Edwards, son of Hen., baker
30 July Wm. Woodward, son of Wm., blacksmith
106 Dan. Parry, app. of Thos. Selwin, cordwainer
Francis Hall, app. of Lawr. Singleton, woollen-draper
13 Aug Thos. Pace, son of Thos., cooper
16 Aug Jas. Gittos, } sons of Wm., glover
Wm. Gittos, }
7 Sept John Rutter, maltster, by fine of £5

107 **Thomas Price, esq., mayor 1666–7**

5 Oct Sam. Lye, son of Giles, chandler, late of Gloucester
2 Nov John Lugg, son of John, haberdasher
12 Nov John Gardner alias Mashfield, yeoman, by fine of £6 13*s* 4*d*
15 Nov Thos. Barnes, son of Thos., joiner, late of Gloucester
19 Nov John Whitson, app. in turn of Margaret Tyler, widow, late of Gloucester, and Francis Yates, cordwainers
3 Dec Geo. Filder, app. of Thos. Voyers, farrier and blacksmith
108 21 Dec Thos. Partridge, son of Thos., baker
24 Dec Chas. Pine, app. of John Smallwood, barber-surgeon
1667 5 Jan Ric. Humphris, son of Ric., butcher
6 Jan Jas. White, app. of John Nicholls, tanner
11 Jan John Hanx, app. of Edw. Clayfeild, tanner
28 Jan John Cudd, app. of Sam. Mills, silkweaver, decd.
109 4 Mar Josiah Randle, app. of John Perkes, baker
29 Mar Thos. Laurence, app. of John Brown, butcher, decd.

[1] Compiler of the first detailed history of the city and county: *Trans. B.G.A.S.* xcix. 170–2.
[2] Having married a freeman's daughter: GBR B 3/3, p. 177.

6 Apr Patrick Clarveato, gent., (by gift).[1] Paid fee of 5*s* 4*d**
22 Apr Wal. Winston, app. of Ric. Humphris, butcher
6 May Jas. Woodiatt, app. of John Bradford, button-maker
110 13 May Jas. Harris, son of Edw., tailor
28 June Jasper Taylor, app. of Wm. Lugg, combmaker, late of Gloucester
1 July Isaac Wood, son of John, tanner, decd.
5 Aug Sam. Berrowe, son of Geo., tailor
26 Aug Edm. Rea, gent., by fine of £5*[2]
Jas. Browne, son of John, butcher
Ric. Bradgate, son of Ric., barber-surgeon, decd.
30 Aug Sam. Sisemore, son of Sam., barber-surgeon, decd.
111 Edm. Gregory, app. of Marian, widow of Dan. Clutterbooke, skinner
16 Sept Isaac Manning, app. of Wm. Powell, pinmaker
23 Sept Giles Randle, app. of John Beard, silkweaver

112
113 **John Woodward, esq., mayor 1667**

14 Oct Wm. Barrett, son of Thos., cutler, decd.
Jos. Byford, son of Jos.*
Ric. Jones, app. of Giles Reeve, gunsmith
4 Nov Ric. Till, son of Ric., cutler[3]
11 Nov Wm. Reeve, son of Wm., butcher, decd.[3]
20 Dec Edw. Smith, son of Wm., feltmaker[3]

114 **Anthony Arnold, esq., mayor 1667–8[4]**

1668 9 Feb Thos. Stephens, son of Thos., pinmaker
6 Apr John Roberts, app. of Wm. Wood, mercer
10 Apr Dan. Washbourne, son of Dan., maltster
20 July John Pace, son of Thos., cooper
Wm. Sisemore, son of John, barber-surgeon
John Rodway, app. of Wm. Blicke, mercer
John Yeedinge, app. in turn of Margaret Paine, widow, and Ric. Pigg, pinmakers
115 27 July Wm. Goode, son of Thos., tailor
Wm. Turner, son of John, cook, decd.
John Freame, app. of Ric. Partridge, baker
Jacob Underhill, app. of John Bell, silkweaver
7 Aug Ric. Jefferis, app. of John Wager,[5] glazier, decd.
Wm. Woodinge, app. of John Bradford, button-maker, late of Gloucester[6]
14 Aug John Wintle, blacksmith, by fine
116 17 Aug Geo. Phillips, son of Thos., trimmer of hats, late of Gloucester
Winston Cox, son of Winston, cordwainer
31 Aug Thos. Best, } sons of Thos., tanner
John Best, }
John Hornedge, app. in turn of Hen. Eckly and John Bennett, button-makers

[1] Having married a freeman's daughter: ibid. p. 334.
[2] Having married a freeman's daughter: ibid. p. 339.
[3] Entry belongs to following mayoralty.
[4] Elected 4 Nov 1667 after Woodward's death: GBR B 3/3, p. 343.
[5] Rob. Wager: ibid. p. 362.
[6] Entry by apprenticeship although not indentured: ibid.

Ric. Price, app. of John Price, wiredrawer
25 Sept Rob. Younge, app. of Augustine Loggins the elder, mason
117 2 Oct Francis Springe, app. of Augustine Gwin the younger, cordwainer
118

119 **Henry Ockold, esq., mayor 1668–9**

8 Oct John Heaven, app. of Rob. Paine the younger, mercer
12 Oct Ric. Smith, son of Ric., gent.
14 Oct (Sir) Baynham Throckmorton, Bt.,† by gift[1]
19 Oct Thos. Vaughan, son of Thos., joiner
2 Nov Thos. Gardner, app. of John Coutcher, pinmaker, late of Gloucester[2]
Dan. Gardner, app. of Wm. Hartland, pinmaker
120 12 Nov Wm. Reeve, app. of Humph. Hiron, chandler, decd.
2 Nov Morgan Thomas, app. of Edw. Charleton, wiredrawer
6 Nov John Gwilliam, son of John, tanner
9 Nov Jos. Bullocke, app. of Ric. Cox, cordwainer
Geo. Chapman, app. of Wm. Colliar, gunsmith
16 Nov And. Beard, son of Wm., tailor
1669 8 Jan Wm. Jeffes, app. of Dan. Syre, ropemaker
121 15 Mar Humph. Heard, app. in turn of Sam. Cripps and Geo. Moore, butchers
19 Mar Humph. Watson, app. of Humph. Hutchins, tailor
22 Mar Giles Wilse, app. of Hen. Abbotts, baker
2 Apr Thos. Chamlyn, son of Thos., turner, late of Gloucester[3]
Thos. Witcombe, app. in turn of Wm. Beard, Jas. Winniatt, and Thos. Chapman, tailors
122 5 Apr Chas. Peirson, son of Wm., gent., decd.
Wm. Warwicke, app. of Wm. Warwicke the elder, vintner
9 Apr Thos. Sparkes, app. of Thos. Sparkes, sievemaker, decd.
23 Apr Thos. Hathway, app. of Ant. Hathway, ironmonger, decd.
26 Apr John Wadly, son of John, haulier
7 May John Simons, button-maker, by fine of £3[4]
John Allen, app. of Geo. Baker, butcher, decd.
123 3 May Giles Marden, app. of Ric. Broade, baker
14 June Godfrey Fawnes, son of Godfrey, cordwainer
Ric. Smarte, app. of Thos. Merrett, cordwainer
22 June Sam. Ham, app. of Wm. Ham, butcher
19 July John Kinge, app. of Jas. Kinge, scrivener
28 July Isaac Williams, son of Nic., joiner
2 Aug Nat. Amos, app. of Wm. Bumford, bodice-maker
124 Nat. Ferrett, app. of Jas. Cordell, glover
13 Sept Gregory Wilshire, son of Lawr., gent., late of Gloucester
John Jenings, son of Wm., barber-surgeon, decd.
Geo. Berrowe, son of Geo., tailor
Hen. Knight, son of Hen., innholder
27 Sept John Beard, son of Ric., tailor, decd.

[1] Of Clearwell, Newland, formerly a commissioner for Gloucester under the 1661 Corporations Act: ibid. C 8/1, *passim; Complete Baronetage*, i. 66.
[2] Entrant had been bound app. to Coutcher and his wife.
[3] The words *by fine* have been added.
[4] Son of John, porter, decd., having served Edw. Eckly for several years: GBR B 3/3, p. 406.

125 **John Wagstaffe, esq., mayor 1669–70**

11 Oct John Bradgate, son of Ric., barber-surgeon, decd.
Thos. Weaver, son of Thos., butcher
22 Nov John Ricketts, app. of Thos. Pedlingham the elder, saddler, decd.
Ric. Cooke, app. of Ric. Cooke, blacksmith
29 Nov John Bingle, son of John, cooper
126 6 Dec John Palmer, son of John, cooper
Jas. Evans, app. of Wm. Peirson, victualler, decd.
13 Dec Jas. Price, son of Ric., pewterer, decd.
1670 21 Feb Wm. Randle, app. of Wm. Bicknell, tailor
John Soule, app. of Wm. Warwicke, vintner
14 Mar Thos. Gibbins, son of Thos. wiredrawer, decd.
126–7 25 Mar Sam. Eckly,[1] son of Thos., chandler, late of Gloucester, and app. of Thos. Yate, apothecary, decd., by apprenticeship[2]
127 11 Apr John Hancocke, app. of Dan. Colericke, bodice-maker
18 Apr Ric. Cawdle, son of Wm., maltster
2 May Thos. Cowles, app. of John Hughes, cordwainer
16 May Sam. Evans, app. of Winston Cox, cordwainer
Geo. Ricketts, app. of Sam. Freeman, jersey-comber
128 John Chapman, son of Thos., tailor, decd.
30 May John Hill, app. of Hen. Davis, cordwainer
4 July Thos. Eldridge, son of Thos., joiner, decd.
Thos. Stephens, son of Thos., victualler
11 July Wm. Watts, app. of Wm. Madocke, tailor*
8 Aug Hen. Church, son of Hen., tailor, decd.
129 22 Aug Hen. Cooke, app. of Geo. Pharley, cutler
Jos. Nash, app. of Jas. Ricketts, tanner*
19 Sept Nat. Cooke alias Castle, app. of John Perkes, baker
Rob. Cawdale, son of Rob., turner
John Edwards, yeoman, by fine*
26 Sept Nic. Perry, upholsterer, by fine of £10*
130 Jas. Jones, son of Arthur, gent., decd.
Rob. Savory, son of Wm., farrier
Hen. Ven, son of John, feltmaker
April Dudley, app. of John Baker, butcher, late of Gloucester
Hen. Bicke, app. of Augustine Gwin the elder, cordwainer
3 Oct Thos. Turbett, app. of Wm. Day, tanner
Wm. Ackson, yeoman, porter (*janitor*) in the city, by gift*[3]

131 **Henry Fowler, esq., mayor 1670–1**

7 Oct Wm. Andros, musician, by gift[4]
17 Oct Alan Kilmister, app. of Wal. Vaisie, tailor*
Jas. Wood, app. of Lawr. Lugg, baker*
24 Oct Ric. White, app. of Ric. Hands, bricklayer
132 Rob. Cooke, son of Jas., sawyer*
7 Nov Wal. Longe, app. of John Singleton, innholder
Dan. Hughes, son of John, cordwainer
14 Nov Thos. Reeve, son of Wm., butcher, late of Gloucester

[1] Knighted by Queen Anne: Fosbrooke, *Glouc.* 166.
[2] Last year of apprenticeship remitted by Yate's widow Elizabeth.
[3] Had married a freeman's daughter: GBR B 3/3, pp. 431, 455.
[4] Elderly, blind, and 'in a low condition': ibid. p. 456.

		13 Dec	Ric. Huntley, app. of Jesse Nash, feltmaker
		22 Dec	Nat. Gwin, clerk, son of Augustine the elder, cordwainer*
133	1671	10 Jan	Giles Holliday, app. of John Beard, silkweaver
		20 Jan	Giles Freeman, app. of Giles Smith, baker
		13 Feb	John Harrell,[1] son of John, tailor
			Hen. Cleevely, son of Rob., chandler, decd.
			Jeremiah Harris, son of Thos., gunsmith
		20 Feb	Thos. Cooke, son of Ric., chandler
		21 Feb	Brian Price, app. of Wm. Powell, pinmaker
134		27 Feb	Giles Longe, heelmaker, by fine of £10
			Benj. Hiett, gent., by gift[2]
		20 Mar	John Whitterne, son of Ric., gent., decd.*
			Ric. Underwood, app. of John Baker the younger, butcher*
		10 Apr	Ric. Gibbins, app. of Wal. Dowsinge, farrier and blacksmith, late of Gloucester*
		15 May	Rob. Perry, son of Rob., cordwainer
			Aaron Samson, } sons of Wm., horner and combmaker
			Dan. Samson, }
135		22 May	Rob. Punter, app. of Rob. Laurence, mercer, late of Gloucester[3]
		5 June	Wm. Hancockes, app. of Toby Bubb, cordwainer, decd.
			Hen. Norwood, esq., of Tuffley by gift[4]
		17 July	John Hall, app. of Hen. Fowler, surgeon
			John Marten, son of John, baker
136		31 July	Edm. Best, } sons of Thos., tanner*
			Sam. Best, }
		7 Aug	Thos. Yarnold, son of Thos., mariner
			Thos. Meeke, app. of Thos. Meeke the elder, currier
		15 Sept	Jos. Humphris, app. of Ric. Nash, grocer

137 **Henry Fowler, esq., mayor 1671–2**

	1672	9 May	Wm. Cooke, esq.,[5] ald. appointed by king,	}
			Duncombe Colchester, esq.,[6] ald. appointed by king,	}
			Wm. Selwyn, esq.,[7] ald. appointed by king,	}
			Rob. Halford, gent.,[8] common councillor appointed by king,	} by gift[10]
			John Cromwell, gent.,[9] common councillor appointed by king,	}
		13 May	Thos. Dobbs, app. of John Dobbs, barber-surgeon, decd.	
		n.d.	Thos. Homes, app. of Thos. Mills, baker	
138		n.d.	Cressey Dymocke, app. of John Webb, mercer	
		n.d.	Francis Reeve, app. of Steph. Baldwin, stonecarver, late of Gloucester	

[1] Also spelt *Horrell.*

[2] Servant to the town clerk for several years: GBR B 3/3, p. 470.

[3] Entrant had served his apprenticeship with Lawrence and with John Beard, mercer.

[4] Ald. by royal mandate in 1672 and M.P. for the city 1675–9: Rudder, *Glos.* App. p.v; Williams, *Parl. Hist. of Glos.* 201; *V.C.H. Glos.* iv. 110, 113, 378, 394.

[5] Of Highnam, M.P. for Gloucester 1679 and 1689–95: *V.C.H. Glos.* x. 19; Williams, *Parl. Hist. of Glos.* 201.

[6] Of Westbury-on-Severn, knighted in 1674 and M.P. for Gloucester 1689–90: *V.C.H. Glos.* x. 87–8; Glos. R.O., D 36/T 54–5; Williams, *Parl. Hist. of Glos.* 203.

[7] Of Matson: *V.C.H. Glos.* iv. 441.

[8] Attorney, of Barton Street: ibid. 393, 395; GBR B 3/3, p. 530.

[9] Carrier and innkeeper, later pinmaker, of Gloucester: *V.C.H. Glos.* iv. 107–8.

[10] On instruction from the Crown following their appointment 18 Apr 1672 to the common council: Rudder, *Glos.* App. p.v.

	n.d.	John Rogers, app. of Thos. Rogers, baker
	n.d.	Wal. Atkins, son of Rob., cordwainer
	n.d.	Wm. Dawsinge, son of Wal., blacksmith
139		**Henry Norwood, esq., mayor 1672–3**
	n.d.	Wm. Byrd, son of Dan., feltmaker
	n.d.	Ant. Smart, son of Ric., cordwainer
	n.d.	John Shipton, son of John
	n.d.	Thos. Childe, app. of Thos. Childe, maltster, decd., [by patrimony][1]
	n.d.	Thos. Parker the younger [by patrimony][1]
	n.d.	Ric. Barnelme, son of Ric., victualler, late of Gloucester
140	n.d.	Thos. Stephens, son of Thos., pinmaker
	n.d.	Rob. Murrell, app. of Thos. Barrett, cutler, decd.
	n.d.	John Wadley the younger [by apprenticeship][1]
	n.d.	Sam Ives† by apprenticeship*
	n.d.	John Higgins† by apprenticeship*
	n.d.	John Higgs, app. of Ric. Cooke, chandler, late of Gloucester
141	n.d.	Wm. Barnes [by apprenticeship][1]
	n.d.	Hen. Holliday, app. of Ric. Morris, carpenter, late of Gloucester
	n.d.	John Hyett, app. of Rob. Payne, mercer
	n.d.	Thos. Hill† by apprenticeship*
	n.d.	Wm. Wadley, app. of Jas. Slicer, tanner
142	n.d.	Geo. Cooke, son of Ric., chandler
	n.d.	Leigh James, son of Leigh, baker
	n.d.	John Wood, son of John, tanner, late of Gloucester
	n.d.	Peter Haines, son of Peter, grocer
	n.d.	Ric. Edwards, son of Ric., baker, decd.
	n.d.	John Lugg the younger [by patrimony][1]
	n.d.	John Woodward the younger [by patrimony][1]
143	n.d.	Ric. Nash the younger [by patrimony][1]
	n.d.	Rob. Yarnold, son of Thos., mariner, decd.
	n.d.	Thos. Greene the younger [by patrimony][1]
	n.d.	John Sparrowhawke, son of Rob.†*
	n.d.	Chas. Sisemore, son of Sam., barber-surgeon, decd.
	n.d.	Rob. Horward,[2] son of Geof., woollen-draper, late of Gloucester
144	n.d.	Gustavus Swayne, son of Wm., late of Gloucester*
	n.d.	Thos. Clutterbooke, son of Amity, late of Gloucester*
	n.d.	Wm. Barker, son of a pinmaker*
	n.d.	John King, app. of Jas. King, scrivener
	n.d.	Wm. Brocke [by apprenticeship]*[3]
	n.d.	John Coopy, app. of John Niccolls, tanner, decd.
145	n.d.	Nat. Byford, tailor, [by apprenticeship][3]
	n.d.	Thos. Panter, app. of Ric. Stephens, tobacconist
	n.d.	John Webb, app. of a baker*
	n.d.	Francis Symes, app. of a tailor*
	n.d.	John Bickarton, app. of Giles Reeve, gunsmith
	n.d.	Thos. White, app. of Ric. White, cordwainer

[1] GBR F 4/7, p.v.

[2] Also spelt *Harward*.

[3] GBR F 4/7, p.v.

146		n.d.	Jas. [Butler], duke of Ormonde,†[1]
		n.d.	John [King], Baron Kingston,†[2]
		n.d.	Sir Wm. Coventry, [Kt.],†
		n.d.	Reginald Bray, esq.,†[3]
		n.d.	Wm. Dutton, esq.,†[4]
		n.d.	John Sackvill, esq.,† [by gift][7]
		n.d.	Fleetwood Dormer, esq.,†
		n.d.	Edw. Selwyn, gent.,†[5]
		n.d.	Dennis Cooke, gent.,†[6]
		n.d.	Jas. Clarke, gent.,†
		n.d.	John Wilcocks, gent.,† (of Newnham by fine)
		n.d.	Thos. Wilcocks, gent.,† (of Newnham by fine)
147		n.d.	Hen. [Somerset], marquess of Worcester,† (by gift)[8]
		n.d.	Ferdinando Meighen, gent.,† (by gift)[9]
		n.d.	Wal. Younge† (by gift)
		n.d.	John Powell, esq.,† common councillor appointed by king, by gift[10]
148			**William Cooke, esq., mayor 1673–4**
		n.d.	John Morse, son of Thos., cordwainer
		n.d.	Wm. Perry, app. of Wm. Madocke, tailor
		n.d.	Wm. Phelpes, son of Ric., (glover, decd.)*[11]
		n.d.	Sam. Hodges, app. of Jesse Nash, feltmaker
		n.d.	Thos. Barrett† [by apprenticeship]*[12]
149		n.d.	Wm. Goodcheape, app. of Thos. Goodcheape, cordwainer
		n.d.	Thos. Ady, app. of John Perkes, baker
	1674	3 Apr	John Heaven, app. of John Beard, silkweaver
		n.d.	Thos. Wilmott, app. of Thos. Lane, chandler
		n.d.	Wm. Stowell, app. of Wm. Stowell, pinmaker
150		n.d.	Geo. Horne, app. of Ric. Williams, cooper
		n.d.	Thos. Dewxell, app. of John Welstead, blacksmith
		n.d.	Thos. Bicke, app. of Lawr. Lugg, baker
		n.d.	Rob. Berry, app. of Jas. Phillips the younger, tailor
		n.d.	Thos. Longden, son of Rob., ironmonger
151		n.d.	Ric. Greene, son of Rowland, brewer, late of Gloucester
		n.d.	Thos. Hamonds, app. of Ric. Swett, glazier
		n.d.	Rob. Greene, son of Ric., baker, late of Gloucester
		n.d.	Thos. Davis, son of Thos., wiredrawer, late of Gloucester by gift

1 *Complete Peerage*, x. 152.
2 Ibid. vii. 297.
3 Of Great Barrington: *V.C.H. Glos.* vi. 19.
4 Of Sherborne: ibid. 123.
5 Son of Wm., of Matson: ibid. iv. 442.
6 Son of Wm., of Highnam: *Visit. Glos. 1682–3*, 47–8.
7 GBR F 4/7, p.v; by act of 29 Nov 1672 the mayor was to award the freedom to the duke and 'persons of honour or quality' attending him on his visit to Gloucester: ibid. B 3/3, p. 547.
8 High steward of Gloucester, awarded the freedom by act of 8 Sept 1673 during a visit to the city: ibid. B 3/3, pp. 576–7; cf. *Complete Peerage*, xii (2), 863.
9 By act of 14 Aug 1672, ? attorney, of Gloucester, 'having well deserved of this city': GBR B 3/3, pp. 510–1, 529.
10 On instruction from the Crown following his appointment 18 Apr 1672 to the common council: Rudder, *Glos.* App. p.v. Powell, town clerk 1674–85 and 1687–92 and a justice of Common Pleas, was M.P. for Gloucester 1685–7 and was knighted in 1691: *V.C.H. Glos.* iv. 105; Williams, *Parl. Hist. of Glos.* 202–3.
11 By act of 1 Dec 1673: GBR B 3/3, p. 595.
12 Ibid. F 4/7, p. 5.

		n.d.	Hen. Partridge, son of Thos., baker
		n.d.	John Elliotte, son of John, wiredrawer
152		n.d.	Wm. Beale, app. of Thos. Goodcheape, cordwainer
		n.d.	Thos. Cowcher, son of John, pinmaker, late of Gloucester
		n.d.	Jonathan Dubberly, app. of Cecily Cowcher, pinmaker
		n.d.	Steph. Blissard, app. of Isaac Lumbard, sergeweaver and woolcomber
		n.d.	Thos. Webb, Sergeant Webb, } sons of Sergeant, yeoman, decd.
153		n.d.	Hen. Ashmeade, app. of Ric. Humphris, butcher, decd.
		n.d.	Edm. Hartland, app. of Ric. Davis, glover, late of Gloucester
		n.d.	Geo. [Berkeley], Lord Berkeley,†[1] (by gift)[2]
		n.d.	Jas. de Moulyn, M.D.,† (by gift)[3]
		n.d.	Edm. Allen, son of Edm., yeoman
		n.d.	Chas. Anstee, son of Chas., butcher
154		n.d.	Hen. Cox, son of Ric., cordwainer
		n.d.	Rob. Porter, son of Rob., mercer, decd.
		n.d.	John Guy, son of Ric., butcher
		n.d.	Sam. Palmer, son of Edm., baker
		n.d.	Thos. Snell, gent., son of Nic., gent.
		n.d.	Thos. Baker, app. of Ric. Nash, feltmaker
		n.d.	Jacob Lumbard, app. of Isaac Lumbard, sergeweaver
155		n.d.	Jas. Bidle, son of Jas., haberdasher
		n.d.	Thos. Cleevely, son of Wm., woollen-draper, decd.
		n.d.	Jasper Lugg, son of Lawr., baker
		n.d.	Wm. Mathewes, apothecary, [by apprenticeship][4]
		n.d.	John Knowles, son of Hen., brazier
		n.d.	Jos. Hanckes, app. of John Heyward, feltmaker
		n.d.	Wm. Scudamore, son of Wm., gent.
156		n.d.	Wm. Dawe, app. of Abel Lewis, tiler and plasterer
		n.d.	John Langford, son of Toby, gent.
		n.d.	John Drue, app. of John Greene the elder, cooper
		n.d.	Chas. Tony, son of Chas., gent., decd.
		n.d.	John Longden, son of Rob., ironmonger
		n.d.	Wm. Randle, haulier, (by fine)
157		n.d.	Jos. Munday, victualler, (by fine)[5]
		n.d.	John Longe, app. of John Bennett, button-maker, late of Gloucester
158			**Duncombe Colchester, esq., mayor 1674–5**
	1674	12 Oct	Wm. Bradgate, son of Ric., barber-surgeon, decd.
		n.d.	John Fewtrell, son of Wm., tailor
		n.d.	Thos. Turner, son of Thos., victualler, late of Gloucester
		n.d.	Wm. Wall, carpenter, [by apprenticeship][6]
		n.d.	Rob. Fewtrell, son of Edw., tailor, decd.
159		n.d.	Geo. Marshall, app. of Jesse Nash, feltmaker
		n.d.	John Bradley, son of Hen., feltmaker
		n.d.	Geo. Warde, son of Phil., victualler, late of Gloucester

[1] Of Berkeley: *Complete Peerage*, ii. 139–40.
[2] By act of 29 July 1674: GBR B 3/3, p. 612.
[3] By act of 3 Aug 1674: ibid. p. 615.
[4] Ibid. F 4/7, p. 5.
[5] Having married a freeman's widow: ibid. B 3/3, pp. 563, 617.
[6] Ibid. F 4/7, p. 28.

		n.d.	Wm. Haies, son of Josiah*
		n.d.	John Harris, son of Thos., gunsmith
		n.d.	John Greene, son of John, cooper
160		n.d.	Nic. Williams, son of Nic., joiner, late of Gloucester
		n.d.	John Sowdley, woolcomber, (by fine)[1]
		n.d.	Dan. Byrd, son of Dan., feltmaker
		n.d.	Thos. Elliote, son of John, wiredrawer
		n.d.	Ric. Quench, victualler, (by fine)[2]
		n.d.	Dan. Lysons, gent., son of Dan., gent., late of Gloucester
		n.d.	Jos. Holder, app. of Ric. Holder, pinmaker
161		n.d.	John Drinkwater, app. of John Lugg, pinmaker, decd.
		n.d.	Edw. Heyward, app. of John Beard, silkweaver
	1675	15 Mar	John Hobson, son of John, mercer, decd., [by gift][3]
			John Smallwood, son of John, barber-surgeon, decd.
			Rog. Willy, tailor, by fine of £8
			Thos. Iles, son of Thos., blacksmith, late of Gloucester
162			Ant. Davis, son of John, cobbler, late of Gloucester
		12 Apr	Ric. Parsons, John Mericke, } apps. of Wal. Harris, cordwainer, late of Gloucester
			Thos. Hale, app. of Jas. Tyler, cordwainer
			Chris. Haies, son of Hen., cordwainer
			John Hobbs, son of John, feltmaker, decd.
163			John Hamonds, gent., son of a woollen-draper, late of Gloucester*
			Nic. Webb, son of Nic., gent.
			Wm. Clarke, son of Wm., mercer
			Francis Woodward, app. of a mercer, late of Gloucester*
			John Wells, son of a cobbler, late of Gloucester*
			John Wilmotts, son of John
			Thos. Beard, son of John, mercer, late of Gloucester
			Thos. Tainton, son of Wal., grocer, decd.
164			Giles Grevile, son of Giles, mercer, decd.
			Nat. Lye, clerk,[4] son of Giles, chandler, decd.
			Jas. Powell, gent., son of John, ald., decd.
			Sam. Smi[th],[5] app. of John Thomas, cordwainer, late of Gloucester
			Wm. Pitt, app. of Ric. Stephens, tobacconist
			Sam. Pitt, app. of Francis Yates, cordwainer
			Wm. Kinge, son of Wm., pinmaker, [by gift][6]
165			Thos. Webb, son of Nic., gent.
			Benj. Beard, son of a gent., decd.*
			Edw. Whittingham, son of Thos., baker
			Ric. Ayleway, app. of Thos. Belcher, baker, decd.
			Wal. Bosly, app. of Ric. Bosly, feltmaker
			Wm. Savory, son of Wm., farrier
166			Thos. Berry, app. of Abel Lewis, plasterer, late of Gloucester
			Thos. Winiard, wiredrawer, as if an apprentice
			Wm. Humfras, tailor, as if an apprentice[7]

[1] By act of 21 Oct 1674: ibid. B 3/3, p. 624.
[2] By act of 16 Sept 1674, tailor: ibid. p. 616.
[3] Ibid. F 4/7, p. 28.
[4] Rector of Cowley and Kemerton and later archdeacon of Gloucester and rector of Dursley: *Alumni Oxon. 1500–1714*, iii. 953.
[5] GBR F 4/7, p. 28.
[6] Ibid.
[7] By patrimony: ibid.

John Hawthorne, app. of Edw. Charleton, wiredrawer
21 June Sam. Browne, app. of Hen. Clarke, glazier
9 Aug Thos. Rogers, app. of Wm. Jordan, apothecary
167 Wm. Phelpes, son of Nic., gent.
5 July Wm. Lacy, app. of Humph. Hiron, vintner, late of Gloucester
Geo. Broad, app. of Thos. Lugg the younger, mercer, decd.
Dan. Bryan, app. of Sam. Whitle, cordwainer
168 16 Aug Wm. Powell, son of Wm., haulier, decd.
30 Aug Benj. Plott, son of Cornelius, gent.
John Engly, app. of Ric. Whitfeild, baker, late of Gloucester
27 Sept Moses Vaughan, son of Thos., joiner
John Browne, son of John, mercer, decd.
169–70
171 **William Selwyn, esq., mayor 1675–6**

25 Oct Tristram Lodge, app. of John Greene the elder, cooper
Thos. Baylee, son of Thos., serjeant-at-mace
6 Dec Wm. Harris, son of John, mercer, decd.
26 Nov Jos. Baker, gent.† by gift[1]
172 29 Nov Sam. Atkins, son of Rob., gardener
1676 12 Jan (Sir) John Guise, Bt.,†[2] (by gift)
14 Jan John Heyford, paver, (by fine)[3]
21 Jan Wm. Cromleholme, gent., (by fine)
24 Jan Hen. Bubb, app. of Wm. Russell, skinner, ald.
14 Feb Wm. Atkins, app. of John Heyward, feltmaker
Wm. Kent, son of Wm., cordwainer, decd.
173 Wm. Endall, son of Wm., butcher, decd.
3 Apr Thos. Clarke, app. of Wm. Kinge, wiredrawer
Thos. Joseph, app. of John Niccolls, tanner, decd.
Ric. Turner, app. of Winston Cox the elder, cordwainer
Thos. Conon, app. of Edw. Cripps, butcher
174 26 July (Chas.) Osbourne, esq.,† brother of [Thos.] Osbourne, [earl of Danby], Lord Treasurer of England, by gift*[4]
John White, app. of Edw. Clayfeild, tanner
20 Sept (Wm.) Howard† (by gift)
Jasper Lugg, son of Lawr.
175 Jos. Humfras, app. of Ric. Nash, grocer
Giles Rodway, app. of John Rodway, mercer
John Bucke, app. of John Williams, ropemaker
8 May Thos. Vaisey, son of Wal., gent.
Rob. Reade, app. of Francis Singleton, ironmonger
176 John Clarvoe, app. of Hen. Abbotts, baker
21 July Wm. Price, app. of John Tyler, cordwainer
7 Aug Jos. Palmer, son of Geo., baker
25 Sept John Stephens, app. of David Griffin, tailor
4 Sept Wm. Merry, app. of Jos. Phelps, grocer
177–9

[1] Servant of John Dorney, former town clerk, on his appointment as attorney in the city's hundred and piepowder courts: ibid. B 3/3, pp. 643–4.

[2] Of Brockworth: Glos. R.O., D 326/F 13. Whig, disfranchised 13 Feb 1685 for having, among other things, 'upon all occasions slighted the government' of the city and readmitted by act of 18 Nov 1686: GBR B 3/3, pp. 876, 915, 918; cf. *V.C.H. Glos.* iv. 114.

[3] 'Necessary workman to this city': GBR B 3/3, p. 646.

[4] By act of 27 July 1676: ibid. p. 658; cf. below: ibid. C 9/7, p. 183. For the earl of Danby, *Complete Peerage*, vii. 507–9.

180			**William Russell, esq., mayor 1676–7**
		16 Oct	Thos. Webly, app. of Thos. Partridge the younger, baker
		30 Oct	Rob. Stone, app. of Thos. Robins, tanner
			Thos. Probert, app. of Wm. Day, tanner
		3 Nov	Giles Webly, app. of Ric. Nash
181		6 Nov	Phil. Hughes, app. of Wal. Beard, tailor, decd.
		11 Dec	Wm. Haines, son of Thos., late of Gloucester*
		6 Nov	John Clifford, app. of Wm. Day, tanner
	1677	15 Jan	Ric. Lane, app. of Toby Jordan, stationer, decd.
			John Mathewes, son of John, butcher, decd.
182			Ric. Jenings, app. of David Griffin, tailor
		22 Jan	John Painter, son of John, glazier, late of Gloucester
		29 Jan	Mat. Mathewes, son of John, brewer
			John Prince, son of Thos., gent., decd.
183		5 Feb	Steph. West, app. of Jacob Hague, grocer
		11 Feb	Hen. Grevile, app. of Dan. Lysons, draper
	1676	21 July	John Vaughan, joiner, by gift[1]
	1677	19 Feb	John Ludnam, musician, by gift
			Thos. Williams, app. of Wm. Williams, butcher
	1676	27 July	Chas. Osborne, esq.,† by gift[2]
184	1677	23 Apr	Thos. Ravenor, app. of Wm. Eldridge, silkweaver
		7 May	Thos. Freeman, app. of John Hancoke, bodice-maker
		30 Apr	Thos. Probert, app. of Jas. Phillipps the younger, tailor
		14 May	Ric. Quench, app. of Thos. Chamlyn, turner, late of Gloucester
185			John Hartland, app. of John Dobbs, barber-surgeon, late of Gloucester
		18 May	Thos. Baker, app. of Edw. Clayfield, tanner
		28 May	Thos. Cooke, son of Thos., butcher, decd.
			Edw. Vaughan, vintner, by fine of £10
186			Geo. Bowler, victualler, by fine of £10
		7 June	Ric. Hoskins, victualler, by fine of £10
			Wm. Redwood, victualler, by fine of £10
		18 June	John Fones, son of Godfrey the elder, cordwainer
		3 July	Thos. Hale, son of Wm.
187			Mat. Vaus, victualler, by fine of £10
		18 July	Sam. Fletcher, victualler, by fine of £10
			Thos. Pace, app. of Thos. Merrett, cordwainer
		23 July	Lawr. Dunne, son of Edw.*
188		2 Aug	Giles Hayward, app. of David Griffin, tailor
		27 Aug	Mat. Phelps, app. of John Gwilliam, feltmaker
			Thos. Turner, son of John, cook, decd.
		24 Sept	Isaac Skillum, son of Wm., tanner
	1681	21 Dec[3]	Ric. Corsnet, vintner, (by fine)
188–91			
192			**Thomas Price, esq., mayor 1677–8**
	1677	8 Oct	Nat. Iles, victualler, by fine of £10
			Wal. Powell, silkweaver, by gift
		15 Oct	Wm. Sparks, (footpost between Gloucester and Bristol), by fine of £8
			John Merry, app. of John Pirkes, baker, decd.
193		22 Oct	Giles Kent, app. of John Tyler, cordwainer

[1] Entry belongs to previous mayoralty.
[2] Entry belongs to previous mayoralty; cf. above: GBR C 9/7, p. 174.
[3] Date incorrect; by act of 21 Dec 1677: ibid. B 3/3, p. 692.

			Dan. Haward, app. of Dan. Collericke, bodice-maker
			Dan. Collericke, son of Dan., bodice-maker
		29 Oct	Job Dowle, son of Clement, mercer
194		12 Nov	Thos. Pembridge, app. of Ric. Nash, grocer
		26 Nov	Benj. Freeman, app. of Wm. Niccolls, tanner
		3 Dec	Wm. Bubb, app. of Ric. Partridge, baker
195		21 Dec	Abraham Clarke, esq.,†[1] by gift
			Rob. Frampton, S.T.P., (dean of Gloucester cathedral),† by gift
			Abraham Gregory, S.T.P., (prebendary of Gloucester cathedral),† by gift
196	1678	1 Mar	Sam. Collett, app. of Thos. Lugg, haberdasher
			Edw. Downebell, son of Steph., vintner, decd.
		29 Mar	John Thayer, app. of Wm. Burt, tailor
197			Jas. Phillips, son of Jas., tailor
		29 Apr	Thos. Bowler, app. of Edw. Swaine, collar-maker
		6 May	Hen. Meadway, son of Hen., hosier
198		13 May	John Shortt, app. of Ant. Mutlow, horner
			Wm. Horrold, son of John, tailor
		27 May	Moses Cooke, app. of John Wealsteed, blacksmith
		1 July	John Hiron, app. of Hen. Lea, cordwainer
199			Thos. Price, app. of Ant. Lea, cordwainer
			John Smith, app. of Ric. Nash, feltmaker
		5 July	John Williams, son of Nic., joiner
		15 July	Sam. Webly, app. of John Atkins, cordwainer
200		29 July	John Mount, app. of John Perkes, baker, decd.
			John Greene, son of Rowland, brewer, decd.
			Ambrose Weyman, app. of Winston Cox, cordwainer
201		16 Aug	John Lane, app. of Wm. Brymyard, tobacco-pipemaker
		19 Aug	John Lovett, app. of Sam. Heath, silkweaver
			John Whitehead, dyer, by fine of £15
202		26 Aug	Thos. Fones, son of John, glover
		2 Dec	Rob. Lane, app. of Wm. Brymyard, pipemaker[2]
	1679	4 Feb	Chas. Berkley, K.G. (*praenobilis ordinis periscellidis*),†[3] by gift[2]
			Edw. Slaughter by gift[2]
		10 Feb	Ric. Sparkes, son of Thos., sievemaker[2]
203–6			
207			**John Wagstaffe, esq., mayor 1678–9**
		1 Mar	Edw. Till by patrimony*
		4 Apr	Thos. Bonfield, app. of John Marston and his wife Rebecca†
	1681	1 May[4]	Wm. Baldwyn, silkweaver, (by fine)
	1679	26 May	Jos. Keys, app. of Rob. Payne and his wife†*
		16 June	John Wyman, shoemender, [by apprenticeship][5]
208		4 Aug	Edw. Charlton, son of Edw.
			Ric. Gelf by gift
		8 Aug	Wm. Smith, son of Ric., gent.
			John Ward, son of Phil.†
			Jos. Young, app. of Sam. Pitt, pinmaker

[1] Of Flaxley: P.R.O., E 179/247/13, rot. 24d.; cf. A.W. Crawley-Boevey, *Perverse Widow* (1898), 60–3.

[2] Entry belongs to following mayoralty.

[3] Of Berkeley, M.P. for Gloucester 1679–81: Williams, *Parl. Hist. of Glos.* 202.

[4] Date incorrect; by act of 1 May 1679: GBR B 3/3, p. 724.

[5] Ibid. F 4/7, p. 160.

209		11 Aug	John Clarke, son of Ric. [and] app. of Wm. Fewtrell,† [by apprenticeship][1]
			Edw. Tyler, son of John, cordwainer
			Jas. Hazelwood, son of Chris.†
			John Turner, son of Thos.†
			Edw. Elliotts, son of John†
			John Morris, app. of Thos. Aram, ald.
210		18 Aug	Hugh Prosser, app. of Cornelius Plott, tailor
			Wm. Cowcher, son of John†
			Rowland Freeman, app. of John Beard, mercer
			Wm. Holford, gent., son of Rob., gent., ald.,† (by gift)
			Wm. Arnell, son of Thos.
			John Nurse, son of John, cooper
211		19 Aug	Edw. Smith, esq.,† by gift
		22 Aug	Herbert Rogers, son of John, ald.
			John Aram, son of Thos., ald.
			Wm. Hays, son of Hen., cordwainer
			John Grafstock, son of John, butcher
			Geo. Moor, son of Geo. butcher
212		30 Aug	(Sir) Gabriel Low, Kt.,†[2] (by gift)
			John Keene, app. of Hen. Gilbert, cordwainer
	1680	7 Sept	John Crumpe, innholder, (by fine)[3]

Henry Fowler, esq., mayor 1679–80[4]

	1679	8 Dec	Dan. Ferrett, app. of Nat. Ferrett*
	1680	26 Jan	John Ward, app. of John Washford, blacksmith
213		9 Feb	Arthur Gunn, app. of Augustine Gwin, cordwainer
			Ric. Fords, app. of John Greene, cooper
		23 Feb	John Washborne, son of Dan.
		24 Mar	Hen. Jefferis, app. of Sam. Kent, joiner
214		28 July	Sam. Pembridge, app. of Mary Parker, baker
		9 Aug	John Madocks, } sons of Wm., tailor
			Rob. Madocks, }
		6 Sept	Dan. Hinton, app. of Wm. Sampson, cordwainer
215		7 Sept	Wm. Baker, innholder, (by fine)
			Ric. Steight, innholder, (by fine)
			Jas. Lander, woolcomber, (by fine)
216–20			

221 **John Gythens, esq., mayor 1680–1**

	1681	17 Jan	Steph. Gythens, son of John, mayor
		24 Jan	John Rogers, son of John, ald.
		17 Jan	John Bell, son of John, silkweaver
			Thos. Williams, son of Nic., joiner
	1680	15 Nov	Simon Lawrence, app. of Thos. Sellwyn, cordwainer
222			John Bicknell, son of Wm., tailor
	1681	14 Feb	Francis Pace, son of Sam., baker
			John Badger, son of Albert, pinmaker
			Giles Nourse, son of Jos., cordwainer
			Thos. Edding, son of John, pinmaker

[1] Ibid.
[2] Of Newark, Ozleworth: *Visit. Glos. 1682–3*, 118.
[3] Entry belongs to following mayoralty.
[4] MS. gives Wagstaffe as mayor until p. 214 where the mistake is corrected.

223		Giles Stephens, } sons of Thos., pinmaker
		Sam. Stephens, }
		Dennis Jones, son of Thos., pinmaker
		John Wright, app. of John Bell, silkweaver
		John Hickman, son of John, gent.
224		Thos. Chewett, app. of Thos. Sellwyn, cordwainer
		Isaac Aldrington, app. of Thos. Pace, cooper
		Abraham Thomas, son of John, feltmaker
		John Nicholls, son of Rhys, brewer
		Sam. Heyward, son of John, feltmaker
225		John Jones, app. of Wm. Jones, cobbler
		Wm. Thomas, app. of John Gwinn, silkweaver
		Ric. Beaven, app. of Jas. Walker, button-maker
		Thos. Bowridge, app. of Isaac Lumbard, sergeweaver
		Ric. Knight, app. of Thos. Meek, cordwainer
226		Sam. Elliott, son of John, wiredrawer
		Edw. Newman, son of Edw., butcher
		Phil. Greene, son of Phil., brickmaker
		Wm. Burton, app. of Wal. Hill, cobbler
		John Price, son of John, ald.
227		Ric. Rathbone, app. of Wm. Brymyard, pipemaker
		Thos. Ready, app. of John Cox, cordwainer
		Thos. Loggins, son of Augustine, haulier
		Humph. Merry, son of Humph., wiredrawer
		John Mower, app. of John Mower, victualler
228	28 Mar	John Gardner, app. of John Freame, baker
		Sam. Humphris, son of Ric., butcher
	16 May	Dan. Yate, app. of Sergeant White, cordwainer
	18 July[1]	(Sir) Thos. Thynn, Bt.,†[2] by gift
229	1 Aug	Thos. Lewis, clockmaker,† (by gift)
	15 Aug	Thos. Weaver (the younger), pipemaker, (by gift)[3]
		Jos. Harris, app. of Mary Broade, baker
	29 Aug	Wm. Bicknell, son of Wm., tailor
		Wm. Little, son of John, cordwainer, of Maisemore
230	12 Sept	Sam. Willetts, son of Sam., wiredrawer
	15 Sept	John Clutterbooke, LL.D., son of Steph.
		Wm. Gythens, son of John, ald.[4]
		Thos. Trippett by patrimony*
	19 Sept	Ric. Cowcher, son of Ric., pinmaker
231		Thos. Hill, app. of Ric. Nash, feltmaker
	26 Sept	Wm. Jelfe, son of Thos., baker
		John Greene, blackwireman,[5] by gift
		Ric. Puxon (the elder), labourer, by gift
232		
233		**John Rogers, esq., mayor 1681–2**
	5 Oct	(Sir) Rob. Atkins the younger, Kt.,†[6] by gift

[1] Or *14 July*.
[2] Of Kempsford: *V.C.H. Glos.* vii. 99.
[3] By apprenticeship: GBR F 5/24; app. of Wm. Brimiard, pipemaker, to pay fees for enrolling his indentures: ibid. B 3/3, p. 798.
[4] Mayor.
[5] Provost marshal: GBR B 3/3, p. 803.
[6] Of Pinbury Park, Duntisbourne Rouse, author of the first printed history of the county: *Trans. B.G.A.S.* l. 240–6.

		5 Dec	Jas. Keele, app. of John Bell, silkweaver
		10 Dec	Wm. Crasse, app. of John Hancocke, bodice-maker
		12 Dec	Dennis Seysmore, son of John, barber
234		19 Dec	Thos. Soule, app. of John Soule, vintner
	1682	23 Jan	Wal. Wornford, app. of Francis Yate, cordwainer
		11 Jan	(Sir) Chas. Kemmis, Kt.,† by gift
		27 Jan	Wm. Madocks, gent., (by fine)
		27 Feb	Thos. Kersey, app. of Thos. Gardner, pinmaker
		3 Apr	John Taynton, son of Wal., grocer, late of Gloucester
		13 Mar	Francis Harris, son of Thos., gunsmith, late of Gloucester
235		13 Apr	Jos. Howell, app. of John Wasfeild, blacksmith
		7 Apr	Ric. Thorpe, mercer, (by fine)
		1 May	John Bishopp† by apprenticeship*
		5 May	Benj. Rose, app. of Sam. Rose, brewer
		11 May	Wm. Edwards, app. of Arnold Aram, haberdasher of hats
			Mat. Mills† by patrimony
236		19 June	Wm. Nicholls, son of Wm., tanner
			Chas. Turner, son of Thos., labourer, late of Gloucester
			Thos. Williams, app. of Joan Symons, glover
			Thos. Edmunds, son of John, milliner
			Thos. Mathews, son of Wm., of Ledbury, Herefs.
		3 July	Phil. Clarke, app. of Joan Howlett, butcher
			Wm. Whittington, clerk, [by patrimony][1]
			Thos. Pury, gent., of Gloucester, son of Thos.†[2]
			Thos. Fletcher, labourer, by fine of £5
			John Bazard, app. of Nat. Cooke, baker
237		4 Aug	John Barret, app. of John Brocke, glover and fellmonger
			Seth Blanch, app. of Thos. Croker, carpenter[3]
			Thos. Weale, app. of Toby Taynton, grocer
		7 Aug	Geo. Farley, son of Thos., cutler
		14 Aug	Jonathan Brookes, app. of John Cox, cordwainer
238		21 Aug	Francis Burford, app. of John Woodward, combmaker
			Wm. Wellavise, app. of Ric. Nash, feltmaker
		24 Aug	John Soudley, app. of John Soudley, jersey-comber
		11 Sept	Miles White† by apprenticeship
			Rob Davis† by apprenticeship
			Thos. Shipton† by patrimony
239			**John Webb, esq., mayor 1682–3**
		9 Oct	Thos. Gibbs, app. of John Wellsteed, blacksmith
		16 Oct	Mic. Jennings, son of Hen., yeoman, of Hempsted, and app. of Thos. Cooke, butcher, by apprenticeship
			Jos. Pegler, son of John, farmer, of Bledington, and app. of Thos. Robbins, tanner, by apprenticeship
			Thos. Chandler, son of Ric., saddler
			Thos. Oldridge, son of Thos., yeoman†*
		9 Oct	Thos. Sturt, fishmonger, by fine of £15
240		30 Oct	Rob. Walters, woolcomber, by fine
		23 Oct	Francis Reeve, son of Francis, stonecutter, by apprenticeship[4]

[1] GBR F 5/25

[2] M.P. for Gloucester 1656–8: Williams, *Parl. Hist. of Glos.* 198.

[3] Croker previously disfranchised for taking Blanch and his brother Dan. Blanch as apps. solely to enable them to enter the freedom: GBR B 3/3, pp. 674–5.

[4] Cf. below: ibid. C 9/7, p. 241.

		23 Dec	Wm. Cooke, tailor, (by fine)[1]
	1683	8 Jan	Jas. Withinbury, son of Jas., carpenter, by apprenticeship
		12 Mar	John Gwynn, son of Thos., clerk, of Horton
		12 Feb	Ric. Fenn, stationer, by fine
			Rog. Smith, trowman, by fine[2]
241			Francis Reeve, son of Francis, stonecutter[3]
			Dan. Bishoppe, tailor, by apprenticeship
		30 Apr	Adam Colericke,[4] son of Dan., bodice-maker
			Thos. Cox, app. of Thos. Mason, baker
			Alex Readdy, app. of Wm. Bicknell, tailor
			Jas. Man, app. of Thos. Martin, glover
242		20 Apr	John Stanter, innholder, (by fine)
			Aaron Webly, innholder, (by fine)
		7 May	Ric. Nash, app. of Francis Singleton, ironmonger
		2 July	John Tyler, app. of Hester, widow of Edm. Palmer, baker
		8 July	Geo. Nott, app. of Lawr. Not, carpenter
		18 June	Elisha Hathaway, son of Elisha, weaver†
243		23 July	Ant. Goddard, app. of Jas. Price, pewterer
			Jas. Clifford, son of Jas., pinmaker
		4 Aug	John Branch, son of John, merchant, late of Gloucester
			John Brewster, son of Sam., gent., late of Gloucester
		20 Aug	Jas. Crowdey, app. of Wm. Madocks
		11 June	Thos. Pace, son of Sam., baker, of Newent
244		17 Sept	John Browne, son of John, butcher
			Wm. Allen, son of a grocer*
		n.d.	Hen. Wintle, son of Hen., cooper, decd.[5]
		8 Oct	Lawr. Not(t), son of Lawr., carpenter[6]

245 **John Price, esq., mayor 1683–4**

		21 Oct	Hen. Wintle, son of Hen., cooper, late of Gloucester[7]
		9 Nov	Nat. Veysee, app. of Wal. Vaysee, tailor
		16 Nov	Ric. Heming, } sons of Arnold, chandler, decd.
			Rob. Heming, }
	1684	21 Jan	Hen. Gilding, app. of Thos. Mills, baker
	1683	24 Dec	Wm. Baylee[8] by fine of £13 6*s* 8*d*
246	1684	28 Jan	Jonathan Greene, son of Wm., joiner
			Abraham Meadway, son of Hen.
			Thos. Lawrence, app. of Josiah Randle, baker
			Silvanus Dunn, son of Edw., combmaker
		4 Feb	Jacob Conklin, glassmaker, by fine of £13 6*s* 8*d*
247			Rob. Clarke, vintner, by fine of £13 6*s* 8*d*
		11 Feb	Wm. Messenger, son of Wm., gent.
		7 Mar	Ant. Workman, app. of Wm. Williams, butcher

[1] Had served part of his apprenticeship with John Cowdall, tailor, a freeman: ibid. B 3/3, p. 834.

[2] To continue paying the corporation tolls on goods carried on, and landed from, the river Severn: ibid. p. 836.

[3] Cf. above: ibid. C 9/7, p. 240.

[4] Also spelt *Coldricke*.

[5] Entry struck through; cf. below: GBR C 9/7, p. 245.

[6] Entry belongs to following mayoralty.

[7] Cf. above: GBR C 9/7, p. 244.

[8] Baylis: ibid. B 3/3, p. 853.

14 Mar Ric. Robinson, yeoman, by fine of £10
Jas. Rush, yeoman, by fine of £10
248 24 Mar Guy Ellis, app. of Thos. Longdon, ironmonger
John Cowdall, son of John, tailor
11 Apr Thos. Showell, app. of Thos. Rogers
John Phillips, app. of John Grafstock, butcher
John Annett, app. of John Harris, blacksmith
21 Apr Rob. Arrowsmith, app. of Thos. Dobbs, barber-surgeon
Thos. Watkins, app. of Wm. Gregory, butcher
John Browne, app. of Morgan Thomas, wiredrawer
249 12 May Ric. Davis, app. of John Beard, silkweaver
Hen. Turner, app. of Edw. Hayward, silkweaver
26 May Jas. Baker, app. of Geo. Moore, butcher
Abraham Young, app. of his father Wal.[†]
27 May Ric. Yate, maltster, by fine of 20 marks
19 June Chas. Tuf(f)ley, son of Chas., barber-surgeon, late of Gloucester
250 Wm. Stephens, son of Wm., cordwainer
23 June Jas. Marshfeild, fisherman, by fine of £10
7 July Jos. Pitt, app. of Jos. Phelps, feltmaker
11 Aug Edw. Holtham, son of Wm., chandler
13 Aug John Smart, son of John, joiner
251 8 Sept Jos. Felton, cutler, by fine of £10
10 Sept Isaac Watkins, labourer, by fine of £10
252–4
255 **William Lambe, esq., mayor 1684–5**

10 Oct Edw. Knowles, son of Hen., brazier
Jonathan Garway, app. of Jos. Phelps, grocer
1685 16 Feb John Grenden, app. of Jos. Phelps, feltmaker
Thos. Webb, son of John, ald.
John Gythens, son of John, ald.
256 23 Feb Edw. Meadway, son of Edw., hosier
2 Mar Geof. Beale, son of Geof., late of Gloucester
Jas. Hawkins, son of John, yeoman of Huntley, and app. of Hen. Abbotts, baker, [by apprenticeship][1]
Thos. Singleton, clerk, by patrimony
6 Mar Thos. Powell, son of John, gent., late of Gloucester
Jas. Seyer, son of Jas., tailor
257 John Hill, son of John, ald.
Humph. Hutchins, son of Humph., ironmonger
23 Mar John Benson, pargeter, by fine of £10
Wm. Benson, pargeter, by fine of £10
Thos. Mower, son of John, victualler
258 Sam. Clarke, app. of John Clarke, joiner
30 Mar Ric. Mason, son of Edw., saddler, by apprenticeship[2]
Wm. Clarke, app. of Lawr. Lugg, baker
13 Apr John Cox, son of Grey, brewer, late of Gloucester
John Collier, son of Wm., gunsmith
Wm. Cooke, son of Wm., baker, late of Gloucester
259 John Kircombe, son of Thos., blacksmith
Wm. Cowles, son of Wm., butcher
Solomon Sparkes, app. of Dan. Cowldricke, bodice-maker

[1] Ibid. F 4/7, p. 345, where entrant is called Jas. Hopkins.
[2] By patrimony: ibid.

Ric. Swaine, son of Edw., collar-maker, decd.
Ric. Turbett, app. of Thos. Martin, glover
John Ryland, son of John, tanner, decd.
260 27 Apr Rob. Bruckbanke, app. of Thos. Winiate, pinmaker
Rob. Rowles, app. of Edw. Cripps, butcher
John Poole, app. of Wm. Dawe, plasterer
Wm. Winniatte, app. of Thos. Winiatte, pinmaker
Jas. Miles, son of Jas., baker
18 May Thos. Baker, app. of John Hartland, barber-surgeon
261 4 May Thos. Hartland, son of Wm., pinmaker
[John] Birt,[1] son of Wm., tailor*
Wm. Slye, tailor, (by fine)
262
263 6 Sept John Moore, son of Geo., butcher
John Greening, son of a horner, decd.*
John Mathews, clerk, } sons of John, innholder, decd.
Hen. Mathews, }
Geo. Cowcher [by patrimony]*[1]
Edw. Elliott [by patrimony]*[1]
Ant. Walker, app. of Ric. Cooke, smith
264
265 **William Jordan, esq., mayor 1685–6**

23 Oct Jasper Freame, app. of Ric. Partridge, baker
Francis Oatley, app. of Ric. Cooke, feltmaker
13 Nov John Deane, innholder, (by fine)
David Simond, victualler, (by fine)
14 Dec John Dew, victualler, son of John, victualler, late of Gloucester
17 Dec Dan. Bishopp, son of Dan., tailor
31 Dec Chris. Eastham, victualler, (by fine)
266 1686 8 Feb Ric. Mathews, app. of Wm. Mathews, apothecary
20 Feb Wm. Andrews, app. of Wm. Barnes, saddler
29 Mar Wm. George, app. of Rog. Willey, tailor
2 Apr John Nest, app. of Hen. Holliday, carpenter
10 May John Lewis, son of John, pargeter
Wm. Phelpes, son of And., tanner
31 May Giles Bawle, app. of Francis Proben, cooper
14 June Thos. Aram, son of Thos., late ald.
267 26 July Steph. Berrow, son of Thos., tailor
9 Aug Clement Heyward, } sons of John, feltmaker
Sam. Heyward, }
23 Aug Jos. Onion, son of Thos., weaver
1 Oct Sam. Arkwell, victualler, (by fine)
23 Aug Wm. Hathaway, app. of John Mutley, turner
268
269 **John Hill, esq., mayor 1686–7**

8 Nov Abraham Puckeridge, app. of John Tyler, cordwainer
Chas. Jones, son of Thos., haulier, late of Gloucester
15 Nov Wm. Bubb, son of Toby, cordwainer, late of Gloucester
Sam. Wiggett, app. of Thos. Martin, glover
Jas. Hornedge, app. of Nic. Washfield, blacksmith

[1] GBR F 4/7, p. 345.

13 Dec Jas. Daw, app. of Rob. Cheeseman, cooper
1687 22 Jan Jeremiah Bubb, esq., son of Wm., apothecary, late of Gloucester
7 Feb Ric. Fletcher, app. of John Ward, blacksmith
270 John Webb, app. of John Harrold, tailor, decd.
11 Feb Geo. Willetts, son of Sam., pinmaker, decd.
John Sheppard, app. of Wm. Fowler, barber-surgeon
John Dobbs, son of John, barber, late of Gloucester
John Hughes, app. of John Cudd, silkweaver
4 Apr Ric. Weaver, son of Thos., butcher, decd.
11 Apr Thos. Sizemore, app. of Ric. Beard, tailor
18 Apr Jeremiah Whitfeild, app. of Jesse Nash, feltmaker
19 May Humph. Pendris, app. of Thos. Bick, baker
27 May Thos. Phillipps, son of Geo., feltmaker, decd.
13 May John Reeves, app. of Giles Reeve, gunsmith
271 4 July Ric. Carpenter, app. of Leigh James, baker
Geo. Mower, son of John, victualler
John Wintle, son of John, cordwainer, decd.
18 July Dan. Seyre, son of Dan., ropemaker
Chas. Williams, son of Nic., tailor, late of Gloucester
15 Aug Jonathan Clarke, baker [by apprenticeship][1]
John Heyford, app. of John Elliott, wiredrawer
Wm. Bliss, app. of Nat. Castle, baker
272 29 Aug Thos. Pheasant, app. of Wm. Boker, button-maker
And. Beard, app. of Ambrose Weyman, cordwainer
2 Sept Ric. Gwinnett, app. of Josiah Randle, baker
12 Sept Francis Brabant, son of Francis
19 Sept John Cook, son of Thos., cook, late of Gloucester
2 Oct Geo. Perkins, app. of Steph. Doubl[ ],[2] pinmaker
273 Hen. Plott, son of Cornelius, tailor
23 Sept Wm. Bidwell, app. of Ric. Till

John Hill, esq., mayor 1687–8

7 Dec Thos. Browne, esq., } by royal mandate[3]
Sam. Farmer, apothecary, }
274 14 Nov Thos. Farley, son of Thos.
John Gregory, son of John, butcher, late of Gloucester
Wm. Barrow, son of Wm., tailor, late of Gloucester
12 Dec John Essington, esq.,[†] by royal mandate[4]
275 Dan. Weyman, gent., by gift[5]
18 Dec John Carelesse, gent., by royal mandate[6]
23 Dec John Sextee, cheesemonger, (by fine)
Jeremiah Jennings, tailor, of Barton Street (by fine)
276 1688 2 Jan John Porter, app. of John Hayward, feltmaker
9 Jan John Bodnham, esq.,[†] by gift
2 Jan Wm. Birt, app. of Jas. Browne, pewterer
9 Jan John Wright, esq.,[†] by gift

[1] Ibid. p. 417.
[2] ? Doughton; cf. below: ibid. C 9/7, p. 278.
[3] By act of 8 Dec 1687 following the Crown's order for their election to the common council: ibid. B 3/6, f. 175 and v.
[4] Of Gossington Hall, Slimbridge, following the Crown's order for his election as common councillor: ibid.; *Visit. Glos. 1682–3*, 61.
[5] On his appointment as attorney in the city's courts: GBR B 3/6, f. 176v.
[6] Following the Crown's order for his election as common councillor: ibid. f. 175 and v.

		30 Jan	Wm. Wood, app. of Jas. Wood of Barton Street
		n.d.	John Greenwood, esq.,† by gift
		5 Mar	Wm. Maverly the younger, button-maker, (by fine)
		9 Jan	Hen. Trinder the younger, esq.,† by gift
		9 Mar	Ant. Chester, app. of Geo. Chester, baker
		9 Jan.	Wm. Guise, esq.,† by gift
			John Truman by gift[1]
277		12 Mar	John Ralph, labourer, (by fine)
			Thos. Crass, lastmaker, (by fine)
			Sam. Coke, app. of Jas. Jones, silkweaver
		23 Mar	Wm. Pace, app. of Benj. Cooke, tailor
			Jos. Webb, woolcomber, by fine of £10
		30 Apr	Ric. Brodway, } sons of Ric., yeoman
278			Edw. Brodway, }
		4 May	Ric. Webb, woolcomber, (by fine)
		2 May	Geo. Meighen, yeoman, (by fine)
			Edw. Love,[2] gent., (by gift)
		14 May	Chris. Estcourt, app. of Steph. Doughton the younger, pinmaker
279			Thos. Hawker, app. of Jane Watkins, maltster
		28 May	[Ric.] Swett,[3] son of Ric., glazier*
		16 June	Ralph Randle, app. of Giles Smith, baker
			Edw. Elliott, son of John
		28 Aug	Sam. Ham, son of Wm., butcher, late of Gloucester
280		5 Sept	Ric. Reeves, gent., son of a butcher*[4]
			Ric. Reever, M.A., son of a butcher, late of Gloucester*[5]
		19 Sept	Ric. Hill, app. of Albert Badger, pinmaker
			Wm. Bradley, son of Hen., feltmaker
		21 Sept	Ric. Winiatt, son of Thos., pinmaker
281		24 Sept	John Winiatt, pinmaker, [by patrimony][6]
			Toby Freeman, app. of John Bicknell, tailor
			Jos. Edwards, clerk, son of John, clerk†
		1 Oct	Thos. Engley, app. of John Linkinholt, wiredrawer†
			Jas. Bradley, son of Hen., feltmaker†

282 **Anselm Fowler, esq., mayor 1688**

		22 Oct	Nathan Nott, son of Lawr., carpenter, late of Gloucester

283 **William Cooke, esq., mayor 1688–9**[7]

		3 Dec	Sam. Burroughs, son of Sam., merchant
	1689	14 Jan	Edm. Humphris, app. of Thos. Meeke, currier
		11 Mar	Jonathan Davis, son of John, wiredrawer, late of Gloucester
		1 Mar	Hen. Beard, app. of John Longdon, ironmonger
284		20 May	Wm. Merrett, son of Wm.
			Thos. Winston, son of John, tailor, decd.
		9 June	Sam. Newman, app. of Thos. Parker, baker

[1] For payment of £15 for the office of serjeant-at-mace: ibid. f. 182v.
[2] Edw. Low: ibid. f. 194v.
[3] Ibid. F 4/7, p. 455.
[4] Entry struck through; cf. following entry.
[5] Entry replaces preceding entry for Ric. Reeves, who was a Roman Catholic priest: *Alumni Oxon. 1500–1714*, iii. 1244.
[6] GBR F 4/7, p. 455.
[7] Elected 29 Nov 1688 on Fowler's resignation: ibid. B 3/6, f. 219 and v.

17 June Rob. Watts, app. of Wm. Randle, tailor
2 Sept Wm. Hornett, app. of Francis Yates, cordwainer

285 **William Hodges, esq., mayor 1689–90**

20 Sept Edw. Butter, app. of John Horrall, tailor[1]
28 Oct Gabriel Harris, son of Thos., gunsmith, late of Gloucester
Thos. Cooke, son of Thos., butcher
7 Oct John Davis, app. of John Davis, pinmaker
28 Oct Thos. Rogers, app. of John Rogers, baker
22 Nov Thos. Maddocks, app. of Wm. Gyttos, saddler
4 Oct Chas. [Gerard], earl of Macclesfield,[†2] (by gift)
22 Nov Abel Lewis, son of John, pargeter
4 Oct Fitton (*Fitten*) Gerrhard, esq.,[†3] [by gift][x]
2 Dec Thos. Fletcher, app. of Tristram Lodge, cooper
4 Oct [Sir] Ralph Dutton, Bt.,[†4] [by gift][x]
4 Dec John Heming, app. of his father Ric.
4 Oct John Delabeare, esq.,[†5] [by gift][x]
Thos. Pyrke, esq.,[†6] [by gift][x]
286 20 Dec Chas. Bidwell, app. of Wm. Stowell, pinmaker
1690 7 Apr Jos. Hale, son of Thos., feltmaker
7 May Edw. Nourse, gent., son of a gent., late of Gloucester*
19 May Phil. Pinchbacke[†] (by fine)
26 May John Barradell, app. of John Greene and Ric. Williams, coopers
287 21 June Thos. Houghton, app. of Edw. Harris, tailor, late of Gloucester
23 June Wm. Skinner, app. of Thos. Selwyne, cordwainer
Steph. Skinner, app. of Dan. Bishopp, barber
4 Aug Thos. Spencer, app. of Francis Broben, cooper
11 Aug John Arnold, gent., son of Ant., gent., late of Gloucester
Ant. Mutloe, son of Miles, tailor
288 Benj. Robbins, son of Jas., currier
23 Aug Jeremiah Michel, son of Geo., garter-weaver, late of Gloucester
7 Sept Rob. Stephens, son of Rob., innholder
Jas. Collins, app. of Sam. Lye, chandler
Ric. Williams, son of a milliner, decd.*
15 Sept Wal. Clarke, app. of Thos. Clarke, pinmaker

289 **[Sir] John Guise, Bt., mayor 1690–1**

1691 9 Feb Wm. Fisher, app. of Thos. Stephens, pinmaker
13 Feb Ric. Green, maltster, by fine of £10
14 Feb Wm. Rawlins, app. of Jonathan Green, joiner
16 Mar Peter Lugg, son of John, porter, late of Gloucester
22 Mar Ric. Wintle, gent., by gift
15 Mar Ric. Wells, app. of John Wells, cordwainer

[x] By act of 1 Oct 1689 the mayor was empowered to award the freedom to up to six gentlemen attending the earl of Macclesfiedl on a visit to Gloucester: GBR B 3/6, f. 249 and v.; cf. ibid. F 4/7, p. 500.

[1] Entry belongs to previous mayoralty.

[2] *Complete Peerage*, viii. 328–9.

[3] Son of the earl of Macclesfield: ibid. 330–2.

[4] Of Sherborne: *Complete Baronetage*, iv. 104; *V.C.H. Glos.* vi. 123.

[5] Of Southam, Bishop's Cleeve: *V.C.H. Glos.* viii. 10. Unsuccessful candidate in 1690 for one of Gloucester's parliamentary seats: Williams, *Parl. Hist. of Glos.* 203.

[6] Of Littledean: Glos. R.O., D 36/M 54–6.

1 Feb Jos. Felton, app. of Wm. Sysemore, barber
Sam. Heath, son of Sam., silkweaver, by apprenticeship[1]
290 30 Mar John Gregory, app. of Thos. Webb, mercer (*bombicinarii*)
17 Apr Thos. Bright, app. of John Grafstock, butcher
20 Apr Dan. Niblett, app. of Edw. Palmer,[2] baker
27 Apr Nat. Gardner, son of Nat., baker, of Berkeley
n.d. Thos. Nicholson, app. of Wm. Smith, glover
8 May Ric. Corsley,[3] son of Wm., ald., late of Gloucester
25 May Thos. Humphris, son of Ric., apothecary
291 8 June Arnold Davis, app. of Thos. Mills, baker
15 June Hen. Beard, app. of Thos. Dobbs, barber and periwig-maker
13 Aug Ric. Yate, esq., of Arlingham by gift
26 June John Lane, app. of Tristram Lodge, cooper
13 Aug (Captain) Nat. Pyrke, gent., of Littledean[4] by gift
29 June Wm. Puxon, app. of Jas. Lovell, silkweaver
1 Sept Rog. Church, app. of Wm. Perry, tailor
Thos. Vyner, son of Wm., feltmaker, late of Gloucester
Hen. Watts alias Jones, app. of Wm. Watts alias Jones, cordwainer†
292 4 Sept Rog. Church, app. of John Paynter, glazier
Adam Green, app. of John Brock, glover
21 Sept Hen. Hathaway, app. of Thos. Deane, blacksmith
18 Sept John Webb, son of John, ald., decd.
1 Oct Jas. Davis, son of John, pinmaker
20 Nov Abraham Riddall, carpenter, (by gift)[5]
11 Dec Thos. Jones, app. of Thos. Smith*[6]

293 **Thomas Browne, esq., mayor 1691–2**

1692 1 Jan Hen. Abbott, clerk, son of Hen., baker
1691 3 Nov John Rogers, son of John, baker
1692 1 Feb Ric. Drinkwater, app. of Mary Lugg, pinmaker
1 Mar Ric. Weaver, app. of John Wellsteed, blacksmith
2 Apr Thos. Harison, app. of Ric. Nash, feltmaker, late of Gloucester
25 Apr John Ball, son of John, collar-maker
294 30 May Thos. Marshael, app. of John Gwilliam
3 June Thos.*
13 June Hen. Weaver, app. of Ric. Gibbons, blacksmith
Jas. Mutloe, app. of Thos. Smith, glover
15 Aug Thos. Browne, app. of Francis Yate the elder, cordwainer
John Harding, son of John, glover
Ric. Low, son of Ric., wiredrawer, decd.
295 1 Sept Wm. Try, esq.,† by gift[7]
4 Sept Thos. Winston, son of Wal., butcher, by apprenticeship[8]
9 Sept Wm. Cadman, glover, by fine of £6 13*s* 4*d*

[1] By patrimony: GBR F 4/7, pp. 511–2.
[2] Edm. Palmer; cf. above: ibid. C 9/7, pp. 30, 98, 154.
[3] By act of 12 Nov 1695 Corsley, who was using the trade of goldsmith, was to be disfranchised if he failed to join the metalmen's company: ibid. B 3/7, f. 138v.
[4] Also of the Wilderness, Abenhall: Glos. R.O., D 36/M 78, f.61.
[5] Entry belongs to following mayoralty.
[6] Entry belongs to following mayoralty.
[7] Wm. Trye of Hardwicke, M.P. for Gloucester: *V.C.H. Glos.* x. 182; Atkyns, *Glos.* 454; Williams, *Parl. Hist. of Glos.* 203; cf. *V.C.H. Glos.* iv. 115.
[8] By patrimony: GBR F 4/7, p. 536.

		19 Sept	Wm. Abbott, son of Hen., baker
			Nat. Lye,[1] son of Sam., grocer
			Ric. Thomas, son of John, cordwainer
296			Wm. Lawrence, app. of John Tyler, baker
		23 Sept	Thos. Puckson, app. of Thos. Summers, silkweaver
		26 Sept	John Rone, app. of Wm. Sly, tailor
			Sam. Hossington, son of Thos., bodice-maker
		30 Sept	Hen. Jelfe, app. of John Rogers, baker
			John Carsey, app. of Humph. Heard, butcher
			Mat. Caper† (by fine)
		10 Oct	Jos. Browne, son of Jos., mercer, decd.[2]

297 **Robert Payne, esq., mayor 1692–3**

		10 Oct	Jos. Browne, son of Jos., mercer, decd., by apprenticeship[3]
		[ ] Nov	Thos. Fletcher, app. of Giles Wilse, baker
		[ ] Nov	John Jones, app. of Wm. Powell, pinmaker
		5 Dec	John Ewins, son of John, ald.
			Ric. Price, app. of Wm. Dawes, tiler and plasterer, late of Gloucester
		29 Dec	Thos. Rodway, app. of Geo. Moore, butcher, late of Gloucester
	1693	9 Jan	Steph. Reeve, Jos. Reeve, } apps. of their father Francis, stonecarver[4]
298		3 Feb	Thos. Ludlow, son of Jos., milliner or mercer, of Cheltenham
		10 Feb	Abraham Archer, app. of Abraham Meadway, bricklayer
		27 Feb	John Gamon, app. of Lawr. Lugg, baker
		10 Apr	Thos. Davis, app. of Elizabeth Beard, silkweaver
		24 Apr	Ric. Skelton, app. of Wm. Jordan, apothecary
		1 May	John Wright, app. of Wm. Randle, tailor
		2 May	Edw. Cooke, esq., of Highnam by gift
			John Cocks, esq., by gift
299		12 May	Hen. Lugg, son of Jasper, tanner
			Dan. Harris, son of Dan., tobacconist, of Bewdley, Worcs.
		15 May	Thos. Lea, son of Hen., cordwainer
		26 May	Ric. Partridge, Rob. Partridge, } sons of Ric., baker
		26 June	Benj. Beal, app. of Ant. Walker, blacksmith
		3 July	Chas. Pritchard, app. of Sam. Evans, cordwainer
		28 July	John Price, } sons of John, wiredrawer, decd.
300			Thos. Price,
		30 July	Thos. Davis, app. of Wm. Blanch, tailor
		11 Aug	Thos. Field, app. of John Hyett, mercer, ald.
		28 Aug	Edw. Guy, son of Ric., innholder, decd.
		11 Sept	Ric. Gwinnell, app. of Wm. Allen, grocer
		25 Sept	Ric. Kempley, son of Thos., decd.*
			Ant. Williams, app. of Thos. Baker, barber-surgeon
301		28 Sept	Wm. Fletcher, app. of John Allen, butcher
			Nat. Stephens, esq., of Eastington (by gift)
		29 Sept	Ric. Ingly, bricklayer, (by fine)

1 Resigned 6 July and readmitted by act of 12 Aug 1730: ibid. B 3/9, ff. 278, 279v.
2 Entry struck through; cf. following entry.
3 By patrimony: GBR F 4/7, p. 567. Cf. preceding entry.
4 Occupation also given as *stonecutter*.

John Ewins, esq., mayor 1693–4

27 Oct Wm. Fream, app. of Wm. George, feltmaker
30 Oct Wm. Davis, app. of Clement Hayward, tailor
John Corr, son of Rob., surgeon, decd.
302 6 Nov Chas. Hannis, app. of Geo. Rudge, farrier, decd.
13 Nov Wm. Randle, son of Wm., tailor
27 Nov Hen. Bayly alias Baylis, trowman, (by fine)
4 Dec Chas. Moore,[1] son of Geo., butcher, decd.
Ric. Emsly, app. of Thos. Wynniatt, pinmaker
23 Dec Thos. Hayward, son of Sam., grocer
1694 5 Jan Jos. Ravener, app. of Thos. Ravener, weaver
303 10 Jan Ric. Crump, app. of Rob. Davis, brazier
22 Jan Ric. Cooke, app. of John Grabstocke, baker
12 Feb Wm. Hawkins, app. of Jasper Tayler, combmaker
26 Feb John Churches, son of Thos., wiredrawer, decd.
Jas. Okey, app. of Giles Ball, decd., and Francis Braban the younger, coopers
19 Mar Eli Dupree, app. of John Sowdly, woolcomber
304 23 Mar Giles Ham, son of Wm., butcher, decd.
Thos. Rogers, son of Thos., baker, decd.
Thos. Concklyn, app. of Jonathan Garway, grocer
20 Apr Geo. Gwinnett, app. of Thos. Niccolls, plumber
27 Apr Thos. Dudley, son of April, butcher
11 May John Ricketts, app. of Thos. Cowcher, pinmaker
Nic. Lane, son of Nic., apothecary
305 30 May John Abbott, clerk,[2] by gift
15 June Jas. Watts, app. of John Sheppard, barber-surgeon
18 June Jas. Stephens, son of Ric., gent.
2 July John Evenis, app. of Nat. Castle, baker
27 Aug Ric. Buckle, app. of Thos. Bicke and Margaret Carpenter, bakers
25 Sept Thos. Endall, app. of Wm. Sysemore, barber-surgeon

306 **William Tayler, esq., mayor 1694–5**

23 Nov Thos. Young, app. of Thos. Webb, mercer
Jas. Randle, son of Dan., joiner
26 Nov Wm. Gardner, son of Thos., pinmaker
3 Dec Wm. Window, app. of John Parker, tailor
1695 25 Jan John Beach, app. of Mary Mason, widow
8 Feb Ric. Driver, app. of Thos. Gosling, gent.
11 Feb Rowland Pitt, app. of Wm. Scudamore the younger, ald.
307 25 Feb Thos. Davis, son of John, pinmaker
19 Mar Jas. Comelin, son of Dan., gent.
22 Apr Nic. Barnes, app. of Giles Rodway, ald.
3 May Sam. Cooke, son of Wm., victualler, decd.
10 May Geo. Fielder, son of Geo., farrier
20 May Wm. Proben, app. of Jas. Sayer, tailor
24 May Ric. Perrys, son of Wm., butcher
27 May Thos. Selwyn, son of Thos., cordwainer, decd.
7 June Sam. Lucas, app. of Sam. Kent, decd., and Wm. Rawlins, joiners
22 June Hen. Vernon, app. of Sam. Eckly, apothecary

[1] Later clerk, to whom the city corporation gave the benefices of Newnham and Littledean: GBR B 3/8, p. 85.
[2] Rector of Great Witcombe: Hockaday Abs. ccccxiii; *Alumni Oxon. 1500–1714*, i. 1.

308	1 July	Edw. Robinson, app. of Rob. Read, ironmonger
	8 July	Ric. Holton, app. of Jacob Lumbard, sergeweaver
		Sam. Ackson, son of Wm., cordwainer
		John Ryder, apothecary, (by fine)
	12 July	Ric. Townsend, app. of Wm. Maddocks, tailor, late of Gloucester
	5 Aug	Francis Bennett, son of Wm., yeoman, late of Barton Street
		Giles Smith,[1] app. of Giles Smith, baker, decd.
	19 Aug	John Fords, app. of Albert Badger, pinmaker, decd.
	30 Aug	John Hall, son of Francis, woollen-draper, decd.
		Edw. Gregory, son of Edm., furrier
309	5 Sept	Thos. Jeynes, app. of Edm. Pearce, feltmaker, of Tewkesbury, formerly of Gloucester
	12 Sept	Chas. Berkeley, esq.,†[2] } by gift[7]
		Maynard Colchester, esq.,†[3] } by gift[7]
		Geo. Lloyd, esq.,†[4] } by gift[7]
		Wm. Smith, esq.,†[5] } by gift[7]
		Thos. Norwood, clerk,†[6] } by gift[7]
		John Fortune, gent.,† } by gift[7]
	16 Sept	John Seyer, son of Dan., ropemaker, decd.
	27 Sept	Thos. Drew, app. of John White, cordwainer
310		**Thomas Longden, esq., mayor 1695–6**
	1 Oct	Jeremiah Hayward, son of Sam., grocer
	3 Oct	Rob. Longden, son of Thos., mayor
	4 Oct	Thos. Wilcocks, son of Thos., ald.
		Thos. Carill, son of John, hosier, decd.
		Jasper Nelme, app. of Martha Selwyn, widow
	14 Oct	Sam. Woodward, son of Sam., blacksmith, decd.
		Jas. Young, app. of Rebecca Cowcher alias Gardner, widow
		Hen. Aldridge, } sons of Thos., yeoman, of Leigh
		Sam. Aldridge, } sons of Thos., yeoman, of Leigh
	15 Oct	Jas. Niccolls, } sons of Wm., ald., decd.
		Edw. Niccolls, } sons of Wm., ald., decd.
311		Chas. Beard, son of And., cordwainer, decd.
		Giles Lovegrove, app. of Wm. Benson, plasterer
	16 Oct	Rob. Niccolls, clerk,[8] son of Wm., ald., decd.
		John Greene, son of Phil., brickmaker, decd.
		Thos. Price, son of Thos., cordwainer, decd.
		Wm. Beaven, app. of Thos. Martin, tailor
		Hen. Gregory, son of Brice, cordwainer, decd.
	19 Oct	Ric. Baker, son of Benj., feltmaker
		Jacob Young, app. of Wal. Young, currier, decd.
		Rob. Cowdall, son of Rob., feltmaker
		John Heyter, app. of Rob. Wilmott, glassmaker

[1] ? disfranchised 12 Mar 1742 and readmitted by act of 22 Dec 1746: GBR B 3/10, ff. 7, 76v.

[2] Of Berkeley, son of Chas., V. Dursley, high steward of Gloucester: *Complete Peerage*, ii. 140–1; cf. Williams, *Parl. Hist. of Glos.* 202.

[3] Of Westbury-on-Severn: *V.C.H. Glos.* x. 87–8; Atkyns, *Glos.* 799.

[4] Of Wheatenhurst (later Whitminster): *V.C.H. Glos.* x. 292; *Visit. Glos. 1682–3*, 117.

[5] Of North Nibley: *Visit. Glos. 1682–3*, 172.

[6] Of Leckhampton: Atkyns, *Glos.* 532; cf. *Alumni Oxon. 1500–1714*, iii. 1080.

[7] By act of 6 Sept 1695 the mayor was empowered to create up to six freemen when V. Dursley, the high steward, was at the Tolsey: GBR B 3/7, f. 128.

[8] Vicar of Sandhurst: Hockaday Abs. cccxxx.

Wm. Champneys, son of Arthur,[1] cooper, decd.
312 Wm. Smart, son of John, joiner
Miles Mutloe, son of Miles, tailor
Jas. Bicknell, son of Wm., tailor, decd.
Sam. Onyon, son of Thos., silkweaver
John Dudly, son of April, butcher
21 Oct Wal. Fryer, app. of John Cudd and Wal. Powell, silkweavers, decd.
Wm. Brymyard, son of Wm., pipemaker, decd.
Sam. Wheeler, app. of Peter Smith, carpenter and plumpmaker, late of Gloucester
Edw. Barnelme, son of Wm., turner, decd.
Jacob Hague, son of Jacob, grocer
Thos. Hale,[2] son of Thos., cordwainer, decd.
John Pynnocke, app. of Rob. Wilmott, saddler
Thos. Bradshaw, app. of Ric. Sparks, cordwainer
John Lane, son of Thos., grocer
John Jefferys, app. of John Hayward and Francis Oatley, feltmakers
Sam. Stephens, } sons of Thos., pinmaker
Jas. Stephens, }
313 Wm. Nash, son of Wm., feltmaker
Edw. Meeke, son of Thos., currier
Hen. Holliday, son of Hen., carpenter
Wm. Sparrowhawke, son of Wm., garter-weaver
Thos. Wilse, } sons of Giles, baker, of Barnwood, formerly of
Giles Wilse, } Gloucester
Sam. Perkes, son of Wm., pinmaker, late of Barton Street near Gloucester
Jos. Kent, son of Sam., joiner, decd.
Chas. Greenway, app. of Wal. Atkyns, cordwainer
Jos. Robins, son of Jas., currier
Ric. Mans, app. of John Shipton, cordwainer, decd., of Barnwood
John Mamby, app. of Edw. Whitfield, cordwainer
23 Oct John Beedle, }
Geo. Beedle, } sons of Jonah, cordwainer, decd.
Jonah Beedle, }
Ric. Payne, clerk, son of Rob., ald.
25 Oct Giles Cooke, cordwainer, of Maisemore, app. of John Tyler, cordwainer
Hen. Davis, son of John, pinmaker
John Halford, son of Edm., of Maisemore, app. of John Wells, cordwainer
John Mathews, son of John, butcher
314 Lawr. Allen, son of Edm., yeoman, late of Gloucester
Edm. Turner, app. of Rog. Wadman, garter-weaver
Wm. Knott, app. of Wm. Sampson, combmaker
Chas. Watson, son of Humph., tailor
Albert Badger, son of Albert, pinmaker, late of Gloucester
Thos. Green, son of John, cooper, late of Gloucester
Chas. Rudge, app. of Sam. Pembridge, baker
Wm. Hayes, son of Wm., cordwainer
John Hall, app. of Wm. King, pinmaker

[1] Described originally as *yeoman, of Berkeley, formerly of Gloucester.*
[2] ? Thos. Hale, tailor, disfranchised 28 July 1732 for refusing to appear before the mayor and readmitted by act of 22 Mar 1733: GBR B 3/9, ff. 317v., 333v.; cf. below: ibid. C 9/7, p. 462.

315 Thos. Sturmey, son of Thos., glover, late of Gloucester
Isaac Wood, son of John, button-maker
26 Oct Thos. Cooke, } sons of Thos., grocer
Ric. Cooke, }
Price Rogers, son of John, ald., decd.
Arthur Dudley, son of Arthur, butcher, decd.
Herbert Mercer, app. of Chas. Jones, cooper
Wm. Styles, app. of Abraham Meadway, bricklayer
Wm. Beard, app. of John Hyett, ald.
Thos. Hossington,[1] son of Thos., bodice-maker
316 Thos. Sanders, son of Thos., tanner, decd.
30 Oct John Cooke, son of John, woolcomber, of Tetbury, formerly of Gloucester
Nic. Moore, son of Geo., butcher, decd.
John Smith, app. of Thos. Meeke, currier
31 Oct Sam. Matthews, app. of Rob. Lane, pipemaker
1 Nov Hercules Evans, son of Jas., innholder, decd.
8 Nov Thos. Venn, son of John, feltmaker, decd.
13 Nov John Luter, app. of John Matthews, butcher
1696 3 Feb Thos. Weal, app. of Lawr. Lugg, decd., and John Evans, bakers
14 Feb John Atkyns, son of Wal., cordwainer
12 Mar John Rutter, son of John, maltster
317 14 Mar Thos. Fielder, son of Geo., farrier
29 May John Shingler, app. of Thos. Wynniatt, pinmaker
15 June Wm. Skillerne, son of Ric., tailor, decd.
22 June John Collins, app. of Thos. Parker, baker
3 Aug Dan. Walker, app. of Dan. Coldrake, bodice-maker
10 Aug Geo. Bowler, son of Geo., innholder
Hen. Cross, app. of Thos. Farley, cutler
14 Aug Wm. Lawrence, esq., of Shurdington by gift
28 Aug Rob. Jefferyes, son of Giles, late of Gloucester[2]
318 Rob. Freeman, son of Giles, baker
7 Sept Thos. Bosley, son of Ric., feltmaker, decd.
Ric. Bryan, app. of Hen. Knowles, brazier
Edw. Symonds, app. of Wal. Veysey, tailor, decd.
18 Sept Hen. Church, son of Hen., carrier, decd.

John Hyett, esq., mayor 1696–7

17 Oct Dan. Comelin, son of Dan., gent.
23 Nov Thos. Hoar, son of Chas., grocer, decd.
1697 4 Jan Wm. Nest, app. of John Nest the younger, carpenter
319 23 Jan Phil. Hampton, app. of Jos. Pegler, tanner
5 Feb Rob. Bubb, app. of Wm. Gyttos, saddler
27 Feb Sam. Hyeron, son of Nic., bodice-maker
9 Mar Thos. Branch, app. of Sarah Hoar, widow
29 Mar John Parlour, son of Hen., cutler, decd.
9 Apr John Gittos, son of Wm., saddler
John Bishopp, app. of Margaret Marden, widow
320 16 Apr John Hathway, son of Thos., ironmonger, decd.
10 May Wm. Jakeman, app. of Sam. Broad, baker, decd.
31 May John Willy, son of Rog., tailor, decd.

[1] ? Thos. Horsington, disfranchised 12 Mar 1742 and readmitted by act of 22 Dec 1746: GBR B 3/10, ff. 7, 76v.
[2] Entry struck through.

Thos. Berwicke, app. of Wm. Maverly, button-maker, decd.
4 June Jethro Harward, son of Rob., grocer
7 June John Morse, son of John, hornturner
19 June Geo. Greene, son of Phil., hornturner, decd.
321 Ric. Symonds, son of Ric., glover
21 June Edw. Grevile, son of Giles, gent., decd., of Charlton Kings
6 Sept Edw. Clayfield, son of Edw., tanner
20 Sept Thos. Cooper alias Allen, app. of John Webb, tailor
Wm. Butcher, app. of John Elliott, upholsterer, decd.
21 Sept Thos. Perry, innholder, by gift[1]
29 Sept Geo. Smith, esq., of North Nibley by gift
322 4 Oct Wm. Goodwin, app. of Wal. Miles, baker

Giles Rodway, esq., mayor 1697–8

14 Oct Nic. Webb, son of Nic., ald., by gift
4 Nov Jas. Carpenter, app. of Thos. Longden, ald.
1698 7 Jan John Barker, son of Wm., pinmaker
4 Feb Lewis Gwynn, son of John, silkweaver
25 Feb John Singleton, son of Francis, ald., decd.
7 Mar John Barrett, son of Thos., tailor, decd.
323 11 Mar Wm. Evenis, app. of Ric. Wells, cordwainer
28 Mar John Corsley, goldsmith, of Bristol, son of Wm., ald., decd.
7 Apr John Gastrell, app. of Wm. Baldwyn, glassmaker
4 May Wm. Browne, son of Jos., mercer, decd.
6 May Theophilus Hopkins, app. of Sam. Kent, joiner
9 May John Goodwin, } sons of Ric., cordwainer
Sam. Goodwin, }
324 20 May Thos. Merrett, son of Thos., clerk
18 June Rob. Wintle, app. of Thos. Mills, baker, decd.
28 June Isaac Williams, son of Nic., cordwainer
4 July John Carill, son of John, hosier, decd.
15 July John Heyford, son of John, paver
21 July Sam. Witcombe, son of Thos., clothier, decd.
28 July Ric. Corr, son of Edw., button-maker
325 Thos. Launder, app. of Sam. Humphris, butcher
29 July Francis Stephens, app. of John Gwillim, feltmaker
Sam. Davis, son of John, woolcomber, decd.
30 July Thos. Rodway, son of Giles, esq., mayor
John Rodway, son of John, mercer, decd.
Wm. Lodge, son of Tristram, cooper, decd.
Jas. Evans, son of Jas., innholder, decd.
Capel Longden, son of Thos., ald.
Peter Haynes, son of Peter, grocer, decd.
326 Wm. Horrold, son of Wm., tailor, decd.
And. Gardner, app. of John Sowdley, woolcomber, decd.
1 Aug John Grove, app. of Wm. Baldwyn, tobacconist
Wm. Dowson, son of Wm., tailor
Rob. Savory, son of Rob., farrier
John Watkins, app. of Thos. Ready, cordwainer
Jas. Beale, son of Geof., mercer, decd.
Wm. Fowler, app. of Thos. Fletcher, baker
Wm. Price, son of Jas., pewterer, decd.

[1] 'For his good services to the city and government': GBR B 3/7, f. 181v.

			Chas. Tyler, son of John, cordwainer
327			Wm. Brabant, son of Francis, cooper
			Newman Merriman, app. of Clement Hayward, tailor
			Virgil Cripps, son of Sam., butcher, decd.
			John Witcombe, son of John, cordwainer
			Francis Singleton, son of Francis, late ald.
			Jas. Niblett, app. of Wm. Gregory, butcher
			Sam. Street, app. of John Washborne, watchmaker
			(Sir) Wm. Rich., Bt.,[†1] (Brigadier) Wm. Selwyn, esq.,[†2] Rob. Rich, esq.,[†] (son of Sir Wm.), by gift[3]
328		30 Aug	Ric. Cowles, son of John, butcher, decd.
		5 Sept	Wm. Higgs, app. of Francis Broben, cooper
		30 Sept	Ephraim Higgins, app. of Abraham Meadway, bricklayer
			Sam. Bliss, son of John, tanner, late of Gloucester

Thomas Wilcocks, esq., mayor 1698–9

		21 Nov	Thos. Iles, son of Thos., innholder
		9 Dec	Francis Still, maltmaker,[4] (by fine)
	1699	2 Jan	Jas. Lugg, son of John, yeoman, decd.
329		13 Jan	Thos. Bynion, cheesemonger, (by fine)
			Sam. Ricketts, carpenter, (by fine)
		20 Mar	John Cox, son of Winston, cordwainer

William Cooke, esq., mayor 1699[5]

		28 Apr	Sam. Palmer, son of Edm., baker
			John Long, son of John, button-maker
		1 May	Geo. Perkins, app. of Josiah Randle, baker
			Sam. Powell, app. of Giles Smith, baker, decd.
330		5 May	Wm. Branch, app. of Sam. Yate, grocer
		12 May	Jas. Yate, son of Ric., gent.
		23 May	Wm. Blicke Elmes, son of Rob., mercer, decd.
		12 June	Wm. Maddocke, app. of Dan. Bishopp, barber-surgeon, decd.
		19 June	Chas. Hyett,[6] son of Benj., gent.
		21 June	Sam. Sparkes, son of Wm., carrier, decd.
		14 July	Thos. Felton, app. of Jos. Felton, barber-surgeon
331		28 July	John Rush, app. of Thos. Humphris, barber-surgeon, decd.
		14 Aug	Aaron Vaughan, son of Thos., joiner, decd.
		18 Aug	Edw. Corr, son of Edw., button-maker
		26 Aug	Meinhard (*Maynard*) [Schomberg], duke of Schomberg and Leinster,[†] by gift[7]
		4 Sept	Sam. Bower, son of Sam., tanner, decd.
			Nat. Jones, app. of John Browne, tailor
		11 Sept	Ralph Langley, gent., by gift

[1] Of Sonning, Berks.: *Complete Baronetage*, iii. 180. His father Sir Thos. (d. 1667), Bt., had been a benefactor of his native Gloucester: *V.C.H. Glos.* iv. 300, 335–6, 357.

[2] Of Matson and Stonehouse: *V.C.H. Glos.* iv. 441; x. 276, 280 n.

[3] Sir Wm. Rich and Brigadier Selwyn were elected M.P.s for Gloucester the following day: Williams, *Parl. Hist. of Glos.* 204.

[4] Labourer: GBR B 3/7, f. 209v.

[5] Elected 7 Apr 1699 after Wilcocks's death: ibid. f. 215v.

[6] M.P. for Gloucester 1722–7: Williams, *Parl. Hist. of Glos.* 208.

[7] *Complete Peerage*, xi. 527–9; admission to freedom confirmed by act of 29 Aug 1699: GBR B 3/7, f. 220.

15 Sept Sam. Smart, son of John, joiner
332 25 Sept Sam. Makepeace, app. of Ric. Partridge, baker

Thomas Snell, esq., mayor 1699–1700

17 Oct Jos. Holder, app. of Mary Bayly, widow
27 Oct Sam. Sysemore, app. of Ambrose Wyman, cordwainer, decd.
John Snell,[1] son of Thos., esq., mayor
24 Nov Thos. Hemsley, app. of Ric. Sparks, cordwainer
11 Dec Chris. Herbert, app. of Thos. Goodcheap, cordwainer
333 18 Dec Sam. Swayne, app. of Hen. Weaver, farrier
1700 15 Jan John Cowles, son of Thos., cordwainer
John Meeke, son of Thos., currier
22 Jan John Tayler, son of Wm., schoolmaster, decd.
26 Feb Wm. Greene, son of Phil., brickmaker, decd.
4 Mar Jas. King, son of John, scrivener
6 May Jas. Launder, son of Jas., maltster
334 Thos. Gibbons, son of Thos., yeoman
17 May Augustine Gwyn, son of Augustine, cordwainer
31 May John Beal, son of Wm., cordwainer
14 June Thos. Wadley, son of John, haulier, decd.
28 June Ric. Harris, app. of Wm. Bubb, barber
22 July John Watson, son of Humph. the elder, fishmonger
14 Aug John Ashmead, app. of John Hyett, ald.
335 30 Aug Toby Gundey alias Gundimore, app. of Ric. Jennings, tailor, decd.
9 Sept Amity Clutterbucke, son of Dan., baker, decd.
John Best, app. of Jas. Fordes, tailor
20 Sept Jas. Farley, son of Thos., cutler
30 Sept Thos. Eldridge, son of Thos., joiner, decd.

Nicholas Webb, esq., mayor 1700–1

7 Oct Thos. Barker, app. of Lawr. Lugg, decd., and John Tyler, bakers
336 14 Oct John Coopey, son of John, tanner
Thos. Walden, app. of John Reeve, gunsmith
28 Oct Sam. Sparry, app. of Thos. Coxe, baker
4 Nov Wm. Beard, app. of Hen. Elliott the elder, joiner, decd.
11 Nov John Perris, son of Wm., butcher, decd.
25 Nov Wm. Gittos, son of Wm., saddler
13 Dec John Motley, app. of Ric. Corsnett, vintner
337 Wm. Frankis, son of Wm., yeoman, of Upton St. Leonards
16 Dec Thos. Cole, app. of Jas. Collins, grocer
John Wooding, son of Wm., button-maker
Phil. Dyer, son of Jas., glover, decd.
20 Dec Ric. Terrett, app. of Francis Yate, cordwainer, decd.
Wm. Dixe alias Diss, app. of Abraham Meadway, bricklayer
Thos. Swayne, son of Chris., cordwainer, decd.
Edm. Ady, son of Thos., baker
John Freeman, son of Giles, baker
338 Rob. Partridge,[2] son of Rob., baker, decd.
23 Dec Geo. Nurse, son of John, yeoman, of the Rea, Hempsted
Wm. Cowles, app. of Wm. Allen, grocer
Thos. Nest, app. of John Paynter, glazier, decd.

[1] M.P. for Gloucester 1713–26: Williams, *Parl. Hist. of Glos.* 207.
[2] ? disfranchised 12 Mar 1742: GBR B 3/10, f. 7.

Jeremiah Brotherton, app. of Wal. Atkins, cordwainer
John Beard, son of John, clerk, decd.
Geo. Hanks, son of Jos., feltmaker
John Smith, son of John, feltmaker
Ric. Beard, son of Benj., clothier, of Dymock
339 Wm. Savory, son of Rob., farrier
John Vaughan, son of Edw., vintner, decd.
Thos. Symonds, son of Wm., butcher, decd.
Rob. Lea, son of Hen., cordwainer
Eleazer Daws, son of Wm., tiler and plasterer, decd.
24 Dec Ric. Price, son of Jas., pewterer, decd.
Giles Marden, son of Giles, baker, decd.
John King, son of John, feltmaker
John Rogers, clerk, son of John, maltster, decd.
340 Jos. Restall, app. of Jos. Howell, blacksmith, decd.
Giles Jones, son of John, cordwainer, decd.
John Williams, } sons of John, glover
Ric. Williams, }
Francis Best, app. of John Parker, tailor
John Bird, son of Dan., combmaker
John Carter, app. of Dan. Bryan, cordwainer
26 Dec Ric. Harding, son of John, glover
341 Edw. Outing, son of Thos., yeoman, decd.
John Charles, app. of John Wyman, cordwainer
John Shipton, son of John, cordwainer, decd., of Barnwood
Hen. Meadway, son of Hen., sergeweaver, decd.
Wal. Greenway, app. of Ric. Hill, pinmaker, decd.
Capel Wilse, son of Giles, baker, of Barnwood
John Bishopp, app. of Thos. Sparks, silkweaver
Thos. Willis, app. of John Shipton, cordwainer, decd., of Barnwood
342 John Stephens, son of Rob., innholder, decd.
Edw. Grigg, app. of Timothy Rowles and Thos. Woolford, basket-makers
Isaac Puckeridge, app. of Thos. Puckeridge, tailor
Thos. Morse, son of John, hornturner
Wm. Berry, son of Thos., tiler and plasterer, decd.
Edw. Cripps, son of Edw., butcher, decd.
Edw. Sollars, app. of Humph. Heard, butcher
Dan. Bryan, son of Dan., cordwainer
343 John Symonds, son of Wm., butcher, decd.
Mat. Yate, clerk,[1] son of Thos., apothecary, decd.
27 Dec Thos. Sparks, son of Thos., cordwainer
30 Dec Nat. Ferrett, son of Nat., glover, decd.
Wm. Stone, app. of Wm. Randle, tailor
Thos. Lugg, son of John, tanner
31 Dec John Flower, app. of Jas. Crody, tailor
1701 6 Jan John Addams, son of John, weaver, decd.
344 11 Jan Hen. Underwood, son of Ric., yeoman, of Taynton
16 Jan John Fereby, app. of Wal. Veysey, tailor, decd.
20 Jan Giles Townsend, app. of Hen. Elliott, joiner
John Williams, app. of Wm. Crass, bodice-maker
Thos. Barrett, app. of Thos. Martin, tailor

[1] Rector of St. Mary de Crypt and Matson and owner of the Netheridge estate in Quedgeley: Glos. R.O., D 177, Yate family, Quedgeley deeds 1698–1801; P 154/11/CW 2/3; Hockaday Abs. cclxxviii.

31 Jan Wm. Gill, app. of Dan. Sayer, ropemaker
10 Feb John Gardner, app. of Mic. Jennings, butcher
5 Apr Wm. Mason, app. of John Price, gardener
345 7 Apr Thos. Hayward, app. of Thos. Goodcheap, cordwainer
11 Apr Edw. Swayne, son of Edw., collar-maker, decd.
26 Apr Wm. Vyner, app. of Edw. Whittingham, baker
4 Aug Chas. Hawthorne, son of John, wiredrawer, decd.
11 Aug Edm. Wilcocks, son of John, gent., decd.
14 Aug Abraham Rudhall, app. of Abraham Rudhall, bellfounder
29 Aug Rob. Mayoe, app. of Ric. Aylway, baker
346 Sam. Clarke, app. of Phil. Clarke and Thos. Lander, butchers
15 Sept Edw. Hamlett, app. of John Wells, cordwainer
26 Sept Isaac Skillerne, son of Isaac, furrier, of Winchcombe

Thomas Webb, esq., mayor 1701–2

10 Oct Dan. Randle, son of Wm., maltster
13 Oct Hen. Corr, son of Edw., button-maker
18 Oct Maur. Smith, app. of Ric. Chandler, decd., and Wm. Gittoes, glovers
17 Nov Ric. Price, app. of Wm. Parker, cordwainer, decd.
347 18 Nov Ric. Mathews, son of John, butcher
Jos. Young, son of Jos., pinmaker, decd.
21 Nov Jos. Stephens, son of Thos., merchant
Jas. Browne, son of John, mercer, late of Gloucester
Wm. Aylberton, app. of Thos. Veysey, mercer
John Sexty, app. of his father John, cheesemonger
Jas. [Berkeley], Lord Dursley,† by gift[1]
348 22 Nov Thos. Bossom, app. of John Heaven, barber-surgeon
24 Nov Steph. White, son of Ric., mason, of Painswick
John West, son of Steph., mercer, of Painswick
Godfrey Fownes, son of Godfrey, maltster
Wm. Barrett, app. of Ric. Webb, woolcomber
Thos. Clarke, app. of Aaron Jaques, baker
28 Nov Thos. Deane, app. of Wm. Lawrence, baker
15 Dec Hen. Draper, app. of Steph. Greene, woolcomber, of Newent, formerly of Gloucester
349 3 Dec Jas. Kingman, wiredrawer, (by fine)
1702 23 Jan Ric. Barnfield, app. of Jas. Hornage, blacksmith
26 Jan Edw. Horrold, app. of Ric. Williams, cooper
16 Feb Sam. Johnson, app. of John Bell, gent.
19 Feb Geo. Underhill, son of Jacob, silkweaver
23 Feb Ric. Price, } sons of Ric., gardener
Hen. Price, }
4 Mar Hen. Partridge, app. of Thos. Webb, esq., mayor
350 9 Apr John Harris, app. of Rob. Punter, mercer
10 Apr Rob. Fielding, son of Rob., M.D., late of Gloucester
15 Apr [Sir] John Guise, Bt.,†[2] by gift
20 Apr John Hone, app. of Jeremiah Jenings, tailor
24 Apr Thos. Elliott, son of Thos., wiredrawer, decd.
8 May Wm. Sweat, son of Ric., glazier, late of Gloucester
Wal. Young, son of Wal., currier, decd.
Rob. Cleevely, son of Hen., grocer, decd.

[1] In Gloucester as candidate, in the event successful, for one of the city's parliamentary seats: GBR B 3/8, pp. 42–3; *Complete Peerage*, ii. 141.

[2] Of Rendcomb: Atkyns, *Glos.* 303, 429, 612; *V.C.H. Glos.* vii. 221–2.

Rob. Webly, son of Rob., cordwainer, decd.
351 11 May Thos. Whitehead, son of John, innholder, of Barnsley, formerly of Gloucester
Dan. Jackson, son of Edw., pinmaker
Thos. Cowles, son of Thos., cordwainer, decd.
Sam. Estcourt, app. of Thos. Hartland, pinmaker
Hen. Cox, son of Hen., tailor, decd.
Wm. Bradshaw, app. of Dan. Randle, joiner
John Holder, son of Jos., pinmaker
John Nurse, son of Giles, cordwainer, of Upton St. Leonards, formerly of Gloucester
Chas. Butter, app. of Edw. Butter, tailor
12 May John Collett, son of Sam., haberdasher of hats, decd.
Geo. Nott, app. of Chas. Jones, cooper
352 13 May Edw. Lewis, son of Abel, pargeter
14 May Thos. Turner, app. of his father Thos., cordwainer[1]
15 May Jas. Hobson, son of Jas., button-maker
Jas. Ward, son of Geo., gunsmith, decd.
John Powell, app. of Edw. Hicks, tobacco-pipemaker
John Thomas, app. of Sam. Evans, cordwainer, decd.
Dan. Bretherton, app. of Elizabeth Beard, silkweaver
John Woodward, app. of Wm. Sparrowhawke, cotton-weaver
Jos. Smith, son of Thos., pewterer, decd.
Sam. Lane, son of Thos., grocer, decd.
Ric. Lewis, son of Abel, pargeter
353 Jas. Young, son of Jos., pinmaker, decd.
Josiah Hayes, son of Wm. the elder, cordwainer
Sam. Phelps, son of Jos., feltmaker, decd.
Thos. Bramley, son of Wm., glover, decd.
Ant. Gardner, app. of John Gammond, baker
Ric. Engly, app. of his father Ric., bricklayer
John Ellis, app. of Milborough (*Milberrow*) Rudge, widow
Wm. Bicke, app. of Jacob Conklin, salter, decd.
Edw. Addis, son of Edw., cordwainer
John Hooper, app. of John Pace, cordwainer
16 May John Grevile, son of Giles, gent., decd., of Charlton Kings
18 May John Chapman, } sons of Geo., gunsmith, of Hereford, formerly of
354 Geo. Chapman, } Gloucester
Ric. Mathews, app. of Jos. Howell, blacksmith
Edw. Mathews, app. of Ric. Cooke and Ant. Walker, blacksmiths, decd.
John Randle, son of Giles, silkweaver
John Haydon, app. of Wm. Bumford, bodice-maker, decd.
Sam. Hayward, son of Sam., grocer
Ric. Puckson, app. of Wm. Brymyard, tobacco-pipemaker, decd.
Sam. Merrett, app. of Sam. Wiggett, glover
Sam. Crafte, app. of Ric. Sparrowhawke, silkweaver, decd.
Thos. Maverly, app. of Rob. Watts, tailor
John Mayoe, app. of Wm. Fisher, pinmaker
John Symonds, son of Ric., glover
355 John Higgins, son of John, tailor
John Fones, son of Thos., glover, decd., of Tibberton, formerly of Gloucester

[1] By patrimony: GBR F 4/7, p. 769.

1702 Phoenix Badger, app. of Thos. Bayly, pinmaker, decd.
John Pearce, son of Edm., feltmaker, of Tewkesbury, formerly of Gloucester
Ric. Surman, son of Ric., cordwainer, of Tewkesbury, formerly of Gloucester
Geo. Ravener, son of Thos., silkweaver
Edw. Elliott, app. of John Wilcocks, glassmaker, decd.
Jas. Parker, app. of Rob. Wilmott, saddler, formerly glassmaker
Wm. Grove, app. of Thos. Meeke and Edm. Humphris, curriers
Wm. Lambeth, app. of John Wilcocks, glassmaker, decd.
Wm. Gibbons, son of Thos., wiredrawer, decd.
Jas. Griffin, app. of John Bennett, button-maker, decd.
356 John Washborne, son of John, watchmaker
Jas. Knowles, app. of Ant. Davis, pinmaker
Paul Cheesman, son of John, cooper, decd.
Thos. Engly, son of John, baker, decd.
Jonathan Swayne, son of Gustavus, brewer, decd.
Arthur Bradley, son of Hen., feltmaker, decd.
Wm. Wadley, son of Wm., tanner
Adam Mason, app. of Rob. Wilmott, saddler, formerly glassmaker
19 May John Holstead, app. of Geo. Powell, pinmaker, decd.
Thos. Hinton, app. of John Trow, pinmaker
Ant. Arnold, app. of Dan. Gardner, pinmaker
Rob. Lucas, son of Thos., farrier, decd.
357 John Pace, son of John, cordwainer
Thos. King, Sam. King, } sons of John, scrivener
Thos. Mudwell, son of Wm., feltmaker, decd.
Wm. Knight, app. of Jas. Crodye of St. Mary Magdalen's Hospital [near Gloucester]
John Ferrett, son of Nat., glover, decd.
Wm. Grove, app. of John Wilcocks, glassmaker, decd.
Hugh Griffin, app. of Rob. Rowles and Thos. Bright, butchers, of Minsterworth, formerly of Gloucester
Nat. Castle, son of Nat., baker, decd.
20 May Steph. Tench, app. of Jacob Underhill, silkweaver
358 Thos. Griffin, app. of Edw. Dunning, combmaker, decd.
Thos. Colericke, app. of Edm. Pearce, feltmaker, of Tewkesbury
Ric. Hathway, app. of Wm. Wooding, button-maker
Josiah Randle, son of Wm., tailor
22 May John White, son of John, tanner, of Newent, formerly of Gloucester
Thos. Baldwyn, app. of Wm. Skynner, cordwainer, of Newent, formerly of Gloucester
John Gwinn, son of John, silkweaver
Nic. Nelmes, app. of Wm. Gittoes, saddler
John Shaw, app. of Ric. Gibbons, blacksmith, decd.
Thos. Skillerne, son of Isaac, furrier, of Winchcombe, formerly of Gloucester
Wm. Overthrow, app. of Albert Badger, pinmaker, decd.
359 Silvester Lambert, app. of John Moore, tobacco-pipemaker, decd.
Sam. Champneys, son of Arthur, cooper
Wm. Pitt, son of Wm., tobacconist
23 May John Stait, son of Ric., innholder, decd.
25 May Sam. Watkins, app. of Edw. Tyler, cordwainer
John Skillerne, son of Isaac, furrier, of Winchcombe, formerly of Gloucester

Abraham Underwood, app. of Wm. Andrews, saddler
Geo. Paynter, app. of Thos. Maddocks, saddler
Thos. Turbett, son of Thos., tanner
Rob. Perry, son of Rob., innholder, decd.
John Rowles, app. of Wm. Watts, butcher, of Minsterworth
360 Hen. Fords, son of Jas., tailor
Wm. Powell, son of Wm., cordwainer
Mark Lightfoot, app. of Wm. Skynner, cordwainer, of Newent, formerly of Gloucester
Ant. Mutlow, son of Ant., hornturner, decd.
Ric. Greene, son of Ric., clothier, decd., late of Gloucester and of Painswick
Wm. Cugley, son of Thos., cardmaker, decd.
29 May John Roberts, } sons of Thos., skinner, of Ruardean
Edw. Roberts, }
John Barnelme, son of Edw., labourer
John Reynolds, app. of John Cudd, silkweaver
361 John Cudd, son of John, silkweaver
John Cugley, son of Dan., cardmaker, decd.
Wm. Tayler, son of Wm., schoolmaster, decd.
John Jennings, son of John, barber-surgeon, late of Gloucester
Jas. Hampton, } apps. of Josiah Cowles, glover
Wm. Motley, }
Jos. Phelpes, son of Jos., grocer
Rob. Punter, son of Rob., mercer
Isaac Gyles, app. of Thos. Winstone, tailor
John Armitage, app. of Ric. Till, cutler
Thos. Ford, son of Thos., gunsmith, of Newent
362 Thos. Underwood, son of Thos., of Taynton
Thos. Barnard, app. of John Tyler, cordwainer
Toby Munday, app. of Wm. Slyde, tailor
Giles Dawby, app. of John Greene*
Wm. Sparrow, app. of John Gravestocke and Chas. Cooke, butchers
1 June Sam. Lumbard, son of Isaac, weaver, late of Gloucester
John Cheesman, son of John, cooper, decd.
John Man, app. of Jas. Man, glover
John Mathews, app. of Wm. Bubb, baker
2 June John Chapman, son of John, maltster
363 John Price, son of Jas., pewterer, decd.
Thos. Niccolls, son of Thos., cordwainer
Giles Merrett, son of Thos., clerk
Dan. Roberts, son of Thos., skinner, of Ruardean, formerly of Gloucester
5 June Wm. Window, app. of Rob. Rowles, butcher, of Minsterworth
Francis Parry, app. of Jesse Nash, feltmaker
8 June Thos. Cherrington, app. of Jas. Jones, silkweaver
9 June Thos. Child, son of Ric., baker, decd.
12 June John Cowles, son of Wm., butcher, decd.
364 15 June Thos. Lugg, son of Jasper, tanner, decd.
Thos. Chamlyn, son of Thos., turner, of Hereford, formerly of Gloucester
John Lunn, app. of Ric. Cooke, feltmaker
16 June Edm. Browne, son of John, mercer, decd.
Jeremiah Beard, son of Thos., mercer, decd.
Chas. Jones, son of Geo., gent., late of Gloucester
17 June Edw. Cleavely, son of Wm., woollen-draper, decd.

19 June Francis Gythens, son of John, gent.
John Longden, son of John, ironmonger, decd.
365 20 June Chas. Grevile, Francis Grevile, } sons of Giles, gent., decd., of Charlton Kings
22 June Jos. Cowdall, son of John, tailor
24 June John Bridgman, esq., of Prinknash (by gift)[1]
25 June John Barton, app. of Ric. Ingly, bricklayer
John Baldwyn, app. of Francis Brabant and Thos. Spencer, coopers
Wm. Puckeridge, app. of Wm. Bishopp, tailor, decd.
Thos. Lane, app. of Jas. Walker, button-maker, decd.
Jas. Cooke, app. of Jas. Randle, joiner
366 Bernard (*Barnard*) Cooke, son of Geo., grocer
Abraham Roach, app. of Wm. George, feltmaker, decd.
26 June John Washbourne, app. of Nic. Wastfield, blacksmith, decd.
Hen. Bradley, son of John, butcher
Thos. Keare, app. of Jos. Ludlow, mercer, late of Gloucester
27 June John Randle, son of Dan., joiner
Wm. Bamford, son of Wm., bodice-maker, decd.
Ric. Wintle, app. of Edw. Whittingham, baker, of Westbury, formerly of Gloucester
John Hornage, son of Thos., bodice-maker, decd.
367 29 June Thos. Nott, Wm. Adams, } apps. of Francis Pace, cordwainer, of Newent, formerly of Gloucester
1 July Thos. Tannar, app. of Wm. Jordan, apothecary
3 July Geo. Forty, John Ellis, Ric. Beckett, } apps. of Geo. Chestroe, cordwainer, decd., of Cheltenham
Rob. Woones, app. of Jas. Marshfield, fisherman
John Cooke, son of Sam., innholder, decd.
Sampson Longden, son of John, ironmonger, decd.
368 4 July Steph. Palmer, app. of Ric. Mills, wiredrawer
6 July John Wooding, app. of Geo. Farley, cutler, decd.
John Dole, app. of Thos. Meeke, currier, decd.
John Whithorne, son of John, cordwainer
Wm. Greene, app. of Ric. Greene, clothier, decd., of Painswick
8 July Wm. Humphris, app. of Wm. Cooke, chandler, decd., of Cheltenham
Sam. Steele, app. of Jas. Hornage, blacksmith, decd.
10 July Francis Hutchings, app. of Benj. Robins and Wm. George, tailors
Thos. Baker, son of Thos., tanner, decd.
369 13 July Thos. Bradley, app. of Wm. Reeve, butcher, of Standish, formerly of Gloucester
Wm. Colericke, app. of Rob. Powell, cordwainer, of Tewkesbury
14 July Sam. Child, son of Ric., baker, decd.
16 July Hen. Elliott, son of John, wiredrawer, decd.
18 July John Priest, app. of Steph. Doughton the younger and [ ] Perks, wiredrawers, both decd.*
John Jones, app. of Thos. Hale and John Hayward, feltmakers
21 July Thos. Etkins, app. of Thos. Mason, baker, decd.
Thos. Ravenhill, app. of Joan Howlett, widow
Acton Hale, son of Ric., cordwainer, decd.
370 Sam. Tyler, son of John, cordwainer

[1] By act of 21 Nov 1701, having been M.P. for Gloucester, not to be sworn until the parliamentary election then in progress was over: ibid. B 3/8, p. 42; cf. Williams, *Parl. Hist. of Glos.* 205.

			Nat. Allard, app. of Sam. Evans, cordwainer
			Edw. Prichard, app. of Jos. Byford, glazier
			Jonathan Churches, app. of Thos. Partridge, baker, decd.
			John King, son of John, scrivener
		22 July	Rob. Longden, son of John, ironmonger, decd.
			John Hopkins, app. of Ric. Williams, cooper
		3 Aug	John Hope, app. of Thos. Mathews, apothecary
		3 Sept	John Corsnett, son of Ric., vintner, decd.
371			**Sir Samuel Eckley, Kt., mayor 1702–3**
		5 Nov	Alex. Griffithes, app. of John Hyett, ald.
		30 Nov	Ric. Darke, app. of John Reeve, gunsmith
			Clement Job Dowle, app. of Job, mercer
		16 Dec	Joshua Brotherton, app. of Ric. Quench, hornturner
		29 Dec	Cowcher Shipton, son of Thos., bodice-maker, decd.
	1703	6 Jan	Ric. Sparks, app. of John Seyer, ropemaker
			Edw. Barnes, app. of Ric. Crump, brazier, late of Gloucester
			Thos. Beal, son of a cordwainer*
372		31 May	Jas. Smith, app. of Francis Brabant the younger, cooper
		16 July	John Keyse, app. of Jas. Seyer the elder, tailor
		19 Aug	Sampson Archer, silkweaver,[1] (by gift)
		23 Aug	Wm. Carter, gent.,[2] (by fine)
		28 Sept	Hen. Niccolls, maltster, (by fine)
			Sam. Collett, son of Sam., haberdasher of hats, late of Gloucester
			Robert Payne, esq., mayor 1703–4
		8 Oct	David Symon, app. of John Beedle, collar-maker
			Hen. Brymyard, son of Wm., pipemaker
373		1 Nov	Benj. Hopkins, app. of Thos. Field, gent.
	1704	7 Jan	Nat. Hardwicke, app. of Aaron Jaques, baker
		7 Feb	Thos. Hannis, app. of Wm. Brymyard, pipemaker, decd.
			John Cowles, son of John, butcher, decd.
		6 Mar	Sam. Hawkins, app. of Thos. Hoare, grocer
		24 Apr	Thos. Hornedge, son of John, button-maker, decd.
			Jos. Coopey, son of John, tanner
			Thos. Hughes, app. of John Trow, pinmaker
374		8 May	Thos. Hutchins, son of Wm., tailor, decd.
		27 May	Wm. Collett, son of Sam., haberdasher of hats, decd.
		22 June	Thos. Williams, app. of John Guy, maltster, decd.
		28 June	John Lugg, son of John, pewterer
		3 July	John Stock, app. of Thos. Edwards, grocer
		11 July	Sam. Seyer, son of Dan., ropemaker, decd.
		25 July	Chas. Price, son of Thos., salter, decd.
375		26 July	Wm. Shaw, app. of Sam. Lucas, joiner
		28 July	Jas. Derham, app. of Thos. Webb, ald.
		7 Aug	Humph. Gregory, son of Edm., gent., sheriff
		4 Sept	Thos. Best, son of John, gardener
		11 Sept	Ric. White, son of Ric., cordwainer
		25 Sept	John Wadley, son of John, haulier, decd.
		29 Sept	Thos. Skynner, app. of Mary Mason, widow

[1] One of the city's porters: GBR B 3/8, p. 103.
[2] Excise officer: ibid. p. 101.

John Hyett, esq., mayor 1704–5

		10 Oct	Wm. Launder, son of Jas., maltster
376		16 Oct	Wm. Haynes, app. of Sam. Burroughes, gent.
		26 Oct	Wm. Mason, app. of Wm. Window, tailor
		12 Nov	Jos. Edwards, son of Jos., decd.*
		4 Dec	Thos. Gardner, app. of John Tyler the younger, baker
		11 Dec	Wm. Powell, app. of Thos. Niccolls, gent.
		15 Dec	Dan. Pawling, app. of John Gammond, baker
	1705	12 Jan	Sam. Hayford, son of John, paver, late of Gloucester
		17 Jan	Nic. Clarke, son of Thos., pinmaker
377		19 Jan	John Vyner, son of Wm., feltmaker, decd.
		22 Jan	Geo. Fewtrell, son of John, cordwainer, decd.
		29 Jan	Ric. Webb, app. of Rob. Wilmott, saddler
		30 Jan	Hen. Fewtrell, son of John, cordwainer, decd.
		5 Feb	Chas. Hooper, app. of John Graffstocke, butcher
			John Hornedge, son of Jos., ropemaker
		10 Feb	Reginald Pyndar, esq., by gift
			Abel Wantner, son of Abel*
		20 Feb	John Gardner, son of a pinmaker*
378		12 Mar	Sam. Hendy, app. of Anne Thorp, widow
		19 Mar	Ric. Finch, app. of Dan. Collericke, bodice-maker
			Thos. Rogers, son of John, baker, decd.
		20 Mar	Jonathan Browne, app. of Thos. Sparks, silkweaver
			Hen. Ingly, bricklayer, [by fine][1]
			John Ingly, bricklayer, [by fine][2]
		27 Mar	Thos. Wells, son of Ric., yeoman, of Bristol
			Ric. Whithorne, son of Wal., baker, decd.
		28 Mar	Jonathan Browne, app. of Thos. Sparks, silkweaver[3]
379		31 Mar	Jonathan Hooke, app. of Rob. Freeman, joiner
			Edw. Haynes, app. of Wm. Gardner, pinmaker
		2 Apr	Giles Long, son of Giles, maltster
			John Lugg, son of John, pinmaker
			Thos. Maddocks, son of Thos., gent., decd.
			Wm. Welch, son of Wm., yeoman, of Badgeworth
			Thos. Gythens, son of John, gent.
			Thos. Smith, son of Thos., glover
			Ric. Woodward, son of Ric., pinmaker, decd.
380			Ric. Webly, son of Giles, feltmaker
			Chas. Dowsing, son of Wm., tailor
			John Philipps, son of Thos., tailor
			Dan. Bird, son of Dan., combmaker
			Rob. Burridge, son of Thos., weaver
			Thos. Ward, son of Geo., gunsmith, decd.
			Thos. Bullocke, son of Thos., scrivener, decd.
			John Benson, app. of John Benson, tiler and plasterer
			Sam. Grove, app. of Wm. Hornage, cordwainer
381			Nat. Veysey, app. of Nat. Veysey, tailor
			Thos. Lye, app. of Thos. Berwicke, button-maker
			Wm. Watts, son of Thos., gent., of Highnam
		3 Apr	Thos. Ravener, son of Thos., gardener
			Jos. Medway, son of Hen., silkweaver, decd.

[1] Ibid. F 4/7, p. 832.
[2] Ibid.; resigned 6 July and readmitted by act of 12 Aug 1730: ibid. B 3/9, ff. 278, 279v.
[3] Entry struck through; cf. above: ibid. C 9/7, p. 378.

John Merchant, app. of John Brocke, glover, decd.
4 Apr Ric. Bullocke, app. of Jas. Marshfield, fisherman
5 Apr Rog. Pitt, app. of John Jones, pinmaker
Hen. Hayes, son of Chris., cordwainer
Nat. Iles, son of Nat., woolcomber, decd.
382 6 Apr Sam. Washborne, son of John, clockmaker†
Nic. Nott, son of Geo., carpenter, decd.
Thos. Phelps, son of Jos., feltmaker, decd.
9 Apr Thos. Stephens, son of Thos., tailor, decd.
Wm. White, son of John, tanner, of Newent
Jos. Nourse, son of John, currier
Jesse Nash, son of Jesse, feltmaker, decd., of Shrewsbury (*Salop*), formerly of Gloucester
Nat. White, app. of Francis Pace, cordwainer, of Newent
383 11 Apr John Wiltshire, son of Gregory, gent.
12 Apr John Harris, son of John, gunsmith
13 Apr Ric. Newton, gent.,†[1] by gift
16 Apr John Baker, son of Thos., of Ledbury, Herefs.*
Thos. Webb, son of Sergeant, yeoman, decd., of Eldersfield (*Elsfield*), Worcs.
Wm. Window, app. of Chas. Greenway, cordwainer[2]
17 Apr Thos. Cannon, son of Thos., butcher, decd.
18 Apr Wm. Sexty, app. of John Sexty, cheesemonger
384 19 Apr Steph. Cooke, son of John, haberdasher of hats, decd.
21 Apr Rowles Scudamore, gent., son of Wm., ald., decd.
Thos. Lye, clerk,[3] son of Sam., ald.
2 May Ric. Gardner, app. of Anne Humphris, widow
5 May Thos. Wood, son of Jas., baker, late of Gloucester
11 May John Hall, son of John, apothecary, decd.
Phil Panter, son of Phil., skinner, decd.
385 14 May Benj. Atkins, son of John, cordwainer, decd.
Thos. Longden, son of Thos., gent., ald., decd.
19 May Wm. Mills, son of John, wiredrawer, of Wick Rissington, formerly of Gloucester
21 May Lawr. Whithorne, son of John, cordwainer, decd.
Dan. White, son of Sam., tanner, decd.
22 May Sam. Bryan, son of Dan., cordwainer
Wm. Cooke, esq., of Highnam by gift[4]
Chas. Whitehead, son of John, innholder, of Barnsley, formerly of Gloucester
386 23 May Hen. Cleavly, son of Hen., grocer, decd.
24 May Josiah Bland, app. of Rob. Payne, ald.
Thos. Fownes, son of Godfrey, maltster, decd.
Wm. Baker, app. of Thos. Probert, tailor
John Bayly, son of Thos., barber-surgeon, decd.
John Hawkins, app. of Dan. Sayer, ropemaker
Nat. Harris, son of Thos., gunsmith, decd.
25 May Lawr. Griffin, son of David, tailor, decd.
387 4 June Hen. Grevile, son of Hen., woollen-draper, late of Gloucester

[1] 'Clerk to Justice Powell': ibid. B 3/8, p. 163.
[2] Described originally as *silkweaver*.
[3] Became vicar of Broadhempston, Devon, in 1705 and of South Petherton, Som., in 1706: *Alumni Oxon. 1500–1714*, iii. 953; cf. Fosbrooke, *Glouc.* 179.
[4] Three days before election as M.P. for the city: Williams, *Parl. Hist. of Glos.* 206.

		16 July	Ric. Hale, maltster, (by fine)
		20 July	Dan. Brocke, son of Wm., collar-maker
		7 Aug	Hen. Ireton, esq.,[†1] by gift
		13 Aug	Thos. Bower, app. of Wm. Niccolls, tanner
		23 Aug	Mat. Ducie (*Ducey*) Moreton, esq.,[†2] by gift
		17 Sept	Jonathan Vice, app. of Sam. Wiggett, glover

Samuel Lye, esq., mayor 1705–6

		6 Oct	Jos. Brocke, app. of John Hyett, gent., ald.
388		10 Dec	Thos. Stephens, son of Thos., pinmaker, decd.
		17 Dec	Sam. Ady, son of Thos., gent.
	1706	11 Jan	Thos. Kearsy, son of Thos., pinmaker
			Wm. Fryer, son of Wal., labourer
		25 Feb	Wm. Freeman, app. of Abraham Archer, bricklayer
		8 Mar	Thos. Mills, app. of John Pool, tiler and plasterer
		15 Apr	Hen. Hyett, app. of Hen. Platt, grocer, decd.
389		1 May	Wm. Stephens, son of Thos., pinmaker
		2 May	Thos. Hornage, son of Wm., pinmaker
		3 May	Geo. Bishopp, son of Dan., tailor
			John Stephens, son of John, tailor, decd.[3]
			John Barrett, son of John, woolcomber
		13 May	Thos. Veysey, son of Nat., tailor
		12 July	Wm. Hyett, son of Benj., gent.
		9 Aug	Thos. Stephens, gent., by gift[4]
390		30 Aug	Thos. Bound, app. of Ric. Lane, grocer
			Thos. Willy, son of Rog., tailor, decd.
		10 Sept	Wal. Winstone, son of Wal., butcher
		12 Sept	Geo. Lloyd, esq., of Berkeley } by gift[5]
			(Captain) Chas. Weston, esq., of Berkeley }
		28 Sept	Jos. Wells, app. of Ric. Partridge, baker and maltster, decd.

John Bell, esq., mayor 1706–7

		14 Oct	Wm. Gregory, app. of Jonathan Davis, tailor
			John Rosse, app. of Jas. Bicknell, tailor, decd.
391		28 Oct	Ric. Walker, app. of Wm. Nest, carpenter
		4 Nov	Jas. Lovett, son of Jas., silkweaver
		2 Dec	John Brimyard, son of Wm., pipemaker, late of Gloucester
		6 Dec	Chas. Vaughan, app. of Theophilus Hopkins, joiner
			Jas. Ravenhill, app. of John More, butcher
	1707	10 Mar	Wm. Pace, app. of Sam. Yate, decd., and Jas. Yate, grocers
		12 Mar	John Collett, app. of Rob. Punter, mercer
392		19 Mar	And. Pegler, app. of Rob. Wilmott, saddler, decd.
		21 Mar	Wm. Leighton, app. of John Barker, barber-surgeon
		8 Apr	Knightly Chettwood, S.T.P., dean of Gloucester cathedral, by gift[6]
		29 Apr	Wm. Hayes, son of Wm., cordwainer
		5 May	Wm. Aycrigg, app. of Wm. Jordan, apothecary
		5 June	Giles Ashmead, app. of Wm. Beard, mercer

[1] Of Williamstrip, Coln St. Aldwyns: Atkyns, *Glos.* 364; *V.C.H. Glos.* vii. 48.

[2] Of Tortworth: Atkyns, *Glos.* 785; cf. *Complete Peerage*, iv. 474.

[3] Entry originally was incomplete and gave entrant's father as *Wm., combmaker*.

[4] Clerk of the peace for the county, at the request of the earl of Berkeley, high steward and lord lieutenant of the city: GBR B 3/8, p. 192; *V.C.H. Glos.* iv. 133.

[5] At the request of the earl of Berkeley: GBR B 3/8, p. 192.

[6] On his installation as dean: Fosbrooke, *Glouc.* 108.

23 June Wm. Bicknell, son of John, gent., decd.
393 4 July Jas. Man, son of Jas., glover
7 July John White, app. of John Rogers, glover
17 July (Captain) Wal. Nourse, esq., of Newent by gift
1 Sept John Philipps, son of Thos., tailor
Jas. Read, son of Rob., ironmonger
John Elliott, son of Edw., yeoman, of Barton Street
12 Sept John Wintle, gent., } by gift[1]
Posthumus Bell, gent., }
394 John King, dyer, (by fine)
John More, son of Nic., of Sandhurst
Thos. Smith, porter,[2] by gift
15 Sept Thos. Silly, app. of Thos. Bright, butcher, decd., of Tibberton
19 Sept Francis Wyndham,[3] esq., of Clearwell (*Clowerwall*) by gift
27 Sept Thos. Cleevely, son of Thos., gent., decd., of Over
1 Oct Sam. Whittington, son of Wm., clerk, decd.

395 **Capel Payne, esq., mayor 1707–8**

20 Oct Thos. Land, app. of Sam. Humphris, butcher
24 Oct Jas. Fords, son of Jas., tailor
25 Oct Sam. Sermon, app. of John Blizzard, baker
30 Oct Thos. Randle, son of Giles, silkweaver
28 Oct Capel Scudamore, son of Wm., gent., ald., decd.
31 Oct Thos. Lugg, son of Jasper, tanner, of Hereford, formerly of Gloucester
Wm. Marden, app. of John Gwillim, gent.
396 Jas. Long, son of John, button-maker
Wm. Engly, son of John, baker, decd.
1 Nov Mat. Phelps, son of Mat., feltmaker, decd.
3 Nov John Parker, son of Thos., baker
Ric. Mills, app. of Dan. Colericke, gent., sheriff
Thos. Cowles, son of Thos., cordwainer
Ric. Cox, son of Hen., tailor, decd.
Jesse Hale, son of Wm., pinmaker
397 Thos. Davis, app. of Thos. Winstone, tailor
Rob. Hunt, app. of Ric. White, mason and bricklayer
5 Nov John Lovett, son of Jas., silkweaver
6 Nov John Mason, son of Ric., bricklayer
7 Nov Thos. Tyler, app. of Thos. Cooke, tailor
John Welladvise, son of Wm., feltmaker, decd.
Thos. Butt, app. of John Greene, cordwainer, decd.
John Cowles, son of Jos., glover
Wm. Stephens, son of Thos., tailor, decd., of Barton Street in Gloucester
398 10 Nov Wm. Chapman, son of Geo., gunsmith, of Hereford
Wm. Long, app. of Francis Pace, cordwainer, of Newent
Thos. Pace, son of John, cordwainer
Jas. Gunn, son of Arthur, cordwainer, of Painswick
Chas. Ward, son of Geo., gunsmith, decd.
John Mamby, app. of Sam. Davis, butcher
Thos. Symon, son of David, victualler, decd.
Dan. Greening, app. of Humph. Heard, butcher

[1] Attorneys in the city's courts: GBR B 3/7, f. 167; 8, p. 246.
[2] One of the city's porters: ibid. 8, p. 246.
[3] M.P. for Gloucester 1709–10: Williams, *Parl. Hist. of Glos.* 206.

1707 John Lord, son of Ric., baker, decd.
399 Thos. Lugg, son of John, pinmaker
Wm. Twyning, app. of Wm. Fowler and Nat. Castle, bakers
Wm. King, son of John, scrivener
Jos. Cowles, son of Jos., glover
11 Nov Matthias Welch, son of Wm., yeoman, of Badgeworth
Chas. Workman, app. of Francis Pace, baker
12 Nov Nic. Wilkins, son of Thos., butcher, decd.
14 Nov Thos. Webley, son of Thos., baker, decd.
Wm. Welladvise, son of Wm., feltmaker, late of Gloucester
400 Steph. Lodge, son of Tristram, cooper, decd.
17 Nov Ric. Witcombe, son of Sam., weaver
21 Nov John Lee alias Lea, app. of his mother, widow*
Grey Stayte, son of Ric., innholder, decd.
28 Nov Steph. King, app. of Wm. Bliss, baker
Wm. Turner, son of John, button-maker
2 Dec Jos. Merrett, app. of Francis Yate the elder, cordwainer, decd.
5 Dec Wm. Lawrence, son of Thos., baker, of Ledbury, Herefs.
401 Hen. Merrett, son of Thos., clerk, decd.
8 Dec Francis Harris, son of Dan., tobacconist, decd.
12 Dec John Lovegrove, app. of Giles Lovegrove, tiler
29 Dec Jos. Harris, son of Jos., baker, decd.
Thos. Wyly, son of Thos., baker
1708 15 Jan Sam. Merrett, app. of Dan. Perry, decd., of Leonard Stanley*
16 Jan Leon. Pates, app. of Thos. Fletcher, baker
24 Jan John Hale, son of Wm., pinmaker
402 26 Jan John Greene, app. of Ric. Lane, grocer
6 Feb Jos. Goodwin, son of Ric., decd., of Over*
9 Feb Jos. Atkyns, son of Wal., cordwainer
25 Feb John Hawkins, son of Jas., baker, of Newent
10 Mar Wm. Scudamore, son of Wm., gent., ald., decd.
11 Mar Thos. Birch, son of Thos., feltmaker, decd.
12 Mar Chas. Toney, son of Chas., gent., decd.
Francis Cowdall, son of John, gent.
403 Chas. Dymocke, son of Cressey, mercer, decd.
John Drew, app. of Wm. Sysemore, barber-surgeon, late of Gloucester
Jos. Longden, son of Thos., gent., ald., decd.
John Palmer, son of Edm., baker
29 Mar Sam. Best, son of Sam., gardener, decd.
30 Mar Jas. Walker, son of Ant., blacksmith
2 Apr John Jones, app. of Wm. Skynner, cordwainer, of Newent, formerly of Gloucester
John Wheeler, app. of Rob. Freeman, joiner
404 5 Apr Wm. Jelfe, son of Thos., baker
Lawr. Nott, app. of John Nest, carpenter
Wm. Edwards, son of Wm., gent.
Ric. Edwards, app. of Thos. Webb, gent., ald.
Geo. Philipps, son of Thos., tailor
6 Apr Dan. Washborne, son of John, of Barton Street near Gloucester
Ric. Webb, son of John, baker
Jeremiah Jennings, son of Jeremiah, tailor
John Hayward, son of Sam., gent.
405 Isaac Fewterell, son of John, cordwainer, decd.
Ric. Nest, app. of John Nest, carpenter
Thos. Archer, app. of Thos. Farley, cutler, decd.
Edm. Allen, son of Edm., yeoman, decd., of Maisemore

	7 Apr	Jas. Edwards, son of Ric., cordwainer, decd.
		Jos. Puxon, son of Thos., silkweaver
		Jonathan Greene, son of Jonathan, joiner
		Jas. Greene, son of Ric., woolcomber, decd.
		Hen. Medway, son of Edw., hosier
		Ric. Williams, son of Ric., cooper, decd.
406		Hen. Toney, son of Chas., fiddler,[1] decd.
		Ric. Kersy, son of Thos., gardener, of Kingsholm
		John Brocke, son of John, skinner, decd.
		Thos. Mathews, son of Thos., baker, decd.
	8 Apr	Wm. Hathway, son of Wm., combmaker, decd.
	9 Apr	Wm. Cooke, son of Chas., butcher
	10 Apr	Wal. Mason, app. of John Mathews, tanner
	12 Apr	Wal. Fryer, app. of Jas. Pitt, pinmaker
	13 Apr	Thos. Perkins, app. of Thos. Meeke, currier
407	17 Apr	Jos. Gardner, son of Dan., mason, of Upton St. Leonards
	19 Apr	Jas. Bosley, app. of Edw. Whittingham, baker, of Westbury
		Jas. Gregory, son of Edm., gent., ald.
		John Greene, son of John, cordwainer, decd.
	21 Apr	Thos. Jones, son of Dennis, yeoman
		Sam. Ball, app. of John Gammond, baker
		Dan. Greening, app. of Jos. Phelps, grocer
	22 Apr	Wm. Hutchings, son of Wm., tailor, decd.
	23 Apr	Wm. Langford, son of Nic., mercer, decd.
408	24 Apr	Thos. Puxon, son of Thos., silkweaver
	26 Apr	Sam. Blizzard, son of Steph., sergeweaver and woolcomber, of Chipping Norton, Oxon.
	1 May	Ric. Drinkwater, app. of Thos. Drew, cordwainer
	3 May	Thos. Synocks, app. of Wm. King, pinmaker
		John Myles, son of Jas., baker, decd.
		Thos. Haynes, app. of Isaac Wood, tailor
		Hen. Wadley, son of John, tanner, decd.
		Wm. Toms, app. of John Gregory, mercer
	4 May	John Everett, son of Ambrose, woollen-draper, decd.
409	5 May	Thos. Perry, son of Thos., innholder, decd.
	6 May	Wm. Hartland, son of Thos., pinmaker, of St. Margaret's Hospital near Gloucester
	7 May	John Ward, son of John, blacksmith
		John Williams, son of Nic., cordwainer
		Giles Webley, son of Giles, feltmaker
	8 May	John Eckley, son of Thos., chandler, decd.
		John Keene, app. of John Sheppard, barber-surgeon
	10 May	John Baker, son of Jas., butcher
		Jas. Young, son of Jas., pinmaker
		Sam. Glowe, son of Wm., cooper, of Weston under Penyard, Herefs.
		Geo. More, son of Geo., butcher, decd.
410		Ric. Yarnold, app. of Nic. Lane the younger, apothecary
		Geo. Packer, son of Wm., tanner, decd.
		Wm. Okey, app. of Francis Brabant the elder, cooper
		Wm. Wilkins, app. of Thos. Selwyn, cordwainer, decd.
		Benj. Long, son of Giles, patten-maker
		Sam. Cooke, son of John, woolcomber, of Tetbury

[1] Cf. above: GBR C 9/7, p. 402, where he is described as *gent.*

			Giles Nurse, son of Giles, cordwainer, decd.
			Thos. Ashmead, son of Hen., butcher, of Cheltenham
			Steph. Blizzard, Thos. Blizzard, } sons of Steph., sergeweaver and woolcomber, of Chipping Norton, Oxon.
			Wm. Hall, app. of Aaron Jaques, baker
411			Phil. Tayler, app. of Jasper Tayler, combmaker
			Ebenezer Child, son of Thos., cordwainer, late of Bristol
			Owen Griffith, app. of Humph. Smith, glover, late of Gloucester
			Nic. Hieron, son of Nic., bodice-maker
			Hen. Jenings, app. of Nat. Veysey, tailor
			Thos. Harris, son of John, gunsmith
		11 May	Ric. Bickerton, son of John, gunsmith, of Evesham, Worcs.
		28 May	Isaac Oatley, Josiah Fitchew, } apps. of Francis Oatley, feltmaker
		28 June	Giles Young, app. of Rog. Church, tailor
		2 July	Jas. Philipps, son of Jas., saddler, decd.
412		2 Aug	Ric. Greene, son of Ric., gent.
		1 Sept	Joshua Worrall (the elder), silkweaver, (by fine)
		2 Sept	John Cage, app. of Jos. Jones, barber-surgeon

Giles Rodway, esq., mayor 1708–9

	1709	14 Jan	Thos. Hayes, son of Wm., cordwainer
		15 Jan	Wm. Ham, son of Wm., butcher, decd.
		17 Jan	Ric. Gooding, son of Ric., yeoman, decd., of Over
		7 Feb	Sam. Kemmis, app. of Wm. Barrett, woolcomber
		28 Feb	Ric. Welch, son of Wm., yeoman, of Badgeworth
413			John Heaven, son of John, dyer
			John Hayes, son of Wm., cordwainer
			Thos. Hathaway, son of Wm., turner
			Chas. Wantner, son of Abel, innholder
			Geo. Long, app. of Wm. Sparrowha[wke], cordwainer
			Wm. Burdocke, app. of Jonathan Davis, tailor
		4 Mar	John Tyler, son of Edw., cordwainer
		22 Mar	Isaac Watkins, son of Isaac, yeoman, of Barton Street
414		16 May	Jas. Burgis, app. of Thos. Niccolls, plumber
		20 June	Dan. Remington, app. of Giles Rodway, esq., mayor
		27 June	Wm. Still, app. of Francis Still, maltster
			Phil. Philipps, app. of Sam. Lucas, joiner
		1 July	Wm. Phelps, son of Wm., tanner
		18 July	Chas. Harding, son of John, glover, decd.
			Thos. Winniatt, son of Wm., pinmaker, late of Gloucester
			Sam. Powell, son of John, silkweaver
415		19 July	Jos. Phelps, son of And., tanner, late of Gloucester
		22 July	Geo. Cole, app. of Thos. Cooke, tailor
			John Mathews, app. of John Davis the younger, pinmaker
		25 July	John Adams, app. of Ric. Cowcher, pinmaker
			Jos. Cother, app. of Ric. Wells, cordwainer, decd.
			Thos. Phillipps, son of Thos., tailor
		29 July	Hen. Stephens, son of Wm., combmaker, late of Gloucester
		22 Aug	Sam. Stocke, app. of Geo. Perkins, baker
		9 Sept	Chas. Young, app. of Wm. Gardner, pinmaker
		30 Sept	Chas. Fielding, son of Rob., gent., decd., of Withington

416 **Edmund Gregory, esq., mayor 1709–10**

		5 Oct	John Gardner, son of John, yeoman, of Sheepscombe, Painswick

6 Oct John Newman, app. of John Smith the younger, currier. Disfranchised 28 Nov 1709[1]
24 Oct Thos. Payne, app. of Chas. Tyler, plumber
31 Oct John Eastham, son of Chris., victualler, decd.
Wm. Niccolls, son of Wm., ald.
John Bishopp, app. of Thos. Carill, hosier
John Browne, son of John, innholder
Thos. White, son of Miles, tanner, of Newland
John Fisher, app. of Wm. Barnes, saddler, decd.
11 Nov Edw. Lugg, son of John, tanner, decd.
417 14 Nov Edm. Holford, app. of John Holford, cordwainer
Thos. Davis, son of Rob., brazier
Thos. Rolfe, son of John, yeoman, decd.
Thos. Aldridge, son of Thos., yeoman, decd., of Longford
Wm. Symon, son of David, innholder, decd.
John Cooke, app. of Sam. Sparry, baker
Hen. Smith, app. of Thos. Maddocke and Sam. Cooke, saddlers
15 Nov John Cowles, son of Thos., cordwainer, decd.
16 Nov Dan. Lea, son of Edw., cordwainer
18 Nov Geo. Cowcher, son of Geo., mercer
Geo. Cook, son of Geo., grocer
418 19 Nov John Torkington, son of Jos., tailor, decd., of Monmouth
21 Nov Wm. Mathews, son of Ric., apothecary, late of Ledbury, Herefs.
Hen. Miles, app. of Thos. Fletcher, baker
John Mower, son of Thos., barber, decd.
Thos. Elms, son of Rob., mercer, decd.
Toby Mills, son of Mat., mercer, decd., of Birdlip
Lawr. Nott, son of Nathan, glazier
Chas. Turner, son of John, cordwainer
Wm. Perks, son of Wm., pinmaker, decd., of Barton Street in the parish of St. Michael
22 Nov Edw. Bleeke, app. of Wm. Allen, grocer
24 Nov Giles Estcourt, son of Chris., pinmaker, decd.
419 25 Nov Sam. Burford, app. of John Bell, ald.
29 Nov Benj. Filder, son of Geo., farrier
30 Nov John Showell, son of Thos., baker, decd., of Longford
2 Dec John Cowdall, son of John, grocer. Disfranchised [6 Dec 1709][2]
Dan. Blanch, app. of John Ricketts, pinmaker
Ric. Bosley, app. of John Bosley, feltmaker
3 Dec Jas. Price, son of Thos., cordwainer
5 Dec Edw. Pheasant, son Thos., button-maker
420 John Bayly, son of John, innholder, decd.
6 Dec John Perks, son of Wm., pinmaker, decd., of Barton Street
9 Dec Sam. Welladvise, son of Wm., feltmaker, late of Gloucester
10 Dec Chas. Snell, son of Thos., ald., decd.
12 Dec Little Wintle, son of John, cordwainer
Sam., Monning, son of Isaac, pinmaker
John Lugg, son of John, vintner, decd.
Jas. Cowdall, son of John, gent.
Wm. Myles, son of Jas., baker, decd.
Wm. Painter, son of John, glazier, decd.
Lawr. Eckly, app. of John Trow, pinmaker

[1] Entry struck through.
[2] Entry struck through; disfranchised for having obtained the freedom by fraud: GBR B 3/8, p. 335.

421 John Chappell, app. of John Elliotts, wiredrawer, decd.
13 Dec Hen. King, son of Wm., pinmaker, decd.
Thos. Wilcox, son of Thos., tailor, decd.
Geo. Bradford, app. of Francis Brabant the younger, cooper
Giles Kent, son of Giles, cordwainer, decd.
Jas. Hornidge, son of Jas., blacksmith
Thos. Hill, son of Rob., clerk, of Condicote
Thos. Trustram, Phil. Trustram, John Trustram, } sons of Thos., cordwainer, of Duntisbourne
422 Edw. Jones, son of Chas., woolcomber, of Tibberton
Jasper Lugg, app. of Jasper Lugg, woolcomber, late of Gloucester
Sam. Hendrick, son of Sam., ironmonger, decd.
John Gregory, son of Edm., esq., mayor
1710 10 Mar Thos. Stephens, esq., of Lypiatt[1] by gift
Kynard de la Bere, esq., of Southam by gift
20 Mar Nic. Lechmere, esq., of the Middle Temple, London, by gift
Ric. Southby,[2] esq., of Carswell, Berks., by gift
10 Apr John Selwyn,[3] esq., of Matson by gift
423 Chas. Selwyn,[4] esq., of Matson by gift
(Dr.) Wm. Beavoir, gent., by gift
20 Apr Thos. Tyler, son of Edw., cordwainer
24 Apr Thos. Blake, app. of Wm. Lawrence, baker
8 May Wm. Tomlins, app. of Hen. Davis, pinmaker
31 May Rowland Pitt, app. of Wm. Tayler, ald.
1 July John Wood, son of John, carrier
22 July Obadiah Lawrence, app. of Wm. Lodge, cooper
Geo. Dowding, app. of Sam. Rickards, carpenter
1 Aug Wm. Corsnett, son of Ric., gent., decd.
14 Aug Dennis Cooke, esq., of Highnam by gift
424 Roynon Jones, esq., of Nass by gift
Wm. Kingscott, esq., of Kingscote by gift
John Downes, clerk, of Painswick by gift
25 Aug Jas. Hawkins, son of Jas., baker, of Newent
31 Aug John Dutton, esq., of Sherborne by gift
1 Sept Chas. Lander, son of Jas., maltster
9 Sept Jas. Serjeaunt, app. of Jane Elliott, widow
11 Sept Thos. Saunders, app. of John Matthews, tanner, decd.
Thos. Whittingham, son of Edw., baker, of Westbury
425 And. Allen, app. of Sam. Farmer, apothecary
15 Sept John Hatton, app. of John Way, butcher
Edw. Hayward, son of Edw., weaver
Jos. Holder, app. of Wm. Benson, tiler
Wm. Benson, son of Wm., plasterer
Jos. Davis, son of Jos., cordwainer
Wm. Stirt, son of Thos., fishmonger
Rob. Cooke, son of Rob., cordwainer
Wm. Ady, app. of Thos. Jeanes, feltmaker
Thos. Bosse, app. of John Best, tailor

[1] Lypiatt Park, Stroud: *V.C.H. Glos.* xi. 112.
[2] Son-in-law of Nat. Lye, archdeacon of Gloucester: Burke, *Land Gent.* (1846), ii. 1264; Fosbrooke, *Glouc.* 178 names Lye's son-in-law as Chas. Southby.
[3] M.P. for Gloucester 1734–51: Williams, *Parl. Hist. of Glos.* 209–10.
[4] M.P. for Gloucester 1727–34: ibid. 209.

John Hem(m)ing, son of John, innholder
18 Sept Sam. Sheppard, son of John, barber-surgeon
426 Wm. Kearsey, app. of Wm. Horrold, pewterer
Wm. Little, son of Wm., yeoman, decd., of Ashleworth
Lawr. Churches, son of Jonathan, baker, of Woodchester
John Webb, app. of Thos. Vaughan, joiner, late of Gloucester
Jonathan Churches, son of Jonathan, baker, of Woodchester
John Wells, son of Ric., yeoman, decd.
22 Sept Ric. Phewterell, app. of Mic. Jennings, butcher
Wm. Weaver, son of Ric., butcher
Wm. Allen, son of Edm., yeoman, decd., of Maisemore
Thos. Bradley, son of John, butcher
23 Sept Geo. Daw, app. of Edw. Tyler, cordwainer
427 Jas. Maverly, app. of Thos. Berwicke, button-maker
John Watts, app. of Ric. Bryan, brazier
25 Sept Wm. Wood, son of Jas., maltster, of Cheltenham
Edw. Charleton, son of Edw., gent., of Churchdown
Hen. Nurse, son of John, yeoman, of the Rea, Hempsted
Jos. Pegler, son of Jos., tanner
Thos. Jones, son of Chas., cooper, decd.
Thos. Bowler, son of Thos., collar-maker
Wm. Hale, son of Wm., pinmaker
26 Sept Wm. Saunders, son of Thos., tanner
Thos. Stirt, son of Thos., fishmonger
29 Sept John Stratford, app. of Jas. Lander, baker
428 Abraham Smith, app. of Jas. Smith, cooper

Capel Payne, esq., mayor 1710–1

2 Oct Thos. Pyrke, esq., of the Middle Temple, Mdx., by gift
John Leighton, app. of John Parker, tailor[1]
3 Oct Thos. Stone, son of Rob., tanner, decd.
5 Oct Wal. Marshall, gent., of Eastington by gift
6 Oct Josiah Hathway, son of Elisha, weaver, decd.
Ric. Weeksey, app. of Capel Longden, ironmonger
Geo. Hill, son of John, gent., of Edge (*the Rudge*), Painswick
9 Oct Thos. Mamby, son of John, bricklayer, decd.
Thos. Blisse, son of Wm., baker, of Painswick
John Hornell, app. of John Nest, carpenter
429 10 Oct Jas. Hermitage, app. of John Turner, cordwainer
Hen. Young, app. of Wm. Hornadge, cordwainer
Isaac Elton, merchant, of Bristol by gift
Jacob Elton, merchant, of Bristol by gift
13 Oct Thos. Cox, son of Hen., tailor, decd.
Jas. Arnold, son of Thos., wagoner
John Edwards, son of Thos., gent.
16 Oct Ebenezer Hathway, son of Elisha, dyer, of Powick, Worcs.
Wm. Mathews, app. of Jas. Robins the younger, currier
19 Oct Edw. Stephens, esq., of Alderley by gift
20 Oct Nat. Harris, son of Francis, apothecary, of Bristol
430 Jas. Edwards, app. of Thos. Weal, baker
Wm. Dewxell, } sons of Wm., brewer, decd., of Barton Street
Dan. Dewxell, }

[1] Originally named as *John Barker, barber-surgeon.*

John Cowcher, son of Wm., cordwainer, decd.
Ant. Suffield, son of Ant., cordwainer, decd.
John Partridge, son of Hen., baker, decd.
John Baldwyn, son of Wm., glassmaker, decd.
Geo. Myon alias Meighen, son of Geo. Meighen, grocer, decd.
Ric. Sweat, son of Ric., glazier, decd.
Ric. Beard, son of John, clerk, decd.
John Thomas, son of John, cordwainer
431 Dan. Hughes, son of Dan., cordwainer, of London
Edm. Collett, son of Edm., haberdasher of hats, decd.
Wm. Pace, son of Wm., tailor, decd.
Jos. Hanks, son of Jos., feltmaker
Thos. Bliss, son of John, tanner, decd.
21 Oct John Monnington, app. of Rob. Sparrowhaw[ke], silkweaver, decd.
Steph. Tench, son of Steph., weaver, of Tewkesbury
John Williams, app. of Thos. Stephens, pinmaker, decd.
23 Oct Ric. Bosely, John Bosely, } sons of Ric., feltmaker, decd.
Wm. Cooke, son of Wm., cordwainer, decd.
Ric. Stait, son of Ric., innholder, decd.
432 Clement Bubb, son of Wm., baker, decd.
Jas. Bray, son of Hen., mercer, decd.
Guy Warwicke, son of Wm., scrivener, decd.
Wal. Gardner, son of Nat., baker, decd., of Berkeley
Ric. Lewis, son of Thos., gent., decd.
Nat. Careles, son of John, gent., decd.
Thos. Hemming, app. of Rob. Syms, mercer, decd.
Chris. Ludlow, app. of Jos. Ludlow, mercer, late of Gloucester
John Shatford, app. of Theophilus Hopkins, joiner
John Bullocke, son of John, glover
Thos. Higgins, son of Nic., saddler, of Abergavenny, Mon.
Jesse Paynter, son of John, glazier, decd.
433 Chas. Evans, son of Jas., innholder, late of Gloucester
Rob. Baldwyn, son of Wm., tobacconist, decd.
John Dobbs, son of John, smith, decd.
John Staniford, son of Chas., mercer, decd.
16 Dec Job Cowly, app. of Rog. Church, glazier
1711 17 Feb Rob. Greene, app. of Wm. Randle, weaver
19 Mar Wm. Hayns, app. of John Rogers, baker
19 Apr Edm. Nelme, app. of Nat. Castle, baker
7 May John Smith, app. of Ant. Williams, barber-surgeon
11 June Edw. Addis, app. of Thos. Puckeridge, tailor
29 June John Price, app. of Ric. Heming, tailor
434 3 Sept And. Whitfield, app. of Anne Bishopp, widow
12 Sept Ralph Ady, app. of John Graffstocke, butcher
2 Oct Edw. Hare, app. of Wm. Fletcher and John Lutre, butchers

Samuel Hayward, esq., mayor 1711–2

31 Dec John Penrice, son of Humph., baker, decd.
1712 19 Jan Wm. Roberts, app. of Sam. Ricketts, carpenter
4 Feb Chas. Beal, app. of Sam. Ricketts, carpenter
8 Feb John Ricketts, carver, by gift[1]
19 May Thos. Baker, son of Thos., barber-surgeon

[1] For carving a statue of the monarch for the corporation: GBR B 3/8, pp. 377–8, 414.

3 Aug Benj. Hyett, son of Benj., gent., decd.
435 25 Aug Hen. [Somerset], duke of Beaufort,†[1] by gift
Thos. Chas. [Tracy], Lord Tracy,†[2]
[Sir] Ric. How, Bt.,†[3]
John Berkley, esq.,†[4]
John How the younger, esq.,†[5] [by gift][7]
John Cotherington, esq.,†
Chas. Coxe, esq.,†[6]
2 Oct Zachariah Stephens, son of Thos., merchant

James Furney, esq., mayor 1712–3

13 Oct Zachariah Stephens, son of Rob., innholder, decd.
17 Oct Thos. Newton, app. of Dan. Seyer, ropemaker
Wm. Cooke, son of Wm., tailor
24 Nov Thos. Bishopp, app. of John Gregory, barber-surgeon
436 19 Dec Ric. Beckett, app. of John Gregory, mercer
1713 5 Jan Thos. Lewis, app. of Wm. Mason, gardener
19 Jan Wm. Gold, app. of Eleanor Tyler, widow
20 Jan Chas. Roberts, app. of Wm. Collett, grocer
6 Feb John Hellyard, app. of Rob. Savory, farrier
2 Mar John Monnington, app. of Edm. Humphris, currier
27 Mar Sam. Pawling, app. of Dan. Pawling, baker, late of Gloucester
10 Apr Wm. Perry, son of Wm., tailor, decd.
15 May John Cooke, son of Chas., butcher
13 July John Chestroe, son of Ant., baker, of Cheltenham
437 17 July Jos. Serman, app. of Ric. Wells, cordwainer, decd.
Jas. Hill, son of John, gent., decd., of Edge, Painswick
21 July Edw. Bayly, woolcomber, [by fine][8]
23 July Rob. Futter, gent., by gift
24 July Arthur Engly, son of John, baker, decd.
Sam. Hossington, son of Sam., bodice-maker
Sam. Millard, app. of John Price, gardener
Ric. Cowcher, son of Ric., pinmaker
John Archer, app. of Abraham Archer, bricklayer
438 1713 John Grindle, son of John, feltmaker, decd.
John Birch, son of Thos., feltmaker, decd.
Thos. Knight, son of Ric., currier, decd.
Wm. Dunning, app. of Thos. Cowles and Thos. Swayne, tilers and plasterers
Thos. Hardwicke, app. of Ric. Cowcher, pinmaker
Thos. Hartland, son of Thos., pinmaker
Sam. Brotherton, app. of Abraham Archer, bricklayer
Geo. Ireland, son of Ric., brickmaker

1 Of Badminton: *Complete Peerage*, ii. 53.
2 Of Toddington: ibid. xii (2), 4.
3 Of Cassey Compton, Withington, and Wishford, Wilts.: *Complete Baronetage*, iii. 123.
4 ? of Stoke Gifford: Atkyns, *Glos.* 691.
5 Of Stowell, M.P. for Gloucester Feb–Aug 1727: Williams, *Parl. Hist. of Glos.* 208; cf. *Complete Peerage*, iii. 156–7.
6 ? of Nether Lypiatt, M.P. for Gloucester 1713–22; Williams, *Parl. Hist. of Glos.* 207; Atkyns, *Glos.* 701.
7 GBR F 4/8, p. 95; by act of 12 Aug 1712 the mayor was empowered to admit to the freedom up to six men nominated by the duke of Beaufort, lord lieutenant of the city, when attending the assizes: ibid. B 3/8, p. 455.
8 Ibid. F 4/8, p. 140.

1713 Thos. Cowcher, son of Rob., pinmaker, decd.
Sam. Perkins, app. of John Benson, tiler and plasterer
439 John Lane, son of John, pipemaker, decd.
Jos. Hale, son of Jos., feltmaker, decd.
Thos. Merry, son of John, baker, decd.
Jacob Lumbard, son of Jacob, sergeweaver
Abraham Archer, son of Abraham, bricklayer
Wm. Phelps, son of Jos., feltmaker, decd.
Thos. Gardner, son of Thos., pinmaker, decd.
Jacob Kirby, app. of Thos. Summers, silkweaver
Wm. Perry, app. of John Cowles, tailor
Rob. Fords, son of Jas., tailor
Jos. Pitt, son of Jos., feltmaker
John Mower, son of Geo., pewterer, decd.
440 Thos. Deane, app. of Edw. Cripps and Sam. Humphris, butchers
Sam. Field, app. of Rob. Freeman, joiner
Jos. Mitchell, app. of John Benson, tiler and plasterer
John Hopkins, app. of Sam. Ricketts, carpenter
Thos. Pembruge, son of Sam., baker, decd.
Wm. Nurse, son of Giles, cordwainer, of Upton St. Leonards
John Pool, son of John, tiler and plasterer
27 July Rob. Harding, app. of John Heaven, barber-surgeon
Ric. Church, app. of Jas. Mutlow, glover
John Wadley, son of Wm., tanner, decd.
Ric. Skey, app. of Edm. Humphris, currier
441 John Man, son of Jas., glover
John Hornage, son of John, pinmaker, decd.
Thos. Browne, son of Thos., cordwainer
Nathan Nott, son of Nathan, glazier
Ric. Man, app. of Mat. Capper, innholder
John Reband, son of Ric., pipemaker, decd.
Wm. Shatford, app. of Thos. Jones, glover
Francis Lye, son of Hen., blacksmith, decd.
John Jeffes, app. of Ric. Weaver, blacksmith
Jacob Medway, son of Abraham, bricklayer, decd.
John Woodward, app. of Ric. Woodward and Thos. Stephens, pinmakers
442 Giles Blake, app. of John Nurse and Ant. Walker, blacksmiths
Jos. Merry, son of John, baker, decd.
Jas. Baker, son of Jas., butcher
Sam. Jefferyes, son of Hen., joiner
Benj. Heming, son of John, innholder
Thos. Rooke, app. of John Collett, joiner
Edw. Elliott, son of Edw., innholder, of Barton Street near Gloucester
Jas. Wiley, son of Thos., baker
Sam. Bishopp, son of Dan., barber-surgeon, decd.
John Aylway, son of Ric., baker
443 John Tyler, son of Jas., plumber and glazier, decd.
29 July John Prinn, esq., of Charlton Kings by gift
31 July John Way, son of John, butcher, decd.
Griffith (*Griffantius*) Philipps, app. of Rob. Watts, tailor
Guy Winniatt, son of John, pinmaker, decd.
Wm. Herring, app. of Jos. Pegler, tanner
John Preece, app. of John Heaven, barber-surgeon
Wal. Miles, son of Wal., baker
Edm. Long, app. of Aaron Jaques, decd., and Sam. Stocke, bakers

Thos. Paynard, app. of Nic. Lane the younger, gent.
Gregory Niccolls, son of Wm., ald.
John Pembruge, son of Thos., grocer
444 Ric. Reeve, innholder, (by fine)
3 Aug Jasper Freame, } sons of Jasper, baker, of Newent
Wm. Freame, }
Ric. Draper, app. of Thos. Drew, cordwainer, decd.
John Wood, app. of John Reeve, gunsmith
John Phelps, son of Wm., tanner
John Webb, son of Sergeant, yeoman, decd., of Eldersfield, Worcs.
Jos. Punter, son of Rob., gent.
Sam. Burroughes, son of Sam., gent.
5 Aug Chas. Bloxom, innholder, (by fine)
Jos. Toms, ostler, (of the Swan inn by fine)
John Vaunt, ostler (at the Crown and Sceptre, by fine)
445 7 Aug Thos. Cother, app. of Dan. Bryan, cordwainer
Florence (*Florice*) Cooke, app. of Jas. Sayer the younger, writing-master
Ric. Greene, son of Ric., cordwainer, decd.
Wm. Gorton, app. of Thos. Selwyn, cordwainer, decd.
John Edding, son of Thos., pinmaker, decd.
8 Aug Geo. Archer, tailor,[1] (by fine)
13 Aug Wm. Hitchman, app. of John Green, cordwainer, decd.
John Kingman, son of John, wiredrawer
10 Aug Ven. Hen. Penrice, LL.D., chancellor of Gloucester diocese,[†] by gift
Edm. Bray, esq., of Barrington[2] by gift[x]
Ant. Lechmere, esq., of Hanley,[3] Worcs., by gift[x]
Thos. Whorwood, esq., of [?Holton], Oxon.,[4] by gift[x]
446 15 Aug Thos. Andrews, gent., son of Wm., saddler
17 Aug Jas. Dencox, carpenter, (by fine)
Thos. How, yeoman,[5] (by fine)
John Brooks, app. of John Pace, cordwainer, decd.
Thos. Draper, app. of Hen. Draper, blacksmith
Wm. Skinner, son of Wm., cordwainer, of Newent
Abraham Winniatt, son of Wm., pinmaker, decd.
Geo. Harrison, salt merchant, of Droitwich, Worcs., [by fine][6]
20 Aug Thos. Bingham, woolcomber, (by fine)
Rob. Davis, grocer, (by fine)
21 Aug John Hall, app. of Thos. Weal, baker
447 Rob. Stephens, son of Rob., innholder, decd.
John Lander, son of Jas., maltster, late of Gloucester
22 Aug Sam. Sexty, son of John, cheesemonger
Nat. Harris, woolcomber, (by fine)
24 Aug John Engly, son of John, baker, decd.
John Hickman, son of John, tailor, decd.
Jas. Knowles, app. of Jos. Howell, blacksmith

[x] Date incorrect; among six men nominated under act of 11 Aug 1713 by the earl of Berkeley, the high steward, then in Gloucester: GBR B 3/8, p. 506.
[1] Son of Sampson, serjeant-at mace: ibid. p. 505.
[2] Great Barrington: *V.C.H. Glos.* vi. 19.
[3] Hanley Castle: Nash, *Worcs.* i. 560.
[4] Cf. *V.C.H. Oxon.* v. 172.
[5] Servant of John Snell and formerly of Justice Powell, decd.: GBR B 3/8, p. 509.
[6] Ibid. F 4/8, p. 139.

26 Aug John Horseman, gent., [by fine][1]
Thos. Witcombe, woolcomber and weaver, of Barton Street [by fine][2]
27 Aug Mat. Bradgate, son of Wm., innholder
31 Aug Ric. Wadley, son of John, haulier, late of Gloucester
4 Sept Thos. Webb, gent., son of Thos., gent., decd.
448 Chas. Yate, esq., son of Ric., esq., decd., of Arlingham
5 Sept Moses Dyer, app. of John Shingler, pinmaker
25 Sept John Webb, app. of Sam. Powell, baker
28 Sept Thos. Hill, victualler, (by fine)
1 Oct John Nurse, barber-surgeon, (by fine)

Richard Greene, esq., mayor 1713–4

12 Oct Edw. Bennett, app. of Thos. Mathews, apothecary
1714 18 Feb Edw. Fletcher, app. of John Barker, barber-surgeon
21 June Wm. Attwood, yeoman, (by fine)
Wm. Howlett, app. of John Harris, mercer
18 June Wm. Billings, app. of John Charles, cordwainer
449 6 Aug Ric. Bishopp, son of John, gent.
Thos. Palmer, son of Edm., baker
1715 8 Jan John Fryer, app. of Abraham Archer, bricklayer[3]
1714 1 Oct John Cowcher, son of Geo., gent.
Wm. Greene, app. of Thos. Drew, cordwainer, decd.
Ric. Woodward, app. of Wm. Gardner, pinmaker
Joshua Worrall the younger, gent., } by gift[4]
Wm. Robins, gent., }

Samuel Browne, esq., mayor 1714–5

23 Nov Ant. Workman, son of Ant., butcher
1715 8 Jan John Fryer, app. of Abraham Archer, bricklayer (*blacklayer*). Entered in Ald. Green's year[5]
450 28 Jan Jas. Wood, son of Jas., maltster, of Cheltenham
John Bicknell, son of Wm., tailor
John Wilks, app. of Jacob Lumbard, sergeweaver
4 Feb Wm. Mills, app. of Jonathan Voice and John Man, glovers
Wal. Harris, app. of Nat. Hardwicke and Dan. Palling, bakers
5 Feb Francis Farmer, son of Francis, feltmaker, decd.
Thos. Mills, app. of John Ricketts, pinmaker
Dan. Collericke, son of Adam, barber-surgeon
Sam. Wintle, son of Hen., maltster
Nat. Washborne, son of John, watchmaker
John Jefferyes, son of John, feltmaker
451 Hen. Clayton, app. of John Wiltshire, tailor
Thos. Harding, son of John, glover
Wm. Merry, son of John, baker, decd.
Thos. Hayes, son of Chris., cordwainer
John Roffe alias Ralph, son of John Ralph, labourer, decd.
Jas. Caldwell, app. of John Carter, cordwainer

[1] Ibid.; according to ibid. B 3/8, p. 509, Horseman, servant of Justice Powell, decd., was awarded the freedom by gift.
[2] Ibid. F 4/8, p. 139.
[3] Entry struck through; cf. below: ibid. C 9/7, p. 449.
[4] Attorneys in the city's courts: ibid. B 3/8, p. 539.
[5] Cf. above: ibid. C 9/7, p. 449.

7 Feb John Webb, son of Thos., esq., ald.
Wm. Baker, son of Thos., tanner, decd.
Nat. Taynton, son of John, grocer
John Engly, app. of Nat. Jones, tailor
Geo. Nurse, son of John, cooper, late of Hempsted
Wal. Young, son of Abraham, pipemaker, of Ludford, Herefs.
Thos. Nest, son of John, carpenter
452 Sam. Webley, son of Giles, feltmaker
John Perris, son of Ric., butcher
Alex. Ready,[1] gent., son of Thos., cordwainer, decd.
John Graffstocke, son of John, butcher
Godfrey Fownes, son of John, distiller
Ric. Jones, son of Dennis, yeoman
Sam. Keene, app. of Wal. Young, cordwainer
John Beard, son of Benj., clothier, decd., of Newent
Jas. Gunter, app. of Sam. Lucas, joiner
Hen. Weaver, son of Hen., farrier
Thos. Eldridge, app. of John Cowles, butcher
John Harris, son of Jos., baker, decd.
453 John Hayward, son of Clement, tailor, decd.
John Merrett, son of Thos., clerk, decd.
John Kemmis, app. of Thos. Puckeridge, tailor
Wm. Birt, son of John, gent., of Leominster, Herefs.
Edw. Church, son of John, pinmaker
Nat. Badger alias Bale, app. of Thos. Swayne, tiler and plasterer
Wm. Puxon, son of Wm., silkweaver
John Little, app. of John Singleton, pinmaker
Hen. Grigg, app. of John Trow, decd., and John Singleton, pinmakers
John Davis, app. of John Halford, cordwainer
Wm. Wheeler, app. of Ephraim Higgins, bricklayer, decd.
John Spiller, app. of John Wadley, baker
Jas. Mutloe, son of Jas., glover
454 Jos. Brimyard, app. of Thos. Harrison, feltmaker, decd.
Jas. Cobb, son of Thos., cordwainer
Wm. Harris, app. of Thos. Stephens, pinmaker
Wm. Ireland, son of Ric., innholder, decd.
Thos. Vaughan, son of Aaron, joiner
Sam. Salcombe, } sons of Sam., ropemaker, decd., of Defford,
Jas. Salcombe, } Worcs.
John Hartland, app. of John Pace, cordwainer
Hen. Bubb, son of Wm., baker, decd.
Thos. Harris, son of Jos., baker, decd.
Ric. Swayne, son of Ric., collar-maker
Thos. Humphris, son of Thos., barber-surgeon, decd.
Ric. Phipps, app. of Francis Steel, maltster
455 Wm. Webley, son of Jos., tailor
John Bradford, app. of Capel Payne, gent., ald.
John Cowles, son of Wm., gardener, of Kingsholm
Wm. Elliott, son of Edw., yeoman, of Barton Street
Jos. Webb, son of Jos., woolcomber, decd.
Sam. Bradley, son of John, grocer
John Kersey, son of Thos., gardener, decd., of Kingsholm

[1] Later assumed the surname Colston; cf. below: ibid. 8, pp. 229, 256; Burke, *Land. Gent.* (1846), i. 247.

Dan. Gardner, son of Thos., pinmaker, decd.
Wm. Humphris, son of Edm., currier
Ric. Window, app. of Wm. Hayes, decd., and Ric. Drinkwater, cordwainers
Thos. Woolford, son of Thos., basket-maker, decd.
Titus Hopley, app. of Ric. Baker, haulier
456 Wm. Milton, app. of Theophilus Hopkins, joiner
Duncombe Pyrke, son of Nat., esq., of Littledean
Wm. Stone, son of Rob., tanner, decd.
Dan. White,[1] son of John, tanner, of Newent
14 Feb Thos. Hobbs, app. of John Nest, carpenter
21 Feb Wm. Cooke, app. of Thos. Niccolls, plumber
11 Mar Rob. Watts, son of Rob., tailor
18 Mar Giles Watts, son of Rob., tailor
16 Apr John Moutlow, app. of John Bell, gent., ald.
27 June John Humphris, app. of Humph. Heard, butcher
10 Aug John White, clerk,[2] son of John, gent.
457 25 Aug Thos. Roberts, app. of John Reeve, gunsmith
24 Sept Maj.-Gen. [Chas.] Wills,[3] esq.,† by gift*
Brigadier [? Thos.] Stanwix,[4] esq.,† by gift*
(Col.) [ ] Weld, esq.,† by gift*
(Major) [ ] Macklean, esq.,† by gift*
26 Sept John Blizzard, son of John, baker

Thomas Ludlow, esq., mayor 1715–6

14 Oct Thos. Gardner, app. of Sam. Wygate, glover
28 Oct Thos. Trinder, app. of Francis Oatley, feltmaker, decd.
12 Dec Ric. Ball, app. of Francis Brabant, cooper
458 1716 17 Feb John Carter, app. of Thos. Weal, baker
10 Mar John King, merchant, of Bristol by gift
6 Apr Ralph Freak, esq., of Westbury by gift
Geo. Townsend the younger, esq., of Lincoln's Inn, Mdx., by gift
13 Apr Francis Cole, app. of John Rogers, baker, decd.
30 Apr John Freame, son of Jasper, baker, of Newent
28 May Giles Smart, app. of Thos. Carill, hosier
22 June Jos. Cole, app. of John Hale, barber-surgeon
16 July Lt.-Col. Moses Leathes, esq.,† by gift
Benj. Newton, clerk,[5] by gift

459 **Thomas Niccolls, esq., mayor 1716–7**

3 Dec Rob. Arnold, son of Thos., wagoner, decd.
1717 4 Jan Nat. Sanders, app. of Edw. Swayne, joiner
14 Mar John Iremonger, app. of Dan. Bryant, apothecary
1 Apr Jos. Gooding, son of Jos., cordwainer, of Minsterworth
4 Apr Wm. Sparks, app. of Wal. Young, cordwainer
25 Apr Jasper Keylocke, app. of John Halford, cordwainer
20 May Sam. Heath, son of Sam., innholder

[1] Cf. below: GBR C 9/7, p. 478.
[2] Curate of Newnham and Littledean by the corporation's gift: ibid. B 3/8, p. 557.
[3] *D.N.B.*: later in 1715 he led troops against the Jacobite forces at Preston, Lancs.
[4] Cf. ibid. s.v. Stanwix, John.
[5] Master of the College (later the King's) school, curate of St. Nicholas, and rector of Taynton: B. Newton, *Sermons on Several Occasions* (1736), i, pp. ix–xiii.

		13 June	Thos. White, son of John, ge[nt.]
		24 June	Ric. Crowdy, son of Jas., tailor, decd.
460		10 Aug	Edw. Machen, gent., by gift
		12 Aug	Thos. Chewett, son of Thos., labourer
		19 Aug	John Warne, app. of Dan. Lea, cordwainer
		23 Sept	John Perrocke, gent., of Highnam by gift
		28 Sept	Edw. Stephens, gent., by gift
			Edw. Quarrington, maltster, (by fine)
			Ric. Parker, maltster, (by fine)

John Bell, esq., mayor 1717–8

		1 Oct	Sam. Worrall,[1] app. of Joshua Worrall, gent.
		12 Oct	(Sir) John Rushout, Bt.,† by gift[2]
		21 Oct	Moses Davis, app. of Dan. Lea, cordwainer
			Geo. Moore, son of John, butcher
461		2 Nov	Ric. Evans, ropemaker, of Gloucester, formerly of Cirencester, (by fine)
		11 Nov	Wm. Yeend, app. of Ant. Williams, barber-surgeon
		25 Nov	Wm. Cooke, app. of Jas. Robins, currier
	1718	18 Jan	John Gibbs, son of Thos., blacksmith, of Dursley
		28 Feb	Dan. Trotman, app. of Jeremiah Jennings, tailor
		17 Mar	John Price, son of Wm., cordwainer
		22 Mar	John Kent, son of Sam., joiner, decd.
462		12 May	Ambrose Weyman, app. of John Wadley, baker
		6 June	Nat. Brocke, son of Wm., collar-maker
		16 June	Sam. Spencer, son of Thos., cooper
		27 June	Thos. Weaver, son of Ric., butcher
		11 Aug	John Crump, son of John, innholder, decd.
		22 Aug	Thos. Hale,[3] son of Jos., pinmaker
		29 Aug	John Ellis, son of Guy, ironmonger, decd.
		1 Sept	Humph. Bowyer, app. of Timothy Rowles, basket-maker
		11 Sept	Sam. Jennings, son of Mic., butcher
463		19 Sept	Thos. Wheeler, app. of Sam. Wheeler, carpenter
		22 Sept	John Bonnett, app. of Ric. Engly, bricklayer
		29 Sept	Jas. Cooke, son of Wm., tailor
		3 Oct	Dan. Bishopp, son of Dan., barber-surgeon, decd.

James Furney, esq., mayor 1718–9

		7 Oct	Rob. Bicke, app. of Wm. Rawlings, joiner
		27 Oct	Ric. Baker,[4] son of Ric., beadle
			Jas. Myles, son of Wal., baker, decd.
		17 Nov	Jas. Rogers, app. of Hen. Engley, bricklayer
		28 Nov	John Mason, app. of Wm. Mason, tailor
464		5 Dec	Humph. Smith, son of a glover, decd.*
		8 Dec	Nic. Lane, son of Nic., apothecary
	1719	9 Jan	Benj. Cole, app. of Wm. Jackeman, baker
		9 Feb	Thos. Moore, son of John, butcher

[1] Proctor: *V.C.H. Glos.* iv. 379.

[2] Of Northwick Park, Blockley, Worcs., one of six men nominated under act of 11 Aug 1713 by the earl of Berkeley: GBR B 3/8, p. 506; *Complete Baronetage*, iii. 211.

[3] ? Thos. Hale, tailor, disfranchised 28 July 1732 for refusing to appear before the mayor and readmitted by act of 22 Mar 1733: GBR B 3/9, ff. 317v., 333v.; cf. above: ibid. C 9/7, p. 312.

[4] Innholder, resigned 6 July and readmitted by act of 12 Aug 1730: ibid. B 3/9, ff. 278, 279v.

20 Feb John Gardner, son of John, butcher
13 Apr Jas. Window, app. of Dan. Lea, cordwainer
22 May Thos. Pace, son of Wm., tailor
12 June John Stephens, son of Rob., vintner, decd.
29 June Thos. Ellis, app. of his father John, farrier
465 21 Aug Nat. Mills, app. of Geo. Dowdin, carpenter
Thos. Dudley, son of Thos., butcher
Gregory Perris, son of Ric., butcher
4 Sept Hen. Wintle, son of Hen., distiller
11 Sept Wm. Bayly, son of Wm., waterman, decd.
18 Sept Ric. Rogers, son of John and app. of Ralph Addy, butcher, by apprenticeship
28 Sept Thos. Wilcocks, son of Thos., gent., decd.

Richard Cossley, esq., mayor 1719–20

6 Nov Jos. Bullocke, app. of Dan. Bryan, cordwainer
466 9 Nov Thos. Bicke, app. of Joan Greene, widow
18 Nov John Webb, son of Thos., gent., decd.
31 Nov John Smyth, son of Thos., currier
4 Dec Francis Brabant, son of Francis, cooper
9 Dec Thos. Presbury, app. of John Stock, grocer
1720 21 Jan Sam. Tomlins, app. of Ric. Engly, bricklayer
8 Feb John Baldwyn, app. of Sam. Pawlin, baker
29 Feb Geo. Bishopp, app. of Thos. Bishopp, barber-surgeon
467 1 Mar Chas. Moore, son of Chas., clerk, decd., of Newnham
20 Mar John Clifford, son of John, decd.*
13 May John Read, app. of Thos. Pace, cordwainer
18 May Isaac Bennett, app. of Sam. Richards, carpenter
25 June Wm. Kendall, painter, (by fine)
22 June Hen. Beard, son of John, innholder
Edw. Gregory, son of Humph., gent., of London
1 July Jos. Bird, son of Dan., hornturner
468 13 Aug Wm. Bubb, son of Rob., yeoman, late of Hempsted
16 Aug John Waugh, S.T.P., dean of Gloucester [cathedral],† by gift[1]
Ric. Cossley, son of Ric., gent., ald.[2]
1 Sept Wm. Cooke, son of Wm., barber-surgeon, decd.
7 Sept John Porter, app. of John Bonner, grocer
12 Sept Thos. Jordan, app. of John Vaughan, vintner, decd.
Dan. Lysons, esq., of Hempsted (by gift)
Thos. Archer, son of Abraham, bricklayer
469 Reuben Fletcher, son of Ric., blacksmith
[ ] Childs, son of [ ], late of Minchinhampton*
16 Sept Wm. Dean, app. of John Nest, carpenter
John Fream, son of Wm., feltmaker
Thos. Lambeth, app. of Hen. Brimyard, cordwainer
12 Sept Nic. Webb, son of Thos., esq.
John Archer, son of Abraham, bricklayer
19 Sept John Keyse of Scollupp Court, Puddledocke Hill, London, son of Jos., mercer, decd.
Miles Mutlow, son of Ant., tailor, decd.
470 Thos. Brampton, app. of Hen. Draper, ironsmith

[1] Soon after his appointment as dean: Fosbrooke, *Glouc.* 108.
[2] Mayor.

Dan. Forty of Cheltenham, son of Dan., brazier, decd.
Winston Moore, son of John, butcher
Wm. Graffstocke, son of John, butcher, decd.
23 Sept Thos. Wells, son of John, cordwainer, decd.
Ric. Overthrow, app. of Ric. Weaver, blacksmith
Benj. Beal, son of Benj., blacksmith, decd.
John Knight, son of Ric., currier, decd.
Ric. Weaver, } sons of Hen., farrier
Mat. Weaver, }
471 Wal. Warnford, son of Wal., cordwainer
Sam. Fowle, app. of Hen. Brimyard, cordwainer
Geo. Clarke, app. of John Holder, pinmaker
Wm. Clarke, app. of Cowcher Shipton, pinmaker
Thos. Ollfett, app. of John Collett, joiner
John Marshfield, son of Jas., fisherman
26 Sept Giles Venn, son of Thos., labourer, late of Longford
Hen. Holyday, son of Hen., carpenter
Ant. Mowtloe, son of Ant., tailor
Wm. Ricketts, son of John, pinmaker
Edw. Armitage, app. of Ant. Mowtloe, tailor
472 Thos. Hayward, son of Edw., tailor
Wm. Cooke, son of Sam., saddler, late of Gloucester
Jas. Crowdey, son of Jas., tailor, late of Gloucester
Geo. Mamby, son of John, brickmaker
Jos. Haines, app. of John Gregory, barber-surgeon
Jos. Browne, son of Jos., limner, late of Gloucester
Thos. Witcombe, son of Thos., tailor, late of Gloucester
Leigh Langley, son of Ralph, gent., decd.
Phil. Pinchback, son of Phil., tailor, late of Gloucester
Thos. Gardner, son of John, baker, of Sheepscombe
John Hill, } sons of John, gent., late of Painswick
Chas. Hill, }
473 29 Sept Wm. Idding, son of Thos., pinmaker
30 Sept Thos. Gifford, app. of Wm. Long, cordwainer
Wm. Daw, son of Eleazer, carpenter
Benj. Robins, } sons of Benj., tailor
Jas. Robins, }
Geo. Cowdall, son of Rob., labourer
Jas. Hartland, son of Thos., pinmaker
Thos. Young, son of Jas., pinmaker
1 Oct John King, app. of Ric. Engly, bricklayer
Moses Long, app. of Giles Long, salter, decd.
Thos. Bamford, son of Wm., yeoman, of Westbury
3 Oct Thos. Ratcliffe, gent., by gift
474 Sam. Lawrence, clerk, of Highnam by gift[1]
Wm. Bamford, son of Wm., yeoman, of Westbury
John Puxon, son of Wm., labourer
John Ricketts, son of John, pinmaker, decd.
Wm. Clifford, son of Jas., pinmaker, decd.
Wm. Dancey, app. of Hen. Engley, bricklayer
n.d. John Clarke, son of Wal., wiredrawer, decd.

[1] Rector of Lassington, by act of 5 Nov 1716 thanking him for a sermon he preached in the cathedral that day: GBR B 3/9, f. 9v.; Hockaday Abs. cclv.

John King, esq., mayor 1720–1

	4 Oct	Wm. Ball,[1] app. of Thos. Bosom, barber, of Mitcheldean
		Wm. Williams, app. of John King, esq., mayor
		Thos. Cooke, son of Thos., tailor, decd.
		Wm. Holton, son of Ric., weaver
475	7 Oct	Chas. Smith, app. of Francis Pace, cordwainer, of Newent
		John Makepeace, son of Sam., baker, decd.
		Abraham Medway, son of Abraham, bricklayer, decd.
		John Garrett, app. of Thos. Symon, currier
		Thos. Mason, son of Ric., baker
	10 Oct	John Churches, son of John, wiredrawer
		Thos. Bromley, app. of Rob. Partridge, cordwainer
		Albert Badger, son of Albert, pinmaker
		Thos. Clifford, son of Jas., pinmaker, decd.
		Wm. Heming, son of John, gent.
		John Swayne, son of Thos., pargeter
		Sam. Haynes, app. of Rob. Savory, farrier
		Ric. Dower, app. of Wm. Hayes, cordwainer
476		Steph. Reeve, app. of Steph. Reeve, mason
		Hen. Berkley,[2] esq.,† by gift
	14 Oct	John Bicke, app. of Wm. Bicke, tiler and plasterer
		Geo. Cowles, innholder, (of the Red Lion by fine)
		Hen. Wintle, son of John, cordwainer
		John Winston, son of Thos., tailor
		Thos. Skey, app. of Sam. Powell, baker
		John Barnes, innholder, (of the Nag's Head by fine)
		Amity Medway, son of Abraham, bricklayer, decd.
		Jos. Morris, innholder, (by fine)
		Sam. King, app. of Dan. Jackson, plasterer
		John Reeve, } sons of Steph., stonecutter
		Nat. Reeve, }
477	21 Oct	John Hayford, son of John, pitcher, decd.
	24 Oct	Wm. Barrett, son of Wm., woolcomber, decd.
		Wm. Bullocke, app. of Miles Mutlow, cordwainer, decd.
	31 Oct	Edm. Everett, son of Ambrose, woollen-draper, decd.
	29 Oct	Wm. Frankis, son of Wm., yeoman, of Upton St. Leonards
	4 Nov	Wm. Nest, son of John, carpenter
		And. Gardner, son of And., woolcomber
	7 Nov	Sam. Bayly, son of John, waterman, decd.
	9 Nov	Chas. Greenway, son of Wal., wiredrawer
	14 Nov	John Bamford, son of Wm., yeoman, of Westbury
		Moses Wingate, app. of Ric. Engly, bricklayer, decd.
	17 Nov	Rob. Mutlow, son of Miles, cordwainer, of Huntley
	18 Nov	John Glow, son of Wm., cooper, of Weston under Penyard, Herefs.
478	28 Nov	Ebenezer Careles (by fine)[3]
	2 Dec	Wm. Maverly, app. of John Hone, tailor
	10 Dec	Hen. Harris, innholder, (by fine)
	17 Dec	Dan. White, cordwainer, (by fine)[4]

[1] Disfranchised 31 Aug 1727, when of Ross, Herefs., for obtaining the freedom by fraud: GBR B 3/9, f. 222.

[2] Son of Chas., earl of Berkeley (d. 1710), and M.P. for the county: Williams, *Parl. Hist. of Glos.* 64.

[3] On his appointment as serjeant-at-mace: GBR B 3/9, f. 99v.

[4] Evidently previously disfranchised, not to use his trade in the city: ibid. f. 100; cf. above: ibid. C 9/7, p. 456.

			Wm. Bevan, innholder, (by fine)
			Thos. Bevan, innholder, (by fine)
	1721	31 Jan	Wm. Wood, son of John, wagoner, decd.
		18 Feb	Geo. Wilcox, app. of Nic. Lane the elder, apothecary
		24 Feb	Adam Collericke, son of Adam, barber-surgeon, decd.
		24 Mar	Lawr. Crump, son of John, brewer (*binarii*), decd.
		3 Apr	John Blackwell, app. of Sam. Powell, baker
		8 Apr	Wm. Garner, weaver of Over, Churcham, (by fine)
479		17 Apr	John [Brydges], marquess of Carnarvon, son of [Jas.], duke of Chandos,†[1] (by gift)
			Jas. West, esq.,† (by gift)
			Chas. Stewart, esq.,† (by gift)
			John Bruges, esq.,†[2] } (by gift)[4]
			Humph. Lloyd, clerk,†[3] } (by gift)[4]
			Wm. Crossby, esq.,† } (by gift)[4]
		1 May	Jeremiah Hawkins, app. of John Harris, barber-surgeon
		15 May	Francis Gooding, son of Wm., baker, decd.
		19 May	Thos. Clarke, app. of John Hall, baker
		9 June	Geo. Rayer, app. of John Barker, barber-surgeon, decd.
		10 June	Wm. [Capell], earl of Essex,†[5] } (by gift)[10]
			(Sir) Thos. Read, Bt.,†[6] } (by gift)[10]
			Wm. Bromley, esq.,†[7] } (by gift)[10]
			Geo. Read, esq.,† } (by gift)[10]
			Ric. Nash, esq.,†[8] } (by gift)[10]
			Wm. Diston, esq.,† } (by gift)[10]
			Reginald Morgan Bray esq.,†[9] } (by gift)[10]
		26 June	John Fletcher, currier,[11] (by fine)
480		25 Aug	Jos. Fownes, son of John, distiller

Gabriel Harris, esq., mayor 1721–2

		10 Oct	Jos. Everard, app. of John Ashmead, mercer
		3 Nov	Wm. Pembruge, son of Wm., baker, decd.
		10 Nov	John Heath, son of Sam., silkweaver, decd.
		20 Nov	John Tranter, app. of Jas. Lovett, barber-surgeon
		28 Dec	Wm. Salcomb, app. of John Greene, cordwainer, decd.
	1722	5 Jan	Ric. Elly, gent., by gift
		26 Jan	Wm. Smart, app. of Mary Wells, cordwainer
		29 Jan	Thos. Hampton, app. of Rog. Church, tailor
481		2 Feb	Jas. Lambeth, app. of Thos. Stephens, pinmaker, decd.
		26 Feb	Thos. Porter, app. of Thos. Hill, apothecary
		15 Mar	Jos. Whittingham, son of Edw., baker, decd.
		19 Mar	Sam. Etheridge, app. of Wm. Lodge, cooper

[1] Of Canons, Whitchurch, Mdx.: *Complete Peerage*, iii. 131.

[2] ? of the Mythe, Tewkesbury, relative of the marquess of Carnarvon: *V.C.H. Glos.* viii. 136; *Glos. N.&Q.*, iv. 328; *Complete Peerage*, iii. 128–31.

[3] Became vicar of Oakley, Bucks., in 1721: *Alumni Oxon. 1500–1714*, iii. 925.

[4] At the request of the marquess of Carnarvon: GBR B 3/9, f. 106.

[5] *Complete Peerage*, v. 146–7.

Of Shipton Court, Shipton-under-Wychwood, Oxon.: *Complete Peerage*, iii. 173.

[7] Of Upton upon Severn, Worcs.: Nash, *Worcs.* ii. 445.

[8] Of Kempsey, Worcs.: ibid. 21; *Alumni Oxon. 1715–1886*, iii. 1008, s.v. Nash, Treadway.

[9] Of Great Barrington: *V.C.H. Glos.* vi. 19.

[10] The earl and Sir Thos. by act of 11 June 1721 and the others, being gentlemen attending the earl on his visit to Gloucester, by act of the following day: GBR B 3/9, f. 108v.

[11] Of Barton Street: ibid. f. 109v.

1722 Edw. Haines, app. of Thos. Puckeridge, tailor
Sampson Glendall, app. of Thos. Jones, glover
Thos. Mathews, app. of Ric. Church, glover
Adam Bennet, app. of Ric. Williams, glover
Ric. Weal, app. of Thos. Weal, baker
Jos. Jones, son of Thos., glover
John Nourse, son of John, cooper, decd.
482 Thos. Greene, son of Thos., cooper
Jas. Brotherton, son of Jeremiah, cordwainer
n.d. John Motlow, son of Ant., tailor
19 Mar Francis Ashmead, app. of Chas. Dymocke, mercer
John Noakes, app. of Dan. Brian, cordwainer
John Griffin, app. of Wm. Hale, pinmaker
Elisha Pytt, son of Rowland, draper
Ric. Messinger, son of Ric., draper
Wm. Fowler, son of Wm., baker
Hen. Elliott, son of Hen., joiner
Jos. Heming, son of John, gent., decd.
Sam. Fewterell, son of John, cordwainer
483 Thos. Adams, son of John, weaver
Wm. Slye, son of Wm., tailor, decd.
Jas. Fords, son of John, pinmaker
Wm. Bright, son of Thos., innholder
Jonathan Badger, app. of Phoenix Badger, pinmaker
Thos. Wood, app. of Wm. Window, tailor
20 Mar Ric. Harding, son of Ric., gardener
Hen. Addis, son of Edw., button-maker
Hen. Davis, son of Hen., pinmaker
Jos. Reeve, son of Steph., stonecutter
Wm. Trye, son of Wm., esq., decd., of Hardwicke
484 Chas. Bidwell, son of Wm., cutler
John Dowell, app. of Jas. Marshfield, fisherman, late of Gloucester
John Weston, app. of Jonathan Swaine, pargeter (*spargiter*)
Thos. Browne, app. of Dan. Lea, cordwainer
Nat. Perrin, app. of Nat. Harris, woolcomber
Sam. Graffstocke, son of John, butcher
Moses Cowdall, son of Rob., brickmaker
Ant. Layton, app. of Joan Davis, widow
Edw. Cryps, son of Edw., butcher
Thos. Lea, app. of John Lea, tailor, by patrimony[1]
John Wilton, app. of John Shingler, pinmaker, by patrimony[2]
John Lewis, app. of Edw. Haynes, pinmaker
485 Thos. Drinkwater, app. of Jos. Hornidge, ropemaker
Ric. Davis, app. of Wm. Nest, carpenter
Mic. Arundell, app. of Edw. Haynes, pinmaker
John Williams, app. of Ric. Darke, gunsmith
Ric. Nourse, app. of John Nourse, barber
Phil. Greene, son of Phil., hornturner
Rob. Cowles, son of Rob., butcher
John Ellis, son of John, farrier
John Carpenter, app. of Thos. Niccolls, saddler
Chas. Hoare, son of Thos., grocer

[1] By apprenticeship: ibid. F 4/8, p. 372.
[2] By apprenticeship: ibid.

Brandon Trye, son of Wm., esq., of Hardwicke
Giles Webb, app. of Hen. Vernon, apothecary
21 Mar Thos. Price, son of John, smith
486 (Sir) Edw. Fust,[1] Bt., of Hill by gift
John Nourse, clerk,[2] by gift
John Ricketts, son of Sam., carpenter
Jos. Price, son of John, smith
Hen. Weaver, son of Wm., cordwainer, of Churchdown
Thos. Hornidge, son of Wm., cordwainer, decd.
Sam. Weaver, son of Wm., cordwainer, of Churchdown
Jas. Kingman, son of Jas., wiredrawer
22 Mar Miles Bell, son of John, gent., decd.
Thos. Broughton, app. of Mary Wells, widow
Geo. Phipps, app. of John Beard, cutler
Ric. Baldwyn, son of Wm., silkweaver, decd.
487 Jas. Young, son of Jas., pinmaker, late of Gloucester
Ric. Townsend, son of Ric., tailor
John Corr, son of John, surgeon, decd.
John Shipton, son of John, cordwainer
Jas. Clifford, son of Jas., pinmaker
John Williams, } sons of Elisha, ropemaker, decd.
Dan. Williams, }
23 Mar Geo. Lander, son of Jas., weaver
Thos. Crump, son of Ric., brazier
Sam. Tyler, } sons of John, baker
John Tyler, }
Chas. Tyler, son of Chas., plumber
John King, son of Jas., bricklayer
488 Thos. Gwyn, son of Lewis, pinmaker, late of Gloucester
John Hathaway, son of Hen., smith, decd.
Benj. Okey, app. of Rog. Church, tailor
Wm. Jeffs, app. of Thos. Cocks, baker
Jas. Evenis, } apps. of Wm. Evenis, cordwainer
Abraham Hale, }
Wm. Lisle, app. of Wm. Allen, grocer
Ric. Furney, clerk,[3] son of Jas., gent.
Ric. Lane, } sons of Ric., bookseller, late of Gloucester
Wm. Lane, }
Benj. Randle, son of Wm., weaver
Nat. Jones, app. of Edw. Braddis, bricklayer
Wm. Williams, app. of Thos. Swaine, tiler and plasterer
489 Thos. Endall, son of Thos., barber
Geo. Washbourne, son of John, clockmaker
John Turner, app. of Thos. Jones, glover
Francis Reeve, son of Francis, stonecutter, late of Gloucester
Thos. Locke, app. of John Cooke, baker
Thos. Yate, son of Ric., maltster, decd.
Isaac Darke,[4] app. of Ric. Lane, grocer
24 Mar Wm. Nest, son of Wm., carpenter

[1] Unsuccessful parliamentary candidate for Gloucester in 1722: Williams, *Parl. Hist. of Glos.* 208.
[2] Rector of St. Mary de Crypt: Hockaday Abs. ccxvi.
[3] Master of the Crypt school, who compiled a history of the city: Gray, *Antiquaries*, 59–61; Austin, *Crypt School*, 113–4.
[4] Described as of Campden 4 Aug and disfranchised 2 Sept 1727 for obtaining the freedom by fraud: GBR B 3/9, ff. 217v., 222v.–223.

Thos. Gulliford, app. of Ric. Drinkwater, cordwainer
Thos. Guy, son of John, innholder, decd.
Jos. Phelps, son of Wm., tanner, decd.
Ric. Wheeler, app. of John Halford, cordwainer
Mic. Jennings, son of Mic., butcher
Jas. Roberts, son of John, stonecutter, of Ruardean
490 Wm. Stone, son of Wm., tailor, of Newent
Ant. Williams, son of Ant., barber
Francis Lea, son of John, tailor, late of Gloucester
Chas. Butter, son of Chas., tailor, late of Gloucester
Thos. Braddis, son of Hen., pinmaker, decd., of Barton Street
John Spillman,[1] app. of Thos. Cowles, tiler and plasterer
John Price, son of Thos., maltster, decd.
Thos. Rogers, son of Thos., saddler
26 Mar John Randle, app. of Jas. Randle, joiner
John Luther, son of John, butcher
John Jones, son of Chas., cooper, decd.
John Greene, son of Ric., woolcomber, decd.
John Cudd, son of John, weaver
Francis Harris, son of John, gunsmith
Wm. Andrews, son of Wm., saddler
491 John Brotherton, app. of Jeremiah Brotherton, cordwainer
Thos. Greene, app. of Thos. Stephens, pinmaker, decd.
Wm. Bell, gent., of Sandhurst by gift
Hen. Barrett, app. of Thos. Elliott, cordwainer, decd.
Wm. Scott, app. of Nic. Lane, apothecary
John Mountague, app. of Ric. Drinkwater, cordwainer
John Batchford, app. of Edw. Fletcher, barber-surgeon
Hen. Gilding, son of Hen., baker, decd.
Wm. Lucas, son of Sam., joiner
Chas. Bradgate, son of Wm., button-maker
Nat. Hyeron, app. of Thos. Freeman, bodice-maker, decd.
Jos. Small, app. of Ric. Driver, haberdasher, decd.
Capel Payne, esq., son of Capel, ald.
Wm. Townly, app. of John Cowles, tailor
Wm. Randle, son of Wm., weaver
492 Gerard Smith, app. of John Heaven, barber-surgeon
Thos. Bradley, app. of Thos. Ward, pinmaker
Rob. Browne Gittoes, son of Wm., saddler, decd.
Elisha Hathway, son of Elisha, tailor
Aaron Smith, app. of Abraham Smith, cooper
Wm. Barrett, app. of Wm. Swett, tobacco-pipemaker, decd.
Wm. Chewett, son of Thos., cordwainer
Thos. Rich, esq., son of [Sir] Rob., Bt.†[2]
Thos. Pulton, app. of Jas. Furney, ald.
Thos. Cugley, app. of Wm. Cugley, cardmaker, decd.
Ric. Winniatt, son of Ric., pinmaker
Jos. Hornage, son of Jas., blacksmith
Ric. Crump, son of Ric., brazier
Godfrey Fownes, son of John, distiller, decd.
John Parsons, esq., of Kemerton by gift
Sampson Harris, son of Gabriel, esq., mayor

[1] The younger, disfranchised 2 Sept 1727 for obtaining the freedom by fraud: ibid.
[2] Of Sonning, Berks.: *Complete Baronetage*, iii. 180.

493			Benj. Hall, son of John, apothecary, decd.
			Geo. Dun, app. of Jos. Ravener and Jacob Lumbard, sergeweavers
			John Ward,[1] app. of Rog. Pytt, carpenter
			Oliver Jelfe, son of Thos., baker, decd.
			Francis Skelton, son of Ric., apothecary, of Malvern, Worcs.
			John Holder, app. of Edm. Halford, cordwainer
			John Nott, son of Lawr., joiner, decd.
			Wm. Furney, son of Jas., ald.
		27 Mar	Wm. Nash, son of Wm., carpenter, of London
			Thos. Lugg, son of Jasper, combmaker, of Hereford
			Jas. Pinchbacke, app. of Phil. Pinchbacke, victualler
			Thos. Cooke, esq.,†[2] by gift
			John Stephens, esq.,†[3] by gift
494			John Beal, app. of Capel Payne, gent., ald.
		11 May	Thos. Cowles, son of Thos., plasterer, of London
		18 May	Thos. Hawkins, son of Jas., baker, decd., of Newent
		21 May	Wm. Buckley, collier and waterman, of Broseley, Salop., (by fine)
		2 July	John Williams, app. of Wm. Long, cordwainer
		30 July	Theodore Winston, son of Thos., tailor
		20 Aug	Thos. Jones alias Watts, app. of Jas. Workman, butcher
		24 Aug	Meshach Charleton, son of Edw., yeoman, of Cheltenham
		29 Sept	Martin Lloyd, clothier, (by fine)
495			John Riddall, maltster and distiller, (by fine)
			Daniel Washbourn, esq., mayor 1722–3
	1723	1 Mar	Thos. Burridge, son of Thos., weaver, decd.
		28 Mar	Jas. Swaine, son of Ric., collar-maker
		29 Mar	Wm. Bond, app. of Gabriel Harris, bookseller
		1 Apr	John Farmer, son of Sam., gent., decd.
		27 May	Thos. Price, son of Thos., maltster, decd.
		31 May	John Niccolls, app. of Hen. Niccolls, maltster, late of Gloucester
496		17 June	Thos. Weaver, son of Hen., farrier
		10 July	John Hawkins, app. of Wm. Sparrowhawke, cordwainer
		5 Aug	Jos. Phipps, app. of Wm. Lodge, cooper
		16 Aug	John Richards, app. of Wal. Young, cordwainer
		28 Sept	Jas. Thomas, maltmaker, by gift[4]
		30 Sept	Wm. Broughton, app. of John Ellis, farrier
			John Rodway, esq., mayor 1723–4
	1724	10 Jan	Thos. Still, son of Francis, maltster
497		20 Jan	Dan. Webb, son of Thos., gent., decd.
		24 Feb	Jeremiah Brotherton, son of Jeremiah, cordwainer
		8 May	John Man, son of Ric., cordwainer, decd.
		18 May	Guy Ellis, son of Guy, ironmonger, decd.
		6 July	John Hopkins, son of Theophilus, joiner
		24 July	John Smith, son of John, feltmaker, late of Gloucester
		10 Aug	Nic. Webb, son of Thos., gent., decd.
		13 Aug	Thos. Smith, gent.,[5] (by fine)

[1] Wheelwright, disfranchised 2 Sept 1727 for obtaining the freedom by fraud: GBR B 3/9, ff. 222v.–223.

[2] Of Leigh: *V.C.H. Glos.* viii. 62; *Trans. B.G.A.S.* vi. 157.

[3] Of Lypiatt Park, Stroud: *V.C.H. Glos.* xi. 112; *Visit. Glos. 1682–3*, 177.

[4] At the mayor's request: GBR B 3/9, f. 152v.

[5] Of 'near the high cross': ibid. f. 163v.

498			Ric. Butt, gent., by gift
			Thos. Butt, gent., by gift
		17 Sept	(Col.) Archibald Hamilton, esq.,[†] by gift
			Mic. Bayley, gent., of Uley by gift
			Jos. Coleborne, app. of Nic. Lane the elder, apothecary
		21 Aug	Wm. Gregory, app. of John Heaven, barber-surgeon
			Sam. Grove, app. of Jacob Lumbard, weaver
		28 Aug	Wm. Smith, app. of Rog. Church, glazier

499 **Richard Greene, esq., mayor 1724–5**

		12 Oct	John Parker, app. of Wm. Mason, tailor
		30 Oct	Jas. Jennings, son of Mic., butcher
		14 Dec	Geo. Worrall, app. of Joshua Worrall, merchant
	1725	4 Feb	John Gardner, son of And., tailor
		27 Apr	John Gregory, son of John, mercer
		11 May	Sampson Stephens, son of Thos., pinmaker, decd.
	1724	[ ] Dec	Wm. Rudge by apprenticeship*
	1725	9 July	Ric. Taylor, app. of John Gregory, barber-surgeon
			Thos. Parker, app. of Sam. Bishopp, barber-surgeon
		12 July	Geo. Graffstocke, son of John, butcher, decd.
500		13 Aug	Wal. Little, son of Wm., yeoman, decd., of Ashleworth
		23 Aug	Hen. Bradley, son of Hen., butcher
		30 Aug	Wm. Holder, app. of Hannah Drew, widow, and Ric. Draper, cordwainer
		6 Sept	John Goodwyn, son of John, tailor, of St. Aldgate, London
		13 Sept	John Lindsey, app. of Rob. Arnold, pinmaker
		20 Sept	Wm. Hale, app. of Hen. Wilton, pinmaker

Samuel Browne, esq., mayor 1725–6

		27 Nov	John Grimmett, app. of Wm. Billings, cordwainer
		14 Dec	Geo. Beard, son of John, cutler, decd.
501	1726	27 June	Edw. Barnes, son of Edw., brazier, decd.
		12 Aug	Edw. Barnes, app. of Nic. Barnes and John Beal, mercers
		22 Aug	Wm. Rogers, app. of Edw. Bennett, apothecary
			Lawr. Price, son of Thos., salter
		29 Aug	John Cole, son of Thos., grocer, decd.
			Thos. Bower, son of Thos., tanner, of Newent, formerly of Gloucester
		12 Sept	Lawr. Ravenhall, app. of John Tyler, tailor
		19 Sept	John Shingler, son of John, pinmaker
			Hen. Guise, esq., by gift
		1 Oct	Zachariah Venn, son of Thos., yeoman, decd., of Longford
502			John Williams, son of John, cordwainer
		3 Oct	Wm. Williams, son of John, cordwainer
			Wm. Clarke, app. of Ric. Cowcher, pinmaker, decd.
			John Davis, son of Thos., pinmaker, decd.
			John Pace, son of Wm., tailor, decd.
			John Estcutt, son of Sam., pinmaker
			Thos. Powell, app. of John Shingler, pinmaker
			Rob. Simpson, app. of Thos. Stephens, decd., and John Woodward, pinmakers

Thomas Ludlow, esq., mayor 1726–7

		7 Oct	Hen. Fuller, app. of John Benson, plasterer
		10 Oct	John Marshall, app. of Sam. Ricketts, carpenter

Thos. Davis, son of Thos., tailor, decd.
503 John Canning, app. of Wal. Young, cordwainer
Jas. Hoskins, app. of Ric. Draper, cordwainer
Thos. Bradgate, son of Wm., button-maker, decd.
11 Oct Wm. Skillerne, son of John, furrier, of Winchcombe. Disfranchised 1 Feb 1727
18 Oct John Rudhall, son of Abraham the younger, bellfounder
25 Oct Wm. Rowles, son of John, butcher, of Minsterworth
31 Oct Thos. Shipton, son of Cowcher, pinmaker, decd.
Steph. Swayne, son of Thos., plasterer
Thos. Fuller, app. of John Benson, tiler and plasterer
Sam. Pembruge, son of Sam., baker, decd.
Ellis Tayler, son of Wm., tailor
Wm. Brobend, son of Wm., tailor
504 Wm. Price, son of Wm., cordwainer
Hen. Stone, son of Rob., tanner, decd.
John Clifford, son of Jas., pinmaker, decd.
John Cox, son of Hen., labourer
Thos. Barnard, son of Thos., cordwainer, of Hardwicke
John Badger, son of Phoenix, labourer
8 Nov Isaac Barker, son of Thos., baker, of Tirley[1]
Jos. Bloxom, app. of Wm. Stephens, weaver
John Ellis,[2] app. of Thos. Hale, tailor
(Sir) Wm. Codrington, Bt., of Dodington by gift
11 Nov Chas. Annis, son of Chas., blacksmith
Jas. Baker, son of Edw., wiredrawer
14 Nov Jos. Skillerne, son of Isaac, skinner
Ric. Herring, app. of And. Pegler, saddler

GBR C9/8[3]

1
City of Gloucester

Burgesses made in the time of Thomas Ludlow, esq., mayor.

1726 14 Nov Sam. Buckle, son of Ric., baker, decd.
15 Nov John Barnelme, son of John, labourer
17 Nov Freeman Partridge, son of Hen., mercer, decd.
18 Nov Wm. Man, app. of John Wadley, baker
21 Nov Sam. Gardner, son of John, baker, of Sheepscombe, Painswick
25 Nov Ric. Bryan, son of Ric., brazier, decd.
John Watts, app. of Thos. Webley, brazier
Aaron Cowdall, son of Rob., brickmaker, decd.
Thos. Savory, son of Thos., farrier, decd.
Thos. Hawkins, app. of Francis Brabant, cooper
2 28 Nov John Cooke, son of Thos., tailor, decd.
Ric. Cooke, son of Ric., bricklayer
5 Dec Jas. Butter, son of Chas., tailor, decd.
12 Dec Josiah Randall, son of Jas., joiner
16 Dec John Chapman, son of John, flaxdresser
19 Dec Geo. Bennett, app. of Hen. Engly, bricklayer

[1] *alias Trinley*.
[2] Disfranchised 31 Aug 1727 for obtaining the freedom fraudulently: GBR B 3/9, f. 222.
[3] Index of entrants at front.

		23 Dec	John Bright, app. of Sam. Jefferyes, joiner
			Thos. Bower, } sons of Sam., pipemaker, decd.
			Wm. Bower,
			Wm. Dix, son of Wm., bricklayer
3		27 Dec	Thos. Shipton, son of John, cordwainer, decd.
		30 Dec	Ric. Goodwyn, } sons of Sam., yeoman, of Linton, Churcham
			Sam. Goodwyn,
			Wm. Wheeler,[1] app. of Thos. Wheeler, wheelwright, decd.
	1727	2 Jan	Dan. Jackson, son of Dan., pinmaker
		4 Jan	John Small, esq., of Pudhill (by gift)
		5 Jan	Giles Robinson, app. of Abraham Smith, cooper
		9 Jan	Nat. Bubb, app. of Thos. Niccolls, saddler
		16 Jan	Edw. Prestbury, app. of Geo. Perkins, baker, decd.
4		20 Jan	Edw. Norman, son of Edw., butcher, decd.
		10 Mar	Rob. Hyett, app. of Wm. Hyett, trowman (*troughman*)
		3 Apr	Jonathan Webb, son of John, butcher, decd., of Newnham by apprenticeship
		5 May	Wm. Crowdy, son of Jas., tailor, of Barnwood
		15 May	Thos. Maddox, son of Thos., husbandman
		5 June	Hen. Church, son of Hen., carrier, decd., of Hereford
			Thos. Windham, esq., of Clearwell by gift
		30 June	Wm. Wright, son of John, silkweaver, decd.
		10 July	Ric. White, } sons of Steph., mason, decd., of Painswick
			Steph. White,
5			John Cooke, son of Jas., joiner
		11 July	Jos. Jeffs, app. of Wm. Sparks, cordwainer
			Thos. Swayne, } sons of Thos., tiler and plasterer
			Jas. Swayne,
			John Hayes,[2] son of Jos., cordwainer
			Wm. Arnold, app. of Abraham Archer, bricklayer
			Ric. Dicks, son of Wm., bricklayer
			Thos. Badger, son of Albert, pinmaker
			John Sheppard, son of John, labourer, decd.
			Geo. Fewterell, son of Geo., pinmaker
6			Jas. Middleton, app. of Wm. Rawlins, joiner, decd.
			Posthumus Underhill, son of Jacob, weaver, decd.
			Virgil Cripps, son of Edw., butcher, decd.
			John Wingate, app. of Chas. Greenway, cordwainer
			Steph. Workman, son of Ant., butcher, decd.
			Wm. Gill, son of Wm., ropemaker, decd.
			Phil. Greene, son of Geo., feltmaker, decd.
			John Bond,[3] app. of Jas. Baker, cordwainer
			John Bullocke, son of Ric., fisherman
			John Barton, son of John, bricklayer
7			John Ireland, app. of Sam. Kemmis, woolcomber
			Edw. Overthrow, son of Wm., yeoman, of Minsterworth
			Jas. Ward, son of Jas., labourer
			Benj. Mutlow, son of Miles, cordwainer
			Edw. Griggs, son of Edw., basket-maker
			John Davis, son of Sam., woolcomber

[1] Joiner, disfranchised 2 Sept 1727 for obtaining the freedom by fraud: GBR B 3/9, ff. 222v.–223.

[2] Disfranchised 28 July 1781 to enable him to give evidence in a cause between the mercers' company and Jas. Hayward, a non-freeman: ibid. 11, ff. 298v., 344.

[3] Disfranchised 31 Aug 1727 for obtaining the freedom by fraud: ibid. 9, f. 222.

Thos. Jones, } sons of Thos., glover
Geo. Jones,
Jos. Webley, son of Jos., tailor
18 July Ric. Charles, son of John, cordwainer, decd.
8 Isaac Gyles, son of Isaac, tailor, decd.
Jas. Woodcocke, app. of Jeremiah Jennings, tailor
Ric. Vickeridge, app. of Dan. Bird, hornturner, decd.
Edw. Elliott, son of Edw., glassblower
John Yate, esq., son of Ric., esq., decd., of Arlingham
John Greenway, son of Wal., pinmaker
John Mayoe[1] son of John, pinmaker
John Holder, son of John, pinmaker
Jas. Wilson, app. of Francis Hutchins, tailor
John Wickham, app. of Jas. Smith, distiller and maltster
Wm. Mills, son of Thos., cordwainer, of Hucclecote
Wm. Lodge, son of Wm., cooper
9 Thos. Puxon, app. of John Baker, carpenter
Thos. Merrett, son of Wm., barber-surgeon
Wm. Fords, app. of Giles Watts, tailor, decd.
Wm. Overthrow, } sons of Wm., yeoman, decd., of Minsterworth
Sam. Overthrow,
Thos. Fletcher, app. of Thos. Fletcher, baker
John Bullock, app. of Jos. Pegler, tanner
John Coopy, } sons of John, cooper, of Churchdown
Ric. Coopy,
Thos. Bossom, son of Thos., barber-surgeon, of Mitcheldean
10 Wm. Rush, son of John, barber-surgeon, decd.
Benj. Piffe, app. of Wm. Cooke, barber-surgeon
Wm. Ham, son of Giles, yeoman, decd., of Haresfield
Chas. Cowdall, son of Rob., bricklayer, decd.
John Sexty, son of John, cheesemonger
Thos. Hayward, app. of Mary Cox, widow
John Baylis, app. of Edw. Baylis, woolcomber
Thos. Drew, app. of Dan. Pawling, baker
Geo. Cooke, son of Thos., tailor, decd.
Thos. Arnold, son of John, gent., decd.
John Pitt, son of Rog., carpenter
11 Thos. Lucas, son of Sam., joiner, decd.
Francis Tyler, son of Chas., plumber (*plummer*), decd.
John Evans, son of Hercules, yeoman, of Maisemore
Sam. Sparry, son of Sam., baker
Hen. Jones, app. of Ric. Church, glover
Dan. Ellis, app. of Hen. Corr, tailor, decd.
John Swayne, son of Edw., joiner
Rob. Longden, son of Rob., mercer, decd., of Worcester
19 July Wm. Swayne,[2] app. of John Wheeler, joiner
Edw. Swayne, app. of Wm. Freame, decd., and Josiah Fitchew, hatmakers
20 July Hen. Jelfe, son of Hen., baker, of Ruardean, formerly of Gloucester
12 Peter Chewett, son of Thos., cordwainer, decd.
Silvanus Lambeth, son of Wm., glassmaker, decd.
Jas. Reeve, son of Steph., stonecutter, decd.

[1] Disfranchised 4 Aug and readmitted by act of 22 Dec 1746: ibid. 10, ff. 68, 76v.
[2] Disfranchised 31 Aug 1727 for obtaining the freedom by fraud: ibid. 9, f. 222.

1727 Jos. Mutlow, son of Miles, cordwainer
Dan. Sayer, son of Dan., ropemaker, decd.
Jas. Nott, son of Lawr., carpenter
John Hobson, son of Jos., bodice-maker, late of Gloucester
Thos. Brotherton, app. of John Randle, plasterer[1]
Thos. Parrett,[2] app. of Wm. Randle, barber-surgeon, decd.
Jos. Jeanes,[3] app. of Jas. Cooke, joiner
13 Edw. Pearce, son of John, feltmaker, of Tewkesbury
Wm. Collericke, son of Thos., feltmaker, of Tewkesbury
Wm. Beard, son of Wm., mercer, decd., of Painswick
Thos. Winston, son of Thos., haulier
24 July Sam. Flower, son of John, tailor, decd.
Thos. Watts, app. of Nat. Veysey, tailor, decd.
Ralph Critchley, app. of Rob. Byrke, joiner
Wm. Gundy alias Gundimore, son of Toby, tailor, of Thornbury
John Child, son of Thos., tailor, of Minchinhampton
Wm. Yate, app. of And. Pegler, saddler
14 25 July John Salcomb, son of Sam., ropemaker, decd., of Defford, Worcs.
Ric. Reynolds,[4] son of John, silkweaver, decd., of Coleford
Ric. Child, son of Thos., tailor, of Minchinhampton
Thos. Roberts, } sons of John, stonecutter, of Ruardean
Dan. Roberts, }
John Maverley, app. of Eleanor Tyler, widow
John Steel, son of Sam., blacksmith, of Littledean
Wm. Pearce, app. of Lawr. Dunn, cordwainer
27 July Wm. Harris, app. of Wm. Evenis, cordwainer
Thos. Clarke, son of Jonathan, baker, decd., of Barnsley
15 John Wright, son of John, button-maker
Geo. Hanks, son of Geo., feltmaker, decd.
Jos. Felton, son of Jos., barber-surgeon, decd.
John Playdell, app. of Sam. Pawling, baker
Ric. Elliott, son of Edw., glassmaker
Francis Carpenter, son of Jas., ironmonger
Chas. Grevill, son of John, gent., decd., of Charlton Kings
Wm. Clarke, son of Wm., gent., decd., of Newtown, Mont., formerly of Gloucester
Ric. Underwood, son of Hen., decd., of Taynton
John Wintle, son of Rob., barber-surgeon, of Blaisdon
16 Wm. Mathews, son of John, barber-surgeon, of Newnham
Vicesimus Watts, son of Thos., gent., decd., of Highnam
Thos. Colericke, son of Thos., feltmaker, of Tewkesbury
Wm. Lane, son of Ric., bookseller, of Norton
Wm. Grevill, son of Hen., woollen-draper, decd.
John Meighen, app. of John Engley, bricklayer
28 July Edw. Robinson Payne, son of Capel, ald.
John Higgins, son of John, cordwainer, decd.
31 July Jos. Cowdall, son of Jos., tailor, decd.
Giles Grevill, son of Chas., apothecary, decd., of Bristol
17 John Rogers, son of John, baker, decd.
1 Aug John Garway, son of Jonathan, grocer, decd.

[1] *No right* subsequently written in margin.
[2] Of Tewkesbury: GBR B 3/9, f. 217v.
[3] Of Tewkesbury, disfranchised 31 Aug 1727 for obtaining the freedom by fraud: ibid. f. 222.
[4] Disfranchised 31 Aug 1727 for obtaining the freedom by fraud: ibid.

3 Aug Giles Grevile, son of John, yeoman, decd., of Charlton Kings
Hen. Fewterell, son of Geo., labourer
Wm. Wools alias Woones, son of Rob., fisherman, of Minsterworth
4 Aug Sam. Hathway, son of John, saddler, decd.
Thos. Cooke, son of Wm., tailor, decd.
Hen. Lugg, son of Jasper, combmaker
Chas. Smith, app. of John King, gent., ald.
Wm. Weaver, son of Hen., blacksmith
7 Aug Thos. Ades, app. of Jas. Baker, cordwainer
8 Aug Thos. Merrett, son of Giles, ship's carpenter, decd., of Tewkesbury
18 Giles Long, app. of Geo. Dowdy, carpenter
Isaac Wood, son of Abraham, button-maker, of Bristol
Thos. Harrison, son of Thos., feltmaker, decd.
John Dowle, son of Job., mercer, decd.
Wm. Sparry, son of Sam., baker
Francis Child, } sons of Sam., weaver, of St. Philip and St. Jacob
Sam. Child, }
John Carter, son of John, cordwainer
John Wheeler, app. of Sam. Spencer, cooper
Wm. Kemble, app. of John Hale, barber-surgeon†
John Driver, son of Ric., haberdasher of hats, decd.
Thos. Jefferyes, son of John, feltmaker
Thos. Taynton, son of John, grocer, decd.
19 9 Aug Thos. Cudd, son of Wm., weaver
10 Aug Ant. Gilding,[1] son of Hen., baker, decd.
11 Aug John White, son of Steph., mason, decd., of Painswick
Thos. Iles, son of Thos., glazier, decd.
Wm. Viner, son of Wm., yeoman, of Westbury
Edw. Hopkins, son of John, cooper, of Tetbury
Thos. Farley, son of Jas., cutler
Sam. Champneys, son of Wm., pinmaker, decd.
Sam. Harris, son of Jos., baker, decd.
Thos. Cooper, son of Thos. Cooper alias Allen, tailor, decd.
12 Aug John Birt, son of John, gent., decd., of Leominster, Herefs.
15 Aug Thos. Harris, son of Francis, apothecary, of Bristol
John Hale, son of Ric., maltster and distiller
20 Benj. Fownes, son of John, distiller
Hen. Groves, son of Wm., glassblower, decd.
Hen. Heane, app. of Sam. Hayward, barber-surgeon
Wm. Hartland alias Jones, app. of Jane Davis, widow
17 Aug Wm. Perkes, son of Sam., woolcomber, decd.
Jos. Stone, son of Wm., tailor, of Newent
Thos. Ady, son of Edm., baker
Thos. Lane, son of Ric., bookbinder, late of Gloucester
18 Aug Rob. Freeman, son of Rob., joiner
Jos. Fowles, app. of Grey Staytes, tailor, decd.
Thos. Wood, son of Wm., yeoman, of Barton Street
19 Aug John Mathews, son of John, tanner, decd.
Hen. Crump, son of Ric., brazier
21 John Haynes, son of Edw., pinmaker
John Buckle, app. of Wm. Lawrence, baker

[1] Of Tewkesbury, disfranchised 31 Aug 1727 for obtaining the freedom by fraud: ibid.

1727 Jas. King, Nat. King, } sons of Jas., bricklayer, of Cardiff[1]
John Greene, son of Thos., cooper, decd.
Wal. Maddocks, son of Wm., barber, decd.
22 Aug John Carill, son of Thos., gent.
John Ashmead, son of John, mercer
John Bubb, app. of John Cowles, butcher
Humph. Smith, son of John, currier
Jos. Wintle, son of Hen., distiller
Geo. Nurse, son of Geo., cooper, of Standish
Sam. Fielder, son of Geo., yeoman, of Haresfield
22 23 Aug Wm. Winniott, son of Ric., pinmaker
John Meeke, son of John, currier, decd.
John Veisey, son of Nat., tailor, decd.
Peter Hampton, son of John, innholder, late of Gloucester
John Bowler, son of Geo., tailor, of London
Rob. Webly, son of Giles, feltmaker, decd.
Thos. Beale, John Beale, } sons of Benj., smith, decd.
Aaron Cowdall, son of Rob., hatter, decd.
John Wintle, Jas. Wintle, } sons of John, cordwainer
24 Aug Thos. Ready, son of Thos., cordwainer, decd.
25 Aug Chas. Norwood, son of Thos., clerk, of Leckhampton
John Joy, app. of John Davis, pinmaker
Sam. Winniott, son of Ric., pinmaker
23 28 Aug John Kane, app. of John Wyman, cordwainer, decd.
Hen. Frankis, son of Wm., baker, decd.
Jos. Winniott, son of Ric., pinmaker
John Phelpes, app. of Hen. Corr, tailor, decd.
Thos. Dowle, son of Job, mercer, decd.
Hen. Benson, son of Wm., plasterer
Chas. Carrill, son of John, vintner, decd.
30 Aug Job Beale, son of John, cordwainer
Thos. Rodway, son of Thos., mercer, decd.
John Bower, son of Sam., tanner, decd.
Sam. Bower, John Bower, } sons of Sam., pipemaker, decd.
Ric. Emsley, son of Thos., shoemaker, decd.
24 John Hutchins, son of Thos., fishmonger, of London
Phil. Birt, app. of Ric. Darke, smith
Thos. Fords, app. of Thos. Ford, jacksmith
Edw. Fielders, son of Thos., tinman
Luke Seaberne, app. of Wm. Sparks, cordwainer
John Hornidge, son of Jas., smith
Wm. Smith, son of Giles, porter
Ric. Leyton of London by apprenticeship
John Reddy, son of Thos., cordwainer
Sam. Gill, son of Wm., decd.*
John Merricke, app. of Steph. Barrow, tailor, decd.
Jos. Bicknell, gent., of London, son of Wm.†
Ric. Cooke, app. of Jos. Howell, blacksmith
25 Hanbury Heath, son of Sam., packer, of London

[1] County given as *Carms.* rather than Glam.

John Stephens, app. of Thos. Stephens, pinmaker
Wm. Graffstocke, son of John†
Hen. Browne, son of Jas., pewterer, decd.
John Allen, son of Lawr., yeoman, of Maisemore
Rob. Carpenter, son of Jas., smith
Hen. Cole, } sons of Thos., grocer
Wm. Cole, }
Hen. Cross, son of Hen., cutler
Thos. Price, son of Thos., corkcutter
John Bliss, son of Sam., tanner, decd., of Berkeley
Arnold Wintle, son of Ric., baker, decd., of Berkeley
Giles Townsend, son of Giles, joiner, of Minsterworth
26 Chas. Gythens, app. of Thos. Peace, cordwainer
31 Aug John Elliott, son of Edw., pinmaker, decd., of Marlborough, Wilts.
Sam. Farmer, son of Sam., apothecary, decd.
John Badger, son of John, pinmaker, decd.
Wm. Window, son of Wm., tailor
Abraham Gregory, clerk, son of John, mercer
Ric. Window, son of Wm. the elder, tailor
Geo. Mountague, app. of John Browne, tailor, late of Gloucester
Ric. Church, son of Rog., glazier
Steph. Child, son of Thos., tailor, decd.
John Tench, } sons of Steph. wiredrawer, of Tewkesbury
Luke Tench, }
John Pearce, }
Thos. Pearce, } sons of John, feltmaker, of Tewkesbury
27 Nat. Pearce, }
Edm. Pearce, son of Edm., yeoman, of Tewkesbury
Jas. Price, son of Jas., pewterer, decd.
Sam. Merry, son of Wm., woolcomber, of London
Wm. Ford, son of Ric., yeoman, decd., of Highworth, Wilts.
Wm. Palmer, son of Jos., tailor, decd.
John Herbert, son of Chris., cordwainer, decd.
John Clement, app. of John Harris, mercer
Ric. Weaver, son of Ric., butcher, late of Gloucester
John Norman , son of Edw., butcher, late of Gloucester
John Sparrowhawke, son of Wm., garter-weaver, decd.
Cornelius Prichard, son of Thos., saddler, decd.
Edw. White, son of Steph., mason, decd., of Painswick
28 Rob. Sparrowhawke, son of Rob., garter-weaver, decd.
Thos. Braddis, son of Ric., bricklayer, decd.
1 Sept John Rogers, app. of Thos. Rogers, baker
Jos. Kent, son of Sam., joiner, decd.
Wm. Smith, son of Thos., glover, decd.
Geo. Ady, app. of Thos. Cox, baker, decd.
Jas. Harris, son of Jos., baker, decd.
Sam. Hodges, app. of Ric. Aylway, baker, decd.
Nat. Seyer, son of Dan., ropemaker, decd.
29 Rob. Gwin, son of Augustine, gent., decd.
Wm. Bradshaw, son of Wm., joiner
Thos. Fisher, app. of Hen. Brimyard, cordwainer
Wm. Cowcher, son of Wm., cordwainer, decd.
Rog. Church, son of Rog., tailor
John Williams, son of Ant., barber-surgeon
Wm. Hornage, son of Thos., bodice-maker, decd.
2 Sept Jas. Young, son of Sam., pinmaker, decd.

30		John Chandler, son of Nat., baker, decd.
		Wm. Little, Thos. Little, John Little, } sons of Wm., plasterer, of London
		John Cheeseman, son of John, cooper, of Highworth, Wilts.
		John Havard, app. of Thos. Hill, apothecary
		Wm. Elliotts, app. of Jos. Hale, cordwainer
		Isaac Meadway, son of Abraham, bricklayer, decd.
		Rupert Lugg, son of John, tailor
		Ric. Driver, son of Ric., haberdasher, decd.
31		John Grafstocke, son of John, baker, decd.
		Wm. Bubb, son of Wm., baker, decd.
		Job Higgins, son of Ric., saddler, decd.
		Wm. Phelp(e)s, Hen. Phelps, } sons of Wm., gent.
		Ric. Sparks, son of Thos., silkweaver, decd.
		Ric. Ireland, son of Ric., yeoman
		Hen. Heming, son of John, innholder, decd.
		John Price, son of John, smith
32	4 Sept	Dan. Brocke, son of Dan., gent., decd.
		Edw. Bevan, app. of Jas. Clifford, pinmaker, decd.
		Thos. Stayte, son of Ric., gilder, decd., of London
		Wm. Spencer, son of Thos., cooper
		Wm. Wadley, app. of Wm. Jordan, apothecary, late of Gloucester
		Edw. Corr, son of Edw., gunsmith, of London
		John Higgins, son of Nic., saddler, decd.
33		Job Charleton, Shadrach Charleton, } sons of Edw., grazier, decd., of Cheltenham
		John Roberts, son of John, labourer, of Ruardean
		Thos. Williams, son of Ant., barber-surgeon
		John Ford, son of Thos., tailor, decd.
		John Browne, son of Thos., joiner, decd.
		Peter Birt, app. of John Barker, barber-surgeon, decd.
		Edw. Wattson, son of Humph., tailor, decd.
		Sam. Kent, son of Sam., joiner, decd.
34		Giles Bridges, son of Ric., yeoman, decd., of Coberley
		Joshua Little, son of Wm, yeoman, decd., of Ashleworth
		Ric. Salcombe, son of Sam., yeoman, decd., of Defford, Worcs.
		Jonathan Smith, son of Thos., clerk, decd., of Bristol
		Mic. Johnsons, son of Sam., mercer, late of Bristol
		Thos. Beard, app. of John Beard, silkweaver, decd.
		John Skillerne, son of John, furrier, of Winchcombe
35		Wm. Wood, Jas. Wood, } sons of Wm., yeoman, of Barton Street
		John Drinkwater, son of Ric., pinmaker, decd.
		Sam. Willey, son of John, grocer, decd.
	6 Sept	Benj. Tench, son of Steph., weaver, of Tewkesbury
	8 Sept	Ric. Hartland, John Hartland, } sons of John, barber-surgeon, decd.
		Giles Symes, woolstapler, of Stroud, Amity Symes, woolstapler, of Stroud, } brothers, by gift
		John Rogers, yeoman, by gift[1]
		Rob. Phelps, son of Wm., innholder, decd.

[1] Servant of Posthumus Bell, by act of 19 Sept 1727: GBR B 3/9, f. 223v.

36 **John Selwyn, esq., mayor 1727–8**

28 Oct Ric. Arundell, app. of Sam. Stocke, baker
1728 26 Feb Wm. Mayoe, app. of John Harris, barber-surgeon
1 Mar Wm. Axon, son of Sam., cutler, decd.
3 June Wm. Vyner, app. of John Stocke, grocer
17 June Jos. Cheston, app. of John Cowcher, apothecary
Sam. Wilkes, app. of Wm. Haynes, mercer, decd.
23 Aug Thos. Bond, app. of Jas. Edwards, baker
26 Aug Hen. Hunt, gardener, of Kingsholm by gift

37 **4 September 1727**[1]

Lewis (Ducie) Morton, esq.[†2]
Chas. (Ducie) Morton, esq.[†3]
Jos. Clarke of [the] Hill,[4] Herefs.
Maynard Colchester, esq., of Westbury[5]
Peter Wheeler, gent.[†]
Herbert Westfaling, esq., of Rudhall, Herefs.
Wal. Ridler, esq., of Syde
John Pritchard, esq., (of Kempstone), [?Norf.][†]
Thos. Hayward, esq., of Quedgeley
Thos. Rous, esq., (of Wotton under Edge)[†]
Ric. Cambridge, esq., (of Pudhill)[†]
38 Sam. Ridler, gent., (of Syde)[†]
Abraham Ridler, gent., (of Syde)[†]
John Turner, gent., (of Ebley)[†]
Kedgwin Hoskins, gent., (of Clearwell)[†]
Wm. Baggott, esq., (of Prestbury)[†]
Edw. Baggott, gent., (of Prestbury)[†]
Thos. Bayly, gent.[†]
Giles Nash, gent., (of Stonehouse)[†]
Sam. Bruton, gent., (of Wotton under Edge)[†]
John Andrews, gent., (of Stonehouse)[†]
John Ball, esq., (of Stonehouse)[†]
Sam. Hawker, gent., (of Wallbridge)[†]
Thos. Daunt, esq., (of Owlpen)[†]
39 Jasper Selwyn, esq., (of Frampton on Severn)[†]
Giles Clutterbuck, gent., (of Eastington)[†]
Ric. Clutterbuck, gent., (of Bristol)[†]
Wm. Fortune, gent., (of North Nibley)[†]
Sam. Peach, gent., (of Chalford)[†]
Jasper Clutterbuck, gent., (of King's Stanley)[†]
Thos. Careles, gent.,[†6]
Thos. Toms, gent., (of Cromhall)[†]
Thos. Winstone, gent., (of Wotton under Edge)[†]
Thos. Winstone the younger, gent., (of Wotton under Edge)[†]

[1] Under this heading are listed men to whom the corporation gave the freedom, mostly by acts of 25 July and 9 Aug 1727, for electoral purposes: ibid. ff. 214v.–215v., 218v.; cf. Williams, *Parl. Hist. of Glos.* 208.
[2] Son of Mat. Ducie Moreton, Lord Ducie, of Tortworth: Glos. R.O., D 340A/Z 6.
[3] Son of Mat. Ducie Moreton, Lord Ducie, of Tortworth: ibid.
[4] In Walford, later called Hill Court: Heref. R.O., F 8/III/214–7; W.H. Cooke, *Continuation of Duncumb's Hist. of Herefs.* iii (1882), 188, 204.
[5] Westbury-on-Severn: *V.C.H. Glos.* x. 87.
[6] Excise officer: GBR B 3/9, f. 215.

1727 4 Sept Jas. Rous,[1] gent., (of Wotton under Edge)†
Wm. Tayloe, gent., (of Chalford)†
Wm. Gyles, gent., (of Wickwar)†
40 Wm. Payne, gent., (of King's Stanley)†
Jos. Dancy, gent., (of Wotton under Edge)†
Randall Playdell, gent., (attorney, of Gloucester)†
Wm. Haward, gent., (of Gloucester)†
Wm. Lane, esq., (of Apperley)†
Wm. Greene, gent., (of Newent)†
Benj. Collett, esq., (of Tewkesbury)†
Rob. Moore, gent., (of Gloucester)†
John Shipway, gent., (of Rodborough)†
Nat. Beard, gent., (of Stroud)†
Rob. Ellis, gent., (of Ebley)†
Sam. Cole, gent., (of Salmon's Mill)†
Wm. Tayloe the younger, gent., (of Chalford)†
Wm. Caple, gent., (of Stroud)†
Steph. Phillips, clerk, (of Bisley)†
Francis Wells, clerk, (of Prestbury)†[2]
41 Thos. Wells, clerk, (of Prestbury)†[3]
Jackman (*Jakeman*) Morse, clerk, (of Awre)†
John Summors, clerk, (of Stonehouse)†[4]
Dan. Caple, clerk, (of Dursley)†[5]
Thos. Savage, clerk, (of Gloucester)†[6]
Thos. Chamberlayne, clerk†[7]
Sam. Gwinnett, clerk†[8]
Peter Lewis de Bons, clerk†
Jeremiah Davis, gent., (of Stroud)†
Nat. Pool, gent., (of Stonehouse)†
Thos. Small, gent., (of Nailsworth)†
John Thomas, gent., (of Uley)†
42 Steph. Burcomb, gent., (of Stinchcombe)†
John Wilkins, gent., (of Frocester)†
Rob. Webb, gent., (of Cromhall)†
Giles Nash the elder, gent., (of Stonehouse)†
Sam. Cockerell, gent.†
John Walker, gent., (of Yate)†
Ric. Hill, esq., (of Yate)†
Jeremiah Tidcombe, gent.†
Thos. Pettat, gent., (of Ebley)†
Nic. Webb, gent., (of Wotton under Edge)†
John Wingfield, clerk†[9]
Rob. Hayward the younger, gent.†
43 Edw. Bearpacker, gent., (of Wotton under Edge)†
John Phillimore, gent., (of Cam)†
Wm. Holborough, gent., (of the Green, Uley)†

[1] Jas. Rowe: ibid.
[2] Became rector of Earl's Croome, Worcs., later in 1727: Nash, *Worcs.* i. 269.
[3] Rector of Cowley: *V.C.H. Glos.* vii. 198.
[4] Rector of Nympsfield: Hockaday Abs. cccii.
[5] Vicar of Cam: ibid. cxxxix.
[6] Rector of Hinton on the Green: ibid. ccxliv.
[7] Rector of Little Rissington and Wick Rissington: ibid. cccxxiii.
[8] Later appointed curate of St. Nicholas by the corporation: GBR B 3/9, f. 365.
[9] Curate of Newnham and Littledean by the corporation's gift: ibid. f. 210.

Geo. Gibbons, gent., (of Gloucester)†
Ric. Webb, gent., (of Nailsworth)†
Edw. Webb, gent., (of Nailsworth)†
Edw. Adderley, gent., (of Alderley)†
Rob. Cocks, esq., (of Dumbleton)†
(Captain) Jas. Bissell, gent., (of Redmarley D'Abitot), [Worcs.]†
(Captain) Wm. Clarke, gent., (of Berkeley Castle)†
Wm. Cooke, gent., (of Longford)†
Thos. Cole, gent., (of Gloucester)†[1]
44 Edw. Lloyd, esq.
Giles Lawrence, esq.†[2]
(Major) John Suckling, esq.†[3]
Mat. Ducie (*Ducy*) Morton, esq.†[4]
John How, esq.†[5]
John Temple, esq., (of Sudgrove)†
Thos. Warner, esq., (of Paganhill)†
Thos. Holder, gent., (of Frampton on Severn)†
Major Jos. Mason (of Barnwood)†
Wm. Johnson, gent., (of Barnwood)†
Captain [?Thos.] Dolman[6] of Bristol
Geo. Lillington, esq., (of Bath)†
45 Godfrey Elly, clerk†[7]
Ric. Parks, clerk†[8]
Wm. Lane, gent., of Mitcheldean
Geo. Gwinnett, gent., (of Shurdington)†
Dan. Lysons the younger, esq.†[9]
Nat. Iles, clothier, (of Randwick)†
Thos. Philipps, gent., (of Stonehouse)†
Revd. [Thos.] Baker[10] of Bibury
Jos. Pinfold, gent., of Rodborough
Dan. Bond, clerk†[11]
Giles Gardner, esq.†[12]
Thos. Vernon, gent., of the Inner Temple, London
Thos. Roberts of Stonehouse

46 **John King, esq., mayor 1728–9**

1729 20 Jan Moses Clarke, app. of John Hall, baker
23 June John Ipsley, app. of Edw. Fletcher, barber-surgeon
4 Aug Geo. Cowles, app. of Ric. Draper, cordwainer
10 Aug Thos. Taylor, app. of Abraham Rudhall, bellfounder

[1] Independent minister: *V.C.H. Glos.* iv. 323–4.
[2] By act of 27 Sept 1722: GBR B 3/9, f. 130.
[3] By act of 11 Aug 1724: ibid. f. 164.
[4] Of Tortworth, one of four candidates in the 1727 general election who agreed, after the poll on 5 Sept, to share the city's seats: *Complete Peerage*, iv. 474–5; Williams, *Parl. Hist. of Glos.* 208–9; cf. *Trans. B.G.A.S.* lxxviii. 139.
[5] ? of Stowell, same as John Howe the younger admitted to the freedom 25 Aug 1712 and M.P. for Gloucester Feb–Aug 1727: cf. above: GBR C 9/7, p. 435; Williams, *Parl. Hist. of Glos.* 208.
[6] Cf. *Trade of Bristol in 18th Cent.* ed. W.E. Minchinton (Bristol Rec. Soc. xx), 18, 21, 143.
[7] Rector of Tibberton: Hockaday Abs. ccclxxiv.
[8] Vicar of Tirley: ibid. ccclxxvi.
[9] ? of Hempsted: *V.C.H. Glos.* iv. 423.
[10] Cf. Hockaday Abs. cxxi.
[11] Master of the Crypt school: GBR B 3/9, f. 158v.; Austin, *Crypt School*, 114–5.
[12] ? of Stroud: *V.C.H. Glos.* xi. 118.

		11 July	Benj. Harris, app. of John Engly, tailor
		7 Nov	Thos. Branch, tinman, (by fine)[1]
47		15 Aug	Jas. Meighen, app. of Jos. Pegler, tanner
		25 Aug	Francis Gythens, son of Francis, mercer, decd., of Bristol
		1 Sept	Dan. Quarrington, app. of his father Edw., distiller
48		4 July	Thos. Fawlks, app. of Ralph Ady, butcher[2]
		15 Sept	Joshua Counsell, gent., of Bristol by gift
			Steph. Box, saddletree-maker, (by fine)[3]

Thomas Carrill, esq., mayor 1729–30

		19 Nov	Littleton Lawrence, esq., of Painswick by gift
49		15 Sept	Steph. Box, saddletree-maker[4]
	1730	2 Feb	John Darke, app. of Sarah Cooke, widow
		13 Apr	Rob. Evenis, app. of Hen. Brimyard, cordwainer
		1 June	Gabriel Harris the younger, bookseller, by patrimony
		3 Apr	Chas. Selwyn, app. of John Heaven, barber-surgeon
		5 June	John Barnes, app. of Jas. Baker, cordwainer
		3 Apr	Ric. Webb, app. of Sarah Collins, widow
50	1729	4 July	Thos. Fawlks, app. of Ralph Ady, butcher[5]
	1730	27 July	Jas. Tyler, son of Jasper, combmaker, decd.
		29 July	Giles Rodway, son of Thos., mercer, decd.
			Benj. Phelps, son of Wm., tanner, decd.
51		7 Aug	Thos. Beach, app. of John Carter, baker
		12 Aug	Nat. Lye, gent., }
			John Engley, bricklayer, } by gift[6]
			Ric. Baker, yeoman, }
			John Engley, son of John, bricklayer
		17 Aug	John Rowles, son of John, butcher, of Minsterworth
52			Jos. Chester, app. of Jas. Wood, mercer
		31 Aug	Kirkham Weaver, son of Hen., smith
		7 Sept	Wm. Hayes, son of Wm., cordwainer
		2 Oct	John Perks, son of John, dyer, decd.

John Small, esq., mayor 1730–1

		23 Oct	John Keyse, app. of Thos. Weaver, pinmaker
53		20 Nov	Wm. Garne,[7] son of Wm., weaver
	1731	11 Jan	Thos. Perris, son of John, butcher
		25 Jan	Thos. Bonnor, app. of Ric. Lane, chandler and grocer
			Wm. Tanner, carpenter, (by gift)[8]
		1 Feb	Wm. Hooper, app. of Francis Brabant, cooper, decd.
		22 Mar	John Benson, son of John, tiler and plasterer
54			Paul Stephens, son of Francis, feltmaker, decd.
			Thos. Bright, app. of Ric. Beard, decd., and Ant. Williams, barber-surgeon
			Ric. Spillman, app. of Sam. Pawling, baker

[1] Entry belongs to following mayoralty.
[2] Cf. below: GBR C 9/8, p. 50.
[3] Cf. below: ibid. p. 49.
[4] Entry struck through; cf. above: ibid. p. 48.
[5] Entry struck through; cf. above: ibid.
[6] Readmitted, having resigned the freedom 6 July 1730: ibid. B 3/9, ff. 278, 279v.
[7] Disfranchised 28 July 1781 to enable him to give evidence in a cause between the mercers' company and a non-freeman: ibid. 11, ff. 298v., 344.
[8] For discharging a debt owed him by John Crump, serjeant-at-mace: ibid. 9, f. 290.

3 May Ephraim Higgins, son of Ephraim, bricklayer
17 May Benj. Baker, son of Ric., butcher
26 July Thos. Man, son of Thos., baker
55 6 Aug John Ashworth, app. of Wm. Tomlins, pinmaker
John Cowles, son of Ric., grazier
27 Aug Martin Lloyd, app. of Martin Lloyd, butcher
30 Aug Thos. Price, son of John, barber-surgeon, late of Bristol
4 Sept Lt.-Gen. Wm. Evans† by gift
56 20 Sept Jonathan Dugmore, app. of Jos. Goodwin and Mic. Jennings, butchers

William Bell, esq., mayor 1731–2

25 Oct Ric. Lewis, app. of Rob. Arnold, pinmaker
11 Oct Dan. Newcome, S.T.P., dean of Gloucester cathedral, by gift
1732 9 Feb Benj. Bulkley, S.T.P., of Dewchurch,[1] Herefs., by gift
27 Mar John Washborne, son of John, clockmaker, late of Gloucester
57 24 Apr Thos. Chandler, app. of Thos. Still, grocer
John Price, app. of Edw. Bennett and Wm. Rogers, apothecaries
5 May Thos. Spencer, son of Thos., cooper
10 July Jonathan Millington, app. of Sam. Spencer, Francis Brabant the elder, decd., and Francis Brabant, coopers
14 July Hen. Cleevely, son of Hen., tailor
28 July Thos. Whale, app. of John Hale, barber
58 4 Aug Mat. Garne, app. of his father Wm., weaver
21 Aug Thos. Bushell, esq., of Cleeve,[2] Worcs., by gift
15 Sept Dan. Carter, son of John, cordwainer
19 Sept Wm. Moseley, clerk, of Hasfield (*Haresfield*)[3] by gift
25 Sept Dan. Mathews, app. of Chas. Dymocke, mercer

Gabriel Harris, esq., mayor 1732–3

2 Oct Hen. Gally, S.T.P., prebendary of Gloucester cathedral, (by gift)
14 Oct John Baylis, gent., by gift
59 16 Oct Sam. Maverley, app. of Wm. Maverley, tailor
3 Nov John Weston, app. of John Hickman, Rob. Motlow, and Thos. Ades, cordwainers
Wm. Ashmead, son of Giles, mercer, decd., of Cheltenham, formerly of Gloucester
Jas. Smith, son of Jas., cooper, decd.
1733 12 Feb Luke Hooke, son of Jonathan, joiner
2 Apr Benj. Hyett,[4] esq., } sons of Chas., esq.,
Nic. Hyett, esq., }
11 Apr Ric. Beard, son of Ric., clothier
60 8 June Sam. Millard the younger, app. of Sam. Millard, gardener
Ric. Hathway, son of Ric., button-maker
Geo. Rickards,[5] app. of Sam. Palling, baker
Jas. Cooke, son of Jas., joiner
22 June Ric. Hayle, app. in turn of Jos. Pegler the elder and Thos. Bower, tanners

[1] Much Dewchurch: *Alumni Oxon. 1500–1714*, i. 207.
[2] Cleeve Prior: Nash, *Worcs.* i. 237 and n.; *V.C.H. Worcs.* iii. 311.
[3] Cf. Hockaday Abs. ccxxxvi.
[4] Candidate in 1741 for one of Gloucester's parliamentary seats: Williams, *Parl. Hist. of Glos.* 210; cf. *Trans. B.G.A.S.* lxxviii. 140.
[5] Disfranchised 28 July 1781 to enable him to give evidence in a cause between the mercers' company and a non-freeman: GBR B 3/11, ff. 298v., 344.

2 July Sam. Bonner, son of John, gent., decd.
61 30 July Thos. Skinner, son of Thos., baker
Jeremiah Williams, app. of Thos. Merry, cordwainer
3 Aug Ric. Barton, son of John, bricklayer
6 Aug Wm. Collett, son of Wm., grocer, decd.
Benj. Freeman, app. of John Price, whitesmith
27 Aug Edw. Bower, son of Thos., tanner, of Newent
7 Sept Jos. Beard, son of Jas., woolcomber, and app. of Thos. Hayward, weaver, late of Gloucester, by apprenticeship
62 Ric. Evans, son of Ric., ropemaker
Wm. Rogers, son of John, baker
10 Sept Jos. Phelps, son of Jos., grocer
17 Sept Isaac Brotherton, son of Jeremiah, shoemaker
1 Oct John Harris, son of Gabriel, esq., mayor

John Selwyn, esq., mayor 1733–4

8 Oct Wm. Cossley, son of John, goldsmith, of Bristol
10 Oct Jas. Grevile, son of Francis, gent., of Bristol
12 Nov Giles Browne, app. of Rob. Bicke, joiner
63 24 Dec Caleb Wells, app. in turn of Dan. Bryan and John Price, apothecary
1734 7 Jan Micah (*Mico*) Wagstaffe, app. of Ric. Lane and Wm. Holtham, grocers and chandlers
14 Jan Chas. Wilton, son of Hen., pinmaker
Thos. Humphris, son of Thos., currier
25 Jan John Wheeler, son of John, joiner, late of Gloucester
4 Feb John Turner, app. in turn of Guy Ellis and Wm. Lander, grocers
Thos. Hill, app. of Jas. Lovett, barber-surgeon
18 Feb John Harmer, app. of Jos. Fownes, distiller
64 11 Feb Wm. Merricke, app. of Zachariah Stephens, tailor
Jas. Webley, son of Jos., tailor
15 Mar Wm. Smith, son of Maur., saddler, of Dursley
8 Apr Hen. Skynner, Chas. Skynner, } sons of Thos., baker
26 Apr Wm. Coopey, son of John, cooper, decd., of Churchdown
4 May Sam. Steel, son of Sam., gent., of Littledean
65 24 May Wm. Stephens, son of Wm., weaver
4 May Thos. Stephens, esq., of the Inner Temple, London, by gift
Thos. Barrow, esq., of Quedgeley by gift
Dan. Small, esq., of Wheatenhurst by gift
Thos. Rogers, clerk, of Wheatenhurst by gift
Rob. Breton, clerk, (of Lydney)† by gift[1]
6 May Wal. Jones, D.D., (of Upton upon Severn, Worcs.),† by gift[2]
66 Thos. Longden, son of Capel, ironmonger
Leon Pitt, son of Rowland, linen-draper
Thos. Smith, son of Abraham, cooper
Jas. Cleeveley, son of Hen., tailor
Thos. Barrett, son of John, labourer
Edw. Stephens Estcourt, clerk,[3] by gift
Thos. Branch, son of Wm., gent., decd.
67 John Woore, app. of Sarah Oatley, widow, decd.

[1] By act of 25 July 1727: ibid. 9, f. 215; cf. Hockaday Abs. cclxix.
[2] By act of 9 Aug 1727: GBR B 3/9, f. 218v.
[3] Master of the Bluecoat Hospital (or Sir Thomas Rich's school): ibid. ff. 333v., 341.

Jas. Commelin, clerk,[1] son of Jas., gent., decd.
Chas. Hanbury-Williams, esq., } sons of John Hanbury,[2] esq., of
Capel Hanbury, esq., } Pontypool, Mon.
Jas. Wintle, son of Hen., maltster
Timothy Webb, app. of Martha Perkins, widow
68 Thos. Lewis, app. of Thos. Lewis, gardener
Hen. Greville, son of Hen., barber-surgeon, of London
John King, son of John, ald.
Thos. Lander, son of Thos., innholder
John Greene, son of Phil., brickmaker
Wm. Norwood, esq., son of Thos., clerk, of Leckhampton
69 John Selwyn, esq., son of John, esq.[†3]
Thos. Dibble, clerk, of Woodchester by gift
Ric. Silly, son of Thos., yeoman, decd., of Tibberton
Sam. Turbett, son of John, carpenter, decd.
Sam. Hayford, son of Sam., pitcher, decd.
Wm. Hampton, app. of John Stephens, glazier
70 John Hayward, clerk, of Withington by gift
Wm. Hayward, son of Jeremiah, grocer, decd.
7 May Ric. Roberts, esq., by gift
John Wiltshire, clerk, of Painswick by gift
Wm. Cossley, son of Ric., ald.
Jos. Twemloe, gent., of Dursley by gift
71 Francis Nash, esq., of Stonehouse by gift
Nat. Fowler, gent., of Stonehouse by gift
Reginald Winniatt, esq., of Stanton by gift
Jos. Bowly, app. of Hen. Engly, bricklayer
Hen. Engly, son of John, collar-maker
Hen. Furly, app. of Chas. Dimocke, mercer
72 Holman Hope, app. of Ant. Gardner, baker
Ric. Beckett, son of Ric., gent., decd., of Cheltenham
Knightly Benson, } sons of John, pargeter[4]
Rob. Benson, }
Edw. Nicholls, clerk, son of Edw., woollen-draper
Jos. Smith, app. of Thos. Parker and Wm. Cook, barber-surgeons
73 Thos. Pembruge, app. of John Hawkins[†*]
Phil. Reading, app. of Sam. Spencer, cooper
Wm. Bennett, app. of John Hickman, Wm. Evenis, and Rob. Evenis, cordwainers
Hen. Window, } apps. of Ric. Cowcher, pinmaker
Wm. Drake, }
Ric. Maule, app. of Jas. Cooke, joiner
74 Wm. Lewis, app. of Sam. Grove[†*]
Hen. Drake,[5] app. of Hen. Wilton*
Thos. Swaine, app. of Josiah Fitshew*
Ric. Price, app. of John Davis, pinmaker
Sam. Darby, app. of John Cowles, butcher
Thos. Beard, app. of John Price*

[1] Usher of the Crypt school: ibid. f. 323; Fosbrooke, *Glouc.* 152.
[2] M.P. for Gloucester 1701–2 and 1702–8: Williams, *Parl. Hist. of Glos.* 205–6.
[3] Mayor, owner of Matson House near Gloucester: *V.C.H. Glos.* iv. 441–2; cf. above: GBR C 9/7, p. 422.
[4] Cf. below: GBR C 9/8, p. 96.
[5] Pinmaker, of Wotton, disfranchised 28 July 1781 to enable him to give evidence in a cause between the mercers' company and a non-freeman: ibid. B 3/11, ff. 298v., 344.

75 1734 Ric. Powell, app. of Wm. Barrett*
Wm. Drinkwater, app. of Jos. Hale and Jos. Cother, cordwainers
Francis Gregory, app. of Thos. Jaines, feltmaker
Sam. Johnson,[1] app. of Wm. Hayes and Jas. Brotherton, cordwainers
Thos. Wilton, app. of John Singleton, pinmaker
Sam. Blocksom, app. of Wm. Lodge*
76 Jos. Hill, app. of Rob. Longden*
Wm. Chamberlayn, app. of Jas. Brotherton*
John Latham, app. of John Best*
Thos. Humphris, app. of John Ricketts*
John Box, app. of Cowcher Shipton, pinmaker
John Child, app. of John Jelfe and Ric. Weaver*
77 Francis Hembly, app. of Wm. Stephens*
Thos. Selwyn, app. of Geo. Edwards, heelmaker
Thos. Evans, app. of Thos. Jones, glover
Thos. Jeffs, app. of John Holder, pinmaker
Jas. Oldacre, app. of Thos. Fletcher*
Ric. Young, app. of Nic. Wilkins†*
78 Benj. Spillman, app. of Abraham Smith*
Cornelius Gardner, app. of Ric. Taylor, barber-surgeon
Thos. Child, app. of Sam. Ricketts, carpenter
John Lane, app. of Ric. Weaver, farrier
John Lake, app. of Hen. Draper and Ric. Weaver, farriers
Wm. Simonds, app. of Wm. Sparrowhawke*
79 Rob. Buckle, app. of Thos. Puckeridge*
Clement Fisher, app. of Thos. Browne*
Ric. Purton,[2] app. of Jos. Collier, cordwainer
Ric. Wintle, app. of Thos. Humphris, currier
Thos. Gaze, app. of Wm. Roberts, carpenter
Jas. Cull, app. of Geo. Edwards*
80 Thos. Hathaway, son of Wm.†*
John Wood, son of Wm.†*
Ric. Gill, son of Wm.*
Thos. Holder,[3] son of John*
Rog. Church, son of Rog., glazier
Thos. Randle, son of Thos., pargeter
81 Jeremiah Harris, son of Nat.*
John Cowles, son of John*
Wm. Swayne, son of Thos., pargeter
Edm. Ady, son of Edm., baker
Wm. Hayward, son of Edw., weaver
John Gamond, son of John, baker
82 Ric. Cook(e), son of Ric.*
Wm. Bishop, } sons of John*
John Bishop, }
Wm. Gunn, son of Jas., glazier
Jas. Church, son of Rog., glazier
Edw. Baker, son of Edw.*
83 Thos. Engly, son of Thos., butcher
John Barnfield, son of Ric., whitesmith, decd.

[1] Disfranchised 28 July 1781: ibid.
[2] Disfranchised 28 July 1781 and readmitted 5 Dec 1783: ibid.; below: ibid. C 9/9, p. 13.
[3] Pinmaker, disfranchised 28 July 1781 and readmitted 5 Dec 1783: ibid.

Dan. Palling, John Palling, sons of Dan., baker
Wm. Welch, son of Ric.†*
Sam. Cripps, son of Edw.*
84 Ric. Hale, son of Ric.*
Wm. Tainton, son of John†*
Thos. Peace, son of John*
Wm. Child, son of Sam., weaver, decd., of Bristol
John Shaw, son of John, blacksmith, of Blakeney
Thos. Mathews, son of Thos.*
85 John Bennett, son of Francis*
Jas. Bradly, son of Hen.*
Thos. Randle, son of Wm., weaver
Jas. Randle, son of John*
Thos. Stephens, son of Jos.*
John Best, son of John, tailor
86 John Viner, son of John, sawyer
Wm. Hayes, son of Hen.*
Geo. Phillips, son of Geo.†*
Thos. Williams, son of John*
Thos. Merrett, son of John*
Thos. Barrett, son of Thos., tailor
87 Thos. Lea, son of Rob*
Aurelius Nurse, son of Geo., cooper
Dan. Niblett, son of Dan.†*
Jos. Holder, son of John, pinmaker
Thos. Saunders, Ric. Saunders, sons of Thos.†*
88 Wm. Powell, John Powell,[1] sons of John*
Abraham Howell, son of Abraham, cordwainer
Sam. Burdock, son of Wm., tailor
Wm. Hayes, son of John*
Chris. Estcourt, son of Sam.†*
89 Wm. Merry, son of Wm.*
Phil. Phillips, son of John*
Rob. Bossly, son of Jas.*
Sam. Washbourne, son of John, whitesmith
Thos. Fownes, son of Thos., clothier, of Minchinhampton
Sam. Coldrick, son of Wm.*
Steph. Churches, son of Steph., clothworker, of Minchinhampton
90 Geo. Griggs, son of Edw.*
John Tomlins, son of Wm.*
Wm. Stephens, son of Wm.*
John Garne, son of Wm.*
Ric. Cox, son of Ric.†*
Thos. Sparks, son of Thos.*
91 Thos. Smith, son of Jos., woolcomber
John Davis, son of Hen., pinmaker
Thos. Hornedge, son of John*
Ric. Darke, son of Ric., gunsmith
Chas. Williams, son of Ant., barber

[1] Pipemaker, disfranchised 28 July 1781: ibid. B 3/11, f. 298v.

			Sam. Merrett, son of Sam., glover
92			Hen. Engly, son of John*
			John Viner, son of Wm.*
			Mic. Arnold, son of Mic.*
			Hen. Merrett, son of Hen., baker
			John King, son of John*
			Jas. Ricketts, son of John*
93			Wm. Messenger, son of Wm.†*
			John Cheesman, son of Paul†*
			John Birch, son of Thos.†*
			Sam. Sair, son of Dan.†*
			Hen. Brimyard, son of John, cordwainer
			Hen. Dowl, } sons of John, currier
94			Thos. Dowl, }
			Hen. Smith, } sons of Hen.†*
			Wm. Smith, }
			Isaac Skillerne, son of John, furrier, of Winchcombe
			Joshua Skillerne, son of Thos.†*
			Wm. Bick, son of Wm., labourer
95			Thos. Holford, son of John*
			Lawr. Lane, son of Ric., bookseller, decd., of Norton
			John Cleeveley, son of Hen., tailor
			John Trustrum, son of John†*
			Jas. Engly, son of Thos.*
			Ric. Gardner, son of And., woolcomber
96			Knightly Benson, } sons of John, pargeter. Both entered before[1]
			Rob. Benson, }
			Thos. Mayoe, son of Rob.†*
			Hen. Beard, } sons of Wm., mercer
			Halliday (*Holliday*) Beard, }
			Thos. Ward, son of Thos., pinmaker
97			Abraham Motlow, son of Miles*
			John Jelfe, son of Hen.†*
			John Haynes, son of John†*
			Thos. Wilkins, son of Nic.†*
			John Holford, son of John*
			Hen. Hervey, esq., by gift†
98		5 July	Thos. Bingham, son of Thos., maltster
		5 Aug	Benj. Rider, app. of John Rathbone, farrier
		6 Sept	Ric. Greene, son of John, grocer, decd.
			Jas. Edwards, son of Jas., baker
			Jas. Cullerne, app. of John Heaven, barber-surgeon
		9 Sept	Benj. Aycrigg, son of Wm., apothecary, decd., of Upton upon Severn, Worcs.

John Hayward, esq., mayor 1734–5

	1735	16 Jan	John Washbourne, } sons of John, blacksmith, decd., of Evesham,
99			Nic. Washbourne, } Worcs.
			Ric. Reeve, app. of Ric. Reeve, innholder
		17 Feb	Adam Fletcher, app. of John Fletcher, currier
		21 Mar	Wm. Wharton, app. of Edw. Norman, butcher
		21 July	Ralph Vaughn, son of John, vintner, decd.
		18 Aug	Sam. Perkins, son of Geo., baker, decd.

[1] Entries struck through; cf. above: ibid. C 9/8, p. 72.

		28 July	Martin [Benson], bishop of Gloucester,[1] by gift
100		12 Sept	Wm. Harding, son of Chas., pinmaker, decd.

Richard Lewis, esq., mayor 1735–6

		n.d.	Thos. Fownes*
		15 Oct	Edm. Rudhall, Abel Rudhall, } sons of Abraham the younger, bellfounder
	1736	8 Mar	Jos. Wells, Ant. Wells, } sons of Jos., baker, decd.
			Francis Brotherton, app. of Jas. Rogers, bricklayer
		19 Mar	Edw. Grevile, son of Francis, haberdasher, decd., of Bristol
101		5 Apr	Jas. Dancocks, son of Jas., innholder
			Wal. Hooper, son of Chas., butcher
		12 Apr	Ric. Ashworth, app. of Jas. Collwell, cordwainer
		4 June	John Reen, app. of Jacob Kirby, weaver
		29 June	Jas. Herbert, gent., by gift
		9 July	Ric. Engly, son of Ric., bricklayer, decd.
		13 Sept	Wm. Shatford, app. of Wm. Rogers, apothecary
			John Hathaway, son of Ric., button-maker
102		2 Oct	Humph. Cox, yeoman, by gift

Charles Selwyn, esq., mayor 1736–7

		15 Oct	Chas. Pool, app. of John Graffstocke, butcher
	1737	11 Feb	Edw. Vaughan, son of John, innholder, decd.
		18 Feb	John Garne, app. of Jos. Cother, cordwainer
			John Clarke, app. of John Webb, baker
			Wm. Wood, app. of Giles Robinson, cooper
			Thos. Millard, son of Sam., gardener
103		13 May	John Quarrington, app. of John Ellis, ironmonger
		20 May	Jas. Gunn, son of Jas., glazier
		14 June	Ant. Ellis, D.D., prebendary of Gloucester cathedral, by gift
			Jos. Atwell, D.D., prebendary of Gloucester cathedral, by gift
		1 July	Wm. Bell, gent., by gift
			John Knight, gent., by gift
104		28 July	Jas. Elly, gent., by gift
		1 Oct	John Nicholas, yeoman, by gift
			Chas. Lewis, yeoman, by gift

Thomas Hill, esq., mayor 1737–8

		21 Oct	Ric. Stephens, app. of John Carter, baker
		4 Nov	Sam. Cooke, son of John, baker
		18 Nov	Sam. Niblett, son of Dan., baker, of Haresfield
		9 Dec	Thos. Wadley, son of John, baker, decd.
105	1738	24 Mar	Thos. Wagstaffe, app. of Ellis Taylor, baker
		17 Apr	John Vaughan, son of John, vintner, decd.
		28 Apr	Geo. Gwinet, app. of Geo. Cooke, grocer
		12 May	Edw. Fox, app. of Ann Jones, widow, late of Gloucester, and John Jones, cooper
		15 May	Sam. Wadley, son of John, baker, decd.
		9 June	John Restall, app. of Wm. Mason, tailor
		21 June	John Way, son of John, butcher
106		31 July	Geo. Stephens, son of Wm., pinmaker, decd.

[1] Fosbrooke, *Glouc.* 137.

4 Aug Thos. Knight, son of Thos., labourer, decd.
22 Sept John Williams, app. of John Wilshere, tailor
John Greene, son of Rob., weaver
29 Sept Wm. Reeve, son of Ric., innholder, decd.

William Niccolls, esq., mayor 1738–9

20 Nov John Ready, app. of Thos. Hill, apothecary, ald.
1739 29 Jan Nat. Cowles, app. of Ric. Spillman, baker
107 26 Feb John Cliff, app. of Thos. Weaver, pinmaker
Thos. Davis, son of Moses, cordwainer
30 Mar John Barrett, app. of Mic. Jennings, butcher
11 May Dan. Yates, app. of Thos. Adey, grocer
25 May Wm. Window, button-maker, by gift
22 June John Hardwicke, son of Nat., baker
6 July Dennis Hutchins, app. of Wm. Broughton, farrier
108 16 July Jas. Lye, son of Francis, cooper, decd.
Thos. Marshfield,[1] app. of John Jeffs, blacksmith
20 July Seth Cocks, app. of Chas. Dymock, decd., and Jos. Chester, mercers
14 Aug Augustus [Berkeley], earl of Berkeley,[†2]
Hen. Berkeley, esq.,[†]
Wm. Young, esq.,[†]
Steph. Jenner, clerk,[†3]
} by gift[4]
109 10 Sept Giles Webley, son of Sam., labourer
29 Sept Wm. Cooke, victualler, by gift

Edward Machen,[5] esq., mayor 1739–40

2 Nov John Jennings, son of Hen., carpenter, decd.
7 Nov Powell Snell,[6] esq., son of John, esq., decd. Sworn at five in the evening
16 Nov Thos. Gardiner, son of And., woolcomber
14 Dec Sam. Weladvise, son of Sam., glazier
17 Dec Mat. Smith, son of Jas., distiller, decd.
110 1740 7 Jan Willoughby Bannaster, app. of John Ricketts and Ric. Cowcher, pinmakers, both decd.
Ant. Brotherton, app. of his father Thos., tiler and plasterer
11 Feb Benj. Bonner, app. of Thos. Webley, brazier
25 Feb Winston Cox, son of John, barber-surgeon, decd.
4 Apr Arthur Yarnold, son of Ric., apothecary, decd., of Ledbury, Herefs.
21 Apr Chas. Clarke, son of Nic., pinmaker, decd.
5 May Geo. Hall, app. of Thos. Bower and Ric. Hayle, tanners
111 19 May Jacob Kirby, son of Jacob, weaver
14 Apr Nat. Pyrke, son of Duncombe, mercer, decd., of Bristol
23 May John Smith, son of Maur., saddler, decd., of Dursley
6 June Edw. Griffiths, app. of Sam. Heath, joiner

[1] Whitesmith, disfranchised 28 July 1781 and readmitted 5 Dec 1783: GBR B 3/11, ff. 298v., 344; below: ibid. C 9/9, p. 13.

[2] *Complete Peerage*, ii. 142.

[3] Vicar of Berkeley: Hockaday Abs. cxix.

[4] By act of 10 Aug 1739 the earl, high steward of Gloucester, and up to six of his attendants of his choice were to receive the freedom when he visited the city on 14 Aug, the day of the nomination of the next mayor: GBR B 3/9, f. 435.

[5] Also spelt *Machin*.

[6] Candidate in 1761 for one of Gloucester's parliamentary seats: Williams, *Parl. Hist. of Glos.* 210–1.

Ric. Shurmar, app. of Martha Perkins, widow, Ant. Gardner, baker, both decd., and Ric. Stephens, baker
11 Aug Jas. Rich, esq., son of Sir Rob., Bt., decd.[†1]

(John Hayward, esq., mayor 1740)[2]

4 Oct Sam. Roberts, innholder, by gift

112 **Samuel Worrall, esq., mayor 1740–1**

17 Oct Ric. Perrin, app. of John Cowles, decd., and John Gardner, butchers
Josiah Cooke, son of Jas., joiner
20 Oct Ric. Perkins, son of Geo., baker, decd.
31 Oct Thos. Hale, son of Jos., cordwainer
3 Nov Wm. Millard, son of Sam., gardener, decd.
27 Nov Edw. Baylis, son of Edw., woolcomber, decd.
1741 2 Jan Jacob Guest, app. of Chas. Cowdall, butcher, decd.
9 Jan Wm. Stephens, son of Wm., combmaker, decd.
113 23 Jan Chas. Barton, son of John
6 Feb Wm. Coles, app. of Rowland Pytt, ironmonger
John Moore, son of John, yeoman, decd., of Sandhurst
9 Feb Wm. Niccholls, son of Wm., ald.
Thos. Hannis, son of Thos., pinmaker, late of Gloucester
Francis Rowly, app. of Sarah Cooke, saddler
Jas. Walker, son of Jas., blacksmith
Thos. Stephens, son of Wm., weaver
13 Feb Wm. Powell, son of Wm., plumber
16 Feb Wm. Roberts, son of Wm., carpenter
Geo. Dean, son of Thos., baker, decd.
114 20 Feb John Mills, } sons of Thos., tiler and plasterer
Thos. Mills, }
Roynon Jones, clerk, son of Roynon, esq., decd., of Nass
Jas. Keys, app. of John Keys and John Jefferys, pinmakers
23 Feb Nat. Saunders, son of Nat., joiner
Sam. Perkins, son of Sam., tiler and plasterer
Thos. Puckeridge, son of Thos., tailor
Ric. Woodward, son of Ric., pinmaker
115 9 Mar Thos. Fane, esq., of Bristol (by gift)
11 Mar Wm. Freake, esq., son of Ralph, esq., of Hannington, Wilts., formerly of Westbury
Wm. Jones, esq., of Nass (by gift)[3]
12 Mar Thos. Gwillim, esq., of Whitchurch, [?Herefs.], (by gift)
16 Mar Jacob Rudhall of Bristol, son of Abraham, bellfounder, decd.
Thos. Phillips of Friday Street, London, son of Thos., pinmaker
John Wilkes,[4] son of John, weaver
Turpin Stephens, son of Thos., pinmaker
John Flower, son of John, tailor
Edw. Barnard, son of Thos., cordwainer, of Quedgeley
Adam Gardiner, son of John, yeoman, of Highnam

[1] Of Sonning, Berks.: *Complete Baronetage*, iii. 180.
[2] Elected 22 Sept after Machen's death: GBR B 3/9, f. 449v.
[3] By act of 30 Aug 1731, son of Roynon: ibid. f. 301v.
[4] Wiredrawer, disfranchised 28 July 1781 to enable him to give evidence in a cause between the mercers' company and Jas. Hayward, a non-freeman, and readmitted 5 Dec 1783: ibid. 11, ff. 298v., 344; below: ibid. C 9/9, p. 13.

116 1741 Theophilus Hopkins, son of Theophilus, joiner, decd.
Rob. Gregory, son of Wm., tailor
John Merry, son of Thos., cordwainer
Jas. Foords, } sons of Hen., tailor
Hen. Foords, }
John Lovett, son of Jas., barber-surgeon
John Ireland, son of Wm., gent., decd.
Jas. Saunders, son of Thos., tanner
Thos. Swaynes, app. of John Holder, pinmaker, decd.
Thos. Mills, app. of Wm. Stephens, pinmaker, decd.
117 Chas. Wheeler, app. of John Shingler the younger, pinmaker
John Hickman, son of John, cordwainer
Thos. Ashmeade of Charlton Kings, son of Thos., decd., of Cheltenham
John Merrett, son of John, tailor, of Stonehouse
20 Mar Wm. Oakey, son of Wm., cooper, of St. Philip and St. Jacob
John Baker, son of Ric., joiner, decd.
Wm. Gardiner, son of Wm., labourer, decd., of Highnam
Edw. Gardiner, son of Nat., baker, decd., of Berkeley
Edw. Mann, son of John, glover
118 John Baldwin, son of John, cabinet-maker, decd.†
Thos. Harris of Whaddon, son of Giles, decd., of Haresfield
Benj. Welch, } sons of Ric., yeoman, of Badgeworth
John Welch, }
John Stratford, son of John, baker, of Barnwood
Ric. Crowdy, son of Ric., yeoman, of Barton Street
Thos. Underwood, } sons of Thos., butcher, decd., [of] Taynton
Rob. Underwood, }
Wm. Hale, son of Jesse, pinmaker, decd.
119 Edw. Hoskins, app. of John Randall, pargeter
Chas. Bloxam, }
John Junele, } apps. of Jacob Lumbard, shagmaker
John Jennings, }
Jas. Bingley, app. of And. Pegler, saddler, decd.
Thos. Cheeselet, app. of John Holder and Thos. Weaver, pinmakers
11 May Wm. Howlett, clerk, son of Wm., mercer, decd.
15 May Hubert Bower, son of Thos., tanner, decd., of Newent
Jasper Freame, son of Jasper, baker, of Newent
120 18 May Hen. Mason, son of Wal., tanner
Wm. Dunn, son of Wm., tiler
13 May John King, } sons of Sam., labourer
Sam. King, }
Hen. Stephens, son of Nat., esq., decd., [of] Eastington
Hen. Collett, son of Wm., grocer, decd.
John Lander, son of Jas., baker, decd.
Sam. Brotherton, son of Sam., bricklayer, decd.
Dan. Hornidge, son of Thos., bodice-maker, decd.
121 Sam. Mathews, son of John, pinmaker
Ric. Bower, son of Sam., pipemaker, decd.
Edm. Best, son of Sam., gardener, decd.
20 May Nat. Harris, son of Nat., woolcomber, decd.
18 May Wm. Hanman, app. of Ric. Weaver, blacksmith and farrier
20 May Nat. Toomer, app. of Jacob Lumbard, weaver
Thos. Worgan, app. of Chas. Dimmock, decd., and Sam. Burroughs, mercers
21 May Abel Pride, app. of John Shingler the younger, pinmaker

Benj. Simmons, app. of Sam. Ades, cordwainer, of Mitcheldean, formerly of Gloucester
122 Jas. Bennett, app. of John Greemott, cordwainer
Jos. Colesman, app. of Thos. Ades and Rob. Evenis, cordwainers, late of Gloucester
Sam. Underwood, app. of Jos. Cother, cordwainer, decd.
22 May Wm. Cowcher, app. of John Lindsey, pinmaker
John Rudge, app. of John Shatford, joiner
Isaac Broadwell, app. of Wm. Mason, tailor
Thos. Partridge, son of Rob., cordwainer
John Vaughan, son of Thos., glassgrinder, of London
Josiah Ady, son of Edm., baker, decd.
123 21 May Wm. Bamford, son of Wm., gardener, of Westbury
Zachariah Stephens, son of Zachariah, tailor
Nat. Castle, son of Nat., baker, decd.
Geo. Bosley, son of Jas., baker, of Redmarley [D'Abitot, Worcs.]
22 May John Palmer, clerk, son of John, bookseller, decd.
Jos. Chapman, son of Wm., gunsmith, of Hereford
Wm. Barker, son of Thos., baker, of Tirley
Wm. Gardner, son of John, baker, of Sheepscombe
Jasper Lugg, son of Jas[per], combmaker, of Hereford
124 Thos. Skillerne, son of Thos., furrier, of Winchcombe
Steph. Skillerne, son of John, furrier, of Winchcombe
John Smith, son of Hen., saddler, of Mitcheldean
Wm. Hale, son of Ric., sugar-baker, of Dublin, formerly of Gloucester
Chas. Holder, son of John, joiner, decd.
John Newton, son of Thos., ropemaker, of Newent
Lawr. Nott, son of Lawr., glazier, of St. Giles, formerly of St. James, Mdx.
Chas. Watson, son of Chas., fishmonger
John Browne, app. of Thos. Weaver, pinmaker, late of Gloucester
125 Ric. Greville, gent., son of Chas., apothecary, decd., of Bristol
John Ward, son of Thos., pinmaker
Wm. Simon, son of Thos., currier, decd.
Wm. Long, cordwainer, of London, son of Wm., cordwainer
Jos. Maverly, son of Jas., button-maker
Rob. Longden, } sons of Rob., gent., decd.
John Longden, clerk, }
Wm. Pace, son of Wm., grocer, decd.
John Iremonger, son of John, apothecary, decd.
John Oakey, app. of Ant. Workman, butcher
126 Hen. Lovett, son of Jas., barber-surgeon
Ric. Walker, plasterer, of London, son of Ric., carpenter, decd.
Thos. Land, son of Thos., butcher
Ric. Knight, son of Thos., labourer, decd.
Sam. Pitt, son of Rog., carpenter
Wm. Hornidge, son of John, pinmaker, late of Gloucester
Rob. Mayo, son of Rob., baker, decd., of Newent
Ric. Lane, son of John, cordwainer
Dan. Dix, son of Wm., bricklayer
127 Wm. Draper, son of Ric., cordwainer
John Green, son of John, gent., decd.
Wm. Bryan, son of Ric., brazier, decd.
John Crump, son of John, serjeant-at-mace
Benj. Rogers, gent., of Lyon's Inn, London, son of Thos., hatter, of London

1741 Thos. Merry, son of Thos., cordwainer
Hen. Lye, son of Francis, cooper, late of Gloucester
Rowles Scudamore, son of Capel, gent.
Jas. Cowcher, son of Cowcher Shipton, pinmaker
John Birch, cordwainer, of Gloucester, son of John, broadweaver, decd., of Rodborough
128 23 May John Bower, son of Thos., tanner, of Newent
Joshua White, son of John, tanner, of Newent
Thos. Motlow, son of Ant., tailor
John Keel, son of Jas., yeoman, of Newent
Jos. Beal, son of Benj., smith
25 May Gabriel Fownes of Bristol, son of Godfrey, by apprenticeship
Rog. Horseman, baker, of Bristol, son of John, gent., decd.
Somerset Blake of Bristol, son of Thos.†*
Thos. Rogers, son of John, clerk, of Bradford,[1] [Wilts.]
129 Ric. Mathews, son of Thos., pipemaker
Humph. Mathews, son of Thos., of Malmesbury, [Wilts., and] app. of John Shatford, joiner, by apprenticeship
Berkeley Conklin, son of Thos., grocer, late [of] Bristol
Jas. Mann, son of John, skinner, late of Barton Street
Ambrose Wyman, son of Ambrose, baker
Jas. Workman, butcher, son of Jas., butcher, late of Gloucester
Geo. Lawrence of London, app. of Jeremiah Hawkins, peruke-maker
Jas. Collins, excise officer at Abingdon, [Berks.], son of Jas.†*
Wm. Trotman, son of Wm., tailor
130 Dan. Trotman, app. of his father Wm., tailor
Thos. Jeans, feltmaker, of Tewkesbury, son of Thos., feltmaker, late of Gloucester
John Nelmes, tinplate-maker, of London, son of Edm., baker, late of Gloucester
Wm. Stock, carpenter, of Bristol, son of Sam., baker, late of Gloucester
Bright Mathews, smith, of Bristol, son of Edw., blacksmith
John Hale, son of John, barber-surgeon
Jas. Bosly, son of Jas., of Redmarley [D'Abitot, Worcs.]
Wm. Stait, blockmaker, of Bristol, son of Gray, tailor, late of Gloucester
131 Wm. Ireland, glassmaker, of Bristol, son of Geo., glassworker, of St. Philip and St. Jacob
John Child, cordwainer, son of Sam., weaver, of Bristol
Capel Wilse, son of Capel, of Highnam
Job Cowly, son of Job, glazier
Jos. Stephens of Bristol, son of Jos., huckster, late of Gloucester
Wm. Jones, son of Edw., husbandman, of Thornbury
Joshua Brotherton, son of Joshua, horner
Ric. Pope of London, app. of Ric. Engley, bricklayer
Geo. Archer, plumber and glazier, son of Geo., tailor, late of Gloucester
132 Ric. Barnard, yeoman, of London, son of Thos., yeoman, of Hardwicke
Geo. Harrison, bargemaster, of Bewdley, [Worcs.], son of Geo., of Droitwich, [Worcs.]
Ralph Ady, soldier in the Guards, son of Wm., hatmaker, of Stroud
Sampson Hale, son of John, barber-surgeon
Jos. Partridge, haberdasher of small wares, of Bristol, son of Hen., mercer, late of Gloucester

[1] Bradford-on-Avon: *V.C.H. Wilts.* vii. 47.

Jas. Long, carpenter, of London, son of Jas., pinmaker, decd.
Thos. Trustram,
John Trustram, } sons of Thos., yeoman, of Duntisbourne
Rob. Trustram,
133 Thos. Trustram, son of Phil., yeoman, of Duntisbourne
John Cox, barber, son of John, barber, late of Gloucester
Jos. Darke, app. of Thos. Harrison, carpenter
Jos. Mayo of London, son of Rob., yeoman, late of Minsterworth
Thos. Browne, carpenter, son of Jonathan, weaver, of Bristol
Thos. Brimyard, } sons of Hen., shoemaker
Sam. Brimyard,
Jas. Reeve, son of John, bricklayer
Thos. Workman, butcher, son of Jas., butcher
134 Hen. Townsend, cabinet-maker, son of Giles, joiner, of London
Thos. Bryan, son of Ric., brazier
Thos. Bubb, baker, app. of John Pleydell
Ric. Armitage, combmaker, of Worcester, app. of Jas. Reeve, combmaker
John Cox, plumber, of Evesham, [Worcs.], son of Thos., porter
Jos. Whitfield of London, app. of And. Whitfield, barber, late of Gloucester
Wm. Cooke, tailor, son of Giles, cordwainer, of Maisemore
135 Jas. Pace, son of John, cordwainer
Geo. Phillips of Tetbury, app. of Sam. Spencer, cooper
Ric. Washbourne, butcher, son of John, tanner, decd., of Evesham, [Worcs.]
Wm. Fletcher of Barton Street, app. of Ric. Draper, cordwainer
Wm. King, weaver, son of Steph., weaver, of Bristol
John Thynne (*Thynn*) How, esq., son of John, Lord Chedworth†[1]
Ric. Corr, gunsmith, of London, son of Edw., button-maker
Benj. Pearce, carpenter, of Longford, son of John, hatter, decd., of Tewkesbury
136 Jos. Cowles, pipemaker, son of John, skinner, of Bristol
Thos. Pyrke, son of Thos., esq., of Littledean
John Powell Snell, son of John, esq., decd.
Wm. Cooke, son of Wm., barber
Steph. Blizard, butcher, of London, son of [ ], of Chipping Norton, [Oxon.]*
Chas. Weston, gent., son of Chas., esq., of Berkeley
John White, son of John, clerk, decd.
Webb Weston, gent., son of Chas., esq., of Berkeley
137 Wm. Scudamore, son of Capel, gent., late of Gloucester
John Bradshaw, carpenter, of London, son of Wm., carpenter
John Gardiner, pinmaker, son of Dan., pinmaker
Paul Cheeseman of Reading, son of John, cooper, of Highworth, [Wilts.]
Chas. Stanniford, } sons of John, mercer, of Highworth, [Wilts.]
John Stanniford,
Hen. Church, son of Rog., glazier, late of Gloucester
Hen. Hone, son of John, tailor, decd.
138 Hen. Clayton, son of Hen., tailor, of Wormington
Thos. Jelf, son of Hen., baker, of Ruardean
Edw. Mathews, son of Edw., blacksmith, of London

[1] Of Stowell and Cassey Compton, Withington: *Complete Peerage*, iii. 156–7.

1741 Rob. Savory, son of Rob., blacksmith, late of Gloucester
Geo. Ward of the Guards, son of Chas., pinmaker, late of Gloucester
Thos. Ricketts, son of John, decd.
Jos. Hopson, son of Jos., bodice-maker
Luke Skinner, app. of Jos. Pegler, tanner
Wm. Baldwin, tailor, of London, son of John, cabinet-maker, decd.
139 Wm. Ricketts, app. of John Ricketts, carver, late of Gloucester
Thos. Stephens, son of Wm., pinmaker
Jacob Underhill, app. of Thos. Winniate, pinmaker
John Barrett, son of John, late of Gloucester*
John King, house-carpenter, son of Thos., carpenter, of Bristol
Ric. Partridge, baker, of London, app. of Mat. Weaver, baker
Sam. Ball, baker, son of Sam., baker, decd.
Ric. Thurston Stait, swordcutter, of London, son of Ric., painter, decd.
140 Rob. Stephens, son of Francis, hatter
Thos. Gravestock of London, son of John, baker
Wm. Hill of London, app. of Francis Ricketts, pinmaker
Wm. Shaw, } sons of John, blacksmith, of Blakeney
Thos. Shaw, }
Edw. Harewell, maltster, of Tetbury, } sons of Edw., of Hankerton,
Geo. Harewell, } Wilts.
Nat. Gardner, ship's carpenter, of Bristol } sons of Nat., baker, decd.
141 Wal. Gardner of Berkeley, }
Thos. Long of St. Martin le Grand, London, son of Wm., victualler
Peter Fewtrell,* }
Isaac Fewtrell, }
Geo. Fewtrell, } sons of Isaac, of London
Jas. Fewtrell, }
John Stone of Minchinhampton (*Hampton*), son of Thos., joiner, of Tewkesbury
n.d. Thos. Keylock, son of Jasper*
142 25 May John Weller, son of Jos., baker, of Walton Cardiff
Gregory Niccolls of Westerleigh, son of Thos., saddler, of Hucclecote
Thos. Cowles, son of John, skinner, of Bristol
Pyrke Nat. Gibbs, app. of Jas. Brotherton, cordwainer
Mat. Hayford, son of Sam.
Jas. Lander, vintner, of London, son of Jas., baker
Rob. Mathews, pinmaker, of London, son of John, farrier
Wal. Hardwicke[1] of London, app. of Wm. Lander, grocer
143 Thos. Spiller of the Guards, son of John, decd.
Thos. Parker, son of John, feltmaker
Thos. Chestroe, son of John, yeoman, of Cheltenham
Wm. Davis, shoemaker, of Standish, son of John, shoemaker, of Longney
Wm. Lane of Chaceley (*Chavely*), [Worcs.], app. of Thos. Drew, baker, by patrimony
Geo. Ravenhill, son of Thos., labourer
Ric. Rathband, farrier, of Stroud, son of Ric., farrier
Jas. Rogers, son of Jas., bricklayer
Wm. Hatton, app. of Ric. Church, glover
144 Sam. King, } sons of Wm., cooper
Isaac King, }

[1] Occupation given as *grocer and tallow-chandler*.

Jas. Pytt, son of Rog., carpenter
26 May Thos. White, mercer, of Birmingham, son of Thos., glover, of London
Ric. Brimyard, shoemaker, of Birmingham, son of Hen., shoemaker
Thos. Washborn, watchmaker, of London, son of John, clockmaker
Jos. Young of the Guards, son of Giles, tailor
Caleb Lodge, baker, of Bristol, son of Wm., cooper
145 Edw. Smith of London, app. of John Washborne, clockmaker
Thos. Remington, staymaker, of Norwich, son of Dan., mercer
Dan. Winniate, cabinet-maker, of London, son of Ric., pinmaker, decd.
Jeffs Little, husbandman, of Ashleworth, son of Wm., decd.*
Chas. Pheasant, soldier, son of Edw., labourer, decd.
Thos. Overthrow, son of Wm., decd., of Minsterworth
n.d. Jas. Drinkwater, son of Ric., cordwainer, late of Gloucester
146 26 May Thos. Fletcher, son of Thos., cooper
Thos. Holford, app. of Wm. and Elizabeth Ricketts, pinmakers
Thos. Critchly, app. of John Woodward, pinmaker
Sam. Byard, app. of Thos. Fletcher the younger, baker
Wm. Hen. Harris, app. of Hen. Harris, waterman
Edw. Bickerton, broadweaver, son of Ric., glover, decd., of Worcester
Thos. Pritchard, joiner, of Bristol, son of Edw., glazier, decd.
147 Lewis A Dean, gent., of Temple Guiting, app. of Sam. Hendy, mercer, decd.
Hen. Muskett, soldier, son of Thos., labourer, decd.
Thos. Pace, bricklayer, of London, son of Thos., cordwainer
Wm. Stephens, cordwainer, of Callow near Ledbury, [Herefs.], son of Thos., tailor, late of Gloucester
Sam. Bevan, weaver, son of Edw., pinmaker, of Coventry
Chas. Williams, soldier, } sons of John, gardener
John Williams, pinmaker, of London, }
Edw. Parker of Wheatenhurst, app. of Ann Jones, cooper
148 Jas. King, son of Sam., dyer
Jas. Winstone, son of Thos.*
Hen. Nelmes, app. of Francis Brabant, cooper
Jas. Hicks, } apps. of Wm. Ricketts, pinmaker
Wm. Hare, }
John Loxly, app. of John Shingler the elder, pinmaker
Jos. Allen, son of Lawr., coachman, of London
Jonathan Hook, son of Jonathan, joiner
149 Geo. Dean, son of Wm., carpenter, decd.
Thos. Herbert, app. of Jos. Smith, pipemaker
Jas. Parsons, son of John*
Isaac Bassett, app. of John Collett, joiner
John Robins of Cheltenham, app. of John Ricketts, carver
Dan. Bird, son of Dan., of Peterchurch, Herefs.
John Sparks, app. of John Chapman, silkweaver
Rob. Tracy, esq.,†[1] (by gift)
150 Ant. Keck Tracy, esq.,†[2] (by gift)
Thos. Freeman† (of Laverton by gift)
Jas. Wheeler, app. of Geo. Worrale, pinmaker
John Wadly, son of John, butcher

[1] Of Stanway: Glos. R.O., D 2311/T 1; *V.C.H. Glos.* vi. 226.
[2] Ant. Keck of Great Tew, Oxon., brother of Rob. Tracy of Stanway: Glos. R.O., D 2311/T 1; D 4582/1/6; *V.C.H. Oxon.* xi. 231.

Thos. Walford of Dumbleton, app. of Jos. Phipps, cooper, decd.
Thos. Edwards,[1] app. of Ric. Draper, shoemaker
Hen. Hayes, app. of Hen. Weaver and Thos. Hampton, staymakers
151 25 May Dan. Randle, son of John, pargeter
Thos. Chestroe, son of [John], of Cheltenham.* Entered before[2]
20 May Edw. Gregory, distiller, of Bristol by gift[3]
Ric. Cambridge, esq., of Wheatenhurst by gift
25 May Corsley Rogers, merchant, of Bristol by gift
Mic. Becher, esq., of Bristol by gift
Edw. Cooper, merchant, of Bristol by gift
Francis Rogers, merchant, of Bristol by gift
Hen. Franklin, merchant, of Bristol by gift
Wm. Reeve, merchant, of Bristol by gift
Wm. Swymmer, esq., of College Green, Bristol, by gift
Cranfield Becher, merchant, of Bristol by gift
Hen. Casamajor, merchant, of Bristol by gift
Wm. Swymmer, esq., of Marshfield by gift
Hen. Swymmer, merchant, of Bristol by gift
26 May Nigel Kingscote, esq., son of Wm., esq., decd.†[4]
152 16 June Sir John Guise, Bt., son of Sir John, Bt., decd.†[5]
8 Oct Sir Francis Fust, Bt., of Hill by gift[6]
Wm. James,[7] gent., of Soilwell by gift[6]
27 Nov Ric. Peachey, app. of John Playdell, baker[6]
7 Dec Wm. Jeynes, app. of Thos. Bond, baker[6]

Thomas Hayward, esq., mayor 1741–2

1742 14 May Wm. Curtis, app. of Wm. Rogers, apothecary
Thos. Humphris, son of John, butcher, decd.
153 24 May Chas. Hooper, son of Chas., butcher, decd.
21 June John Cother, son of Jos., cordwainer, decd.
2 July Thos. Ashmeade, son of Giles, mercer, decd., of Cheltenham
30 Aug John Wilkins, son of Nic., butcher, of Westbury
2 Oct John Griffitts, yeoman, by gift

Richard Finch, esq., mayor 1742–3

15 Oct John Bevan, app. of Jas. Cooke, baker[8]
23 Oct Hopewell Hayward, gent., of Forthampton by gift
154 1743 17 Jan Ric. Jennings, son of Hen., carpenter, decd.
4 Feb Giles Fowler, app. of Sam. Harris, barber-surgeon
18 Feb Thos. Smith, app. of Mic. Jennings, butcher
11 Mar Jas. Perkins, son of Geo., baker, decd.
30 Mar Ric. Rogers, esq., of Dowdeswell by gift
John Prinn, clerk,[9] of Charlton Kings by gift
18 Apr Jarvis Sayer, app. of Jos. Cother, cordwainer, decd.

[1] Disfranchised 28 July 1781 to enable him to give evidence in a cause concerning the mercers' company and readmitted 5 Dec 1783: GBR B 3/11, ff. 298v., 344; below: ibid. C 9/9, p. 14.
[2] Entry struck through; cf. above: ibid. C 9/8, p. 143.
[3] Entry preceded by heading *Honorary Burgesses Sworn*.
[4] Of Kingscote: Atkyns, *Glos.* 492; *Visit. Glos. 1682–3*, 104.
[5] Of Rendcomb and Elmore: *V.C.H. Glos.* vii. 221–2; *Complete Baronetage*, iii. 219.
[6] Entry belongs to following mayoralty.
[7] Chas. James: GBR B 3/9, f. 464v.
[8] Entry struck through.
[9] Rector of Shipton Oliffe and of Shipton Solers: Hockaday Abs. cccxxxvii.

153		19 Apr	John Stephens, son of Wm., tailor
		23 May	Wm. Prinn, gent., of Charlton Kings by gift
		8 July	Josiah Fitchew, son of Josiah, feltmaker, decd.
		29 July	John South, app. of Thos. Fletcher the younger, baker
		26 Aug	Dan. Remington, clerk,[1] son of Dan., mercer
		30 Sept	Ric. Phelps, son of Jos., grocer, decd.
			Lawrence Crump, esq., mayor 1743–4
		4 Nov	Wm. Mathews, son of Ric., butcher, decd.
156		7 Nov	Geo. Cowcher, son of John, apothecary, decd.[2]
	1744	20 Jan	Jos. Gardiner, son of Ant., baker, decd.
			Rob. Hammond, app. of John Jones, cooper
		10 Feb	Hen. Wilton, son of Hen., pinmaker
		13 Feb	Dan. Greening, son of Dan., butcher
		11 Mar	Ant. Gardiner, app. of Cornelius Gardiner, barber-surgeon
157		2 Apr	Benj. Baylis, son of Edw., woolcomber, decd.
		13 Apr	Thos. Browne, son of Thos., cordwainer[3]
			John Twyning, app. of Thos. Browne, cordwainer
			John Bishop, son of Sam., barber-surgeon, decd.
			Sam. Sanders, son of Thos., tanner, decd.[4]
			John Stephens, son of Wm., pinmaker, decd.
			Sam. Bullocke, son of John, cordwainer
158			Wm. Jelfe, son of John, blacksmith, decd.
			John Alford, app. of Thos. Price, blacksmith
		16 Apr	Sam. Estcott, son of Sam., pinmaker, decd.
		20 Apr	Chas. Festus Fletcher, app. of Rob. Evenis, cordwainer
		23 Apr	Thos. Donn, son of Wm., pargeter
		25 May	Jas. Window, son of Jas., cordwainer
		2 July	Thos. Rich Stocke, son of John, grocer
159			Maur. Smith, son of Maur., saddler, decd., of Dursley
		20 July	Wm. Jenkins, app. of John Cowles, butcher, decd., and Mary Cowdall, widow
		3 Aug	John Hayward, son of Thos., weaver, decd.
		6 Aug	John Kerby, son of Jacob, weaver
		20 Aug	Abel Welladvise, son of Sam., glazier
		28 Sept	John Gulliver, yeoman, of Churchdown by fine[5]
			Jos. Relph, gent.,[†] by gift
160			Wm. Crump, son of John, serjeant-at-mace
			John Blackwell, esq., mayor 1744–5
		15 Oct	Wm. Felton, app. of Ric. Nurse, barber-surgeon, decd.
		22 Oct	Thos. Cole, son of Geo., tailor
		26 Oct	John Maverly, son of Jas., button-maker
		17 Dec	John Engley, son of Arthur, bricklayer
		21 Dec	Sam. Sayer, clerk,[6] son of Sam., upholsterer, decd.
161	1745	7 Jan	Elton Wantner, son of Chas., barber-surgeon, decd.
		25 Feb	Wm. Bird, app. of John Lane, blacksmith and farrier
		15 Mar	Wm. Rodway, app. of Moses Clarke, baker

[1] Rector of St. John the Baptist: ibid. ccxv.
[2] Entry struck through.
[3] Entry struck through.
[4] Entry struck through.
[5] Entry struck through.
[6] Master of Bristol grammar school: *V.C.H. Glos.* ii. 375.

7 May Thos. Winniatt, son of Abraham, weaver, of Stroud
14 June Hen. Hitchman, son of Wm., of St. James, Westminster
17 June Ric. Coxe, app. of Mat. Weaver, baker
28 June Jas. Gurner, app. of Benj. Beale, blacksmith
162 John Mountague, son of John, cordwainer, of Over
30 Aug Wm. Kendall, son of Wm., painter, decd.
Chas. Dimock, son of Chas., mercer, decd.
2 Sept Jas. Sadler, app. of Ric. Spillman, baker

Benjamin Saunders, esq., mayor 1745–6

18 Oct Abel Wantner, saddler and ironmonger, of Barnstaple, Devon, son of Abel, decd.
Wm. Mills, son of Wm., glover
163 Thos. Dew, app. of Thos. Drew and Thos. Bubb, bakers
1746 7 Feb Thos. Bromley, app. of Rob. Hyett, decd., Sam. Bloxom, and Hen. Nelme, coopers
2 May Wm. Welles, son of Jos., baker, decd., of Walton Cardiff
Rob. Wood, app. of Guy Ellis, ironmonger
30 May Ric. Moy, app. of Edw. Bower, currier
2 June Wm. Barrett, son of Hen., cordwainer, of Stroud
23 June Ambrose Wadley, son of John, baker, decd.
164 1 Aug Job Williams, app. of Francis Brabant, cooper
15 Aug John Goodwin, son of Ric., yeoman, decd., of Over
1 Sept Wm. Reeve, app. of Jas. Baker, cordwainer
5 Sept Thos. Barrett, baker, (by fine)[1]
3 Oct Ric. Coleman, gent., by gift
Abraham Clark, vintner, by gift
Sam. Heath,[2] son of John, gent.

165 **Gabriel Harris, esq., mayor 1746–7**

13 Oct Wm. Hale, son of Jos., cordwainer
17 Nov Wm. Tayloe, clothier, of Chalford Bottom by gift
22 Dec Thos. Davis, schoolmaster, of Moreton-in-Marsh by patrimony
1747 5 Jan Jas. Innell, app. of Wm. Mason, tailor
20 Feb Thos. Yate, app. of Dan. Yate, grocer
20 Mar Wm. Dymock, son of Chas., mercer, decd.
1 June Wm. Phelps, app. of Winston Moor, butcher[3]
166 27 Mar Wm. Elmes, son of Thos., gent., decd.
Ric. Payne, son of Thos., gent., decd.
John Elliott, son of Edw., butcher, decd.
18 Apr Ric. Ellis, glazier, of London by gift
1 May Edw. Charlton, apothecary, of Bristol, son of Meshach, feltmaker
4 May Sam. Okey, app. of Ant. Workman and John Oakey, butchers
1 June Wm. Phelps, app. of Winston Moor, butcher[4]
167 John Yeend, app. of Mic. Jennings, butcher
(Lieut.) Jas. Doake† by gift[5]
5 June Jas. Launder, son of Wm., grocer, decd.

[1] Entrant had served only part of an apprenticeship to Ellis Taylor, baker: GBR B 3/10, f. 70v.
[2] Brazier, resigned 9 Mar 1795 to enable him to give evidence in a cause concerning the city's common meadows and readmitted 17 Aug 1795: ibid. 12, ff. 220, 227v.; below: ibid. C 9/9, p. 122.
[3] Entry struck through; cf. below: ibid. C 9/8, p. 166.
[4] Cf. above: ibid. p. 165.
[5] For his presentation to the corporation of French colours captured by his ship, the *Gloucester*: ibid. B 3/10, f. 77v.; cf. below: ibid. C 9/8, p. 169.

19 June John Turner, son of John, glover
Jonathan Hooper, son of Chas., butcher, decd.
John Cooke, son of John, butcher, decd.
Chas. Newton, son of Benj., clerk, decd.
22 June Wm. Humphris, son of John, butcher, decd.
168 21 June Geo. Sexty, app. in turn of Wm. Hayward and Ann Luther, widow, butchers
29 June Chas. Cooke, son of Jas., joiner
Wm. Perkins, son of Sam., pargeter
Geo. King, son of John, bricklayer
Hugh Bishop, son of Geo., barber-surgeon
Steph. Hall, son of John, baker
Wm. Engley, son of Arthur, bricklayer
Wm. Taylor, son of Wm., baker
169 Sam. Spiller, son of John, baker
Jas. Doake[†] by gift[1]
Ric. Wood, son of Jas., mercer
Antioch Stoner, app. of Mat. Weaver, baker
John Hartland, app. of John Clarke, baker
Jas. Sparrow, app. of Giles Robinson, cooper
Jas. Lovett, son of Jas., barber-surgeon
Thos. Braddis, son of Thos., yeoman, of Barton Street
170 Chas. King, son of John, bricklayer
Hen. Dark, son of Ric., gunsmith
2 July Wm. Ashmead, gent., by gift
21 Aug Wm. Webley, son of Wm., yeoman
24 Aug John Hutchins, app. of Giles Robinson, cooper
2 Oct Wm. Bayly, son of Hen., waterman, decd.
Sam. Salcomb, son of Wm., cordwainer, decd.
171 John Cole, son of Geo., tailor
John Dean, son of Wm., carpenter, decd., of Barton Street
Wm. Nelson[†] (by fine)

Michael Bayly, esq., mayor 1747–8

9 Nov Wm. Nest, son of Wm., carpenter
11 Dec Chas. Cole, victualler, by fine
18 Dec Ric. Whitefield, app. of Capel Longden, ironmonger, decd.
22 Dec John Favell,[2] excise officer,[†] by fine
30 Dec Methuselah Jeynes, victualler, (of the Duke of Gloucester) by fine
Chas. Perry, victualler, by fine
172 Ric. Pearce, victualler, by fine[3]
Wm. Rayor, victualler, (of the Boothall) by fine
David Sayse, victualler, by fine
Wm. Houlton, victualler, (of the Black Dog) by fine
Thos. Hooper, victualler, (of the Old Bear) by fine
Thos. Chartres, victualler, (of the Horse and Groom) by fine
Edw. Jones, victualler, by fine
John Greenhalf, victualler, (of the Three Kings) by fine
Thos. Evans, victualler, (of the Green Dragon) by fine
1748 8 Jan Ric. Price, victualler, (of the Fleur de Lis) by fine
Jos. Mason, victualler, (of the Lamb) by fine

[1] Entry struck through; cf. above: ibid. C 9/8, p. 167.
[2] John Flavell: ibid. B 3/10, f. 92.
[3] Entry struck through.

173 Ric. Poulson, victualler, (of the Saracens Head) by fine
Thos. Organ, victualler, (of the Talbot) by fine
John Sparks, victualler, by fine
Wm. Daniel, victualler, by fine
Ric. Felton, victualler, (of the Swan and Falcon) by fine
18 Jan Dan. Jolliman, victualler, (of the Dog, the Quay), by fine
Ric. Ellis, app. of Thos. Price, goldsmith†
5 Feb John Webb, app. of Jas. Swayne, butcher, and his wife Elizabeth†
15 Feb Wm. Tovey, victualler and innholder, (of the Ram) by fine
Jos. Spillman, victualler, (of the Fox) by fine
26 Feb Jos. Perris, son of John, grazier, of Llanthony, formerly of Gloucester
174 16 May Jos. Hawkes,[1] app. of Thos. Browne, cordwainer
8 Sept Thos. Atkinson, innholder, (of the Golden Heart) by fine
Ric. Robins, innholder, (of the Cock) by fine
Geo. Nelson, innholder, (of the New Inn) by fine
Jas. Middleton, victualler, (of the Dog in the Green) by fine
Hen. Harris, victualler, (of the Duke of Gloucester, the Quay), by fine
Jos. Gracebrooke, innholder, (of the Bolt) by fine
15 Sept Edm. Wadley, victualler, (of the Welsh Harp) by fine[2]
Thos. Linnell, victualler, (of the Three Mariners) by fine[3]
John Brooks, victualler, (of the Fleece) by fine
Thos. Stroud, victualler, by fine
175 16 Sept John Kemeys, son of John, tailor
n.d. Benj. Newton, son of Benj., clerk, decd.
n.d. Jos. Baylis, clerk,[4] son of Edw., woolcomber, decd.
n.d. Thos. Dark, son of Ric., gunsmith
29 Sept Wm. Rogers, son of Ric., esq., by gift

William Bell, esq., mayor 1748–9

10 Oct Jas. Colerick,[5] bodice-maker, by fine
14 Oct Wm. Jones,[6] app. of Rob. Evenis, cordwainer
14 Nov Ant. Boulton, app. of John Pleydall, baker
25 Nov Wm. Machin, app. of Ric. Draper, cordwainer
7 Dec Thos. Ridler, victualler, (of the Leather Bottle) by fine[7]
16 Dec Jos. Fletcher, victualler, (of the Cock, the Alvin gate), by fine
176 Ric. Mugg, victualler, (of the Bakers Arms) by fine
Rob. Ladbrooke, victualler, (of the Black Swan) by fine
1749 9 Jan Newton Lewis, carpenter, by fine
14 Jan Thos. Harris, app. of Wm. Wood, cooper
17 Feb Edw. Norman, son of Edw., butcher
20 Feb Wm. Barrett, app. of John Box, pinmaker
8 Apr Mat. Cooke, pargeter, by fine
14 Apr Rob. Gransmore, app. of Ant. Workman, butcher

[1] Resigned 9 Mar 1795 to enable him to give evidence in a cause concerning the city's common meadows and readmitted 17 Aug 1795: GBR B 3/12, ff. 220, 227v.; below: ibid. C 9/9, p. 122.

[2] To pay £10 on taking up the freedom and £10 on using the trade of cordwainer: ibid. B 3/10, f. 109v.

[3] To pay £10 on taking up the freedom and £10 on using the trade of cordwainer: ibid. f. 110.

[4] Curate of Kingswood, Wilts.: Hockaday Abs. cclii.

[5] Disfranchised 28 July 1781 to enable him to give evidence in a cause between the mercers' company and a non-freeman and readmitted 5 Dec 1783: GBR B 3/11, ff. 298v., 344; below: ibid. C 9/9, p. 13.

[6] Disfranchised 28 July 1781 and readmitted 5 Dec 1783: ibid.

[7] Entrant to pay £10 on taking up the freedom and £10 on using the trade of cordwainer: ibid. B 3/10, f. 117.

			John Beale Price, app. of Thos. Bond, baker
		5 May	Wm. Millard, app. of Hester Workman, widow, butcher
177		8 May	Thos. Dix, app. of John Ashmeade, mercer
		2 June	Hen. Curtis, app. of John Turner and Thos. Steele, grocers
		12 June	Sam. Wilson, app. of Jas. Wood, mercer
		15 June	Wm. Crump, son of Lawr., ald.
		23 June	Thos. Clifford, son of John, writing-master
		7 July	Wm. Farren, app. of Winston Moore, butcher
			Wm. Prestbury, son of Edw., baker, late of Gloucester
		4 Sept	Thos. Pembruge, son of Thos., baker, late of Gloucester
178		6 Sept	Wm. Ellis, victualler, (of the New Bear) by fine
		7 Sept	Wm. Beard, victualler, (of the Bull) by fine
		11 Sept	Sam. Salcombe, } sons of Sam., yeoman, late of Powick, Worcs.
			John Salcombe, }

Samuel Farmer, esq., mayor 1749–50

		16 Oct	Sam. Farmer the younger, apothecary, son of John, mercer, decd.
		23 Oct	Thos. Smith, son of Humph., glover
		11 Dec	Mark Everard, son of Jos., mercer
	1750	19 Jan	Thos. Rudge, son of Thos., carpenter, decd.
179		22 Jan	John Ireland, app. of Wm. Cowcher and John Keyse, pinmakers
		30 Mar	Ric. Rayor, son of Geo., barber
		6 Apr	Wm. Goodwin, son of Ric., yeoman, decd., of Over
		4 May	Wadley Way, son of John, butcher
		29 May	Thos. Mee, esq., (of Gloucester)† by gift
			Wm. Smith, app. of Jas. Cooke and Thos. Barrett, bakers
		1 June	Ric. Billings, son of Wm., cordwainer, decd.
		15 June	Joshua Councill, app. of Wm. Rogers, apothecary
		16 July	Thos. Parker, clerk, son of John, tailor
180		10 Aug	Rowland Pytt, son of Rowland, ironmonger
		17 Aug	Geo. Blackwell, app. of Cornelius and Ant. Gardiner, barbers
		27 Aug	Geo. Dowding, son of Geo., carpenter, late of Gloucester
			John Tanner, app. of Ric. Engley, goldsmith[1]
		14 Sept	Jos. Bayse, app. of Thos. Browne, cordwainer
		28 Sept	John Webb, app. of his father Ric., grocer

Lawrence Crump, esq., mayor 1750–1

		18 Oct	Ric. Worrall, son of Sam., ald., decd.
		2 Nov	John May, app. of Jacob Guest, butcher
		5 Dec	Wm. Salcombe, son of Wm., cordwainer
181	1751	25 Jan	Ric. Harris, son of John, coachman
		28 Jan	Ric. Cox, son of John, barber
		1 Feb	Ant. Bond, app. of Chas. Hooper, butcher
		14 Feb	Rob. Stock, son of John, grocer. Misentered[2]
		4 Feb	John Heming, son of Benj., gent.
			Thos. Price, son of Thos., broker
		22 Feb	Thos. Crump, son of John, serjeant-at-mace
		18 Mar	Wm. Alexander, app. of Giles Robinson, cooper
		29 Mar	Ant. Motlow, son of Ant., tailor, decd.
		15 Apr	Geo. Boseley, son of Jas., baker, of Redmarley [D'Abitot], Worcs.
182		22 Apr	Sam. Hayward, son of John, ald.

[1] *Now dead* subsequently added.
[2] The correct place for this entry, after that for Thos. Price, is indicated.

26 Apr Thos. Hartland, son of John, cordwainer
2 Sept Wm. Smith, app. of Thos. Fletcher, baker
27 Sept John Hillman Gransmore, app. of Rob. Sadler, baker

Richard Roberts, esq., mayor 1751–2

7 Oct Benj. Hare, app. of John Lindsey, pinmaker
25 Oct Jas. Nest, son of Wm., joiner
11 Nov Wm. Man, son of Wm., baker, of Tirley
Wm. Axon, son of Wm., cutler
183 22 Nov Hen. Dunn, son of Wm., pargeter, decd.
Thos. Badger, son of Nat., pargeter
Gustavus Swayne, son of John, pargeter
Jos. Reeve, son of Jos., stonecutter
Rob. Freeman, son of Rob., joiner
John Wilton, Jas. Wilton, } sons of John, pinmaker
John Fletcher, son of Thos., cooper, decd.
Mat. Man,[1] son of John, skinner
Thos. Bretherton, son of Thos., pargeter, decd.
Wm. Simpson, son of Rob., pinmaker, decd.
John Woodward, son of Ric., pinmaker, decd.
Jas. Phillips, son of Geo., pinmaker, decd.
Wm. Ricketts, son of Wm., pinmaker, decd.
John Phillips, son of Thos., wiredrawer
Ric. Webb, son of Jonathan, butcher, decd.
Thos. Harris, son of Wm., decd.*
Sam. Adey, son of Edm., tailor, decd.
Wm. Rich Stock, son of John, grocer, decd.
Wm. Randle of Elmore, son of Josiah, decd.†
Edw. Hopkins, son of John, carpenter, decd.
John Rudge, son of Thos., carpenter, decd.
John Bullock, son of John, cordwainer
Ralph Ady, son of Ralph, butcher, decd.
Jas. Badger, son of Nat., pargeter
184 Thos. Webley, son of Jos., huckster
John Cole, son of Benj., baker
Wm. Welsh, Thos. Welsh, Simon Welsh, } sons of Matthias, yeoman, of Bisley
Ralph Fletcher, app. of Jos. Gardiner, baker
Jas. Beard, app. of Jos. Beard, weaver
Jos. Richards, app. of Wm. Stephens, weaver
John Swetman, app. of Thos. Weaver, pinmaker, decd.
9 Dec Nat. Mallett James, app. of Thos. Bonnor, grocer
13 Dec Thos. Jolliman, app. of Abraham Smith and John Jones, coopers, both decd.
30 Dec Sam. Taylor, son of Ric., barber-surgeon
1752 10 Jan John Fley, yeoman,[2] by fine
Ric. Swayne, son of Jas., butcher
John Nelson (of the New Inn)† by fine
185 7 Feb Wm. Elliott, app. of Ant. Gardiner and Geo. Blackwell, barber-surgeons

[1] *now a dragoon in Sir John Ligonier's regiment* subsequently added.
[2] ? servant of Gloucester cathedral: Fosbrooke, *Glouc.* 143.

10 Feb Wm. Brabant, son of Wm., cooper, decd.
Jos. Mann, app. of Elizabeth Weaver, pinmaker
21 Feb Wm. Bullock of Coleford, son of Wm., yeoman, of Longhope
King Edward Huzzley† by fine[1]
16 Mar Thos. Branch, app. of Thos. Branch, tinman
13 Apr Wm. Bower, son of Thos., tanner, decd., of Newent
8 May Wm. Keys, son of John, pinmaker, decd.
18 May Geo. Ward, son of John, whitesmith, of London
25 May Wm. Instocke, app. of Geo. Washborne, clockmaker
10 July Benj. Hickman, son of John, cordwainer
186 31 July Rob. Ellis, son of John, ironmonger
Wm. Lane, son of Wm., yeoman
Ric. Webley, son of Sam., bellfounder
21 Aug Jos. Wood,[2] app. of Thos. Wadley, baker
14 Sept Geo. Augustus Selwyn,[3] esq., son of John, esq.†
15 Sept Sam. Lysons, esq.,[4] son of Dan., esq., of Hempsted

James Herbert, esq., mayor 1752–3

25 Oct Chas. Kemys, son of John, tailor
18 Dec Geo. Rayer, son of Geo., barber
28 Dec Sam. Worrall, son of Sam., late ald.
187 1753 29 Jan Thos. Roberts, son of Thos., gunsmith, decd.
23 Feb John Heath, son of John, sword bearer to this corporation
20 Apr Rob. Sextie, son of Wm., wine merchant, of Worcester
13 May Jos. Goodwin, son of Ric., yeoman, decd., of Over
John Sextie, son of Wm., wine merchant, of Worcester
28 May Sacheverell Lander, son of Jas., baker, decd.
4 June John Rayer, son of Geo., barber
8 June John Taylor, app. of Wm. Axon, cutler
25 June Wal. Rowles, son of Wm., yeoman, of Longney
20 July John Sole, app. of Thos. Merrett, cordwainer
Hen. Wintle, son of Hen., cordwainer, decd.
188 23 July John Arnold, son of Thos., innholder, decd.
Chas. Bishop, clerk, son of Sam., barber, late of Gloucester
6 Aug John Puxon, son of John, weaver, of Barton Street
20 Aug Ric. Chandler, (woolstapler, of Gloucester)† by gift
31 Aug[5] Nat. Bond, son of Wm., bookbinder
Thos. Woodward, son of John, pinmaker
Ellis Tayler, son of Ellis, baker
Guy Ellis, son of Guy, grocer, decd.
24 Aug Thos. Leech (of the Red Lion)† by fine
3 Sept Wm. Vyner, son of Wm., grocer
7 Sept John Spillman, son of Ric.†
10 Sept Thos. Wheeler, son of Peter, gent.†
n.d. Sam. Wooley, M.A., prebendary of Gloucester [cathedral], by gift[6]
189 10 Sept John Adams, son of John, pinmaker, late of Gloucester

[1] Entry, which has been interlined and belongs to following mayoralty, is for King Edward Ursell, stonecutter, by act of 26 Oct 1752: GBR B 3/10, f. 173; F 4/10, p. 273.
[2] Resigned 9 Mar 1795 to enable him to give evidence in a cause concerning the city's common meadows and readmitted 17 Aug 1795: ibid. 12, ff. 220, 227v.; below: C 9/9, p. 122.
[3] Owner of the Matson estate and M.P. for the city 1754–80: *V.C.H. Glos.* iv. 442; Williams, *Parl. Hist. of Glos.* 211.
[4] Clerk: *Alumni Oxon. 1715–1886*, iii. 887.
[5] Date struck through.
[6] By act of 25 Sept 1753: GBR B 3/10, f. 182v.

Benj. Collett, Jos. Collett, Waterworth Collett, } sons of Benj., esq., late of Tewkesbury
Rob. Barrett, son of Hen., cordwainer, of Stroud
29 Aug Jas. Lamb, esq., of Fairford by gift
Thos. Bush, esq., of Cirencester by gift
14 Sept John Jeffrys, son of John, pinmaker
Thos. Skey, son of Thos., baker, decd.
24 Sept Wm. Rudge, app. of Wm. Coles and Hester Freeman, smiths[†]
John Price, son of John, cordwainer, decd.
1 Oct John Penoyre[†1] by fine

190 **Thomas Hill, esq., mayor 1753–4**

5 Oct Moses Randall, son of John, pargeter
12 Oct Edw. Elton, app. of Peter Haynes, grocer
Wm. Price, app. of Wm. Sparks, cordwainer
19 Oct Thos. Glendall, son of Sampson, glover
2 Nov Nest Havard, son of John, apothecary, of Tewkesbury
12 Nov Wm. Baylis, son of Sam., broadweaver, of Painswick
Hen. Baker, son of John, joiner, decd.
Thos. Dix, son of Wm., porter, decd.
Benj. Cooke, son of Wm., butcher, decd.
191 Thos. Stephens, son of Thos., tailor, decd.
16 Nov Wal. Harris, John Harris, } sons of Wal., baker, of Walford, Herefs.
Sam. Field, son of Sam.[†2]
19 Nov Jos. Cleaveley, son of Hen., tailor, decd.
26 Nov Jas. Estcutt,[3] son of John, pinmaker
Thos. Webb, son of Nic., mercer
1 Dec Thos. Bamford, son of Thos., yeoman, of Upton Bishop, Herefs.
Jas. Butter, Wm. Butter, } sons of Chas., yeoman, of Brampton Abbotts, Herefs.
3 Dec Wm. Wellavize, son of Sam., glazier
192 Wm. Harris, Sam. Harris, } sons of Wm., pinmaker, decd.
Jonathan Badger, son of Jonathan, labourer
Rob. Savory, son of Wm., blacksmith, decd.
John Remington, son of Dan., serjeant-at-mace, decd.
Thos. Garner, son of Dan., labourer
Jos. Fuller, son of Hen., pargeter, decd.
Sam. Ricketts, son of John, pinmaker, decd.
Rob. Gorton, son of Wm., decd.
John Richards, son of John, cordwainer
Wm. Powell, son of Wm., farrier, late of Gloucester
193 Benj. Holdford, app. of Thos. Holford, pinmaker
Jos. Bright, son of Wm. Wood, cooper
John Woodward, app. of John Keys, pinmaker, decd.
Josiah Cantrill, app. of John Lindsey, decd., and John Holder, pinmakers
7 Dec Thos. Mathews, son of Wm., baker, of Littledean

[1] The city's water bailiff: ibid. f. 116.
[2] Entry struck through and *now dead* added.
[3] Resigned 9 Mar 1795 to enable him to give evidence in a cause concerning the city's common meadow and readmitted 17 Aug 1795: GBR B 3/12, ff. 219v., 227v.; below: C 9/9, p. 121.

			Wm. Layton, [son][1] of Ant., weaver
			Ric. Wheeler, son of Ric., cordwainer, decd.
			Thos. Corr, son of John, weaver
			Thos. Bromley, son of Thos., cordwainer
			John Spillman, son of John, tiler
			Thos. Lock, son of Thos., baker, late of Gloucester
			Sam. Jeffs, son of John, blacksmith
			John Jeffs, son of Wm., baker, late of Gloucester
194			Ric. Middleton, app. of John Jennings, blacksmith
			Ric. Bullock, son of John, fisherman, decd.
			Jas. Best, son of Sam., gardener
			Edw. Addis, son of Edw., tailor, decd.
			Ric. Humphris, son of Thos., currier, decd.
			Hen. Harding, son of Ric.[2]
		10 Dec	Thos. Bamford, John Bamford, } sons of Wm., yeoman, of Westbury
			Edw. Quarrington, son of Dan., maltster
			Wm. Randle, son of Wm., weaver, of Tewkesbury
195			John Motlow, son of Miles, labourer
			Wm. Bloxholm, son of Jos., weaver†
			Wm. Price, son of Wm., cordwainer
		17 Dec	Wm. Puxon, son of Wm., tailor
		24 Dec	Ric. Steele, son of John, carpenter, of Littledean
	1754	7 Jan	Wm. Winniatt, Abraham Winniatt, Jasper Winniatt, } sons of Abraham, weaver, of Stroud
			Steph. White, son of Steph., mason, of Painswick
			Wm. Motlow, Jos. Motlow, } sons of Jos., cordwainer, decd., of Dursley
			John Smith, son of John, feltmaker, decd.
196		14 Jan	Jas. Smith, son of John, feltmaker, decd.
			John Philpot, app. of Thos. Bond, baker
		18 Jan	Thos. Underwood, son of Ric., yeoman, of Taynton
		21 Jan	Wm. Puxon, son of John, weaver, of Barton Street
			Nat. Elliot, son of Wm., cordwainer, decd., of Stroud
			Ant. Wilkins alias Wilton, app. of John Keyse, decd., and Wm. Clarke, pinmakers
			John Rodway, son of Giles, gent., decd.
			Giles Smart, app. of Ant. Barrett and John Lindsey, pinmakers, decd.
197		28 Jan	John Hawkins, Hen. Hawkins, } sons of John, cordwainer, decd.
			Chas. Morris, son of Jos., innholder
			Steph. White, John White, } sons of John, mason, of Painswick
			Hen. Freeman, son of Rob., joiner
		1 Feb	Sam. Head, app. of John Shatford, joiner, decd.
		4 Feb	Nat. Merry, son of Thos., cordwainer
			Benj. Stock, app. of John Hippesley, barber-surgeon
		8 Feb	Thos. Venn, son of Giles, yeoman, of Norton
198		4 Mar	Ralph Critchley, son of Ralph, joiner
		8 Mar	Wm. Sextie, son of Wm., merchant, of Worcester
		22 Mar	Ebenezer Fownes, son of Benj., wine cooper, of Bristol

[1] Cf. ibid. F 4/10, p. 317.

[2] Entry struck through and *now dead* added.

John Brock, son of John, skinner, decd.
29 Mar Chas. Cox, son of John, barber, decd.
1 Apr John Gilden, Wm. Gilden, } sons of Hen., yeoman, of Hanley, Worcs.
6 Apr Thos. Steele, Sam. Steele, } sons of John, carpenter, of Littledean
8 Apr Thos. Maverly, app. of Sam. Maverly, tailor
Wm. Window, app. of Wm. Haynes and Wm. Crump, joiners
Rob. Ball, esq.,† by gift
199 Chas. Aylway, son [of ?John],[1] mercer, of Cheltenham
Jos. Jeffs, son of John, whitesmith, decd.
Hen. Stone, son of Hen., cordwainer
Ric. White, son of Nat., cordwainer, of Newent
Jas. Brotherton, son of Thos., plasterer
John Davis, app. of Thos. Ward, pinmaker
Jas. Bourn, app. of Sarah Price, widow, pinmaker
Giles Horsington, son of Thos., bodice-maker
Phil. Pinchbeck, son of Phil., wiredrawer
12 Apr Ric. Crump, son of Lawr., ald.
Edw. Weaver, son of Thos., pinmaker, decd.
Wm. Jeffs, Jos. Jeffs, } sons of Jos., cordwainer, decd.
200 Nat. Washborn, son of Geo., watchmaker
Wm. Gwinnett Hornage, app. of Ric. Spillman, baker
Ric. Rogers, son of Wm., apothecary
John Cooke, app. of Wm. Rogers, [apothecary]
John Wingate, son of John, cordwainer
John King, son of Sam., labourer, decd.
Ric. Webb, Thos. Webb, Jas. Webb, } sons of Ric., grocer
13 Apr John Scudamore, esq.,† by gift
John Wade, esq., (of Gloucester)† by gift
Thos. Smith, son of Thos., gent., decd.
John Bicknell, son of John, tailor
201 John Davis, son of Rob., grocer
John Porter, son of Thos., apothecary
Rob. Green, son of Rob., weaver, decd.
John Holder, son of Thos., gent., of Frampton on Severn
Ric. Perry, son of Wm., tailor
Jas. Bromley, son of Thos., cordwainer
Jas. Wilkins, son of Nic., yeoman, decd., of Westbury
John Hyett, app. of Francis Brabant and Job Williams, coopers
Thos. Stroud, app. of John Box, pinmaker
Wm. Warren, app. of Phil. Reading, cooper
John Gardiner, son of John, yeoman, decd., of Sheepscombe
Ric. White, son of Ric., carpenter, decd., of Painswick
202 Ralph Lewis, son of Thos., gardener
Wm. Bubb, son of Hen., innholder
Ric. Webb, son of Ric., shopkeeper, of Newnham
15 Apr Sandys Longden, son of Rob., glover
John Fords, Wm. Fords, } sons of John, tailor, of Newent

[1] Cf. above: GBR C 9/7, p. 442.

Wm. Holder, son of Wm., gent., of Frampton on Severn
Hen. Priest, son of John, of Ledbury, Herefs.*
Thos. Browne, son of Thos., cordwainer, of Worcester
John Barker, son of Isaac, yeoman, of Upleaden
John Boseley, son of Jas., yeoman, of Redmarley [D'Abitot], Worcs.
203 Wm. Harrison the younger, gent., of Newnham by gift
Geo. Fownes, son of Godfrey, colourman, of Bristol
Giles Long, son of Giles, cordwainer, of Bristol
Jas. Cleavely, son of Hen., ropemaker, of Bristol
Wm. Harris, son of Wm., cabinet-maker, of Bristol
Ric. Dowell, } sons of Ric., cordwainer, of Bristol
John Dowell, }
Thos. Nest, son of Wm., joiner
Thos. Taynton, son of Thos., pewterer, of Bristol
Wm. Taynton, son of Wm., wine cooper, of Bristol
John Child, } sons of Francis, of Bristol*
Sam. Child, }
Wal. Taynton, son of Nat., of Bristol*
204 Sam. Wood, son of John, cordwainer, of Bristol
Thos. Palmer, son of Thos., cordwainer†
Wm. Williams, son of Wm., dyer†
Thos. Hall, son of Benj., skinner, of the same city
John Engley, son of John, tailor, decd.
Thos. Child, son of John, yeoman, of Chalford
Jas. Mills, son of Wm., glover
Thos. Holder, } sons of Wm., cordwainer, of Dursley
Josiah Holder, }
Thos. Gibbs, son of John, blacksmith, of Dursley
Wm. Perks, } sons of Wm., yeoman, of Little Washbourne, [Worcs.][1]
Sam. Perks, }
205 Sam. Bond, son of Ant., yeoman, of Eldersfield, Worcs.
29 Apr John Fream, son of John, butcher, of Newent
6 May Chas. Pleydell, son of John, baker
14 June John Harris, app. of Wm. Draper, cordwainer
1 July Sam. Morris, app. of Edw. Bower, tanner, and his widow Elizabeth
29 July Thos. Window, app. of Ant. Gardiner and Geo. Blackwell, barbers
6 Sept Wm. Whitaker, merchant, of London by gift
13 Sept Whetham Hill, clerk,†[2] by gift
20 Sept Wm. Butt, victualler, by fine
John Innell, app. of Wm. Mason, tailor
Wm. Stephens, gent., son of Zachariah, tailor, decd.

206 **John Blackwell, esq., mayor 1754–5**

20 Dec Wm. Brook, son of Nat., skinner†
1755 3 Feb Rob. Arnold, son of Rob., pinmaker†
14 Feb John Pace, son of Thos., cordwainer†
28 Feb Geo. Holder, app. of John Ready, apothecary
7 Mar Geo. Harrison, app. of Ric. Perrin the younger, butcher
18 Apr Wm. Bush, app. of Wm. Weaver, saddler
14 July Geo. Jas. Williams, esq., of London by gift
John Harcourt, esq., of Dan y Parc (*Daney Park*), Brec., by gift
8 Aug Ishod (*Izod*) Rayer, son of Geo., barber†

[1] County given as *Glos.*; cf. *Kelly's Dir. Glos.* (1870), 666; *V.C.H. Glos.* vi. 232.
[2] Curate of Newnham and Littledean by the corporation's gift: GBR B 3/9, f. 433.

Benj. Thomas, son of Jas., maltster[†]
5 Sept Dan. Ellis, son of Guy, decd.[†]

207 **Thomas Hayward, esq., mayor 1755–6**

24 Oct Ric. Dix,[1] son of Ric., bricklayer
7 Nov Sam. Roberts, app. of Jas. Wintle, brushmaker, by fine
Thos. Harmar, (app. of John Harmer), distiller, by fine
1 Dec Wm. Vail, victualler, by fine
1756 19 Jan Wm. Harris, son of Thos., peruke-maker, late of Gloucester
9 Feb Ric. Coopey, son of Ric., yeoman, of Churchdown
Sam. Gwinnett, son of Sam., clerk
8 Mar Thos. Goodwin, son of Ric., yeoman, decd., of Over
John Jones, app. of Giles Robinson, cooper
12 Mar John Clarke, feltmonger,[2] by fine
208 Jas. Crowdey, son of Jas., carpenter
Wm. Crowdey, son of Wm., yeoman
John Mountford, app. of Jacob Guest, butcher
15 Mar Wm. Ward, son of Thos., pinmaker
Thos. Swaine, son of John, pargeter
Jas. Crowdey, son of Wm., yeoman
Edw. Jones, son of Edw., yeoman
Wm. Commins, app. of Thos. Bond, baker
22 Mar Sam. Overthrow, son of Ric., smith, decd.
Wm. Evans, son of Thos., victualler, of Upton St. Leonards
209 John Rogers, son of Ric., butcher, decd.
29 Mar Chas. Randle, son of Wm., weaver, of Tewkesbury
John Boulton, app. of John Pleydell, baker
9 Apr John Rogers, son of John, upholsterer, decd., of Hereford
Dan. Nest, son of Wm., joiner, decd.
3 May John Davis, son of John, pinmaker
25 June Ric. Bond, son of Wm., bookbinder
2 July John Buckingham, app. of Thos. Farley, cutler
John Cooke, son of John, grocer, decd.
2 Aug John Smith, son of John, barber, decd.
210 31 Aug Wm. Rogers,[3] son of Ric., esq., of Dowdeswell (by gift)
15 Sept Wm. Selwyn, esq., of London (by gift)
16 Sept Arthur Cook, innkeeper, by fine
John Matthews, innkeeper, by fine
17 Sept John Hannington, gent., (by gift)
John Pitt,[4] gent., (by gift)
29 Oct Wm. Singleton, merchant, of London (by gift)[5]

211 **Benjamin Saunders, esq., mayor 1756–7**

1757 24 Jan Chris. Cooke, son of John, joiner
4 Feb Ric. Price the younger, app. of Thos. Fletcher, baker, decd.
7 Feb Nic. Barnes, son of Edw., barber, decd.
Thos. Gale, app. of Ric. Wood, mercer

[1] In 1795 he resigned on 9 Mar and, after being readmitted, on 15 July to enable him to give evidence in a cause concerning the city's common meadows. Readmitted the second time 17 Aug 1795: ibid. 12, ff. 219v., 222v., 226, 227v.; below: ibid. C 9/9, pp. 119, 122.

[2] Fellmonger, of Barton Street St. Michael, Gloucester: ibid. B 3/10, f. 213v.

[3] John Rogers: ibid. f. 221v.

[4] M.P. for Gloucester 1789–1805: Williams, *Parl. Hist. of Glos.* 211–2.

[5] Entry belongs to following mayoralty.

25 Feb Thos. Rea, app. of Thos. Drew, baker
6 June John Bradford, Phil. Bradford, sons of John, mercer, of Newent
10 June Mic. Jennings, son of Jas., skinner, of Ross, Herefs.
Wm. Faucks, son of Thos., butcher
13 June Jos. Pew, app. of Winston Moore, butcher
212 27 June Ric. Merrett, app. of Ric. Weaver
1 July Ant. Workman, son of Ant., butcher
5 Aug Rob. Smith, app. of Wm. Jones, grocer, and Hen. Grevile, mercer
9 Aug Thos. Bullock the younger, son of John, cordwainer
Edw. Smith, son of Jos., barber, decd.
23 Sept Hen. Barrett, son of Hen., victualler, of Stroud
26 Sept Wm. Merrett, son of Thos., cordwainer

213 **Gabriel Harris, esq., mayor 1757–8**

7 Oct Thos. Draper, maltster, by fine
Abraham Saunders, wine merchant, (by gift)[1]
Thos. Humphries, innholder, of Frogmill (by gift)
14 Oct Rob. Wyndowe, app. of Geo. Cooke, grocer
17 Oct John Gardiner, son of And., tailor
24 Oct Button Gwinnett,[2] son of Sam., clerk
2 Dec Thos. Kendall, son of Wm., painter, decd.
1758 2 Jan John Roberts, esq., Ric. Roberts, gent., sons of Ric., esq., ald., (by gift)[3]
6 Jan Ric. Wintle, innholder, by fine
16 Jan John Purton, son of Ric., cordwainer
214 13 Feb John Guise, esq., son of Hen., esq., decd.
20 Feb Hen. Miles, son of Hen., baker, of Brimpsfield
10 Apr Edw. Clutterbuck, app. of Chas. Hooper, butcher
Jos. Spillman, app. of Geo. Blackwell, barber-surgeon
5 May Lyndon Chas. Browning, app. of Mat. Weaver, baker
8 May Jos. Lewis, son of Thos. the younger, gardener
Thos. Tayloe the younger, clothier, of Chalford (by gift)
22 May John Coopey, son of Ric., yeoman, of Churchdown
26 June Giles Greenaway, innholder, by fine
3 July Wm. Cother the younger, app. of Ric. Cope and Thos. Bubb, bakers
17 July Wm. Wood, son of Thos., yeoman, decd., of Barton Street
215 8 Aug John Thomas, son of Jas., maltster
11 Sept Jos. Goodwin, son of Francis, butcher, of Upton St. Leonards
18 Sept John Ridgley, innholder, by fine
29 Sept Jas. Williams, innholder, by fine
Josiah Tucker, D.D., dean of Gloucester [cathedral], (by gift)
Jos. Ellis, clothier, of Ebley (by gift)

George Augustus Selwyn, esq., mayor 1758–9

30 Oct John Machen, app. of Wm. Machen, cordwainer
6 Nov Thos. Bannister,[4] innholder, by fine
216 8 Dec Nic. Browne, app. of Jas. Sparrow, cooper

[1] By act of 30 Sept 1757 on recommendation of Benj. Saunders, mayor: GBR B 3/10, f. 234v.
[2] Signatory of the 1776 Declaration of American Independence: *Dict. American Biog.* viii. 65–6.
[3] By act of 6 July 1752 on recommendation of their father Ric., mayor: GBR B 3/10, f. 167.
[4] Resigned 9 Mar 1795 to enable him to give evidence in a cause concerning the city's common meadows and readmitted 17 Aug 1795: ibid. 12, ff. 220v., 227v.; below: ibid. C 9/9, p. 122.

1759 23 Mar Ric. Tombs, app. of Ric. Weaver, blacksmith
6 Apr Ric. Green, son of Ric., gent., of Churcham
30 Apr Thos. Faucks, son of Thos., butcher, decd.
25 July John Rosse, app. of John Hardwicke, tailor
10 Sept Jos. Paulling Taylor, son of Ric., tobacconist
17 Sept John Lea, son of Thos., yeoman, of Leigh (*the Lye*)
21 Sept Geo. Cowles, son of Geo., haulier
Wm. Lane, son of Wm., gent., late of Mitcheldean
217 24 Sept Ric. Frankis, Thos. Frankis, } sons of Ric., yeoman, of Upton St. Leonards
Wm. Haviland, innholder, by fine

Joseph Cheston, esq., mayor 1759–60

15 Oct Geo. Moore, son of Geo., butcher
Thos. Watts, app. of John Webb, butcher
13 Dec Brig.-Gen. Geo. Townsend, commander of H.M. forces at the taking of Quebec,[†1] (by gift)
1760 25 Jan Ric. Child, son of Thos., carpenter, decd., of Hempsted
11 Feb Jos. Bennett, app. of Kirkham Weaver, collar-maker
218 22 Feb John Barnes, son of Edw., barber, decd.
17 Mar Chas. Wilton, Hen. Wilton,[2] } sons of Chas., pinmaker
4 Apr Jas. Puxon, son of John, weaver, of Barton Street
5 May Thos. Saunders, app. of Hen. Curtis and Wm. Hayward, grocers
9 June Jas. Lewis, son of Thos., gardener
n.d. Jos. Ellis, clothier, of Ebley (by gift). Entered last year[3]
23 June John Beale, son of John, gent., of Worcester
27 June Chas. Wyndham,[4] esq., son of Thos., esq., decd., of Clearwell
219 Maynard Colchester, esq., Ric. Colchester, esq., } sons of Maynard, esq., late of the Wilderness, Abenhall (*Abinghall*)
Roynon Jones, esq., son of Wm., esq., late of Nass
30 June Ric. Ward, son of Thos., pinmaker
Francis Hamblin, son of Francis, barber
18 July Ric. Baker, son of Benj., cordwainer
5 Sept Wm. Clark, innholder, (by fine)
18 Aug Thos. Birt, haberdasher, of London, son of John, gent., decd., of Leominster, Herefs.
220 22 Aug Hen. Davis, son of John, pinmaker
Thos. Adey, son of Thos., grocer, late of Gloucester
1 Sept Wm. Webley, son of Jos., huckster
5 Sept Thos. Crump, son of [Lawr.],[5] ald.
22 Sept Thos. Bonnor, son of Thos., grocer
3 Oct Ric. Browne Cheston, son of Jos., esq., mayor
22 July John Simmons[†] by fine
Wm. Gardiner[†] by fine
26 Sept Wm. Higgins[†] by fine
Thos. Baker the younger, gent., of Larport, Herefs., by gift

1 Geo. Townshend of Raynham, Norf.: *Complete Peerage*, xii (1), 808–10.
2 Disfranchised 28 July 1781 to enable him to give evidence in a cause between the mercers' company and a non-freeman and readmitted 5 Dec 1783: GBR B 3/11, ff. 298v., 344; below: ibid. C 9/9, p. 13.
3 Cf. above: ibid. C9/8, p. 215.
4 Later called Chas. Edwin: Rudge, *Hist. of Glos.* ii. 103.
5 Cf. above: GBR C 9/7, p. 478; 8, p. 177.

221			**Richard Webb, esq., mayor 1760–1**
		31 Oct	Jos. Webb, son of Ric., esq., mayor
		3 Nov	Jas. Kearsey, app. of Jas. Kingman, wiredrawer
		24 Nov	Hen. Wintle, son of Jas., brushmaker
			Edw. Barnes, son of Edw., barber
			Jos. Bloxam, son of Jos., sergeweaver
			John Powell, son of Thos., pinmaker
			Hen. Bradley, son of Hen., butcher
			Phoenix Badger, son of Jonathan, labourer
			Jos. Elliotts, son of Edw., carpenter
			Thos. Gardiner, app. of Hester Workman, widow, butcher
		1 Dec	Jas. Rogers, son of Wm., apothecary
222		11 Dec	Sam. Blackwell, esq., of Williamstrip[1] (by gift)
	1761	22 Jan	Benj. Heming,[2] son of Benj., gaoler
			Thos. Wintle,[3] son of Jas., brushmaker
		26 Jan	Wm. Clark, son of Wm., pinmaker
		6 Feb	Benj. Wood, app. of Jos. Holder, tailor
			Jas. Dowell, app. of Wm. Draper, cordwainer
			Jos. Mason, app. of Chas. Hooper, butcher
			Sam. Dutton, app. of Chas. Wilton, pinmaker
			Jas. Lewis, app. of Wm. Jones, cordwainer
223			Jos. Powell, app. of Benj. Baker, cordwainer
		16 Feb	Rob. Simpson, son of Rob., pinmaker, decd.
			Ric. Powell, son of Thos., pinmaker, decd.
			Chas. Holder, son of John, pinmaker, decd.
			Wm. Wood, son of Wm., cooper
			Thos. Stratford, son of John, barber, decd.
			John Wheatstone, son of John, cordwainer, decd.
			John Mann, son of Thos., porter
			Jas. Gunn, son of Jas., cordwainer
			Wm. Smith, } sons of Chas., dyer, decd.
224			Gerard Smith, }
			John Powell, } sons of Wm., farrier, decd.
			Thos. Powell, }
			Jeremiah Clarke, son of Wm., pinmaker
			John Glendall, son of Sampson, glover, decd.
			Nic. Webb, son of Nic., mercer
			Thos. Price, } sons of Wm., cordwainer
			John Price, }
			Thos. Perry, son of Wm., tailor
			Humph. Clarke, son of Wm., pinmaker
225			Dan. Drake, son of Hen., pinmaker
			Wm. Bright, son of John, joiner
			Jonah Brotherton, son of Thos., plasterer, decd.
			Thos. Garn, son of John, cordwainer
			John Gaze, son of Thos., carpenter
			Chas. Merrett, son of Thos., cordwainer
			Ric. Maverley, son of Sam., tailor
			Dan. Bloxsome, son of Sam., cooper
			Wm. Bower, son of Wm., labourer, decd.

[1] Of Painswick: ibid. B 3/10, f. 261v.
[2] Later clerk: *Alumni Oxon. 1715–1886*, ii. 643.
[3] Clerk: ibid. iv. 1591; Fosbrooke, *Glouc.* 215.

1761 Thos. Dicks alias Dix, son of Ric., bricklayer
226 John Bishop, son of Wm., cordwainer
John Simpson, son of Rob., pinmaker, late of Gloucester
Thos. Simpson, app. of Ric. Stephens and Dan. Palling, bakers
Sam. Baskerville, app. of Thos. Chandler, grocer
Wm. Lander, app. of Wm. Cowcher, pinmaker
John Watts, app. of John Cheeseman, tailor
20 Feb Nat. Reeve, son of Jos., stonecutter
Abraham Smith, son of Thos., cooper, decd.
John Clark, son of Moses, baker, decd.
Thos. Pace, son of Thos., cordwainer
Jas. Adey, son of Edm., tailor, decd.
227 Geo. Nott, son of Geo., cooper, decd.
Jas. Reeve, son of Jas., combmaker, decd.
Wm. Wingate, son of John, cordwainer
Jas. Garn, son of Wm., weaver
Giles Viner Cooke, son of John, joiner
Wm. Hamblin, app. of John Hipsley, barber-surgeon
23 Feb Wm. Box, son of John, pinmaker
27 Feb John Moore, son of Chas., saddler, late of Gloucester
Hen. Collett, son of Hen., barber, late of Gloucester
Chas. Aycrygg,[1] son of Benj., apothecary, decd., of Upton upon Severn, Worcs.
John Hinton, app. of John Jennings, whitesmith
228 John Frankis, son of Ric., yeoman, of Upton St. Leonards
Jos. Pyrton, son of Ric., cordwainer
John Hamblin, son of Francis*
2 Mar Thos. Engley, son of Ric., goldsmith, decd.
Jas. Randall, son of Jas., pargeter
Thos. Sparks, son of Thos., pargeter, late of Gloucester
Geo. Washbourne, son of Geo., watchmaker
Sam. Bower, son of Thos., weaver, decd.
Thos. Venn, son of Zachariah, labourer
John Southall, app. of Thos. Branch, tinplate-worker
6 Mar Hen. Dymock, son of Chas., mercer, decd.
229 Benj. Webb, clerk, son of Ric., esq., mayor
John Barton, son of Ric., plumber, decd.
Ric. Crowdy, son of Wm., labourer, of Wotton
Sam. Gooding, son of Ric., yeoman, decd., of Linton
9 Mar John Darke, son of John, innholder, decd.
Ric. Clayton, son of Hen., tailor, late of Wormington, Herefs.[2]
14 Mar John Chaunler Ready, esq., } sons of Alex. Colston, formerly called
Edw. Colston Ready, esq., } Alex Ready†[3]
John Pegler, clerk, son of And., saddler, decd.
Wm. Gyse, esq., son of Sir John, Bt., of Rendcomb
Thos. Roberts, son of Thos., clothier, of Lightpill, Painswick
230 Wm. Cossley, son of Ric., goldsmith, decd.
John Parsons, son of John, esq., decd., of Kemerton
20 Mar Edw. Brotherton, son of Jas., cordwainer, decd.
John Chester, son of Jos., mercer
John Hampton, son of Wm., glazier, of Woodchester

[1] Also spelt *Aycrigg*.
[2] ? Wormington, Glos., or Wormbridge, Herefs.
[3] Of Filkins, Oxon.: Burke, *Land. Gent.* (1846), i. 247.

Nestor Nest, son of Wm., joiner, decd.
Bernard Cooke, son of John, excise officer, late of Bristol
Job Boseley, son of Jas., baker, late of Redmarley [D'Abitot], Worcs.
Geo. Mutlow, son of Miles, labourer, decd.
Thos. Porter, son of Thos., apothecary
231 Wm. Bright, Thos. Bright, } sons of Thos., barber
Chas. Powell Snell, son of Powell, esq., of Guiting[1]
Wm. Rogers, son of John, upholder, decd.
21 Mar Dan. Lea, son of Thos., yeoman, of Leigh
Sam. Overthrow, son of Edw., yeoman, of Highnam
Wm. Rowles, son of John, yeoman, of Longney
Ric. Price, son of Thos., bookseller
Wm. Bradley, son of Sam., tailor, decd.
Thos. Savory, son of Thos., labourer, decd.
Josiah Salcomb,[2] son of Wm., cordwainer
232 John Colborne,* Sam. Colborne, Benj. Colborne, } sons of Jos., apothecary, of [Stroud],[3] Glos.
Wm. Hayward Roberts, clerk,[4] son of Ric., esq., decd.
Thos. Merrett, son of Hen., baker, of Mitcheldean
Wm. Morse, son of Jackman, clerk, of Awre
Benj. Roberts, son of Wm., carpenter, decd.
23 Mar John Quarrington, son of John, ironmonger
Sergeant Webb, son of Thos., brazier, of Hereford
Ric. Barton, son of Ric., plumber, decd.
233 Thos. Long, app. of Ric. Moye, currier
Thos. Wadley, app. of Josiah Fitchew, barber
Edw. Bower, son of Edw., currier
John Bower, son of Thos., tanner, of Newent
Wm. Barton, son of Ric., plumber, decd.
Sam. Rogers, son of Wm., apothecary
Edw. Bloxsome, son of Sam., cooper
Edw. Gardiner, app. of Jacob Lumbard, weaver
John Johnsons, son of Sam., yeoman, of Newent
Wm. Harris, son of Wal., yeoman, of Walford, Herefs.
234 John Drinkwater, son of Ric., cordwainer, decd.
Hen. Heane, Wm. Heane, } sons of Hen., coalminer, of Ruardean
Ric. Young, Rob. Young, } sons of Ric., butcher, of Westbury
John Moore, clerk,[5] son of Thos., gent.
Thos. Cheeseman, son of John, cooper, decd., of Highworth, Wilts.
Geo. Cooke, son of Wm., butcher
Ric. Harris, son of Wal., yeoman, of Walford, Herefs.
Chas. Tomlins, son of John, pinmaker, decd.
235 1761 Sam. Guilding, son of Hen., yeoman, of Strensham, Worcs.

[1] Guiting Power: Rudder, *Glos.* 464.
[2] Woolcomber, resigned 9 Mar 1795 to enable him to give evidence in a cause concerning the city's common meadows and readmitted 17 Aug 1795: GBR B 3/12, ff. 220v., 227v., below: ibid. C 9/9, p. 122.
[3] Cf. below: ibid. C 9/8, p. 265.
[4] Assistant master of Eton College, Bucks.: *Alumni Cantab. 1752–1900*, v. 320; *D.N.B.*
[5] Archbishop of Canterbury 1783–1805: *Alumni Oxon. 1715–1886*, iii. 975.

1761 John Phelps, son of Benj., tailor, decd., of Gotherington, Bishop's Cleeve
Thos. White, son of Edw., shearman, decd., of Painswick
Wm. Venn, son of Zachariah, labourer, of Norton
Wm. Holder, } sons of Jos., tailor
Rob. Holder, }
John Lake, son of John, farrier, late of Hartpury
Chas. Butter, son of Chas., blacksmith, of Breinton (*Branton*), Herefs.
Geo. Harrison, app. of Jacob Lumbard, weaver
Ric. Taynton, son of Nat., flaxdresser, of Ross, Herefs.
236 Geo. Smyth, esq., son of Geo., esq., decd., of North Nibley
John Higgins, } sons of John, gardener, of Abergavenny, Mon.
Nic. Higgins, }
Ric. Lane, }
Thos. Lane, } sons of Thos., labourer, of Kempsford
Wm. Lane, }
Thos. Gyde, app. of Jas. Sparrow, cooper, decd.
Aaron Smith, son of Aaron, cooper, late of Slimbridge
Jos. Mitchell, son of Jos., pargeter
Ric. Perkes, son of Wm., labourer, of Little Washbourne, [Worcs.][1]
24 Mar Jos. Reeve, son of Francis, stonecutter, late of Staunton
237 Chas. Battsford, } sons of John, barber, decd., of Winchcombe
John Battsford, }
Dan. Caple, son of Wm., gent., of Painswick
Steph. Swayne, son of Steph., pargeter, decd.
Shadrach Charlton, son of Meshach, feltmonger, decd.
Thos. Poulton, son of Thos., ironmonger, decd.
Hen. Woolves, son of [ ], sailmaker, decd., of Bristol*
John Ferebee, son of John, tailor, of Uley
Lawr. Nott, son of Jas., woolcomber
Chas. Ferebee, }
Dan. Ferebee, } sons of John, tailor, of Uley
238 Jos. Ferebee, }
Wm. Woodward, app. of Jacob Kirby, weaver
Sam. Commeline, gent., son of Jas., linen-draper, decd., of Bristol
Theophilus Morris, son of Jos., victualler
Ric. Crump, son of Thos., pinmaker, decd.
John Lodge, son of Wm., distiller, decd., of London, formerly of Gloucester
Wm. White, son of Ric., carpenter, decd., of Painswick
Caleb Garraway, son of John, gent., of Worcester
Wm. Clark, son of Moses, baker, decd.
John Rogers, son of John, clerk, decd., of Bradford,[2] Wilts.
Paul Porter, son of John, grocer
239 John Jelfe, son of Hen., carpenter, decd., of Ruardean
John Randall, son of John, mason, decd.
John Pettat, clerk, son of Thos., gent., of Stonehouse
Thos. Ferebee, son of John, tailor, of Uley
Thos. White, son of John, clerk, decd., of Newnham
Wm. Smith, son of Hen., saddler,[3] of Ross, Herefs.

[1] County given as *Glos.*
[2] Bradford-on-Avon: *V.C.H. Wilts.* vii. 47.
[3] *should be cordwainer* subsequently added.

John Butter, son of Chas., blacksmith, of Brampton Abbotts, Herefs.
Thos. Niccolls, app. of Edw. Bennett and Wm. Curtis, apothecaries, both decd.
Hen. Baldwin, son of Rob., apothecary, of Faringdon, Berks.
Ric. Baldwin, son of Ric., bookseller, of London
John Coopey, son of Wm., cooper, decd., of Churcham
240 Sam. Phillimore, son of John, gent., of Cam
John Clark, son of Wm., pinmaker
Dan. Freeman, son of Benj., blacksmith, decd.
Thos. Hall, son of John, saddler, decd., of Ross., Herefs.
Francis Gregory, son of Francis, hatter, of Birmingham
Thos. Laurence, son of Wm., gent., decd., of Newbury, Berks.
25 Mar Chas. Jasper Selwyn, clerk,[1] son of Hen., esq., decd.
Sam. Holder, son of Thos., of Frampton on Severn
Wm. Hall, son of Benj., skinner, decd., of Thornbury
Thos. Dunn, son of Geo., sergeweaver, decd., of Bristol
241 Thos. Blanch, son of Thos., heelmaker, of Tewkesbury
Thos. Webb, son of Ric., esq., mayor
Hen. Howe, esq., } sons of John, Lord Chedworth, [decd.][†2]
Wm. Howe, esq., }
Geo. Hanbury-Williams, esq.,[3] son of John Hanbury, esq.[†4]
Rob. Benson, son of Rob., pargeter
Theophilus Bridges, son of Giles, decd., of Upton St. Leonards
Wm. Freame, son of John, butcher, of Newent
Wm. Whitehead, son of Chas., glazier, of Barnsley
Thos. Collerick, son of Thos., labourer, of Tewkesbury
Wm. Trustram, son of Thos., yeoman, of Duntisbourne Abbots
242 Brian Brampton, son of Thos., blacksmith, decd., of Cirencester
John Box, son of Steph., saddletree-maker, of London
Thos. Preece, son of John, barber, of Ledbury, Herefs.
Dan. Brocke, son of Nat., skinner, decd.
Thos. Pettat, son of Thos., gent., of King's Stanley
Peter Hawker, clerk,[5] son of Sam., esq., decd., of Rodborough
Wm. Matthews, son of Wm., baker, of Newnham
Jos. Perkes, son of Wm., yeoman, of [Little] Washbourne, [Worcs.][6]
Wm. Milton, son of Wm., yeoman, of Cheltenham
Thos. Bryan, son of Thos., gent., of Bassaleg, Mon.
243 Rob. Yanworth, app. of Ric. Hayle, tanner
John Steel, son of Sam., surgeon, of Coleford
Edw. Holtham, son of Wm., grocer
Ric. Crowdy, son of Jas., carpenter, of Wotton near Gloucester
Geo. Lander, son of Geo., mercer, of Painswick
Chas. Beard, app. of Jos. Beard, weaver
Wm. Greville, son of Edw., yeoman, of Charlton Kings
John Young, son of Ric., butcher, decd., of Westbury

[1] Assistant curate, later vicar, of Blockley, Worcs.: H.E.M. Icely, *Blockley Through Twelve Centuries* (Kineton, 1974), 89–91, 106–7; *State of Bishopric of Worcester 1782–1808*, ed. M. Ransome (Worcs. Hist. Soc. N.S. vi), 69.
[2] Of Stowell and Cassey Compton, Withington: *Complete Peerage*, iii. 156–7.
[3] Of Coldbrook Park, Abergavenny, Mon.: Burke, *Land. Gent.* (1846), ii. 1598.
[4] Decd., of Pontypool, Mon.: ibid. 1597; cf. above: GBR C 9/8, p. 67.
[5] Rector of Woodchester: Hockaday Abs. ccccxv.
[6] County given as *Glos.*; cf. above: GBR C 9/8, pp. 204, 236.

1761 Treadway Nash,[1] D.D., son of Ric., esq.†[2]
Sam. Cugley, son of Thos., cardmaker, of Stroud
244 John Roberts, son of Jas., labourer, of Ruardean
Jas. Nott,[3] son of Jas., woolcomber
Thos. Bossom, son of Thos., barber, of Mitcheldean
Thos. Freame, son of John, butcher, of Newent
Wm. Hanks, son of Geo., hatter, decd.
Cartwright Maddox, app. of Thos. Wadley, baker
Thos. Roberts, son of Thos., cordwainer, of Mitcheldean
John Perks, son of Wm., labourer, of [Little] Washbourne, [Worcs.][4]
Wm. Lane, son of Ric., labourer, late of Norton
John Birch, [son of ?John],[5] carpenter, decd., of Leigh
245 Jas. Howe, son of John, Lord Chedworth, [decd.]†[6]
Jas. Gardiner, son of And., tailor, decd.
Jas. Smart, son of Wm., cordwainer, decd.
Jas. Pryor, son of Jas., cordwainer, decd., of Bristol
John Smith, son of Thos., cooper, decd.
Anselm Woones alias Wools, } sons of Rob., fisherman, late of
Rob. Woones alias Wools, } Minsterworth
Thos. Bishop Child, son of Thos., carpenter, decd., of Hempsted
Jas. Jennings, son of Jas., skinner, decd., of Ross, Herefs.
Jonathan Hobbs, son of Thos., carpenter
246 Wm. Washbourne, son of Geo., clockmaker
Chas. Lindsey, son of John, pinmaker, decd.
Sam. Jones, son of Thos., breeches-maker, decd.
Wm. Dicks, son of Wm., bricklayer
Thos. Ashmeade, son of Wm., mercer and chandler, of Alcester, Warws.
Jos. Causon, app. of Sam. Harris, barber
John Dower, app. of Jos. Holder, tailor
John Golder, app. of Thos. Barrett, Wm. Smith, and Jos. Wood, bakers
Ric. Weaver, son of Ric., tailor, of London
John Hall, son of John, baker
247 John Keylock, son of Jasper, cordwainer
Wm. Pace, son of John, pinmaker
Wm. Hall, son of John, baker
John Ward, son of Jas., bricklayer
Sam. Smith, son of Thos., baker, of Framilode
Thos. Skillern, son of John, tailor, of London
Thos. Browne, app. of Wm. Jeynes and John Pleydell, bakers
John Gunn, son of Wm., tailor
Steph. Phillips, clerk,† by gift
26 Mar Sam. Maverley,[7] son of Sam., tailor

[1] Later of Bevere, Claines, Worcs., historian of Worcestershire: *Alumni Oxon. 1715–1886*, iii. 1008; Nash, *Worcs.* i. 205.
[2] Of Kempsey, Worcs.: cf. Nash, *Worcs.* ii. 21; *Alumni Oxon. 1715–1886*, iii. 1008, s.v. Nash, Treadway.
[3] Yeoman, disfranchised 28 July 1781 to enable him to give evidence in a cause between the mercers' company and a non-freeman and readmitted 5 Dec 1783: GBR B 3/11, ff. 298v., 344; below: ibid. C 9/9, p. 13.
[4] County given as *Glos.*; cf. above: ibid. C 9/8, pp. 204, 236.
[5] Cf. above: ibid. C 9/8, p. 93; F 4/11, p. 96.
[6] Of Stowell and Cassey Compton, Withington: *Complete Peerage*, iii. 156–7.
[7] Disfranchised 28 July 1781 to enable him to give evidence in a cause between the mercers' company and Jas. Hayward, a non-freeman: GBR B 3/11, ff. 298v., 344.

248 Wm. Rudge, app. of Rob. Simpson, pinmaker
Jos. Skillern, son of Jos., salesman
Jas. Cole, app. of John Keyse, pinmaker, decd.
Harry Jennings, app. of Francis Tyler and Ric. Barton, plumbers
Wm. Heming, son of Hen., clothier, decd.
Hale Lodge, son of Wm., tailor, decd.
Thos. Fitchew, } sons of Josiah, hatter, decd.
Jas. Fitchew, }
Jas. Broadways alias Braddis, }
Thos. Broadways alias Braddis, } sons of Thos., weaver, decd.
249 Sam. Broadways alias Braddis, }
Thos. Pearce, son of Nat., cutler, decd., of London
Thos. Price, son of Lawr., carrier, late of Gloucester
Ric. Bennett, app. of John Shatford, joiner, decd.
Benj. Randle, son of Benj., weaver, decd.
Sam. White, son of Thos., carpenter, of St. Briavels
Wm. Mason, son of John, tailor
John Cheeseman, } sons of John, of Highworth, Wilts.
Thos. Cheeseman, }
John Mason, son of John, tailor
John Bright, son of Thos., barber
250 Wm. Longdon, son of Rob., gent., decd.
Thos. Jones, son of Jos., glover, decd.
Wm. Bond, son of John, cordwainer
John Holder,[1] son of Thos., pinmaker
Edw. Barrett, son of John, labourer, decd.
Thos. Hall, son of John, baker
Ric. White, } sons of Ric., cordwainer, decd.
Sam. White, }
Cornelius Little, son of Wm., yeoman, of Ashleworth
John Fewtrell, son of Ric., butcher
251 Abraham Smith, son of Abraham, cooper, decd.
John Young, son of Jas., pinmaker, decd.
John Hellyard, son of John, farrier, decd., of London
Hen. Barrett, son of Wm., pinmaker, decd.
Josiah Hathaway, }
John Hathaway, } sons of Ebenezer, joiner, late of Beckenham, Kent
Ebenezer Hathaway, }
Giles Long, son of Benj., mariner, decd.
Jas. Ford, son of John, tailor, decd., of Newent
Ric. Barrett, son of Hen., innholder, of Stroud
Nat. Taynton, son of Nat., of Ross, Herefs.
252 Sam. Bower, son of John, pipemaker, decd.
Wm. Workman, son of Ant., butcher
27 Mar Rob. Downes Moore, } sons of Chas., saddler, decd.
Chas. Moore, }
Chas. Cowcher, }
John Cowcher, } sons of Wm, plasterer, of London
Geo. Cowcher, }
Wm. Church, son of Rog., tailor, decd., of London
Chas. Church, son of Rog., glazier, decd.
Wm. Drinkwater, son of Wm., cordwainer, decd.
253 Solomon Brotherton, son of Francis, bricklayer

[1] Disfranchised 28 July 1781 and readmitted 5 Dec 1783: ibid.; below: ibid. C 9/9, p. 13.

			Wm. Holder, son of John, cordwainer
			John Hampton, son of Peter, pinmaker, decd., of London
			Wm. Barrett, son of Wm., pinmaker, decd.
			Thos. Wolford, son of Thos., basket-maker, decd.
			Thos. Kemble, esq.,† by gift[1]
		10 Apr	Wm. Hathaway, son of John, baker, decd.
			Wm. Clark, son of John, wiredrawer, decd.
		13 Apr	Thos. Barrett, son of Ant., pinmaker, of London, formerly of Gloucester
		23 Nov	Rob. Derry, innholder, by fine[2]
254		28 Aug	Wm. Moore, app. of Jas. Wintle, brushmaker, by fine[3]
		14 Sept	Wm. Murcutt, joiner, by fine
		2 Oct	Wm. Middleton, maltster, by gift
			Thos. Lewis, son of Thos., gardener
			John Hoskins, son of Edw., pargeter

John Baylis, esq., mayor 1761–2

	1762	7 May	Wm. Buchanan, app. of Dan. Yates, grocer
			Thos. Rudge, app. of Moses Randle, vintner
		9 July	Thos. Young, app. of Jas. Lovett the younger, barber
		10 Sept	Wm. Park, son of Paul and app. of Rob. Arnold and Thos. Branch the younger, tinmen, by apprenticeship
255		17 Sept	Thos. Moore, son of John, yeoman, late of Hardwicke
		27 Sept	Wm. Wells, son of Ant., tailor, decd., of Twyning
			Wm. Jeanes, innholder, by fine
			Wm. Williams, innholder,[4] by fine
		1 Oct	Mary Hopkins, victualler, by fine

Edward Baylis, esq., mayor 1762–3

		22 Oct	Benj. Hyett, son of Nic., esq.
			John Probyn, esq., by gift
	1763	17 Jan	Thos. Bird, victualler,[5] by fine
		11 Apr	John Window, son of Hen., pinmaker
		10 June	John Arch, app. of Thos. Bond, baker
		23 June	Jos. Wathen, clothier, of Thrupp, Stroud, by gift

256 **Samuel Farmer, esq., mayor 1763–4**

		29 Sept	Edw. Linnell, (app. of Thos. Swayne), hatmaker, by fine[6]
		14 Oct	Wm. Stephens, son of Thos., pinmaker
		22 Aug	Wm. Browning, innholder, by fine. Omitted[7]
		4 Nov	Sam. Manning, wagoner,[8] (by gift)
		25 Nov	Price Cleaveley, son of John, tailor, late of Gloucester
		2 Dec	Alex. Colston,[9] son of Alex. Colston, formerly called Alex. Ready†
		16 Dec	Wm. Perris, son of Thos., butcher

[1] Of Tewkesbury, by act of 25 Sept 1753 when sheriff of Gloucestershire: ibid. B 3/10, f. 183; Glos. R.O., D 2957/302.16, 152.

[2] Of London: GBR B 3/11, f. 13v.; entry belongs to following mayoralty.

[3] By fine of 5*s*: ibid. f. 8.

[4] Drawer of the Golden Heart inn: ibid. f. 25.

[5] Porter: ibid. f. 31v.

[6] By fine of 5*s*: ibid. f. 41v.; entry belongs to preceding mayoralty.

[7] i.e. in preceding mayoralty.

[8] Carrier: GBR B 3/11, f. 42v.

[9] Later clerk: *Alumni Oxon. 1715–1886*, i. 282; cf. Hockaday Abs. ccxlii.

	1764	10 Feb	Benj. Burroughs, app. of Sam. Burroughs, linen-draper
		30 Mar	Ric. Clements, app. of John Davis, pinmaker
257		14 May	Newton Braban, app. of John Box, pinmaker
		6 July	John Perkins, app. of John Ward, pinmaker
		16 July	John Dudley, son of Thos., butcher, decd.
		23 July	Geo. Savage, esq., son of Thos., clerk, decd.
		20 Aug	John Adey, son of Thos., grocer, late of Gloucester
		31 Aug	Rob. Fitzharding Kingscote, esq., son of Wm., esq., decd., [of] Kingscote
		1 Oct	Marshall Rowles, yeoman, by fine

Thomas Branch, esq., mayor 1764–5

		7 Dec	Jas. Wintle, son of Jas., gent., decd.
258	1765	11 Jan	Jos. Grasing, app. of Winston Moore, butcher
		21 Jan	Wm. Cowcher, son of Wm., pinmaker
			Jos. Quarrington, son of John, ironmonger
			Wm. Hinton, app. of Wm. Cowcher, pinmaker
			Francis Mayo, app. of Edw. Elton, grocer
		8 Feb	John Hill, app. of Thos. Lee, tailor
		4 Mar	Hen. Holder, son of Jos., tailor, decd.
		15 Mar	Thos. Mutlow, son of Thos., tailor
		1 Apr	Chas. Cole the younger, app. of Rob. Smith, mercer
		19 Apr	John Fendall, esq., of Bampton (*Bampton on the Bush*), Oxon., by gift
		1 June	Rob. Ellis, clothier, of Paganhill, Stroud, by gift
259		22 Apr	Jos. Coopey, son of Ric., yeoman, of Churchdown
		24 May	Wm. Wheatstone, son of John, cordwainer, decd.
		26 July	John Adey, app. of Thos. Ward, pinmaker
		26 Aug	Rob. Faucks, son of Thos., butcher, late of Gloucester
		20 Sept	Edw. Quarrington, son of John, ironmonger
			Benj. Spillman, son of Ric., baker
		27 Sept	Ric. Jeffes, son of Jos., cordwainer, late of Gloucester
			John Price by fine
			Wm. Ward by fine
			Thos. Trickey by fine
		28 Sept	Ric. Hill the elder, gent., of Dymock by gift
260			Miles Astman the elder, gent., of Newent by gift

George Augustus Selwyn, esq., mayor 1765–6

		14 Oct	Thos. Crowdy, son of Wm., husbandman, of Wotton [near Gloucester][1]
		29 Nov	Jas. Hyatt, innholder, of Tewkesbury by fine
		13 Dec	Phil. Jones by fine
		23 Dec	Steph. Skinner, son of Wm., yeoman, decd., of Newent
		30 Dec	Thos. Cox, son of Thos., porter, decd.
			Rob. Cowcher, app. of Wm. Axon, cutler, decd.
261	1766	18 Apr	Thos. Hill the younger, app. of Wm. Farren, butcher
			Wm. Phelps, son of Benj., tailor, late of Gotherington, Bishop's Cleeve
		21 Apr	Thos. Spire, app. of Thos. Ward, pinmaker
		26 May	Rob. Wathen, } apps. of Ralph Critchley, pinmaker
			Wm. Wathen, }
		10 June	Jas. Birt, son of John, barber, decd., of Leominster, Herefs.

[1] *the hamlet of Wotton.*

16 June Thos. Dunn, app. of Ric. Bond, bookseller
28 July Wm. Freame, son of John, feltmaker
8 Aug Thos. Stock, app. of Ric. Swayne, butcher
11 Aug Benj. Elliotts, son of Edw., carpenter
18 Aug Dan. Bishop, app. of Thos. Drew, baker
262 20 Aug Elisha Washbourn, son of Geo., clockmaker
29 Aug Ric. Jones the younger, app. of Wm. Price, cordwainer
5 Sept Sam. Jennings, Mic. Jennings, } sons of Sam., butcher, decd.
8 Sept Wm. Ireland, son of John, cordwainer, decd.
Hen. Draper Lye, son of Hen., victualler
Thos. Bevan, son of John, baker, decd.
26 Sept Rob. Spillman, son of Ric., baker
Thos. Okey of Barton Street by fine
Thos. Pitcher by fine
John Spire by fine
263 2 Oct Thos. Weaver, son of Thos., pinmaker, late of Gloucester
3 Oct John Bush, woolstapler, by gift
Wm. Kendall, by fine

Joseph Cheston, esq., mayor 1766–7

3 Nov Wm. Baldwin, son of Wm., tailor, of Gloucester, formerly of London
14 Nov John Yarnold, son of Arthur, innholder, of Ledbury, Herefs.
24 Nov Jos. Lewis, tiler and plasterer, son of Ric., pinmaker
1 Dec John Welch, yeoman, of Boddington, son of Benj., yeoman, of Badgeworth
5 Dec Hopewell Hayward, gent., son of Hopewell, gent., decd., of Forthampton
264 22 Dec Wm. Welch, cordwainer, of Hucclecote, Churchdown, son of Wm., cordwainer, decd., of Badgeworth
1767 2 Feb Hen. Frankis, yeoman, of Quarhouse, Painswick,[1] Benj. Frankis, yeoman, of Quarhouse, Painswick, } sons of Ric., yeoman, decd., of Upton St. Leonards
23 Feb Wm. Bonnewell, app. of Hen. Nelme, cooper
2 Mar Ric. Lane, pinmaker, son of Ric., sheriffs' officer, of Littleworth [near Gloucester][2]
Rob. Soloway, app. of Wm. Cowcher, pinmaker
6 Mar Elias Jeffes, farrier, of All Hallows, London, son of Jos., cordwainer, late of Gloucester
23 Mar Jas. Cooke, pinmaker, son of Josiah, innholder, of Long Ashton, Som.
21 Apr John Drake, pinmaker, of Bristol, son of Hen., pinmaker
25 Apr Lieut. John Barnes, R.A., son of Edw., gent., decd.
265 8 May Wm. Watts, carpenter, son of John, brazier, decd.
11 May Ric. Bonnor, weaver, son of Thos., grocer, decd.
18 May Francis Ursell, app. of Wm. Powell, plumber and glazier
5 June Ric. Hawker, app. of Wm. Ward, pinmaker
15 June Rob. Gregory, brassfounder, of London, son of Rob., corkcutter, late of Gloucester
22 June Thos. Gibbs of Blenheim, Oxon., formerly of Gloucester, app. of Thos. Window, Thos. Parker, and Elton Wantner, barbers and peruke-makers

[1] ? Quarhouse, Stroud: *P.N. Glos.* (E.P.N.S.), i. 141.
[2] *the hamlet of Littleworth.*

20 June Thos. Yeats, esq., of Hampton Road, Minchinhampton,[1] by gift
3 July Rob. Morrison of London, app. of Jas. Wintle, brushmaker, decd.
20 July Thos. Colborne, gent., of London, son of Jos., apothecary, of Stroud
31 Aug John Holtham, victualler, by fine
266 14 Sept Abraham Rudhall, mercer, son of Abel, bellfounder, decd.
18 Sept Wm. Baylis, son of Benj., woolstapler
Thos. Woore, [son of ?John],[2] feltmaker, decd., of Monmouth
Jas. Broughton, app. of Wm. Webley and Thos. Pembruge, barbers
21 Sept Wm. Coopey, yeoman, son of Wm., cooper, decd., of Churcham
25 Sept Jacob Rudhall, gent., son of Jacob, haberdasher of hats, decd., of Bristol

Richard Webb, esq., mayor 1767–8

3 Oct Wm. Stephenson, gent., of Bristol by gift
9 Oct Hen. Cole, wireworker, son of Wm., coalmeter, of Cannon Street, London
267 13 Nov John Webb,[3] esq., of Cowley, son of Nic., mercer
4 Dec Sam. Wintle, skinner, of Upton upon Severn, Worcs., son of Jas., gent., decd.
1768 11 Jan Geo. Crump, surgeon and apothecary, of Lichfield, Staffs., son of Hen., victualler
15 Jan Chas. Taylor, tinman, son of Ellis, baker, decd.
Ric. Chandler, app. of his father Ric., woolstapler
18 Jan Thos. Cole, clothier, son of Thos., pinmaker, of Bristol
8 Feb Wm. Deane, joiner and carpenter, son of Geo., joiner and carpenter, late of Gloucester
15 Feb Sam. Mason, app. of Ric. Weaver, blacksmith
4 Mar John Merrett, coalminer, of Midsomer Norton, Som., son of Hen., baker, decd., of Bristol
268 9 Mar John Perks, son of John, corkcutter, decd.
John Skinner Stock, son of Thos. Rich Stock, grocer
John Colchester, son of Maynard, esq., decd., of Westbury[4]
Merrot (*Merrett*) Stephens, son of Ric., baker, of Ebley, formerly of Gloucester
John Mills, son of Thos., tiler and plasterer, decd.
John Pitt, app. of Nic. Webb, mercer
John Woore, son of John, hatter, of Monmouth
Francis Reeve, son of Jos., stonecutter
Hen. Hale, app. of Chas. Hooper, butcher
Wm. Stephens, son of Wm., pinmaker
269 Thos. Bower, son of Edw., tanner, decd.
John Baker, son of John, joiner, decd.
Sam. Hicks, son of Jas., pinmaker
Wm. Gardiner, son of Wm., labourer, of Barton Street
Seth Haines, son of John, barber, decd.
Thos. Smith, } sons of Thos., cooper, decd.
Rob. Smith, }
John Drinkwater, son of Jas., cordwainer, decd.

[1] Clothier, of Nailsworth: GBR B 3/11, f. 71.
[2] Cf. above and below: ibid. C 9/8, pp. 67, 268.
[3] M.P. for Gloucester 1780–95: Williams, *Parl. Hist. of Glos.* 211.
[4] Westbury-on-Severn: *V.C.H. Glos.* x. 87.

1768 Sam. Millard, son of Wm., gardener
Wm. Bradley, Ric. Bradley, sons of Hen., butcher
270 Thos. Jackson, son of Dan., labourer
Thos. Stephens, son of Thos., innholder
Thos. Yates, app. of Wm. Harris, barber
Geo. Phillipps, son of Geo., pinmaker
Thos. Gunn, son of Jas., cordwainer, of St. Margaret's Hospital near Gloucester
Geo. Bower, son of Thos., weaver, decd.
Jas. Browne, app. of Jos. Holder and Abel Wellavize, tailors
Thos. Jelfe, son of Thos., pinmaker
Ric. Welch, son of Wm., cordwainer, decd., of Badgeworth
Jos. Cother, son of John, cordwainer
John Jennings, app. of Thos., Swayne, hatter and feltmaker
271 Wm. Knight, son of Thos., pinmaker
John Cheesman, Wm. Cheesman, sons of John, tailor
John Maverley, son of Sam., tailor
Geo. Chapman, son of Jos., blacksmith, of Kempley
Wm. Drake, son of Hen., pinmaker
Ric. Poulson, app. of Mary Worrall, pinmaker
Peter Price, son of Wm., cordwainer
Steph. Reeve, app. of John Adams, cordwainer
Thos. Merrett, son of John, tailor, decd., of Rodborough
10 Mar Edw. Jones, son of Wm., esq., of Nass
272 Jeremiah Williams, son of Jeremiah, cordwainer
Hen. Holder, son of John, pinmaker, of St. Mary Magdalen's Hospital near Gloucester
John Woodward, son of Ric., pinmaker
Jos. Longden, son of Jos., grocer
Thos. Wilkins, son of Thos., yeoman, decd., of Maisemore
Wm. Barker, son of Wm., carpenter, decd., of Hasfield
John Ricketts, son of John, pinmaker, decd.
Phil. Merrett, son of John, tailor, decd.
John Birch, son of John, broadweaver, of Rodborough
Wm. Hanman, son of Wm., blacksmith
273 Thos. Millington, son of Jonathan, cooper, decd., of Cirencester
John Washbourne, clerk, son of John, clockmaker, decd.
14 Mar John Griffitts,[1] son of John, yeoman
John Ashmeade, son of John, mercer
Wm. Hughes Vernon, son of Thos., esq.
Thos. Deane, son of Geo., carpenter, decd.
Wm. Brobant, app. of Elizabeth Weaver, pinmaker
Thos. Adey, app. of Jas. Lovet the younger, barber and peruke-maker
Thos. Winniatt, clothworker, son of Thos., weaver, of Stroud
Chas. King, app. in turn of John Jefferies and Geo. King, pinmakers
Jas. King, carpenter, son of Jas., bricklayer
274 Wm. Atkins, app. of Wm. Cowcher, pinmaker
John Organ, app. of Ric. Weaver, blacksmith and farrier
Wm. Swayne, woolcomber, son of Wm., pargeter, decd.
Chas. Williams, combmaker, son of Chas., glover, decd., of Worcester

[1] Later clerk; cf. below: GBR C 9/9, p. 106.

Hayward Vernon, app. of Benj. Bonner, brazier
Jas. Oakey, app. of John Davis the younger, pinmaker
John Workman,[1] butcher, son of Ant., butcher
Thos. Bower, yeoman, son of Hubert, tanner, of Newent
Benj. Mutlow, son of John, labourer, decd.
Ric. Bunce, app. of Abraham Saunders, vintner
275 John Lewis, gardener, son of Thos., gardener, decd.
Chas. Cole, app. in turn of Jas. Sparrow, decd., and Wm. Wood the younger, coopers
Thos. Coleman, cordwainer, and Jas. Coleman, cordwainer, sons of Jos., cordwainer
Hen. Bossom, cordwainer, of Blakeney, son of Thos., barber, of Mitcheldean
John More, yeoman, of Great Witcombe, son of John, yeoman, decd., of Hardwicke
Dan. Bubb, baker, son of Thos., baker, decd.
Wm. Wells the younger, app. in turn of John Grimmett, decd., and Elizabeth Grimmett, spinster, cordwainers
Thos. Smith, butcher, son of Thos., butcher, decd.
276 John Merry, app. of Hen. Wintle, brushmaker
Ric. Ford, barber, son of Hen., bricklayer, decd.
Benj. Price, cordwainer, son of Wm., cordwainer
Thos. Batsford, labourer, of Temple Guiting (*Upper Guiting*), son of John, barber, decd., of Winchcombe
Thos. Lea, yeoman, and Hen. Lea, yeoman, sons of Thos., carpenter, decd., of Leigh
Ric. Pettat, gent., of Ryeford, Stonehouse, son of Thos., gent., decd., of Ebley
Sam. Dalby, butcher, son of Sam., butcher, of Ombersley, Worcs.
17 Mar Thos. Ashmeade,
277 Edw. Ashmeade, and Giles Ashmeade, sons of Thos., butcher, of Charlton Kings
Wm. Ashmeade, son of Wm., ironmonger and mercer, decd., of Alcester, Warws.
Sam. Cripps,[2] son of Sam., cordwainer
Elmes Steel, son of Sam., gent., of Coleford
John Ellis, son of John, victualler, decd.
Sam. King, son of Jas., bricklayer
18 Mar Sam. Harris, ship's carpenter, of Bridgnorth, Salop., and Wm. Harris, forgeman, of Madeley, Salop., sons of Wm., waterman
John Wilks, dragoon, Gen. [Hen. Seymour] Conway's regiment, son of John, wiredrawer[3]
Jas. Maverley, organist, of West Wycombe, Bucks., son of Jas., barber
278 John Latham, painter and stonecutter, of Mitcheldean, son of John, tailor
Benj. Freeman, whitesmith, of Warmley, son of Benj., whitesmith, decd.
Rob. Boseley, and John Boseley, sons of Jas., yeoman, of Redmarley [D'Abitot], Worcs.

[1] Resigned 9 Mar 1795 to enable him to give evidence in a cause concerning the city's common meadows and readmitted 17 Aug 1795: ibid. B 3/12, ff. 219v., 227v.; below: ibid. C 9/9, p. 121.

[2] Journeyman shoemaker, disfranchised 28 July 1781 to enable him to give evidence in a cause between the mercers' company and a non-freeman: ibid. B 3/11, ff. 298v., 344.

[3] For Conway, *D.N.B.*

Jas. Clark, tinplate-worker, of London, son of Moses, baker, decd.
22 Apr John Smith, haberdasher, of St. Martin le Strand, Mdx., son of Maur., mercer, decd., of Dursley
25 June John Niblett, grocer, son of Sam., grocer
25 July Moses Rayer, grocer, of Southwark, app. of Hen. Curtis, grocer, soapboiler, and chandler
9 Sept Thos. Cox of Tewkesbury, app. of Ambrose Wadley, baker
279 12 Sept Wm. Organ, app. of Elizabeth Weaver, pinmaker
19 Sept Sam. Viner, clerk, of Oxford University, son of Wm., grocer
Ric. Smeeths, late ostler to Giles Greenaway, innholder, by fine
23 Sept Thos. Jones, saddler, of Tewkesbury by fine
26 Sept Thos. Pruin, innholder, of Cheltenham by fine
30 Sept Wal. Price, victualler, of Barton Street by fine

Edward Baylis, esq., mayor 1768–9

1769 17 Feb John Bethell, victualler, of Chepstow, Mon.,[1] by fine
Jos. Hawkins of Corse, app. of John Webb, butcher
Thos. Parker, app. of Jos. Cheston, apothecary
22 May Jonathan Frankis, husbandman, of Painswick, son of Ric., yeoman, decd., of Upton St. Leonards
280 16 June Thos. Plaistead of Newnham, app. of Wm. Farren, butcher
11 July Jas. Gardiner, servant-man, of Coventry, son of Ric., tailor
28 July Jos. Baylis, mercer, of Bewdley, Worcs., son of Benj., woolstapler
25 Aug John Jones, cordwainer, son of Edw., yeoman
John Stephens, pinmaker, son of Wm., pinmaker
1 Sept Wm. Hill, app. of Wm. Cummins and Thos. Rea, bakers
29 Sept Thos. Saunders, victualler, by fine
Wm. Binning, hosier, by fine
Jas. Middleton, woolcomber, by fine
Hen. Greening by fine

281 **John Jefferis, esq., mayor 1769–70**

6 Oct Thos. Bower, waterman, son of Thos., plushweaver, decd.
10 Nov Jas. Walker, app. of Thos. Saunders, soapboiler and tallow-chandler
12 Dec Maur. Smith, haberdasher, of Bow Lane, Cheapside, London, son of Maur., saddler, decd., of Dursley
1770 1 June Thos. Acock, app. of Ambrose Wadley, baker
11 June John Morse, clerk, of Sutton St. Mary, Lincs., son of Jackman, clerk, decd., of Awre
John Jones, app. of Chas. Wilton, pinmaker
Edm. Boughton, app. of Ric. Moye, currier, decd.
18 June John Kirby, merchant's clerk, of Chepstow, Mon., son of John, schoolmaster, late of Gloucester
282 17 Aug Pettat Gardiner, son of Cornelius, timber merchant, late of Gloucester
27 Aug John Stephens, husbandman, of Barton Street, son of Wm., weaver, late of Gloucester
24 Sept Jas. Smart, app. of Wm. Ward, Jas. Wintle, and John Adey, pinmakers
29 Sept John Hargest by fine
Jas. Cole by fine
Sam. King, (app. of Thos. Branch, tinplate-worker), by fine
John Cooke, pargeter, by fine

[1] Of the Upper George, Gloucester: GBR B 3/11, f. 107; cf. ibid. f. 95.

John Webb, esq., mayor 1770–1

15 Oct Wm. Parker, gent.,[1] by gift
16 Nov Jos. Drew, baker, son of Thos., baker, decd.
John Selwyn, app. of Nat. Washbourne the younger, baker
10 Dec Sam. Jones, app. of Chas. Wilton, pinmaker
283 17 Dec Jas. Brotherton,[2] whitesmith, son of Jas., victualler, decd.
1771 5 Jan Jas. Innell, yeoman, son of Jas., porter, of Lincoln's Inn, Mdx., formerly tailor, of Gloucester
11 Jan Thos. Taylor Mans, porter, son of Thos., porter, decd.
28 Jan Wm. Turner, grocer, son of John, grocer, decd.
25 Feb Wm. Greening, barber, son of Dan., cordwainer
1 Mar Benj. Matthews, pipemaker, son of Ric., pipemaker
15 Apr John Caruthers of Randwick, app. of Rob. Smith, mercer
19 Apr Dan. Smith, app. of Thos. Yates, grocer
26 Apr John Ricketts, app. of Jas. Lovett, barber
1 July Wm. Salcomb of Sandhurst, app. of Mic. Jennings, butcher
284 19 Aug Wm. Blanch, heelcutter, of Tewkesbury, son of Thos. Blanch alias Selwyn†
5 Aug Edw. Baylis, clothier, of Kingswood, Wilts., son of Jos., clerk, of Ludgershall, Wilts.
16 Sept John Lamb, confectioner, by gift
20 Sept Thos. Organ, wine cooper, second son of Thos., innkeeper
28 Sept Rob. Bathorne, gent., of Broadoak by gift
20 Sept Wm. Man, cooper, third son of Thos., porter, decd.
Chas. Hooper, butcher, only son of Chas., butcher, decd.
30 Sept Geo. Hinks† by fine
Chas. Peart† by fine

285 **John Baylis, esq., mayor 1771**

4 Oct Nat. Biddle, app. of Wm. Viner, grocer
4 Nov Thos. Stock of Pembroke College, Oxford University, son of Thos. Rich Stock, grocer, decd.
8 Nov John Labeter by fine
Ric. Haviland by fine
11 Nov Wm. Peace, cordwainer, son of Thos., cordwainer

Thomas Branch, esq., mayor 1772[3]

1772 3 Feb Thos. Webb,[4] app. of John Hays, cordwainer
1 May Geo. Davis, victualler, by fine
8 May John Derrett, son of Wm., of Badgeworth, and app. of Thos. Watts and Chas. Hooper, butchers, by apprenticeship
Thos. Abell, app. of Wm. Murcutt, joiner and cabinet-maker
286 Wm. Gammond of Welland, Worcs., app. of Rog. Horseman, baker
25 May Thos. Gransmore, butcher, son of Rob., butcher
15 June Edw. Roberts, app. of Thos. Branch, tinplate-worker
3 July Wm. Smith, stationer, of St. Dunstan, Stepney, Mdx., youngest son of Maur., mercer, decd., of Dursley
10 July Wm. Rayer, wine cooper, son of Wm., innholder

[1] Of Hasfield: ibid. f. 122.
[2] Jas. Bretherton, resigned 9 Mar 1795 to be able to give evidence in a cause concerning the city's common meadows and readmitted 17 Aug 1795: ibid. 12, ff. 220v., 227v.; below: ibid. C 9/9, p. 122.
[3] Elected 6 Jan 1772 after Baylis's death: ibid. B 3/11, f. 138.
[4] Resigned 9 Mar and readmitted 17 Aug 1795: ibid. 12, ff. 219, 227v.; below: ibid. C 9/9, p. 121.

21 Aug John Gurney of Littleworth, app. in turn of Ralph Critchley and Wm. Cowcher, pinmakers
14 Sept Ric. Cowcher, pinmaker, son of Wm., pinmaker
Wal. Woore, hatmaker, of Gloucester, son of John, hatmaker, of Monmouth
287 18 Sept Wm. Skillern, cook, of St. Clement, Mdx., eldest son of Isaac, furrier, decd., of Winchcombe
3 Oct Thos. Bamford, yeoman, by fine

Benjamin Baylis, esq., mayor 1772–3

19 Oct Wm. Powell, cooper, of St. Nicholas, Gloucester, son of Ric., pinmaker, late of Gloucester
1773 29 Jan Noah Neale, esq., by gift
8 Feb Thos. Woodward, app. of John Woodward, pinmaker
Sam. Daniel, joiner and carpenter, son of Wm., victualler
26 Mar Jas. Lander, pinmaker, son of Jas., grocer
288 22 Apr Wm. Lane, cabinet-maker, son of John, farrier
21 May Thos. Bennett of Southwark, app. in turn of Mary Worrall and John Woodward, decd., pinmakers
14 June John Ward, labourer, of Minsterworth, son of John, cordwainer, late of Down Hatherley
23 Aug Edwin Jeynes,[1] app. of Sam. Wilson, mercer
17 Sept Jas. Rudge, gent., son of Thos., gent.
Hen. Lawrence of Leigh, app. of Ellis Taylor, baker
20 Sept John Cooke, saltman, son of Sam., glassman, decd.
1 Oct Wm. Gray, flaxdresser, by fine
Butler Rene, bricklayer, by fine
289 2 Oct Sam. Bowyer, victualler, of Minchinhampton by fine
Thos. Wilcox, labourer, by fine
4 Oct Martin Barry, clerk, by gift[2]

Abraham Saunders, esq., mayor 1773–4

15 Oct Ric. Draper Yates, son of Dan., grocer
22 Oct John Organ, bookbinder, son of Thos., innholder
Rob. Ladbrooke, organist, son of Rob., victualler, decd.
1 Nov Jas. Bower, glover and breeches-maker, of Tewkesbury, son of Thos., plushweaver, late of Gloucester
12 Nov Chas. Adey, bricklayer, of St. George, Hanover Square, Westminster, son of Edm., tailor, late of Gloucester
290 15 Nov Wm. Tomson, app. of Edw. Elton, grocer
22 Nov Chas. Clark, blacksmith, son of Chas., blacksmith, late of Arlingham
1 Dec Lawr. Crump, gent., son of Lawr., esq., ald.
17 Dec Wm. Draper, plumber and glazier, son of Wm., cordwainer, decd.
1774 14 Jan John Pearce, baker, son of Benj., postmaster, of Tewkesbury, formerly carpenter, of Longford
28 Feb Peter Gardiner of Stroud, app. of Thos. Garner, butcher
18 Mar Chas. Tyler, grocer, son of Francis, plumber and glazier, late of Gloucester
7 Mar Thos. Ellis, clothier, of Ebley, Randwick, by gift
291 25 Apr Jonathan Lake, gardener,
Benj. Lake, gardener, } sons of John, victualler, of Hartpury, formerly app. of Hen. Draper and Ric. Weaver, farriers

[1] Knighted in 1800: cf. ibid. B 3/12, f. 315v.
[2] Entrant was later perpetual curate of St. Nicholas by the corporation's gift: Hockaday Abs. ccxx.

2 Apr Ric. Cooke, clothier, of Lodgemore, Stroud,[1] by gift

29 Apr Edw. Hawkins, merchant, son of Thos., merchant, of Newnham, formerly app. of Francis Brabant, cooper

Thos. Moye, cabinet-maker, son of Ric., currier, formerly app. of Edw. Bower, currier

2 Apr Hen. Cooke, clothier, of Wallbridge, Rodborough, by gift

29 Apr John Wilce, app. in turn of Bernard Cook and, following his bankruptcy, Francis Mayo, grocers

2 May Wm. Sexty, butcher, son of Geo., butcher, of Hailes, formerly app. in turn of Wm. Hayward, decd., and Ann Luther, widow, butchers

292 13 June Wm. Hardwick(e), painter, John Hardwick, mercer and draper, of Alcester, Warws., } sons of John, tailor

18 July Isaac Skillern, excise officer, of Abingdon, Berks., son of Isaac, stonecutter, late of Winchcombe

9 Aug John Pegler, clothier, of Steanbridge, Painswick, by gift

26 Aug Wm. Dunn,[2] pargeter, son of Hen., pargeter

29 Aug Thos. Wadley, baker, son of Ambrose, baker, decd.

5 Sept Thos. Rudhall, bellfounder, son of Abel, bellfounder, decd.

9 Sept Hilly Crump, cabinet-maker, of London, son of Wm., joiner

Hen. Bayly alias Baylis, stocking-framework-knitter, of Tewkesbury, son of Wm., ship's carpenter, late of Gloucester

293 Wintour Harris, accountant, son of Thos., cooper, decd., of Bristol

12 Sept Thos. Rodway, app. of Wm. Price, cordwainer

Thos. Parker, gent.,[3] son of Thos., clerk

Rowland Hean, yeoman, son of Hen., victualler

Wm. Bubb, carpenter, son of Thos., baker, decd.

John Okey, butcher, son of John, butcher, of Westbury

23 Sept Wm. Selby, labourer, by fine

John Chandler, labourer, by fine

Chas. Doggett, bricklayer, by fine

Josiah Hale, stocking-framework-knitter, of Tewkesbury, son of Wm., pinmaker, decd.

294 Thos. Dew, brushmaker, son of Thos., baker, late of Gloucester

Josiah Boughton, baker, son of Ant., baker, late of Gloucester

24 Sept Rob. Campbell, esq., of Creed Place,[4] Upton St. Leonards, by gift

Rob. Baldwin, bookseller, of Paternoster Row, London, son of Rob., apothecary, decd., of Faringdon, Berks.

26 Sept Sir Wm. Strachan, Bt., of Hucclecote by gift

Thos. Chartar, app. of his father Thos., weaver

John Matthews, app. of Ric. Weaver, farrier, decd.

30 Sept Chas. Bishop, gent., of Oxford University, son of John, tallow-chandler and soapboiler, late of Gloucester

295 **John Jefferies, esq., mayor 1774–5**

6 Oct John Saunders Hayward, esq., of Merton College, Oxford University, son of Sam., esq., of Wallsworth Hall, Sandhurst

John Baylis, woolstapler, son of Edw., esq., ald.

[1] Lodgemore Mill, Rodborough: *V.C.H. Glos.* xi. 225–6.

[2] Resigned 12 Mar 1795 to enable him to give evidence in a cause concerning the city's common meadows and readmitted 17 Aug 1795: GBR B 3/12, ff. 222, 227v.; below: ibid. C 9/9, p. 122.

[3] Later clerk: *Alumni Oxon. 1715–1886*, iii. 1068.

[4] Later called Bowden Hall: Bigland, *Glos.* iii, no. 277.

Thos. Bonnor Bishop, gent., of London, son of John, tallow-chandler and soapboiler, decd.
17 Oct Midshipman Thos. Jeynes, R.N., son of Thos., feltmaker, decd., of Tewkesbury
24 Oct Ric. Bevan, pinmaker, of Southwark, son of John, baker, decd.
1775 16 Jan Luke Church, (app. of Ric. Evans), flaxdresser, by fine
13 Jan Dan. White, app. of Sam. Roberts, brushmaker
19 Jan John Lane, farrier, son of John, farrier
27 Jan Wm. Cook, chinaman, son of Sam., chinaman, decd.
296 Wm. Stock, druggist, of London, son of Thos. Rich Stock, grocer, decd.
13 Feb Wm. Walker, whitesmith, son of Jas., whitesmith
John Ready, gent., son of John, apothecary, decd.
13 Mar Jas. Collerick, cooper, son of Jas., bodice-maker
10 Apr Edw. Holder, app. of Sam. and John Niblett, grocers and co-partners
8 May John Lewis, app. of Mary Bevan, baker
2 June Wm. Edw. Rogers, corn factor, of Lewisham, Kent, son of Wm., baker, of London
17 June John Saunders, gent., of Grafton Lodge, Worcs., by gift[1]
297 26 June Geo. Martin, app. of Ric. and John Webb, grocers
John Pleydell, baker, of Bristol, son of Chas., baker
7 July Ambrose Wadley, baker, son of Ambrose, baker, decd.
17 July Wm. Daniel, app. of his father Wm., joiner
21 Aug Ric. Coopey, cordwainer, son of Wm., cordwainer, decd., of Churcham
Jas. Workman, butcher, son of Ant., butcher, decd.
18 Sept Wm. Artis, (late) waiter at the King's Head inn, by fine
Ann Randle, spinster, by fine
29 Sept John Tovey, ironmonger, by fine
26 Sept Sam. Woodcock, esq., by gift
298 29 Sept Selwyn James, gent., of Chepstow, Mon., by gift
Jos. Holder, grocer, son of Jos., tailor, late of Gloucester
Jas. Sadler, mercer, son of Jas., gent.

William Crump, esq., mayor 1775–6

6 Oct Sam. Gwinnett, innholder, by fine
30 Sept Rob. Pyrke, gent., of Newnham by gift[2]
20 Oct Jas. Ruck of Hawling (*Halling*), app. of Steph. Hall, baker
10 Nov Benj. Bonner, brazier, of Ross, Herefs., son of Benj., brazier
4 Dec Edm. Stock, grocer, son of Thos. Rich Stock, grocer, decd.
15 Dec Wm. Woodward, cabinet-maker, of Wotton, son of Ric., pinmaker, late of Gloucester
299 1776 15 Jan Elton Wantner, serjeant-at-mace, son of Elton, serjeant-at-mace, decd.
Jas. Hill, app. of Hen. Wintle, brushmaker
9 Feb Wm. Johnson, app. of Sam. and John Niblett, bankers, formerly grocers
15 Apr Wm. Butt the younger, app. of Wm. Humphrys, butcher
22 Apr John Surman, app. in turn of Thos. Bevan and Thos. Brown, bakers
29 Apr John Betteredge, victualler, by fine
Jas. Butt of Standish, app. of Ric. Swayne, butcher

[1] By act of 30 Sept 1774 on the recommendation of his brother Abraham, mayor: GBR B 3/11, f. 174.
[2] Entry belongs to preceding mayoralty.

8 May Rob. Ready, clerk, of Buscot, Berks., son of Alex. Colston, formerly called Alex. Ready, esq., decd., of Filkins, Oxon.

300 3 June Wm. Cooke, plasterer, son of Mat., pargeter

13 June John Small, gent., Jos. Atwell Small, clerk, } sons of Jos., gent., of Cirencester

24 June Chas. Thos. Cox, barber, son of Ric., barber, decd.

15 July Jas. Man, flaxdresser, son of Thos., porter, decd.

Thos. Dowden, innholder, son of Geo., maltster, decd., of Cirencester

23 July Thos. Crauford, esq., of Bristol by gift

16 Aug Jas. Daniel, carpenter, son of Wm., victualler, decd.

David Arthur, captain in the East India service,† by gift

301 23 Aug Jos. Chester, clerk,[1] son of Jos., mercer, decd.

Thos. Rogers, maltster, by fine

2 Sept Jas. Herbert of Colesbourne, app. of Elizabeth Faucks, widow, butcher

23 Sept Powell Chandler, wine merchant, son of Thos., grocer

John Webb, esq., mayor 1776–7

15 Nov Chas. Spencer, bricklayer, by fine

4 Nov Ralph Badnedge, currier, by fine

15 Nov John Rogers, maltster, by fine

18 Nov Francis Draper Lye, upholder, son of Hen., victualler

9 Dec Francis Bradford, app. of Francis Mayo, grocer

302 1777 17 Feb Abel Pride, pinmaker, son of Abel, pinmaker, decd.

Sam. Wilton, pinmaker, son of Chas., pinmaker

21 Mar Doctor Cowcher, victualler, of St. Anne, Soho, Mdx., son of Wm., plasterer, late of St. George, Hanover Square, Mdx.

31 Mar John Gardiner, baker, Thos. Gardiner, baker, of Gloucester, } sons of Wm., baker, of Painswick

2 May John Selwyn Pitt, printer, son of Leon., gent., decd.

23 May Ric. Ellis, silversmith, of London, John Ellis, jeweller, of London, } sons of Ric., silversmith, decd.

303 9 June Geo. Fielder, yeoman, son of Sam., yeoman, decd., of Putloe, Standish

23 June Wm. Jones, wine merchant, of Worcester, son of John, cooper, decd.

30 June Ric. Dunn, app. in turn of Ric. Cox, peruke-maker, and his widow Mary

4 July Chas. Launder, cooper, of Newnham, son of Jas., grocer

7 July Isaac Thompson, innholder, by fine

21 July Ric. Wood, cabinet-maker, son of Wm., cooper, decd.

4 Aug Ric. Hall, innholder, by fine

John Pitcher, victualler, by fine

304 Edm. Pembruge, peruke-maker, son of Thos., peruke-maker

28 Aug Wm. Price, victualler, by fine

8 Sept Thos. Jones of London, app. of John Hardwick, tailor, decd.

Jas. Dancocks, haberdasher, of London, son of Jas., apothecary, decd.

Wm. Wells, mercer, son of Wm., innholder

12 Sept Ric. Reade, gent., of Goodman's Fields, Whitechapel, Mdx., app. of Thos. Rudge, writing-master

John Reade, app. of Chris. Cooke, grocer

19 Sept Ric. Hale, coppersmith, son of Wm., coppersmith, of Bristol

20 Sept John James, yeoman, of Highnam by gift

[1] Vicar of Longney and perpetual curate of Elmore: Hockaday Abs. cclxiv, cxciii.

305 4 Oct Jos. Perrin, servant of Moses Randall, wine merchant, by fine
John Marshall, gent., of Hasfield by gift

John Box, esq., mayor 1777–8

24 Oct John Arundell, clothier, } sons of Ric., baker, decd.,
Ric. Arundell, soapboiler, of Painswick, } of Stroud
1 Dec Ric. Weaver, farrier, son of Ric., farrier, decd.
1778 12 Jan Thos. Rudge, clerk,[1] son of Thos., gent.
26 Jan Jas. Wilks, wiredrawer, son of John, wiredrawer
23 Feb Sam. Giles, app. of Rob. Smith, mercer
306 9 Mar Thos. Perris, pinmaker, son of Thos., butcher, late of Gloucester
27 Mar John Perris, tinplate-worker, of Ross, Herefs., son of Thos., butcher, decd.
30 Mar Jos. Taylor, app. of Sam. Flower, tailor, decd.
18 Apr Thos. Bradshaw, watch manufacturer, of London by gift
8 May John Archer, plumber and glazier, son of Geo., plumber and glazier
27 May Thos. Hopkins of Hucclecote, Churchdown, servant of Sir Wm. Strachan, Bt., by fine
1 June John Pain, innholder, of Frocester by fine
19 June Thos. Ivey Binning, app. of Edw. Bloxsome, cooper
John Phillips, brushmaker, son of John, pinmaker, decd.
307 22 June Jas. Rogers, baker, son of Wm., baker, decd., of St. Sepulchre, London
26 June Nat. Millard, maltster, by fine
3 July John Webb by fine
15 July David Evans by fine
24 Aug Thos. Evans, skinner, of Mitcheldean, son of Thos., victualler
31 Aug Thos. Heath, woolstapler, son of John, sword bearer, decd.
Geo. Wheeler, cabinet-maker, of Bristol, son of Ric., wheelwright
11 Sept Sam. Worrall, gent., son of Sam., gent., of Bristol
14 Sept John Evans, fellmonger, of Mitcheldean, son of Thos., victualler
308 John Wilkins Jepson, gent.,[2] by gift. Sworn same day
19 Sept Hen. Jones, minor canon of Gloucester cathedral, by gift
21 Sept Ingram Ball, esq., by gift
22 Sept Sam. Gunn, tavern waiter, of Hackney, Mdx., son of Wm., tailor, late of Gloucester
29 Sept Wm. Gough, yeoman, of Maisemore by fine
Thos. Thornton, yeoman, late of Redmarley D'Abitot, Worcs., by fine

James Sadler, esq., mayor 1778–9

7 Dec Thos. Platt, app. of Wm. Cowcher, pinmaker
18 Dec Sam. Jones Horseman, son of Rog. (*Rogers*) and Elizabeth, baker
309 1779 22 Jan Thos. Mount, app. of Shadrach Charleton, apothecary
15 Feb Benj. Aycrigg, apothecary, son of Benj., apothecary, late of Upton upon Severn, Worcs.
26 Feb Chas. Elliott, carpenter and joiner, son of Edw., snuffmaker, decd.
8 Mar Hubert Bower, tanner, son of Hubert, tanner, decd., of Newent
Benj. Wilkes, bricklayer, son of John, wiredrawer
15 Mar Chas. Matthews, servant, of Reading, son of Sam., pinmaker, decd.
7 May Wm. Wood the younger, cheese factor, of Tetbury by gift

[1] Vicar of Frampton on Severn and later author of histories of the county and city: ibid. cc; *V.C.H. Glos.* iv. 158–9; x. 153, 196.
[2] Deputy town clerk: GBR B 3/11, f. 230v.

10 May Rob. Greetwood, app. of Ric. Green, grocer, tallow-chandler, and soapboiler

310 17 May Ric. Hayle, tanner, son of Ric., tanner, decd.

Wm. Jeynes, flaxdresser, son of Wm., baker

Hen. Curtis, grocer, son of Hen., grocer, decd.

Chas. Mutlow, bookseller, son of Thos., tailor

John Holt, app. of Ric. Webb, soapboiler

31 May Wm. Perry, gent., son of Wm., tailor, late of Gloucester

14 June Jas. Rich Keys, tinman, of London, son of Jas., pinmaker, decd.

Rowland Pitt (*Pytt*) Coles, potter, of Swansea,
Edw. Coles, ironmaster,
311 John Coles, ironmonger,
} sons of Wm., ironmaster, decd.

12 June John Chandler, son of Thos., grocer

2 June Ric. Jeynes, brazier, son of Wm., baker, decd., of Bristol

19 June Jos. Broughton, app. of Jos. Lewis, barber and peruke-maker, and his wife Elizabeth

2 July Wm. Hill, yeoman, by fine

Abraham Saunders, esq., mayor 1779[1]

10 Sept Gabriel Holt, app. of Merrot Stephens, mercer

13 Sept Jas. Wood, mercer, son of Ric., mercer

Aaron Knight, victualler, by fine

17 Sept Edw. Cowcher, pinmaker, son of Wm., pinmaker

312 25 Sept Norman Hill, glazier, of St. James, Bristol, son of Jos., glass-bottle-maker, decd., of St. George near Bristol

27 Sept Thos. Goodwin, app. of Thos. Saunders, soapboiler, tallow-chandler, and grocer

1 Oct Chas. Tyrell Morgan, esq., of Hempsted by gift[2]

Thos. Mee, esq., by gift

Thos. Paytherus, surgeon, by gift

22 Nov Chas. Howard, earl of Surrey,[†3] by gift[4]

313 **William Lane, esq., mayor 1779–80**

5 Oct Jas. Lane,[5] gent., of King Street, St. Paul, Covent Garden, Westminster, by gift

15 Nov Sam. Taylor, app. of Ralph Fletcher, baker

6 Dec Wm. Fords, cordwainer, son of Jas., waterman

1780 3 Jan John Fords, private, North Glos. Militia, son of Jas., waterman

7 Feb John Newton, flaxdresser, son of John, flaxdresser, of Ross, Herefs.

6 Mar Wm. Smart, app. in turn of John Adams, cordwainer, late of Gloucester, and his wife Anne

25 Mar Chas. Hayward, esq., eldest son of Thos., esq., senior ald., of Quedgeley

314 n.d. Thos. Watts, husbandman, son of Vicesimus, husbandman, decd., of Highnam

10 Apr Wm. Jones, peruke-maker, son of Wm., cordwainer

Thos. Way, butcher, son of John, butcher, decd.

Nat. Harris of London, app. of Ambrose Wadley, baker

[1] Elected 19 Aug 1779 after Sadler's death: ibid. f. 249v.
[2] On his election to the common council: ibid. f. 253v.
[3] Of Holme Lacy, Herefs.: ibid. f. 162.
[4] Entry belongs to following mayoralty.
[5] John Lane: GBR B 3/11, f. 236v.

			Thos. Fords, private, North Glos. Militia, son of Jas., waterman
	1780	14 Apr	Geo. Washbourne, baker, son of Nat., baker
315			Wm. Fletcher, app. of John Spillman, baker
		5 Apr	Joshua White, tanner, } sons of Joshua, tanner, of Newent Wm. White, tanner, }
		28 Apr	Sam. Ricketts, app. of Jas. Wintle, pinmaker
		5 May	Geo. Woolley, app. of Francis Mayo, grocer
		8 May	Nat. Seyer, salesman, son of Sam., salesman
		12 May	Josiah Gardiner, baker, of Stonehouse, son of John, baker, of Sheepscombe
		13 May	Chas. Bradgate, confectioner, of Ross, Herefs., son of Chas., peruke-maker, decd.
316		15 May	John Smith of Worcester, servant of Chas. Trubshaw Withers, esq., and son of Hen., cordwainer, of Ross, Herefs., by patrimony
			Geo. Butter, blacksmith, of Llandinabo, Herefs., son of Chas., blacksmith, of Brampton Abbotts, Herefs.
		22 May	John Hen. Baker, bellfounder, son of Hen., bellfounder
			Hen. Price, pinmaker, son of Ric., pinmaker, decd.
			John Humphris, carpenter, son of Ric., carpenter, now or late of Gloucester
			Wm. Okey, app. of Thos. Stock, butcher
			Chas. Williams, flaxdresser, } sons of Jeremiah, cordwainer
317			Jos. Williams, cordwainer, }
			Jas. Mann, collar-maker, son of Mat., fellmonger
			Thos. Jelf, brushmaker, son of Wm., blacksmith, decd.
			Ralph Critchley, pinmaker, son of Ralph, pinmaker, decd.
			Ric. Gardiner, baker, son of Wm., baker, of Sheepscombe
		24 May	Jas. Heane, cordwainer, of Ruardean, third son of Hen., victualler, decd., of Gloucester, formerly of Ruardean
		26 May	Kedgwin Hoskins, gent., son of Kedgwin, gent., decd., of Clearwell
318			John Gardiner, corporal, North Glos. Militia, son of Thos., pinmaker
			Thos. Glendall, private, North Glos. Militia, son of Thos., carpenter
			Thos. Suffield Lander, corporal, North Glos. Militia, } sons of Jas., soapboiler Hen. Lander, corporal, North Glos. Militia, }
			Sam. Lane, private, North Glos. Militia, app. of Newton Brabant, pinmaker
			Thos. Merrett, private, North Glos. Militia, son of Wm., cordwainer, decd.
			Chas. Maverley, pinmaker, son of Wm., tailor, decd.
319			Wm. Williams, cordwainer, son of Jeremiah, cordwainer, of St. Bartholomew's Hospital, Gloucester
			Chas. Hanman, labourer, son of Wm., blacksmith, decd.
			Dan. Dix, labourer, } sons of Thos., porter, decd. John Dix, peruke-maker,[1] }
			Jas. Ireland, porter, son of John, cordwainer, decd.
		27 May	Francis Richards, private, North Glos. Militia, son of Jos., weaver
320		30 May	Jos. Bayse, husbandman, of Ruardean, } sons of Jos., cordwainer, late of Gloucester John Bayse, husbandman, of Ruardean, }
			Wm. Hatton, breeches-maker, son of Wm., breeches-maker
		2 June	Hen. Dunn, tiler and plasterer, son of Hen., tiler and plasterer
		5 June	Wm. Freeman, app. of Wm. Pace, cordwainer
		9 June	Ric. Matthews, pipemaker, son of Ric., pipemaker

[1] Private, North Glos. Militia, disfranchised 28 July 1781 to enable him to give evidence in a cause between the mercers' company and a non-freeman: ibid. ff. 298v., 344.

12 June John Rudge, carpenter, son of John, carpenter, of Frocester
321 23 June Isaac Barker, labourer, of Norton, son of Wm., carpenter, late of Hasfield
24 July Hen. Fords, tailor, son of Hen., tailor, decd.
Jas. Price, shoemaker, son of Ric., pinmaker, decd.
Geo. Ravenhill, sackweaver, son of Geo., labourer, decd.
John Reade, gent., by gift[1]
25 July John Smith, gent., of London, son of John, clothier, decd., of Dursley
31 July Thos. Gardiner, baker, son of Thos., decd., of Painswick
322 7 Aug Chas. Wantner, peruke-maker, of Wotton under Edge, son of Elton, peruke-maker, decd.
18 Aug Wm. Bishop, tailor, son of Wm., cordwainer
Wm. Mutlow, pinmaker, son of John, carpenter, decd.
Ric. Allen, app. of Virgil Cripps, cordwainer
Ric. Harding, flaxdresser, son of Ric., gardener, decd., of Kingsholm
25 Aug John Wathen, app. of Ralph Critchley, pinmaker, decd.
John Badger, pinmaker, of Gloucester, son of Jonathan, pinmaker, of St. Mary Magdalen's Hospital [near Gloucester]
Jas. Roston, app. in turn of John Davis, pinmaker, decd., and his wife Elizabeth
Wm. Davis, pinmaker, son of John, pinmaker, decd.
323 Dan. Dix, pinmaker, son of Dan., pinmaker
Ric. Bower, pinmaker, son of Wm., labourer, decd.
28 Aug King Edward Ursell, victualler, son of King Edward Ursell, victualler, decd.
John Davis, cordwainer,
Jos. Davis, labourer, of Wheatenhurst,
Wm. Davis, labourer,
Jas. Davis of South Hamlet, servant of Wm. Cother, yeoman, of the Sheephouse,
} sons of Wm., cordwainer, decd., of Longney
324 Ric. Hopkins, app. of Wm. Baldwin, tailor
Sam. Best, cordwainer,
Jos. Best, cordwainer,
} sons of Edw.,[2] cordwainer
Wm. Wadley, app. of Jos. Hawkes, cordwainer
Benj. Hare, pinmaker, son of Benj., pinmaker
Ric. Gardiner, tailor, son of Ric., tailor, decd.
Wm. Mann, cordwainer, son of Jos., pinmaker
Sam. Spicer, app. of Wm. Price, cordwainer, decd.
325 Thos. Knight, pinmaker, son of Thos., pinmaker
Jas. Bourne, cordwainer, app.[3] of Jas. Bourne, cordwainer, decd., by patrimony
Wm. Bourne, cooper, son of Jas., cordwainer, decd.
Chas. Hartland, pinmaker, son of Thos., pinmaker
Wm. Dark, pinmaker, son of Jos., carpenter, decd.
John Shaw Stephens, tailor, son of Thos., pinmaker, decd.
Chas. Fettiplace, esq., of Llantarnam, Mon., son of Thos. Bushel, esq., decd., of Cleeve,[4] Worcs.
326 1 Sept Wm. Boseley, breeches-maker, son of Geo., victualler, decd.
Wm. King, pargeter, son of Geo., pinmaker

[1] On his election to the common council: ibid. f. 270.
[2] ? Edm.; cf. above and below: ibid. C 9/8, p. 121; 9, pp. 13, 17.
[3] Or *son*.
[4] Cleeve Prior: Nash, *Worcs.* i. 237 and n.; *V.C.H. Worcs.* iii. 311.

1780 Thos. Adams, farrier, son of John, cordwainer, decd.
4 Sept Wm. Richards, peruke-maker, son of Jos., peruke-maker
Wm. Salcomb, silk mercer, of Worcester, }
Sam. Salcomb, victualler, } sons of Sam., victualler
Jas. Mutlow, tailor, son of Thos., tailor
Jos. Price, brazier and coppersmith, of Tewkesbury, son of Jos., cordwainer, decd.
327 Wm. Smith, cabinet-maker, son of Thos., butcher, decd.
Jos. Wells of Tewkesbury, app. of John Hyett, cooper, }
Thos. Gale of Monmouth, app. of Thos. Simpson, baker, late of Gloucester, }
John Moulder, app. of Mary Bevan, baker, decd., } claim the freedom by apprenticeship
Sam. Ricketts, gent., son of Sam., pinmaker, decd.
Sam. Hyett, app. of Wm. Price, cordwainer, decd.
Jas. Hawkes, cordwainer, son of Jos., cordwainer
328 Rob. Philips, soldier, 1st Marines, son of Geo., decd.
Wm. Hooper, app. of John Wheatstone, cordwainer
Ric. Barrett, painter, son of Wm., tobacco-pipemaker, decd.
Ric. Moore, app. of Ric. Green of Churcham, formerly soapboiler, of Gloucester
Thos. Wood, cooper, son of Wm., cooper, decd.
John Bourn, app. of John Bourne, cordwainer, decd.
John Engley, tavern waiter, son of John, peruke-maker
329 Thos. Walker, victualler, son of Jas., whitesmith
Thos. Jeffs, victualler, of the Naight (*Height*),[1] North Hamlet, son of Jos., corkcutter
Rob. Coleman, woolstapler, son of Jos., cordwainer
Thos. Corr, labourer, son of Thos., plushweaver, decd.
8 Sept Benj. Baylis, woolstapler, son of Benj., woolstapler, decd.
Rob. Weeksey Ellis, mercer, son of Rob., ironmonger
John Jones, app. of Nat. Washbourne, baker
Elisha Farmer Sadler, mercer, son of Jas., esq., decd.
330 Ric. Goodwin, wheelwright, of Tibberton, son of Ric., yeoman, decd., of Linton, Churcham
Thos. Leech, app. of Abel Wellavize, tailor
Thos. Webley, tailor, son of Wm., peruke-maker, decd.
Thos. Cowles, grazier, son of John, grazier
Thos. Cooke, app. of Chas. Cole, mercer
Jas. Kirby, grocer, of Rosemary Lane, London, }
Chas. Kirby of Lincoln's Inn, London, } sons of John, writing-master, of Chepstow, Mon.
Chas. Crump, tinplate-worker, son of Thos., mayor's officer
331 Jas. Bower, painter, son of Ric., porter, decd.
Jas. Crump, tailor, son of Thos., mayor's officer
Phil. Welch, tailor, of Brockworth, son of Benj., tailor, of Boddington
Thos. Welch, mason, of Hucclecote, son of Wm., cordwainer, decd., of Badgeworth
Wm. Welch, labourer, of Elmstone Hardwicke, son of John, labourer, decd., of Boddington
John Adams, brushmaker, of Beer Lane, Tower Street, London, son of John, decd., cordwainer

[1] Island in the river Severn's eastern channel below Gloucester castle: *V.C.H. Glos.* iv. 383.

332 John Coleman,[1] combmaker, of Whitechapel Road, Mdx., son of Jos., cordwainer

Wm. Puxon, carpenter, } sons of John, carpenter, decd., of Bow
John Puxon, carpenter, } Street, Westminster

John Hartland, brushmaker, of St. Thomas, Southwark, son of Thos., pinmaker

Ric. Bubb, brushmaker, of Snow Hill, London, son of Thos., baker, decd.

Benj. Welch, labourer, of Stoke Orchard, Bishop's Cleeve, son of Benj., tailor, of Boddington, formerly of Badgeworth

333 Ric. Hathaway, pinmaker, son of Ric., victualler, decd.

Thos. Welch, labourer, of Churchdown, son of Benj., tailor, of Boddington, formerly of Badgeworth

Jas. Hunman, butcher, son of Wm., blacksmith, decd.

Ant. Browne, wine cooper, son of Nic., wine cooper, of Chepstow, Mon.

Ant. Gardner, tobacconist, of Chepstow, Mon., son of Ant., gent., of London

334 Thos. Hartland, pinmaker, of Barton Street, son of Thos., pinmaker

Thos. Fowler of Bristol, app. of Wm. Cheeseman, brushmaker

Isaac Kirby, pinmaker, of Gloucester, son of Jacob, weaver, decd., of Bristol

John Clark, blacksmith, son of Chas., blacksmith, decd., of Arlingham

Wm. Smart, pinmaker, son of Giles, pinmaker, decd.

John Ireland, woolcomber, son of John, cordwainer, decd.

335 Chas. Woodward, plasterer, son of Ric., victualler, decd.

Mat. Cooke, pargeter, son of Mat., pargeter

11 Sept Thos. Trustram, labourer, of Chedworth, son of John, labourer, of Poulton, Wilts.

Thos. Wilkins, husbandman, son of John, butcher, decd., of Westbury

Jos. Mutlow, cordwainer, son of Wm., wiredrawer, of Dursley

Wm. Vail, husbandman, son of Wm., husbandman, of Fretherne

336 Jos. Flower, gent., of Chick Lane, West Smithfield, London, son of John, tailor, decd.

John Bower, plushweaver, of Banbury, Oxon., son of Thos., plushweaver, decd.

Dan. Dix, bricklayer, of Wapping, Mdx., son of Ric., bricklayer, decd.

Ric. Woodward, pinmaker, son of Ric., pinmaker, decd.

Wm. Venn, pinmaker, of Churchdown, son of Thos., labourer, of Sandhurst

337 Thos. Hornidge, combmaker, of Worcester, son of Wm., tailor

Jos. Badger, pinmaker, of Gloucester, son of Jonathan, pinmaker, of St. Mary Magdalen's Hospital near Gloucester

Chas. Bonner, brazier, son of Benj., brazier

John Wells, silversmith, son of Wm., innholder

John Webb Pinfold Palmer, surgeon, son of John, clerk

Capel Bond, gent., of Lincoln's Inn, Mdx., son of Ric., printer, of London

David Bond, printer, of St. John, Clerkenwell, Mdx., son of Wm., bookbinder, decd.

338 John Holder, surgeon, of Gloucester, son of Geo., surgeon, decd., of Cirencester

[1] Also spelt *Coalman*.

1780 John Ashmeade, labourer, son of Thos., husbandman, decd., of Charlton Kings
Wm. Higgins, clerk, of St. Pancras, London, son of John, chandler, of Abergavenny, Mon.
Wm. Wood, carpenter, of Gloucester, son of Wm., yeoman, of Barton Street St. Mary
Chas. Hutchings, fishmonger, son of Dennis, farrier, decd.
339 Edw. Taylor, carpenter,
John Taylor, yeoman, of Broadway, Worcs., } sons of John, cutler, of Cirencester
Paul Cheeseman, gent., of Whittington (*Wittington*), son of John, tailor
Thos. Smith of Aldersgate Street, London, app. of John Perkes, corkcutter, decd.
Thos. Bubb, hairdresser, of London, son of Thos., baker, decd.
Ric. Lane, farrier, son of John, farrier, decd.
John Ursell, plumber, of Worcester, son of King Edward Ursell, victualler, decd.
340 Chas. Williams, cordwainer, of Tothill Fields, Westminster,
Watkin Williams of St. George, Hanover Square, Westminster, } sons of John, glovecutter, late of Westchester[1]
Hen. Norwood, esq., son of Chas., esq., decd., of Leckhampton
Chas. Murrell, app. of Chas. Hooper, butcher
Humph. Matthews, shopman, of St. Giles, Cripplegate, London, son of Humph., grocer, decd., of St. Giles in the Fields, Mdx.
Benj. Collerick, tinplate-worker, of Worcester, son of Jas., earthenware man
341 John Seyer, pinmaker, of Christchurch, Southwark, son of Dan., flaxdresser, decd.
Wm. Trustram, labourer, of Stratton, son of John, labourer, of Poulton, Wilts.
Wm. Powell, plumber, son of Wm., plumber, decd.
Jas. Beard, silkweaver, of St. Leonard, Shoreditch, Mdx.,
Thos. Beard, silkweaver, } sons of Jas., weaver and woolcomber, of Spitalfields, Mdx.
Steph. Steel, tiler, of Blakeney, son of John, carpenter, decd., of Littledean
342 Chas. Norwood, esq., son of Chas., esq., decd., of Leckhampton
Geo. Barrett, pinmaker, of Christchurch, Surr., son of Wm., pinmaker, decd.
Steph. Skillerne, labourer, of Twyning,
Mat. Skillerne, cordwainer, } sons of Steph., schoolmaster, decd., of Winchcombe
Thos. Smith, servant, of Newland, son of Wm., baker, decd.
343 Wm. Davis, pinmaker, son of John, pinmaker, decd.
John Maverley, private, Surr. Militia, app. of John Davis, pinmaker, decd.
Benj. Bannister, wiredrawer, son of Willoughby, wiredrawer, of St. Saviour, Southwark
Wm. Smith Bartlett, app. of Jas. Wintle, pinmaker
Thos. Powell, apothecary, son of Wm., plumber, decd.
Steph. Stroud, wireworker, son of Thos., pinmaker, decd.

[1] ? Westminster.

Chas. Gate Baylis, customs officer, of Beachley, Tidenham, son of Jos., clerk, late of Ludgershall, Wilts.

344 Thos. Clark, weaver, of Cripplegate, London, son of Moses, baker, decd.

Edw. Heene, waterman, son of Hen., victualler, decd.

Wm. Boseley, husbandman, son of Jas., husbandman, decd., of Flaxley

12 Sept Ric. White, husbandman, of Cugley, Newent, son of Ric., carpenter, of Oxenhall

Chas. Palmer of Pembroke College, Oxford [University], son of John, clerk

345 13 Sept John Taynton, son of Wal., skinner, of Ross, Herefs.

Jas. Smith, snuffmaker, of Wolverhampton, Staffs., son of Jas., cooper, late of Gloucester

Chas. Bathurst, clerk, of Barcombe, Suss., son of Benj.,[1] esq., late of Gloucester

John Blanch, heelmaker, of Coventry, son of Thos., heelmaker, late of Gloucester

Francis Keys, gent., of Plymouth, son of Wm., gent., late of Gloucester

Chas. Elliott, soldier in the Guards, of Westminster, son of Wm., barber, late of Gloucester

Hen. Lugg, plumber and glazier, son of Hen., combmaker, late of Hereford

346 Jas. Lugg, labourer, son of Jasper, labourer, late of Hereford

Wm. Palmer of London, app. of John Cook, apothecary

Wm. Wheeler, pinmaker, of London, son of Chas., pinmaker, late of Gloucester

Chas. Knight, yeoman, son of Ric., flaxdresser, late of Gloucester

Jas. Maverly, corkcutter, of London, son of John, innholder, late of Gloucester

Albert Badger, gent., of London, son of Albert, pinmaker, late of Gloucester

347 John Staight, fanmaker, son of Thos., silkweaver, decd., of London

Ric. Overthrow, butcher, son of Sam., fisherman, decd.

Nat. Harris of London, app. of Ambrose Wadley, baker, decd.

Ric. Thurston Stayte, servant, son of Thos., silkweaver, late of London

Thos. Harmar, engraver, of London, son of Thos., hosier

Hen. Barrett, cooper, son of Rob., cooper, of Stroud

Ric. Cutlack Partridge, staymaker, son of Rob., baker, decd., of London

348 Wm. Kirby, pinmaker, son of Jacob, weaver, decd., of Bristol

Wm. Parsons,[2] clerk, of Frampton on Severn, son of John, esq., decd., of Kemerton

Chas. Lea of Worcester, app. of Wm. Stephens, upholder, and his wife Martha

Rowles Scudamore, clothier, of Stroud, son of Rowles, brushmaker, late of Birmingham

Wm. Heath, private in the Guards, [of] London, son of John, innholder, late of Gloucester

349 Ant. Ellis, ironmonger, son of Rob., ironmonger

Ric. Ades, cordwainer, son of Thos., cordwainer, decd., of Mitcheldean

[1] M.P. for Gloucester 1727–54: Williams, *Parl. Hist. of Glos.* 209.

[2] From 1817 called Wm. Hopton: Burke, *Land. Gent.* (1846), i. 590.

1780 John Yeend, yeoman, of Rous Lench, Worcs.,
Wm. Goodwin Yeend, yeoman, of Little Comberton, Worcs.,
Loveridge (*Lewrindge*) Yeend, yeoman, of Great Malvern, Worcs.,
} sons of John, bonesetter, of Pershore, Worcs.

350 John Charles, pinmaker, son of Ric., pinmaker, late of London
John Phillipps, buckle-maker, of Birmingham, son of Phil., tailor
Wm. Gardner, whitesmith, of Birmingham, son of Ric., tailor, decd.
Nat. Mills, painter, of Lambeth, Surr., son of Thos., plasterer, decd.
Wm. Chandler, grocer, son of Thos., grocer
Capel Hanbury-Williams, esq., of Abergavenny, [Mon.,] son of Geo.,[1] esq., late of Llanfoist, Mon.
351 John Harris, yeoman, of Awre, son of Ric., labourer
Wm. Hathaway, carpenter, son of Thos., labourer, decd., of Ripple, Worcs.
John White, currier, of Stroud, son of Joshua, tanner, of Newent
Rob. Longden, clothier, of Painswick, son of Geo., clerk, of Winstone
Thos. Nest, plasterer, son of Thos., plasterer
Chas. Fletcher, brassfounder, son of John, plasterer, decd., of London
Chas. Barrett, cordwainer, of London, son of Thos., baker, decd.
352 Jos. Gardner, pinmaker, of Bristol, son of Wm., gardener
Hen. Cleeveley, hairdresser, son of Jos., hairdresser, decd., of Bristol
Wm. Peters of Bristol, app. of Edw.Roberts, tinplate-worker
Job Marshall, sawyer, of Bristol, son of Job, carpenter, decd., of Tidenham
John Tayloe, clothworker, son of Thos., clothworker, of Chalford
Rob. Bossley, miller, son of Jas., miller, decd., of Flaxley
353 Chas. Burton King, bricklayer, son of Sam., bricklayer, decd., of London
Rob. Freeman, button-maker, son of Rob., buckle-maker, of Birmingham
John Welch, cordwainer, of Brockworth, son of Wm., cordwainer, of Badgeworth
John Jeffs, farrier, of London, son of John, blacksmith, decd.
John Swain, pinmaker, son of Thos., pinmaker, decd., of Southwark
Jas. Steel, carpenter, of Frampton on Severn, son of Sam., surgeon, decd., of Coleford
354 Wm. Perks, servant, of Bretforton (*Bradforton*), Worcs., son of Sam., yeoman, decd., of Beckford
Wm. Gibbs, servant, son of Thos., blacksmith, of Dursley
John Child, tailor and staymaker, of Chalford, son of Thos., tailor, of Bisley
Sam. Gilding, labourer, of Leigh, Worcs., son of Wm., labourer, of Hanley, Worcs.
Jas. Page, hairdresser, of London, app. of Jos. Jeffs, barber and peruke-maker
Thos. Gibbs, labourer,
355 John Gibbs, labourer,
} sons of Thos., blacksmith, of Dursley
Jas. Barnard, app. in turn of Francis Mann and Jas. Clark, feltmongers, decd.
Wm. Powell of Southwark, app. of John Box, pinmaker

[1] Surname given as Hanbury, presumably Geo. Hanbury-Williams (d. 1764); cf. ibid. ii. 1598; above: GBR C 9/8, p. 241.

Rob. Hawkes of Minsterworth, app. of Benj. Hickman, cordwainer
John Gregory, labourer, of Upton St. Leonards, son of Wm., barber, late of Painswick
14 Sept Sam. Nelme, vintner of Bishopsgate Street, London, son of John, tinplate-worker, late of St. Sepulchre, London

356 Wm. Ashmeade, labourer, Hen. Ashmeade, breeches-maker, of Fairford, Ric. Ashmeade, labourer,	sons of Thos., farmer, decd., of Charlton Kings
Wm. Bamford, cordwainer, of Mangotsfield, Thos. Bamford, labourer, John Bamford, wiredrawer, of Mangotsfield,	sons of Wm., labourer of Siston

357 Merchant Kemys, labourer, of Withington, son of Sam., woolcomber, decd.
Wal. Taynton, pewterer, son of Thos., pewterer, decd., of Bristol
John Boseley, husbandman, of Abenhall, son of Jas., yeoman, decd., of Flaxley
John Spillman, cooper, son of Benj., cooper, decd., of Berkeley
Ric. Lane, ironmonger, son of Wm., brushmaker, of Bristol
Septimus Stroud, pinpointer, of Bristol, son of Thos., pinmaker, decd.
358 Thos. Harris, baker, of Bristol, son of Sam., carpenter, decd.
Adam Gardiner, wiredrawer, of Bristol, son of Wm., gardener, of Barton Street
Rob. Bennett of Bristol, app. of Jas. Wintle, brushmaker
John Lewis, carver, son of Newton, bedstead-maker, late of Bristol
Sam. Gardiner Price of Bloomsbury, London, app. of Benj. Hickman, cordwainer
Sam. Wilkes, private, Surr. Militia, son of John, pinmaker
359 Wm. Leighton, weaver, of Kent Street, Southwark, son of Ric., pinmaker, of Redcross Street, Southwark
John Bamford, watchmaker, son of John, tailor, decd., of Clerkenwell, Mdx.
Thos. Hickman, sergeant, South Glos. Militia, son of Benj., cordwainer
Wm. Gibbs, butcher, of Butcher Row Temple Bar, London, son of Pyrke Nat. Gibbs, cordwainer, decd., of Bristol

Edw. Heath, cordwainer, of Portland Street, St. Marylebone, Mdx., *360* Rob. Heath, private, South Glos. Militia, Ric. Heath, saddler, of St. Marylebone, Mdx.,	sons of Sam., brazier
Jos. Ashmeade, hatter, of St. Mary Overy, Surr., Benj. Ashmeade, breeches-maker, of St. George, Westminster,	sons of Wm., ironmonger, decd., of Alcester, Warws.

John Keylock, cordwainer, of James Street, Covent Garden, Westminster, son of Thos., cordwainer, of Bow Street, Westminster

Giles Brown(e), cordwainer, of St. George, Southwark, *361* Wm. Browne, cordwainer, of Bermondsey, Southwark,	sons of Giles, carpenter, decd.

Jas. Pytt,[1] cordwainer, son of Jas., cordwainer, of Bermondsey Street, Southwark
John Hooper of Ripple, Worcs., app. of Phil. Reading, wine cooper, decd., of Barton Street

[1] Also spelt *Pitt*.

John Child of St. Marylebone, Mdx., app. of John Lane, farrier, decd.
Wm. Powell of Wathing Street, London, app. of Wm. Evans, carpenter, now or late of Gloucester
John Ravenhill, hatter, of Bucklersbury, London, app. of Sam. Buckle, hatmaker, decd.
362 Jas. Taynton, wine cooper, son of Wm., wine cooper, decd., of Bristol
Nat. Hieron, oil-leather-dresser of Long Lane, Southwark, son of Nat., bodice-maker, decd., of Wotton under Edge
Wm. Bullock, cordwainer, of Carnaby Street, Westminster, son of Wm., cordwainer, of Coleford
Wm. Viner, limeburner, of Bristol, son of John, carpenter, decd.
Giles King, corporal, 15th Light Dragoons, son of Jas., bricklayer, decd.
Jas. Bromley, ropemaker, of Hereford, son of Thos., cooper, decd., of Barton Street
Hen. Harris, private, South Glos. Militia, app. in turn of Thos. Merrett and Virgil Cripps, decd., cordwainers
363 15 Sept Jas. Crowdy, gent., of Highworth, Wilts., son of Ric., yeoman, of Longford
Jas. Lloyd Bradley, whitesmith, of Sedgley, Staffs., son of Hen., butcher, decd.
John Cliff, wiredrawer, } sons of John, wiredrawer, decd., of Castle
Thos. Cliff, wiredrawer, } Lane, Southwark
Geo. Gardiner, ribbon-weaver, of St. Bartholomew the Great, London, son of Ant., gent., of London
Thos. Fowler, watchmaker, of St. Luke, Mdx., son of Giles, barber, decd., of Clerkenwell, Mdx.
364 Rob. Kirby, gent., of Pontypool, Mon., son of John, writing-master, of Chepstow, Mon.
Thos. Venn, private, South Glos. Militia, son of Thos., labourer, of Sandhurst
Hen. Mutlow, engraver, of Snow Hill, London, son of Thos., tailor
Steph. Skillerne, tailor, of Arundel Street, Strand, Mdx., son of Isaac, furrier, decd., of Winchcombe
Jos. Perris, saddler, son of Jos., butcher, decd.
John Reeve, bricklayer, of Bishopsgate Street, London, son of Jas., combmaker, decd.
365 Wm. Aycrigg, private, Surr. Militia, son of Benj., decd., of Upton upon Severn, Worcs.
Thos. Porter, baker, of Covent Garden, Westminster, son of John, grocer, decd.
Thos. Ellis, hairdresser, of St. Botolph, London, } sons of Ric.,
Dan. Ellis, jeweller, of Foster Lane, Westminster, } silversmith, decd.
John Guest, potter and glass-seller, of St. John Street, Mdx., son of Jacob, butcher, decd.
Wm. Billings, labourer, of Powick, Worcs., son of Wm., cordwainer, decd., of Charlton Kings
366 Sam. Lucas, drummer, South Glos. Militia, son of Thos., joiner, decd., of Thornbury
Wm. Goodwin, porter of Newgate Street, London, son of Wm., yeoman, of Leigh
Jas. Matthews, whitesmith, son of Edw., blacksmith, decd., of Whitechapel, Mdx.
Job Jefferis of Berkeley Square, Mdx., app. in turn of Chas. Browning, decd., and Thos. Read, bakers

Geo. Rogers, servant, of Hackney, Mdx., son of Benj., gent., decd., of Lyon's Inn, London

367 John Crowdy, baker, of Lincoln's Inn Fields, Westminster, son of Wm., decd., of St. Mary Magdalen's Hospital near Gloucester

Thos. Bower, private, South Glos. Militia, son of Sam., cordwainer

18 Sept Wm. Felton, lottery office keeper, of Leadenhall Street, London, Jos. Felton, broker, of Change Alley, London, Thos. Felton of 44, Leadenhall Street, London, } sons of Jos., shoemaker, decd., of Cheltenham

Benj. South, cordwainer, of Portsmouth, son of John, baker, decd.

368 Chas. Rudhall, ironmonger, of Brighton (*Brighthelmstone*), Suss., son of Abel, bellfounder, decd.

Wm. Baker, soldier, 1st Dragoon Guards, son of John, joiner, decd.

Edw. Ricketts of Piccadilly, Mdx., app. of Jos. Bennett, collar-maker

Jos. Reeve, private, North Glos. Militia, son of Jos., soldier, Worcester Volunteers[†]

Wm. George of the Light Dragoons, app. of Jos. Wood, baker

Benj. Beard of Windsor, Berks., app. of John Adams, cordwainer, decd.

N.B. The four next folios [pp. 369–72] being entered irregularly the entries are crossed through and carried to the new book [G.B.R., C9/9].[1]

GBR C9/9[2]

1 **William Lane, esq., mayor**

1780 20 Sept John Steel, ship's joiner, of Rotherhithe, Kent, son of John, carpenter, late of Littledean

29 Sept Jas. Window, gent., of Charing Cross, Westminster, son of Thos., peruke-maker, late of Gloucester

30 Sept John Jones, cider merchant, by fine

2 Oct Wm. Fendall, fellow of Merton College, Oxford University, by gift

Thos. Crawley-Boevey of Flaxley Abbey by gift

2 **John Bush, esq., mayor 1780–1**

23 Dec Sam. Syer,[3] clerk, of Redland, son of Sam., clerk, decd., of Bristol

1781 15 Jan John Jas. Hough, stationer, app. of Thos. Dunn, bookbinder

Ephraim Hall, collar-maker and coach-harness-maker, of Bristol, app. of Jos. Bennett, collar-maker

13 Mar Meredith Price, assize clerk on the Oxford circuit,[†] by gift

Abraham Saunders, esq., mayor 1781[4]

22 June Wm. Farren, butcher, son of Wm., butcher, decd.

6 July Wm. Jenkins, tailor, (by fine)

3 10 Aug Chas. Pace, apothecary, son of Thos., bricklayer, decd.

[1] Compared with GBR C 9/9, pp. 1–9 the entries in ibid. 8, pp. 369–72 are an incomplete record of admissions to the freedom between 20 Sept 1780 and 10 Mar 1783.

[2] Index of entrants at front.

[3] Sam. Sayer, historian of Bristol: Gray, *Antiquaries*, 74.

[4] Elected 5 June after Bush's death: GBR B 3/11, f. 228v.

3 Sept Thos. Bradley Pagett of Chipping Norton, Oxon., app. of Edw. Elton, grocer
29 Sept Edw. Rogers, esq., by gift
John Heathfield Hicks, M.D., by gift
1 Oct Sam. Jeynes, esq., of Tewkesbury by gift
Jas. Martin, esq., of Overbury, Worcs., by gift[1]

4 **Thos. Weaver, esq., mayor 1781–2**

19 Oct John Selfe, esq., of Sudgrove by gift
Sir Wm. Codrington, Bt., of Dodington by gift[2]
2 Nov John Raymond, esq., of Fairford by gift
n.d. Wm. Smith, chairman,[3] by fine
9 Nov Rob. Pleydell Wilton, gent., son of Hen., gent.
John Hinton, app. of Jos. Lewis, peruke-maker
1782 5 Jan Wm. Lloyd Baker of Castle End, Herefs., rector of Aston Ingham, Herefs., son of Thos. Baker, clerk, decd., of Bibury
5 7 Jan Thos. Phelps of Bulley (*Bullow*), app. of Ant. Workman, butcher
11 Jan Thos. Cam, yeoman, by fine
21 Jan Edw. Jas. Hector Jones of Monmouth by gift
25 Feb Wm. Binning, app. of John Ricketts, barber, peruke-maker, and hairdresser
11 May Powell Snell, esq., of Guiting Grange by gift
17 May Rob. Ladbroke, app. of Wm. Cheeseman, brushmaker
2 Aug Benj. Price, esq., associate on the Oxford circuit,† by gift. Sworn same day
16 Aug Rob. Sexty, yeoman, son of Geo., yeoman, of the Hill House, Ledbury, Herefs.
6 Wm. Hicks, pinmaker, son of Jas., pinmaker, late of Gloucester
2 Sept Wm. Window, app. of Jos. Wood, baker
9 Sept Jos. Bubb, saddler, son of Thos., baker, decd.
27 Sept Sam. Castle, victualler, late of the Salutation[4] by fine
28 Sept John Martin, esq., of Ham Court, Worcs., by gift
John Philpotts, merchant, of Bridgwater, Som., by fine
Jas. Morris, innholder, of Gloucester, formerly of Cheltenham, by fine
Rob. Hulbert, gardener, by fine

7 **Richard Webb, esq., mayor 1782–3**

1 Oct Thos. Went, clothier, of Uley by gift
John Cooke, wine merchant, by gift. Sworn same day
Geo. Dineley Goodyer, esq., by gift
John Carter, woolstapler, by gift
Thos. Hopkins Merrick, esq., of Bollitree (*the Bolley Tree*), Weston under Penyard, Herefs., by gift
14 Oct Mat. Paul, gent., of Newent by gift
8 2 Nov Wal. Wilkins, esq., of Maesllwch (*Maieslough*), Radnors., by gift
18 Nov Chas. Parsons, esq., of Kemerton, formerly of Worcester, son of John, gent., decd., of Kemerton

[1] M.P. for Tewkesbury, for helping to obtain an improvement Act for the city (21 Geo. III, c. 74): ibid. f. 303; Williams, *Parl. Hist. of Glos.* 250–1; cf. *V.C.H. Glos.* iv. 245.
[2] M.P. for Tewkesbury, for helping to obtain the improvement Act of 1781: GBR B 3/11, f. 303; Williams, *Parl. Hist. of Glos.* 250.
[3] Labourer, by act of 5 Nov 1781: GBR B 3/11, f. 310.
[4] In Barnwood: *V.C.H. Glos.* iv. 411.

22 Nov Edw. Vernon,† rector of Bourton-on-the-Water, by gift
9 Dec John Parker, esq., of Hasfield by gift
Thos. Clarke Bretherton, hairdresser, son of Jas., whitesmith
1783 2 Jan Hen. Smith, esq., of Minchin Lane, London, by gift
7 Jan Captain Thos. Raymond,[1] 1st battalion of Glos. Militia,† by gift
9 10 Jan John Smith, app. of Rob. Benson, glover, breeches-maker, and fellmonger
17 Feb Jacob Riddle, esq., of St. Philip in or near Bristol[2] by gift[3]
10 Mar Ric. Hill, app. of Jos. Boughton, currier
22 Mar Hen. Toye, esq., of Bristol by gift[3]
24 Mar Ric. Selwyn, app. of Jas. Lewis, collar-maker
28 Mar Sam. Span, esq., of Bristol by gift[3]
Alex. Edgar, esq., of Bristol by gift[3]
10 5 May Thos. Watts, son of Thos., butcher
12 May Thos. Hale, pewterer, son of Wm., coppersmith, decd., of Bristol
Ric. Perkins, pewterer, son of Ric., haberdasher, decd., of Bristol
6 June Thos. Mott by fine
3 July Ric. Clarke of Hasfield, app. in turn of Ric. Swayne, decd., and Mary Fauckes, butchers
26 July Chas. Parker of Madeley (*Madderly*), Salop., by fine
28 July Sam. Halifax, bishop of Gloucester, by gift
11 31 July Lucy Salcombe, victualler,[4] by fine
5 Aug Sir Geo. Onesiphorus Paul, Bt., of the Hill House, Rodborough, by gift
23 Aug John Herman Kater, sugar-baker, of Bristol by gift. Sworn same day
25 Aug John Olney,[5] app. of John Bush, woolstapler, decd.
John Way, butcher, son of John, butcher, decd.
29 Aug Thos. Cooke, shopkeeper, of Blakeney by fine
3 Oct Wm. Rogers, app. of Ric. Webb, grocer, tallow-chandler, and soap-boiler
4 Oct Dan. Wiley, gent., of Moreton Valence by gift
1 Nov Job Watts, gent., of Bristol*[6]

12 **[Charles Howard], earl of Surrey,[7] mayor 1783–4**

7 Oct Rob. Kingscote, esq., of Kingscote by gift. Sworn same day
8 Oct Thos. Brodrick of Lincoln's Inn, [Mdx.], by gift
20 Oct Wm. Musto, peruke-maker, by fine
1 Nov Job Watts, gent., of Bristol by gift[8]
8 Nov John Mayo of Stroud by fine
2 Dec Thos. Reynolds Moreton, Lord Ducie,†[9] by gift. Sworn same day
5 Dec John Wilkes, wiredrawer, of Wotton [near Gloucester]
13 John Holder, pinmaker, of Wotton [near Gloucester]
Thos. Holder, pinmaker, of Wotton [near Gloucester]
Ric. Perton, cordwainer, of Wotton [near Gloucester]
} by gift[10]

[1] From 1797 called Thos. Raymond Symons: Burke, *Land. Gent.* (1898), ii. 1436.
[2] i.e. the parish of St. Philip and St. Jacob.
[3] In return for the gift of the freedom of Bristol to John Webb, M.P. for Gloucester: GBR B 3/11, f.328.
[4] Spinster: ibid. f. 337v.
[5] Later called John Harvey Ollney: ibid. 12, f. 53; *V.C.H. Glos.* iv. 356, 408.
[6] Entry struck through; cf. below: GBR C 9/9, p. 12.
[7] *Complete Peerage*, ix. 633.
[8] Cf. above: GBR C 9/9, p. 11.
[9] Of Woodchester: *Complete Peerage*, iv. 475.
[10] Previously disfranchised, 28 July 1781, to enable them to give evidence in a cause between the mercers' company and a non-freeman: GBR B 3/11, ff. 298v., 344.

Edm. Best,[1] cordwainer, of Wotton [near Gloucester]
Wm. Jones, cordwainer, of Wotton [near Gloucester]
Hen. Wilton, wiredrawer,
Jas. Nott, labourer,
Thos. Marshfield, whitesmith,
Jas. Collerick, bodice-maker,
14 Thos. Edwards, } by gift[2]

1784 7 Jan Thos. Purnell Purnell, esq., of Kingshill by gift
26 Jan Jas. Commeline, esq., of Pembroke College, Oxford University, son of Jas., clerk, decd.
11 June Wm. Elliott, pinmaker, son of Wm., peruke-maker, decd.
18 June Steph. Nash, esq., of Bristol by gift
2 July Wm. Capel, esq., of Stroud, son of Wm., clothier, decd., of the Grove, Painswick
15 July Winchcombe Hen. (*Hen. Winchcomb*) Hartley, esq., of [Sodbury][3] by gift*[4]
15 16 July Sam. Critchley[5] by gift
John Belcher, victualler, of Gloucester, formerly of Norton, by fine
Wal. Bowcott by fine
23 July John James, mariner, by fine
12 Aug Wm. James, app. of Merrot Stephens, mercer
14 Aug Geo. [Cranfield] Berkeley†[6]
23 Aug Dan. Cox, surgeon and apothecary, son of Ric., barber, decd.
13 Sept Chas. Gwinnett, innholder, by fine
Sam. Lilly, yeoman, by fine
1 Oct Jas. Walwyn, esq., of Longworth, Herefs., by gift[7]
16 Thos. Erskine, barrister,† by gift[8]

Samuel Colborne, esq., mayor 1784–5

12 Nov Chas. Jeffs, tailor, son of Sam., pinmaker
Thos. Webb, app. of his father Thos., cordwainer
10 Dec Wm. Barnfield, app. of Dan. Smith, grocer
20 Dec Thos. Meek, app. of Ric. Dunn, peruke-maker
1785 19 Jan John Turner, banker,
John Hope, gent., of Barton Street, } by gift[9]
17 Benj. Saunders, wine merchant, eldest son of Abraham, esq., ald.
28 Mar Wm. Best, flaxdresser, son of Edm., cordwainer, of Wotton
4 Apr Thos. Nest, carpenter, son of Jas., pinmaker
22 Apr Chas. Wilkes, pinmaker, son of John, wiredrawer
Jas. Badger, pinmaker, son of Phoenix, labourer, decd.
Sam. Bower, pinmaker, son of Sam., cordwainer, decd.

[1] Edw. Best: ibid.; above: ibid. C 9/8, p. 324.

[2] Previously disfranchised, 28 July 1781, to enable them to give evidence in a cause between the mercers' company and a non-freeman: ibid. B 3/11, ff. 298v., 344.

[3] Also of Bucklebury, Berks.: Rudder, *Glos.* 674, 677–8.

[4] By act of 24 Sept 1781, for helping, while M.P. for Berkshire, the city obtain the improvement Act of 1781 (21 Geo. III, c. 74): GBR B 3/11, f. 303; Williams, *Parl. Hist. of Glos.* 68.

[5] Victualler, resigned 12 Mar 1795 to enable him to give evidence in a cause concerning the city's common meadows and readmitted 20 Mar 1795: GBR B 3/12, f. 222 and v.; below: ibid. C 9/9, p 119.

[6] Entry, interlined, originally recorded below: ibid. C 9/9, p. 71.

[7] For 'the unabated zeal with which he has opposed the ruinous system which has been so ruinous to the interest of this country': ibid. B 3/11, f. 350.

[8] For arguing, during the trial of the dean of St. Asaph, the rights of juries in libel cases: ibid. f. 367; cf. *D.N.B.*

[9] On their election to the common council: GBR B 3/12, f. 11 and v.

John Hambling, labourer, son of John, cooper, decd.
Ric. Harris, labourer, son of Ric., labourer
Wm. Ricketts, cordwainer, son of Wm., pinmaker, decd.
18 Jas. Escott, pinmaker, son of Jas., pinmaker
Jos. Bower, pinmaker, son of Sam., cordwainer, decd.
Wm. Maisey, app. of Wm. Bubb, carpenter
2 May Jas. Dadd, app. of John Wheatstone, cordwainer
Jos. Lewis, collar-maker, son of Thos., gardener, decd.
Thos. Meek, gardener, } apps. of Newton Brabant, pinmaker
Wm. Floyd, pinmaker, }
Wm. Dix, bricklayer, son of Thos., porter, decd.
6 May Thos. Holder, cordwainer, son of Chas., cordwainer
19 Thos. Wilton, tailor, son of Jas., pinmaker
9 May Wm. Davis, app. of Wm. Cowcher, pinmaker
John Boughton, staymaker, son of Ant., baker, decd.
John Hare, wiredrawer, son of Benj., pinmaker
John Matthews, cordwainer, son of Ric., pipemaker
Wm. Webley, labourer, son of Wm., yeoman, decd.
13 June John Tovey the younger, ironmonger, by fine
1 Aug Thos. Rogers, app. of John Moulder, baker
4 Aug Sam. Commeline, esq.,[1] son of Jas., clerk, decd.
29 Aug Ric. Addis, peruke-maker, app. in turn of Mary Cox, peruke-maker, and Chas. Thos. Cox, hairdresser

20 **Edwin Jeynes, esq., mayor 1785–6**

8 Oct Ric. Hill, gent., of Dymock by gift
12 Oct John Noble, esq., of Bristol by gift[2]
1786 27 Feb Thos. Wells, yeoman, by fine
Elizabeth Carter, widow, by fine
17 Mar Wm. Seyer, merchant, son of Sam., clerk, decd., of Bristol
30 Mar John Hollings, esq., of Stroud by gift
5 May John Wadley, baker, son of Ambrose, baker, decd.
8 May Ric. Wakefield of Newent, } apps. of Wm. Lane,
Thos. Ursell of West Smithfield, London, } cabinet-maker
21 10 June Ant. Keck, architect, of King's Stanley by gift
12 June Wm. Browning of Vere Street, Clare (*Clear*) Market, Mdx., app. of Wm. Bower, cordwainer
John Estcourt, hairdresser, son of Jas., pinmaker
Thos. Swayne Reeve, cordwainer, son of Jos., stonecarver, late of Gloucester
Thos. Jeynes, fisherman, son of Methuselah, victualler, decd.
16 June Chas. Glendall, cooper, of Gloucester, son of Thos., carpenter, of Wotton near the city
17 June Ric. Wood, victualler, by fine
10 July Nat. Taynton, tailor, son of Wal., feltmonger, of Ross, Herefs.
12 July Nat. Peach, esq., of Bownhams by gift
22 14 July Rob. Morgan, ship's captain in the East India Company's service,† by gift
15 July John Matthews, gent., of Newnham by gift
21 July John Calcott, victualler, by fine
24 July Wm. Wingate, drummer, North Glos. Militia, son of Wm., tailor
8 Sept Benj. Holford, labourer, son of Benj., wiredrawer

[1] Later clerk: *Alumni Oxon. 1715–1886*, i. 284; Hockaday Abs. ccxl.
[2] By act of 4 Nov 1782, in return for the gift of the freedom of Bristol to John Webb, M.P. for Gloucester: GBR B 3/11, f. 328.

			John Mann, cordwainer, son of Mat., skinner, decd.
		20 Sept	Thos. Andrews, app. of (Thos.) Adey, grocer*
23		22 Sept	Ric. Nayles, surgeon, by gift

John Webb, esq., mayor 1786–7

		2 Oct	Thos. Pear, victualler, by fine
		3 Oct	Hen. Fowke, gent.,[1] of Tewkesbury by gift. Sworn same day
		6 Oct	Thos. Medlicott, victualler, by fine
		9 Oct	Jos. Coopey, baker, son of Jos., yeoman, of Churchdown
			Hen. Wilton, gent., son of Hen., gent.
		20 Oct	Edw. Colston Grevile, clerk, son of Giles, apothecary, decd., of Bristol
24		6 Nov	Edm. Probyn, esq., of Newland by gift
		10 Nov	Jas. Gunn, brazier, son of Jas., cordwainer
		17 Nov	Thos. Gregory, corkcutter, of Gloucester, son of Rob., corkcutter, late of London
	1787	26 Mar	Geo. Powell, app. of Hen. Davis, pinmaker
			Thos. Harbert, app. of John Adey, pinmaker
		22 June	John Rudhall, bellfounder, son of Abel, bellfounder, decd.
			Wm. Hen. Cavendish Bentinck, duke of Portland,† by gift[2]
25			Wm. Bentinck, marquess of Titchfield,†[3] by gift
		19 July	Elijah Hill, victualler, by fine
		23 July	John Saunders, yeoman, by fine
			John Marshall, baker, by fine
		30 July	Chas. Organ, currier, son of Thos., innholder, decd.
		13 Aug	John Buckingham, yeoman, by fine
		17 Aug	Thos. Price, gent., son of Thos., gent., decd.
			Wm. Lawrence, esq., of Shurdington by gift
26		20 Aug	Thos. Long, currier, son of Thos., innholder, of Over
		17 Sept	Dennis Hutchings, button-maker, of Birmingham, son of Dennis, blacksmith, decd.
			John Overthrow, victualler, } sons of Sam., fisherman, decd.
			Thos. Overthrow, waterman, }
		29 Sept	Sam. Parkes, yeoman, by gift
		1 Oct	Jos. Harford, esq., of Bristol by gift[4]
			Chas. Hen. Wilton, musician, of York, son of Hen., gent.

27 **Sir John Guise, Bt., mayor 1787–8**

		2 Oct	Sam. Bowyer the younger, Chancery clerk,† by gift[5]
		8 Oct	John Lewis, app. of John Machen, cordwainer
			John Harper, app. of John Wheatstone, cordwainer
		22 Oct	Benj. Sadler, gent., son of Jas., esq., ald., decd.
		2 Nov	Geo. Elward, upholder,[6] of London by gift
			Edw. Fishwick, esq., of London by gift
		10 Nov	John Probyn, clerk, of Newland[7] by gift

[1] Attorney: ibid. 12, f. 53.

[2] For 'his inviolable attachment and steady adherence to the true constitutional principles of this country': ibid. f. 71v.

[3] Son of the duke of Portland: *Complete Peerage*, x. 595.

[4] By act of 4 Nov 1782, in return for the gift of the freedom of Bristol to John Webb, M.P. for Gloucester: GBR B 3/11, f. 328.

[5] By act of 29 Sept 1780, of the Exchequer Office, Inner Temple, London: ibid. f. 281v.

[6] Upholsterer: ibid. 12, f. 53.

[7] Rector of Abenhall: Hockaday Abs. xcv.

		16 Nov	Ric. Smith, weaver, son of Jas., weaver, of Painswick
28	1788	14 Jan	Wm. Salcomb, waterman, son of Sam., waterman, decd., of Tirley, formerly of Defford, Worcs.
			Thos. Drinkwater, cordwainer, son of John, labourer
		21 Jan	Wm. Hinton, pinmaker, son of Wm., pinmaker
		28 Jan	Geo. Church, app. of Ric. Evans, ropemaker, decd.
			Thos. Matthews the younger, farrier, app. of his brother John, blacksmith
		15 Feb	Sam. Farmer Sadler, clerk, of Sandhurst, son of Jas., esq., ald., decd.
			Thos. Lewis, app. of Chas. Peart, cordwainer
29		29 Feb	Jos. North, victualler, by fine
		15 Mar	Chas. King, bricklayer, of Tewkesbury, son of Jas., bricklayer, decd.
		26 Mar	Benj. Loscomb, esq., of Bristol by gift[1]
		19 May	Edw. Griffiths, victualler, by fine[2]
		30 May	Cartwright Maddocks, app. of Cartwright Maddox, baker
		20 June	Thos. Woodward, cabinet-maker, son of Ric., victualler, decd.
		11 July	Wm. Piffe, app. in turn of Jas. Herbert, Ant. Workman, butchers, and Workman's widow Elizabeth
30		14 Aug	John Thos. Townsend[†3] by gift[4]
		18 Aug	Geo. Worrall, gent., son of Sam., esq., of Clifton
		5 Sept	Chris. Mayall by fine
		8 Sept	Jas. Broughton, app. of his father Jas., peruke-maker
		17 Sept	John Nash of Broseley, Salop., app. of Wm. Lane, joiner and cabinet-maker
		26 Sept	John Mountain, app. of Francis Mayo, grocer, decd.
		29 Sept	Benj. Aycrigg, gent., son of Chas., surgeon, of Newent
31		3 Oct	Thos. Fream, app. of Wm. and Ric. Cowcher, pinmakers
			Wm. Drinkwater, victualler, by fine

Samuel Woodcock, esq., mayor 1788–9

		10 Oct	Jas. Bower, carpenter, son of Sam., cordwainer, decd.
			Elijah King, victualler, by fine
		13 Oct	Hen. Cruger, esq., of Bristol by gift[5]
		3 Nov	Spencer Thompson, app. of Wm. Washbourn, apothecary
		14 Nov	Thos. Shea, victualler, by fine
32		17 Nov	Thos. Probyn, esq., of Newland by gift
		5 Dec	Chas. Escutt, pinmaker, son of Jas., pinmaker
		15 Dec	Wm. Craddock, app. in turn of Jas. Page and Mary Cox, hairdressers
		19 Dec	Ric. Hinton, app. in turn of Ralph Critchley, decd., Elizabeth Critchley, late of Gloucester, and John Adey, pinmakers
		24 Dec	Edm. Probyn the younger, esq., of Newland by gift
	1789	3 Jan	Hen. Burgh, esq., of Stroud by gift
33	1789	15 Jan	Dodington Hunt, esq., of Charlton Kings by gift. Sworn this day
		16 Jan	Jos. Bonnor Cheston, gent.,[6] son of Ric. Browne Cheston, M.D.
		17 Jan	Chas. Pleydell, yeoman, son of Chas., baker, decd.

[1] By act of 4 Nov 1782, in return for the gift of the freedom of Bristol to John Webb, M.P. for Gloucester: GBR B 3/11, f. 328.

[2] Fine of £5, his wife having purchased the freedom for £20 before their marriage: ibid. 12, f. 89.

[3] ? of Chislehurst, Kent: *Complete Peerage*, xii (1), 592.

[4] By act of 24 Sept 1781 the freedom was granted to his father Thos., M.P. for Whitchurch, Hants., for helping obtain the improvement Act of 1781 (21 Geo. III, c. 74): GBR B 3/11, f. 303; *Complete Peerage*, xii (1), 590–2.

[5] By act of 4 Nov 1782, in return for the gift of the freedom of Bristol to John Webb, M.P. for Gloucester: GBR B 3/11, f. 328.

[6] Later clerk: *Alumni Cantab. 1752–1900*, ii. 25.

1789 John Bullock, cordwainer, son of Sam., cordwainer
John Roberts, app. in turn of Edw. Bayliss, decd., and John Baylis, woolstaplers
Thos. Wood of Gloucester, servant of Jas. Commeline and son of Wm., yeoman, of the outhamlet of St. Mary,[1] by patrimony
34 Wm. Simpson, carpenter, son of Wm., pinmaker, decd.
John Jeffs, corkcutter, son of Jos., corkcutter, decd.
Wm. Bower, cordwainer, son of Wm., cordwainer
Wm. Dowell, pinmaker, son of Jas., pinmaker
Wm. Hickman, cordwainer, son of Benj., cordwainer
Paul Mutlow, tailor, son of Thos., tailor, decd.
Benj. Newton, clerk, of Defynnog (*Devynnock*), [Brec.],[2] son of Benj., clerk, decd.
35 John Merrett, baker, of Gloucester, } sons of Thos., baker,
Thos. Merrett, hairdresser, of Gloucester, } of Mitcheldean
Ric. Turberville, app. of Ralph Fletcher, baker, decd.
Dan. Toysom, app. of John Bush, woolstapler, decd.
Thos. Stephens, app. of Ric. Weaver, blacksmith
Thos. Commeline, gent., son of Jas., clerk, decd.
Thos. Rudge, cheesemonger, son of Thos., wine cooper
36 Wm. Okey, brushmaker, son of Thos., innholder
Wm. Byard, app. of Pettat Gardiner, brushmaker
Wm. Labetter, app. of Wm. Dunn, tiler
Chas. Eldridge, app. of Pettat Gardiner, brushmaker
Sam. Wadley, hairdresser, son of Ambrose, baker, decd.
Thos. Gunn, hairdresser, son of Jas., cordwainer
Chas. Wheeler, carpenter, son of Ric., carpenter, decd.
Sam. Arch, stonemason, son of John, baker, decd.
37 John Hyett, cooper, son of John, cooper
Nat. Dadd, app. of Chas. Taylor, tinplate-worker, late of Gloucester
Thos. Powell, pinmaker, son of Wm., tailor, decd.
John Best, hairdresser, son of Jas., wiredrawer, decd.
John Hutchings, app. of Wm. Evans, joiner
Wm. Wilton, app. of John Wilton, pinmaker, decd.
38 19 Jan Wm. Mutlow, organist,[3] son of Thos., tailor, decd.
Rob. Mutlow, } sons of Wm., of Dursley
Wm. Mutlow, }
Geo. Hawker of Rodborough, son of Peter, clerk, of Woodchester
John Boughton of Broadoak, app. of Ric. Wood, mercer
Sam. Lewis, gardener, son of Ralph, gardener, decd.
John Washbourn, stationer, } sons of Nat., confectioner
39 Nat. Washbourn, confectioner, }
Wm. Winnett, labourer, son of Wm., labourer, decd., of Stroud
Dan. Carter Lewis, clerk, son of Jos., hairdresser
Miles Price, gent., son of Thos., broker, decd.
Sam. Coldrick, labourer, of Ashchurch, son of Thos., labourer, decd., of Tewkesbury
Wm. Randall, collar-maker, son of Chas., tailor, decd., of Tewkesbury
Wm. Smith, gent., of Warwick Lane, London, son of John, clothier, decd., of Dursley

[1] Part of St. Mary de Lode parish outside the city: *V.C.H. Glos.* iv. 382.
[2] *South Wales.*
[3] Of Gloucester cathedral: D. Lysons, *Origin and Progress of the Meeting of the Three Choirs* (1812), 231.

40 John Perks, labourer, of Conderton, Overbury, Worcs., son of Wm., labourer, of Beckford[1]
Thos. Richardson, surgeon, of Newent by gift. Sworn this day
Jos. Young, labourer, son of John, yeoman, of Westbury-on-Severn
Sam. Wathen, esq., son of Jos., clothier, of Thrupp, Stroud
Benj. Perris, cordwainer, son of Thos., pinmaker, decd.
Wm. Ricketts, app. of Wm. Wathen, pinmaker
41 Wm. Holder, app. of Nat. Biddle, grocer
Sam. Vail, yeoman, son of Wm., yeoman, of Bulley
Giles Venn, labourer, of Norton, son of Thos., labourer, of Sandhurst
Jas. Wal. Cook, son of Bernard, grocer
Reginald Winniatt, clerk,[2] son of Reginald, esq., decd., of Stanton
Jas. Vail, yeoman, son of Wm., yeoman, of Bulley
Ric. Dole, app. of John Wheatstone, cordwainer
42 Wal. Harris, yeoman, son of Wal., yeoman, of Walford, Herefs.
John Young, labourer, of Newnham, son of John, yeoman, of Westbury-on-Severn
Wm. Fletcher, baker, son of Ralph, baker, decd.
Thos. Butt, yeoman, son of Wm., yeoman, of Over
Wm. Young, son of Ric., labourer, of Westbury-on-Severn
Rob. Philips, esq., of Hereford by gift. Sworn this day
Josiah Jenner Jordan, app. of Edm. Stock and Edw. Holder, grocers
43 Chas. Venn, labourer, of Blaisdon, son of Thos., labourer, decd., of Sandhurst
Jos. Young, pig dealer, son of Rob., labourer, decd., of Westbury-on-Severn
John Crump, brushmaker, son of Thos., serjeant-at-mace
Wm. Clark, schoolmaster, app. of his father Wm., woolcomber, of Churchdown
20 Jan Rob. Cook of Saintbridge, app. of Wm. Baldwin, tailor
Hen. Heane, collier, son of Hen., collier, of Ruardean
Thos. Ady, attorney, son of Thos., gent.
44 John Scudamore, esq., son of John, esq., of Kentchurch, Herefs.
Thos. Dix, carpenter, of Cheltenham, son of Thos., porter, late of Gloucester
Francis King, bricklayer, of Brislington, Som., son of Jas., bricklayer, late of Gloucester
Francis Child, heelmaker, of Bristol, son of John, weaver, decd., of St. Philip and St. Jacob
John Fownes, wine cooper, son of Godfrey, colourman, decd., of Bristol
Wm. White, cordwainer, of Walford, Herefs., son of Ric., carpenter, late of Newent
John Ireland, pinmaker, of Southwark, son of John, pinmaker, of Birmingham
45 1789 Wm. Badger, wiredrawer, app. of his father Jonathan, pinmaker
Hen. Jelfe, porter, of Clifton, son of Hen., carpenter, decd., of Weston under Penyard, Herefs.
Dan. Smith, cooper, of Stonehouse, son of Aaron, cooper, of Leonard Stanley
Chas. Tomlins, glover, of Worcester, } sons of Chas., glover, decd.
John Tomlins, glover, of Worcester, }

[1] County given as *Worcs.*
[2] Landowner and rector of Stanton with Snowshill: Rudder, *Glos.* 688; Hockaday Abs. cccxlix.

1789 Thos. Blanch, heelmaker, son of Thos., heelmaker, of Bristol
Wm. Bennett of Longford, app. of Wm. Barton, plumber
46 Isaac Barker, glover, } sons of John, labourer, decd., of Hereford
John Barker, tailor, }
Thos. Bond, collar-maker, of Birmingham, son of Sam., collar-maker
Chas. Price, cordwainer, of Ledbury, Herefs., son of Wm., cordwainer
Phil. Allard Ward, glasscutter, son of Ric., pinmaker, of St. Philip and St. Jacob
Jas. Bosley, husbandman, of Abenhall, son of Jas., miller, decd., of Flaxley
Wm. Perry, organist, } sons of Ric., wine merchant, decd.,
47 John Perry, wine merchant, } of Hereford
Geo. Derrett of Badgeworth, } apps. of John Derrett, butcher
Jas. Derrett of Brockworth, }
Wm. Wintle, breeches-maker, son of Ric., victualler, decd.
John Osborne, app. of Sam. Bond, collar-maker
Chas. Beard, gauzedresser, son of Jas., sackweaver and woolcomber, decd., of Bell Lane, Spitalfields, London
Wm. Evans, caulker, of London, son of Wm., carpenter
48 John Dowell, cordwainer, son of Ric., cordwainer, of Bristol
Jos. Brown, soapboiler, son of Nic., wine cooper, of Chepstow, Mon.
Jos. Coopey, husbandman, son of Ric., yeoman, of Badgeworth
Jas. Smith, weaver, son of Jas., weaver, of Painswick
John Rowles, cordwainer, of Brookthorpe, son of Wm., cordwainer, of Bulley
John Bamford, labourer, of Stapleton, son of Thos., labourer, of Littledean
John Dower, tailor, son of John, tailor, of Whitechapel, London
49 John Woore, gent., son of Thos., hatter
John Jones, cooper, son of John, cooper, of Newent
Jas. Cole, tailor, of Rodborough, son of John, cordwainer, decd., of Hasfield
Jos. Lewis, gent., of Dinchill,[1] Herefs., son of Jos., tiler and plasterer
John Paull, app. of Virgil Cripps, cordwainer, late of Gloucester
Jas. Crowdy, porter, of Gloucester, son of Jas., labourer, of St. Mary Magdalen's Hospital near Gloucester
Thos. Charter, app. of his father Thos., woolstapler, decd.
50 Chas. Ward, bricklayer, of Cheltenham, son of Jas., bricklayer, late of Gloucester
John Phelps, cordwainer, son of John, staymaker, of Woodmancote
Thos. Rudge, cordwainer, of Frampton on Severn, son of John, joiner, decd., of Frocester
Nat. Taynton, pewterer, son of Thos., pewterer, late of Bristol
Wm. Harris, farrier, of Bristol, son of Sam., carpenter, decd.
Jas. Hoskins, beam-maker, son of Jas., cordwainer, decd., of Bristol
Wm. Broadway, weaver, } sons of Thos., weaver, of London
51 John Broadway, weaver, }
Sam. Broadway, weaver, son of Sam., weaver, of London
Edw. Jenner, surgeon, son of Steph., clerk, decd., of Berkeley
Nat. Gardiner, baker, of Eastleach, son of John, baker, of Sheepscombe
John Fletcher of Hempsted, app. of Geo. Mutlow, wiredrawer
Rob. Hammonds, cooper, son of Rob., cooper, decd., of Stroud

[1] Altered from *Donnington*.

52 21 Jan Ric. Phil. Scudamore, esq., of the Inner Temple, London, son of John, esq., of Kentchurch, Herefs.

Jos. Hill, carpenter, son of Jos., glass-bottle-maker, decd., of Bristol

Jos. Innell, cook, of St. Dunstan, Mdx.,
John Innell, seaman, of Chancery Lane, London,
} sons of John, porter of Lincoln's Inn, London

John Geo. Hannington, clerk, of Eton, Bucks., son of John, gent., decd.

Jas. Heane, coalminer, of Ruardean, son of Hen., victualler, decd.

Thos. Fream, broker, of Worcester, son of John, butcher, decd., of Newent

Wm. Badger, breeches-maker, of Worcester, son of Jas., pargeter, decd.

53 Marks Barrett, baker, of Worcester,
Wm. Humphris Barrett, baker,
Edm. Barrett, glover, of Worcester,
} sons of Wm., baker, decd., of Cheltenham

Wm. Bond, glover, son of Nat., stationer, decd., of Worcester

Jas. Wingate of Bristol, app. of Hen. Wintle, brushmaker, decd.

Jasper Selwyn of Shoreditch, Mdx., app. of Dan. Freeman, whitesmith

Wm. Badnedge of Cirencester, app. of his father Ralph, currier, decd.

54 Thos. Partridge of Worcester, app. of Wm. Woodward, cabinet-maker

Wm. Trotman, draper and tailor, of Bristol, son of Wm., cutler, decd.

Wm. Taylor, labourer, son of John, cutler, of Cirencester

Ferdinando Niccolls, sawyer, son of Gregory, schoolmaster, of Westerleigh

John Batchford, stocking-framework-knitter, son of John, labourer, of Tewkesbury

John Fletcher of Bristol, app. of Edw. Bloxham, cooper

Ric. Child, glass-master, son of John, cordwainer, of Bristol

55 Thos. Cooper, baker, son of Thos., baker, decd., of St. Philip and St. Jacob

Thos. Wells, clerk, of Worcester College, Oxford University, son of Thos., clerk, decd., of Cowley

Dan. Trotman, pinmaker, of Birmingham, son of Dan., tailor, decd.

Wm. Alexander, gent., son of Wm., cooper

Wm. Hartland, turner, of George Street, Grosvenor Square, London, son of Thos., pinmaker, decd.

Jas. Long, cordwainer, son of Giles, cordwainer, of Bedminster, Som.

Wm. Percival Clark, pinmaker, of St. Giles in the Fields, Mdx., son of Wm., pinmaker

56 Thos. Powell, turner, son of John, pinmaker, decd., of Bermondsey Street, Surr.

Thos. Hartland, hairdresser, of Islington, Mdx., son of Thos., pinmaker, decd.

Rob. Hare, hairdresser, of Birmingham, son of Benj., pinmaker

Jas. Crowdy, gent., of Swindon, Wilts, son of Wm., yeoman, of Wotton near Gloucester

Nat. Bond, glover, son of Nat., stationer, decd., of Worcester

Thos. Smith,[1] esq., son of Rob., esq.

Jos. Gunn, cordwainer, of London, son of Jas., cordwainer

57 Thos. Nest, baker, of Swallow Street, Piccadilly, Westminster, son of Nester, late of Brentford (*Branford*), Mdx.

[1] Later called Thos. Smith Crawfurth: Glos. R.O., D 4453, Gloucester (Clarence Street) deeds 1758–1886.

1789 John Perks, labourer, of Bretforton, Worcs.,
Thos. Perks, labourer, of White Ladies Aston, Worcs.,
Sam. Perks, labourer, of Old Shottery, Warws., } sons of Sam, labourer, late of Beckford

Edm. Wadley, hairdresser, of Bristol, son of Thos., hairdresser, of Newnham

Wm. Harris, sailmaker, of Woolaston, son of Wal., yeoman, of Walford, Herefs.

58 Rob. Williams, brazier, of Worcester, son of Jas., innholder, decd.

John Cole, pinmaker, son of Jas., pinmaker, of London

Ric. Merrett, saddler, of Bath,
Peter Merrett, goldsmith, of Bath, } sons of Ric., farrier, decd.

Jos. Coules, china riveter, of St. Luke, Mdx., son of Jos., pipemaker, decd., of Bristol

Ellis Taylor Farren, butcher, son of Wm., butcher, decd.

Chas. Ferebee, clothdrawer,
59 Wm. Ferebee, cordwainer, } sons of John, clothdrawer, of Uley

Wm. Lewis, cordwainer, son of Jas., cordwainer

John Jeynes, cabinet-maker, of Bristol, son of Wm., baker, decd.

Geo. Worrall Counsell, gent.,[1] son of Joshua, apothecary, decd.

Wm. Price, surgeon, of London, son of Wm., cordwainer, decd.

22 Jan Jas. Gibbs, labourer, of Llangarron, Herefs., son of Thos., blacksmith, decd., of Dursley

60 Steph. Child, tailor, son of Thos., tailor, decd., of Chalford

John Guilding, labourer, of Powick, Worcs., son of Wm., labourer, of Hanley, Worcs.

Jas. Yeend, tinplate-worker, of Gloucester, son of John, butcher, decd., of Little Comberton, Worcs.

Jos. Harrison, plushmaker, of Banbury, Oxon.,
Wm. Harrison, plushmaker, of Banbury, Oxon., } sons of Geo., plushmaker, of Adderbury (*Hathabury*), Oxon.

Wm. Elliott, clerk, of Westcott Barton, Oxon., son of Nat., esq., of Oxford

61 Marmaduke Engley, bricklayer, of St. Marylebone, Mdx., son of Wm., bricklayer, decd., of St. George, Mdx.

John Birt, glass manufacturer, of London, son of John, cider merchant, late of [ ] (*Leimsten*),[2] Worcs.

Jas. Smith, tailor, son of Hen., saddler, decd., of Coleford

Jas. Elliott, servant, of Dowdeswell, son of Wm.,, peruke-maker, decd.

Wm. Merry, cordwainer, of Hackney, Mdx., son of Wm., pinmaker, decd.

John Gurner, brassfounder, of Moorfields, London, son of Jas., smith, decd.

62 John Pitt, cordwainer,
Ric. Pitt, cordwainer, } sons of Jas., cordwainer, of Bermondsey Street, St. Mary Magdalen, Surr.

Mat. Pitt, waterman, son of Sam., carpenter, decd., of St. George in the East, Mdx.

Ric. Young, waterman, of Upton upon Severn, Worcs., son of John, labourer, of Westbury-on-Severn

[1] Attorney and historian of Gloucester: *V.C.H. Glos.* iv. 159, 168.

[2] Not identified.

John Rudge, jacksmith, of Bulls Rents, the Park, Southwark, son of Wm., pinmaker, of 3, Mango Yard, Castle Lane, Southwark

Miles White, sawyer, of Oxford Road, Mdx., son of Thos., carpenter, decd., of St. Briavels

63 Geo. Harmar, gent.,
Jas. Harmer, gent.,
Ric. Harmar, banker, of Stangate Street, Lambeth, Surr., } sons of Thos., wharfinger

Sam. Mutlow, apothecary, of Pall Mall, Westminster, son of Thos., tailor, decd.

Wm. Probyn, clerk, of Goodrich, Herefs.,[1] by gift. Sworn this day

Wm. Venn, labourer, of Eldersfield, Worcs., son of Wm., labourer, of Ashleworth

Wm. Greville, labourer, of Eldersfield, Worcs., son of Wm., labourer, of Charlton Kings

64 Chas. Bassett, glazier and painter, of Southwark, son of Isaac, joiner, decd.

Ric. Smith of Coberley, app. of Jas. Middleton, woolcomber

Wm. Child, accountant, son of John, cordwainer, of Bristol

John Turner, hatter, of Gloucester, son of John, gent., of King's Stanley

Arthur Yarnold, hairdresser, son of John, cabinet-maker, decd., of Ledbury, Herefs.

Ric. Dix, bluemaker, of Whitecross Street, St. Luke, Mdx., son of Thos., porter, decd.

Ric. Wintle, baker, of Wellclose Square, Mdx., son of Ric., innholder, decd.

65 Berkeley Concklin, gent., of Queen's Square, Bristol, son of Berkeley, gent., decd., of Bristol

Wm. Ferebee, yeoman, son of Jos., yeoman, decd., of Uley

John Child, whitesmith, of Petty France, Westminster, son of John, weaver, decd., of St. Philip and St. Jacob

Ric. Coopey, grocer, of Gloucester, son of Ric., yeoman, of Badgeworth

Dan. Cope, waterman, son of Ric., baker, decd.

Chas. Elmes, mercer, of Gloucester, son of Wm., banker, of Hereford

Wm. Rea, app. of Thos. Rea, baker

Thos. Pearce, button-maker, of Pools Building, Mount Pleasant, Cold Bath Fields, Mdx., son of Thos., button-maker, decd., of Cold Bath Fields, Mdx.

66 Jos. Colborne, esq.,[2] son of John, esq., of Stroud

John Higgins, clerk, of Llandinabo, Herefs., (by gift). Sworn this day

John Griffiths of Hackney, Mdx., app. of Cartwright Maddox, baker

Wm. Harris, painter, son of Thos., farrier, decd.

Phil. Addis of Weston under Penyard, Herefs., app. of Cartwright, Maddox, baker

Geo. Holder, apothecary, of Gloucester, son of Geo., surgeon, decd., of Cirencester

John Pearce, mercer, of Lombard Street, London, son of Thos., button-maker, decd., of Cold Bath Fields, London

Thos. Foster of Bristol, app. in turn of Thos. Branch and Chas. Taylor, tinplate-workers

[1] Of Newland: GBR B 3/12, f. 53; vicar of Longhope: *Alumni Oxon. 1715–1886*, iii. 1156.

[2] Later clerk: *Alumni Oxon. 1715–1886*, i. 273; Glos. R.O., D 1722/15.

67 1789 Thos. Broadway alias Braddis, silkweaver, of Shoreditch, Mdx., son of Jas., silkweaver, of Bedlam Green, Mdx.

Jas. Jennings, printer, son of Sam., printer, of Fleet Market, London

Jas. Clutterbuck, cordwainer, of Southwark, son of Edw., butcher, decd., of Bettle Bridge, Southwark

Jas. Ward, farrier, of St. Catherine, Tower Hamlets, Mdx., son of Jas., bricklayer, decd.

Chas. Child, corn factor, son of Thos., tailor, decd., of Bisley

23 Jan Thos. Skillerne, cordwainer, of Highgate near London, son of Isaac, furrier, decd., of Winchcombe

68 Chas. Skillerne, currier, of Berkeley Street, Clerkenwell, Mdx., son of Steph., schoolmaster, decd., of Winchcombe

Wm. Higgins, cordwainer, of [the] Crown [and] Anchor, Strand, London, son of John, cabinet-maker, of Abergavenny, Mon.

Chas. Aycrigg, apothecary, of Hereford, son of Chas., surgeon, of Newent

Jas. Clark, gent., of Lincoln's Inn, London, son of John, pinmaker, decd.

Francis Welles, gent., of Upton upon Severn, Worcs., son of Thos., clerk, decd., of Cowley

Wm. Long, butcher, of Kenchester, Herefs., son of Thos., victualler, of Over

69 Wm. Maisey, app. of Mat. Cooke the elder, plasterer

Thos. Roberts, postboy, of Bath, son of Thos., baker, decd., of Upton upon Severn, Worcs.

Jas. Ellis, goldsmith, of Old Change, London, son of Ric., silversmith, decd.

Wm. Smith, hairdresser, of Brecon (*Brecknock*), son of Abraham, flaxdresser

Thos. Bamford, silversmith, of 6, Cortin Road near Shoreditch, Mdx., son of Thos., silversmith, decd., of London

Thos. Holder, mercer, of Marlborough, Wilts., son of Geo., surgeon, decd., of Cirencester

Wm. Stoner, clothier, of Kingswood, Wilts., son of Antioch, baker, late of London

70 Obadiah Griffith of Llanrumney, Mon., app. of Phil. Reading, cooper, decd.

Wm. Gardiner, tobacconist, of Chepstow, Mon., son of Ant., gent., of London

Wm. Barrett, cordwainer, of Wardour Street, Soho, Westminster, son of Ric., factor, decd., of Leather Lane, Holborn, Mdx.

Wm. Brook, esq., of Grove House, Bromsberrow, by gift. Sworn this day

Jos. Stratford, coachman, of Gloucester, son of John, baker, decd., of Barnwood

John Child, carpenter, of Longdon, Worcs., son of Ric., carpenter, of Southwark

71 Wm. Browning,[1] labourer, of Longney,[2] son of Chas. Lyndon (*Lindle*) Browning, baker, decd.

Wm. Jones, cooper, of Hereford, son of John, cooper, of Newent

[1] Wm. Browning, son of Leon., baker, decd.; GBR B 3/12, f. 159v.

[2] County given as *Worcs.*

Elias Clevely, cordwainer, of Cheltenham, Jas. Cleevely, cordwainer, of Whitechapel, London, } sons of Price, cordwainer, of London

Jos. Welch, tailor, of Oxford, son of Benj., tailor, decd., of Hayden

24 Jan Geo. Cranfield Berkeley, son of Augustus Berkeley, earl [of Berkeley, decd.].†[1] Sworn 14 Aug 1784[2]

Jas. Lane of St. Martin's Lane, Westminster, son of Wm., brushmaker, of Bristol

Dan. Mayo, stonemason, of Stratford, Essex, son of Thos., butcher, decd.

72 Wm. Webley, hairdresser and perfumer, of Bath, son of Ric., perukemaker, of Cheltenham

Geo. Baylis, butler, of Bath, son of Wm., comber, of Painswick

Rob. Clark, joiner, of Strand, Westminster, son of Chas., blacksmith, decd., of Arlingham

Rob. Sextie, hairdresser, son of Rob., schoolmaster, decd., of Lower Marsh, Lambeth, Surr.

Wm. Barrett, pinmaker, son of Wm., pinmaker, of St. Saviour, Southwark

Wm. Freame, glazier, son of Wm., glazier, of St. Luke, Chelsea

John Tracy, D.D., of Oxford University,[3] son of Thos. Chas., V. Tracy, decd., of Toddington

73 Benj. Phelps, tailor, of Soho Square, Mdx., son of John, staymaker, of Bishop's Cleeve

Thos. House of Tothill (*Tottell*) Street, Westminster, app. of Wm. Bubb, carpenter

Thos. Baylis, servant, of 9, Old Bond Street, Piccadilly, Westminster, son of Wm., comber, of Painswick

John Turner, fisherman, son of John, yeoman, decd., of Elmore

Wm. Gardiner, servant, of London, son of Thos., butcher, decd.

John Wood, carpenter, of Battersea, Surr., son of Wm., yeoman, of Barton Street St. Mary near Gloucester

Thos. Elliott, cordwainer, of Fleet Street, London, son of Wm., barber, decd.

74 Rob. Haviland, distiller, of London, son of Wm., yeoman, of Coberley

Wm. Augustus Holder, linen-draper, of Gloucester, son of Geo., surgeon, decd., of Cirencester

John Guilding, yeoman, son of Sam., yeoman, of Defford, Worcs.

John Hall, portrait painter, son of Benj., skinner, decd., of Bristol

Francis Drake, wiredrawer, son of Dan., wiredrawer, of Queen Street, the Park, Southwark

Zachariah Venn, labourer, of Cheltenham, son of Zachariah, labourer, decd., of Norton

John Brookes, app. of John Cooke, pargeter

75 Wm. Wheeler, baker and miller, of St. Anne, Limehouse, Mdx., John Wheeler, pinmaker, of St. Anne, Limehouse, Mdx., } sons of Wm., millwright and wheelwright, decd.

Thos. Stephens, carpenter, of Windmill Lane, London, son of Wm., barber, decd.

[1] *Complete Peerage*, ii. 146.
[2] Cf. above: GBR C 9/9, p. 15.
[3] Warden of All Souls: *Complete Peerage*, xii (2), 4.

1789 Lewis Fletcher of George Street, Portman Square, Mdx., app. of Wm. Draper, plumber and glazier, decd.

Sam. Merrett, cordwainer, son of Sam., cordwainer, decd.

Wm. Elmes, ship's master, of St. George in the East, Mdx., son of Wm., mercer, decd.

76 Thos. Ireland, saddler, of Piccadilly, Westminster, son of Wm., cooper

Wm. Bick of Gravel Lane, Southwark, son of Wm., cordwainer, decd., of Northampton

Jos. Pegler Cummings, cheesemonger, of Bishopsgate Street, London, son of Wm., baker, of Carmarthen

26 Jan And. Foley of Haseley,[1] Oxon., by gift. Sworn this day

Jas. Hereford, esq., of Sufton, Herefs., by gift. Sworn this day

Thos. White, builder, of Bristol, son of Thos., clothworker, of Stroud

77 Thos. Baker, gent., of London, son of Thos., esq., of Lugwardine, Herefs.

Thos.Turner, clerk, of Sherston (*Sherston Magna*), Wilts., son of John, gent., decd., of King's Stanley

John Harmar, gent., of Piccadilly, Westminster, son of Thos., wharfinger

Dan. Bond, printer, son of Ric., printer, of London

Rog. Longden, gent., son of Rob., gent., of Doctors' Commons, London

Edw. Francis Coulston, esq., son of Alex., clerk, of Filkins, Oxon.

Thos. Fuller, app. of Jos. Fuller, pargeter, decd.

78 Ant. Boughton, baker, of High Street, Southwark, son of Ant., baker, decd.

Sam. Steel, cordwainer, of Dursley, son of John, cooper, decd., of Coleford

Thos. Hayward, esq., son of John, clerk, of Withington

John Randall, apothecary,
Josiah Randall, mercer, of London, } sons of John, mason, of Oxford

Chas. Bubb, linen-draper, of London, son of Hen., victualler, decd.

Thos. Ridgeley, brushmaker, of Uxbridge, Mdx., son of John, gent.

79 John Terrett, surgeon, of Tewkesbury by gift. Sworn this day

Sam. Cook, glover, son of Thos., glover, decd., of Dursley

Francis Tyler, currier, of London, son of Chas., plumber, decd., of Bristol

Thos. Wyndham, esq., of Dunraven Castle, Glam., son of Chas. Wyndham Edwin, esq., of Clearwell

Thos. Young, private, 15th or King's Light Dragoons, app. of John Wheatstone, cordwainer

Wm. Woolles alias Woones, waterman, son of Rob., waterman, decd., of Minsterworth

80 Thos. Jones, app. of his father Thos., saddler

Wm. Hopkins, gent., son of Edw., carpenter, decd.

Thos. Webb, waterman, of Didbrook, son of Sergeant, tinman, late of Ross, Herefs.

Jos. Hickman, yeoman,
Frank Hickman, yeoman, of Ilton, Som., } sons of John, yeoman, of Isle (*High*) Abbotts, Som.

Wm. Batsford, button-maker, of Birmingham, son of Chas., tanner, of Henley-in-Arden (*Henley Harding*), Warws.

Thos. Longden, woolstapler, son of John, clerk, of Winstone

[1] Haseley Court: Glos. R.O., D 2957/116, 26–9.

81 27 Jan Ric. Crowdy, cabinet-maker, of Duke's Street, Bloomsbury, Westminster, son of Ric., yeoman, of Longford

Wm. Bradley, corkcutter, of Leather Lane, Holborn, Mdx.,
Sam. Bradley, cabinet maker, of Leather Lane, Holborn, Mdx., } sons of Wm., victualler

Giles Taylor, waiter, of Hereford, son of John, cutler, of Cirencester

Chas. Woodward, app. of Thos. Price, cordwainer

Isaac Brown, cordwainer, of Whitechapel, London, son of Thos., cordwainer, decd., of Worcester

Ric. Baghott-De la Bere, esq.,
Thos. Baghott-De la Bere, esq., } sons of Wm. Baghott, esq., decd., of Southam

82 John Webley, hairdresser, of Southampton, son of Wm., hairdresser, decd.

Wm. Bamford of Uxbridge, Mdx., app. of John Mills, apothecary

Francis Child, carpenter, of Clement's Lane, Clare Market, Mdx., son of Francis, weaver, decd., of St. Philip and St. Jacob

John Wilkins, farmer, son of Jas., butcher, decd., of Westbury-on-Severn

Dan. Smith, app. of Thos. Rea, baker

John Butt, baker, of Bristol, son of Wm., farmer, of Over

Sam. Jones of St. John Street, West Smithfield, Mdx., app. of Sam. Roberts, brushmaker

83 Thos. Gaze of Leominster, [Herefs.], app. of his father Thos., joiner, decd.

28 Jan John Dark, haberdasher, of Holborn, Mdx., son of John, mercer, decd., of Hereford

Geo. Brimyard, baker, of Evesham, Worcs., son of Jos., hatter, decd., of Cheltenham

Francis Welles, clerk, son of Francis, clerk, decd., of Earl's Croome, Worcs.

John Ellis, app. of Wm. Cowcher, pinmaker, decd.

Phil. Lovegrove, schoolmaster, son of Giles, schoolmaster, late of Bristol

Wm. Cowles, grazier, of Odiham, Hants., son of John, grazier, decd.

John Ashmeade, baker, of King's Lynn, Norf., son of Wm., ironmonger, decd., of Alcester, Warws.

84 Edw. Friend of Southampton, app. of Wm. Draper, plumber and glazier, late of Gloucester

Jas. Rene, app. of Rob. Solloway, pinmaker

Jas. Blanch, patten-maker, of Castlebar, Ealing (*Castle Bear, Heeling*), Mdx.,
Wm. Blanch, patten-maker, of Castlebar, Ealing, Mdx., } sons of Thos., patten-maker, of Bristol

Jas. Allford, wheelwright, of Tibbles Lane, Bloomsbury, Mdx., son of John, whitesmith, late of Gloucester

John Webb, cabinet-maker, of Tooley Street, Southwark, son of Ric., ironmonger, decd., of Newnham

85 29 Jan Jas. Tombs, labourer, son of Ric., farrier, late of Gloucester

Captain Sam. Steel, 34th Foot, son of Sam., surgeon, decd., of Coleford

Chas. Barton, gent., of Oxford University, son of Wm., plumber and glazier

Ric. Harrison, gent., of Sandbach, Ches.,
Hen. Harrison, gent., of Middlewich, Ches., } sons of Geo., bargemaster, decd., of Bewdley, Worcs.

1789 Lieut. Sam. Hawker, 16th Light Dragoons, of Kinson, Dors., son of Peter, clerk, of Woodchester

John Wassell of Wolverhampton, Staffs., app. of Thos. Saunders, soapboiler, decd.

86 Bevis Blizard, butcher, of Oxenton, son of John, butcher, decd., of Gotherington

Steph. White, organ-builder, son of Thos., organ-builder, of Stephen Street, Tottenham Court Road, Mdx.

Wm. Read Lawrence, gent., of Picccadilly, Mdx., son of Thos., gent., of Bristol

Thos. Hornidge, surgeon, of Hatton Garden, Mdx., by gift. Sworn this day

30 Jan Jos. Brown Cull, tailor, son of Jas., heelcutter, decd.

Dan. Lysons, clerk, son of Sam., clerk, of Rodmarton

Hen. Tracy of Portman Street, London, son of Thos. Chas., V. Tracy, decd., of Toddington (*Toddenham*)[1]

87 John Richards, labourer, son of John, pinmaker, late of Gloucester

Hen. Williams of Llancarfan (*Llangarvon*), Glam., app. of John Washbourn, clock and watchmaker, decd.

Wm. Gardiner, baker, son of Sam., victualler, decd., of Sheepscombe

31 Jan Chas. Hobbs, steel-toyman, of Birmingham, son of Jonathan, organist, decd., of Warwick

John Webb, surgeon, of Doynton, son of John, butcher, decd.

John Phillipps of Broadway, Westminster, app. of Jas. Gunn, cordwainer

John Ward, cordwainer, of Gray's Inn Lane, Holborn, Mdx., son of Geo., peruke-maker, decd., of Holborn

88 Wm. Roberts, clerk, } sons of Wm. Hayward Roberts, clerk,
Ric. Roberts, clerk, } of Eton College, [Bucks.]

John Ferebee, labourer, son of Jos., labourer, decd., of Uley

Wm. Coleman of Warminster, Wilts., app. of Wm. Barton, plumber and glazier

Sam. Webb, esq., of the Hill, Painswick, by gift. Sworn this day

Congreve Selwyn, clerk, son of Chas. Jasper, clerk, of Blockley, Worcs.

Thos. Friend of Hadlow, Kent., app. of Jas. Lewis, collar-maker

Ric. White, broadweaver, son of Ric., carpenter, of Painswick

89 Hen. Dimock, gent., of Oxford University, son of Hen., clerk

Thos. Broadway alias Braddis, weaver, of Cock Alley, Norton Folgate, Mdx., son of Thos., weaver, of Shoreditch, Mdx.

Sam. Freeman, button-maker, son of Rob., button-maker, of Birmingham

2 Feb Lord Geo. Hen. Cavendish† by gift.[2] Sworn this day

Lord Frederick Townshend, son of Geo., Marquess Townshend†

Chas. Heming, hardwareman, of Oxford Street, London, } sons of Wm., officer
Jas. Nat. Heming, cooper, of St. Dunstan's Hill, London, } of the marshal's court, decd., of Holborn, Mdx.

90 Dan. Bond, painter and japanner, of Birmingham, son of Wm., bookbinder, decd.

John South, hairdresser, of Rochester, [Kent], son of John, baker, decd.

[1] Cf. above: GBR C 9/9, p. 72.

[2] By act of 4 Apr 1782, for upright conduct in parliament: ibid. B 3/11, f. 313v.

John Isaac Sextie, hairdresser, of Lincoln's Inn Fields, London, son of Rob., schoolmaster, decd., of Lambeth, Surr.

Elias Jeffs., farrier, son of Elias, farrier, of London

Ric. Felton, servant, of Cardiff, son of Wm., peruke-maker, decd., of Cowbridge, Glam.

Hen. Bathurst, LL.D., of Oxford University,[1] son of Benj., esq., decd., of Lydney

Sam. Groves, glassblower, son of Hen., glassmaker, decd., of Bristol

Jos. Marchant, private, 17th Foot, app. of Thos. Saunders, soapboiler, decd.

91 Thos. Harding of Gardiner's Lane, King Street, Westminster, app. of John Perks, corkcutter, decd.

Ric. Nelme, vintner, of Clapton, Mdx., son of John, tinplate-worker, decd., of Snow Hill, London

Benj. Baldwin, apothecary, of Minchinhampton, son of Rob., apothecary, decd., of Faringdon, Berks.

3 Feb Hen. Seymour-Conway† }
Lord John Cavendish† } by gift.[2] Sworn this day

[Thos.] Chas. [Tracy], V. Tracy, son of Thos. Chas., V. Tracy, [decd.]†[3]

Wm. Houlton, cordwainer, of Upton upon Severn, Worcs., son of Wm., victualler, decd.

Lieut. Rob. Smith, [R.]M., son of Rob., esq.

92 Wm. Cummins, baker, son of Wm., baker, of Carmarthen

Wm. Dorsett of Chertsey, Surr., app. in turn of Jos. Cheston, decd., and Thos. Parker, apothecaries

Thos. Hawker, esq., of Berners Street, Oxford Road, London, son of Peter, clerk, of Woodchester

Wm. Kendall, upholder, of High Street, Southwark, son of Thos., carpet manufacturer, of Cirencester

Dan. Quarington, gent., of Lant Street, Southwark, son of Dan., wine merchant, decd.

Wm. Freame, butcher, son of Thos., butcher, of Westbury-on-Severn

93 Francis Barton, plumber and glazier, of Pembroke, son of Ric., plumber and glazier, decd.

Wm. Rudge, draper, of Stafford, son of Wm., ironmonger, decd.

Phil. Hayes, professor of music, of Oxford University, son of Wm., professor of music, of Oxford University, decd.

Edw. Hare, weaver, of Leominster, Herefs., son of Edw., butcher, decd.

Wm. Bamford, cordwainer, of Dursley, son of Thos., labourer, of Littledean

Phil. Bosley, barge carpenter, of Stourport, Worcs., son of Geo., victualler, decd.

John Hayward, baker, of Winstone, son of Thos., victualler, decd., of Northleach

Wm. Gardiner, baker, of Mile End, Mdx., son of Wm., baker, of Sheepscombe

94 Thos. Hayward, maltster, of Coln St. Dennis, son of Thos., victualler, decd., of Northleach

[1] Bishop of Norwich 1805–37: *Alumni Oxon. 1715–1886*, i. 75.

[2] By act of 4 Apr 1782, for upright conduct in parliament: GBR B 3/11, f. 313v.

[3] Of Toddington: *Complete Peerage*, xii (2), 4.

Wm. Felton, cordwainer, son of Wm., hairdresser, decd., of Cowbridge, Glam.[1]

Edw. Felton, tailor, son of Wm., hairdresser, decd., of Bristol[2]

4 Feb John Cook of Blackwall, Mdx., app. of Ellis Taylor, baker, decd.

Hen. Jennings, gent., of Silver Street, Fleet Street, London, son of Hen., gent., of Lambeth, Surr.

John Gardiner, oilman, of 17, Whitechapel, Mdx., }
Geo. Gardiner, sawyer, of Holborn, Mdx., } sons of Ant., peruke-maker, of St. Martin's Lane, Mdx.

95 John Cotterel Price, surgeon, son of Ric., esq., decd.

Thos. Bishop, labourer, of Haresfield, }
Ric. Bishop, nailer, of Littledean, } sons of John, yeoman, decd., of Harescombe

John Ford, sailor, son of John, tailor, decd., of Newent

Chas. Batsford, tanner, son of John, miller, of Tewkesbury

Ric. Hobbs, musician, of Hampstead, Mdx., son of Thos., carpenter, late of Gloucester

John Cowles, yeoman, of Wheatenhurst, son of John, yeoman, decd., of Framilode

Geo. Griffiths, sawyer, of St. Briavels hundred,[3] son of John, yeoman, decd., of Mitcheldean

96 Thos. Underwood, whitesmith, of Churchdown, }
Hen. Underwood, blacksmith, of Sherborne, } sons of Ric., whitesmith, decd., of Over

Wm. Hoddinott of Birmingham, app. of Rob. Cowcher, cutler, decd.

Wm. Moore, yeoman, of Hardwicke, son of John, yeoman, decd., of Berkeley

John Blake, coachmaker, son of Somerset, baker, decd., of Bristol

Thos. Griffiths, quarryman, son of John, yeoman, decd., of Mitcheldean

Wm. Tayloe, clothier, of Chalford, by gift.[4] Sworn this day

97 Chas. Gardiner, carpenter, of Holborn, Mdx., son of Ant., peruke-maker, of St. Martin's Lane, Mdx.

John Greville, yeoman, of Hucclecote, son of John, yeoman, decd., of Charlton Kings

John Carter, worsted-weaver, of Coventry, son of John, husbandman, decd., of Bishop's Cleeve

10 Feb Hen. Howard,[5] esq., of Thornbury Castle by gift. Sworn this day

25 Feb Sam. Whitcombe, gent.,[6] by gift. Sworn this day

25 May Jas. Jelf, gent., app. of Sam. and John Niblett, bankers and co-partners

98 22 June John Holder, bellfounder, son of Chas., cordwainer

24 July Wm. Davis, hairdresser, son of Thos., cordwainer, decd.

4 Sept John Salcomb, waterman, son of Sam., waterman, decd., of Tirley

5 Sept Wm. Bowyer, esq., Exchequer clerk,[†7] by gift. Sworn this day

[1] The fathers of this and the following entrant were presumably the same person: cf. GBR C 9/8, p. 160.

[2] Above, preceding note.

[3] i.e. the Forest of Dean.

[4] By act of 26 Sept 1755: GBR B 3/10, f. 204v.

[5] M.P. for Gloucester 1795–1818, adopted the additional surnames of Molyneux and of Howard in 1812 and 1817 respectively: Williams, *Parl. Hist. of Glos.* 212.

[6] Knighted in 1816: Glos. R.O., GE 95.

[7] ? of Minchinhampton: GBR B 3/12, ff. 78v., 106.

7 Sept John Bishop, yeoman, by fine
25 Sept Chas. Simpson, baker, son of Thos., baker, decd.
1 Oct Hen. Chas. Selwyn, esq., by gift. Sworn this day
99 28 Sept Ric. [Beadon], bishop of Gloucester, } by gift
Ric. Beadon, esq.,† son of the bishop of Gloucester, }
30 Sept John Palmer, esq., comptroller-general of the Post Office, London, by gift. Sworn this day
6 Oct Chas. Bonnor, esq., deputy comptroller-general of the Post Office, London, by gift. Sworn this day

James Sadler, esq., mayor 1789–90

20 Oct Jas. Wintle, apothecary, son of Sam., brandy merchant, decd.
16 Nov Sam. Badger, pinmaker, son of Phoenix, wiredrawer, decd.
100 1790 2 Feb Sam. Heath, private, 30th Foot, son of Sam., brazier
8 Feb John Powell, tailor, son of John, beadle
Jas. Bishop, app. of John Wheatstone, cordwainer
12 Feb John Hinton, tailor, son of Wm., pinmaker
15 Feb Jas. Woodward, carpenter and joiner, son of John, pinmaker
26 Feb Geo. Coopey, pedlar, of Somerton, Som., son of John, yeoman, late of Churchdown
17 Mar Isaac Barrow, millwright, of Gloucester, formerly of Cheltenham, by fine
20 Mar Wm. Holt, tea dealer, of Holborn Hill, St. Andrew, Mdx., app. of Elizabeth Cooke, grocer
101 25 Mar Watkin Crowther, innkeeper, by fine
31 Mar Wm. Jones, esq., son of Roynon, esq., of Hayhill
1 Apr Wm. Dovey, grocer, by fine
10 May Jas. Dowell, tailor, son of Jas., cordwainer
17 May Rob. Hicks, tailor, son of Sam., pinmaker
John Bick of Wotton, app. of Newton Brabant, pinmaker
30 July Chas. Crowdy, labourer, son of Ric., yeoman, of Longford
11 Sept H.R.H. [Prince Wm. Hen.], duke of Gloucester,†[1] by gift
Prince Wm. Frederick, son of the duke of Gloucester,† by gift
6 Sept Abraham Saunders, wine merchant, son of Abraham, esq., ald.
27 Sept Dan. Spencer the younger†[2] by fine
[ ] Oct Thos.Piffe, innholder, by fine[3]
2 Oct Benj. Williams, innholder, by fine

102 **Giles Greenaway, esq., mayor 1790–1**

19 Oct Jas. Drinkwater, labourer, by fine
12 Nov Chas. Cooke, apothecary, son of John, apothecary
1791 17 Jan Chas. King, waterman, son of Chas., porter
28 Jan Sam. Roberts, brushmaker, son of Sam., brushmaker
11 Feb Jos. Baylis, clerk,[4] son of Jos., clerk, decd., of Ludgershall, Wilts.
Ric. Woodward, app. of Chas. Cox, hairdresser
18 Feb Wm. Rowles, cordwainer, son of Wm., cordwainer, of Bulley
102A 21 Mar Jos. Spillman, tailor, son of Jos., hairdresser, decd.

[1] *Complete Peerage*, v. 744.
[2] Bricklayer, of Gloucester, resigned 12 Mar 1795 to enable him to give evidence in a cause concerning the city's common meadows and readmitted 17 Aug 1795: GBR B 3/12, ff. 221v., 227v.; below: ibid. C 9/9, p. 122.
[3] Entry possibly belongs to the following mayoralty, Piffe's fine being accounted for on 8 Oct 1789: ibid. B 3/12, f. 130v.
[4] Rector of St. Mary de Crypt: Hockaday Abs. ccxvi.

Thos. Simpson, pinmaker, son of Wm., pinmaker, decd.
John Maisey, app. of Thos. Rodway, cordwainer
30 May Ric. Base of Rodborough, app. of Thos. Webb, cordwainer
19 July John Keysall, clerk, of Long Melford, Suff., by gift
15 Aug Wm. Fitzharding[e] Berkeley of Berkeley Castle by gift. Sworn 23 Sept 1816[1]
Frederick Maur. Fitz[hardinge] Berkeley[2] of Berkeley Castle by gift. Sworn 28 Oct 1816[3]
Augustus Fitzharding[e] Berkeley of Berkeley Castle by gift. Sworn 28 Oct 1816[4]
103 Sam. Pickering, clerk, of Cleeve[5] by gift
Bartholomew Fox, wine merchant, by gift[6]
19 Aug David Arthur Saunders,[7] wine merchant, son of Abraham, esq.
30 Sept Chas. Stock, surgeon and apothecary, son of Thos., butcher
Thos. Wogan, esq., of Wiston, Pemb., by gift
Hugh Barlow, M.P. for Pembroke,† by gift
104 Thos. Scott, esq., of [ ] (*Shipperton*),[8] by gift*
Chas. Howard, V. Andover,†[9] by gift
Thos. Howard,[10] esq., of Charlton, Wilts., by gift. Sworn 29 Sept 1799
Edw. Howard, son of Hen., esq., of Glossop, Derb., by gift
Ralph Bigland,[11] Richmond Herald, of the Heralds' Office, London, by gift. Sworn 12 Oct 1816: p. 335[12]
Geo. Caesar Hopkinson, esq., of Hempsted by gift
105 Wm. Peacey, gent., of Eastington by gift
Wm. Pickering Reid, esq., of Prestbury by gift
And. Sprowle, esq., of Swindon by gift
Chas. Higgs, gent., of Cheltenham by gift
Wm. Fox, gent., by gift
Jos. Symonds, clerk, of Dymock by gift
106 John Stone, gent., of Pull Court, Worcs., by gift

William Middleton, esq., mayor 1791–2

14 Oct Hen. Wintle of Pembroke College, Oxford [University], son of Sam., distiller, late of Gloucester
7 Oct Wm. Bishop, yeoman, by fine
Mic. Peyton by fine
14 Oct John Pickering, app. of Sam. Roberts, brushmaker
17 Oct Wm. Hambling, pargeter, son of John, cooper, decd.
19 Dec Lieut. Anselm John Griffiths, R.N., son of John, clerk, decd., of Kingston-upon-Thames, [Surr.]
1792 27 Feb Wm. Dix, bricklayer, son of Ric., bricklayer
27 Apr Chas. Faucks, grocer, of Cirencester, son of Wm., butcher, late of Gloucester

[1] Entry repeated below: GBR C 9/9, p. 277.
[2] M.P. for Gloucester for three periods between 1831 and 1857: Williams, *Parl. Hist. of Glos.* 214.
[3] Sworn 6 Nov 1812: GBR B 3/12, f. 145.
[4] Entry repeated below: ibid. C 9/9, p. 337.
[5] Bishop's Cleeve: *V.C.H. Glos.* viii. 20–1.
[6] On his election to the common council: GBR B 3/12, f. 145v.
[7] On his election to the common council: ibid.
[8] Place not identified.
[9] Of Tittleshall, Norf.: *Complete Peerage*, xii (1), 479.
[10] Brother of V. Andover: ibid. 479–80.
[11] Antiquary and historian of Gloucestershire: Gray, *Antiquaries*, 64–6.
[12] Sworn 23 Jan 1792: GBR B 3/12, f. 152v.

107 Wm. Holtham, son of John, victualler, decd.

21 May Sam. Salcombe, excise officer, of Tirley, son of Sam., waterman, decd.

22 June Thos. Clarke, tailor, of the College precincts, Gloucester, son of John, pinmaker, decd.

6 Aug Wm. Perkins of Aston Ingham, Herefs., app. of Edm. Boughton, currier

27 Aug Wal. Price, baker, son of Wal., victualler, decd.

Jas. Buchanan, grocer, son of Wm., grocer, decd.

108 Wm. Bury, yeoman, by fine

28 Aug John Wheatstone, gent., son of John, cordwainer

3 Sept John Rea, pinmaker, son of Thos., baker

7 Sept Wm. Harbert, pinmaker, app. of Edm. Stock and Edw. Holder, grocers and co-partners

21 Sept Chas. Jones, cordwainer, } sons of Ric., cordwainer
Jas. Jones, pinmaker, }

John Owen Bower, cordwainer, son of Wm., cordwainer

109 Thos. Crawley-Boevey, esq., son of Sir Thos., Bt., by gift

John Hawker, esq., of Dudbridge by gift

Ant. Austin, esq., of Wotton under Edge by gift

John Hurford, esq., by gift

Wm. Davis, esq., of Cooper's Hill, Upton St. Leonards,[1] by gift[2]

110 Wm. Fowler, esq., of Newnham by gift

Geo. Nayler, genealogist of the Order of the Bath and Blanc Coursier Herald, of the College of Arms, London, by gift. Sworn 22 Sept 1792

Wm. Chandler the younger, gent., of Apperley by gift

25 Sept Sam. Browning, cordwainer, by fine

27 Sept Thos. Holbrow, esq., of Leonard Stanley by gift

Edw. Parker, clerk, of Durham by gift

111 Chas. Morris, esq., of Charlotte Street, Rathbone Place, London, by gift

1 Oct Sam. Escott, tailor, son of Jas., pinmaker

Thomas Weaver, esq., mayor 1792–3

5 Oct Luke Holford, bricklayer, son of Benj., labourer, of Birmingham, formerly of Gloucester

12 Oct Rob. Davis, tailor, son of John, pinmaker, decd.

27 Nov Ric. Peyton, mercer, of Birmingham by gift

7 Dec John Stroud, gent., app. of Sam. and John Niblett, bankers

1793 21 Jan Wm. Bonnewell, cooper, of Tewkesbury, son of Wm., cooper, decd.

112 18 Feb Wal. Castle of Tewkesbury, app. of Nat. Washbourne, baker and confectioner

22 Feb Thos. Smith of Brookthorpe, app. of Ric. Wood, decd., and Jas. Wood, mercers

10 June Wm. Davis of Cooper's Hill, Upton St. Leonards, by gift[3]

15 July Benj. Watts, butcher, son of Thos., butcher, decd.

5 Aug Benj. Jennings, cordwainer, son of John, hatter and feltmonger

Wm. Knight, app. of Ric. Heath, saddler

15 Aug John Spencer, bricklayer, by fine

113 Ric. Pitt, victualler, by fine

3 Sept John Heath, innholder, by fine

[1] Cooper's Hill, Brockworth: Rudder, *Glos.* 312.
[2] Cf. below: GBR C 9/9, p. 112.
[3] Entry struck through; cf. above: ibid. p. 109. Entrant sworn 10 June 1793: ibid. B 3/12, f. 169.

9 Sept Chas. Ireland, hairdresser, of Kingsland, Hackney, Mdx., son of Wm., cooper
24 Sept Sam. Flower Button, surgeon, son of Sam., gent.
27 Sept Jas. Wintle, pinmaker, son of Jas., pinmaker, decd.
Ric. Baldwin, app. of Jas. Lewis, collar-maker
Brian Hodgson, esq., of Macclesfield, Ches., by gift
Jas. Dalby, gent., of Tetbury by gift
114 Abraham Mills, esq., of Macclesfield, Ches., by gift
Jas. de Visme, esq., of Newent by gift. Sworn 28 Feb 1800
Wm. Russell, esq., of Wotton [near Gloucester] by gift
Sam. Skay, merchant, of Bewdley, Worcs., by gift
John Wall, esq., of Tewkesbury Park by gift
Rob. Lawrence,[1] clerk, of Shurdington by gift. Sworn 19 June 1795

Thomas Mee, esq., mayor 1793–4

15 Oct Chas. Theomartyr Crane, merchant, of London by gift
115 4 Nov Jas. Dalloway, clerk,[2] by gift. Sworn 12 Nov 1793
8 Nov Ric. Goodwin, tailor, of Gloucester, son of Sam., yeoman, of Cowley
16 Dec Chas. Batchford, tanner, son of John, tanner, of Tewkesbury
23 Dec Lieut. Lyde Brown, North Glos. Militia,[†] by gift. Sworn 17 Feb 1794
Wm. Moor Ady, esq., of Wotton under Edge by gift. Sworn 17 Feb 1794
1794 9 Feb John Baylis, yeoman, by fine
17 May Wm. Baker, esq., of Christ Church, Mdx., by gift
John Baker, esq., of Christ Church, Mdx., by gift
19 July Chas. Bridges Woodcock, esq., of Brentford Butts, Mdx., by gift
25 Aug Wm. Window, cabinet-maker, son of John, cabinet-maker
12 Sept Ric. Webb, gent., son of Ric., staymaker, decd.
116 1 Oct Hen. Gorges Dobyns Yate, clerk, of Bromsberrow by gift. Sworn 15 June 1795
Jas. Parsons, clerk, by gift
(Morgan) Price, clerk, of Knebworth, Herts., by gift*
Chas. Turner, tea dealer, of London by gift
Jas. Wellington, esq., of Ross, Herefs., by gift. Sworn 14 Feb 1800
Thos. Cook, clerk, of Wickwar by gift
Chas. Evans, esq., of Highgrove[3] by gift. Sworn 17 Oct 1794

117 **John Turner, esq., mayor 1794–5**

28 Oct Ric. Stiles of Cheltenham, app. of John Wheatstone, cordwainer
Sam. Lane, cordwainer, of Gloucester, son of Ric., pinmaker, of Littleworth
31 Oct Wm. Lewis, plumber, son of Thos., gardener, decd.
1790 29 Sept Chas. Harris, merchant, of Bristol by gift[x]
Edw. Chas. Symonds Powell, gent., by gift[x]
Lieut. Sam. Higgs, 4th Foot, of Charlton Kings by gift[x]
118 Ant. Keck, clerk, of King's Stanley by gift[x]
Rob. Morris,[4] esq., of Barnwood by gift[x]
Edw. Turner, gent., of Dowdeswell by gift[x]

[x] Entry belongs to Jas. Sadler's mayoralty.
[1] Later called Rob. Lawrence Townsend: *Alumni Oxon. 1715–1886*, iv. 1431.
[2] Jas. Dallaway, curate of Rodborough and historian of Gloucestershire and Sussex: *Trans. B.G.A.S.* lxxxi. 208–10; *Alumni Oxon. 1715–1886*, i. 333.
[3] In Minsterworth: Fosbrooke, *Glos.* ii. 206.
[4] M.P. for Gloucester 1805–16: Williams, *Parl. Hist. of Glos.* 212.

			Wm. Dillon, surgeon, of Tewkesbury by gift.[x] Sworn 7 Aug 1805
			Thos. Powell Symonds, esq., of Eltham, Kent, by gift.[x] Sworn 15 July 1792
	1794	5 Dec	Moses Binning, tailor, son of Wm., woolcomber
		22 Dec	Jas. Herbert, butcher, of Gloucester, son of Wm., yeoman, of Pamington by gift
119	1795	23 Jan	Chris. Rowles,[†] late servant of Sir Howe Hicks, Bt.,[†1] by gift
			Jos. Bennett, app. of Newton Brabant, pinmaker
		13 Feb	Hen. Barrett, app. of Wm. Hardwick, painter
		16 Feb	Chas. Hale, app. of Wm. Bubb, carpenter and joiner, decd.
		2 Mar	John Hawkins, husbandman, son of Jos., butcher, decd., of Staunton, Worcs.
		16 Mar	Dan. Bloxsome, cooper, son of Edw., cooper
		20 Mar	Sam. Critchley, victualler, } readmitted by gift[2]
			Ric. Dix, bricklayer, } readmitted by gift[2]
		27 Mar	Ric. Woodward, tailor, son of John, pinmaker
120			Wm. Holder, app. of Hen. Dunn, pargeter
			Wm. Brown, tailor, son of Jas., tailor
			Thos. Lewis, tailor, son of Jos., tiler and plasterer
			Wm. White, joiner and carpenter, } sons of Wm., joiner and carpenter
			John White, joiner and carpenter, } sons of Wm., joiner and carpenter
			John White, joiner and carpenter, of Gloucester, son of Ric., carpenter, of Painswick
			Wm. Bradley, tailor, son of Wm., tailor, decd.
		20 Mar	Benj. Kibble, app. of Jos. Bower, pinmaker
		23 Mar	John Freame, cordwainer, son of Wm., feltmaker
121		7 Apr	Chas. Daniell, cordwainer, of Westminster, son of Sam., joiner and carpenter
		13 Apr	Wm. Caudle, app. of Ric. Weaver, farrier
		15 July	John Smith, late ostler at the Boothall inn, by fine
		31 July	Wm. Ward, printer, of Westminster, son of Wm., printer, and app. of Nat. Washbourne, baker and confectioner, by apprenticeship
		14 Aug	John Brown, app. of Jas. Bourn, cordwainer
		17 Aug	Thos. Webb, cordwainer, } readmitted by gift[3]
			John Workman, butcher, }
			Jas. Estcourt, pinmaker, }
122			Ric. Dix, bricklayer, }
			Jos. Hawkes, cordwainer, }
			Sam. Heath, brazier, }
			Jos. Wood, baker, }
			Thos. Bannister, gent., }
			Jas. Bretherton, whitesmith, }
			Josiah Salcomb, woolcomber, }
			Dan. Spencer the younger, bricklayer, }
			Wm. Dunn, pargeter, }
		21 Aug	Edw. Walker, victualler, by fine. Sworn 2 Oct 1795
			Wm. Taynton, hairdresser, son of Wal., skinner, of Ross, Herefs.
		31 Aug	Thos. Driver, app. of Ric. Dunn, hairdresser
123		2 Oct	Hen. Francis Wintle, grocer, of St. Gregory, London, son of Hen., brushmaker, decd.

[x] Entry belongs to Jas. Sadler's mayoralty.

[1] Of Witcombe: *Complete Baronetage*, i. 126.

[2] Readmitted after resigning to be able to give evidence in a cause concerning the city's common meadows: GBR B 3/12, ff. 219v., 222 and v.

[3] Readmitted after resigning to be able to give evidence in a cause concerning the city's common meadows: ibid. ff. 219–22, 227v.

Edm. Jones, esq., of Fawley, Herefs., by gift. Sworn 8 Aug 1805
Phil. Jones, attorney, of Ross, Herefs., by gift. Sworn 5 Oct 1816[1]
Amos Jones, grocer, of Ross, Herefs., by gift. Sworn 28 Aug 1801
Thos. Smith, esq., of Pudhill by gift. Sworn 10 Nov 1795
Wm. Houlston, surgeon, of Chancery Lane, London, by gift
Thos. Nayler, esq., of Preston, Lancs., by gift
124 Alex. Townsend, esq., of Theescombe (*Thievescomb*) by gift. Sworn 12 Feb 1796
John Remington, esq., of Barton End[2] by gift. Sworn 5 Oct 1795
Hen. Hooper Fryer, attorney, of Tewkesbury by gift. Sworn 3 Oct 1795

John Cook, esq., mayor 1795–6

26 Oct Wm. Stephens, musician, North Glos. Militia, son of John, sergeant in the same regiment, formerly pinmaker
2 Nov John Howes, innkeeper, by fine. Sworn 7 Nov 1795
13 Nov Ellis Taylor, cordwainer, of Gloucester, son of Chas., tinman, of Frome, Som.
125 16 Nov Wm. Hicks, carpenter, son of Sam., pinmaker
John Baker, cordwainer, of Minsterworth, son of John, bricklayer
23 Nov Thos. Saunders, soapboiler, Dan. Ellis Saunders, cheesemonger, of Frocester, } sons of Thos., soapboiler, decd.
1796 11 Jan Benj. Peart, private, North Glos. Militia, son of Chas., cordwainer, of London, formerly of Gloucester
27 Jan Ric. Draper, plumber and glazier, son of Wm., plumber and glazier, decd.
126 5 Feb Wm. Roberts, private, South Glos. Militia, formerly app. of John Derrett, butcher, decd., by patrimony
12 Feb Thos. Mann, cooper, son of Wm., cooper
15 Feb Warren Stephens, cabinet-maker, son of Wm., upholsterer
29 Feb Wm. Grafton, mercer, app. of Edwin Jeynes, mercer and linen-draper, and his wife Elizabeth
John Pleydell Wilton, surgeon and apothecary, son of Hen., gent.
4 Mar Geo. Davis, carpenter, son of Geo., victualler, decd.
11 Mar Wm. Cook, plasterer, son of John, pargeter
127 Wm. Wathen, pinmaker, son of Wm., pinmaker, decd.
17 Mar Jos. Rudge, yeoman, by fine
John Allen,[3] late servant of the bishop of Gloucester, by gift
29 Apr Thos. Davis, gent., son of Hen., pinmaker, decd.
6 May Chas. Bonnewell, servant, son of Wm., cooper, decd.
17 June Wm. Jeffs, tailor, son of Wm., mercer, decd.
8 Aug Wm. Westwood, cordwainer, by gift
128 12 Aug Edm. Boughton, currier, son of Edm., currier, decd.
Jas. Davis, carpenter and joiner, of Chelsea, Mdx., son of Geo., victualler, decd.
2 Sept Wm. Coopey, pig dealer, son of Wm., pig dealer, of Churcham
21 Sept Hen. Phillipps, late coachman to Sir John Guise, Bt.,† by fine. Sworn 10 Oct 1796
30 Sept Sir Ric. Neave, Bt., of Westminster by gift
Captain Hen. Howard, West Yorks. (*York*) Militia,† by gift

[1] Entry repeated below: ibid. C 9/9, p. 322.
[2] In Horsley: *V.C.H. Glos.* xi. 179.
[3] Nic. Allen: GBR B 3/12, f. 246v.

Alex. Adair, esq., of Pall Mall, Westminster, by gift
129 Thos. Kingscott, esq., of Randalls Park, Surr., by gift. Sworn 28 Sept 1802
Phil. Godsall, esq., of Hampstead, Mdx., by gift
Alex. Bunn Haden, clerk, of Wednesbury, Staffs., by gift. Sworn 1 Oct 1796
Wm. Morris, esq., of Hempsted by gift. Sworn 1 Oct 1796
Paul Wathen,[1] esq., of Woodchester by gift. Sworn 3 Oct 1796
Philo Maddy, currier, by gift. Sworn 3 Oct 1796
Thos. Astill Davis, gent., by gift. Sworn 3 Oct 1796
130 John Higgs, yeoman, of Leigh by gift. Sworn 3 Oct 1796
John King, gent., of Barton Street by gift. Sworn 3 Oct 1796
3 Oct Wal. Bosley Woore, hatmaker, of Gloucester, son of Thos., hatmaker, of Tewkesbury, formerly of Gloucester

John Ready, esq., mayor 1796–7

12 Oct Josiah Tippetts, app. of Penelope Powell, plumber and glazier, decd.
28 Oct John Westron Vaughan, upholsterer, son of John, upholsterer, of Prince's Street, St. James, Westminster, Mdx.
Francis Lye, son of Hen. Draper Lye, schoolmaster
131 7 Nov Wm. Wicks by fine
Hen. Fitzharding[e] Berkeley, esq., of Berkeley Castle by gift[2]
Lloyd Crawley, esq., by gift. Sworn 11 Nov 1805
1797 23 Jan Edw. Weaver, esq., son of Thos., esq.
Sam. Jeynes, esq., son of Edwin, esq.
10 Feb Wm. Manns, tailor, son of Wm., cooper
27 Feb Geo. Elliott, carpenter, son of Wm., barber, decd.
Geo. Jones, tailor, son of Ric., cordwainer
132 12 May Ric. Barber, app. of Sam. Wilton, pinmaker, decd.
Wm. Greening, hairdresser, son of Wm., decd.
30 May Hen. Hall Gage, son of [Hen.], V. Gage,[3] of Highmeadow by gift
4 Aug Edw. Bower, currier, son of Thos., pinmaker, late of Gloucester
18 Aug John Wintle, distiller, son of Sam., distiller, decd.
21 Aug Wm. Cook Ireland, waterman, son of Wm., cooper
4 Sept Thos. Frankis, husbandman, son of Ric., husbandman, of Upton St. Leonards
133 27 Sept Rob. Martin Popham Wall, esq., of Tewkesbury Lodge by gift. Sworn 16 Jan 1812[4]
John Crewe, esq., of Crewe Hall, Ches., by gift
Edw. Hinchcliffe, clerk, of Barthomley, Ches., by gift
Wm. Dix., esq., of Top-y-fron (*Vron*), Flints., by gift
Herbert Brace, esq., of the Middle Temple, London, by gift
Sir Francis Molineux, Bt., of Wellow, Notts., by gift
134 Thos. [Reynolds] Moreton[5] of Tortworth by gift. Sworn 29 Sept 1801
Ebenezer King, esq., by gift. Sworn 30 Oct 1797
Rob. Stephens, gent., of Little Barrington by gift. Sworn 27 Oct 1797
Thos. Smith,[6] gent., of Highnam by gift. Sworn 9 Nov 1797
6 Oct Shadrach Charleton, grocer, of Alcester, Warws., son of Meshach, hatmaker

[1] Later knighted and from 1812 called Paul Baghott: *V.C.H. Glos.* xi. 112, 300.
[2] Entry repeated below: GBR C 9/9, p. 366.
[3] Burke, *Peerage* (1963), 969.
[4] Entry repeated below: GBR C 9/9, p. 251.
[5] *Complete Peerage*, iv. 476.
[6] Awarded freedom under name of Wm. Smith: GBR B 3/12, ff. 277, 282v.

10 Oct Benj. Blewett, app. of Steph. Stroud, pinmaker[1]

135 **Samuel Colborne, esq., mayor 1797–8**

6 Nov Jas. Yearsley, innkeeper, by fine. Sworn 5 Dec 1797
John McLaren, seedsman, by fine
1798 26 Jan Ric. Lane, cordwainer, son of Ric., pinmaker, of Littleworth
Benj. Gurney, pinmaker, son of John, pinmaker, of Littleworth
Jas. Ricketts, app. of Wm. Smith Bartlett, pinmaker
Jas. Nest, app. of Thos. Rodway, cordwainer
Rob. Phillipps, cordwainer, son of Geo., pinmaker, late of Gloucester
136 2 Feb Chas. Cother, app. of Merrot Stephens, mercer
14 Feb Thos. Lewis, victualler, by fine. Sworn 21 May 1795
22 June Wm. Dunn, son of Wm., pargeter
6 July Hen. Merrett, baker, of Milford Haven, Pemb., son of Thos., of Mitcheldean
17 Aug Jas. Bretherton, minister, } sons of Jas., smith
Edw. Bretherton, hairdresser, }
20 Aug Ric. Seyer, bricklayer, by fine. Sworn same day
137 24 Aug John Biddle, grocer, son of Nat., grocer
7 Sept John Perring, gent., son of Ric., butcher, decd.
Jas. Stock, butcher, son of Thos., butcher
21 Sept Chas. Gabriel Woodcock, banker, of Lombard Street, London, son of Sam., esq.
27 Sept Wm. Kilmister, stonemason, by fine
Wm. Roberts, M.B., (of Upton St. Leonards)[†] by gift. Sworn 13 Feb 1799
138 Thos. Bayly Howell, esq., of Prinknash by gift. Sworn 19 Oct 1798
Edw. Jones, clerk, by gift. Sworn 29 Sept 1798
Edw. Davis, surgeon, by gift. Sworn 5 Oct 1798
Hugh Taylor, grocer, by gift. Sworn 1 Oct 1798
Ric. Palmer, gent., of Moreton Valence by gift. Sworn 28 Feb 1806
Thos. Bayly Villiers, master of the Bluecoat Hospital,[2] by gift. Sworn 1 Oct 1798

139 **Charles [Howard], duke of Norfolk, mayor 1798–9**

12 Nov Wm. Lander, pinmaker, son of Wm., pinmaker
23 Nov Jos. Rea, searcher of customs, son of Thos., baker
21 Dec Thos. [Boulden] Thompson,[†] late captain of the *Leander*, } by gift[3]
Alex. Ball,[†] captain of the *Alexander*, }
1799 14 Jan Thos. Washbourn, druggist, son of Wm., druggist, decd.
1 Feb Chas. Cole, tinman, of Gloucester, son of Jas., gent., of Barton Street
4 Feb Thos. Salcombe, waterman, son of Sam., waterman, decd., of Tirley
140 25 Apr Lt.-Col. (Wm.) Christmas, 18th Light Dragoons,[†] by gift[4]
4 May Hen. Frankis, baker, of Gloucester, son of Ric., yeoman, of Upton St. Leonards
Chas. Okey, tinplate-worker, son of Thos., victualler
24 May Wm. Wheatstone, cordwainer, son of John, cordwainer

[1] Entry belongs to following mayoralty.
[2] Sir Thomas Rich's school: *V.C.H. Glos.* iv. 335–8.
[3] Both entrants had family ties with Gloucester and had served under Nelson at the battle of the Nile in 1797: *D.N.B.* Entry for Thompson, created a baronet in 1806, is repeated below: GBR C 9/9, p. 260.
[4] With a purse of 20 guineas to be distributed among his soldiers for their good behaviour while quartered in the city: GBR B 3/12, f. 299.

14 Aug Chas. Church, ropemaker, son of Luke, ropemaker
16 Aug Chas. Fletcher, baker, son of Ralph, baker, decd.
19 Aug Thos. Okey, attorney, son of Thos., victualler
23 Sept Wm. Halling, yeoman, by fine. Sworn 24 Sept 1799
Jos. Davis, yeoman, by fine. Sworn 18 Oct 1799
141 Lot Clotterbuck, yeoman, by fine. Sworn 24 Sept 1799
Ric. Beck, innholder, by fine. Sworn 24 Sept 1799
Geo. Mander, vict[ualler], by fine. Sworn 24 Sept 1799
Dan. Hopton, yeoman, by fine. Sworn 24 Sept 1799
Chas. Pugh, yeoman, by fine. Sworn 24 Sept 1799
Jas. Green, esq., of Llansantffraed, Mon., by gift
John Elwes, esq., of Colesbourne by gift. Sworn 29 Sept 1799
Revd. Ric. Collier of Blockley, Worcs.,[1] by gift
142 Geo. Rolph, gent., of Thornbury by gift
Wm. Montague, gent., by gift. Sworn 18 Oct 1799
24 Sept Jas. Barton, grocer, son of Wm., plumber and glazier

Edwin Jeynes, esq.,[2] mayor 1799–1800

30 Sept Frederick Augustus [Berkeley], earl of Berkeley, by patrimony.[3] Came this day and was admitted
7 Oct Thos.Wintle, gent., son of Thos., clerk, of Brightwell, Berks.
Thos. Spier, mercer, son of John, victualler, decd.
Wm. Deane, carpenter, son of Wm., carpenter
143 11 Oct Chas. James, gent., of Gray's Inn, Mdx., son of Selwyn, gent., of Chepstow, Mon.
4 Nov Thos. Meek, ostler, by fine
21 Dec Geo. Wadman by fine. Sworn 30 Dec 1799
Benj. Hobhouse, esq., of Cottles House, Wilts., by gift. Sworn 9 Oct 1801
Geo. Hen. Mason, esq., of Nass by gift. Sworn 3 Feb 1800
Thos. Marsh the younger, victualler, by fine. Sworn 22 Mar 1800
1800 4 Apr John Cook, gent., } sons of John, pargeter
144 Phil. Cook, gent., of St. Clement Danes, Westminster, } sons of John, pargeter
9 May Wm. Gwinnett Hornidge, clerk,[4] son of Wm. Gwinnett Hornidge, baker, decd.
Benj. Mutlow Rea, baker, son of Thos., baker
John Hooper, app. of Jas. Wood, mercer
21 May Sir John Douglas, R.M.,[†] by gift. Sworn 7 Jan 1803
11 July Ric. Tolley, victualler, by fine[5]
145 16 June Thos. Hawkins, yeoman, of Staunton, Worcs., son of Jos., butcher, late of Corse
23 June Wm. Haviland, victualler, son of Ric., victualler
11 July Thos. Baylis, app. of John Wadley, baker
Ric. Tolley, victualler, by fine
15 Aug Thos. Bonner, paymaster, 15th Foot, formerly app. of Sam. Colborne, apothecary
146 3 Oct Thos. Hudson, tailor, by fine

[1] Vicar of Upton Snodsbury, Worcs.: H.E.M. Icely, *Blockley Through Twelve Centuries* (Kineton, 1974), 104.
[2] Knighted during mayoralty: cf. GBR B 3/12, f. 315v.
[3] Son of Augustus (d. 1755), earl of Berkeley: *Complete Peerage*, ii. 142.
[4] Usher of the College (later the King's) school: *Glouc. New Guide* (1802), 54.
[5] Entry struck through and repeated below: GBR C 9/9, p. 145.

John Russell, victualler, by fine. Sworn 13 Oct 1800
John Wilkinson, esq., of New Bond Street, London, by gift
Wm. Marsh, esq., of South Street, Grosvenor Square, London, by gift
Jas. Hammond, esq., of Woolaston by gift. Sworn 10 Feb 1802
Edw. Freeman, esq., of Ledbury, Herefs., by gift. Sworn 6 Nov 1800
147 Revd. John Neale of Staverton by gift. Sworn 13 Oct 1800
John Otter, esq., by gift. Sworn 6 Oct 1800
20 Oct John Hen. Frankis, gent., of Bristol, } sons of Hen., husbandman, of
Wm. Frankis, husbandman, } Upton St. Leonards[1]

148 **John Jefferis, esq., mayor 1800–1**

28 Nov Jas. Taylor, brushmaker, of St. Mary, Whitechapel, Mdx., son of Chas., tinman, decd.
1 Dec Ric. Frankis, husbandman, } sons of Ric., yeoman, decd., of Upton
John Frankis, butcher, } St. Leonards
5 Dec Wm. Gunn, pinmaker, son of Jas., cordwainer
1801 2 Jan John Hatch, yeoman, by fine
12 Jan John Stephens, patten-maker, son of John, pinmaker
19 Jan Jas. Wood, cabinet-maker, of Gloucester, son of Wm., yeoman, decd., of Barton Street
9 Mar Mic. Jennings, tailor, son of John, hatmaker
149 1 May Jos. Wood, cutler, son of Jos., baker
22 May Wm. Marshfield, yeoman, by fine. Sworn 17 Sept 1801
John Workman, hairdresser, by fine
Wm. Fowler[2] of Newnham by gift
Jas. Pitt, clerk,[3] by gift. Sworn 12 June 1801
John Phillimore, esq., of Symondshall by gift. Sworn 13 July 1801
17 July John Spire, app. of Pettat Gardiner, brushmaker
150 24 Aug John Mic. Saunders, soapboiler, son of Thos., soapboiler, decd.
7 Sept Thos. Pruen, gent.,[4] of Prestbury, son of Thos., innkeeper, late of Gloucester
14 Sept John Hewlett, app. of Thos. Woodward, cabinet-maker
29 Sept Rob. Hen. Pytt, surgeon, son of John, printer
Gilbert Davis of Bristol, app. of Geo. Martin, grocer, by fine. Sworn 1 Oct 1801
Revd. Rob. Symonds of Hinton,[5] Berks., (by gift)
Captain Jas. Matthews, Royal North Glos. Militia,[†] by fine.[6] Sworn 7 Jan 1802
151 Hen. Sharpe Pocklington, esq., of Tibberton by gift. Sworn 20 Dec 1802
Thos. Palmer, gent., of Moreton Valence by gift. Sworn 29 Sept 1801
Hen. Stephens, esq., of Chavenage by gift. Sworn 4 Aug 1802
Phil. Godsall the younger, of Hampstead, Mdx., by gift. Sworn 3 June 1803

152 **Samuel Woodcock, esq., mayor 1801–2**

23 Oct Wm. Heane, tailor, son of Wm., porter
6 Nov Thos. Dix, app. of Ric. Goodwin, tailor

[1] Entries belong to following mayoralty.
[2] *Esquire* struck through.
[3] Rector of Brimpsfield and Cranham: *V.C.H. Glos.* vii. 148, 209.
[4] Later clerk: Hockaday Abs. clxxxvi, 1817; below: GBR C 9/9, p. 466.
[5] Hinton Waldrist: *V.C.H. Berks.* iv. 465.
[6] By gift: GBR B 3/12, f. 334.

Thos. Clifford Lane, app. of Sam. Lane, cordwainer
Sam. Harris, saddletree-plater, son of Sam., carpenter, decd.
Dan. Freeman, son of Dan., whitesmith, late of Gloucester
Sam. Turner, esq., of Gloucester, formerly of Bengal, the East Indies, son of John, grocer, decd.
4 Dec Thos. Taylor, victualler, by fine
16 Dec Sir Berkeley Wm. Guise, Bt., of Fulham, Mdx., son of Sir John, Bt., decd., of Highnam
153 21 Dec Lieut. John Fisher Hope, North Glos. Militia,† by gift.[1] Sworn 26 Dec 1801
1802 18 Jan Wm. Bourn, app. of Jas. Bourn, cordwainer
29 Jan Jas. Bradley, baker, } sons of Wm., victualler
Thos. Jas. Bradley, watchmaker, of Newent, }
Wm. Beard, app. of Chas. Spencer, bricklayer
Jas. Knight, pinmaker, son of Wm., pinmaker
12 Feb Chas. Garratt Ridgeley, hairdresser, son of John, victualler
154 John Eccles of Northleach, app. of Elisha Farmer Saddler, mercer and linen-draper
Wm. Maverley, pinmaker, son of John, pinmaker
Chas. Jaques, app. of Jas. Daniell, joiner
19 Feb Edm. Phillips Stock, gent., of Hereford, son of Edm., grocer
9 Apr Jas. Bower, musician, South Glos. Militia, son of Wm., cordwainer
26 Apr John Wood, private, 2nd Life Guards, of St. Marylebone, Mdx., son of Jos., baker
Thos. Gray, yeoman, of Sandhurst, son of Wm., flaxdresser, decd.
155 Sam. Maverley, baker, } sons of Sam., cordwainer
Lewis Maverley, cordwainer, }
10 May Thos. Miles, yeoman, by fine. Sworn 17 May 1802
Wm. [Eden], Lord Auckland†[2] by gift
Lord Chas. Spencer† by gift
Francis Freeling, secretary (to) the Post Office, London, by gift
18 May Thos. Hastings, yeoman, by fine. Sworn 9 Aug 1802
156 25 June Benj. Matthews, pipemaker, of Hereford, son of Benj., pipemaker
2 July Wm. Fords, app. of his father Wm., cordwainer
Ric. Ford, app. of Chas. Woodward, cordwainer
Jos. Mann, pinmaker, son of Jos., pinmaker, decd.
Wm. Edwards, app. of Chas. Spencer, bricklayer
Thos. Bower, waterman, son of Thos., victualler, decd.
Thos. Greening, hairdresser, son of Wm., hairdresser, decd.
157 3 July John Price, cabinet-maker, son of John, victualler, decd.
Benj. Gunn, hairdresser, son of Jas., cordwainer
5 July John Wright Guise, esq., } sons of Sir John, Bt., decd., of Highnam
Powell Colchester Guise, esq., }
Sam. Gunn, tailor, son of Jas., cordwainer
Chas. Harding, bag-weaver, son of Ric., flaxdresser, of Kingsholm
Jas. Johnson, app. of Thos. Woodward, cabinet-maker
158 Thos. Bossom, cordwainer, } sons of Hen., cordwainer, of Mitcheldean, formerly of Blakeney
Harry Bossom, cordwainer, }
John Vaughan, app. of Rob. Benson, fellmonger
Francis Reeve, brushmaker, son of Francis, gent.
Thos. Stephens, brushmaker, } sons of John, shopkeeper, of Gloucester, formerly husbandman, of Barton Street
Wm. Stephens, tinman and brazier, }

[1] Entrant was son of John, a former member of the corporation, decd.: ibid. f. 340.
[2] *Complete Peerage*, i. 333–4.

159 Sam. Jeffs, tailor, son of Sam., pinmaker, decd.
John Lewis, cooper, son of John, baker
John Lewis, pargeter, son of Jos., tiler and plasterer
Jos. Young, bricklayer, of Gloucester, son of Ric., labourer, of Westbury-on-Severn
Thos. Bennett, app. of Thos. Ady, hairdresser, decd.
19 July Hen. Church of Chepstow, Mon., app. of Dan. Spencer, bricklayer
160 30 July Adm. [Horatio Nelson], Lord Nelson,[†1] by gift
(Hen.) Augustus Berkeley Craven[†2] by gift
9 Aug Chas. Lewis, tailor, of Cirencester, son of Chas., cordwainer, decd.
Ric. Young, labourer, of Gloucester, son of Ric., labourer, of Flaxley
16 Aug Thos. Daniel, carpenter, son of Jas., carpenter
Fream Window Sparks, cordwainer, son of Thos., pargeter, decd.
20 Aug Jos. Wadley, private, 9th Foot, son of Thos., hairdresser, decd., of Newnham
161 23 Aug Wm. Frankis, yeoman, son of Hen., yeoman, of Upton St. Leonards, formerly of Painswick
Sam. Bennett, app. of Thos. Clarke, tailor
Thos. Quarington, wine merchant, son of Edw., wine merchant, decd.
6 Sept Ric. Powell Chandler, tobacconist, of Barton St. Michael, son of Powell, tobacconist, decd.
21 Sept Sam. Bond, collar-maker, of Birdlip, son of Sam., collar-maker, decd.
1 Oct John Dancer, yeoman, of Hardwicke by fine. Sworn 15 Aug 1803
Sam. Haynes, yeoman, by fine
162 Benj. Morgan, yeoman, by fine. Sworn 10 June 1803
Wm. Haynes, yeoman, by fine
Mic. Hanley, yeoman, by fine. Sworn 18 Oct 1802
Sarah Okey, daughter of Thos. Okey, victualler, decd., by fine
Sir Steph. Lushington, Bt., of Harley Street, London, by gift
Hen. Hope, esq., of Cavendish Square, London, by gift
Jos. Thos. Brown, esq., of Calcutta by gift
Thos. Jefferies, esq., of Creed Place[3] near Gloucester by gift. Sworn 30 July 1805
163 Rear-Adm. Edw. Thornborough[†] by gift
Townshend Selwyn, esq.,[4] by gift
Benj. Claxson, mercer, by gift

James Sadler, esq., mayor 1802–3

18 Oct John Gurney, cordwainer, son of John, pinmaker, of Littleworth
29 Oct John Hale, app. of Thos. Rodway, cordwainer
19 Nov John Dicks, app. of Thos. Bretherton, hairdresser
21 Dec John Avery, cordwainer, of Gloucester, son of Edw., decd.,[†] by gift. Sworn 23 Jan 1804
164 1803 28 Jan Wm. Woodward, app. of Jas. Browne, tailor
Wm. Haylin, app. of Chas. Woodward, cordwainer
4 Feb John Favill, app. of Thos. Weaver, pinmaker
7 Feb Thos. Ashmeade, breeches-maker, } sons of Giles, breeches-maker, of Charlton Kings
Ric. Ashmeade, carpenter, }
John Ashmeade, breeches-maker, }

[1] Ibid. ix. 462.
[2] Owner of Elmbridge Court, Hucclecote, and other estates in the county: *V.C.H. Glos.* iv. 433; vii. 213; viii. 72.
[3] Later called Bowden Hall: Bigland, *Glos.* iii, no. 277.
[4] Later clerk: *Alumni Oxon. 1715–1886*, iv. 1273; Fosbrooke, *Glouc.* 115.

21 Feb Geo. Thos. Jones, app. of Thos. Woodward, pinpointer
14 Mar Thos. Merrett, pinmaker, son of Thos., private, North Glos. Militia, decd.
165 18 Mar Geo. Daniell, painter, } sons of Sam., carpenter
John Daniell, carpenter, }
Hen. Dunn Matthews, farrier, of Tewkesbury, son of John, farrier, of London, formerly of Gloucester
22 Apr Wal. Wilkins the younger, esq., of Maesllwch (*Maeslough*), Radnors., by gift. Sworn 15 June 1803
Ric. Donovan, esq., of Redmarley D'Abitot, Worcs., by gift. Sworn 15 July 1803
Revd. Wm. Mills of Miserden by gift. Sworn 24 Sept 1803
166 John Elton, esq., by gift
23 May Benj. Wilkes, pinmaker, son of Jas., pinmaker
Jas. Williams, flaxdresser, son of Jeremiah, cordwainer
24 June Chas. Cook(e), plumber and glazier, son of John, pargeter
22 Aug John Merrot Stephens, esq., of Maisemore, son of Merrot, esq.
30 Aug H.R.H. Prince Ernest Augustus, duke of Cumberland,†[1] by gift
John Penton, yeoman, by fine. Sworn 2 Sept 1803
167 John Tyers by fine. Sworn 2 Sept 1803
John Dowling, victualler, by fine. Sworn 2 Sept 1803
22 Sept Abraham Wintle by fine
John Wombwell, esq., of Golden Square, London, by gift. Sworn 23 July 1805
Captain Mat. Windey, North Glos. Militia,† by gift. Sworn 10 Feb 1806
Chris. Caple, esq., of Prestbury by gift. Sworn 28 Sept 1803
Wm. Caple the younger, esq., of Prestbury by gift. Sworn 20 Sept 1804
168 Wm. Symonds, M.D., of Hereford by gift. Sworn 7 Aug 1805
Jas. Symonds, esq., of Castle End near Ross, Herefs., by gift. Sworn 7 Aug 1805
Wm. Robins, esq., of London by gift. Sworn 13 Sept 1816[2]

Giles Greenaway, esq., mayor 1803–4

1804 25 Jan Sir Wm. Sidney Smith†[3] by gift
Peter Moore, esq., of St. John's College, Cambridge [University], by gift. Sworn 6 Oct 1806
Nigel Kingscote, esq., 17th Foot,† by gift. Sworn 2 Aug 1805
169 23 Mar Jas. Nicholls, app. of Thos. Saunders, soapboiler, decd.
Chas. Boseley, waterman, son of Wm., breeches-maker
Jas. Haynes, app. of Jas. Cole, tinplate-worker
9 Apr Wm. Bourn, cordwainer, of Birmingham, son of Wm., cooper, decd.
16 Apr John Crook, app. of Wm. Jeffs, tailor
9 July John Bell Wilkins, tailor, son of Thos., upholder, decd.
170 16 July John Welch, tailor, of Stoke Orchard, son of John, of Boddington
7 July Wm. Gurney, private, 56th Foot, son of John, pinmaker, of Littleworth
24 Aug Geo. Bullock, app. of Ric. Hayle, tanner, decd.
7 Sept Ric. Lea, yeoman, of Evington, Leigh, son of Thos., yeoman, decd., of Leigh
John Holtham, innholder, son of John, victualler, decd.

[1] King of Hanover from 1837: *Complete Peerage*, iii. 575.
[2] Entry repeated below: GBR C 9/9, p. 272.
[3] Cf. *D.N.B.*: naval commander, known as Sir Sidney Smith.

171		25 Sept	Captain Wm. Hotham, R.N.,[1]† by gift. Sworn 8 Oct 1804
			Thos. Bowen, esq., 10th Light Dragoons,† by gift. Sworn 3 June 1813[2]
			Noah Hill Neale, esq., by gift[3]
			David Walker, printer, by gift.[4] Sworn same day
			John Pearce, gent., of Frampton on Severn by gift
			John Dunford, yeoman, of Little Barrington by gift
		23 Nov	Ric. Ridler, victualler, by fine[5]
172			**Thomas Mee, esq., mayor 1804–5**
		30 Nov	John Green, gent., son of Ric., gent., decd., of Churcham
		3 Dec	Thos. Dance of Ross, Herefs., app. of Ric. and Jas. Wood, mercers
	1805	21 Jan	Wm. Monk, victualler, by fine. Sworn 25 Jan 1805
		28 Jan	Jos. Mitchell, saddler, of Birmingham, son of Jos., plasterer, decd.
			Thos. Morgan, victualler, by fine
		31 Jan	Thos. John Lloyd Baker, esq., of Uley by gift. Sworn 11 Oct 1805
173		11 Feb	John Badham, app. of Paul Mutlow, tailor
			Thos. Stroud, joiner, son of Steph., wireworker
		15 Feb	Abednego Ireland, cordwainer, son of Jas., labourer
		18 Feb	Thos. Jordan, app. of Edm. Stock, grocer
		22 Apr	Captain John Jefferis, 33rd Foot,† son of John, esq.
		24 May	Jas. Drinkwater of Sandhurst, } apps. of Thos. Woodward,
174			Jas. Sessions, } cabinet-maker
			Thos. Townsend, app. of Thos. Herbert, pinmaker
			Dan. Greening, tailor, of Cheltenham, son of Wm., barber, decd.
		8 July	Edw. Jones, vicar of Brockworth,† son of Roynon, esq., of Hayhill
		12 July	John Woodward, labourer, son of Thos., pinmaker
			Jas. Ford, labourer, son of Wm., cordwainer
175			Chas. Woodward, painter, son of Chas., painter
			Sam. Bonnerwell, cordwainer, son of Wm., cooper, decd.
			Adam King, pargeter, son of Chas., pinmaker
			Hen. Wm. Hickes, pinmaker, son of Wm., pinmaker
			Thos. Venn, labourer, son of Thos., labourer
			Jas. Darke, pinmaker, son of Wm., pinmaker, decd.
			Wm. Wathen, servant, son of John, pinmaker, decd.
176			Giles Smart, cordwainer, son of Wm., cordwainer
			John Trickey, basket-maker, son of Thos., basket-maker
			Wm. Smart, tailor, son of Wm., cordwainer
			Wm. Watts, butcher, son of Thos., butcher, decd.
			Thos. Davies Jones of Colchester, Essex, app. of Nat. Biddle, grocer
			John Prothero, app. of Geo. Powell, pinmaker
			Thos. Merrick, app. of Wm. Smith Bartlett, pinmaker
177			Thos. Lewis, app. of John Rea, pinmaker
			Thos. Humphris, app. of Thos. Rodway, cordwainer
			Thos. Pool, app. of Ric. Baldwin, collar-maker
		15 July	Wm. Read, app. of John Read, upholder
			Wm. Barrett, carpenter and joiner, of Littleworth, son of Ric., painter
			Thos. Taylor, app. of Chas. Bonnor, brazier
			Adam Gardiner, pinpointer, son of Adam, wiredrawer
178			John Morris of Bibury, app. of Wm. Evans, carpenter and joiner

[1] Later knighted: *D.N.B.*
[2] Entry repeated below: GBR C 9/9, p. 258.
[3] On his election to the common council: ibid. B 3/12, f. 384v.
[4] On his election to the common council: ibid.
[5] Entry belongs to following mayoralty.

16 July Jos. Reeve, brushmaker, son of Francis, carpenter
John Lander, pinmaker, son of Jas., pinmaker
John Davis, labourer, son of Wm., labourer, of Longney
Edw. Clarke, accountant, of Stepney, Mdx., son of Wm., pinmaker, decd.
Thos. Bower, breeches-maker, of Gloucester, son of Jas., breeches-maker, of Tewkesbury
John Perris, blacksmith, son of Thos., pinmaker, decd.
179 Thos. Swayne, baker and confectioner, son of Wm., woolcomber, decd.
John Davis, app. of Jas. Smart, pinmaker
Jas. Smart, app. of Jas. Brown, tailor
18 July Sam. Farmer Sadler, gent., of Winchcombe, son of Elisha Farmer Sadler, mercer, decd.
Peter Hawker, clerk, son of Peter, clerk, of Woodchester
Ric. Jeynes, ostler, of Cheltenham, son of Wm., flaxdresser, late of Gloucester
John Matthews, pipemaker, son of Benj., pipemaker
180 Ant. George, app. of Powell Chandler, tobacconist, late of Gloucester
Francis Brown of Kingsholm, app. of Thos. Gardner, baker
Peter Cooke, yeoman, of Woolhope, Herefs., son of John, pargeter
Wm. Bubb, liquor dealer, son of Wm., carpenter, decd.
Benj. Lane, cabinet-maker, son of Wm., cabinet-maker
Wm. Cullis, } apps. of Dan. Spencer, bricklayer
Jas. Daw, }
181 Wm. Phillips, app. of Ric. Lane, farrier
20 July Ant. Ashmead, linen-draper, } sons of Giles, breeches-maker,
Giles Ashmead, glover, } of Charlton Kings
Edw. Ashmead, carpenter, son of Thos., yeoman, of Charlton Kings
Wm. Westmancote Ashmead, yeoman, son of John, yeoman, of Charlton Kings
22 July Jonathan Frankis, yeoman, of Painswick, son of Ric., yeoman, decd., of Upton St. Leonards
John Wilce, private, North Glos. Militia, son of John, grocer, decd.
182 Thos. Window, private, North Glos. Militia, son of John, cabinet-maker
Sam. King, gent., } sons of Sam., gent.,
Thos. King, gent., of Frampton on Severn, } of Wheatenhurst
Revd. Wm. Bushell,[1] son of Wm., saddler
Geo. Elton, M.A., son of Edw., esq., of Burley Hill, Glam.
Thos. Gardner, gent., son of Thos., baker, decd.
Abel Wellavize Coleman, surgeon, of Cheltenham, son of Thos., victualler
John L(e)ake, bricklayer, of Wheatenhurst, son of Benj., gardener, of Hartpury
183 Chas. Hough, stationer, son of John Jas., stationer
Jos. Davis, labourer, son of Jos., labourer, of Wheatenhurst
Thos. Wathen, app. of John Wathen, pinmaker, decd.
Wm. Davis, labourer, son of Jos., labourer, of Wheatenhurst
Sam. Pinching of Cranham, app. of Ric. Heath, saddler
John Welch, yeoman, son of Wm., yeoman, of Hucclecote, Churchdown
23 July Thos. Haynes, app. of Sam. Wilton, pinmaker, decd.

[1] Rector of Tibberton: Hockaday Abs. ccclxxiv.

184 1805 Chas. Parker, gent., son of Chas., coal merchant

Wm. Merrett, joiner and carpenter,
Steph. Merrett, cordwainer, of Woodchester,
Phil. Merrett, clothier, of Woodchester,
John Merrett, tailor, of Nailsworth,
Thos. Merrett, joiner and carpenter,
} sons of Phil., clothworker, of Minchinhampton

Wm. Vick, app. of Geo. Washbourn, baker

185 Benj. Frankis, yeoman, of Painswick Lodge, son of Ric., yeoman, decd., of Upton St. Leonards

Thos. Gardner Cole, victualler, of Upton St. Leonards, son of Jas., gent., of Barton Street St. Mary

John Hawkins White, joiner and carpenter, of Cheltenham, son of Wm., tanner, decd., of Newent

Jas. Crowdy, butcher, of Ebley, son of Ric., yeoman, decd., of Wotton

24 July Thos. Welch, bricklayer, son of Thos., bricklayer, of Quedgeley

Wm. Bevan, baker, of Upton St. Leonards, son of Thos., baker, decd.

186 26 July Jos. Jones, gent., son of Thos., gent., of [Barton] St. Michael,[1] formerly victualler, of Gloucester

Jas. Wilkes, tailor, son of Jas., wiredrawer

Ric. Adey, pinmaker, son of John, pinmaker

Wm. Draper, brazier, son of Wm., plumber and glazier, decd.

Wm. Washbourn, druggist, son of Wm., druggist, decd.

Edw. Roberts, app. of Edw. Roberts, tinplate-worker, decd.

Ric. Harris, yeoman, son of Wal., yeoman, decd., of Walford, Herefs.

187 Hen. Wakeman of Tewkesbury, app. of Wm. Evans, carpenter, decd.

Rob. Phelps, tailor, son of John, tailor, of Woodmancote, Bishop's Cleeve

Wm. Bowkott, chaise driver, of Clifton, son of Wal., victualler, decd.

John Coopey, dealer, son of Wm., dealer, late of Churcham

John Cox, yeoman,
Wm. Cox,
Chas. Cox, yeoman,
} sons of Thos., of Apperley, formerly baker, of Tewkesbury

188 Jas. Swayne, tailor, of Bridgnorth, Salop., son of Wm., woolcomber, decd.

Thos. Ashmead, sawyer, son of Thos., labourer, of Charlton Kings

Jos. Welch, tailor, of Barrow, Boddington, son of John, tailor, of Hayden, Boddington

Jas. Butt, yeoman, of Woodmancote, Bishop's Cleeve, son of Jas., yeoman, of Southam

Geo. Bridges, cordwainer, son of Theophilus, carpenter, of Upton St. Leonards

Peter Phelps, tailor, of Broadway, Worcs., son of Wm., tailor, of Gotherington

Wm. Skillern, tailor, of Winchcombe, son of Isaac, excise officer, late of Abingdon, Berks.

189 Thos. Harris, app. of John Rea, pinmaker

29 July Jos. Gransmore, butcher, son of Thos., butcher

Chas. Reynolds Wilkes, tinplate-worker and brazier, of Tewkesbury, son of Jas., wiredrawer

Isaac Lane, tailor, son of Ric., pinmaker, decd., of Littleworth

Chas. Gardiner, cordwainer, son of Thos., baker, decd.

John Chris. Capel Astman Hartland, gent., son of John, gent., decd., of Newent

[1] *the hamlet of St. Michael*: cf. *V.C.H. Glos.* iv. 382.

John Deane, yeoman, of Frocester, son of Wm., victualler, decd.
190 Wm. Rea, baker, son of Thos., baker
30 July John James, gent., of Gloucester, son of John, gent., decd., of Highnam
Chas. Wilkes, pinmaker, son of Chas., pinmaker
Rob. Clarke, yeoman,
Jos. Clarke, yeoman, } sons of Chas., blacksmith, of Arlingham
Geo. Clarke, yeoman,
Chas. Weaver, gent., son of Thos., esq.
Jas. Heane, carrier, son of Rowland, carrier
191 Jos. Abell, surgeon, } sons of Thos., victualler
Wm. Abell, gent.,
Ric. Solloway Skillern, clerk,[1] son of Jos., gent.
31 July Jos. Newton, ropemaker, son of John, flaxdresser, of Ross, Herefs.
Nat. Hooper, clothdrawer, of Eastington, son of Chas., butcher
Wm. Guilding, baker, of Tewkesbury, app. of Geo. Washbourn, baker and confectioner
Rob. Trustram, blacksmith, of Fairford, } sons of Wm., labourer,
192 John Trustram, fellmonger, of Stratton
Thos. Young, collier, son of John, labourer, of Westbury-on-Severn
John Clarke, cordwainer, of Berkeley, } sons of Chas., blacksmith,
Chas. Clarke, blacksmith, of Arlingham
Thos. Frankis, yeoman, son of Hen., yeoman, of Upton St. Leonards
John Perris, cordwainer, son of John, tinplate-worker, of Gloucester, formerly of Ross, [Herefs.]
Thos. Hughes, surgeon, of Stroud (by gift).[2] Sworn same day
193 Jas. Young, labourer, son of John, labourer, decd., of Westbury-on-Severn
1 Aug Chas. Hawker, clothier, son of Peter, clerk, of Woodchester
Jasper Selwyn Hawkins, grocer, of Cainscross, Stonehouse, son of Hen., clothier, decd., of Wheatenhurst
Geo. Daniell, banker's clerk, son of Wm., joiner, decd.
Thos. Wadley, bricklayer, of Shrewsbury, son of Thos., hairdresser, decd., of Newnham
Ric. Yarnold, labourer, } sons of John, victualler, decd.,
194 John Yarnold, yeoman, of Ledbury, Herefs.
2 Aug Cartwright Elliotts of Huntley, app. of Cartwright Maddocks, baker
Wm. Daniell, pinmaker, of Limehouse, London, son of Jas., carpenter
John Venn, labourer, of Minsterworth, son of Wm., labourer, of Ashleworth
Sam. Taylor, app. of Sam. Jones, brushmaker
Jas. Collerick, tinplate-worker, of 14, Bird Street, Oxford Street, London,
Benj. Collerick, glasscutter, of 1, Rolls Buildings, Fetter Lane, London, } sons of Benj., tinplate-worker, decd., of Worcester
195 Ric. Dunn, private, Coldstream Guards, son of Ric., hairdresser
3 Aug Wm. Capel, gent., of Painswick, son of Dan., gent., of Warminster, Wilts.
Chas. Jas. Cooke, brushmaker, of Bristol, son of Jas., corn factor
5 Aug Geo. Jones, esq., son of Roynon, esq., of Hayhill

[1] Master of the Crypt school: Fosbrooke, *Glouc.* 152.
[2] By act of 30 Sept 1785: GBR B 3/12, f. 18v.

1805 Wm. Price, ropemaker, of 4, George Street, Bethlam Green, Mdx., son of John, cordwainer, decd., of Queen Street, the Park, Southwark

John Cocks Bower, gent., son of John, gent., of Newent

196 John Davis, pinmaker, of Siston, son of Hen., pinmaker, decd.

John Quarrington, clerk,[1] son of Edw., wine merchant, decd.

Chas. Lindsey, plasterer, of 61, Duke Street, Southwark,
Ric. Lindsey, horse dealer, of Waltham Abbey, Essex,
} sons of Chas., plasterer, decd., of Forty Hill, Enfield, Mdx.

Wm. Watts, carpenter, of Bermondsey New Road, St. George, Southwark,
197 Isaac Watts, tailor, of 48, St. Martin's Lane, London,
Thos. Watts, carpenter, of 3, Little Compton Street, Soho, London,
John Watts, carpenter, of Fulham, Mdx.,
Benj. Watts, cabinet-maker, of 3, Little Denmark Street, St. Giles, London,
} sons of Wm., carpenter, decd.

Benj. Elliot(t), cordwainer, of 22, James Street, Grosvenor Square, London, son of Wm., peruke-maker, decd.

198 John Bevan, cordwainer, of 39, James Street, Oxford Street (*Road*), [London], son of Ric., baker, decd.

John Wilkes, pinmaker, of 33, Worcester Street, Queen Street, Southwark, son of John, dragoon, Gen. [Hen. Seymour] Conway's regiment, decd.†[2]

John Hampton, needle-maker, of Duke Street, Gravel Lane, Southwark, son of John, pinmaker, decd., of Gravel Lane

Sam. Bowers, weaver,
Jas. Thos. Bowers, copperplate-printer, of 12, Providence Row, St. George Fields, Surr.,
} sons of Sam., weaver, of 3, Falcon Court, Shoe Lane, Fleet Street, [London]

Wm. Jones, wiredrawer, of 22, Gravel Lane, Southwark, son of Thos., breeches-maker, late of St. Giles, London*

199 Hen. Knowles, leather-dresser, of Bermondsey New Road, Mdx., app. of Rob. Benson, fellmonger

Ric. Cleaveley, cordwainer, of 4, New Court, George Yard, Whitechapel, London, son of Price, cordwainer, of 24, Cock Hill, Bishopsgate Street, London

6 Aug John Powell, tanner, of 82, Redcross Street, Southwark,
Ric. Powell, ironplate-worker, of 10, Tailors Row, St. John Street, Clerkenwell, Mdx.,
} sons of John, pinmaker, decd., of St. Mary Magdalen, Bermondsey, [Surr.]

Ric. Moye, carpenter and joiner, of 163, Sloane Street, Knightsbridge, Mdx., son of Thos., cabinet-maker, late of Gloucester

200 Hen. Perrin, cutler, of Drury Lane, London, son of Jos., victualler, decd.

John Matthews, farrier, of Whitechapel Road, London,
Thos. Matthews, salesman, of the Minories, London,
} sons of John, farrier, of [St.] Marylebone, Mdx., formerly of Gloucester

[1] Vicar of Shopland, Essex: *Alumni Oxon. 1715–1886*, iii. 1167.

[2] Cf. above: GBR C 9/8, p. 277.

John Parsons, gent.,[1] son of the Revd. Wm., of Stretton Grandison, Herefs.

Thos. Mott, bootmaker, of Strand, London, son of Thos., victualler, decd.

Sam. Francis Jennings, printer, of Drury Lane, London,
201 John Jennings, printer,
} sons of Sam., printer, of Shoe Lane, Fleet Street, London

Chas. Stephens, gent., son of Wm., gent., decd., of Kencott, Oxon.

Jas. Nest, carpenter, of Windsor, [Berks.],
John Nest, carpenter, of Windsor, [Berks.],
} sons of Dan., carpenter, decd., of Farnborough, Hants.

Rob. Greatwood, grocer, son of Rob., grocer, of Birmingham

Jas. Maverly, tailor, of 22, Duke Street, Union Street, Bishopsgate Street, London, son of John, tailor. 17 Nov 1826 – Jas. Amos Maverly, son of Jas., applied for his freedom, when it appeared from the statement of Wm. Maverly, his uncle, that although he was christened on 11 Aug 1805 he was born a year and a half before that date

Jas. Powell, turner, of Redcross Street, Southwark, son of John, pinmaker, decd., of St. Mary Magdalen, Bermondsey, [Surr.]

202 Thos. Adey, sergeant, 3rd Foot, son of Thos., late sergeant, South Glos. Militia

Geo. Edwards of Bishopsgate Street, London, app. of Wm. Holt, grocer

Wm. Ham, groom and quartermaster, Light Horse Volunteers, of Gray's Inn Lane Road, Mdx., son of Thos., decd., of Whaddon

Jasper Chandler, weaver, of Pitchcombe, app. of Merrot Stephens, mercer

7 Aug Maur. Smith, merchant, of Newgate Street, London, son of John, gent., of London

Geo. Dowden, maltster, son of Thos., innholder, decd., of Cirencester

203 Jas. Wm. Drinkwater Guest, gent., of Hoxton, Mdx.,
Jonathan Shield Guest, gent., of Islington, Mdx.,
} sons of John, potter and glassworker, decd., of St. John Street, Mdx.

Thos. Pettat, clerk, of Hatherop, son of John, clerk, of Stonehouse

Chas. Millman Mount, gent., son of Thos., apothecary, decd., of Cirencester

John Hill of 21, Fish Street Hill, London, app. of Newton Brabant, pinmaker

Wm. Lane, private, 3rd Foot, son of Wm., cabinet-maker

204 Wm. Steel, tiler and plasterer, son of Steph., tiler and plasterer, of Blakeney

Wm. Flatcher, gunstock-maker, of the Minories, London, son of Chas., brassfounder, of London

Ric. Steel, surgeon, of Abergavenny, Mon., son of Elmes, surgeon, of Coleford

Jos. Bamford, pin-wiredrawer, son of John, pin-wiredrawer, of Siston

Jeremiah Bamford, nailmaker, of Pucklechurch, son of Thos., labourer, late of Littledean

Jas. Bamford, wiredrawer, son of Thos., wiredrawer, of Siston

[1] Later clerk and called John Hopton: *Alumni Oxon. 1715–1886*, ii. 690; Burke, *Land. Gent.* (1846), i. 590.

205 1805 Geo. Nicholls, haulier, son of Ferdinando, sawyer, of Westerleigh

Geo. Welch, bricklayer, of Kennington, Surr.,
Ric. Welch, private, 11th Light Dragoons,
} sons of Ric., bricklayer, late of Badgeworth

Wm. Bond, gent., of Wolverhampton, [Staffs.], son of Wm., gent., decd.

John Capel,[1] clothier, of Painswick, son of Dan., gent., of Warminster, [Wilts.]

Sam. Jennings, private, South Glos. Militia, son of John, hatter and feltmonger

Rob. Hawkes, private, South Glos. Militia, son of Rob., cordwainer, late of Minsterworth

206 8 Aug Elisha Farmer Sadler, surveyor, of Hereford, son of Elisha Farmer Sadler, mercer, decd.

Wm. Binning, cabinet-maker, of 42, Ironmonger Lane, London, son of Thos. Ivey Binning, cooper, decd.

Thos. Miles Haviland, coal dealer, of 17, Fetter Lane, London, son of Wm., innholder, decd.

Chas. Bradgate, confectioner, son of Chas., confectioner, of Bristol

Wm. Cowles, cooper, of Gloucester Street, Commercial Row, Mdx.,
Nat. Cowles, broker, of Cornhill, London,
} sons of Geo., silversmith, of Newent

207 Wm. Ashmead Pruen, gent.,[2] of Worcester College, Oxford [University],
John Pruen, lieut. in the East India Company's service,
} sons of Thos., gent., decd., of Worcester

Chas. Williams, private, 1st Foot, son of Chas., combmaker, decd., of Worcester

John Long, hairdresser, son of Giles, cordwainer, decd., of Bedminster, Som.

Wm. Pember Crowdy, attorney,
Jas. Crowdy of Hannington, Wilts.,
} sons of Jas., gent., of Highworth, Wilts.

208 Benj. Taynton, pewterer,
Thos. Taynton, pewterer,
} sons of Wal., pewterer, decd., of Bristol

Wm. Adey, sergeant, 3rd Foot, son of Thos., late sergeant, South Glos. Militia[†]

Wm. Derrett, yeoman, of Merthyr Tydfil, Glam., son of John, butcher, decd.

Wm. Webley, japanner, of 46, Compton Street, Clerkenwell, London, son of Thos., tailor, decd.

Thos. Ric. Beard, labourer, of Brick Lane, Spitalfields, London, son of Jas., decd., of Worship Street, Shoreditch, London

209 Jas. Drinkwater, private, 3rd Royal Battalion, of Jersey, son of John, labourer, decd.

Hen. Prowse Jones, clerk, of Mitcheldean, son of Roynon, esq., of Hayhill

John Pitcher, private, South Glos. Militia, son of John, victualler, decd.

Wm. Ellis, turner, of Spitalfields, Mdx., son of Ric., silversmith, decd., of London

Hen. Barrett, cooper, of 2, Prince's Place, St. George in the East, London, son of Hen., cooper, late of Stroud

[1] Also spelt *Caple*.

[2] Later clerk: *Alumni Oxon. 1715–1886*, iii. 1158.

Ant. Hinton, private, South Glos. Militia, son of Wm., pinmaker
John Ellis, jeweller, of Hoxton, London, son of Ric., silversmith, decd., of London
John Hinton, coach-wheelwright, of 25, Little Earl Street, Seven Dials, Westminster, son of John, whitesmith, of Cheltenham
210 Thos. Bamford, cheesemonger, of 39, Wych Street, London, son of Thos., labourer, decd., of Littledean
Thos. Barnard, private, South Glos. Militia, son of Jas., feltmonger, decd.
Thos. Ric. Ellis, clothworker, of 40, Little Britain, [London], son of Thos., hairdresser, decd., of St. Botolph, London
Wm. Bayley, farrier, of Grafton Street, Fitzroy Square, London, son of Hen., stocking-framework-knitter, late of Tewkesbury
Thos. Engley, jeweller, of 16, Goswell Place, Islington, Mdx., son of Thos., jeweller, of Bridgewater Gardens, Barbican, London
Chas. Dean, clothworker, of Broadwall near Blackfriars Road, London, son of John, flaxdresser, decd.
211 John Harris, baker, of Chepstow, Mon., son of Wal., yeoman, decd., of Walford, Herefs.
John Hulbert Lane, cordwainer, son of Ric., pinmaker, decd., of Littleworth
John Wilcox, clerk, of Prestbury, son of Thos., victualler
Wm. Taynton, mealman, son of John, mealman, decd., of Ross, Herefs.
9 Aug Sam. Lane, cabinet-maker, of Westminster Road, Surr., son of Wm., brushmaker, decd., of Bristol
Edw. Matthews, corporal, 52nd Foot, son of Benj., pipemaker
Captain Dan. Perrin, York Hussars, son of Ric., decd.
212 John Roberts, clerk, of Sonning, Berks., son of Wm. Hayward Roberts, clerk, decd.†
Jas. Clarke, printer, of Crane Court, Fleet Street, London, son of Jas., tinplate-worker, decd.
Wm. Barnard, private, South Glos. Militia, app. of Sam. Bond, collar-maker
Thos. Randall, linen-draper, }
Chas. Randall, statuary and mason, } sons of John, stonemason,
of New Road, Fitzroy Square, Mdx., } of Oxford
John Maverly, gent., of Bristol, son of John, pinmaker
Jas. King, upholsterer, of Brislington, Som., son of Sam., bricklayer, decd.
213 Benj. Mutlow, wiredrawer, of Bristol, son of Wm., wiredrawer, of Dursley
John Roberts, tinplate-worker, of Windsor, [Berks.], son of Edw., tinplate-worker, decd.
Roynon Jones, esq., son of Roynon, esq., of Hayhill
Wm. Woodward, pinmaker, of Warrington, Lancs., son of Thos., pinmaker
Chas. Woodward, cabinet-maker, of Bath, son of Wm., cabinet-maker
Thos. Ashmeade, apothecary, of Bristol, son of John, mercer, decd.
Jas. Fowler, chairmaker, of Wilst Street, Somers Town, Mdx., son of Thos., watchmaker, decd., of St. Luke, Mdx.
Adam Holder of Worcester, app. of Hen. Dunn, plasterer
214 Benj. Fowler, cabinet-maker, of Wilst Street, Somers Town, Mdx., son of Thos., watchmaker, decd., of St. Luke, Mdx.
John Greening, joiner, of Ross, Herefs., son of Wm., barber, decd.

1805 Geo. Dean, plasterer, of 15, Tuttle Street, Mount Pleasant, London, app. in turn of Wm. and Hen. Dunn, pargeters

Levi Ball, esq., of Bath, son of Rob., esq., of Stonehouse

Wm. Woodward, cabinet-maker, of Wells, [Som.], son of Wm., cabinet-maker

Chas. Fream, butcher, of Westbury-on-Severn, son of Thos., butcher

Jos. Cleaveley, tailor, Hen. Cleaveley, turner, } sons of Hen., hairdresser, decd., of Bristol

215 Thos. Hornidge, combmaker, of Kenilworth, Warws., John Hornidge, combmaker, } sons of Thos., combmaker, of Worcester

John Kirby, merchant, son of John, decd., of Chepstow, Mon.

Thos. Griffiths, gent., of Bristol, son of John, shopkeeper, decd.

Thos. Hicks, tailor, of Sheerness, Kent, son of Sam., pinmaker

Thos. Basford, bellows-maker, of Birmingham, John Basford, plumber and glazier, } sons of Chas., tanner, of Henley-in-Arden, Warws.

216 Chas. Powell, cooper, of Birmingham, son of Wm., cooper

John Lawrence, wine cooper, of Greenwich, [Kent], app. of Edm. Stock, wine merchant

Wm. Steel, surgeon, son of Elmes, surgeon, of Coleford

Wm. Holder Cooke, cordwainer, of Oxford Street, London, son of Wm., plasterer, decd.

Wm. Hathaway, carpenter, son of Wm., carpenter, decd., of Ripple, Worcs.

Wm. Randle, tailor, son of Wm., tailor, decd., of Tewkesbury

217 Geo. Goodyer Bower, sergeant, South Glos. Militia, son of Jas., breeches-maker, of Tewkesbury

Jas. Taynton, pewterer, of Bewdley, [Worcs.], son of Thos., pewterer, decd., of Bristol

Ric. Lane, labourer, of Maiseyhampton, son of Ric., labourer, of Marston, Wilts.

John Brock, engraver, of Camden Town, Mdx., son of John, victualler, decd., of Great Earl Street, Seven Dials, London

John Freame, linen-draper, of Worcester, son of Thos., butcher, of Westbury-on-Severn

Thos. Lane, gunsmith, Sam. Lane, gunsmith, } sons of Sam., pinmaker, of Birmingham

218 10 Aug Nat. Wathen, clothier, of Stroud, son of Jos., clothier, decd., of Thrupp, Stroud

John Washbourn, haberdasher, of Holborn, London, Sam. Washbourn, silversmith, Geo. Washbourn, silversmith, of Bristol, Dan. Washbourn, clerk, of Wellingborough, Northants., } sons of Geo., silversmith

Wm. Ashmead, gent., of 6, Mount Street, Grosvenor Square, London, son of Benj., hatter, of St. George, Westminster

219 11 Aug Wm. Fletcher, corkcutter, of Knightsbridge, Mdx., son of Wm., baker

Hen. Harris, moulder, of Coalbrookdale, Salop., son of Wm., forgeman, of Madeley, Salop.

Wm. Coopey, yeoman, son of Ric., yeoman, decd., of Badgeworth

12 Aug Thos. Bamford, son of Thos., victualler, of Kingston's Inn, Kingston, Berks., formerly of Gloucester

Geo. Cooke, D.D., of Tortworth, son of John, surgeon, decd.

Sam. Goodwin, victualler, of Tottenham Court Road, Mdx., son of Sam., victualler, decd.

220 Sam. Hawkins of 52, Webber Row, Blackfriars Road, Southwark, son of Hen., clothier, decd., of Wheatenhurst

Wm. Hardwick, livery stable keeper, of Coleman Street, London, son of John, draper, decd., of Newent

Thos. Lugg, labourer [and] private, Herefs. Militia, son of Jas., labourer, decd., of Hereford

Benj. Pearce, oilman, of Mill Pond Bridge, Bermondsey, Surr., son of John, postmaster, of Tewkesbury

Francis Pearce, button-maker, of Lombard Street, London, son of Thos., button-maker, decd., of Cold Bath Fields, Mdx.

Benj. Hickman, sergeant, 35th Foot, son of Thos., cordwainer, of London

221 John Hickman, sawyer, of Stoke under Ham, Som., Rob. Hickman, sawyer, } sons of John, yeoman, decd., of Isle Abbotts, Som.

Wm. Lugg, labourer [and] private, Herefs. Militia, son of Jas., labourer, decd., of Hereford

Thos. Taylor, labourer [and] private, Herefs. Militia, son of John, cutler, decd., of Cirencester

John Hickes, private, South Glos. Militia, of Brighton, Suss., son of Sam., pinmaker

13 Aug Francis Lye, gent., of Charing Cross, London,
222 John Lye, gent., of College Street, Westminster, } sons of Francis Draper Lye, corn dealer, of Whitechapel, London, formerly upholder, of Gloucester

Edw. Cooke, chairmaker, of Wardour Street, Soho, London, son of Wm., pargeter, decd.

14 Aug Thos. Rogers, oyster merchant, of Little King Street, St. James, Mdx., son of Thos., maltster, decd.

Chas. Wheatstone, music seller, of Strand, Mdx., son of John, cordwainer, decd.

16 Aug Benj. Derrett, yeoman, of Merthyr Tydfil, Glam., son of John, butcher, decd.

John Davis, private, 40th Foot, formerly soapboiler, son of Jos., labourer, of Wheatenhurst

223 Thos. Birch, chaise driver, of Clifton, son of John, broadweaver, of Pitchcombe

Jos. Williams of Stamford Hill near [Stoke] Newington, Mdx., app. of Thos. Webb, cordwainer

9 Sept Wm. Davis, grocer, of College Street, Westminster, son of Geo., victualler, decd.

14 Sept Wintour Harris, gent., son of Wintour, merchant, of Small Street, Bristol

23 Sept John Gardiner, app. of Thos. Bretherton, hairdresser

Thos. Westfaling,[1] esq., of Rudhall, Herefs., by gift. Sworn 20 Feb 1806

224 Chas. James, esq., of Upper Wimpole Street, London, by gift. Sworn 2 Nov 1805

John Phillpotts the younger,[2] esq., by gift. Sworn 24 Sept 1805

Jos. Pyrke, esq., of Littledean by gift. Sworn 10 May 1806

[1] Formerly called Thos. Brereton: Glos. R.O., D 1804/13–4; *V.C.H. Glos.* xi. 42–3.

[2] M.P. for Gloucester for three periods between 1830 and 1847: Williams, *Parl. Hist. of Glos.* 214.

John Coxwell, esq., of Charlton Kings by gift. Sworn 30 Sept 1805
Thos. Turner, esq., by gift. Sworn 24 Sept 1805
John Snowdon, esq., of Stroud by gift. Sworn 19 Oct 1805
225 Rob. Raikes the younger, esq., by gift. Sworn 22 Apr 1811
Captain Geo. Blake, R.N., by gift. Sworn 30 Sept 1805
Chas. Thomas Ellis, esq., of the Inner Temple, London, by gift. Sworn same day[1]
John Wilkinson, esq., of Leigh Street, Red Lion Square, London, by gift. Sworn 18 May 1810[2]
Ric. Smith, esq., of Basinghall Street, London, by gift. Sworn 24 Oct [1805][3]
Hen. Cooke, esq., of Lodgemore (*Ledgemore*) by gift. Sworn 19 Oct 1805

226 **John Turner, esq., mayor 1805–6**

1806 10 Mar Edw. Webb,[4] esq., of Stoke Bishop, son of John, esq., decd., of Cote House
25 Mar Susannah Salcomb, spinster, by fine
14 Apr Sam. Gwinnett, writer, son of Chas., victualler
15 Aug Ralph Fletcher, surgeon, son of Ralph, baker, decd.
John Mann, pinmaker, son of Jos., pinmaker, decd.
22 Aug Edw. Church, attorney, son of Luke, flaxdresser, decd.
227 Thos. Trickey, tailor, son of Thos., basket-maker
Ric. Butt, app. of Shadrach Charleton, grocer
John Hoskins, staymaker, by fine. Sworn same day
Wm. Jordan, maltster, by fine. Sworn same day
John Aston, victualler, by fine. Sworn same day
Jas. Walker, victualler, by fine. Sworn same day
Benj. Chapman, victualler, by fine. Sworn same day
228 John Craddock, app. of Thos. Gunn, hairdresser
Thos. Brimmall, app. of John Bullock, cordwainer
22 Sept Paul Walker, son of Paul, soapboiler, and app. of Elisha Farmer Sadler, (mercer, by apprenticeship).[5] Sworn same day
John Turner, clerk, by gift. Sworn same day
Hen. Wm. Harris, gent., by gift. Sworn same day
Benj. Davis, gent., by gift. Sworn same day
229 27 Sept Rob. Morris the younger, esq., of Barnwood Court by gift. Sworn same day
Hen. Rosser, esq., of Mitcheldean by gift. Sworn same day
1 Oct Hen. Cay Adams, clerk, of Painswick, formerly of Shrewsbury, by gift. Sworn same day

230 **Richard Nayler, esq., mayor 1806–7**

20 Oct Jos. Jordan, gent., of Ross, Herefs., by gift. Sworn 20 Oct 1806
10 Nov Thos. Phelps, butcher, son of Thos., butcher, of Rudford
1807 18 Feb Lieut. Martin Geo. Guise, R.N., son of Sir John, Bt., late of Highnam
24 Apr Wm. Jeffs, brushmaker, son of Thos. Jeffs alias Jelf
15 May Rob. Cooke, plasterer, son of Wm., plasterer, decd.

[1] Sworn 22 Sept 1806: GBR B 3/13, f. 13v.
[2] Entry repeated 19 May 1810: ibid. C 9/9, p. 246.
[3] Ibid. B 3/13, f. 13v.
[4] M.P. for Gloucester 1816–32: Williams, *Parl. Hist. of Glos.* 213.
[5] Entrant prevented from completing his apprenticeship by Sadler's insolvency: GBR B 3/13, f. 27v.

7 Aug Wm. Mann, chaise driver, of Rodborough, formerly cordwainer, of Gloucester, son of Wm., cordwainer

231 Sam. Best, tailor, son of Sam., cordwainer

14 Aug Jas. Lea, yeoman, son of Thos., yeoman, decd., of Leigh

8 Oct Wm. Harmar, attorney, of Mangotsfield, son of Thos., hosier, decd.

It would appear from the common council house book (no. 1463) that at a common council house held on 2 Oct 1807 a resolution was passed presenting the freedom of the city to H.R.H. the Prince of Wales and also to his brother Prince Augustus Frederick, duke of Sussex.[1]

232 **David Willey, esq., mayor 1807–8**

16 Nov Wm. Goodrich, esq., of Maisemore by gift. Sworn same day

21 Nov Thos. Smith of Cheltenham by gift. Sworn 21 Nov 1807

27 Nov John Hughes, clerk, of Berkeley by gift. Sworn same day

18 Dec Wm. Floyd, tailor, son of Wm., pinmaker, decd.

Shadrach Pomfry Jas. Ireland, cordwainer, son of Jas., chairman

233 1808 1 Jan John Baker, esq., of Woodlands near Bristol by gift. Sworn same day

21 Jan John Jepson, gent., son of John Wilkins Jepson, gent., decd.

1 Feb Ric. Woodward, painter, son of Chas., painter

Chas. Launder, tailor, son of Chas., cooper

John Stephens, cordwainer, son of John, baker

234 John Holbert, upholder, son of Rob., gardener and victualler, late of Gloucester

11 Mar Rob. Hobbes, attorney, of Stratford-upon-Avon, Warws., son of Jonathan, organist, late of Warwick

13 May Jas. Cooke, stonemason, son of John, pargeter

11 June Jos. Hawker, esq.,[2] of the College of Arms, London, by gift. Sworn same day

27 June Ric. Hawker, esq., of Dudbridge by gift. Sworn same day

235 1 Aug Wm. Lea, app. of Jas. Nest, cordwainer

29 Aug Wm. Maddox, app. of Cartwright Maddox, baker, late of Gloucester

19 Sept Sam. Arundel, gent., of Dursley, son of Ric., soapboiler, decd., of Painswick

8 Oct Edm. Hopkinson, esq., of Wotton by gift. Sworn same day[3]

21 Oct Edw. Fream, yeoman, of Newnham, son of Thos., butcher, of Westbury-on-Severn[4]

236 21 June Ric. Willis of Tump House, Mon., by gift

23 Sept Jacob Osborne, gent., by gift

24 Sept Sam. White the younger, gent., of Cam by gift

John Barron, esq., of Longney by gift

27 Sept Chas. Brown, gent., of Leonard Stanley by gift

237 28 Sept John Mabbett, esq., of Moreton Valence by gift

1 Oct John Earle, surgeon, of Frampton on Severn by gift

Wm. Smith, gent., of Linton by gift

238 **David Arthur Saunders, esq., mayor 1808–9**

21 Oct Edw. Fream, yeoman, of Newnham, son of Thos., butcher, of Westbury[5]

[1] Later note inserted at pp. 231–2; cf. ibid. B 3/13, f. 44 and v.

[2] Richmond Herald: *College of Arms* (Surv. of London Cttee. 1963), 93–4, 150.

[3] Entry belongs to following mayoralty.

[4] Entry struck through and repeated below: GBR C 9/9, p. 238.

[5] Westbury-on-Severn; cf. above: ibid. p. 235.

8 Dec Hen. Clifford Clifford, esq., son of Nat., esq., of Frampton on Severn
15 Dec Thos. Blaney, esq., of Evesham, Worcs., by gift. Sworn same day
19 Dec Chas. Greenaway, esq., son of Giles, esq.
1809 9 Jan Sam. Wilks, pinmaker, son of Chas., pinmaker, late of Gloucester
239 Wal. Jelf, yeoman, by fine. Sworn same day
16 Jan Chas. Bower, private, Surr. Militia, formerly carpenter, of Gloucester, son of Jos., pinmaker
20 Feb Thos. Sherry alias Sherring, app. of Jas. Bourne, cordwainer
Edm. Best, private, 96th Foot, son of Wm., flaxdresser, of Gloucester, formerly of Wotton
27 Feb Chas. Glendall, wheelwright, son of Thos., private, North Glos. Militia, decd.
240 Ant. Bretherton, hairdresser, son of Thos. Clark Bretherton, hairdresser, decd.
Thos. Woodward, cabinet-maker, son of Wm., cabinet-maker, decd., of Wotton
28 Feb Calvert Ric. Jones, esq., of the Virando, Glam., by gift
23 Mar John Piffe, baker, by fine. Sworn same day
19 May Thos. Constance of Bristol, app. of Ric. Dunn, hairdresser
241 26 June Thos. Jeffs, hairdresser, son of Thos., brushmaker
14 Aug Sam. Woodward, app. of Mic. Jennings, tailor
25 Aug Jas. Bubb, baker, son of Wm., carpenter, late of Gloucester
4 Sept Wm. Gwinnett, victualler, by fine. Sworn same day
Jos. Terry Hone, esq., by gift. Sworn same day
8 Sept Thos. Jenkins, esq., of Mount Pleasant[1] by gift. Sworn same day
9 Sept Jas. Tyers, esq., of Field Place by gift. Sworn same day
242 Chas. Hopkinson, esq., of St. Alban's Street, St. James, Westminster, by gift. Sworn same day
19 Sept Wm. Bellamy, farmer, of Bidfield Farm by fine. Sworn same day
Sam. Brown, yeoman, by fine. Sworn same day
29 Sept Thos. Fords, grocer, son of Thos., private soldier, decd.
Chas. Frederick Parker, esq., of Oxford University, son of Revd. Thos., decd., of Churcham

243 **Charles [Howard], duke of Norfolk,[2] mayor 1809–10**

9 Oct Hen. Croft Burgh, esq., of Stanley Park by gift
20 Oct Jas. Lander, cooper, son of Chas., cooper
Wm. Hicks, pinmaker, son of Wm., pinmaker
Jas. Fream, butcher, son of Thos., butcher, of Westbury-on-Severn
Chas. Hen. Hale of Cheltenham, app. of his father Chas., music master
23 Oct Ric. Holliday, app. of Thos. Rodway, cordwainer. Sworn 6 Nov 1809
244 27 Oct Jas. Bloxsome, gent., son of Edw., cooper. Sworn 1 Nov 1809
13 Nov Jos. Mann, cordwainer, son of Wm., cordwainer
24 Nov John Bagley, gent., of Highnam by gift. Sworn same day
15 Dec Decimus Best, tailor, son of Sam., cordwainer
1810 2 Jan Jas. Palmer, gent., of Frampton on Severn (by gift). Sworn same day
Wm. Palmer, gent., of Moreton Valence (by gift). Sworn same day
8 Jan Geo. Hough, B.A., of Oxford University, son of John Jas., stationer
245 Wm. Evans, whitesmith, by fine. Sworn same day
John Penn, waiter, by fine. Sworn same day

[1] ? customs collector, of Castle Grim near Gloucester: *Glouc. New Guide* (1802), 154.
[2] *Complete Peerage*, ix. 633–4.

12 Jan John Young, carpenter, of Cheltenham, son of Ric., labourer, of Flaxley. Sworn 15 Jan 1810
29 Mar Wm. Jones, surgeon, 43rd Foot,† by gift. Sworn same day
9 Apr Thos. Robins of Ruardean, app. of Edm. Stock and John Mountain, grocers
11 May Revd. Caleb Carrington of Berkeley by gift. Sworn same day
18 May Wm. Fisher Shrapnell, esq., of Berkeley (by gift). Sworn same day
246 19 May John Wilkinson, esq., of Leigh Street, Red Lion Square, Westminster, London, by gift. Sworn same day[1]
8 June Chas. Jones, victualler, by fine. Sworn same day.
13 July Hen. Cooke, pargeter, son of Wm., pargeter, decd.
3 Sept Hen. Butt, butcher, son of Jas., yeoman, of Hucclecote
7 Sept Wm. Browning, app. of John Mic. Saunders, soapboiler and tallow-chandler
John Weaver, tanner, son of Ric., farrier, decd.
12 Sept Wm. Heanes, victualler, by fine. Sworn 14 Sept 1810
John Beard, victualler,[2] by fine. Sworn 14 Sept 1810
John Mason, victualler, by fine. Sworn 14 Sept 1810
247 Wm. Blick, victualler, by fine. Sworn 14 Sept 1810
Nic. Prime, victualler, by fine. Sworn 14 Sept 1810
28 Sept Sir Sam. Wathen, Kt., of Woodchester by gift. Sworn same day

248 **Sir Berkeley William Guise, Bt., mayor 1810–1**

5 Oct Geo. Meadows, hairdresser, by gift. Sworn same day
19 Oct John Arkell, gent., of Boddington by gift. Sworn same day
5 Nov Lieut. John Jas. Hough, R.N., son of John Jas., stationer
Alex. Walker, gent., (by gift). Sworn same day
John Price, chimney-sweeper, son of Hen., pinmaker
Revd. John Duncombe[3] of Hereford (by gift)
17 Dec Chas. Greatwood, confectioner, of Birmingham, son of Rob., grocer
1811 24 May Jos. Coopey, dealer, son of Wm., yeoman, late of Churcham
12 July John Print Field, brushmaker, of Cirencester, formerly of Gloucester, (by apprenticeship).[4] Sworn same day
19 July Thos. Steel, surgeon, son of Elmes, surgeon, of Coleford
249 John Bower, carpenter, son of Jos., pinmaker
30 Aug Sam. Watts, tinplate-worker, son of Wm., carpenter
19 Sept Geo. Yates, barge-owner, by fine. Sworn same day
Rob. Morley, yeoman, by fine. Sworn same day
Wm. Jenkins by fine. Sworn same day

Thomas Commeline, esq., mayor 1811–2

9 Oct John Paul Paul, esq., of Highgrove near Tetbury (by gift)
250 25 Oct Ric. Bower, pinpointer, son of Sam., pinpointer
4 Nov Jas. Nest, baker and confectioner, son of Thos., baker and confectioner, of Gloucester, formerly of Swallow Street, Piccadilly, London
John Reece Fleming, app. of Rob. Phillips, cordwainer. Sworn 8 Nov 1811

[1] Originally recorded above: GBR C 9/9, p. 225.
[2] Barge-owner: ibid. B 3/13, f. 88.
[3] Historian of Herefordshire: *Trans. B.G.A.S.* xxxvii. 170 and n.
[4] Entrant, following bankruptcy of his master Sam. Roberts, completed his apprenticeship with Sam. Jones: GBR B 3/13, f. 88v.

John Andrews, grocer and soapboiler, }
Jos. Andrews, grocer and soapboiler, } sons of Thos., grocer, decd.
11 Nov Jas. Woodward, gent., son of Chas., painter
9 Nov Thos. Gray, esq., of Cheltenham (by gift). Sworn same day
11 Nov Wm. Cook, }
Edm. John Cook, } sons of John, gent., of Churcham, formerly salt merchant, of Gloucester
251 18 Nov Thos. Draper, cordwainer, of Cheltenham, son of Wm., plumber, decd.
23 Nov Wm. Gore Langton, esq., of Newton Park near Bath (by gift). Sworn same day
30 Nov John Jones, gent., of Cooper's Hill (by gift)
2 Dec Ant. Gard(i)ner, maltster, son of Ant., merchant, of Chepstow, Mon.
23 Dec Kingsmill Evans, esq., of the Hill[1] near Ross, Herefs., (by gift). Sworn same day
1812 13 Jan Jos. Herbert, innholder, by fine. Sworn same day
16 Jan Rob. Martin Popham Wall, esq., of Tewkesbury Lodge (by gift). Entered in page 133: freedom voted 27 Sept 1777.[2] Sworn 16 Jan 1812
20 Jan Edw. Youde, esq.,[3] (by gift). Sworn same day
252 31 Jan Jas. Estcourt, cordwainer, son of John, hairdresser
8 Feb John Hodder Moggridge, esq., of Llanrumney, Mon., (by gift). Sworn same day
14 Feb John Matthews of Cirencester, app. of Pettat Gardiner, brushmaker
28 Feb Ric. Coopy, pig dealer, of Bulley, son of Wm., yeoman, late of Churcham
6 Mar John Hanman, app. of Nat. Biddle, grocer
John Matthews, son of John, cordwainer, of Bristol
13 Mar Wm. Drinkwater, son of Thos., cordwainer
20 Mar Jas. Harris, attorney, }
John Cooper Harris, Blackwell Hall factor, of London, } sons of Wintour, accountant, of Bristol
253 7 Apr Wm. Jeynes, horse dealer, of Gloucester, son of Wm., flaxdresser, lately of Leeds, Yorks., formerly of Gloucester
10 Apr John Baron, M.D., (by gift).[4] Sworn same day
4 May John Bullock, yeoman, by fine. Sworn same day
25 May Jas. Wingate, cooper, son of Wm., wine cooper, formerly drummer, South Glos. Militia, decd.
22 June John Richards, carpenter, son of Jos., carpenter
26 June Lieut. Elmes Steel, R.N., son of Elmes, gent., of Coleford
7 Aug Thos. Mann, servant, of Barnwood, app. of Wm. Smith Bartlett, pinmaker
John Marsh, app. of Thos. Manns, cooper, decd.
14 Aug Jos. Woodward, cordwainer, of Hartpury, son of Chas., of Corse, formerly of Gloucester
254 4 Sept Thos. Platt, tailor, son of Thos., pinmaker
14 Sept Thos. Hyett, yeoman, by fine. Sworn same day
Jos. Waugh, yeoman, by fine. Sworn same day
John Chesterton, yeoman, by fine. Sworn same day
18 Sept Thos. Ward, gent.,[5] by gift. Sworn same day

[1] Hill Court, Walford: Burke, *Land. Gent.* (1846), i. 386.
[2] Freedom voted 27 Sept 1797: GBR B 3/12, f. 276v.; cf. above: ibid. C 9/9, p. 133.
[3] Of Hempsted: ibid. B 3/13, f. 111.
[4] On his election to the common council: ibid. ff. 114–5.
[5] Chinawareman: ibid. f. 120.

19 Sept Wm. Viner Ellis, gent., of Minsterworth by gift. Sworn same day

22 Sept Edw. Reading of Lower Thames Street, London, app. of Wm. Simpson, carpenter and joiner

26 Sept Wm. Cother, esq., of Wotton by gift. Sworn same day

255 **John Pleydell Wilton, esq., mayor 1812–3**

9 Oct Geo. Cooke, tailor, son of Wm., plasterer, decd.

John Ricketts, chairmaker, son of Wm., pinmaker

John Serle, app. of Wm. Stephens, tinplate-worker, and his wife Mary Ann

Wm. Whitehead, app. of Wm. Wheatstone, cordwainer

Hen. Curtis, grocer, son of Hen., grocer, decd.

Wm. Jewsbury, pinmaker, app. of Ric. Allen, cordwainer. Disfranchised[1] 21 Dec 1813

16 Oct Hen. Cowles, tailor, son of Geo., gent., decd., of Newent

Wm. Yeend, butcher, of Hanley, Worcs., } sons of Loveridge (*Larenge*), labourer, of Great Malvern, Worcs.

256 Thos. Yeend, labourer, }

Wm. Billings, cordwainer, of Barbourne, Claines, Worcs., son of Wm., labourer, of Powick, Worcs.

Francis Tucker, app. of Thos. Woodward, cabinet-maker

Edm. Evans, app. of Thos. Cooke, pargeter

19 Oct Ric. Dix, clerk to Messrs. Whitcombe and King, of Serjeants' Inn, Fleet Street, London, son of Ric., bricklayer

23 Oct Jas. Price, private, 89th Foot, son of Hen., pinmaker

Thos. Birt, app. of David Walker, printer

Jos. Holtham of Barnwood, app. of Dan. Spencer, bricklayer

257 Benj. Davis, app. of Edw. Bloxsome, cooper

2 Nov Thos. Davis, app. of Jas. Smart, pinmaker

20 Nov Wm. Humphris Baylis, woolstapler, son of Wm., woolstapler, decd.

Jos. Bower, cordwainer, private, South Glos. Militia, son of Jas., painter, decd.

23 Nov Jos. Carwardine of Newington Row, Kent Road, Surr., app. of Geo. Washbourn, baker

2 Dec John Base, chaise driver, son of Ric., chaise driver, of Gloucester, formerly of Rodborough

Geo. Curtis, app. of Thos. Gunn, hairdresser and peruke-maker

1813 22 Jan Wm. Wilton, musician, North Glos. Militia, son of Wm., wiredrawer, late of Gloucester

258 6 Feb Dan. Mills, esq., of Sudgrove (by gift). Sworn same day

23 Apr John Mitchell, prebendary of Gloucester cathedral, (by gift). Sworn same day

John Thackwell, esq., of Dymock (by gift). Sworn same day

26 Apr Ric. Bourne, cordwainer, son of Jas., cordwainer

Jas. Davis, tailor, son of Wm., pinmaker

3 June Captain Thos. Bowen, Pemb. Militia, formerly 10th Light Dragoons,[†] (by gift). Sworn same day.[2] Entered in p. 171

18 June John Gardiner, grocer, son of Ant., corn dealer, formerly tobacconist, of Chepstow, Mon.

13 Aug Jonathan Lea, app. of Jas. Nest, cordwainer

[1] For obtaining the freedom by fraud. Readmitted by fine 26 May 1816: ibid. ff. 140–2, 206; below: ibid. C 9/9, p. 342.

[2] Entry struck through.

14 Aug Wm. Phelps, yeoman, } sons of Thos., farmer, of Rudford,
Geo. Phelps, yeoman, } formerly of Bulley

259 10 Sept Wm. Medhurst, yeoman, by fine. Sworn same day

13 Sept Geo. Smith, yeoman, by fine. Sworn same day

18 Sept John Somers Cocks of Castleditch, Herefs., son of John Somers [Cocks], Lord Somers,†[1] (by gift). Sworn same day

20 Sept Jas. Somers Cocks[2] of Eastnor Castle, Herefs., (by gift). Sworn 23 Oct 1813

Thos. Griffith, gent., of Cheltenham, son of Edw., victualler, decd.

Sam. Jelf, cordwainer, son of Thos., brushmaker

Wm. Walker, cordwainer, son of Wm., whitesmith

27 Sept Thos. Dowle, gent., of Apperley (by gift). Sworn same day

Geo. Watson, mercer, (by gift). Sworn same day

Jos. Roberts, stationer,[3] (by gift). Sworn same day

Thos. Cunningham, esq., (by gift). Sworn same day

260 Joshua Ellis, app. of John Mountain, grocer. Disfranchised 9 Feb 1814

John Wallop, yeoman, by fine. Sworn same day

Wm. Price the younger, timber merchant, (by gift). Sworn same day

2 Oct Rob. Gordon, esq., of Kemble, Wilts., (by gift). Sworn same day

28 Oct Sir Thos. Boulden Thompson, Bt.,† (by gift)[4]

Edward Weaver, esq., mayor 1813–4

1 Nov Chas. Bonnor, brazier, son of Chas., brazier

John Martin, esq., of Overbury, Worcs., (by gift). Sworn same day

5 Nov John Green, brazier and tinplate-worker, app. of Chas. Bonnor, brazier

8 Nov Geo. Allen, app. of Dan. Spencer, mason and bricklayer

Edw. Gardiner Jones, app. of Thos. Woodward, pinmaker

Hen. Glendall, plasterer, son of Thos., private, North Glos. Militia, decd.

261 Francis Ursell, plumber and glazier, of Gloucester, son of Jos., plumber, decd., of Worcester

17 Nov Ric. Helps, esq., of Barton Street (by gift). Disfranchised by judgment of court of King's Bench Hilary term 1820

1814 24 Jan Lieut. Wm. Greatwood, R.N., son of Rob., tallow-chandler and soapboiler, decd.

9 Feb Thos. Watts, baker, son of Thos., husbandman, decd., of Barton Street, formerly of Highnam

29 Mar John Phillimore Hicks, esq., of Eastington (by gift). Sworn same day

3 June John Fords, labourer, son of John, labourer

27 June Ric. Freame, butcher, of Newnham, } sons of Thos., butcher, late
Thos. Nourse Freame, butcher, } of Westbury-on-Severn

262 8 July Benoni Hill, son of Elijah, victualler, decd.

12 Aug Sam. Jelf Evans, app. of John Lander, pinmaker

22 Aug Jasper Selwyn, mercer, of Gloucester, son of Congreve, clerk, decd., of Blockley, Worcs.

Thos. Halford, brazier and tinplate-worker, of Gloucester, son of Thos., labourer, decd., of Hartpury

[1] Recorder of Gloucester: GBR B 3/13, f. 105v.; *Complete Peerage*, xii (1), 32.

[2] Later clerk, son of Lord Somers: *Alumni Oxon. 1715–1886*, i. 270.

[3] Bookseller: GBR B 3/13, f. 135v.

[4] By act of 21 Dec 1798. Entry, originally recorded above, belongs to following mayoralty: ibid. 12, f. 297; C 9/9, p. 139.

2 Sept Wm. Wilks, hairdresser, } sons of Jas., wiredrawer
John Wilks, wiredrawer, }

19 Sept Edw. Tipton, yeoman, by fine. Sworn same day
Wm. Print Linton, yeoman, by fine. Sworn same day
John Gilbert Clark, butcher, of Gloucester, son of Ric., butcher, of Hasfield

263 Wm. Wingate, carpenter, son of Wm., late drummer, South Glos. Militia

20 Sept Jas. Bullock, yeoman,[1] by fine. Sworn same day

26 Sept Chas. Wingfield, surgeon, of Shrewsbury (by gift). Sworn same day
Geo. Wm. Hall, D.D.,[2] (by gift). Sworn same day
Wm. Cother, surgeon, (by gift). Sworn 26 Sept 1814

Sir James Jelf, Kt., mayor 1814–5

10 Oct Geo. Williams, app. of Mic. Jennings, tailor. Sworn same day
Thos. Cardall, app. of David Walker, printer. Sworn same day

22 Oct Chas. Edw. Hanford, esq., of Strensham, Worcs., (by gift). Sworn same day

24 Oct John Derrett, plumber and glazier, of St. Botolph Without, Aldersgate Street, London, son of John, butcher

264 4 Nov Thos. Lewis, cordwainer, son of Thos., cordwainer, decd. Sworn same day
John Hudson, app. of Mic. Jennings, tailor. Sworn same day. Disfranchised by judgment of court of King's Bench 1819

22 Dec Hen. Purnell Hicks, esq., of Eastington (by gift). Sworn same day.‡ Readmitted 8 Mar 1820: p. 385

1815 6 Jan Abraham Thompson, gent., son of Isaac, innkeeper, decd. Sworn same day

16 Jan John Estcourt, hairdresser, son of John, hairdresser. Sworn same day
John Gardiner of Birmingham, app. of Thos. Woodward, cabinet-maker. Sworn same day

27 Jan Thos. Brabant, tailor, son of Wm., pinmaker, decd. Sworn same day

10 Feb John Lane, son of Sam., pinpointer, formerly private, South Glos. Militia

24 Feb Wm. Carter, esq., of Matson House (by gift). Sworn same day[3]

13 Mar Chas. Barrow Evans, esq., of Highgrove (by gift). Sworn same day

265 Thos. Bretherton, carpenter, son of Thos. Clarke Bretherton, hairdresser

5 Apr Edw. Davies, esq., of Eastbach (by gift). Sworn same day

17 Apr Rob. Hudson, app. of his father Thos., tailor

24 Apr Chas. Wilkinson Barrett, gent., son of Ric., painter

27 Apr Ric. Dobbins, yeoman, by fine. Sworn same day

Daniel Willey, esq., mayor 1815[4]

26 June Wm. Derrett, butcher, son of Jas., butcher, of Cranham
Thos. Best, soldier, 85th Foot, son of Sam., cordwainer

11 July Thos. Evans, yeoman, by fine. Sworn same day

[1] Salesman: ibid. B 3/13, f. 149.

[2] Master of Pembroke College, Oxford University, prebendary of Gloucester Cathedral, and rector of Taynton: Fosbrooke, *Glouc.* 114; Hockaday Abs. ccclxv.

[3] Entry repeated below: GBR C 9/9, p. 267.

[4] Elected 5 June 1815 on Jelf's resignation following bankruptcy: ibid. B 3/13, f. 168; *V.C.H. Glos.* iv. 145.

266 John Lewis, yeoman, by fine. Sworn same day
Jas. Brimall, yeoman, by fine. Sworn same day
14 July Revd. Rob. Wintle of Culham, Oxon., son of Revd. Thos., decd., of Brightwell, Berks.
17 July Hen. Wood, labourer, of Barton Street, son of Ric., victualler, decd.
Jas. Davis, fisherman, } sons of Jas., fisherman, decd., of Elmore
Wm. Davis, fisherman, }
John Turner, waterman, son of John, fisherman, late of Elmore
18 July John Davis, fisherman, son of Jas., fisherman, of Elmore
267 1 Aug Edw. Sheppard, esq., of Uley (by gift). Sworn same day.‡ Readmitted 23 Feb 1820: p. 385
5 Aug Jas. Tew, yeoman, by fine. Sworn same day
1 Aug Wm. Carter, esq., of Matson, (by gift).[1] See p. 264
8 Sept Thos. Smith, gent., (by gift). Sworn same day
14 Sept Thos. Palin, esq., of Bristol (by gift). Sworn same day
19 Sept Wm. Millard, yeoman, by fine. Sworn same day
20 Sept John Baron the younger, gent., of Longney (by gift). Sworn same day.‡ Readmitted 16 Sept 1822: p. 404
21 Sept Peter Radley Jackson, gent., of Wotton (by gift). Sworn same day
23 Sept Wm. White the younger, gent., of Cam (by gift). Sworn same day
25 Sept Chas. Trigge, pinmaker, (by gift). Sworn same day
Rob. Dunn, hairdresser, son of Ric., hairdresser
21 Sept John Tocknell by fine. Sworn same day
26 Sept Wm. Smith by fine. Sworn same day

268 **Charles [Howard], duke of Norfolk,[2] mayor 1815**

18 Oct Thos. Skipp, esq., of Stonehouse (by gift). Sworn same day
24 Oct Jas. Broughton, painter, son of Jas., victualler, decd.
30 Oct Wal. Wood, cordwainer, son of Ric., victualler, decd.
Thos. Taylor Manns, cordwainer, son of Thos. Taylor Manns, porter, decd.
Wm. Rea, cordwainer, son of Wm., baker
Ric. Young, carpenter, son of Wm., carpenter, of Gloucester, formerly of Westbury-on-Severn
1816 29 Feb Thos. Jones Howell, esq., of Prinknash Park (by gift).[3] Sworn same day

269 **Richard Nayler, esq., mayor 1815–6[4]**

30 May Sam. Commeline, gent., son of Thos., esq.
14 June John Davies, labourer, of Coaley, son of Wm., labourer, of Longney[5]
11 July [Arthur Wellesley], duke of Wellington,† (by gift)[6]
15 July Lieut. Francis Hen. Woodcock, R.N., son of Sam., esq., ald., of Wotton
29 July Thos. Critchly, printer, son of Sam., victualler, decd.
9 Aug Thos. Porter Bamford, farmer, of Norton, } sons of Wm., apothecary, decd., of Uxbridge, Mdx.
Francis Bennett Bamford, grocer, of Southampton, }

[1] Entry struck through.
[2] *Complete Peerage*, ix. 633–4.
[3] Son of Thos. Bayley Howell of Prinknash Park: GBR B 3/13, f. 43v. Entry belongs to following mayoralty.
[4] Elected 21 Dec 1815 after the duke's death: ibid. f. 180.
[5] Originally given as *Coaley*.
[6] Presented when the duke visited the city from Cheltenham to dine with the corporation: GBR B 3/13, f. 190 and v.; *V.C.H. Glos.* iv. 157; *Complete Peerage*, xii (2), 451–8.

30 Aug Thos. Browning, cooper, son of Sam., victualler, decd.

270 9 Sept Hen. Craddock, app. of Thos. Wilton, tailor, decd.

Isaac Tooth, plumber and glazier, by apprenticeship*

Wm. Tupsley Washbourn, clerk,[1] son of Geo., baker

Wm. Bourne, cordwainer, son of Jas., cordwainer, decd.

Jas. Smart, tailor, son of Wm., cordwainer

David Walker, } apps. of David Walker, printer
271 Rob. Thackwell, }

John Washbourn, stationer, son of John, stationer

Jos. Bennett, cordwainer, son of Jos., pinmaker

Jas. Price[2] of Gloucester, } apps. of Sam. Lane, cordwainer, of
Jas. Lane, } Littleworth, formerly of Gloucester

272 Geo. Preedy, baker, app. of Thos. Nest, baker and confectioner

13 Sept Wm. Robbins, esq., of London by gift. Entered in p. 168. Freedom voted 22 Sept 1803. Sworn 13 Sept 1816

Benj. Baylis, woolstapler, son of Wm. Humphris Baylis, woolstapler, decd.

Thos. Andrews, gent., son of Thos., grocer, decd.

Thos. Binning, saddler, son of Thos. Ivey Binning, cooper, decd.

John Steele, tiler, } sons of Steph., tiler, of Blakeney
Chas. Steele, tiler, }

John Wingate, carpenter, son of Wm., cooper, formerly drummer, South Glos. Militia

273 Jos. Organ of Barton St. Mary, app. of Thos. and Wm. Washbourn, druggists

Jos. Norris, app. of John Hewlett, cabinet-maker

Hen. Warwick of Barton St. Mary, app. of Wm. Binning, chairmaker. Disfranchised[3] by judgment of court of K[ing's] B[ench]. Readmitted 11 Nov 1819: p. 383

John Hartland of St. White's, Flaxley, Forest of Dean, app. of Paul Mutlow, tailor

16 Sept Sam. Farmer Sadler, esq., } sons of Sam. Farmer Sadler, clerk,
Jas. Hayes Sadler, esq., } of Sandhurst

Ric. Allen, gent., } sons of Ric., cordwainer, decd.
274 Wm. Allen, cordwainer, }

Jos. Welch, tailor, son of Phil., tailor, of Brockworth

Ric. Gardner, printer, son of Ric., baker, of Sheepscombe

Benj. Derrett, servant, of Gloucester, son of Jas., butcher, of Brockworth

Rob. Phelps, tailor, of Gloucester, son of Thos., butcher, of Rudford, formerly of Bulley

Wm. Greville, servant, son of Wm., labourer, of Eldersfield, Worcs.

Chas. Cowles, gent., son of Geo., gent., decd., of Newent

Wm. Selby,† son of Wm., labourer, late of Gloucester

Geo. Woodward, labourer, son of Wm., cabinet-maker, decd.

275 John Spier, gent., son of John, victualler, decd.

Benj. Bevan, baker, son of Ric., baker, decd.

Jeremiah Frankis, yeoman, son of Ric., yeoman, decd., of Upton St. Leonards

Jos. Dike of Barton Street St. Mary, app. of Wm. Mann, cordwainer, decd. Disfranchised by judgment of court of King's Bench Hilary term 1820

[1] Not a clergyman, later a timber merchant: Glos. R.O., D 4270/4/1/13–4.

[2] Ordered in 1819 to be disfranchised for obtaining the freedom by fraud: *Glouc. Jnl.* 22 Feb 1819.

[3] For obtaining the freedom by fraud: ibid.

20 Sept Jas. Lovett, attorney, son of Jas., gent., decd.
Thos. Cother, labourer, of Sudbrook, son of Wm. the younger, decd., app. of Ric. Cope and Thos. Bubb, bakers, formerly of Gloucester
Thos. Bishop, sawyer, } sons of Thos., labourer, of Haresfield
John Bishop, sawyer, }
276 Wm. Smart, cabinet-maker, son of Wm., pinmaker
Wm. Piffe, grocer, son of Wm., butcher
Jos. Coopey, labourer, of Tewkesbury, son of Jos., yeoman, of Churchdown
Ric. Engley, tinplate-worker, of Stroud, son of John the younger, yeoman, of Eastington, formerly waiter, of Gloucester
Jonathan Badger, stonemason, son of Jos., pinmaker
Thos. Wilce, servant, of Bath, son of John, grocer, decd.
Dan. John Niblett, esq., son of John, esq., late of Haresfield
Jas. Woodward, hairdresser, son of Thos., pinmaker
277 John Spencer, gent., son of John, victualler
John Davis, labourer, of Sandhurst, } sons of John, cordwainer,
Alan MacDonall Davis,† } of Longney
Joshua Cooke, tailor, son of Wm., plasterer
Sam. Cocks, app. of Hen. Barrett, painter, decd.
23 Sept Wm. Fitzhardinge Berkeley, esq., of Berkeley Castle (by gift)[1]
John Fendall, esq., of Littledean, son of Wm., esq., decd.
Job Bosley, carpenter, of Hanham, son of Wm., breeches-maker, of Wotton
278 Wm. Cox Buchanan, gent., son of Jas., edgetool-maker
Benj. Bonnor, gent., son of Chas., brazier
Wm. Davis, labourer, of Standish, son of Wm., labourer, of Longney. Sworn 3 Oct 1816
Wm. Blanch, cordwainer, of London Road near Worcester, son of John, heelmaker, late of Coventry
Sam. Pitt, tailor, of Whiteshill near Stroud, son of Ric., victualler, decd.
Chas. Batsford, framework-knitter, son of John, framework-knitter, of Tewkesbury
Frederick Rudge, clerk, of Dursley,[2] son of Thos., clerk, of Haresfield
Steph. Reeve, surgeon, of Bristol, son of Nat., maltster, decd.
Wm. Hayward, labourer, son of John, labourer, of Winstone
279 Jos. Freeman, tailor, of Tirley, son of Wm., cordwainer
Rob. Young, nailer, son of Jos., labourer, of Westbury-on-Severn
Sam. Matthews, farrier, of Cheltenham, son of John, farrier
Thos. Clarke, farrier, son of Chas., farrier, decd., of Arlingham
John Dobbins, baker, app. of Jas. Lamb, baker and confectioner, late of Gloucester
Wm. Butt, tailor, son of Jas., yeoman, of Cheltenham
27 Sept Hen. Hooper Wilton, gent., son of Hen., gent.
Lieut. Wm. Morris, R.N., of Barnwood Court, son of Rob., esq., decd., of Barnwood
280 John Jones, brushmaker, son of Sam., brushmaker
Rob. Hincks, stationer, of Cheltenham, son of Geo., victualler, decd.

[1] Entry originally recorded above: GBR C 9/9, p. 102A.
[2] Became vicar of Eardisland, Herefs., in 1816: *Alumni Oxon. 1715–1886*, iii. 1233.

Mat. Whear Goodwin, labourer, of Norton, son of Wm., porter, decd., of Newgate Street, London

John Hayward, labourer,
Wm. Hayward, labourer,
Thos. Hayward, labourer, } sons of Thos., labourer, formerly maltster, of Coln St. Dennis

John Aubrey Whitcombe, gent., son of Sir Sam., Kt., decd.

281 John Woodward, upholsterer,
Frederick Woodward, gent., } sons of Chas., painter, formerly plasterer

Chas. Turner Cooke, surgeon, son of Chas., surgeon, of Barton St. Michael

Thos. Woodward, private, Royal Horse Guards,[†] son of Thos., pinmaker

Sam. Phelps, tailor, of Cirencester, son of John, cordwainer, of Bishop's Cleeve, formerly of Woodmancote

Isaac Smith, app. of Francis Ursell, plumber and glazier, decd.

282 Ric. Warren Coley, app. of Thos. Parker, surgeon, decd.

Sam. Richardson, esq., of Newent (by gift)[1]

Wm. Hen. Hyett, esq., (by gift)

Peter Butt, grocer, son of Jas., yeoman, of Cheltenham, formerly butcher, of Standish

Thos. Bachford[2] stocking-framework-knitter,
John Bachford,[2] stocking-framework-knitter, } sons of John, stocking-framework-knitter, of Tewkesbury

Maynard Colchester, esq., son of John, esq., decd., of Westbury-on-Severn

283 **Thomas Washbourn, esq., mayor 1816–7**

30 Sept John Arthur Engley, cabinet-maker, of Stroud, son of John the younger, waiter

Ric. Clark, butcher, of Pershore, Worcs., son of Ric., butcher, of Hasfield

Thos. Fletcher, gent., of Cheltenham, son of Ralph, baker, decd.

Sam. Brown, husbandman, of Leonard Stanley, app. of Jas. Wood, banker and mercer

John Kendall, wharfinger, son of Wm., wharfinger, of Gloucester, formerly upholder, of High Street, Southwark

Arthur Hough, bookbinder and stationer, son of John Jas. Hough, bookbinder and stationer

284 Chas. Arthur Pace, letterpress-printer, of Liverpool, son of Chas., surgeon, decd.

Thos. Powell, cordwainer, of Stroud, son of Geo., pinmaker, decd.

Lieut. Chas. Jefferis, R.N., son of John, esq.

Thos. Evans, gent., of Deerhurst,
Rob. Evans, gent., of Bredon, Worcs., } sons of Thos., gent., of Worcester

John Gard(e)ner, servant, of Brownshill, Painswick, son of Ric., baker, of Sheepscombe

285 1816 Ambrose Wadley, gent., of Tewkesbury, son of Ambrose, innkeeper, of Bristol, formerly victualler, of Gloucester

Thos. Butt, tea dealer, of 480, Strand, London, son of Jas., yeoman, of Cheltenham, formerly butcher, of Standish

[1] By act of 1 Oct 1784: GBR B 3/11, f. 367v.; cf. ibid. 12, f. 115.

[2] Also spelt *Backford*.

1816 Ric. Barrett, cooper, son of Rob., cordwainer, decd., of Stroud
John Jas. Rudge, cabinet-maker, son of John, carpenter, of Stroud, formerly of Frocester
Lieut. Thos. Abell, 3rd garrison battalion, son of Thos., victualler, decd.
Thos. Gunn, gent., son of Thos., hairdresser
Geo. Piff, saddler, of 154, Oxford Street, London, son of Thos., innholder, decd.

286 1 Oct Wm. Hasleham Vaughan, stationer, of Orange Court, Rose Street, St. Anne, Westminster, son of John, decd.†
Rob. Wathen, private, 3rd Guards, son of John, pinmaker, decd.
Jas. Broadway, weaver, of 6, Fore Street, Bethnal Green Road, Mdx., son of Thos. Broadway alias Braddis, weaver, of Cock Alley, Norton Folgate, Mdx.
Jas. Gardiner, baker, of Cirencester, }
Hen. Gardiner, baker, } sons of Nat., baker, of Eastleach
Chas. Gardiner, yeoman, }

287 Edw. Lane, gunsmith, of New Thomas Street, Birmingham, son of Sam., formerly private, North Glos. Militia†
Jas. Ellis, jeweller, of 6, White Horse Court, Wheler Street, Spitalfields, London, son of Thos., hairdresser, late of St. Botolph, Aldersgate, London
Sam. Lysons,[1] esq., of the Inner Temple, London, son of Revd. Sam.†
John White, carpenter, son of Joshua, tanner, decd., of Newent
John Cole, shearman, son of Jas., tailor, decd., of Rodborough
Sir Thos. Lawrence,[2] Kt., of Russell Square, London, son of Thos., gent., decd., of London

288 Wm. Hawkes, wood turner, son of Jas., cordwainer, of Birmingham, formerly of Gloucester
Captain Chas. King Rudge, Worcs. Militia,† son of Thos., clerk, late of Gloucester
Mat. Hornidge, combmaker, of Wardour Street, Soho, London, son of Thos., combmaker, of Worcester
John Stroud, wharfinger, of Bristol, son of John, gent., of Cirencester, formerly of Gloucester
John Hall, framework-knitter, son of Josiah, stocking-framework-knitter, of Tewkesbury
Lieut. Frederick Woodcock, R.M., son of Sam., ald.
Aaron Smith, cooper, son of Dan., cooper, decd., of Stonehouse

289 Geo. Sherwood Evans, clerk, of Hinton,[3] Berks., son of Thos., gent., of Worcester, formerly of Mitcheldean
Jos. Spillman, private, Light Dragoons, son of Jos., tailor
Ebenezer Perris, weaver, son of Benj., cordwainer, of Birmingham, formerly of Gloucester
John Way, dyer, of Bristol, son of John, butcher, decd.
Frederick Hinton, tailor, of 21, New Compton Street, London, son of John, tailor, of Westminster, formerly of Gloucester
Edw. Bloxsome, gent., of Dursley, son of Edw.
Jacob Kirby, hairdresser, of Bristol, son of Isaac, pinmaker, decd.

290 Jas. Harris, cordwainer, son of Thos., baker, of Bristol

[1] Antiquary: *D.N.B.*; Gray, *Antiquaries*, 79–81.
[2] Artist: *D.N.B.*
[3] Hinton Waldrist: *Alumni Oxon. 1715–1886*, ii. 433.

Jas. Ellis of Bethnal Green, London, son of Ric., silversmith, decd., of London

Jas. Hoskins, brightsmith, of Magdalen Lane, Bristol, son of Jas., beam-maker, of Bristol

Chas. Randall, saddler, son of Chas., collar-maker, decd., of Tewkesbury

Ric. Price, waterman, of Tipton Green, Staffs.,
Hen. Price, pinmaker, of Tipton Green, Staffs., } sons of Hen., pinmaker, decd.

Ralph Lewis, tailor, of Fairford, son of John, baker

291 2 Oct Chas. Bowyer, Exchequer clerk,
Lieut. Wm. Bohan Bowyer, R.N., } sons of Wm., Exchequer clerk[†]

John Davis, accountant, son of John, tallow-chandler, decd., of Bristol

Geo. Bradgate, accountant, of Bristol, son of Chas., confectioner, of Bedminster, Som., formerly of Ross, Herefs.

Thos. Harris, farrier, of 224, Oxford Street, London, son of Wm., farrier, of Bedminster, Som., formerly of Bristol

John Wood, cheese factor,
Wm. Wood, gent.,
292 Jacob Wood, gent.,
Geo. Wood, grocer, of Oxford, } sons of Wm., cheese factor, of Tetbury

Sam. Carter, gunmaker, of Birmingham, son of John, worsted-weaver, of Coventry

Amos. Woodward, tailor, of Bath, son of Ric., hairdresser, decd.

Rob. Hicks, tailor, of Westminster, son of Sam., pinmaker, decd.

Ebenezer Fownes, japanner, son of Ebenezer, linen-draper, of Birmingham

Wm. Peters, tinplate-worker,
293 Jos. Peters, tinplate-worker, } sons of Wm., tinplate-worker, of Bristol

Thos. Gardiner, cordwainer, of Gloucester Row, Vauxhall, London, son of Thos., butcher, decd.

Jas. Clevely, cordwainer, of Kent Street, Southwark, son of Jas., cordwainer, of Whitechapel, London

Ric. Evans, coachmaker, of the Ship, Vine Street, Westminster, son of Wm., carpenter, decd.

Jeremiah Hooper, carrier, son of Wm., cordwainer, of Ray Street, Clerkenwell, London, formerly of Gloucester

Thos. Saunders, tailor, of Cross Street, Golden Square, Westminster, son of John, yeoman

John Nicholls Ursell, hatmaker, of Lambeth, Surr., son of Thos., cabinet-maker, decd., of West Smithfield, London

294 John Hale, cordwainer, of 12, Bishopsgate Street Without, London, son of Ephraim, collar-maker and coach-harness-maker, of Gloucester, formerly of Bristol

Ric. Nelme, gent., of 9, Bishopsgate Street Without, London, son of Ric., vintner, decd., of Clapton, Mdx.

John Gardner, umbrella-maker, of Cirencester, son of Nat., baker, of Tetbury, formerly of Eastleach

Wm. Critchley of 7, William Street, [St.] Marylebone, Mdx., app. of Wm. Hicks, carpenter

Jas. Hartland of Bristol, app. of John Bell Wilkins, tailor, decd.

John Rudge, blacksmith, of 4, Green's Gardens, Lambeth, London, son of John, jacksmith, of Bules Rents, the Park, Southwark

295 Jos. Owner of Dudley Port Inn, Staffs., app. of Jas. Broughton, peruke-maker, decd.

1816 Wm. Wilkes, pinmaker, son of Chas., pinmaker, decd.
Edw. Aycrigg, gent., of Dymock, son of Chas., surgeon, decd., of Newent
Sam. Bowyer King, gent., son of Elijah, innholder, of Rodborough
Wm. Beard, cordwainer, son of Benj., cordwainer, of 5, Queen Street, Grosvenor Square, London, formerly of Windsor, Berks.
Hen. Ashmead, gardener, of Charlton Kings, son of Hen., breeches-maker, late of Fairford
Wm. Ferebee, clothworker, son of Wm., cordwainer, of Uley

296 Edw. Sam. Selwyn, victualler, of the Wheatsheaf, Clare Market, Westminster, }
Wm. Selwyn, potato merchant, of 22, Clement's Lane, Clare Market, Westminster, } sons of Jasper, whitesmith, decd., of Shoreditch, Mdx.

Thos. Pear, carpenter, son of Thos., carpenter, of Down Hatherley, formerly victualler, of Gloucester
Jas. Willett Clutterbuck, Spanish-leather-dresser, of Russell Street, Bermondsey, Surr., son of Jas., cordwainer, late of Southwark

John Butter, farrier, of Tavistock Mews, Tavistock Square, London, }
Jas. Butter, smith, of 3, Garden Court, Baldwin's Gardens, Leather Lane, London, } sons of Geo., black-smith, of Sevenoaks, Kent, formerly of Llandinabo, [Herefs.]

297 Revd. Jas. Rudge, minister of Limehouse, Mdx., son of Jas., gent., decd.

Ric. Haviland, silversmith, }
Wm. Hen. Haviland, distiller, }
John Francis Haviland, brandy merchant, of Tetbury, } sons of Rob., distiller, of Cirencester, formerly of London

John Overthrow, butcher, of Bristol, son of Ric., butcher, decd.
Thos.Woodward, organist, of Cheltenham, son of Chas., plasterer
Rob. Barrett, surgeon, of Walworth, Surr., son of Ric., factor, decd., of Stroud

298 Nat. Marks Barrett, maltster, son of Wm., baker, decd., of Cheltenham

Thos. Child, carpenter, of 10, Walley Court, [the] Minories, London, }
Chas. Child, carpenter, of Crown and Shears Place, Rosemary Lane, London, }
Ric. Child, carpenter, of 2, Phoenix Court, West Street, West Smithfield, London, } sons of Ric., carpenter, decd., of Norton

Chas. Bonnewell, cooper, son of Wm., cooper, of Cheltenham, formerly of Tewkesbury
Jas. Blanch, ironmonger, son of Wm., patten-maker, of Bristol, formerly of Castlebar, Ealing, Mdx.
John Dutton† (by gift)[1]

299 3 Oct Thos. Newton, joiner, }
Wm. Newton, basket-maker, } sons of John, flaxdresser, of Ross, Herefs.

Edm. Probyn, clerk, of Abenhall, son of Revd. John†
Wm. Atkins of Bath, son of Wm., app. of Wm. Cowcher, pinmaker
Wal. Taynton, tailor, of London, formerly of Ross, [Herefs.], son of Nat., tailor, decd., of Ross

[1] By act of 19 Sept 1808, of Great Barrington: GBR B 3/13, f. 61.

John Jas. Pace, letterpress-printer, of London, son of Chas., apothecary, decd.

Nat. Washbourn(e), clock- and watchmaker, of 60, Great Surrey Street, Blackfriars Road, Surr., son of Geo., baker

300 John Taynton, brewer, of Hotwell Road, Bristol, son of Wm., hairdresser, of Much Marcle, Herefs., formerly of Ross, [Herefs.]

Wm. John Magness Steel, ship's joiner, son of John, ship's joiner, decd., of Rotherhithe, Surr.

Chas. Ashmead, hatter,
Geo. Benj. Ashmead, hatter, } sons of Benj., hatter, of Mount Street, Grosvenor Square, London

Geo. Yeend, farmer, son of John, farmer, of Rous Lench, Worcs.

Edw. Jas. Heming, poulterer, of Gracechurch Street, London, son of Jas. Nat., cooper, decd., of Tower Street, London

301 Geo. Butter, farrier, of Tavistock Mews, Russell Square, London, son of Geo., blacksmith, of Sevenoaks, Kent, formerly of Llandinabo, [Herefs.]

Wm. Oakey, coach painter, of Moorfields, London, son of Wm., butcher, decd.

John Rudge, carpenter, of Shortwood near Horsley, son of John, carpenter, decd., of Frocester

John Rudge, mariner, of St. George, son of Thos., cordwainer, of Frampton on Severn

Jas. King, stonemason, son of Francis, stonemason, of Brislington, Som.

302 Ric. Barrett, printer, of Shadwell, Mdx., son of Hen., cooper, decd., of Stroud

Ric. Selwyn, cabinet-maker, of Percival Street, Clerkenwell, London,
Wm. Selwyn, cooper, of Percival Street, Clerkenwell, London, } sons of Ric., collar-maker, decd.

Wm. Sexty, farmer, of Woolhope, Herefs.,
Geo. Sexty, grocer,
303 Rob. Sexty, maltster, } sons of Rob., yeoman, of Ledbury, Herefs., formerly of the Hill House, [Ledbury][1]

John Webb, cabinet-maker,
Ric. Webb, cabinet-maker, } sons of John, cabinet-maker, of Hereford, formerly of Tooley Street, Southwark

Ric. Barton King, coach-harness-maker, of 28, Whitechapel Road, London, son of Chas. Barton King, bricklayer, decd., of London

John Child, last- and boot-tree-maker, of Millbank Street, Westminster, son of Francis, heelmaker, of Bristol

304 John Fowler, accountant, of Clifton, son of Thos., brushmaker, decd., of Bristol

Thos. Bond Moye, carpenter and joiner, of Chelsea, Mdx., son of Thos., carpenter, decd.

Wm. Davis, a blind man, labourer, of Standish, son of Wm., labourer, of Longney

Chas. Skillerne, currier, of Heming's Row, St. Martin's Lane, Westminster, son of Chas., currier, decd., of Berkeley Street, Mdx.

John Skillerne, gent., of Lincoln's Inn, Mdx., son of Steph., labourer, of Twyning

[1] Cf. above: ibid. C 9/9, p. 5.

305 1816 Wm. Watts, waiter, of Cheltenham, son of Thos., husbandman, decd., of Highnam

Geo. Hawker, esq., of Wallbridge, Painswick, son of Geo., esq., of Rodborough

Jos. Baldwin, painter, app. of Ric. Barrett the elder, painter and glazier

Jas. Oakey of Alstone, Cheltenham, app. of Chas. Simpson, baker, decd.

Wm. Wilton Mutlow, clerk, son of Wm., organist

306 Rob. Bossley, miller, son of Rob., miller, of Newnham, formerly of Flaxley

Wm. Hartland commonly called John Hartland, pinmaker, of Birmingham, son of Chas., pinmaker, decd.

Alfred Blanch, patten-maker, son of Thos., heelmaker, of Great Saffron Hill, Holborn, Mdx., formerly of Bristol

Thos. Blanch, patten-maker, son of Jas., patten-maker, of Great Saffron Hill, Holborn, Mdx., formerly of Castlebar, Ealing, [Mdx.]

John Wadley, accountant, son of Edm., hairdresser, of Bristol

307 John Gardiner, tailor, of 1, Charing Cross, Westminster, son of Thos., baker, decd.

Isaac Geo. Smith, clothworker, of Stroud, son of Ric., weaver, of Painswick

Hen. Morgan Knight, servant, of Monmouth, son of Wm., pinmaker

Thos. Ravenhill, flax- and hempdresser, of 4, Farling Street, St. George in the East, Mdx., son of Geo., sackweaver, decd.

Nic. Brown, tallow-chandler and soapboiler, son of Jos., soapboiler, of Chepstow, Mon.

308 Chas. Jennings, corkcutter, of 23, Gilt Street, Limehouse, Mdx., son of Sam., painter, decd., of London

Wal. Bowcott, painter, of Cheltenham, son of Wal., victualler, decd.

John Merrett, tailor, of King's Stanley, } sons of John, tailor,
Phil. Merrett, cordwainer, } of Nailsworth

John Lindsey, coach painter, of 42, Liquor Pond Street, Gray's Inn Lane, London, son of Chas., plasterer, decd., of London

309 Sam. Child, innkeeper, son of Thos., tailor, decd., of Chalford

John Wilkins, cattle dealer, son of Thos., husbandman, decd., of Westbury-on-Severn

Wm. Brabant, printer, of Cheltenham, son of Wm., app. of Elizabeth Weaver, pinmaker

Wm. Stephens, brushmaker, son of Wm., upholder, decd.

310 4 Oct Jas. Randall, architect, of Fitzroy Square, London, son of John, mason, decd., of Oxford

Septimus Stroud, pinpointer, of Waltham Abbey, Essex, son of Septimus, pinmaker, decd., of Bristol

Dan. Perks, labourer, of Stonehall (*Stonehouse*),[1] Kempsey, Worcs., son of Thos., labourer, of White Ladies Aston, Worcs.

Wm. Wood, app. of Wm. Mann, cordwainer

Geo. Cox, dealer, } sons of Thos., baker, decd., of Tewkesbury
311 Hen. Cox of Apperley, }

Jas. Wood, app. of Jos. Richards, carpenter and joiner. Disfranchised[2] by judgment of court of K[ing's] B[ench] 1820

Hen. Gilden, stocking-framework-knitter, son of Wm., labourer, decd., of Hanley, Worcs.

[1] *V.C.H. Worcs.* iii. 403.

[2] For obtaining the freedom by fraud: cf. *Glouc. Jnl.* 22 Feb. 1819.

John Harrison, plushweaver, son of Geo., plushweaver, decd., of Milton, Oxon.
Chas. Dean, carpenter and joiner, of Tewkesbury, son of Geo., carpenter, decd.
312 John Collins Wilkes, hatmaker, of 22, Castle Street, Southwark, son of Benj., bricklayer, of Great Searl Street, Spitalfields, London, formerly of Gloucester
Thos. Hale, stocking-framework-knitter, son of Josiah, stocking-framework-knitter, of Tewkesbury
Ric. Hornidge, whitesmith, of 101, Wardour Street, Oxford Street, London, son of Thos., combmaker, of Worcester
Thos. Wilkins, dealer, son of Thos., husbandman, decd., of Westbury-on-Severn
Phil. Hickman, flaxdresser, of East Coker, Som., son of John, yeoman, decd., of Elborough, Som.
313 Jos. Innell, servant, of Blackheath, Kent, son of Jos., cook, decd., of St. Dunstan, Mdx.
Thos. Hathaway, servant, of Kidderminster, Worcs., son of Wm., carpenter, decd., of Ripple, Worcs.
Ric. Wheeler Crowdy, gent., of Faringdon, Berks., son of Jas., gent., of Highworth, Wilts.
Wm. Morse Crowdy, gent., son of Jas., gent., decd., of Swindon, Wilts.
Jas. Derrett, butcher, of Teanbey's Buildings, Old Street, St. Luke, Mdx., son of John, butcher, decd.
314 Ric. Taylor, app. of John Window, cabinet-maker
John Collerick, tinman, of Worcester, son of Benj., glasscutter, decd., of 1, Rolls Buildings, Fetter Lane, London
John Child, carpenter, of Longford, Harmondsworth (*Armsworth*), Mdx., son of John, farrier, decd., of St. Marylebone, Mdx.
Thos. Mayall, coin dealer, of 11, Sermons Lane, Doctors' Commons, [London], son of Chris, innholder, late of Gloucester
Geo. Lander, esq., of Birmingham, son of Geo., decd., of Painswick
315 David Evans, coal dealer, son of David, victualler, decd.
Geo. Holder, watchmaker, of Colchester, Essex, } sons of Rob., watchmaker, decd.
Jos. Fletcher Holder, carpenter, of Colchester, Essex, } sons of Rob., watchmaker, decd.
Frederick Holder, labourer, of Nailsworth, son of Thos., mercer, decd., of Marlborough, Wilts.
Hen. Heane, bookkeeper, of Friday Street, Cheapside, London, son of Hen., collier, decd., of Ruardean
316 Chas. Mutlow, bookseller, of 19, Edmund Street, St. Pancras, Mdx., son of Chas., bookseller, decd.
Elisha Holford of Hereford, app. of Geo. Daniell, painter
Edw. Clutterbuck, carpenter, of Brentford, Mdx., son of Jas., cordwainer, of Southwark
John Price Kirby, gent., son of Wm., pinmaker, decd., of Bristol
Chas. Rose, shopman, app. of Thos. and Wm. Washbourne, druggists
317 Thos. Roffe of Worcester, app. of Chas. Cooke, plumber and glazier
Hen. Herbert, gent., of Doctors' Commons, London, son of Thos., pinmaker
Thos. Niccolls Stratford, stationer, son of Thos., gent., decd., of Worcester
Hercules Hailes Dancocks, gent., of Dymock, son of Jas., haberdasher, decd., of London

1816 5 Oct Edw. Griffith, grocer, of 48, Piccadilly, London, son of Obadiah, gent., of Sherborne, Dors., formerly of Llanrumney, Mon.

318 Hen. Wm. Barrett, watchmaker, of St. George, Bloomsbury, London, son of Hen., baker, decd., of Hare Square, London

Ric. Jeynes, twine spinner, of Mint Square, Holborn, London, son of Methuselah, victualler, decd.

Ric. Bush Skillerne, saddler, of Kennington Cross, Surr., son of Chas., currier, decd., of Berkeley Street, Mdx.

Thos. Child, cordwainer, of 4, Lowman Street, Southwark, son of John, farrier, decd., of St. Marylebone, Mdx.

Thos. Fream, clerk,[1] of 32, Berners Street, Oxford Street (*Road*), London,
319 Chas. Fream, upholder,
} sons of Thos., baker, of Worcester

Hen. Kater, gent., son of John Herman, sugar-baker, decd., of Bristol

Hen. White, fishmonger, son of Wm., cordwainer, of Walford, Herefs.

Hen. Higgins Cooke, gent., of Kingsholm, son of John, saltman, decd.

Thos. Smith, gent., of 14, Peacock Street, Newington, Surr., son of Thos., glover, decd.

320 Wm. Dobles, gent., of Ash, Goodrich, Herefs., app. of Edw. Holder and Wm. Herbert, grocers, late of Gloucester

Thos. King, son of Elijah, innholder, of Rodborough

Jas. Commeline, clerk, son of Jas., clerk, of Redmarley [D'Abitot], Worcs., formerly of Pembroke College, Oxford University

Chas. Crawley, clerk, minister of Flaxley, son of Sir Thos. Crawley-Boevey, Bt.†[2]

Thos. Long, pawnbroker, son of Thos., pawnbroker, of Dover, Kent, formerly of Over

321 Jas. Edw. Matthews, smith, of Mary Anne Street, Back Church Lane, Whitechapel, London, son of Jas., whitesmith, of Whitechapel

Jas. Mutlow, carpet-weaver, of Kidderminster, Worcs., son of Wm., decd., of Dursley

Thos. Niccolls, coalminer, son of Ferdinando, sawyer, of Westerleigh

John Smith, tinplate-worker, of New Road, St. George in the East, Mdx., son of Wm., cooper, decd., of Bristol

John Bonnor, ironmonger, of Forster Lane, London, son of Chas., brazier

322 Jos. Carwardine of 24, Old Compton Street, Soho, London, app. of Geo. Washbourn, baker, confectioner, and maltster

Sam. Piffe, gent., of Walworth, Surr., son of Thos., innholder, decd.

Dan. Staight, ivory dealer, of 5, East Harding Street, Gough Square, London, son of John, fanmaker, of London

Phil. Jones, esq., of Ross, [Herefs.], (by gift). Sworn a burgess by act of common council voted 2 Oct 1795[3]

Rob. Gardiner, musician, of 32, Charles Street, Hampstead Road, Mdx., son of Jos., baker, of Sheepscombe, Painswick

323 Captain Dan. Capel, 14th Light Dragoons,† son of Wm., esq., of Prestbury, formerly of Stroud

Thos. Cooke, clerk, of Oxford University, son of Chas., apothecary

7 Oct Geo. Rob. Ball, esq., of Gloucester, son of Rob., esq.†

Decimus Cooke, gent., of Leicester, app. of Wm. Rogers, apothecary

[1] ? clergyman.

[2] Of Flaxley Abbey: A.W. Crawley-Boevey, *Perverse Widow* (1898), 318–9 and nn.

[3] Entry originally recorded above: GBR C 9/9, p. 123.

Wm. Kendall, attorney, of Bourton-on-the-Water, son of Wm., upholder, of High Street, Southwark

Jos. Mutlow, engraver, of Pentonville, London, son of Thos., tailor, decd.

324 Chas. Harrison of Milton, Adderbury, Oxon., son of Geo.,† app. of Jacob Lumbard, plushweaver, decd.

Wm. Dunn, attorney, of Thame, Oxon., son of Thos.,† app. of Ric. Bond, bookseller and bookbinder, decd.

John Stephens, esq., of Kencott, Oxon., son of Wm., gent., decd.†

Edw. Gardiner, servant, of Duke Street, St. James, Westminster, son of Josiah, baker, of Stonehouse

Wm. Vaile, spirit merchant, of Great St. Helens, London, son of Wm., husbandman, decd., of Fretherne

325 Wm. Long, cheesemonger, of Lambeth, Surr., son of Thos. the younger, pawnbroker, of Dover, Kent, formerly of Over

Wm. Goodwin, gent., of Cheltenham, son of Wm., porter, decd., of Newgate Street, London

Hen. Green, app. of Geo. Washbourn, baker and maltster, decd.

Hen. Ashmead, esq., of Cheltenham, son of Wm., gent., decd.

Wm. Ward, leather grounder, of 14, Portsea Street, Bermondsey New Road, Surr., son of Jas., of St. Catherine, Tower Hamlets, Mdx.

326 Ric. Houlton, labourer, son of Wm., cordwainer, decd., of Upton upon Severn, Worcs.

John Smith, servant, of Abercamlais, Brec., son of Wm., hairdresser, of Brecon

Lieut. Chas. Crowdy, R.N., son of Jas., gent., of Highworth, Wilts.

John Felton, cordwainer, of Rumney, Brec.,[1] son of Wm., cordwainer, of Cowbridge, Glam.

Benj. John Barrett, watchspring-maker, of Liverpool, son of Hen., baker, decd., of London

327 Wm. Godwin Yeend, yeoman, son of Wm. Godwin Yeend, yeoman, of Little Comberton, Worcs.

John Smith, gent., of Somers Town, Mdx., app. of Edw. Jeynes, mercer, decd.

Thos. Jas. Welles, gent., son of Francis, gent., of Cheltenham, formerly of Upton upon Severn, [Worcs.][2]

Wm. Bromley, ropemaker, of Kidderminster, Worcs., son of Jas., ropemaker, decd., of Hereford

Wm. Pagett, innholder, of Minchinhampton, app. of Ric. Heath, saddler, decd.

328 Thos. Longdon, maltster, of Stratton, son of Thos., woolstapler, decd., of Winstone

Ambrose Lewis Stoner, linen-draper, of Bristol, son of Antioch,† app. of Mat. Weaver, baker

John Hathaway, surgeon, of 114, Drury Lane, London, app. of Thos. Parker, apothecary, decd.

Geo. Harrison, plushweaver, of Milton, Adderbury, Oxon., son of Geo.,† app. of Jacob Lumbard, plushweaver

Giles Long, hatter, of 5, Wellington Street, Blackfriars Road, London, son of Giles, baker, decd., of Plymouth

[1] Rhymney, Mon.

[2] County given as *Glos.*

329 1816 John Cockle of Bristol, app. of Chas. Cole, tinplate-worker, decd.
Ric. Tomson, draper, of Wootton Bassett, Wilts., son of Wm., grocer, decd.
Hen. Crump, surgeon of Albrighton, Salop., son of Geo., surgeon, decd., of Lichfield, Staffs.
8 Oct Benj. Capel Heming, D.D., of Greys,[1] Oxon., son of Benj., clerk†
Edw. Taylor, carpenter, of Bristol, son of Edw., carpenter, decd., of Cirencester
330 Thos. Bradley Pagett, clerk, of Ashby Magna, Leics., John Warren Pagett, clerk, of Atherstone,[2] Warws., } sons of Thos. Bradley Pagett, grocer, late of Chipping Norton, Oxon.
Lieut. Rob. Weaver, R.N., Lieut. Wm. Hen. Weaver, R.A., } sons of Thos., esq., decd.†
Lieut. Wm. Kater, 27th Foot, of Southampton, son of John Herman Cater, sugar-baker, decd., of Bristol
331 Isaac Smith, gent., of Lewisham, Kent, son of Maur., gent., of Islington, Mdx.
Jas. Wilton, gent., of the Inner Temple, London, son of Hen., gent., decd.
Thos. Mutlow, iron finer, of Bilston, Staffs., son of Thos., tailor, decd.
Wm. Friend, cordwainer, son of Edw., plumber and glazier, of Southampton
Wm. Stroud, gent., of Swansea, son of John, gent.
332 Wm. Turner, surgeon, of Manchester Street, Manchester Square, London, son of Thos., clerk, of Sherston, Wilts.
Nat. Harris, gent., of Southampton Buildings, London, son of Nat., baker, of Southampton, formerly of London
Thos. Smith, brewer, of Bath, son of Wm., cooper, decd., of Bristol
Wm. Wiltshire Smith, merchant, son of John, gent., decd., of London
Arthur Jepson, gent., of 14, New Kent Road, Surr., son of John Wilkins Jepson, gent., decd.
333 John Gransmore, sergeant, 89th Foot, son of Thos., butcher
Hen. Fendall, esq., of Littledean, son of Wm., esq.
Wm. Gardiner, sawyer, of Queen Street, Seven Dials, London, son of Adam, wiredrawer, of Nottingham, formerly of Bristol
Hen. Holder, printer, son of Wm., grocer
David Price, tailor, of Cork Street, St. George, Hanover Square, London, son of Sam. Gardner Price, cordwainer, of Strand, London, formerly of Bloomsbury
334 Wm. Cowles, gent., of Blackwall, London, son of Thos., grazier, decd.
Midshipman Geo. Gardiner, R.N., of Walworth, Surr., son of Geo., ribbon-weaver, of Walworth Common, Surr., formerly of St. Bartholomew the Great, London
Jas. Evenis, innholder, of Milford, Pemb., app. of Jas. Lamb, decd.
John Freame, printer, son of Wm., glazier, decd., of Chelsea, Mdx.
Ric. Base, chaise driver, of Kenilworth, Warws., son of Ric., cordwainer, of Gloucester, formerly of Rodborough
335 11 Oct Francis Chris. Mayall, mariner, son of Chris., yeoman, of Bristol, formerly of Gloucester
Hen. Spering Merrett, architect, of Willian near Hitchin, [Herts.], son of Ric., saddler, decd., of Bath

[1] ? Rotherfield Greys, Henley upon Thames.
[2] ? Atherstone-on-Stour.

John Lane, servant, of 16, Warren Street, Fitzroy Square, London, son of Wm., labourer, late of Fairford

Jos. Gardiner, pinmaker, son of Adam, wiredrawer, of Nottingham, formerly of Bristol

Benj. Hen. Innell, servant, of Blackheath, Kent, son of Jos., cook, decd., of St. Dunstan, Mdx.

11 Oct Chas. Lander, private, 14th Light Dragoons, son of Jas., pinmaker

12 Oct Ralph Bigland, Richmond Herald, [of the] Heralds' College, [London], (by gift)[1]

336 18 Oct Revd. Wm. Crawley of Flaxley Abbey by patrimony[2]

Chas. Holder of Kingston upon Hull, [Yorks.], son of Rob., watchmaker, decd., of Colchester, Essex, formerly of Gloucester

25 Oct Wm. Favill, app. of Mic. Jennings, tailor

28 Oct Revd. Wm. Bishop[3] (by gift).¶ Readmitted 14 Aug 1820: p. 390

Lieut. Wm. Joyner of Berkeley (by gift)

Sam. Pearce, gent., of Berkeley (by gift).¶ Readmitted 10 Jan 1823: p. 405

Wm. Clarke of Barton St. Mary[4] (by gift)

Arthur Hammond Jenkins, gent., (by gift)

337 Ric. Hurd Lucas, esq., (by gift).¶ Readmitted 28 July 1820: p. 387

Augustus Fitzhardinge Berkeley, esq.,† (by gift)[5]

29 Oct Wm. Hen. Staunton, esq., of Stroud (by gift). Sworn same day.¶ Readmitted 18 Sept 1820: p. 392

2 Nov Wm. Woods, esq.,[6] of the College of Arms, [London], (by gift). Sworn 2 Nov [1816][7]

4 Nov John Taylor of Barton Street St. Michael, app. of John Hewlett, cabinet-maker

6 Nov Hen. Jones the younger, gent., of Brockworth (by gift). Sworn same day.‡ Readmitted 14 Aug 1824: p. 411

8 Nov Thos. Phillips, esq., of Monmouth (by gift). Sworn 8 Nov 1816.¶ Readmitted 6 Nov 1820: p. 394

Thos. Bird, esq., of Hereford (by gift). Sworn 8 Nov 1816

338 John Smith, victualler, by fine

13 Nov Kedgwin Hoskins, esq., of Strickstenning, Much Birch, Herefs., (by gift). Sworn 13 Nov 1816

18 Nov Wm. Best, labourer, son of Wm., flaxdresser, of Gloucester, formerly of Wotton [near Gloucester]. Sworn 22 Nov 1816

22 Nov Jas. Taylor, ropemaker, (by gift).¶ Readmitted 7 Aug 1820: p. 388

Wm. Playne, saddler, (by gift).¶ Readmitted 12 Aug 1820: p. 389

John Garn, woolstapler, (by gift).¶

Jos. Webb, cheesemonger, (by gift).¶ Readmitted 11 Aug 1820: p. 389

Thos. Wakeman, gent., (by gift).¶ Readmitted 25 Sept 1820: p. 392

339 Geo. Box Drayton, surgeon, (by gift).¶ Readmitted 12 Aug 1820: p. 389

Wm. Morgan Meyler, surgeon, (by gift).¶ Readmitted 13 Jan 1820: p. 384

[1] Entry originally recorded above: GBR C 9/9, p. 104.

[2] Son of Sir Thos. Crawley-Boevey, Bt.: Crawley-Boevey, *Perverse Widow*, 318–20.

[3] Independent minister: *V.C.H. Glos.* iv. 324.

[4] Maltster, of Barton St. Michael: GBR B 3/13, f. 195v.

[5] Entry originally recorded above: ibid. C 9/9, p. 102A.

[6] Knighted 1832: *College of Arms* (Surv. of London Cttee. 1963), 66.

[7] Evidently disfranchised before 18 Aug 1820, when the common council voted not to admit him: GBR B 3/13, f. 282v.

Revd. Rob. Halifax of Standish (by gift)¶
Wm. Davis, victualler, by fine
23 Nov Thos. Jones, builder, of Cheltenham (by gift).¶ Readmitted 4 Dec 1820: p. 395
Paul Hawkins Fisher,[1] gent., of Stroud (by gift).¶ Readmitted 7 Sept 1820: p. 391
29 Nov Steph. Wilkins, gent., of Cirencester (by gift).¶ Readmitted 11 Aug 1820: p. 389
30 Nov Jas. Powell, silversmith, of Worcester (by gift).¶ Readmitted 6 Oct 1820: p. 393
John Francis Augustus Moreton of Tortworth (by gift).¶ Readmitted 7 Nov 1821: p. 401
26 Nov John Willis of Dixton, Mon., (by gift).¶ Readmitted 13 Sept 1820: p. 392
340 4 Dec John Holder of Ross, Herefs., (by gift).¶ Readmitted 11 Feb 1821: p. 397
Revd. Jas. de Visme of Newent (by gift)¶
19 Dec Wm. Rolph, gent., of Thornbury (by gift)
18 Dec Wm. Hughes, yeoman, by fine
1817 20 Jan Sam. Boughton, tanner, of Ross, Herefs., app. of Edm. Boughton, currier, late of Gloucester
1816 26 Dec Steph. John Welch Fletcher Welch, esq., of Painswick (by gift)
27 Dec John Luke, esq., of Shadwell, London, (by gift).‡ Readmitted 15 Apr 1820: p. 387
Phil George, esq., of Bristol (by gift)‡
341 30 Dec Hen. Hicks, esq., of Eastington (by gift).¶ Readmitted 30 Dec 1820: p. 396
Wm. Read King, gent., of Serjeants' Inn, Fleet Street, London, (by gift)
1817 11 Jan Edw. Moulton Barrett, esq., of Hope End, Herefs., (by gift)
17 Jan Wm. Trye, esq., of Leckhampton (by gift)¶
24 Jan Edw. Austin, esq., of Wotton under Edge (by gift).¶ Readmitted 20 Dec 1821: p. 401
Southgate Austin, esq., of Wotton under Edge (by gift).¶ Readmitted 30 Dec 1820: p. 396
28 Feb John Jas. Maisey, painter, son of John, victualler
18 Apr John Venn, private, Plymouth division of marines, son of Thos., labourer, late of Gloucester
342 21 Apr Thos. Hayter Longdon, esq., of Wimpole Street, London, son of Rog., esq., of Doctors' Commons, London
16 May Edwin Maddy, gent., (by gift).¶ Readmitted 8 Sept 1820: p. 391
26 May Wm. Jewesbury, yeoman, by fine[2]
6 June Chas. Clarke, pinmaker, son of Thos., tailor, decd.
Arthur Palmer, esq., of Bristol by gift¶
Mic. Castle, esq., of Bristol by gift.¶ Readmitted 22 Sept 1820: p. 392
7 July Wm. Welch, bricklayer, of Durham, formerly private, 2nd Dragoon Guards, son of Ric., bricklayer, decd., of Badgeworth
343 2 Aug Sam. Peach, esq., of Idlicote, Warws., by gift¶
11 Aug Benj. Alder, app. of John Tovey, ironmonger
1 Sept Rob. Dadd, maltster, son of Jas., cordwainer
13 Sept Wm. Dennison Wilkinson, esq., of Norfolk House near Gloucester by gift¶

[1] Historian of Stroud: Gray, *Antiquaries*, 93.
[2] Previously disfranchised; cf. above: GBR C 9/9, p. 255.

Wm. Chas. Holder, esq., of Taynton by gift.¶ Readmitted 13 Apr 1821: p. 393

15 Sept John Croose, soapboiler, by gift.¶ Readmitted 12 Aug 1820: p. 389

Jas. Powell the younger, watchmaker, of Worcester by gift.¶ Readmitted 6 Oct 1820: p. 393

344 25 Sept Nat. Wm. Peach, esq., of Bownhams by gift¶

Thos. Ridler, soapboiler, by gift.¶ Readmitted 18 Aug 1820: p. 390

27 Sept Wm. Thomson, gent., of Copthall Court, Throgmorton Street, London, by gift.¶ Readmitted 19 Oct 1821: p. 400

3 Oct Thos. Miles, esq.,[1] of Leonard Stanley by gift.¶ Readmitted 8 Sept 1820: p. 391

David Walker, esq., mayor 1817–8

7 Oct Chas. Stephens, esq., of Stanley[2] by gift.¶ Readmitted 21 Nov 1820: p. 395

21 Oct Rob. Kirby, esq., of Cannon Street, London, by gift.‡ Readmitted 6 Sept 1824: p. 412

345 27 Oct Chas. Haines, app. of Ric. Woodward, tailor

Chas. Batchford, hairdresser, of Tewkesbury, son of Chas., maltster, formerly tanner, of Bristol

3 Nov Ric. Allen, gent., son of Nic., apparitor

Jonathan Jones and Chas. Stewart Ruthven were omitted to be entered and their names will therefore be found in p. 381

14 Nov David Ricardo, esq., of Gatcombe Park by gift

24 Nov Ric. Harris, quartermaster, South Glos. Militia, by gift.¶ Readmitted 28 July 1820: p. 388

25 Nov Geo. Aveline, surgeon, of Ross, Herefs., by gift¶

346 29 Nov Captain Wm. Lane, South Glos. Militia, of Maisemore by gift¶

13 Dec Jeremiah Hawkins, esq., of the Haw, Tirley, by gift.¶ Readmitted 14 Aug 1820: p. 390

22 Dec Wm. Smallbridge, saddler, of Oxford Street, London, by gift

29 Dec John Best, hairdresser, son of Sam., cordwainer

Wm. Giles Maysey, app. of John Estcourt, hairdresser

1818 8 Jan Rob. Canning, esq., of Hartpury by gift

24 Jan Thynne Howe Gwynne (the younger), esq., of Llanigon House, Brec., by gift.‡ Readmitted 17 Feb 1820: [p. 385]

347 16 Feb Thos. Hanman, app. of Wm. Herbert, grocer

25 Mar Chas. Jones, app. of Chas. Jaques, carpenter

21 Apr Edw. Williams, esq., of Carmarthen by gift¶

11 May Wm. Hickman, cordwainer, son of Wm., cordwainer, decd.

18 May John Lewis, app. of Pettat Gardiner, brushmaker, decd.

John Harris, app. of Edw. Heath, cordwainer, decd.

8 June Thos. Rudge Clarke, cordwainer, of Gloucester, son of Thos., tailor, decd., of the College precincts, Gloucester

Wm. Boughton, pinmaker, son of Ant., baker, of Gloucester, formerly of High Street, Southwark

348 1818 9 June Hen. Barrett, organist, son of Hen., painter, decd.

John Smart, cabinet-maker, son of Wm., pinmaker

John Hyett, cordwainer, son of Sam., cordwainer

[1] Surgeon: ibid. B 3/13, f. 211.

[2] King's Stanley: *V.C.H. Glos.* xi. 249, 251.

1818 John Welch, labourer, of Deerhurst Walton, son of Wm., labourer, of Tredington, formerly of Elmstone Hardwicke

Edw. Coopey, labourer, of Twigworth, son of Jos., baker, of Churchdown

12 June Thos. Herbert, chinaman, son of Thos., pinmaker

Chas. Griffiths, gent., of Cheltenham, son of Edw., victualler, decd.

349 Wm. Jones, gent., son of Sam., brushmaker, of Gloucester, formerly of St. John Street, West Smithfield, Mdx.

Jas. Clark, pinmaker, of Gloucester, son of Thos., pinmaker, decd., of the College precincts, Gloucester

Thos. Hayward, labourer, son of John, baker, of Winstone

15 June John Adams, esq., by gift

Jas. Ricketts, chairmaker, son of Wm., pinmaker

Jas. Buchanan, gent., son of Jas., grocer

350 Jas. Dadford Spencer, gent., son of John, victualler

John Welch, cordwainer, of Highleadon, son of Benj., labourer, late of Stoke Orchard, Bishop's Cleeve

Wm. Jollyman, app. of Wm. Stephens, tinplate-worker

Chas. Crowdy, labourer, of Saintbridge, Upton St. Leonards, son of Chas., labourer, of the Reddings,[1] formerly of Longford

Jeremiah Rea, baker, son of Wm., baker

351 16 June Ric. Brook,[2] son of Wm., gent., of Bromsberrow

Chas. Whitcombe, gent., son of Sir Sam., Kt., decd.

John Bourne, cordwainer, son of Jas., cordwainer, decd.

Thos. Hinton, tailor, son of John, tailor, of London

John Broadway, weaver, son of Wm., weaver, of Bethnal Green, Mdx.

352 Ric. Ellis, silversmith, son of Ric., silversmith, decd., of London

Edm. Ellis, jeweller, son of John, jeweller, of London

Edw. Orpin of Rugeley, Staffs., app. of Wm. Hatton, breeches-maker, decd.

Sam. Ric. Whitcombe, gent., son of Sir Sam., Kt., decd.

Rob. Fitzharding[e] Jenner, esq., son of Edw., M.D., of Berkeley

353 Thos. Bush Skillern, currier, of 27, Great George Street, Chelsea, Mdx., son of Chas., currier, decd., of Berkeley Street, Clerkenwell, Mdx.

Weston Hickes, esq., of Painswick, son of John Heathfield Hickes, M.D., decd.

John Wm. Wilton, surgeon, son of John Pleydell Wilton, surgeon

17 June Wm. Welch, labourer, son of Phil., tailor, of Brockworth

354 Thos. Gardiner, sawyer, of Newport Market, Westminster, son of Adam, wiredrawer, late of Nottingham

Wm. Hayward Winstone,[3] esq., of Woolstrop, son of Thos. Hayward, esq., decd., of Quedgeley

Edwin Jones, pin manufacturer, of Gloucester, son of John, cooper, of Newent

Chas. Woodward, cordwainer, of Bridgwater Gardens, London, son of Chas., cordwainer

John Weeks, plumber and glazier, son of Wm., plumber and glazier, of King's Stanley

355 Ric. Cupit Wakefield, cabinet-maker, son of Ric., cabinet-maker, of Worcester

[1] ? in Badgeworth.

[2] Later clerk: *Alumni Oxon. 1715–1886*, i. 168.

[3] Formerly called Wm. Hayward: *V.C.H. Glos.* x. 219.

Hen. Oakey, plasterer, of Cheltenham, son of Jas., pinmaker, decd.
Sam. Vail, yeoman, of Westbury-on-Severn, son of Sam., yeoman, of Churcham, formerly of Bulley
18 June Jas. Deeves Ireland, stockbroker, of Tokenhouse Yard, London, son of Chas., undertaker, of Threadneedle Street, London
Thos. Ellis, engraver, of Ironmonger Row, London, son of Ric., jeweller, late of London
356 Isaac Barker, labourer, son of Isaac, labourer, of Norton
John Perris, pinpointer, son of Benj., cordwainer, of Birmingham
Lieut. Wm. Stock, R.N., son of Edm., grocer, decd.
Ric. Fletcher, cooper, son of John, cooper, of Bristol
Peter Hawker, esq., of London, son of Geo., esq., of Stroud
Geo. Conibere Simpson, plumber and glazier, son of Chas., baker, late of Gloucester
357 John Peters, tinplate-worker, son of Wm., tinplate-worker, of Bristol
Geo. Jenkins Okey, servant, of Clifton, son of Wm., butcher, decd., of Bristol
Jos. Davis, mariner, son of John, grocer and soapboiler, decd., of Bristol
Thos. Hall, feltmonger, son of Wm., feltmonger, decd., of Bristol
Wm. Bradgate, coalminer, son of Chas., baker and confectioner, of Bedminster, Som.
358 Edwin Jas. Parker, esq.,[1] of Filton, son of Thos., clerk, decd., of Churcham
Lieut. Hen. Stroud, R.N., son of John, gent., of Cirencester
Isaiah Smith, plumber and glazier, of London, son of Dan., cooper, decd., of Stonehouse
Thos. Ferebee, clothworker, son of Wm., cordwainer, of Uley
Hen. Barrow Evans, esq.,[2] son of Chas., esq.
359 Mat. Skillern, labourer, of Ashchurch, son of Steph., labourer, of Twyning
Thos. Gardiner, umbrella-maker, son of Nat., baker
19 June Rowland Heane, collier, of Lydbrook, son of Hen., collier, decd., of Ruardean
Wm. Hale, pewterer, son of Thos., pewterer, of Bristol
Jas Luke Church, mariner, son of Luke, flaxdresser, decd.
Jos. Sheppard Wathen, clothier, of North Bradley, Wilts., son of Sam., esq., decd., of Stroud
360 Hen. Okey, carpenter, of Glastonbury, Som., son of Wm., butcher, decd., of Bristol
Jas. Barton King, bricklayer, } sons of Chas. Barton King, bricklayer, decd., of Whitechapel, Mdx.
Wm. Barton King of Poplar, Mdx., }
John Rudhall, silk mercer, of Bristol, son of John, bellfounder
John David Clutterbuck, leather-dresser, son of Jas., cordwainer, decd., of Bermondsey, Surr.
John Bowyer, gent., of Somers Town Mdx., son of Sam., esq., of Camden Town, Mdx.
361 Chas. Cook, gent., son of John, salt merchant, decd.
Jas. Mutlow, engraver, son of Hen., engraver, of York Street, Covent Garden, Westminster
John Woodward, tailor, of Bristol, son of Ric., hairdresser, decd.

[1] Later clerk: *Alumni Oxon. 1715–1886*, iii. 1066.
[2] Later clerk: ibid. ii. 433.

1818 Ric. Perkes, labourer, son of John, labourer, of Evesham, Worcs.
Wm. Perks, labourer, of Fladbury, Worcs., son of Wm., labourer, of Bretforton, Worcs.
Jas. Hawkes, labourer, of Little Chelsea, Mdx., son of Jas., decd., of Birmingham
362 Wm. Freeman, labourer, of Bisley, son of Benj., whitesmith, of Southwark
Thos. Davis Rudge, millwright, son of John, joiner and carpenter, of Stroud
Wm. Harding Meek, mason, son of Thos., mason, of Bristol
Phil. Wadley, gent., of Down Street, Piccadilly, Mdx., son of Edm., hairdresser, of Bristol
John Child, boatbuilder, of Christchurch, Surr., son of John, farrier, decd., of St. Marylebone, Mdx.
363 Ric. Solloway, artist, of Colchester, Essex, son of Rob., pinmaker, decd.
Thos. Church of Chepstow, Mon., app. of Paul Mutlow, tailor[1]
Wm. Hooper, gent., of Ross, Herefs., (by gift)¶
Edw. Francis Colston, esq., } sons of Edw. Francis, esq., of
Wm. Colston, esq., } Filkins Hall, Oxon.
364 Chas. Cook Higgs, esq., son of Chas., esq., decd., of Charlton Kings
Jos. Watts, brewer, of Stroud (by gift).¶ Readmitted 30 Dec 1820: p. 396
20 June Thos. Baghott Baghott, esq., son of Sir Paul, Kt., of Lypiatt Park
Geo. Jelf, esq., of Westminster, son of Sir Jas., Kt., of Oaklands (*Oatlands*), Awre
Edw. Burgh, esq., son of Hen., esq., late of King's Stanley
Jos. Child, carpenter, of Marden, Kent, son of John, carpenter, decd., of Longdon, Worcs.
365 Chas. Grevile, attorney, son of Edw. Colston Grevile, clerk, of Bristol
Wm. Perkins, gent., of Bristol, son of Wm., tanner, of Bridgend, Glam., formerly of Aston Ingham, Herefs.
Geo. Capel, tea dealer, of Red Lion Square, London, son of Wm., esq., late of Stroud
Ric. Wm. Moore Child, cooper, of Redcliff Mead Lane, Bristol, son of Wm., accountant, decd., of Bristol
Jos. Browning, plumber and glazier, son of Sam., cordwainer, late of Gloucester
366 Wm. Coates of Wotton, app. of Ric. Baldwin, collar-maker, decd.
Geo. Chandler, gent., of Clapcote, Wilts., app. of Sam. Jones, brushmaker
Wm. Harris of Dursley, app. in turn of Penelope Powell and Francis Ursell, plumbers and glaziers, decd.
Hen. Fitzharding[e] Berkeley† (by gift)[2]
22 June Ric. White, butcher, of Whitchurch, Herefs., son of Wm., fisherman, of Walford, Herefs.
367 Lieut. John Jones, 6th Dragoon Guards, son of Roynon, esq., decd., of Hayhill
Wm. Ashmeade, surgeon, of Blackheath, Kent, son of Wm., gent., decd.
Francis Brooke Wells, clerk, of Prestbury, son of Francis, gent., late of Upton upon Severn, Worcs.

[1] By act of 4 Nov 1805: GBR B 3/13, f. 17v.
[2] Of Berkeley castle, entry originally recorded above: ibid. C 9/9, p. 131.

Edw. Wood, esq., son of Wm. the younger, cheese factor, of Tetbury
Ric. Ward, bedstead-maker, of Rotherhithe, Surr., son of Wm., pinmaker, decd.
368 Chas. Jones, gent., son of John, gent., of Aston, Som.
John Innell, servant, of Blackheath, Kent, son of Jos., victualler, decd., of Greenwich, Kent
Wm. Hen. Davis, gent., of 19, Orange Court, Leicester Square, London, son of Wm., barber, decd., of London
Francis Drake, pastry cook and confectioner, of Lambeth Marsh, Surr., son of Francis, wiredrawer, decd., of King's Bench Walks, Surr.
Wm. Wise Wilton, gent., son of Chas. Hen., gent., of Liverpool
369 Mic. Cowles, horse dealer, of Bath, son of Wm., horse dealer, of Liverpool
Sam. Jasper Selwyn, bricklayer, of Old Fish Street, London, son of Jasper, whitesmith, decd., of Shoreditch, Mdx.
Geo. Newton, ropemaker, of Oxford Street (*Road*), Mdx., son of John, ropemaker, of Ross, Herefs.
Thos. Stroud, pinmaker, son of Septimus, pinmaker, decd., of Waltham Abbey, Essex
Wm. Young, farmer, of Berkeley, son of Jos., labourer, decd., of Westbury-on-Severn
370 Sam. Hawkins, esq., son of Edw., esq., decd., of Neath, Glam.
Wm. Thos. Organ, gent., of Gillingham, Kent, son of Wm., pinmaker, decd.
Wm. Craddock, servant, of Chatham, Kent, son of Wm., hairdresser, of West Ham, Essex
Ric. Weaver, gent., son of Ric., farrier, decd.
Frederick Merrett, saddler, of Berry Street, Oxford Street, Mdx., son of Ric., saddler, decd., of Bath
371 Edw. Grevile, gent., son of Edw. Colston Grevile, clerk, of Bristol
John Tippetts, app. of Josiah Tippetts, plumber and glazier
John Harding of Clerkenwell, Mdx., app. of Ric. Addis, hairdresser, of Cainscross, formerly of Gloucester
23 June Lord Rob. Edw. Hen. Somerset† (by gift)[1]
Benj. Webb, esq., of Melksham, Wilts., son of Nic., gent., decd.
372 Wm. Rayer, clerk, of Tiverton, Devon, son of Wm., wine merchant, of London
Jacob Cowles, mariner, of Islington, Mdx., son of Geo., jeweller, decd., of London
Ric. Blackwell Kendale, currier, of Abingdon, Berks., son of Thos., carpet manufacturer, late of Cirencester
Isaac Skillern, coal merchant, of Blackfriars Road, Surr., son of Chas., currier, decd., of Berkeley Street, Clerkenwell, Mdx.
373 Edw. Hawkins, gent., of Aberdulais (*Dylais*) near Neath, Glam., son of Edw., merchant, late of Newnham,[2] son of Thos., merchant, of Newnham
Frederick Sandys Wall, clerk, of Stoke St. Milborough, Salop., son of John, esq., decd., of Tewkesbury Park
Wm. Jas. Bradford, esq., son of Francis, gent., of Great Westwood, Herts., app. of Francis Mayo, grocer, decd.
Edw. Friend, gardener, son of Edw., plumber and glazier, of Southampton

[1] By act of 7 July 1815, for gallant services in Flanders: ibid. B 3/13, f. 169v.
[2] Esq., decd., of Neath, Glam.; cf. above: ibid. C 9/9, p. 370.

374 Francis Barton, private, 90th Foot, son of John, plumber and glazier, decd.
Sir Geo. Hen. Frederick Berkeley, Kt., of Hurst House, Surr., son of Geo. Cranfield Berkeley, decd., of London
24 June Wm. Hungerford Colston, D.D., of West Lydford, Som., son of Alex., clerk, decd., of Filkins, Oxon.
Wm. Gilding, sawyer, of Kempsey, Worcs., son of Sam., labourer, of Leigh
375 Chas. Wilton, tailor of Sheerness, [Kent], son of Ant. Wilkins alias Wilton, app. of John Keyse, decd.*
26 June Thos. Edwards Colston, vicar of Broadwell, Oxon., son of Alex., decd.†
Chas. Baldwin, printer, of New Bridge Street, London, } sons of Hen., decd.†
Geo. Baldwin, gent., of Walworth, Surr., }
29 June Wm. Randle, gent., of Commercial Road, Mdx., son of Wm., collar-maker, decd., of Tewkesbury
376 3 Aug Wm. Manns, saddler and harness-maker, of St. Martin's Lane, Westminster, son of Wm., tailor, decd.
17 Aug John Macarthur, esq., of Little New Street, Gough Square, London, (by gift).¶ Readmitted 16 May 1820: p. 387
15 Sept Alex. Barth, printer, (by gift).¶ Readmitted 8 Mar 1820: p. 386
Thos. Smith, timber merchant, of Tibberton (by gift)
16 Sept Ric. Sheen, victualler, by fine
17 Sept John Gardner, whitesmith, by fine
21 Sept Jas. Bennett,[1] printer, of Tewkesbury (by gift).¶ Readmitted 26 Feb 1820: p. 385
25 Sept Rob. Jakeman, silkthrowster, of Coleford (by gift).¶ Readmitted 21 Feb 1820: p. 385
2 Oct Chas. Wm. Jones, gent., of Cheltenham, (by gift)

377 **Ralph Fletcher, esq., mayor 1818–9**

6 Oct John Bowden, cutler, (by gift).¶ Readmitted 7 Aug 1820: p. 388
John Dobbins, cordwainer, (by gift).¶ Readmitted 7 Aug 1820: p. 388
9 Oct Wm. Cook (*Cooke*) Ward, gent., (by gift).¶ Readmitted 17 Aug 1820: p. 399
Ric. Hodges Carter, gent., (by gift).¶ Readmitted 7 Aug 1820: p. 388
10 Oct Jas. Withey, surgeon,[2] of Stroud (by gift).¶ Readmitted 24 Aug 1820: p. 390
Thos. Mee Richardson, esq., of Newent (by gift)
Hen. Richardson, esq., of Newent (by gift).¶ Readmitted 6 Aug 1821: p. 399
12 Oct Benj. Butler, esq., of Painswick (by gift).¶ Readmitted 6 Sept 1820: p. 391
Wm. Gordon, esq., of Hereford (by gift).¶ Readmitted 4 Dec 1820: p. 395
378 Jas. Charter, plumber, (by gift).¶ Readmitted 9 Feb 1821: p. 397
13 Oct Geo. Martin, grocer, (by gift)
15 Oct Thos. Player, (cooper), of Tewkesbury (by gift).¶ Readmitted 6 Nov 1820: p. 394

[1] Historian of Tewkesbury: Gray, *Antiquaries*, 98.
[2] Druggist: GBR B 3/13, f. 234v.

16 Oct John Vick, gent., of Elmore (by gift).¶ Readmitted 13 Nov 1820: p. 394

Thos. Davies, esq., of Leominster, [Herefs.], (by gift).¶ Readmitted 1 Apr 1824: p. 410

17 Oct Obadiah Paul Wathen, esq., of Woodchester (by gift)¶

John Partridge the younger, dyer, of Bowbridge (by gift).¶ Readmitted 6 Sept 1820: p. 391

Hen. Chas. Eycott, esq., of Eastington (by gift).¶ Readmitted 23 Sept 1820: p. 392

Frederick Phelps, surveyor, of Evesham, Worcs., (by gift).¶ Readmitted 24 Aug 1820: [p. 390]

Thos. Rudge, gent., of Ross, Herefs., (by gift).¶ Readmitted 12 Aug 1820: p. 389

379 19 Oct Thos. Reddall (*Rudhall*) Haycock,[1] clothier, of Woodchester (by gift).¶ Readmitted 15 Nov 1821: p. 401

Wm. Haycock, clothier, of Woodchester (by gift) •

20 Oct Wm. Hicks, esq., of Berkeley (by gift).¶ Baptist Wm. Hicks admitted 28 Sept 1820: p. 393

Thos. Foley, esq., of Newport, Herefs., (by gift).¶ Readmitted 19 Sept 1821: p. 400

21 Oct Rob. Hughes, esq., of Cheltenham (by gift).¶ Readmitted 25 Jan 1823: p. 405

John Gibson, gent., of Ross, Herefs., (by gift)¶

22 Oct Wm. Bury Wells, esq., of Dursley (by gift).¶ Readmitted 11 Aug 1820: p. 388

23 Oct Jas. Weller, esq., (by gift).¶ Jas. Weller Ladbroke readmitted 12 Feb 1821: p. 397

24 Oct John Allis Hartland, tanner, of Tewkesbury (by gift).¶ Readmitted 5 Sept 1820: p. 390

26 Oct Thos. Hampton Raymond,[2] esq., of Clifton, son of Thos. Raymond Symonds, esq., of the Mynde, Herefs.

380 27 Oct Chas. Stanton, clothier, of Stroud (by gift).¶ Readmitted 3 Oct 1820: p. 393

John Stanton, clothier, of Stroud (by gift).¶ Readmitted 22 Sept 1820: p. 392

29 Oct Chas. Edw. Hicks, esq., of Eastington (by gift).¶ Readmitted 12 Aug 1820: p. 389

30 Oct Geo. Evans Aubrey, gent., of Manchester, formerly of Stroud, (by gift).‡ Readmitted 3 Jan 1822: p. 401

Claude René Villiers, surgeon, of Ledbury, Herefs., (by gift).¶ Readmitted 7 Mar 1821: p. 398

2 Nov Lieut. Geo. Phillpotts, R.E., son of John, merchant, late of Bridgwater, Som.

Thos. Hen. Hastings Davies, esq., M.P. for Worcester,† (by gift).¶ Readmitted 8 Sept 1821: p. 400

6 Nov John Aust, victualler, by fine

381 18 Nov Geo. Madgwick Davidson, esq., of Warmley House (by gift)

Edw. Francis, esq., of Waltham Abbey, Essex, (by gift)

5 Dec Rob. Moore of Cheltenham (by gift).¶ Readmitted 23 Oct 1820: p. 394

1817 7 Nov[3] Jonathan Jones, printer, (by gift).¶ Readmitted 8 Mar 1820: p. 386

Chas. Stewart Ruthven, printer, of Wellclose Square, London, (by gift).¶ Readmitted 18 May 1820: p. 387

[1] Cf. Glos. R.O., D 677/T 6–7.

[2] Later called Thos. Hampton Symons: Burke, *Land. Gent.* (1898), ii. 1436.

[3] This and the following entry omitted from correct place; cf. above: GBR C 9/9, p. 345.

1818 14 Dec Jas. Bower, pinmaker, son of Sam., pinmaker

1819 19 Jan Rob. Price, esq., M.P. for Herefs.,[†1] (by gift).[¶] Readmitted 14 May 1824: p. 410

Edw. Bolton Clive, esq., of Whitfield Lodge, Herefs., (by gift)

382 25 Jan Thos. Baldwin, collar-maker, of Cheltenham, son of Ric., collar-maker, decd.

28 Jan Peter Smith, dyer, of Wallbridge (by gift).[¶] Readmitted 30 Dec 1820: p. 396

11 Feb Thos. Kingscote, esq., of Kingscote (by gift).[¶] Readmitted 30 Dec 1820: p. 396

8 Mar Ric. Smith, clothier, of Wallbridge (by gift).[‡] Readmitted 13 Sept 1822: p. 403

12 Mar Jos. Nicholls, yeoman, by fine

15 Mar Wm. Wood, yeoman, by fine

27 Mar John Altham Graham-Clarke, esq., of Frocester (by gift)

30 Aug Thos. John Wintle Parker, master mariner, of London, son of Thos., clerk, decd., of Churcham, formerly of Gloucester

383 3 Sept Thos. Cox, yeoman, by fine

John Phillpotts, esq., mayor 1819–20

30 Oct Rob. Peacey, esq., of Chedglow, Wilts., (by gift)

Geo. Lambert of Cheltenham, app. of Hugh Taylor, grocer[2]

2 Nov Hen. Edwards, builder,[3] (by gift)

3 Nov Mark Pearman, gent., of Coventry (by gift)

11 Nov Hen. Warwick, victualler, (by gift)[x]

384 17 Nov Edw. Plomer, esq., of George Street, Adelphi, London, (by gift)

20 Dec Wm. Lane, cordwainer, of Gloucester, son of Ric., cordwainer, of Littleworth

22 Dec Percival Boys, gent., of Bridgwater, Som., (by gift)

31 Dec Wm. Jenkins, whitesmith, (by gift)

1820 13 Jan Wm. Dowler, esq., of Uxbridge, [Mdx.], (by gift)

Wm. Morgan Meyler, surgeon, (by gift)[4 x]

31 Jan John Taylor, app. of Hugh Taylor, grocer

385 11 Feb Lieut. Rob. Lawrence Townsend, 4th Light Dragoons, son of Rob. Lawrence Townsend, formerly called Rob. Lawrence, D.D., of Bishop's Cleeve

17 Feb Thynne Howe Gwynne (the younger), esq., of Llanigon House, Brec., (by gift)[x]

21 Feb Rob. Jackman, gent., of Coleford (by gift)[x]

23 Feb Edw. Sheppard, esq., of Uley (by gift)[x]

26 Feb Jas. Bennett, bookseller, of Tewkesbury (by gift)[x]

8 Mar Hen. Purnell Hicks, esq., of Eastington (by gift)[x]

386 Alex. Barth, printer, (by gift)[x]

Jonathan Jones, printer, (by gift)[x]

10 Mar Sam. Davis, wiredrawer, of Fromebridge Mills, son of Jos., labourer, of Wheatenhurst

13 Apr John Suffield, engraver, of Strand, London, (by gift)

[x] Entrant previously disfranchised.

[1] Later Bt., of Foxley, Herefs.: Debrett, *Baronetage* (1836), 426–7.

[2] Entry followed a court case after the corporation had refused Lambert the freedom on the ground that his apprenticeship indentures had not been enrolled: *Glouc. Jnl.* 8 June 1818; 22 Feb, 5 Apr 1819.

[3] Architect: GBR B 3/13, f. 261.

[4] On his election to the common council: ibid. B 3/13, ff. 263–4.

21 Apr Cornet Ric. Harcourt Symons, 6th Dragoon Guards, son of Captain Thos. Symons, formerly called Thos. Raymond, 1st battalion of Glos. Militia[†]

13 Apr Rob. Farr, merchant, of Lothbury, London, (by gift)

387 15 Apr John Luke, esq., of Denmark Hill, Surr., (by gift)[x]

24 Apr Wm. Merrett, cordwainer, of Gloucester, son of Thos., formerly private, North Glos. Militia[†]

26 Apr Thos. Dix, wholesale glover, of Great Suffolk Street, Southwark, son of Ric., bluemaker, of Percival Street, Islington, Mdx.

16 May John Macarthur, esq., of Little New Street, Gough Square, London, (by gift)[x]

18 May Chas. Stewart Ruthven, printer, of Lombard Street, London, (by gift)[x]

28 July Captain Ric. Hurd Lucas, South Glos. Militia,[†] (by gift)[x]

388 Ric. Harris, esq., quartermaster, Royal South Glos. Militia,[†] (by gift)[x]

Captain Edw. Young, adjutant, Royal South Glos. Militia,[†]
Hen. Shrapnell, esq., surgeon, South Glos. Militia,[†]
Captain Abraham Stanley Rawlinson, paymaster, Royal South Glos. Militia,[†]
} (by gift)[1]

Major Phil. Cross, South Glos. Militia,[†] (by gift)

7 Aug Jas. Taylor, ropemaker, (by gift)[x]

John Bowden, cutler, (by gift)[x]

Ric. Hodges Carter, gent., (by gift)[x]

John Dobbins, cordwainer, (by gift)[x]

11 Aug Wm. Bury Wells, gent., of Dursley (by gift)[x]

389 Jos. Webb, cheese factor, (by gift)[x]

Steph. Wilkins, esq., of Cirencester (by gift)[x]

12 Aug Thos. Rudge, gent., of Ross, Herefs., (by gift)[x]

Wm. Playne, saddler, (by gift)[x]

John Croose, soapboiler, (by gift)[x]

Geo. Box Drayton, surgeon, (by gift)[x]

Chas. Edw. Hicks, esq., of Eastington (by gift)[x]

390 14 Aug Revd. Wm. Bishop (by gift)[x]

Jeremiah Hawkins, esq., of the Haw (by gift)[x]

18 Aug Chas. Hardwick, esq., (by gift)

Thos. Ridler, soapboiler, (by gift)[x]

19 Aug Benj. Coffin Thomas, gent., of Malmesbury, Wilts., (by gift)

Frederick Phelps, surveyor, of Cheltenham, formerly of Evesham, [Worcs.], (by gift)[x]

24 Aug Jas. Withey, druggist, of Stroud (by gift)[x]

5 Sept John Allis Hartland, tanner, of Tewkesbury (by gift)[x]

391 6 Sept Benj. Butler, esq., of Painswick (by gift)[x]

John Partridge the younger, dyer, of Bowbridge (by gift)[x]

7 Sept Paul Hawkins Fisher, esq., of Stroud (by gift)[x]

8 Sept Thos. Miles, surgeon, of Stanley[2] (by gift)[x]

Wm. Creese, yeoman, by fine

Edwin Maddy, esq., (by gift)[x]

392 12 Sept John Mills, printer, of Bristol (by gift)

13 Sept John Willis, esq., of Dixton, Mon., (by gift)[x]

[x] Entrant previously disfranchised.

[1] By act of 14 July 1820, on which day the corporation agreed to entertain Col. Berkeley and the officers of the South Glos. Militia at a dinner: GBR B 3/13, f. 273.

[2] Leonard Stanley; above: ibid. C 9/9, p. 344.

		18 Sept	Wm. Hen. Stanton, esq., of Stroud (by gift)[x]
		22 Sept	Mic. Castle, esq., of Bristol (by gift)[x]
			John Stanton, clothier, of Stroud (by gift)[x]
		23 Sept	Hen. Chas. Eycott, esq., of Eastington (by gift)[x]
		25 Sept	Thos. Wakeman, land surveyor, (by gift)[x]
			John Hyett, yeoman, by fine
			Jas. Brown, stonemason, son of Wm., tailor
393		28 Sept	Baptist Wm. Hicks, esq., of Berkeley (by gift)[x]
			Samuel Jones, esq., mayor 1820–1
		3 Oct	Chas. Stanton, esq., of Stroud (by gift)[x]
		6 Oct	Jas. Powell, silversmith, of Worcester (by gift)[x]
			Jas. Powell the younger, silversmith, of Worcester (by gift)[x]
			Rob. Sutton Deighton, app. of Dan. Spencer, bricklayer
394			Benj. Pitt, cabinet-maker, son of Ric., victualler, decd.
		18 Oct	Geo. Dan. Harris, esq., of Stanley[1] (by gift)[2]
		23 Oct	Rob. Moore of Cheltenham (by gift)[x]
		27 Oct	Jos. Court, coachmaker, by fine
		6 Nov	Thos. Phillips, esq., of Monmouth (by gift)[x]
			Thos. Player, cooper, late of Tewkesbury (by gift)[x]
			Geo. Hen. Mason (the younger), esq., (by gift)
		13 Nov	John Vick, gent., of Elmore (by gift)[x]
395		21 Nov	Chas. Stephens, clothier, of Stonehouse (by gift)[x]
		23 Nov	Thos. Watts, surgeon, of Frampton on Severn (by gift)
		28 Nov	Phil. Jones, esq., of Sugwas,[3] Herefs., (by gift)
		1 Dec	Geo. Hollister, surgeon, of Newent (by gift)
		4 Dec	Wm. Gordon, esq., of Hereford (by gift)[x]
			Thos. Jones, architect, of Cheltenham (by gift)[x]
		8 Dec	Ric. Pruen, gent., of Cheltenham (by gift)
		21 Dec	Thos. Russell, esq., (by gift)
396		30 Dec	Jos. Watts, brewer, of Stroud (by gift)[x]
			Peter Smith, dyer, of Wallbridge (by gift)[x]
			Southgate Austin, esq., of Wotton under Edge (by gift)[x]
			Hen. Hicks, esq., of Eastington (by gift)[x]
			Thos. Kingscote of Kingscote (by gift)[x]
	1821	15 Jan	John Freeman Cooke, surgeon and apothecary, son of Chas., apothecary
		22 Jan	Wm. Joy Binning, private, R.M., son of Moses, tailor, decd.
397		31 Jan	Thos. Phillpotts, esq., of Jamaica, the West Indies, son of John, gent., decd.
		9 Feb	Wal. Lawrence Lawrence, formerly called Wal. Lawrence Morris, esq., of Sevenhampton, son of Wm. Morris, esq., formerly of Hempsted[4]
			Jas. Charter, plumber, (by gift)[x]
		10 Feb	John Holder, esq., of Ross, Herefs., (by gift)[x]
		12 Feb	Jas. Weller Ladbroke, esq., late of Gloucester (by gift)[x]
			Wm. Maisey, carpenter and joiner, son of John, victualler
398		26 Feb	John Turner, hatter, (by gift)

[x] Entrant previously disfranchised.

[1] King's Stanley: Glos. R.O., D 873/T 56.

[2] Entrant had resigned freedom 19 May 1820: GBR B 3/13, f. 271.

[3] Sugwas Court: *Pigot's Dir. Herefs.* (1842), 5.

[4] Cf. *V.C.H. Glos.* iv. 395.

7 Mar Claude René Villiers, surgeon, of Bath, formerly of Ledbury, [Herefs.], (by gift)[x]
9 Mar John Lewis, plumber and glazier, son of Wm., plumber and glazier, decd.
19 Mar Lieut. Hen. Frederick Hawker,[†] son of Major [? Sam.] Hawker,[1†] (by gift)
9 Apr Thos. Jervis, barrister,[†] (by gift)
13 Apr Wm. Chas. Holder, esq., of Taynton (by gift)[x]
21 May Jas. Wilkins, app. of Ant. Bretherton, hairdresser
30 July Wm. Bishop, nailer, of Harescombe, son of Thos., labourer, of Haresfield
399 6 Aug Hen. Richardson, esq., of Newent (by gift)[x]
13 Aug Jas. Whalley, mercer, (by gift)
Lt.-Col. Sam. Gordon Higgins, equerry to H.R.H. the duke of Gloucester,[†] (by gift)
17 Aug Wm. Cook Ward, gent.,[2] (by gift)[x]
Thos. Driver, hairdresser, son of Thos., hairdresser
3 Sept John Carter, esq., M.P. for Portsmouth,[†] (by gift)
Geo. Morris, banker, son of Rob., esq., decd., of Barnwood Court
400 Sam. Clift, yeoman, by fine
8 Sept Thos. Hen. Hastings Davies, M.P. for Worcester,[†] (by gift)[x]
12 Sept Jas. Skey, esq., of Hyde, Upton upon Severn, Worcs., (by gift)
15 Sept Sam. Moulton Barrett, esq., M.P. for Richmond, Yorks.,[†] (of Carlton near Richmond by gift)
19 Sept Thos. Foley, esq., of Newport, Herefs., (by gift)[x]
20 Sept John Cooke, yeoman, by fine
21 Sept John Gale Goodwin, printer, of Tetbury (by gift)
24 Sept John Hancock, gent., of Tewkesbury (by gift)

Henry Wilton, esq., mayor 1821–2

16 Oct Wm. Joyner Ellis, esq., late lieut., 23rd Foot, of Berkeley (by gift)
19 Oct Wm. Thomson, esq., late of Copthall Court, Throgmorton Street, London, (by gift)[x]
401 7 Nov John Francis Augustus Moreton of Tortworth (by gift)[x]
15 Nov Thos. Reddall Haycock, clothier, of Woodchester (by gift)[x]
16 Nov Thos. Theach, app. of Jas. Wood, banker
24 Nov Sir Thos. Edw. Winnington, Bt., M.P. for Worcestershire, of Stanford Court, Worcs., (by gift)
4 Dec Wm. Havard Apperley, esq., of Withington, Herefs., (by gift)
20 Dec Edw. Austin, esq., of Wotton under Edge (by gift)[x]
1822 3 Jan Geo. Evans Aubrey, merchant, of Manchester (by gift)[x]
14 Jan Thos. Carpenter, architect, of 58, Frith Street, St. Anne, Westminster, (by gift)

402 **David Arthur Saunders, esq., mayor 1822**[3]

15 Feb John Greening, pinpointer, son of Wm., hairdresser, decd.
18 Feb Hen. Stroud Lane, labourer, of Gloucester, son of Ric., cordwainer, of Littleworth

[x] Entrant previously disfranchised.
[1] Cf. above: GBR C 9/9, p. 85.
[2] Attorney: ibid. B 3/13, f. 274v.
[3] Elected 8 Feb after Wilton's death: ibid. f. 324.

Shadrach Wood, cordwainer, of Barton St. Michael, son of Ric., victualler, decd.
20 Feb Rob. Josias Jackson Norreys, esq., of Davyhulme Hall, Lancs., (by gift)
8 Mar Ric. White, plumber and glazier, } sons of John, joiner and carpenter, of Painswick, formerly of Gloucester
Wm. White, millwright, }
403 1 Apr Wm. Jennings, tailor, son of Mic., tailor
19 Apr John Phillpotts the younger, gent., (by gift)
21 May Geo. Thomas, esq., of Carmarthen (by gift)
24 May Ric. Davies Morgan,[1] yeoman, by fine
10 June Hen. Spillman, tailor, son of Jos., tailor
13 Aug Thos. Morse, esq., of Ashmead House near Dursley (by gift)
4 Sept Rob. Hurst the younger, esq., of Horsham, Suss., (by gift)
11 Sept Thos. Sargeant, gent., of Linton, Herefs., (by gift)
13 Sept Ric. Smith, clothier, of Wallbridge (by gift)[x]
404 Ric. Cowcher Hudson,[†] son of Thos., tailor and victualler, decd.
16 Sept John Baron the younger, gent., of Longney (by gift)[x]
John Forrest, yeoman, by fine
28 Sept John Smith, gent., of Owdeswell (by gift)

William Price, esq., mayor 1822–3

1 Oct Wm. Roberts, gent., of Coleford (by gift)
4 Oct Hen. Bright, esq., M.P. for Bristol,[†] (by gift)
John Gardner, gent., (by gift)
Frederick Cox, app. of Geo. Cooke, tailor
5 Oct Gabriel Goodman, surgeon, of Upton upon Severn, Worcs., (by gift)
405 11 Oct Chas. Spencer Copnor, app. of Chas. Spencer, bricklayer
Thos. Estcourt, cordwainer, son of Chas., pinmaker
Rob. Davis, tailor, son of Rob., victualler
25 Oct John Lovett, druggist, son of Jas., barber and surgeon, late of Gloucester
28 Oct Chas. Pleydell Neale Wilton, clerk,[2] of Blakeney (by gift)
1823 10 Jan Sam. Pearce, gent., of Berkeley (by gift)[x]
25 Jan Rob. Hughes, esq., of Cheltenham (by gift)[x]
406 17 Apr Hen. Phelps, yeoman, of Rudford, son of Thos., butcher, late of Bulley (*Bullow*)
30 Apr Jas. Hickman, victualler, by fine
2 May Rob. Wilton, attorney, son of John Pleydell Wilton, surgeon and apothecary
17 June Thos. Teakel, yeoman, by fine
4 July Chas. Baldwin, tailor, son of Ric., collar-maker, decd.
14 July Cartwright Maddocks, app. of Wm. Maddocks, baker and maltster
407 28 July Jos. Maisey, cordwainer, son of John, cordwainer
Geo. Coates, app. of Giles Smart, cordwainer
15 Aug Thos. Hardy, yeoman, by fine
29 Aug John Llewelling, app. of Chas. Jeffs, tailor
6 Sept Chas. Frederick Williams, barrister, of Lincoln's Inn, Mdx., (by gift)
408 23 Sept Edw. Wood Mason, esq., of Cook's Mill, Painswick, (by gift)
26 Sept John Jacques, carpenter, son of Chas., carpenter
27 Sept Hen. Haines, builder, of Cheltenham (by gift)

[x] Entrant previously disfranchised.
[1] Entered originally as *Ric. Morgan Davis.*
[2] Assistant curate of Awre with the chapelry of Blakeney: Hockaday Abs. cix, cxxvii.

26 Sept Jas. Wingate, builder, (by gift). Sworn 26 Sept 1823
29 Sept Thos. Wynniatt, esq., of Stanton (by gift)
Reginald Wynniatt, clerk,[1] of Guiting Grange (by gift)
3 Oct Nat. Wood, clothier, of Cap Mill, Painswick, (by gift)
6 Oct Wm. Powell Hartley, attorney, of Bristol (by gift)[2]

409 **Sir Berkeley William Guise, Bt., mayor 1823–4**

6 Oct Chas. Moore Lander, painter and glazier, of Cheltenham, son of Hen., late corporal, North Glos. Militia[†]
21 Nov Chas. Kemeys Kemeys Tynte, esq., of Halswell House, Som., (by gift)
24 Nov Rob. Haviland, secretary to the governor of Sierra Leone,[3] of Gloucester, son of Rob., distiller, of Cheltenham, formerly of London
1824 9 Jan Thos. Swinnerton, esq., of Wonastow Court, Mon., (by gift)
Chas. Heath, esq., formerly mayor of Monmouth,[†] (by gift)[4]
410 2 Feb Thos. Hughes, cabinet-maker, of Gloucester, formerly of Wilton, Herefs., (by gift)[5]
9 Feb Thos. Heath Haviland, naval officer and provost marshal of Prince Edward Island,[†] son of Rob., distiller, of Cheltenham, formerly of London
1 Apr Thos. Davies, esq., of Leominster, Herefs., (by gift)[x]
14 May Rob. Price, esq., M.P. for Herefs.,[†] (by gift)[x]
Ric. Williams, yeoman, by fine
Wm. Mealing, yeoman, by fine
John Poole, yeoman, by fine
411 Sam. Greening, hairdresser, son of Thos., hairdresser, late of Gloucester
15 May John Morse, clerk, of Huntley (by gift)
21 June Sam. Heaven, app. of Ant. Bretherton, hairdresser
2 Aug Thos. Gardner, maltster, son of Thos., baker, of Painswick
14 Aug Hen. Jones the younger, gent., of Brockworth (by gift)[x]
412 31 Aug John Jakeman, grocer, (by gift)
6 Sept Geo. Beard, app. of John Beard, coal merchant
Thos. Baylis, baker, son of Thos., baker
Rob. Kirby, esq., of Cannon Street, London, (by gift)[x]

John Cooke, esq., mayor 1824–5

8 Oct Chas. Wathen, victualler, by fine
Jas. Dewey, victualler,[6] by fine
15 Oct Mat. Wood, esq., M.P. for the city of London, of South Audley Street, London, (by gift)[7]
413 16 Oct Wm. Clifford, esq., of Perrystone near Ross, Herefs., (by gift)
21 Oct Edw. Davies, esq., of Ebley (by gift)
23 Oct Edm. Lechmere Charlton, esq., of Ludford near Ludlow, Herefs., (by gift)

[x] Entrant previously disfranchised.
[1] Rector of Stanton with Snowshill, brother of Thos.: ibid. cccxlix; Glos. R.O., D 4262/T 17.
[2] Entry belongs to following mayoralty.
[3] *the Sierra Leone establishment.*
[4] By act of 6 Nov 1820, for his efforts to restore to the burgesses of Monmouth 'their chartered pride': GBR B 3/13, f. 292.
[5] Had been unable to claim the freedom by apprenticeship because his master, Jas. Wood, had moved to the Spa just outside the city in the last months of his apprenticeship: ibid. f. 313.
[6] Yeoman: ibid. 14, ff. 8v., 15.
[7] Entrant had been left a house in Gloucester by Elizabeth, sister of the banker Jas. Wood, for championing the late Queen Caroline: *D.N.B.; Diary of a Cotswold Parson*, ed. D. Verey (1978), 66.

5 Nov Wm. Simpson, hairdresser, son of Wm., carpenter
Wm. Baldwin, baker, son of Ric., collar-maker, late of Gloucester
12 Nov Wm. Thomas, esq., of Chase Cottage near Ross, Herefs., (by gift)
Wm. Warner, app. of John Hewlet, cabinet-maker
414 26 Nov Jos. Jakeman, app. of Ric. Butt, soapboiler
16 Dec Dan. Lloyd, clothier, of Ashcroft (by gift)
22 Dec Jos. Bussell Kirk, upholsterer,[1] (by gift)
1825 24 Jan Rob. Barrett, painter, son of Ric., painter
4 Feb Phil. Boulter Cooke, gent.,[†] son of John, esq.
11 Feb Benj. Bennett, bricklayer, son of Jos., pinmaker
4 Mar Thos. Meek, app. of Jas. Smart, tailor
415 2 Apr Hen. Rob. Kingscote, esq., of Bank Buildings, London, (by gift)
13 May Thos. Lyons Walcott, esq., of Littleworth (by gift)
6 June Jas. Taylor, cabinet-maker, son of Thos., victualler
20 June Hen. Harris, cordwainer, son of Sam., saddletree-plater
4 July Chas. Jones, carpenter and joiner, son of Chas., cordwainer
8 July Elisha King, clothworker, of Rodborough, son of Elijah, victualler, decd.
416 8 Aug Edwin Mutlow, surgeon and apothecary, of Tewkesbury, son of Wm., organist
15 Aug John Campbell, esq., of the Inner Temple, London, (by gift)
22 Aug Hen. Wintle, gent., son of Hen., clerk, of Somerton, Oxon, formerly of Pembroke College, Oxford [University]
5 Sept Geo. Bower, cordwainer, son of Sam., pinpointer
Jeremiah Price, app. of Thos. Nest, baker
14 Sept Wm. Collett, yeoman, by fine
Thos. Jenkins, yeoman, by fine
417 Edw. Jones, yeoman, by fine
Chas. Dobbins, yeoman, by fine
19 Sept Thos. Hyett, cordwainer, of Wotton near Gloucester, son of Sam., cordwainer, of St. Margaret's Hospital, formerly of Gloucester
21 Sept John Dix, indigo-blue manufacturer, son of Ric., bluemaker, of Lower Northampton Street, Clerkenwell, formerly of Whitecross Street, St. Luke, Mdx.

Thomas Commeline, esq., mayor 1825–6

7 Oct John Page Wood, rector of St. Peter, [Cornhill], London,[2] (by gift)
418 Adam Oldham, esq., of Tooting, Surr., (by gift)
8 Oct Jas. Scott, esq., M.P. for Bridport, Dors., of Rotherfield Park near Alton, Hants., (by gift)
14 Oct Hen. Spring, yeoman, by fine
4 Nov Ric. Trustram, mason, son of Wm., labourer, of Stratton, formerly of Poulton, Wilts.
16 Dec Nat. Thos. King, gent., of Gloucester, formerly of Cheltenham, (by gift)
1826 4 Mar Wm. Vail, butcher, son of Jas., yeoman, of Westbury-on-Severn
419 20 Feb Geo. Clarke, wool sorter, son of Thos., tailor, decd.
Ric. Jones, mariner, son of Wm., cordwainer, decd.
Geo. Edwards, bricklayer, of Wotton near Gloucester, son of Wm., bricklayer
6 Mar Wm. Allen, tailor, son of Nic., late servant of the bishop of Gloucester
8 May Chas. Sterry, yeoman, by fine
420 Jos. Wingate, carpenter, son of Wm., wine cooper, formerly drummer, South Glos. Militia

[1] Upholder: GBR B 3/14, f. 20.
[2] *D.N.B.* s.v. Wood, Sir Mat. (1768–1843), father of entrant.

24 May Frederick Lane, cordwainer, of Brockworth, son of Ric., cordwainer
Chas. Best, cordwainer, son of Sam., cordwainer
2 June Thos. Simpson, printer, son of Thos., pinmaker, decd.
5 June Thos. Jones, clerk, } sons of Sam., brushmaker, of Gloucester, formerly
421 Sam. Jones, brushmaker, } of St. John Street, West Smithfield, Mdx.
Geo. Shearman, servant, app. of Philo Maddy, currier
Thos. Spier, woolstapler, of Barton Street, son of Thos., linen-draper, decd.
Jas. Bennett, cordwainer, son of Jos., pinpointer
6 June Edw. Rowland Bower, surgeon, son of Edw., currier
422 Wm. Batsford, maltster, son of Chas., maltster, of Tewkesbury
Jos. Keveren, app. of Chas. Jeffs, tailor
Jas. Darke the younger, app. of Jas. Darke, pinmaker
Rob. Smith, clerk,[1] son of Rob., esq., late of Gloucester
Wm. Halling, cabinet-maker, of Barton Street, son of Wm., yeoman, decd.
Hen. Davis, cabinet-maker, of Barton Street, son of Wm., pinmaker
423 Wm. Williams, cabinet-maker, son of Wm., cordwainer
John Meek, tailor, son of Thos., pinmaker
7 June Chas. Davis, tailor, son of Wm., pinmaker
Edwin Maverley, tailor, son of Wm., mayor's officer
Ric. Harris, labourer, son of Ric., labourer, decd.
Thos. Haynes, cordwainer, son of Jas., tinplate-worker, late of Gloucester
424 Jas. Herbert, butcher, son of Jas., butcher, decd.
Thos. Greening, grocer, son of Thos., hairdresser, late of Gloucester
John Simpson, printer, son of Thos., pinmaker, decd.
Dan. Holder, sawyer, son of John, bellfounder, decd., of Tewkesbury
Jas. Base, chaise driver, son of Ric., cordwainer, decd.
425 Thos. Silvey, app. of Thos. Herbert, pinmaker
8 June John Brooks, cordwainer, of Newent, son of John, pargeter, late of Gloucester
Geo. Davis, carpenter, of Frampton,[2] son of Wm., labourer, of Longney
Geo. Venn, labourer, of Tewkesbury, son of Chas., labourer, decd., of Blaisdon
Jas. Wheeler, carpenter, son of Chas., carpenter, decd.
426 John Lewis, tailor, son of John, cooper, decd.
Geo. Brown, tailor, son of Wm., tailor
Wm. Walney[3] Reeve, stonemason, son of Thos. Swain Reeve, cordwainer, decd.
Chas. Wheeler, baker, son of Chas., carpenter, late of Gloucester
Jos. Draper, plumber and glazier, son of Ric., plumber, decd.
23 June Rob. Biddulph Phillips, esq., of the Middle Temple, London, son of Rob., esq., decd., of Hereford
427 3 July Chas. Parker Price, gent., of Plymouth, son of Wal., baker
28 July Jas. Gittins, gent., (by gift)
31 July Mat. Hutchinson, mercer, (by gift)
Jas. Jacques, carpenter and joiner, son of Chas., joiner
2 Oct John Allaway, yeoman, by fine

[1] Curate of St. Catherine: Hockaday Abs. ccxiv.
[2] Frampton on Severn: *Slater's Dir. Glos.* (1868), 199.
[3] *should be Whatney* subsequently added.

Shadrach Charleton, esq., mayor 1826–7

		7 Nov	Edw. Weight, esq., of Clingre House (by gift)
		14 Nov	Thos. Dance, attorney, (by gift)
428		17 Nov	Edwin White, carpenter and joiner, of Cheltenham, son of John, carpenter and joiner, of Painswick, formerly of Gloucester
			Thos. Bond, collar-maker, of Sheepscombe, Painswick, son of Sam., collar-maker, of Birdlip
		1 Dec	Chas. Hambleton, yeoman, by fine
		7 Dec	Thos. Gitton, esq., of Bridgnorth, Salop., (by gift)
		8 Dec	Wm. Bishop, nailer, of Stroud, } sons of Thos., labourer, of Haresfield
			Ric. Bishop, nailer, of Pitchcombe, }
429		11 Dec	Jos. White, hatter, son of John, carpenter and joiner, of Painswick, formerly of Gloucester
			Geo. Derrett, butcher, son of Geo., butcher, of Badgeworth
			Wm. Brown, tailor, of Painswick, son of Wm., tailor
		15 Dec	Humph. Austin the younger, esq., of Alderley } by gift. See p. 504[1]
			Ant. Austin, esq., of Bradley House near Wotton under Edge }
		27 Dec	Hen. Sikes, gent., of Barton St. Michael (by gift)
			Thos. Morgan, druggist, (by gift)
		29 Dec	John Goulter Dowling, B.A., son of John, victualler
430	1827	12 Mar	Edw. Briansford,[2] yeoman, by fine
			Jos. Davis, cordwainer, of Quedgeley, son of John, cordwainer, of Longney
			Lieut. Benj. Peyton Sadler, R.N., son of Benj., gent.
		19 Mar	Edw. Pruen, attorney, of Cheltenham (by gift)
		26 Mar	Wm. Russell Skey, gent., (by gift)
			Sam. Williams, yeoman, by fine
431		2 Apr	Jonah Clutterbuck, app. of Geo. Washbourn, baker
		23 Apr	Hen. Mitford Boodle, esq., of 42, Lower Brook Street, Grosvenor Square, London, (by gift)
		30 Apr	Jos. Knight, wiredrawer, son of Jas., pinmaker
			Jos. Base, tailor, son of Ric., cordwainer, of Gloucester, formerly of Rodborough
			Geo. Cox, app. of Ric. Woodward, tailor
		28 May	John Harris, labourer, son of Thos., pinmaker
432		4 June	John Wm. Cundy, gent., of the Stock Exchange, London, (by gift)
		23 June	Hen. Williams, gent., of Lincoln (by gift)
		29 June	Marshall Allen, yeoman, son of Nic., formerly servant of the bishop of Gloucester
		6 July	Wm. Welch, tailor, } sons of John, tailor, of Stoke Orchard
			Hen. Welch, tailor, }
		10 July	Jos. Cotton, yeoman, by fine
433		13 July	Hen. Wright, yeoman, by fine
		20 July	Cornelius Taylor, plumber and glazier, son of Thos., victualler
		6 Aug	Jos. Morris, grocer, (by gift)
		3 Sept	Thos. Pick Hartland, gent., of Fish Street Hill, London, (by gift)
		20 Sept	Hen. Weeks, plumber and glazier, of Cheltenham, son of Wm., plumber and glazier, of King's Stanley
		21 Sept	Wm. Griffiths, yeoman, by fine
434			John Halling, barge-owner, by fine
			Hen. Khnust, yeoman, by fine

[1] Entries interlined.
[2] Edw. Brainsford: GBR B 3/14, f. 58.

Chas. Belcher, yeoman, by fine
24 Sept Thos. Brewer, yeoman, by fine
John Colborne, clerk, of Whitminster, son of Jos., esq., decd., of Stroud

John Pleydell Wilton, esq., mayor 1827–8

15 Oct Wm. Young, carpenter and joiner, son of Wm., carpenter, of Gloucester, formerly of Westbury-on-Severn
435 Thos. Young, labourer, } sons of Ric., coalminer, of Coleford, formerly
John Young, labourer, } waterman, of Upton upon Severn, Worcs.
16 Oct John Rob. Townshend, M.P. [for Whitchurch, Hants.],[1] of Frognal, Kent, son of John Thos., Lord Sydney†
9 Nov Thos. Bradley, yeoman, by fine
436 16 Nov Rob. Acutt, app. of Chas. Bonnor the younger, brazier and tinplate-worker, (by gift)[2]
21 Dec Dan. Smith, app. of Jas. Wood, banker and draper
1828 15 Jan Joel John Tanner, yeoman, by fine
28 Jan Wm. Pear, cordwainer, of Ledbury, Herefs., son of Thos., carpenter, of Down Hatherley, formerly victualler, of Gloucester
Hen. Best, billiard marker, son of Sam., cordwainer
437 18 Feb Thos. Welch, farmer, of Stonehouse, } sons of Phil., tailor,
Geo. Welch, tailor, } of Brockworth
Rob. Simpson, yeoman, son of Thos., pinmaker, decd.
3 Mar Thos. Bullock Washbourne, druggist, son of Thos., banker, decd.
Benj. Jaques, painter, son of Chas., carpenter
Wm. Washbourne, gent., son of Thos., banker, decd.
438 17 Mar Jas. Chadnor White of Chaceley, Worcs., app. of Wm. Playne, saddler and harness-maker
24 Mar Geo. Lewis, scrivener, son of Thos., victualler, decd.
11 July Thos. Phillpotts, esq.,[3] son of John, esq.
21 July John White, tailor, of Llansawel, Carms., son of John, victualler, of Painswick, formerly joiner and carpenter, of Gloucester
439 1 Aug Wm. Haviland, chemist, of Liverpool, son of Wm., victualler, decd.
11 Aug Dan. Clutterbuck, yeoman, by fine
Thos. Cooke, yeoman, by fine
Chas. Cooke, yeoman, by fine
5 Sept Ric. Collins, app. of Wm. Stephens, tinplate-worker and brazier
18 Sept Peter Bullock, yeoman, by fine
John Rawlings, yeoman, by fine
440 John Cooke, yeoman, by fine

Ralph Fletcher, esq., mayor 1828–9

3 Nov John Gamlen of Bristol, app. of Thos. Jeffs, hairdresser
Geo. Probyn, captain in the East India Company's service, of Longhope, son of Wm., clerk, decd., of Goodrich, Herefs.
24 Nov Chas. Wilkes, hairdresser, of Newnham, son of Chas., pinmaker
1829 19 Feb Edw. Coxwell Rogers,[4] esq., of Dowdeswell (by gift)

[1] *Complete Peerage*, xii (1), 592.
[2] Entrant had been app. of Chas. Bonnor and Chas. Bonnor the younger without proper indentures: GBR B 3/14, f. 23.
[3] Later clerk: *Alumni Cantab. 1752–1900*, v. 116.
[4] Edw. Rogers Coxwell Rogers, formerly called Edw. Rogers Coxwell: *Visit. Glos. 1682–3*, 146.

441 21 Feb Wm. Trigge, surgeon, of Cainscross (by gift)

13 Apr Sam. Ric. Capel, clerk, son of Wm., esq., decd., of Prestbury

9 June Chas. Lawrence, attorney, of Cirencester (by gift)

25 Aug Maria Critchley by fine

John Griffiths, yeoman, by fine

John Miles, yeoman, by fine

14 Sept Nat. Taynton, tailor, of Ross, Herefs., son of Wm., hairdresser, of Bristol

442 Ric. Driver, labourer, of Littleworth, son of Thos., hairdresser

Jas. Drinkwater, shoemaker, of Littleworth, son of Jas., private, 3rd Royal Veteran Battalion, late of Jersey

William Henry Hyett, esq., mayor 1829–30

9 Nov Thos. Dix, cordwainer, } sons of John, peruke-maker

John Dix, cordwainer, } sons of John, peruke-maker

443 16 Nov John Lloyd, app. of Thos. Lewis, cordwainer

7 Dec Rob. Washbourn(e), surgeon, son of John, bookseller, decd.

14 Dec Ric. White, farmer, son of Ric., husbandman, of Cugley, Newent

John Jackson, app. of Francis Ursell, plumber and glazier

28 Dec John Wellington, yeoman, by fine

444 1830 8 Jan Wm. Lea, huckster, son of Wm., broker

15 June Wm. Bryan Hartland, surgeon, son of John Chris. Capel Astman Hartland, gent., of Newent

1 Feb Ric. Matthews, joiner, son of Benj., pipemaker, decd., of Hereford

26 Feb Wm. Wathen, surgeon, of Chaxhill, Westbury[-on-Severn], son of Wm., victualler, of St. Catherine, Gloucester

1 Mar Sam. Dudfield, veterinary surgeon, (by gift)

445 23 Apr Thos. Hickes, surgeon, (by fine)

28 June Geo. Jones, brushmaker, son of Sam., brushmaker, of Gloucester, formerly of St. John Street, West Smithfield, Mdx.

2 July Edm. Estcourt, hairdresser, son of John, hairdresser, decd.

Thos. Taylor, app. of Benj. Bevan, baker and confectioner

Jas. Knight, pinmaker, son of Jas., pinmaker

446 5 July Wm. Capel the younger, esq., of the Grove, Painswick, (by gift)

Hen. Frankis, butcher, son of John, butcher, of Painswick

Thos. Bower, cordwainer, son of Thos., waterman

Wm. Merrett, tailor, son of Thos., pinmaker

Jas. Tomlins, china painter, son of John, glover, of Worcester

Jos. Young, nailer, son of Jos., yeoman, of St. Briavels hundred,[1] formerly of Westbury-on-Severn

447 Jas. Lewis, app. of Chas. Jeffs, tailor

Dan. Spencer Copner, app. of Isaiah Smith, plumber and glazier

9 July Wm. Way, app. of Ric. Woodward, tailor

Chas. Gilbert Ladkin, app. of Thos. Gunn, hairdresser

Rob. Evans, app. of Thos. Woodward, cabinet-maker and upholder

John Cocks Bower, gent., son of John Cocks Bower, gent., decd., of Newent

448 Jas. Haynes, tailor, son of Jas., tinplate-worker, decd.

Sam. Spillman, tailor, son of Jos., tailor

Jas. Drinkwater, tailor, son of Thos., cordwainer

Hen. Bourn, cabinet-maker, son of Wm., cordwainer

Jas. Brown Cull, sievemaker, son of Jos. Brown Cull, tailor, late of Gloucester

[1] i.e. the Forest of Dean.

Geo. Hen. Bower, mason, } sons of Jas., late musician,
Jas. Bower, cordwainer, } South Glos. Militia

449 Chas. Simpson, pinmaker, son of Thos., pinmaker, decd.

Wm. Herbert, saddler and harness-maker, son of Jas., butcher, decd.

Sam. Roberts, labourer, of Norton, son of Sam., brushmaker

Wm. Watts, tailor, of Cheltenham, son of Wm., butcher, decd.

Chas. Richards, carpenter, son of Jos., carpenter, decd.

450 13 July Wm. Young, miner, son of Ric., of Joyford, St. Briavels hundred, formerly waterman, of Upton upon Severn, Worcs.

Wm. Holder, confectioner and baker, of Worcester, son of Wm., pargeter, decd.

Chas. Washbourn, baker and maltster, } sons of Geo., baker, decd.
Geo. Washbourn, linen-draper, }

Jas. Cole, labourer, of Gloucester, son of Thos. Gardner Cole, victualler, of Upton St. Leonards

451 Thos. Lewis Poole, gent., son of Thos., collar-maker, decd.

Sam. Doggett, labourer, son of Chas., bricklayer, decd.

Sam. Overthrow, bookbinder, son of John, victualler

Edw. Leader Kendall, wharfinger, son of Wm., wharfinger, of Gloucester, formerly upholder, of High Street, Southwark

Wm. Vernon, app. of Jos. Andrews, grocer and tallow-chandler

452 16 July Edw. Bloxsome the younger, attorney, of Dursley (by gift)

John Faville, victualler, son of John, pinmaker, decd.

Jas. Bretherton, plumber and glazier, son of Thos. Clarke Bretherton, hairdresser, decd.

John Mann, joiner, son of Jos., pinmaker, decd.

Chas. Okey, brazier and tinplate-worker, son of Chas., tinplate-worker

John Hen. Greening, labourer, son of Dan., tailor, decd., of Cheltenham

453 John Coopey, dealer, of Huntley, son of John, dealer, of Churcham

Thos. Perris, broker, } sons of John, blacksmith
John Perris, blacksmith, }

Sam. Vail, farmer, of Westbury-on-Severn, son of Jas., yeoman, of Bulley

Wm. Rowles, labourer, of Westbury-on-Severn, son of Wm., cordwainer, of Bulley

454 Geo. Wheeler, druggist, son of Chas., carpenter, decd.

Thos. Gardner, cordwainer, app. in turn of Chas. Cooke, plumber and glazier, and Sam. Jennings, cordwainer

19 July Wm. Fream, carpenter, son of John, cordwainer

Hen. Vaughan, chairmaker, of Worcester, formerly of Evesham, [Worcs.], } sons of John, fellmonger, of Worcester, formerly of Gloucester
455 John Vaughan, whitesmith, }

John Halling, baker, of Worcester, son of Wm., yeoman, decd.

Steph. Merrett, cordwainer, son of Steph., cordwainer, of Woodchester

Jas. Cole, labourer, } sons of Jas., tailor, decd., of Rodborough
Ebenezer Cole, labourer, }

456 Jas. Owen Hale, saddler and harness-maker, son of Ephraim, collar-maker and coach-harness-maker, of Gloucester, formerly of Bristol

Wm. Hitch Venn, labourer, of Churchdown, son of John, labourer, decd., of Minsterworth

1830 Wm. Vail, labourer, Jas. Vail, stonemason, of Cheltenham, } sons of Sam., yeoman, of Westbury-on-Severn, formerly of Bulley

Geo. Welch, carpenter and wheelwright, of Bishop's Cleeve, son of John, tailor, of Stoke Orchard

457 Jas. Vail, butcher, of Westbury-on-Severn, son of Jas., yeoman, of Bulley

Thos. Davis, labourer, of Frampton on Severn, Geo. Davis, blacksmith, of Frampton on Severn, } sons of Jos., labourer, decd., of Wheatenhurst

John Phelps, tailor, of Cheltenham, son of Rob., tailor, late of Woodmancote, Bishop's Cleeve

458 John Wadley, cordwainer, of Upton St. Leonards, son of Thos., baker

Thos. Merrett, clothworker, of Avening, son of Thos., tailor, of Nailsworth

John Long, grocer, app. of John Andrews, grocer and soapboiler

23 July Edwin Nest, baker, of Gloucester, son of Thos., baker, decd., of Swallow Street, Piccadilly, Mdx.

Wm. Wilton, gent., of Maisemore, son of Hen. the younger, gent., decd.

459 Wm. Bond, currier, son of Sam., collar-maker, of Birdlip

Rob. Hayward, baker, son of John, baker, of Winstone

Sam. Merrett, tailor, son of John, tailor, of Nailsworth

John Lane, labourer, of the out-hamlet of St. Mary de Lode,[1] son of Wm., labourer, late of Norton

Benj. Frederick Frankis, surgeon, son of John Hen., gent., decd., of Bristol

John Chamberlin Knill of 31, Alpha Road, Regent's Park, Mdx., app. of Thos. Saunders, tailor, of Gloucester, formerly of Cross Street, Golden Square, Westminster

460 Edw. Roberts, tinplate-worker, app. of Wm. Stephens, tinman and brazier

John Sheppard, app. of Chas. Cooke, plumber and glazier

26 July Chas. Buchanan, edgetool manufacturer, Geo. Newton Cox Buchanan, edgetool manufacturer, } sons of Jas., grocer

Hen. Somerset Whitcombe, gent., Lieut. Thos. Douglas Whitcombe, Madras Artillery, of Llantrithyd, Glam., } sons of Sam., gent.,[2] decd.

461 Edw. Owen Jones, esq., of Hayhill and of Trinity College, Cambridge [University], son of Edw., vicar of Brockworth†

John James, gent., son of John, gent., of Newnham, formerly of Gloucester

Thos. Coxwell, gent., son of John, gent., decd., of Charlton Kings

Heathfield Weston Hickes, clerk, of Mitcheldean, son of John Heathfield Hickes, M.D., decd.

Wm. Clarke, mariner, John Clarke, waterman, } sons of Geo., yeoman, decd., of Arlingham

462 Chas. Watts, labourer, of Hardwicke, son of Thos., husbandman, decd., of Highnam

[1] Part of St. Mary's parish outside the city: *V.C.H. Glos.* iv. 382.

[2] Kt.; cf. above: GBR C 9/9, pp. 280, 351.

Thos. Drinkwater, tailor, son of Jas., private, 3rd Royal Veteran Battalion, late of Jersey
Wm. Frankis, gent., of Bristol, son of Wm., yeoman, decd., of Upton St. Leonards
Hen. Hawkins, gent., of Eastington, son of Sam., of Rodborough, formerly of 52, Webber Row, Blackfriars, Southwark
Jas. Peat Heane, surgeon, son of Jas., carrier
Rob. Draper, tailor, } sons of Ric., plumber and
463 Geo. Draper, plumber and glazier, } glazier, decd.
Jas. Derrett, butcher, of Cranham, son of Jas., butcher, decd., of Brockworth
Wm. Rayner Coopey, farmer, of Bentham, Badgeworth,
Benj. Hyett Coopey, farmer, of Bentham, Badgeworth, } sons of Wm., yeoman, decd., of Badgeworth
Jos. Coopey, farmer, of Bentham, Badgeworth,
464 Ric. Young, miner, of Joyford, son of Ric., waterman, of Upton upon Severn, Worcs.
Hen. Rea, attorney's clerk, son of Wm., baker
Thos. Woodward, attorney's clerk, son of Chas., cordwainer, decd.
Chas. Mutlow Heane, gent., of 50, Upper North Place, Gray's Inn Lane, Mdx., son of Jas., carrier
John Stephens, tailor, son of John, patten-maker
Francis Brown, gent., of Gloucester, son of Francis, gardener, of Kingsholm
Jas. Welch, carpenter and joiner, of Tewkesbury, son of Geo., bricklayer, decd., of Kennington, Surr.
465 Thos. Watts, grocer, of Bristol, son of Wm., butcher, decd.
Edm. Beard, coal merchant, app. in turn of John Beard, coal merchant, decd., and David Evans, coal dealer
Chas. Thos. Lewis, gent., of Ebley (by gift)[1]
29 July Captain John Surman Carden, R.N.,[†] (by gift)[2]
Roynon Mason, gent., son of Geo. Hen., esq., of Gloucester, formerly of Nass
Wm. Wilton, surgeon and apothecary, son of John Pleydell Wilton, surgeon and apothecary
466 John Hatch, carpenter and joiner, son of John, victualler
Jas. Bradley, baker, son of Thos. Jas., watchmaker, of Newent
Edw. Jenner Pruen, attorney, of Cheltenham, son of Thos., clerk, of Bristol, [formerly] gent., of Prestbury
Edw. Lane, goldsmith and jeweller, } sons of Thos., gunsmith,
Thos. Lane, brasscaster, } decd., of Birmingham
Edw. Bretherton, cheese factor, } sons of Edw., hairdresser, decd.
467 Jas. Bretherton, attorney's clerk, }
Wm. Morgan, grocer, son of Benj., victualler, of Wotton near Gloucester, formerly of Gloucester
Hen. Holder Cooke, gent., son of John the younger, gent.
30 July Thos. Cox Buchanan, surgeon, son of Jas., grocer
Wm. Lawrence Townsend, clerk, of Bishop's Cleeve, son of Rob. Lawrence Townsend, formerly called Rob. Lawrence, clerk, decd., of Shurdington

[1] By act of 5 Mar 1819: ibid. B 3/13, f. 244.
[2] By act of 20 Sept 1813: ibid. f. 135v.

468 1830 Wm. Sam. Gwinnett Hornidge, attorney, of Clements Inn New Chambers, Mdx., son of Wm. Gwinnett Hornidge, clerk, decd.
Wal. Jones, surgeon, of Hereford, son of Edw., clerk, decd.
Hen. Hannington, clerk, of Dewchurch, Herefs., son of John Geo., clerk, decd., of Eton, Bucks.
Wm. Hen. Roberts, clerk, of Clewer, Berks., son of Wm., clerk, of Eton College, [Bucks.]
Sam. Harris, chairmaker, of Bedminster, Som., son of Wm., farrier, decd., of Bristol
Jas. Hen. Dowling, gent., son of John, victualler
469 Jas. Jones, pinmaker, son of Jas., pinmaker, of Wickwar, formerly of Gloucester
Wm. Marshall, blacksmith, of Clifton, son of Job, sawyer, decd., of Bristol
Sam. King, cordwainer, son of Francis, bricklayer, decd., of Brislington, Som.
Chas. Reece Bullock, surgeon, of Chepstow, [Mon.], son of Geo., tanner, of Burford, Oxon., formerly of Gloucester
Wm. Hawkins Clevely, tobacconist, son of Jos., tailor, of Bristol
John Jos. Hoskins, scale beam-maker, son of Jas., beam-maker, of Bristol
Jabez Fletcher, cooper, son of John, cooper, decd., of Bristol
470 Chas. Estcourt, tailor, of Birmingham, son of Jas., pinmaker, decd.
Hen. Smith, tallow-chandler, app. of John Andrews, grocer and soapboiler
31 July Jas. Heavingham Jones, printer, high constable of Maidstone, [Kent], son of Thos. Davies Jones, grocer, of Colchester, Essex
Hen. Rudge, surgeon, of Leominster, Herefs., son of Thos., clerk, decd.
Wm. Daniel, shopkeeper, of 124, Kent Street, Southwark, son of Thos., carpenter, decd.
John Chas. Cooke, surgeon, son of John the younger, gent.
John Benj. Watts, carpenter, of Old Kent Road, Surr., son of John, carpenter, of Fulham, Mdx.
471 John McLaren, warehouseman, of Bath Street, Bristol, son of John, seedsman, decd.
Jas. Watts, sashmaker, of 8, Claremont Place, Old Kent Road, Surr., son of Wm., carpenter, of Bermondsey New Road, St. George, Southwark
Thos. Welch, tailor, of Cheltenham, son of Jos., tailor, of Barrow, Boddington
Sam. Skillern, labourer, of Tredington, son of Steph., labourer, of Twyning
John Harrison, plushweaver, son of Wm., plushmaker, of Banbury, Oxon.
Thos. Frankis, coal merchant, of Barton St. Mary, son of Thos., husbandman, of Upton St. Leonards
472 Chas. Ireland, hairdresser, of 8, Finch Lane, Cornhill, London, son of Chas., hairdresser, of Kingsland, Hackney, Mdx.
Sam. Hawkes, wood turner, of Birmingham, son of Jas., cordwainer, decd.
John Young, waterman, son of John, labourer, of Newnham
Chas. Hen. Ellis, pianoforte tuner, of 5, Yeoman's Row, Brompton, Mdx., son of John, jeweller, decd., of London
Jos. Frankis, farmer, } sons of Thos., husbandman, of
Wm. Frankis, farmer, } Upton St. Leonards

Geo. Giles, flour agent, of Chapman Street, Islington, [Mdx.],
473 Sam. Giles, accountant, of Compton Street, London,
Wm. Giles, linen-draper, of Hammersmith, Mdx.,
} sons of Sam., mercer, of St. Albans, Herts., formerly of Gloucester

Geo. Young, labourer,
John Young, labourer,
Jas. Young, labourer,
} sons of Jas., labourer, of Westbury-on-Severn

Geo. Taynton, hairdresser, of Clifton, son of Jas., pewterer, decd., of Bewdley, [Worcs.]

Wm. Fisher Lane, brushmaker, son of Sam., gunsmith, of Birmingham

474 Wm. Billings, cordwainer, of Birmingham, son of Wm., cordwainer, of Barbourne, Claines, Worcs.

Sam. Gardner, yeoman, of the Horsepools, Painswick,
Hen. Gardner, yeoman, of the Horsepools, Painswick,
} sons of Thos., baker, decd., of Painswick

Jas. Hornidge, combmaker, son of Thos., combmaker, of Kenilworth, Warws.

John Spier, cabinet-maker, of Stourbridge, Worcs.,
Hen. Spier, joiner, of Kingswinford, Staffs.,
} sons of John, brushmaker

Thos. Sparks, printer, of Bristol,
Dan. Sparks, painter, of Bristol,
} sons of Fream Window Sparks, cordwainer

475 David Browning, plumber and glazier, of Cheltenham, son of Sam., cordwainer, late of Gloucester

John Wadley, innholder, of Wheatenhurst, son of John, baker, decd.

Wm. Ward, cheesemonger, of 27, East Road, Hoxton, Mdx., son of Wm., printer, decd., of London

John Hugh Pugh, coal merchant, son of Chas., late of Gloucester

Jas. Rogers Heane, printer, son of Edw., waterman

Jas. Hen. Davis, carpenter, of 7, Mills's Buildings, Knightsbridge, Mdx.,
Thos. Davis, compositor, of 7, Princes Street, Drury Lane, Westminster,
} sons of Jas., carpenter and joiner, of Chelsea, Mdx.

Rob. Wilton, comedian, of Liverpool, son of Chas. Hen., musician, of Southport, Lancs., formerly of York

476 Thos. Cowles, livery stable keeper, son of Wm., of Liverpool, formerly of Odiham, Hants.

Edw. Matthews, tailor, of Hereford, son of Edw., late corporal, 52nd Foot[†]

Wm. Watts, porter, of 22, Chandos Street, Covent Garden, London, son of Isaac, tailor, of 48, St. Martin's Lane, London

Sam. Broadway, weaver, of 6, Butlers Buildings, George Street, Bethnal Green, Mdx., son of Thos. Broadway alias Braddis, weaver, decd., of Cock Alley, Norton Folgate, Mdx.

Isaac Turner Glendall, baker, of Bath, son of Chas., cooper, decd.

Powell Chandler, currier, of Gloucester, son of Ric. Powell Chandler, tobacconist, of Barton Street St. Michael

Jas. Briggs King, upholsterer, of Cheltenham, son of Jas., decd., of Brislington, Som.

477 Wm. Pugh, currier, of Cheltenham, son of Chas., late of Gloucester

1830 Geo. Mitchell, accountant, of Bristol, son of Jos., saddler, decd., of Birmingham

Ric. Dillars Jones, cordwainer, of Birmingham, son of Geo., tailor, late of Gloucester

Wm. Perks, labourer, of Naunton Beauchamp, Worcs., son of Thos., labourer, of White Ladies Aston, Worcs.

Chas. Beard, printer, Thos. Beard, printer, of 103, Hoxton Old Town, Mdx., } sons of Thos. Ric., labourer of 16, Nelson Street, Bethnal Green, Mdx., formerly of Brick Lane, Spitalfields, London

John Wadley, cordwainer, of Bristol, son of Ambrose, baker, decd.

2 Aug John Jacob Hyett, cooper, son of John, cooper, decd.

478 John Ricketts, pinmaker, of 104, Bermondsey Street, Surr., Thos. Ricketts, chairmaker, } sons of Jas., pinmaker, of 37, White's Grounds, Bermondsey, [Surr.], formerly of Gloucester

Jas. Bradgate, tailor, of Bath, son of Chas., confectioner, of Bedminster, Som., formerly of Ross, [Herefs.]

Wm. Bonnewell, cooper, of Cheltenham, son of Wm., cooper, decd., of Tewkesbury

Sam. Worrall, esq., of Clifton, son of Sam., gent., decd., of Bristol

Chas. Merrett, printer, Geo. Merrett, tailor, } sons of Ric., saddler, decd., of Bath

479 Chas. Neale, esq., of Queen's College, Oxford [University], son of John, clerk, of Staverton

Wm. Bossom, grocer and tea dealer, John Bossom, ostler, of Birmingham, } sons of Hen., cordwainer, of Mitcheldean

Thos. Wellington, starch manufacturer, of Bristol, son of Jas., gent., of Ross, Herefs.

Hen. Davis, coachmaker, son of John, pinmaker, of Siston, formerly of Gloucester

Geo. Taynton, cordwainer, of Eugene Street, Bristol, son of Wal., pewterer, decd., of Bristol

Hen. Bossom, painter and glazier, son of Hen., cordwainer, of Mitcheldean

480 Ric. Price Cleaveley, cordwainer, son of Ric., cordwainer, of 8, Thomas's Passage, Bethnal Green Road, London, formerly of 4, New Court, George Yard, Whitechapel, London

Philips Perks, butcher, of Evesham, Worcs., son of John, labourer, of Bretforton, Worcs.

Hen. Thos. Howard of Charlton, Wilts., son of Thos., earl of Suffolk†

Edw. Herbert Butt, grocer, of Cheltenham, son of Jas., butcher, decd., of Standish

John Lee Jones, carpenter, of Ross, Herefs., son of John, cooper, of Newent

Geo. Washbourn Charleton, surgeon, of Gloucester, son of Shadrach, grocer, of Wotton near Gloucester, formerly of Alcester, Warws.

481 Hen. Hooper Fryer, gent., of Coleford, son of Hen. Hooper Fryer, attorney, of Newland, formerly of Tewkesbury

Jas. Lake, husbandman, of Welland, Worcs., son of Benj., decd., of Hartpury

Horatio Deane, accountant, of Bristol, son of Wm., of Frocester, formerly of Gloucester

Hen. Baker, baker, of Upton upon Severn, Worcs., son of Jas., cordwainer, of Stepney, Mdx., formerly of Minsterworth

John Maverley, cooper, of Denmark Street, London, son of Wm., pinmaker

Jas. Lane, broker, of Whitecross Street, London, son of Sam., private, North Glos. Militia†

482 Ric. Coopey, corn factor, son of Ric., grocer

Jas. Lane, labourer, of Castle Eaton, Wilts., son of Ric., labourer, of Marston, Wilts., formerly of Maiseyhampton

Thos. Commeline, clerk, of Leckhampton, son of Thos., gent.

Jos. Hayward, labourer, of Cirencester,
Methuselah Hayward, labourer,
Simon Hayward, labourer,
Ric. Hayward, labourer,
} sons of Thos., maltster, of Coln St. Dennis

483 Thos. Birch, starch manufacturer, son of Thos., chaise driver, of Clifton

Sam. Goodwin, victualler, son of Sam., victualler, of Grafton Street, Fitzroy Square, Mdx., formerly of Tottenham Court Road, [Mdx.]

Chas. Perks, labourer, of Great Washbourne,
John Perks, labourer,
Geo. Perks, labourer,
} sons of John, labourer, of Conderton, Overbury, Worcs.

Jos. Hawkins, labourer, of St. Woollos near Newport, Mon., son of John, husbandman of Staunton, [Worcs.][1]

484 Dan. Price, seaman, son of John, cabinet-maker

Thos. Bamford, tailor, of Littledean, son of Jeremiah, nailmaker, of Pucklechurch[2]

Wm. Harris, moulder, of Worcester, son of Hen., moulder, of Coalbrookdale, Salop.

John Beard, coach-lampmaker, of Ironmonger Row, St. Luke, Mdx., son of Benj., cordwainer, decd., of Windsor, [Berks.]

Geo. Merrett, painter, of Worcester, son of Phil., clothier, of Woodchester

Thos. Daniel, baker, of Adam Street West, [St.] Marylebone, Mdx., son of Thos., carpenter, decd.

Wm. Trustram, labourer, son of Rob., blacksmith, decd., of Fairford

485 Jas. Berriman Tippetts, plumber and glazier, son of Josiah, plumber and glazier

Hen. Young, blacksmith, son of John, labourer, of Newnham

John Randle, gent., son of Wm., collar-maker, late of Tewkesbury

John Lye, plumber and glazier, of Commercial Road, Whitechapel, London, son of Francis

Joshua Smith, carpenter and joiner, of Stroud,
Caleb Smith, hairdresser, of Stroud,
Eliazer (*Eliezer*) Smith, tailor, of Stroud,
} sons of Ric., weaver, decd., of Painswick

486 Hen. Draper Lye, Chelsea pensioner, of 28, George Street, Portland Chapel, London, son of Hen. Draper Lye, decd.†

Thos. Savage Clutterbuck, carpenter, of 35, White's Grounds, Bermondsey, [Surr.], son of Jas., cordwainer, decd., of Southwark

Wal. Jones, gent., son of Phil., attorney, of Ross, Herefs.

Hen. Geo. Francis Moreton of Lasborough, son of Thos. [Reynolds Moreton], Lord Ducie†[3]

[1] Given as *Stanton, Glos.*; cf. above: GBR C 9/9, p. 119.

[2] Cf. below: ibid. p. 489.

[3] *Complete Peerage*, iv. 476.

1830 Wm. Salcomb, waterman, son of Thos., waterman, decd., of Tirley
Chas. Baxwell Clutterbuck, labourer, of 20, Parish Street, Horsleydown, Surr., son of Jas., cordwainer, decd., of Southwark
487 Benj. Pearce, baker, of Deptford, Kent, son of Benj., oilman, decd., of Mill Pond Bridge, Bermondsey, Surr.
Ric. Arthur Roberts, clerk, of Christchurch, Mon., son of Wm., clerk, of Eton College, [Bucks.]
Jas. Nest, carpenter, of Marylebone Lane, Mdx., son of Jas., carpenter, of 8, Henrietta Passage, Henrietta Street, Cavendish Square, London, formerly of Windsor, [Berks.]
John Gurney of Birmingham, app. of Wm. Stephens, tinplate-worker
3 Aug Wm. Chandler Grafton, mercer, son of Wm., mercer
Wm. Bowers of the East India Company's horse artillery,† son of Sam., weaver, of 3, Falcon Court Square, Shoe Lane, Fleet Street, London
488 John Hopton, esq., son of John Hopton, formerly called John Parsons, of Canon Frome, Herefs., formerly of Stretton Grandison, Herefs.
Francis King, chaise driver, of Bath, son of Elijah, victualler, decd.
Thos. Rudge Wadman, servant, son of Geo., servant, of 24, Queen Anne Street, Mdx., formerly of Gloucester
John Ward, cheesemonger, of 37, East Road, Hoxton, Mdx., son of Wm., printer, late of London
John Steel, watchmaker, of Oxford, son of Sam., cordwainer, of Dursley
489 Anselm John Griffiths, hairdresser, of Berkeley, son of Thos., gent., of Bristol
Chas. Ridler, innkeeper, of Warwick, son of Ric., victualler, decd.
Jas. Wilton Hulme Powell, jeweller, of 169, High Street, Southwark, son of Jas., turner, of Redcross Street, Southwark
Jonathan Wathen, esq., of Clifton, son of Sam., esq., decd., of Thrupp, Stroud
Geo. Bamford, tailor, of 14, Tottenham Court New Road, London, son of Jeremiah, nailmaker, of Littledean, formerly of Pucklechurch[1]
Frederick Freame, victualler, of Newgate Market, London, son of Thos., broker, decd., of Worcester
490 Thos. Perks, labourer, of Overbury, Worcs., son of John, labourer, of Conderton, Overbury, Worcs.
Wm. Vaughan, chronometer- and watchmaker, son of John Westron Vaughan, upholsterer of Orange Court, Rose Street, St. Anne, liberty of Westminster and Mdx.
Dan. Mills, lieut. in the East India Company's service,
Wm. Yarnton Mills, clerk, of Shellingford, Berks.,
sons of Revd. Wm., of Miserden[2]
Chas. Brown, grocer, of Abergavenny, [Mon.],
491 Benj. Brown, soapboiler,
sons of Jos., soapboiler, of Chepstow, Mon.
Thos. Rea Bamford, cordwainer, of Somers Town, London, son of Thos., cheesemonger, of 39, Wych Street, London
Thos. Nayler, clerk, of South Brent, Som.,[3] son of Ric., surgeon, decd.

[1] Cf. above: GBR C 9/9, p. 484.
[2] Entrant's father was rector of Shellingford: *Alumni Oxon. 1715–1886*, iii. 959.
[3] ? Devon. Entrant was rector of St. Peter at Arches, Lincoln: *Alumni Cantab. 1752–1900*, iv. 516.

Chas. Roberts, clerk in the Record Office, Tower [of] London,† son of Wm., M.B., decd.†

Edm. Spillman, bootmaker, of 31, Great Windmill Street, Haymarket, London, son of Jos., tailor

492 Jas. Mic. Parsons Hopton, esq., Wm. Parsons Hopton, clerk, of Bishop's Frome, Herefs., sons of Wm. Hopton, formerly called Wm. Parsons, clerk, of Kemerton, formerly of Frampton on Severn

Jos. Clarke, butcher, of Bath, son of Ric., butcher, of Hasfield

Arthur Phelps, tailor, of Cheltenham, son of Rob., tailor, of Woodmancote, Bishop's Cleeve

John Cowles, paper-stainer, of 53, Westmoreland Place, London, son of Nat., broker, of Cornhill, London

Geo. White, organ builder,
493 Thos. White, organ builder, of 15, Mary Street, Regent's Park, London, sons of Steph., organ builder, of 34, Henry Street, Hampstead Road, Mdx., formerly of Stephen Street, Tottenham Court Road, Mdx.

Wm. Edm. Harris, sailmaker, son of Wm., sailmaker, of Woolaston

Dan. Bloxsome Wadley, yeoman, of Wheatenhurst, son of John, baker, decd.

Jos. Harper Yeend, wheelwright and carpenter, son of Wm. Goodwin Yeend, yeoman, decd., of Little Comberton, Worcs.

Lieut. Chris. Claxton, R.N., of Bristol (by gift)

494 John Carter Fewster, miller, of Woodchester Park Mill, app. of Geo. Washbourn, baker, confectioner, and maltster, late of Gloucester

4 Aug [Geo. Chas.] Grantley Fitzhardinge Berkeley[1] of Harrold House, Beds., son of Frederick Augustus, earl of Berkeley, decd.†

John Capel, esq., of Gretton, Winchcombe, son of Wm., esq., decd., of Stroud

Chas. Simpson, saddler, of 57, Great Portland Street, London, son of Chas., baker, decd.

Hen. Jasper Toye, gent., of Chelsea, Mdx., son of Hen., esq., decd., of Bristol

495 Ric. Forster, tinplate-worker, Thos. Forster, tinplate-worker, of 19, Chapel Street, Sheerness, Kent, sons of Thos., tinplate-worker, of 6, Allsop Mews, [St.] Marylebone, London, formerly of Bristol

Hen. Jones, clerk, of Lechlade, son of Edw., clerk, decd.

Jas. Abell, attorney, son of Thos., joiner and cabinet-maker, decd.

496 Wm. Nest, attorney's clerk, son of Jas., cordwainer

Jos. Lewis, gent., son of Jos., gent., of Gloucester, formerly of Dinchill, Donnington, [Herefs.]

Jasper Freame, cabinet-maker, of 7, Cornwall Road, Commercial Road, Lambeth, London, son of Thos., broker, decd., of Worcester

Dan. Ferebee, shearman, son of Wm., clothworker but in his copy described as cordwainer,[2] of Uley

Jos. Rea, gent., of Barnwood, son of Jos., searcher of customs

497 Wm. Dolman Wheatstone, music seller, of 20, Conduit Street, London, son of Wm., cordwainer, of Pentonville, London, formerly of Gloucester

Wm. Ham, livery stable keeper, son of Wm., groom and quartermaster, of Gray's Inn Road, Mdx.

[1] *Complete Peerage*, ii. 144 n.

[2] Cf. above: GBR C 9/9, p. 59.

Wintour Harris, gent., of Bristol, son of Wintour, gent., of Small Street, Bristol

John Fletcher, cordwainer, of Clayhill, Bushey, Herts., son of Chas., brassfounder, decd., of London

Chas. Edw. Fletcher, waiter at the Fountain tavern, of 6, Three Kings Court, [the] Minories, London, son of Wm., gunstock-maker, of the Minories

498 Jas. Holtham, letter carrier, of Cheltenham, son of John, innholder

Geo. Wood, grocer, of 29, Great Smith Street, Chelsea, Mdx., son of Thos., servant of Revd. Jas. Commeline

Wm. Harris, brassfounder, of 7, Edwards Place, Seymour Place, London, son of Wm., farrier, decd., of Bristol

John Coopey, private, 23rd Royal Welsh Fusiliers now lying at Plymouth, son of Wm., pig dealer, decd., of Churcham

John Wheeler, whitesmith, of 15, Upper East Smithfield, London, son of Chas., carpenter, decd.

499 Edw. Craddock, tailor, son of Wm., hairdresser, of Stratford, Essex, formerly of Gloucester

Frederick Watts, carpenter and joiner, of 8, Thomas Street, Old Kent Road, Surr., son of John, carpenter, of 14, Earl Street, Westminster, formerly of Fulham, [Mdx.]

Jas. Davis, tailor, of 10, Northampton Street, Clerkenwell, London, son of Rob., tailor

John Baker, cordwainer, }
Dan. Baker, shipwright, } sons of John, cordwainer, of 58, Dempsey Street, Commercial Road, London, formerly of Minsterworth
500 Emanuel Baker, cabinet-maker, }

Dan. Greening, shopman, of 40, Keppel Street, Russell Square, London, son of Wm., hairdresser, decd.

Wm. Parsons, surgeon, of Littledean, son of Jas., clerk

Thos. White, wheelwright, of Painswick, son of John, joiner and carpenter

Sam. Gard(i)ner, sawyer, son of Ric., baker, of Sheepscombe

Geo. Pleydell Wilton, attorney, of Gray's Inn Square, Mdx., son of John Pleydell Wilton, surgeon and apothecary

501 Lt.-Col. Ric. Jones, R.A., of Woolwich, Kent, son of Roynon, esq., decd.[†]

Wm. Lewis, librarian, of Cheltenham, son of Wm., plumber, decd.

Jas. Maverley, corkcutter, of 20, Roberts Place, Commercial Road, Whitechapel, London, son of Jas., corkcutter, decd., of London

John Jacksons of Bath, app. of Wm. Binning, cabinet-maker, decd., of Gloucester, formerly of 42, Ironmonger Lane, London

Gustavus Howell, baker, of 1, Bird Street, Oxford Street, Mdx., app. of Nat. Washbourn, baker and confectioner

502 Thos. Roberts of Liverpool, app. of Dan. Spencer, bricklayer

Nat. Miles, surgeon, of Stroud, app. of Chas. Cooke, apothecary

Israel May Sowle, Baptist minister, of Lewes, Suss., app. of Wm. Maddox, baker

Wm. Crews of James Street, Manchester Square, Mdx., app. of Thos. Taylor Manns, cordwainer

5 Aug Wm. Lewis of Exeter, app. of Geo. Meadows, hairdresser

Geo. Hornidge, combmaker, of Bermondsey, London, son of Thos., combmaker, of Kenilworth, Warws.

503 John Jas. Frankis, attorney, son of John Hen., gent., decd., of Bristol

6 Aug Thos. Cowles, grocer, of 34, Great Arthur Street, Golden Lane, Mdx., son of Thos., grazier, decd.

Chas. Cooke of 79, Bunhill Row, London, app. of John Andrews, grocer

Hen. March Bradgate, mariner, of Devonport, Devon, son of Chas., confectioner, decd., of Ross, Herefs.

Geo. Turton Stroud, gent., of Swansea, son of John, gent., decd.

John Craddock, hairdresser, } sons of Wm., hairdresser, of Stratford,

504 Geo. Craddock, turner, } Essex, formerly of Gloucester

13 Aug Sam. Jones, admiralty mate of H.M. ship the *Semiramis*, of Cheltenham by gift

14 Aug John Wm. Partridge, dyer, of Bowbridge near Stroud by gift

Captain Geo. Hen. Worthington, adjutant, South Glos. Militia,† (by gift)

Wm. Brown, attorney, (by gift)

16 Aug John Tibbitts, tailor, (by gift)

Memorandum made 2 May 1831. The admission of Humph. Austin and Ant. Austin was by mistake omitted to be entered on 15 Dec 1826. They are since entered . . . see page 429

30 Aug Jos. Woodin, esq., of 35, Gerrard Street, London, (by gift)

505 **David Mowbray Walker, esq., mayor 1830–1**

4 Oct Peter Dickson, esq., of Denmark Hill, Surr., (by gift)

8 Oct Wm. Gearing the younger, app. of Chas. Cooke, plumber and glazier

John Morgan, yeoman, by fine

16 Oct Jas. Woodbridge Walters, esq., of Barnwood Court[1] (by gift)

18 Oct Nat. Sam. Marling, clothier, of Stroud (by gift)

11 Nov Thos. Keene, yeoman, by fine

29 Nov Rob. Fitzwilliam Hallifax, rector of Richard's Castle, Herefs. and Salop., eldest son of Sam., formerly bishop of Gloucester, by gift[2]

506 1831 28 Feb Chas. Rideout, esq., of Weston under Penyard, Herefs., by gift

30 Apr Nat. Reeve, surgeon, R.N., son of Nat., maltster, decd.

Jas. Bonnewell, cordwainer, son of Sam., cordwainer

Wm. Hicks, scrivener, son of Wm., pinmaker

2 May Wm. Beard, bricklayer, son of Wm., bricklayer

Hen. Hatch, cabinet-maker, son of John, victualler

507 Craven Fitzhardinge Berkeley of Cheltenham, son of Frederick Augustus, earl of Berkeley, decd.†

Augustus Hen. Moreton[3] of Woodchester Park, son of Thos. [Reynolds Moreton], Lord Ducie†[4]

Wm. Maverley, cordwainer, son of Wm., pinmaker

Ric. Draper, plumber and glazier, son of Ric., plumber and glazier, decd.

Wm. John Diddams of Cheltenham, app. of Thos. Woodward, cabinet-maker, decd.

Ric. Kirk, victualler, app. of John Maclaren seedsman, decd.

508 3 May Wm. Mann, watchmaker, of Gloucester, son of Wm., chaise driver, of Rodborough, formerly cordwainer, of Gloucester

Sam. Harris, plumber and glazier, of Frampton on Severn, son of Sam., saddletree-plater

[1] ? Barnwood House: cf. *V.C.H. Glos.* iv. 414; Glos. R.O., DC/F 3/2.

[2] By act of 22 July 1783: GBR B 3/11, f. 339v.

[3] Later surnamed Macdonald-Moreton: Burke, *Peerage* (1963), 764–5.

[4] *Complete Peerage*, iv. 476.

Wm. Bradley of 18, Grosvenor Square, London, servant of Francis Lawley, esq., M.P. for Warws., son of Jas. Bradley, watchmaker, of Newent

Alex. John Heath, cordwainer, of Gloucester, son of Edw., decd., of Portland Street, St. Marylebone, Mdx.

Edw. Roberts, labourer, of Norton, son of Sam., brushmaker

509 Wm. Phelps, butcher, of Hartpury, son of Thos., butcher, decd., of Rudford

Hezekiah Shadrach Jones, app. of David Walker, decd., Alex. Walker, and David Mowbray Walker, printers

Hen. Merrett, millwright, son of John, tailor, of Nailsworth

10 June Thos. George, app. in turn of Sam. Greening, hairdresser, decd., and his widow Elizabeth

8 Aug Dan. Spencer Wilkins, bookkeeper at Mr. Heath's coach office, son of John Bell Wilkins,[1] tailor, late of Gloucester

510 29 Aug Benj. Denton, yeoman, by fine

12 Sept Rob. Warren, yeoman, by fine

14 Sept Mat. Gatfield, yeoman, by fine

Joshua Thomas, yeoman, by fine

Benj. George, yeoman, by fine

Wm. Mann, yeoman, by fine

Rob. Gooden, yeoman, by fine

511 Jas. Davis, yeoman, by fine

26 Sept Captain John Rodway Stock, 74th Bengal Native Infantry, of Leeds, Yorks., son of Edm. Stock, grocer, decd.

Alexander Walker, esq., mayor 1831–2

7 Nov John Taylor, yeoman, by fine

16 Dec Theophilus Wright, earthenware dealer, by fine

19 Dec Geo. Ames, wharfinger, by gift

1832 11 May John Wintle, wine and spirit merchant, son of Hen., clerk, of Gloucester, formerly of Pembroke College, Oxford [University]

512 4 June Edwin Jaques, carpenter and joiner, son of Chas., joiner

6 July Edw. Charleton, merchant's clerk, son of Shadrach, gent., of Gloucester, formerly grocer, of Alcester, Warws.

9 July John Poulson Rea, baker and maltster, of Barton St. Michael, son of Wm., baker

23 July Edw. Washbourn, gent., son of Thos., druggist, decd.

27 July Sam. Clift the younger, app. of John Badham, tailor

513 Ant. Gilbert Jones, gent., son of Sam., brushmaker, of Gloucester, formerly of St. John Street, West Smithfield, Mdx.

30 July Jas. Bloxsome, coachman, son of Jas., gent., of Wotton near Gloucester, formerly of Gloucester

Geo. Spier, tailor, son of John, brushmaker

10 Aug Geo. Baldwin, cordwainer, son of Ric., collar-maker, decd.

514 Thos. Knight, carpenter and joiner, son of Jas., pinmaker

Geo. Bower, carpenter and joiner, son of Thos., waterman

Hubert Nash Bower, student of surgery, son of Edw., currier

17 Apr Edw. Baker Hawker, student of surgery, of Gloucester, son of Chas. Hawker, clothier, of Uley, formerly of Woodchester

Hen. Dix, tailor, son of John, peruke-maker, decd.

[1] Cf. below: GBR C 9/9, p. 528.

515 Dan. Bloxsome, carpenter and joiner, son of Jas., gent., of Wotton [near Gloucester],[1] formerly of Gloucester

John Rowles, labourer, son of Wm., cordwainer, of Churcham, formerly of Bulley

Dan. Phelps, tailor, of Gloucester, son of Thos. the younger, butcher, decd., of Rudford

20 Aug Wm. John Pitt Goodrich, esq., of Wotton near Gloucester, son of Wm. Goodrich, esq., of Maisemore

516 Wm. Hen. Woodward, printer, of Gloucester, son of Wm., tailor, of Worcester, formerly of Gloucester

Geo. Washbourn, baker, son of Nat., confectioner

Geo. Meadows Morley, app. of Geo. Meadows, hairdresser and peruke-maker

Edwin Hen. Cooke, pargeter, son of Hen., pargeter, of Littleworth, formerly of Gloucester

Chas. Hill Evans, tailor, son of Wm., whitesmith

517 Wm. Evans, app. of his father Wm., whitesmith

24 Aug Thos. Merrett Crowdy, carpenter and wheelwright, of Painswick, son of Jas., butcher, of Ebley

John Chandler, weaver, son of Jasper, weaver, of Painswick, formerly of Pitchcombe

Dan. Vick the younger, yeoman, of Elmore, son of Wm., baker, of Frampton on Severn, formerly of Gloucester

518 24 Sept Dan. Mousell, yeoman, by fine

Edward Bower, esq., mayor 1832–3

2 Oct Thos. Upton, yeoman, by fine

6 Oct John Wilmore, yeoman, by fine

3 Dec Hen. Hopton of Northgate Street, Gloucester, app. of Jos. Bussell Kirk, cabinet-maker

1833 18 Feb Chas. Jas. Tasker, wine merchant, (by gift)[2]

519 22 Feb Jas. Stratton Cole, gent., son of Chas., tinman, decd.

31 May Edwin Smart, tailor, son of Jas., tailor

John Bennett, tailor, son of Sam., tailor, decd.

Chas. Watts, brazier, son of Sam., tinplate-worker

24 June Jas. Sessions, ironmonger, of Westgate Street, Gloucester, son of Jas., cabinet-maker

520 Wm. Moore the younger, gent., of Barton St. Mary, app. of Jas. Wood, banker and draper

Thos. Beard, coal merchant, of the Island, Gloucester, son of John, barge-owner, decd.

28 June John Jeffs, cabinet-maker, son of Wm., brushmaker

8 July Geo. Bullock, gent., of Burford, Oxon., son of Geo., tanner, of Blaisdon, formerly of Gloucester

521 Thos. Elliott Maddocks, maltster and baker, son of Wm., baker

12 July Jas. Arkell, surgeon, of Hayden, son of John, gent., decd., of Boddington

15 July Giles Taylor, butcher, of Gloucester, son of Thos., late private, Herefs. Militia, of Worcester

19 July Thos. Okey, whitesmith, son of Chas., tinman

[1] *the vill of Wotton*: cf. *V.C.H. Glos.* iv. 383.

[2] On his election to the common council: GBR B 3/14, ff. 211, 216.

522 Wm. Drinkwater, labourer, of Barton Street, son of Jas., late private, 3rd Royal Veteran Battalion, decd.†

22 July Hen. Dark, tailor, of Gloucester, son of Jas., pinmaker, of St. Margaret's Hospital near Gloucester

John Lea, servant of Thos. Gunn, } sons of Wm., cordwainer
Jas. Lea, patten- and clogmaker, }

523 John Lake alias Leake, bricklayer, of Ashleworth, son of John, bricklayer, decd., of Wheatenhurst

Ric. Coopey, labourer, son of Ric., pig dealer, of Churcham, formerly of Bulley

Thos. Ellis, pinmaker, of St. Mary's Square, Gloucester, son of John, pinmaker

29 July Thos. Salcomb, waterman, of the Haw, Tirley, son of Thos., waterman, decd., of Tirley

524 26 Aug Jos. Pumfrey, yeoman, by fine

Jas. Rea, yeoman, by fine

Wm. Barrow, yeoman, by fine

Ric. Castle, yeoman, by fine

30 Aug Abraham Gilbert Davis, land surveyor, of Dewchurch, Herefs., son of Gilbert, grocer

Chas. Field Moore, yeoman, by fine

525 **John William Wilton, esq., mayor 1833–4**

1834 13 Jan Sam. Geo. Wintle, currier, } sons of Revd. Hen.
Jas. Wintle, wine merchant, }

11 Apr Ric. Callaway,[1] yeoman, by fine

21 Apr Wm. Sirdefield, innkeeper, by fine

25 Apr Wm. Clay, yeoman, by fine

526 30 May Ant. Ellis Arkell, attorney, of Hayden Villa, Boddington, son of John, gent., decd., of Boddington

Rob. Heane, gent., son of Jas., carrier

4 July Wm. Wingate, chairmaker, son of Jas., plumber and glazier

7 July Hen. Wilkes, cabinet-maker, of Barton St. Mary, son of Chas. the younger, pinmaker

527 Chas. Jeffs, attorney's clerk, son of Thos., hairdresser

Jas. Nicholls, tailor, of Kingsholm St. Mary, son of Jas., soapboiler, decd.

14 July Sam. Hicks, gent., son of Sam., pinmaker, decd.

John Woodward, tailor, of Barton Street, son of Ric., tailor, decd.

528 Jas. Spier, cabinet-maker, son of John, brushmaker

18 July Nat. Phelps, carpenter and wheelwright, son of Thos. the younger, butcher, decd., of Rudford

21 July Jas. Spencer Wilkins, bookkeeper, son of John Bell [*Ball*] Wilkins,[2] tailor, decd.

25 Aug Rob. Long, yeoman, by fine

Edwin Ford, yeoman, by fine

529 Lewis Stinchcombe, app. of John Marsh, cooper

15 Sept Thos. Cother, yeoman, by fine

John Creed, yeoman, by fine

William Morgan Meyler, esq., mayor 1834–5

10 Oct Conway Whithorne Lovesey, yeoman, by fine

3 Nov Geo. Cox, yeoman, by fine

[1] Ric. Calloway: ibid. f. 235v.

[2] Altered from *John Bell Wilkins*; cf. above: ibid. C 9/9, p. 509.

530 17 Nov Chas. Prosser, druggist, (by gift)[1]

24 Nov Frederick Hatch, carpenter and joiner, son of John, innkeeper

28 Nov Wm. Davis, labourer, son of John, labourer, of Longney

15 Dec Wm. Woodward, private, 35th Foot,[†] son of Wm., cabinet-maker, of Churcham, formerly of Gloucester

1835 1 Jan Midshipman Hen. Charleton, R.N., son of Shadrach, gent., of Gloucester, formerly grocer, of Alcester, Warws.

531 2 Jan John Woodward, baker, of Barton Terrace near Gloucester, son of Jos., cordwainer, of Longney, formerly of Hartpury

Hen. Hinton, carpenter and joiner, son of Ant., private, South Glos. Militia, decd.

26 Jan Wm. Merrell the younger of Littleworth, app. of Jas. Wilkins, hairdresser

20 Mar Rob. Phillips, cordwainer, son of Rob., cordwainer, of South Hamlet

532 6 June Hen. Hugh Butt, soapboiler, son of Ric., soapboiler, formerly grocer

Jas. Bower, cordwainer, son of Thos., waterman

Wm. Wilkes, boot- and shoemaker, son of Sam., pinmaker

John Lane, labourer, son of Ric., cordwainer, of Gloucester, formerly of Littleworth

26 June Wm. Rea, cabinet-maker,
533 Thos. Rea, surgeon, } sons of Wm., baker and maltster, of Barton Street, formerly of Gloucester

29 June Jas. Williams, app. of Wm. Hickman, cordwainer

Ric. Wilkins Wilkes, tinman and brazier,
Jas. Wilks, tinman and brazier, } sons of Chas. Reynolds Wilk(e)s, tinplate-worker and brazier, of Gloucester, formerly of Tewkesbury

534 3 July Ric. Wheeler, plumber and glazier, son of Chas., carpenter, decd.

Thos. Phelps, butcher, of Longford, son of Geo., yeoman, of Rudford

Thos. Yates, cabinet-maker,
John Yates, farrier, } sons of Geo., barge-owner, decd.

Thos. Drinkwater, painter, son of Wm., painter, decd.

535 Wm. Hen. Cullis, butcher, son of Wm., baker, formerly bricklayer

John Hayes, app. of Geo. Meadows, hairdresser

Frederick Johnsons, cabinet-maker, son of Jas., cabinet-maker

6 July Geo. Viner Ellis, surgeon, son of Wm. Viner Ellis, esq., of Minsterworth

536 Chas. Daw, bricklayer, son of Jas., bricklayer

Wm. Wathen, pinmaker, son of Wm., pinmaker

10 July Chas. Roberts, labourer, son of Sam., brushmaker, of Norton, formerly of Gloucester

Thos. Merrett, labourer, son of Thos., pinmaker

537 13 July Sam. Bond, collar-maker, son of Sam., collar-maker, of Birdlip

Francis Tucker, printer, son of Francis, cabinet-maker, late of Gloucester

John Hen. Gardner, app. of John Gardner, whitesmith

20 July Wm. Jas. Holt, attorney, of Kingsholm near Gloucester, son of Wm., tea dealer, decd., of Holborn Hill, St. Andrew, Mdx.

538 Chas. Brown, tailor, of Alvin Street, Gloucester, son of Wm., tailor

Chas. Smart, writer (*uriter*), of St. Catherine Street, Gloucester, son of Jas., tailor, decd.

24 July Hen. Davis, fishmonger, son of Gilbert, fishmonger, of Gloucester, formerly of Bristol

27 July John Harper, servant, of Prinknash Park, son of John, cordwainer, decd.

[1] On his election to the common council: ibid. B 3/14, ff. 251, 252v.

Wm. Edward[s] Lawrence,[1] esq., of the Greenway, Shurdington, son of Wm. Lawrence, esq., decd., of Shurdington

539 Frederick Cullis, carpenter, of Wotton near Gloucester, app. of Wm. Cullis, baker

29 July Jos. Lake, labourer, of Ashleworth, son of John, bricklayer, decd., of Wheatenhurst

31 July Chas. Edw. Penton, painter, son of John, yeoman, late of Gloucester

Jos. Coopey, pig dealer, son of Jos., dealer, decd., of Churcham

Jas. Bower, pinmaker, app. of Ric. Bower, pinpointer

540 Wm. Hen. Fletcher, surgeon, of Gloucester, son of Ralph, surgeon, of Barton St. Michael, formerly of Gloucester

3 Aug Dan. Bretherton, printer, of Worcester, son of Edw., hairdresser, decd.

31 July John Baldwin, tailor, son of Ric., collar-maker, decd.

541 21 Sept David Arthur Ric. Saunders, gent., son of David Arthur, wine merchant, decd.

25 Sept Thos. Chas. Church, attorney, son of Edw., attorney, of 22, Spital Square, London

William Cother, esq., mayor 1836[2]

1836 18 July Peter Ellis, pinmaker, of the Island, Gloucester, son of John, pinmaker, decd.

Jas. Wilkes, tailor, of Whitefriars,[3] Gloucester, son of John, wiredrawer

542 Wm. Perris, labourer, of Barton St. Michael, son of John, blacksmith

22 July Chas. Wilkinson Barrett, painter, son of Chas. Wilkinson Barrett, gent.

Chas. Trickey, basket-maker, son of John, basket-maker

25 July Lieut. Jas. [Pitt] Goodrich,[4] 83rd Foot, of Matson House, son of Wm., esq., of Maisemore

543 27 July Thos. Cole, fishmonger, son of Thos. Gardner Cole, victualler, of Upton St. Leonards

28 Oct Joshua Butt, soapboiler, son of Ric., soapboiler

Hardwicke Shute, M.D., mayor 1836–7[5]

1837 17 June Chas. Binning, painter, son of Wm., cabinet-maker, decd.

30 June Wm. Montague, gent.,
544 Arthur Montague, gent., of Parkend, Forest of Dean,
John Montague, gent.,
Chas. Montague, gent.,
} sons of Wm., gent.

5 July Wal. Welch, tailor, son of Jos., tailor, of Staverton, formerly of Boddington

John Coopey, labourer, son of Ric., pig dealer, of Churcham, formerly of Bulley

545 John Holder, labourer, of Barton Street, Gloucester,[6] son of Adam, plasterer, formerly of Worcester

[1] Cf. Glos. R.O., D 2088/2.
[2] Elected 1 Jan 1836: GBR B 3/15, min. 1 Jan. 1836.
[3] Greyfriars was sometimes called Whitefriars mistakenly: *V.C.H. Glos.* iv. 291 n.
[4] Later knighted: Glos. R.O., GE 167.
[5] Elected 9 Nov 1836: GBR B 3/15, min. 9 Nov 1836.
[6] In 1835 an additional part of Barton Street had been taken into the city: *V.C.H. Glos.* iv. 191.

Rob. Crook, hairdresser, of Sweetbriar Street near Gloucester, son of John, tailor
Chas. Chesterton, maltster, of Southgate Street, Gloucester, son of John, innkeeper
Steph. Crowdy, butcher, of Painswick, son of Jas., butcher, of Ebley
Chas. Glendall, labourer, of Hare Lane, Gloucester, son of Chas., wheelwright
546 Arthur Evans, whitesmith, of Hare Lane, Gloucester, son of Wm., whitesmith
Hen. Aldridge Whitehead, writer, son of Wm., cordwainer
13 July John Frederick Rea, baker, of Westgate Street, Gloucester, son of Wm., cordwainer, decd.
Thos. Taylor, butcher, of Westgate Street, Gloucester, son of Thos., labourer, of Ledbury, [Herefs.], formerly of Gloucester
John Overthrow, waiter, of St. Catherine's Knap, Gloucester, son of John, waiter, formerly victualler
547 21 July Ric. Chandler, cabinet-maker, son of Ric. Powell Chandler, wine merchant
Jos. Jeffs, hairdresser, son of Thos., hairdresser
John Randall, tailor, of Tirley, son of Wm., tailor, of Tewkesbury
22 July Jas. Trigge Print Linton, gent., of Chaxhill, Westbury-on-Severn, son of Wm. Print Linton, yeoman, decd.
29 July Thos. Way, app. of Thos. Saunders, tailor, of Gloucester, formerly of Cross Street, Golden Square, Westminster
548 31 July Sam. Lysons, clerk, of Hempsted Court, son of Dan., clerk, decd., of Rodmarton
Octavius Goodrich, esq.,[1] of Matson House, son of Wm., esq., of Maisemore
Thos. Marsh, gent., son of Thos. the younger, victualler, decd.
Wm. Davis, labourer, of Alvin Street, Gloucester, son of John, labourer, of Upton St. Leonards, formerly fisherman, of Elmore
Chas. Workman, mariner, of Littleworth, son of John, hairdresser, decd.
549 Wm. Edwin Brabant, printer, son of Thos., tailor
4 Aug Baynham Newmarch Coopey, wheelwright, of Shurdington, } sons of Wm., yeoman, decd., of Badgeworth
Isaac Sprouce Coopey, farmer, }
3 Oct Jas. Hyett, carpenter, of Grafton Street, Soho, London, son of Thos., yeoman
7 Oct Thos. Drayton Wintle, gent., of Pembroke College, Oxford [University], son of Hen., clerk, of Gloucester, formerly of Pembroke College

550 **Edwin Maddy, D.C.L., mayor 1837–8**[2]

4 Nov Thos. Lea, tailor, of Northgate Street, Gloucester, son of Wm., cordwainer[3]
1838 2 Jan Thos. Gardner of Pierrepoint Place, Bath, app. of Chas. Cooke, plumber and glazier
27 Apr John Coopey, pig dealer, son of Jos., dealer, decd., of Churcham
Jas. Broughton, saddler, son of Jas., painter, late of Gloucester

[1] Later clerk: *Alumni Oxon. 1715–1886*, ii. 538; Hockaday Abs. ccclxxv.
[2] Elected 9 Nov 1837: GBR B 3/15, min. 9 Nov 1837.
[3] Entry belongs to previous mayoralty.

APPENDIX I

The Freeman's Oath in the early 16th Century

Le serment que borgeys fra en la vile de Gloucestr'

'Ceo oyez vous maire, bayliffs, vic[omtes], seneschaux, et altres bones gentz que si sount qe jee W.H. de ceo jour en avaunt serra feal et lial a nostre seigneur le roy, et a ces heires, et a la comune et a la fraunchise de la vile de Glouc[estr'], et loialment par mon poer meyntendra la dite fraunchise, et obeysaunt serra a les meire, vic[omtes], et bailiffs que sount et serrount par mon temps en la dite ville, et a la comune counsail lelement conseleray, et selonc mon poer derray et rendray ovesque mes gildebrethers; et nuls biens ne chateluz d'estraunges gentz ne coevera par ma fraunchise, par quey nostre seigneur le roy, ses heires, ces bailifs ou vic[omtes] de la vile de Glouc[estr'] serrount en ascune choses deshe[r]ites par dauns ou damages; et que jeo ne purchaser[a] nuls terres ne tenementz deins la fraunchise de la dite vile de Glouc[estr'] de abbe, priour, ne de nul alter seigneur par quel purchase joe serray mys en servage pour faire sute al ascun altre court hors de la dite vile mes soulment a la courtz nostre seigneur le roy en ceste place ou as alters courtz par auncient temps tenutz dedeyns la fraunchise de la dite ville; et bon et leuaux serray en toutz alter pointz que apertenent a un loial borgeys si me aide deu et les seyntes' et adonques bassera le lyver.[1]

The oath taken by a burgess in the town of Gloucester

'Mayor, bailiffs, sheriffs, stewards, and other good people who are present, hear that I, W.H., from this day forward will be true and loyal to our lord the king, to his heirs, and to the commune and freedom of the town of Gloucester, will loyally uphold to my power the said freedom, will be obedient to present and future mayors, sheriffs, and bailiffs in my time in the said town, will advise the common council loyally, and will give and render with my guild brothers according to my means; that I will not cover the goods or chattels of strangers by my freedom whereby our lord the king, his heirs, the bailiffs or sheriffs of the town of Gloucester will be prejudiced in any thing by gifts or damages; that I will not buy any lands or tenements in the freedom of the said town of Gloucester from abbot, prior, or any other lord whereby I will be bound to perform suit to any other court outside the said town save only to the courts of our lord the king in this place or to other courts held from time immemorial within the freedom of the said town; and that I will be good and loyal in all other matters which appertain to a loyal burgess, so help me God and the Saints,' *and then he will kiss the book.*

[1] Text, recorded in GBR B 2/2, p. 5, is also given in Hist. MSS. Com. 27, *12th Rep. IX, Glouc. Corp.* pp. 471–2.

APPENDIX II

The Freeman's Oath in 1746[1]

You shall swear that you shall be a true liegeman, and true faith and truth bear unto our sovereign lord the king's majesty, [his heirs, and lawful successors,] and to your power shall aid and assist the mayor and sheriffs of this city of Gloucester for the time being, and to them shall be obedient and attendant concerning such things as they, or any of them, shall lawfully and reasonably will and command you to do: you shall well and truly observe, perform, fulfil, and keep all such orders and rules as are and shall be made and established by the common council of this city, for the good government thereof, in all things to you appertaining. You shall also give, yield, and be contributory to and with the corporation of this city so far forth as you ought or shall be chargeable to do. And you shall not, by colour of your freedom, bear out or cover under you any foreign person or stranger or their goods and chattels: but according to the best of your skill, wit, cunning, and power you shall uphold and maintain all the liberties, franchises, good customs, orders, and usages of this city and corporation. So help you God.[2]

[1] Text given as printed on the certificate of freedom of William Hale, sworn 13 Oct. 1746: Glos. R.O., D 4693/14, p. 158.

[2] Also printed on the same certificate was an injunction not to take an apprentice for a term of less than seven years and to take care that his indentures were enrolled.

APPENDIX III

Honorary Freemen of Gloucester since 1885[1]

1906	9 July	Michael Edward Hicks Beach, Viscount St. Aldwyn, P.C., D.C.L.[2]
1918	15 July	Sir James Bruton[3]
1928	5 July	George Sheffield Blakeway[4]
1928	14 July	H.R.H. Prince Henry William Frederick Albert, duke of Gloucester, K.G., P.C., G.C.V.O.
1933	5 Oct	Alderman John Owen Roberts
1939	4 July	H.R.H. the duchess of Gloucester, G.C.V.O., G.B.E.
1944	26 Oct	Henry Hugh Arthur Fitzroy Somerset, duke of Beaufort, K.G., P.C., G.C.V.O.[5]
1953	21 Nov	Lieutenant-Colonel James Power Carne, V.C., D.S.O.[6]
1959	24 June	Alderman Martha Lilian Edwards
1982	24 Apr	H.R.H. Prince Richard Alexander Walter George, duke of Gloucester, G.C.V.O.
1982	24 Apr	H.R.H. the duchess of Gloucester

[1] List and biographical information based principally on Glos. Colln. N 12.79.
[2] Lord high steward from 1899.
[3] Mayor: Glos. Colln. NR 12.10.
[4] Town clerk 1883–1927.
[5] Lord high steward from 1925.
[6] Commanding officer of the 1st Battalion of the Gloucestershire Regiment at the battle of the Imjin River, Korea, April 1951.

EDITORIAL NOTE ON THE INDEXES

Figures within brackets indicate multiple entries of a personal name, occupation, or place name on the page concerned. The letter 'n' refers to footnotes to the text. As far as possible different spellings of a surname have been brought together in a single entry, either under the name's modern form or the form most commonly used in the registers. Cross-references have been provided from variant spellings, which also appear in brackets in the consolidated entry. The index of occupations includes clergymen, members of parliament, military men, and holders of municipal office, and, as in the personal-name index, asterisks indicate entries recording the start of a new mayoralty. Allied trades and professions are indicated by cross-references. Wherever possible English places have been indexed according to ancient parishes or towns. Entries have been included for those Gloucester parishes and streets specified in the registers' text. Indexing places in the metropolis has proved extremely problematical owing to textual inconsistency and frequent failure to distinguish places belonging to the cities of London and Westminster and the counties of Middlesex and Surrey. To overcome those problems London entries in the index have been simplified with much detail of addresses necessarily omitted and cross-references have been supplied for places within the metropolitan area but not belonging to the cities of London and Westminster. Ancient counties elsewhere, excepting Gloucestershire and including Wales, are indicated and foreign places are identified by the countries in which they lay at the time the place-name index was compiled. Variant forms of place names are given in brackets and uncertain readings in italics.

John Juřica

INDEX OF PERSONAL NAMES

INDEX OF OCCUPATIONS

INDEX OF PLACE NAMES